ULTIMATE HOCKEY

ULTIMATE HOCKEY

GLENN WEIR, JEFF CHAPMAN, AND TRAVIS WEIR

Published in 1999 by Stoddart Publishing Co. Limited
34 Lesmill Road, Toronto, Canada M3B 2T6
180 Varick Street, 9th Floor, New York, New York 10014

Distributed in Canada by:
General Distribution Services Ltd.
30 Lesmill Road, Toronto, Ontario M3B 2T6
Tel. (416) 445-3333   Fax (416) 445-5967
Email customer.service@ccmailgw.genpub.com

Distributed in the United States by:
General Distribution Services Inc.
85 River Rock Drive, Suite 202, Buffalo, New York 14207
Toll-free Tel. 1-800-805-1083   Toll-free Fax 1-800-481-6207
Email gdsinc@genpub.com

03 02 01 00 99 1 2 3 4 5

Canadian Cataloguing in Publication Data

Weir, Glenn
Ultimate hockey

ISBN 0-7737-6057-1

1. Hockey — History. I. Chapman, Jeff. II. Weir, Travis. III. Title.

GV846.5.W44 1999   796.962'09   C99-931464-5

Cover design: Bill Douglas @ The Bang
Text design: Wordstyle Productions
All photos courtesy of the Hockey Hall of Fame

visit the authors at their web site
www.ulthockey.com

THE CANADA COUNCIL | LE CONSEIL DES ARTS
FOR THE ARTS | DU CANADA
SINCE 1957 | DEPUIS 1957

*We acknowledge for their financial support of our publishing
program the Canada Council, the Ontario Arts Council, and
the Government of Canada through the Book Publishing
Industry Development Program (BPIDP).*

Printed and bound in Canada

For Dad

Contents

Acknowledgments . . . . *ix*
Introduction . . . . *xi*

The Earlies 1
The Oughts 37
The Tens 77
The Twenties 131
The Thirties 177
The Forties 231
The Fifties 285
The Sixties 331
The Seventies 377
The Eighties 419
The Nineties 457

Appendix I: The Stanley Cup: A Retrospective *503*
Appendix II: Authors' All-Time Teams *519*

Acknowledgments

From the Hockey Hall of Fame, we would like to thank Craig Campbell for his help in selecting archival photographs; Jane Rodney for putting up with us and accommodating our many requests; Phil Pritchard for helping tie some straggling ends together; Jacqueline Boughazale; Darren Boyko; and finally, Mr. Tommy Gaston for his stories about those who played the game of hockey before we were even born. You're all true professionals!

We'd like to thank the members of the Hockey Research Association (www.hockeyresearch.com), where the true knowledge base for the history of this great sport resides. From the National Library and Archives of Canada, we'd like to thank Mike McDonald for all of his help in securing CBC archival reels, and Mr. Edward Holden for being a friendly face at the security desk. From Stoddart Publishing, we'd like to thank Nelson Doucet for his belief in *Ultimate Hockey* from the very beginning; editor Don Bastian for his guiding hand; and editors Jim Gifford and Lloyd Davis for their valued input and steady hands; Ron Wight, the flawless fact machine; and Carol Anderson, who helped bring the book to life. A thank you goes out to Harry Handapangoda for his help and advice on anything to do with hockey on the international stage.

We (Travis and Glenn) would like to thank our Lord Jesus Christ for blessing us with the strength to undertake our daily tasks and for the knowledge that we're never alone. We give a big slap on the back to Stuart and Audrey Patterson; Carolyn and "Wild Bill" LeSurf; Sarah "Corny" O'Keefe; Kevin and Stephanie Jaeggin; Cuyler Petersen; Reuben Hoffman; Scott Sheedy; Garth Jones; Francis "Eagle" Piva; Triandos (always!); Jim Paquette; Luc Leger; Tony McElrea; Derek Chapman; Dave Allen; and John Sattler. God bless you all.

First and foremost, I (Jeff) thank my family for their love and support. I'd also like to thank my co-authors for helping me score my goal. A shutout goes to the Bishop's crew and all my friends in Mississauga and across Canada. All of you are special to me and without your support, none of this would have been possible. I would be remiss if I didn't thank anyone else who assisted us with the project, either with a helping hand or a kind word of support. We are grateful. Last but certainly not least, a tip of the hat goes to the Dads. Without the love and guidance of Grant Chapman and the late Ken Weir, our very best friends, this book would still be just some crazy idea. Thank you all.

Introduction

Welcome to *Ultimate Hockey*.

As we move into a new millennium, hockey, the game we have come to love so unconditionally, is undergoing a dramatic facelift. What was a simple game between everyday folk has fast become big business, a place where the word "capital" means more than a puck-chaser from Washington, D.C. Nonetheless, we do not lament what some believe to be the death of Canada's game. (Such transition periods rarely leave us empty-handed.) We prefer to look back on our common past in hockey and look forward to hockey's bright future.

Ultimate Hockey celebrates eleven "decades":

- "The Earlies" leave the eternal "Where did hockey begin?" question to those who have a vested interest in the answer (though we have our own ideas). In this chapter, we deal with hockey from the formation of the first bona fide league in Montreal in late 1886 through the time of the powerful Montreal Shamrocks and Victorias at turn of the century.
- "The Oughts" explore the seedier, more frightening aspects of the early game as it started to grow. The chapter begins in 1900 and rumbles through 1909, when the Montreal Wanderers were the class of the hockey universe.
- "The Tens" deal with what may be termed the "teenage" years of hockey. Suddenly, we are looking at a professional sport, a business tended to by a handful of shrewd men. This section takes us from the formation of a super-league in 1910 through the aborted Stanley Cup playoffs of 1919.
- "The Twenties" is largely a collection of snippets about that period. We begin with 1920 and screech to a halt in 1929 and the beginning of the Depression.
- "The Thirties" were a one step forward, two steps back period in hockey history. By mid-decade, the Depression had somewhat dismantled the game, leaving its bigwigs bemused, befuddled, and, in some cases, bankrupt. This chapter takes us from 1930 through 1939 and the beginnings of World War Two.
- "The Forties" deals with World War Two and the ill effects it had on the NHL. From 1940 through 1949 was the beginning of hockey's Golden Era. Like war itself, this chapter is fairly chaotic.
- "The Fifties" takes us to the end of the Golden Era, from 1950 to 1959, and celebrates the might and fanfare of rival dynasties in Detroit and Montreal.
- "The Sixties" shows us a nice linear progression in the game. Unlike many of the earlier decades, from 1960 to 1969 there were no real starts and stops in the Sixties, other than expansion.
- "The Seventies" is the meatiest chapter in *Ultimate Hockey*. From 1970 through 1979, hockey jumped onto the international stage. The World Hockey Association, the Broad Street Bullies, a Montreal dynasty, and the first important games against the Soviets made for a busy time in hockey.

- • "The Eighties" represent hockey's true coming of age. With the rival WHA dead and buried, the NHL found itself free to flex. Wayne Gretzky was the league's strong boy from 1980 through 1989 as new powers in New York, Calgary, Montreal, and Los Angeles fought for a piece of the pie.
- • "The Nineties" have been something of a conundrum. As the NHL suits turned up the juice on their commercial thinking-caps, hockey became an increasingly defensive sport — not the best way to sell the "Coolest Game on "Earth." Enter the flying Wings and the battling Stars. Exit Wayne Gretzky.

In *Ultimate Hockey*, we part ways with many of yesterday's hockey book conventions. We're not interested in teaching you anything, in telling you how hockey history unfolded. We think you're intelligent enough to decide for yourself what happened based on the facts we provide. Often, we allow those who were there to speak for themselves.

Our inspiration in crafting this book is the incomparable Bill James, who for years made people think about the game of baseball, to challenge some long-held but false notions. His work is well worth the read.

Consider this edition but a beginning. Even as you read this, we are digging deeper and deeper. It is our intent to keep pace, to work alongside our peers, until the history of this sport has been completely dusted off.

Glenn Weir
Jeff Chapman
Travis Weir

July 1999

The
Earlies

In a Flash

COMPOSITE REGULAR SEASON STANDINGS
(DECEMBER 1, 1887–DECEMBER 31, 1899)

Amateur Hockey Association of Canada
Canadian Amateur Hockey League

Club	GP	W	L	T	Pts	WPct	GF	GA
Montreal Amateur Athletic Assoc.	87	54	32	1	109	.626	317	224
Montreal Victorias	76	50	25	1	101	.664	331	221
Ottawa Hockey Club	64	38	26	0	76	.594	219	200
Quebec Hockey Club	59	17	41	1	35	.297	159	249
Montreal Shamrocks	35	13	22	0	26	.371	112	134
Montreal Crystals	38	12	26	0	24	.316	89	150
Montreal Britannias	1	0	0	1	1	.500	2	2
Halifax Chebuctos	2	0	2	0	0	.000	2	10
Montreal Dominions	3	0	3	0	0	.000	8	15
McGill University Hockey Club	7	0	7	0	0	.000	7	41

HELLOS

Edouard "Newsy" Lalonde *early scoring ace*	October 31, 1888
Adolf Hitler *German dictator*	April 20, 1889
Frank Nighbor *Senators star*	January 26, 1893
Gordon "Duke" Keats *western Canadian All-Star*	March 1, 1895
Jack Adams *Detroit Red Wings coach/manager*	June 14, 1895
Golda Meir *Israeli prime minister*	May 3, 1898
C.S. Lewis *British novelist and theologian*	November 29, 1898

GOODBYES

Sitting Bull *Native American chief*	December 15, 1890
P.T. Barnum *American promoter*	April 7, 1891
John A. Macdonald *Canadian prime minister*	June 6, 1891
Lord Alfred Tennyson *British poet*	October 6, 1892
Louis Pasteur *French bacteriologist*	September 28, 1895
Horatio Alger *American writer and clergyman*	July 18, 1899

REGULAR SEASON

BEST RECORD
1898 Montreal Victorias, 8-0-0

WORST RECORD
1894 Montreal Crystals, 0-8-0
1899 Quebec Hockey Club, 0-8-0

FAMOUS FIRSTS

ORGANIZED HOCKEY LEAGUE IN CANADA
Montreal City League, 1885

STANLEY CUP WINNER
Montreal AAA (MAAA), 1893

GOALIE TO WEAR LEG PADS
G.H. "Whitey" Merritt, 1896

"WESTERN" STANLEY CUP CHAMPIONS
The Winnipeg Victorias of 1896 were the first team from western Canada — literally, the first from west of Montreal — to win the Cup.

TEAM TO USE GOAL NETS
MAAA, 1899

ARTIFICIAL ICE HOCKEY RINK
North Avenue Rink, Baltimore, Maryland, 1894

SET OF HOCKEY RULES
J.G.A. Creighton's "McGill Rules," 1875

PUBLISHED SET OF HOCKEY RULES
Montreal Shamrock Hockey Club Guide, 1899

MISCELLANEOUS

MOST GOALS, SEASON
19	Haviland Routh, 1895
19	Harry Trihey, 1899

MOST GOALS, DECADE
57   Arthur "Dolly" Swift

COOLEST MIDDLE NAME
John Bower Hutton

COOLEST HANDLES
Tom "Stonewall" Arnton
George "Bunnie" Lowe
"Big" Arthur Scott
"Little" Arthur Scott
Arthur "Dolly" Swift
Harry "Flip" Trihey
Weldy "Chalk" Young

BEST SHOT
Harry Trihey had a shot that was feared around the league. He was the Shamrocks' go-to guy during the club's salad days.

BEST PASSER
Jack Campbell

BEST SKATER
Mike Grant

WORST SKATER
Charles "Baldy" Spittal was nothing of a Nureyev on the blades. Sportswriters referred to him as the "Mule."

FASTEST PLAYER
Jack Brannen was quite possibly the speediest man in organized hockey's first 50 years. In 1900, he was the world's champion 220-yard speed skater. A graduate of McGill University, the good doctor shared center and rover duties with fellow Shamrock Harry Trihey.

BEST SNIPER
Harry Trihey

BEST PENALTY-KILLER
Jack Findlay

BEST BODY-CHECKER
Charlie Johnstone — played for the Winnipeg Victorias for five years between 1896 and 1902.

BEST SHOT-BLOCKER
James Stewart was Allan Cameron's defensive conscience and the first in modern terms, to act as a second goalie. He held the point position like a rock on those celebrated Montreal AAA squads of Stanley Cup hockey's infancy.

BEST GLOVE HAND (GOALIE)
Tom Paton

FINEST ATHLETE

Dan Bain

Dan Bain was named Canada's athlete of the last half of the nineteenth century. He was Winnipeg's top gymnast, Manitoba's roller skating and cycling champion, and Canada's trapshooting king. He also grabbed titles in pairs figure skating and lacrosse. Beyond the gym and the roller rink, he also managed to squeeze in a brilliant hockey career.

BEST DEFENSIVE FORWARD
Jack Findlay was a bloodhound, one of the grittiest and hardest-working forwards in the Amateur Hockey Association of Canada before 1893.

MOST CONSISTENT PLAYER
Mike Grant

TOUGHEST PLAYER
Dan Bain

BALDEST PLAYER
Robert Jones was a goalie with the dynasty Montreal Victorias and a man with a lot of face to wash.

MOST UNDERRATED PLAYER
Clare McKerrow put in five years with the MAAA, scoring 46 goals in 26 total games.

MOST UNPREDICTABLE CAREER
Arthur "Dolly" Swift

SMARTEST PLAYER
Weldy Young played for Ottawa from 1893–99. He hung up his skates only a few years before the blossoming of a dynasty in Ottawa.

BIGGEST FLAKE
Fred Chittick

MOST TRAGIC CAREER
Fred Higginbotham was Winnipeg's brilliant cover-point in the mid to late 1890s. He died in 1897 after being thrown violently from a horse.

PLAYER VERSUS TEAM
Fred Chittick vs. Ottawa Hockey Club, 1899

BEST REGULAR SEASON
The 1888 schedule culminated in an exciting one-game playoff between the MAAA and Montreal Victorias. The former took the title, winning 2–1 on the strength of some fine goaltending by Tom Paton.

BEST STANLEY CUP FINAL
1896
The Winnipeg Victorias hoisted the Cup over their droopy Montreal namesakes.

IMPORTANT RULE CHANGES

1875
• The first set of hockey rules is introduced.

1879
• Teams are reduced to seven players per squad.

EARLY 1880s
• Games consist of two 30-minute halves.

EQUIPMENT CHANGES

1879
• The rubber puck is introduced.

1896
• Goal pads are worn for the first time.

1897
• Hockey gloves are worn for the first time.

1900
• The first modern tube skate is used.

1900
• The first goal net is introduced.

Seeds Were Planted

The first recorded game of ice hockey took place in Montreal in late February 1837. This match, between the Uptowns and Dorchesters, was described by the Montreal *Gazette* as an "ice hurtling" game. The Dorchesters scored the first and only goal of the contest. As if in a scene from a Hollywood film, most of the spectators spilled out onto the ice in a "wild frenzy."

By the time of Canadian Confederation in 1867, ice hockey was still played only in localized pockets and rules had not yet been standardized. Little if any intercity or inter-team play was set up because poor travel and communication links restricted the arrangement of games. The first legitimate game of hockey as we know it, using a (wooden) puck and played under a formal set of rules, was held on March 3, 1875, at Montreal's Victoria Ice Rink. The dimensions of the ice surface were comparable to that of hockey's modern-day facilities: 200 feet by 85. The Montreal *Gazette* reported:

> A game of hockey will be played at the Victoria Ice Rink this evening between two teams from among the members. Good fun may be expected, as some of the players are reported to be exceedingly expert at the game. Some fears have been expressed on the part of the attending spectators that accidents are likely to occur through the ball flying about in a too-lively manner to the imminent danger of onlookers, but we understand that the game will be played with a flat, circular piece of wood . . .

Both clubs were composed entirely of McGill University students, among them J.G.A. Creighton, who drew up a set of rules. This new code of conduct, a hodgepodge of laws from rugby, lacrosse, and field hockey, was entitled the "McGill Rules." They were laid out thus:

- There shall be nine players per side.
- The length of matches shall be dependent on the scoring of three goals.
- There shall be rover, wing, and forward positions.
- A referee shall be present to officiate and to police puck-ragging, particularly on face-offs.
- Some infractions, such as fighting, shall call for a game misconduct penalty.
- The offside rule shall be in effect.

Victoria Ice Rink in Montreal

Some time after 1875, hockey adopted rugby's rule of dividing games into two 45-minute halves, although these halves would later become three 30-minute periods. In 1879, McGill University introduced two very important changes to the McGill Rules:

• Each team shall ice seven players.
• A vulcanized rubber puck shall replace the wooden puck.

The switch to a heavier rubber puck made good sense. Such a disk would be much less likely than wood to fly off in all directions. Clearly, the intent here was to lessen a fan's chance of taking a puck in the kisser.

By the time the MAAA and McGill University clubs were established in 1877, ice hockey had assumed a definite structure and was enjoying ever-widening public support. Two lacrosse clubs in Montreal, and one in Toronto, resolved to organize their own hockey teams. And the McGill Rules were taking on more than just local significance: they were used in the first unofficial world championship hockey match at the 1883 Montreal Winter Carnival. The game, won by McGill, was widely reported and, as such, did wonders for the sport's profile. This exposure was one of the factors inspiring the formation of city leagues and then of teams in two competing cities. The Montreal City Hockey League, the first bona fide hockey league in Canada, was established in 1885 and included Montreal's Victorias, Crystals, Amateur Athletic Association and McGill University. Each team took its nickname either from its sponsor or home rink.

Although the Montreal League was conceived purely as a city league, it wasn't long before officials began discussing the possibilities of including clubs from across Canada in a truly national association. On December 8, 1886, their plans were realized with the birth of the Amateur Hockey Association of Canada (AHAC). Finally there was a hockey league to "improve, foster and perpetuate the game of hockey in Canada and to protect it from professionalism and to promote the cultivation of kindly feeling among the members of the hockey clubs." Although today hockey is one of the world's sporting giants, in 1886 the game was neck-and-neck with snowshoeing as Canada's official winter sport!

The AHAC brass intended to regulate and convene hockey matches throughout Ontario, Quebec, and the Maritimes. But the Association came under intense criticism for representing only the interests of the Quebec clubs. A scathing editorial in the Toronto *Globe* called the AHAC the "Quebec Association." In the fall of 1890, disgruntled Ontario hockey promoters decided to take matters into their own hands, forming their own regulatory body, the Ontario Hockey Association (OHA), to watch over the development of leagues within their province. Among its founders was Arthur Stanley, son of the now-famous Lord Stanley.

The OHA boasted 11 charter members: Queen's University, Royal Military College, "C" Company of the Royal School of Infantry, Toronto Athletic Association, Toronto Lacrosse Club, Osgoode Hall, Toronto Granites, St. George's, Victoria Skating Rink, Rideau Rebels, and Bowmanville. Within a year the OHA had teams representing schools, fire brigades, law offices, and universities.

Unlike the game of baseball, early hockey was socially acceptable. It was a sport for ladies and gentlemen. Every match was a social event, a jamboree. Between periods, a banquet table was spread where one could belly up to piles of ham, roast beef, and pork, and all the trimmings. Some talked hockey, turning tales of mischief and merriment between bites. Some talked business amid billows of cigar smoke. A hometown player might receive a bouquet and a kiss from a doting female fan.

In the early days of organized hockey, prior to 1916, the defensive positions were "point" and "cover-point." Generally, the point man stayed close to his goalie, while the cover-point skated ahead of the point. Typically the point would lob the puck up and out of his home zone or into the rafters. With any luck, the rubber carried into the enemy zone, where a defender would of course try to return the favor. All the while, the forwards skated themselves dizzy trying to position themselves under the falling puck. A team's forwards were usually spread four abreast: one center, two wingers, and a fourth forward, known as a "rover." The rover's role was dependent on the flow of the play and his energy level. The position was akin to that of the midfielder in modern soccer, involving both defense and the creation of plays. Rovers were called upon to be the most offensively creative of the forwards.

The following is an illustration of early team formation:

Goal
Point
Cover-Point
Rover
Wing   Center   Wing

Defenders wore small shin pads that often buckled on the outside while forwards wore even lighter pads under their leggings. Gloves were not introduced until the late 1890s. Early goalies wore shin pads — a patch of fur stuffed down the front of the pants — as well as a pair of light gloves. It was not until the Winnipeg Victorias' G.H. "Whitey" Merritt wore white cricket pads in the 1896 Stanley Cup finals that goalies began to consider heavier protection for their bruised legs.

Years ago, it was not uncommon for a speedy forward to crash between the flag-decorated goal posts, carrying the puck and the goalie with him. The "imaginary line" joining the tops of the posts caused innumerable goal disputes, although the invention of the goal net in 1900 provided the perfect solution.

In the early days, the skates used by most players were single-ended blades tied onto their boots. The double-enders came next, followed by the so-called "tube skates," which were introduced by western teams in the first decade of the twentieth century. The first tube skates, in fact, may have been worn by star forward Jack Marshall when he played for the Winnipeg Victorias in 1900–1901. The skates he used were quite similar to the kind hockey players use today.

Early rinks were far different from the commercial superstructures of today. End and side boards were only a foot high, compelling spectators to be on guard for flying pucks and bodies. If fans became overly belligerent toward players, it was not uncommon to see a hockey player climb over the boards to shut up a loudmouth the old-fashioned way. There was no artificial ice in Canada until 1911, when the Victoria

Arena opened its doors. In the United States, though, man-made hockey rinks were put up as early as 1894. Such modern skating facilities came to replace the outdoor venues, thereby extending the hockey season beyond what the whims of the weather dictated.

Strangely enough, the hottest complaints in early hockey circles were not about low scores, violence during games, or high ticket prices. Rather, they were about hockey clubs' failure to start games on time. Fans found it maddening to have to wait for games to begin, especially when the only heated areas in the rink were the dressing rooms!

Here are a few pre-modern hockey terms along with their modern-day equivalents:

THEN	NOW
bully	face-off at center ice
doing the needful	scoring a goal
face	face-off
fagging	back-checking
fainting	diving
foxing	drawing penalties
winning a game	scoring a goal

That last term is somewhat confusing. Simply put, the time between each goal scored was known as a "game." The team scoring the goal was known to have won that game. Here is an illustration:

- Ottawa is playing Quebec.
- The starting face-off is won by Quebec.
- Play goes on for 12 minutes.
- Ottawa scores.
- Ottawa wins the first game.
- Play goes on for four more minutes.
- Quebec scores.
- Quebec wins their first game of the match.

Perhaps the most enthusiastic booster of pre-1900 hockey was the outgoing governor general of Canada, Sir Frederick Arthur Stanley — Lord Stanley of Preston. He, like the governors general before him, was hotly interested in sports, in how it inspired and entertained people. But the key to Stanley's unflagging support of hockey was the fact that his two sons, Arthur and Algernon, played on the Rideau Rebels. This personal interest led Lord Stanley to sponsor the erection of a large outdoor rink at Rideau Hall and to suggest an awards incentive for the hockey championship of Canada. At a March 18, 1892, banquet at the Ottawa Amateur Athletic Club, it was announced that the absentee Stanley was purchasing a silver "challenge cup." Stanley's proxy, Lord Kilcoursie, stood up and read a speech straight from the horse's mouth: "I have for some time past been thinking that it would be a good thing if there were a challenge cup which should be held from year to year by the champion hockey team in the dominion." After the customary backslapping and glad-handing, Kilcoursie led the crowd in the singing of a most spirited tune, the chorus of which rang:

Then give three cheers for Russell,
The captain of the boys,
However tough the tussle,
His position he enjoys;
And then for all the others,
Let's shout as loud we may:
O-T-T-A-W-A!

So as to be fair and above-board, Stanley appointed a small panel of Cup trustees, the initial members being two prominent Ottawa sportsmen by the name of John Sweetland and Phillip D. Ross. The two men purchased a gold-lined silver bowl, standing on an ebony base, for 10 guineas and brought it to Canada from England.

Lord Stanley

From the very beginning, Stanley's wish was that Cup competitions be wide-open. His intent was to have sporting bodies from all corners of Canada form teams they thought had the best chance of winning and mount a challenge. This system proved workable and eventually there was participation by teams from all quarters of Canada and, later, the United States. In this way, the Stanley Cup was a major contributor to hockey's status as Canada's "national sport."

1894 Montreal AAA

Cup Number One

In over 100 years of Stanley Cup competition, there is only one case in which the silverware has been awarded without a playoff or comparable challenge. It was in 1893, the first year the Cup was awarded, and the first keepers of the Cup were the Montreal AAA, a clean, methodical club led by league-leading 12-goal man Haviland Routh.

After losing its first match to Ottawa, the MAAA swept its remaining seven games to finish ahead of the AHAC pack. Tom Paton was rock-solid between the pipes, or "flags," leading all net-men with a 2.25 goals-against average, while a solid supporting cast of Archie Hodgson, Allan Cameron, and Billy Barlow rallied around Routh.

The MAAA's February 18 meeting with Ottawa turned out to be the championship game as the capital city boys ended up only a hair behind the Montrealers in the standings. It was no contest, though: Barlow potted three second-half goals to lead the MAAA crew to a 7–1 victory. Although the Montrealers were on a roll, a March 3 date with the Montreal Crystals proved a colossal challenge. The A-men fell back 1–0 before scoring two quick "games," after which the Crystals potted the equalizer to round it out at halftime. Early in the second half, a Crystal player was sent off. The team's demand that he be reinstated for the overtime period was met with an equal and opposite reaction by referee Lewis, who refused to budge. The Crystals elected to forfeit the game and the MAAA was handed its fifth win in six games. They would go on to defeat the Montreal Victorias and Crystals (again) to sew up the league title and take the first Cup in hockey history.

Well, not quite yet. Although the MAAA had scratched its way to the top, the Montreal Hockey Club (MHC) was the "official" winner (the Club was connected to the MAAA, albeit partially). At season's end, Cup trustees presented the silverware to the president of the MAAA, who turned it over to the MHC. This is when the MHC refused to take the Cup!

Theories abound regarding this snub. In his outstanding article "The Little Men of Iron," in the *Canadian Journal of History of Sport*, Don Morrow gave pre-modern hockey "second-class status to snowshoeing," so perhaps the MHC didn't think it worth their while to collect the trophy. Others believe the MHC was miffed over not being officially invited to the Cup presentation ceremony. As it turns out, the MAAA took the Cup again in 1894 before being knocked off by the crosstown Victorias in 1895. Soon thereafter, the MHC and MAAA entered into a full merger.

Triple-A for Glory

At the start of the 1894 season, pundits were hailing Quebec as "the" club. The Citadel skaters, disappointed in their 2-5-1 showing of the past season, decided to merge with their intermediate club in an all-out quest for Lord Stanley's mug.

Stars like Arthur "Dolly" Swift and American-born goalie Frank Stocking helped Quebec make a decent lunge out of the starting gates. After losing to the MAAA and Montreal Victorias, Quebec rang off five straight victories, a streak keyed by top-notch defensive work and the stellar play of Stocking.

From the season's outset, the Montreal Crystals were shown to be the league's punching bag. A combination of weak scoring and a porous defense would prove to be their undoing. This did not prevent the Montreal *Gazette* from singing their praises, though: home-team biases were as poorly disguised then as they are today. A perfect example: the day after the Crystals' January 27 match against Quebec, a *Gazette* sportswriter thought the Crystals' defense was "simply superb." The Crystals had lost the game, 8–4.

By the end of the first month of the season, it was clear that the battle for the Stanley Cup would be between Ottawa and the MAAA.

AHAC STANDINGS (January 31, 1894)

Club	GP	W	L	Pts
Ottawa Hockey Club	4	3	1	6
Montreal Amateur Athletic Association	4	3	1	6
Quebec Hockey Club	5	3	2	6
Montreal Victorias	3	1	2	2
Montreal Crystals	4	0	4	0

Through February, the league ledger underwent many changes. The Victorias pulled off two huge wins at home against Ottawa and the MAAA, who stumbled through February at 1-2. Meanwhile, Quebec won both of its February dates and suddenly had a lock on the title with a 5-2 record. Both Ottawa and the A-boys ended up at 4-3 while the Victorias were 3-3 with two games in hand. The MAAA closed their season on March 2 with a cheesy 2–1 victory over the Crystals. They were in the club-house at 5-3 and in desperate need of an Ottawa victory over Quebec. As it turns out, Ottawa blanked Quebec 2–0. Now the AHAC had three teams at 5-3 and the Victorias took their two remaining games against the Crystals to force a four-way tie.

The league convened at Montreal's Queen's Hotel on March 10, 1894, in an attempt to determine the most prudent manner of awarding the Cup. Quebec, for its part, showed little to no interest in a playoff while Ottawa seemed more eager to settle things. As the meeting progressed, Quebec representative A. Laurie came to realize that his team's participation was needed in order to make the playoffs work. All four parties ultimately agreed that Ottawa and the Victorias would play a semifinal in Quebec while Quebec and the MAAA would duke it out in Ottawa. Arrangements were made as such so that no team would enjoy a home-ice advantage. Matter

----

resolved, it was time to make plans for the final match.

Quebec objected hotly to playing their final match at the Crystal Ice Rink. They simply did not want to play there and felt that if the Victorias knocked off Ottawa in the semifinals, they should have a game at the Victorias' rink. Montreal was fully entitled to host a game but Laurie, blind to such notions, withdrew his team from the playoffs. At this time, the AHAC was down to three teams.

Organizing these games had become increasingly difficult. The MAAA wanted to put the names of the teams in a hat and draw for a "bye" into the finals, a suggestion quickly dismissed by Ottawa, who offered to meet the winner of a Victorias–MAAA semifinal. This motion was carried. The MAAA rubbed out the Victorias, 3–2, behind two Billy Barlow goals. In the final match, Archie Hodgson scored twice and Barlow potted the winner as the MAAA struck it 3–1 over the Ottawas.

Ottawa and the Ball Boys

A very long time before Canada began locking horns with the U.S. of A. in huge international hockey competitions, there was a much-heralded three-game series in early 1895 between an American collegiate all-star team and the Ottawa Hockey Club, one of the finest teams in the Dominion of Canada.

The matches were played at the old Rideau Rink in Ottawa on January 2 and 3. At the time of this *tête-à-tête* the American brand of hockey was significantly different from the Canadian game. The Yanks played hockey with a rubber ball instead of a puck, used sticks similar to those used in field hockey, and played on a smaller rink surface. Perhaps queerest of all was the way they lined up their men:

	Goal	
	Quarterback	
Forward	Forward	Forward

Game One, January 2, 1895

"A FOREIGN WINTER GAME PARALYZES THE HOCKEY PLAYERS OF THE CAPITAL"

The Americans arrived in Ottawa from Kingston on the afternoon of the 2nd and registered at the Russell Hotel downtown. The match was played that night under "American" hockey rules, which made for the use of a ball instead of a puck and a shorter distance between the goals.

The Yanks showed themselves to be most deserving of victory, displaying superior ball-handling and fine attention to combination play. At first, it looked as if Ottawa would run away with the game. In good time, though, the Yanks turned it up a notch and had the lead by the end of the first half.

Twenty-one-year-old Alf Smith showed himself to be the "surest and best shot of the forwards" for Ottawa while George Mattison, the American goalkeeper, "won great applause" in nets. Smith opened the scoring at the seven-minute mark, after which the Americans scored thrice. Herbert Russell then counted for Ottawa, making the score 3–2.

Ottawa did nothing to turn the tide back in their favor in the second half. Everyone from Russell to Smith to Chauncey Kirby were rendered impotent as the Yanks took the match 5–3. The happy visitors attended a post-match banquet and, after a good night's sleep, were shown the sights of Ottawa and neighboring Aylmer across the Ottawa River by horse-drawn carriage.

Game Two, January 3, 1895
"THE AMERICAN HOCKEY TEAM AT THE CANADIAN GAME"

Nearly a thousand people showed up to see the second match, this one played under Canadian rules. Ottawa ended up drubbing the American side, 15–1 this time, showing a clear superiority in "simply toying with their opponents."

Despite letting in all 15 goals, George Mattison played well, saving his club from an even more embarrassing defeat. He stood on his head countless times, showing himself to be quite the acrobat. Kirby was the best Ottawan on the ice, although the team as a whole played an excellent passing game. The fabulous Weldy Young led almost every rush the Canadian boys made.

Weldy Loves Dolly

These days, hockey players skilled at drawing penalties are termed "divers" and "actors." Bill Barber and Claude Lemieux are two names that immediately spring to mind. Back in the 1890s, though, penalties, rough play, and tomfoolery were less common. Not many players were known to flagrantly break the rules. Which is not to say there were no bad boys.

Weldon "Chalk" Young, Ottawa's star cover-point, was among the top three defenders in the AHAC from the early to mid 1890s. In his day, diving was referred to as "fainting," so we know it existed. In fact, Young was quite possibly the most skilled fainter of his time.

Star Quebecker Arthur "Dolly" Swift had been carrying on a fierce rivalry with Young for a while. In an 1895 regular-season tussle with Ottawa, Swift decided he'd had his fill of the Ottawa defender's dives, faints, and sneak plays. In the middle of the second half, Young dropped to the ice in a "hot moment" in his end. As if on cue, Swift skated back to his end and grabbed a bucket of water. He then skated back to the prone Young, only to dump the contents of the bucket all over him! Young sprang to his feet, looking like a cross between a drowned rat and a giant ice crystal, and left the ice to change his uniform.

Bonjour, Au Revoir!

The season after refusing to take part in the Stanley Cup playoffs, Quebec again found itself involved in controversy. This time, the club was suspended by league brass prior to their last match of the 1895 season over incidents during a 3–2 loss to Ottawa on February 23.

Throughout the game, Dolly Swift and Weldy Young locked horns with one another. Young was knocked unconscious after the two collided, and Swift was awarded an early ticket to the showers. This skirmish inspired other battles around the rink, resulting in the banishment of Quebec forwards Archie Scott and David Watson. A partisan Quebec crowd grew increasingly ornery over the rulings, screaming bloody murder over what they perceived to be one-sided officiating. They were especially irked that their boys had had a goal called back. At the final bell, spectators grabbed referee Hamilton and umpire Jack Findlay and demanded that the game be declared a draw. Police were called in to save the ruffled officials.

The AHAC convened for a meeting on February 27. President Jack Watson spared no expense in condemning the behavior of the Quebec fans. If their barbarity continued, warned the big cheese, it would be nearly impossible to secure referees for future matches in the city. Ottawa delegate W.C. Young said he had "no complaints to make against the players, but against the barbarian spectators." At length, it was agreed by all that it was no longer fair to ask a man to referee a game in Quebec. The Montreal Crystals' Robert Laing moved that Quebec "be suspended for the balance of the season," a motion of course seconded by Young.

At first glance, Quebec's suspension seems harsh. After all, why should a team have to pay for the sins of its fans? Well, the league brass reasoned that a team is responsible for the conduct of its fans and that, to borrow a tired cliché, desperate times required desperate measures. One must bear in mind that Quebec had few allies among league delegates due to their refusal to play in the 1894 playoffs. Couple this with the fact that the Quebeckers were 2-5 at the time — officially out of the Cup hunt — and the league's decision is not so hard to fathom.

What If?

What follows is a list of the major awards given out today, and our list of hypothetical winners of those trophies. When the NHL started awarding a certain trophy, the list space is left blank. For example, because the NHL first awarded the Hart Trophy in 1924, the post-1923 Hart slots are blank.

Hypothetical awards were based on the following factors:
- Players' abilities, based on a number of reliable sources
- Player statistics
- All-Star Team selections (where possible)

The lists are intended to stimulate good, healthy discussions about those known and those not so known. Feel free to disagree on any of them.

YEAR	HART	VEZINA	NORRIS	SELKE	ART ROSS
1887	J. Campbell	T. Arnton	A. Cameron	F. Dowd	A. Swift
1888	J. Campbell	T. Paton	J. Campbell	J. Findlay	D. Elliott
1889	Tom Paton	T. Paton	A. Cameron	J. Findlay	A. McNaughton
1890	A. McNaughton	T. Paton	A. Cameron	J. Findlay	A. McNaughton
1891	A. Cameron	T. Paton	A. Cameron	B. Barlow	S. Kingan
1892	R. Bradley	A. Morel	J. Stewart	G. Lowe	R. Bradley
1893	H. Routh	T. Paton	W. Young	R. Elliot	H. Routh
1894	Arthur Swift	H. Collins	W. Young	A. Scott	A. Swift
1895	H. Routh	H. Collins	M. Grant	C. Kirby	H. Routh
1896	Mike Grant	F. Chittick	M. Grant	A. Scott	B. McDougall
1897	B. McDougall	F. Chittick	M. Grant	B. Barlow	C. McKerrow
1898	Mike Grant	H. Collins	M. Grant	C. McKerrow	C. Davidson
1899	H. Trihey	J. McKenna	M. Grant	C. McKerrow	H. Trihey
1900	H. Trihey	J. Hutton	H. Stuart	D. Brown	H. Trihey
1901	R. Bowie	J. Hutton	H. Pulford	J. Brannen	R. Bowie
1902	A. Hooper	B. Nicholson / J. Hutton	H. Stuart	H. Westwick	A. Hooper
1903	R. Bowie	B. Nicholson	D. Boon	B. Russell	R. Bowie
1904					
CAHL	R. Bowie	P. Moran	E. O'Brien	B. Russell	R. Bowie
FAHL	J. Marshall	B. Nicholson	B. Strachan	Allen	J. Marshall
1905					
CAHL	R. Bowie	N. Frye	H. Pulford	H. Westwick	R. Bowie
FAHL	F. McGee	D. Finnie	H. Pulford	J. Marshall	F. McGee
1906					
ECAHA	F. McGee	H. Menard	R. Kennedy	H. Westwick	H. Smith
FAHL	P. LeSueur	P. LeSueur	J. Marks	O. McCourt	T. Smith
1907					
ECAHA	E. Russell	R. Hern	H. Stuart	C. Blachford	E. Russell
FAHL	A. Prevost	J. Hunter	A. Lambert	J. Marshall	O. McCourt
1908					
ECAHA	T. Phillips	B. Nicholson	A. Ross	C. Blachford	R. Bowie
OPHL	E. Lalonde	Ellis	J. Marks	E. Lalonde	B. Ridpath
1909					
ECAHA	M. Walsh	R. Hern	F. Taylor	F. Glass	M. Walsh
OPHL	T. Smith	H. Lehman	P. Charlton	D. Smith	T. Smith
1910					
NHA	F. Taylor	R. Hern	F. Taylor	E. Johnson	E. Lalonde
OPHL	O. Frood	H. Lehman	B. Baird	E. Edmunds	O. Frood
1911					
NHA	M. Walsh	G. Vezina	F. Taylor	E. Johnson	M. Walsh
OPHL	T. Smith	J. Jones	G. McNamara	E. Dey	O. Frood
1912					
NHA	E. Ronan	G. Vezina	A. Ross	J. Marks	E. Ronan
PCHA	E. Lalonde	H. Lehman	E. Johnson	T. Phillips	E. Lalonde
1913					
NHA	J. Malone	P. Moran	S. Cleghorn	J. Marks	J. Malone
PCHA	E. Johnson	B. Lindsay	E. Johnson	J. Gardner	T. Dunderdale
1914					
NHA	E. Lalonde	H. Holmes / G. Vezina	H. Cameron	J. Walker	T. Smith
PCHA	T. Dunderdale	B. Lindsay	E. Johnson	G. Poulin	T. Dunderdale

Year	HART	VEZINA	NORRIS	SELKE	ART ROSS
1915					
NHA	T. Smith	C. Benedict	S. Cleghorn	R. Crawford	T. Smith
PCHA	M. MacKay	H. Lehman	L. Patrick	F. Nighbor	M. MacKay
1916					
NHA	E. Lalonde	C. Benedict	H. Cameron	F. Nighbor	E. Lalonde
PCAHA	E. Johnson	T. Murray	E. Johnson	J. Walker	B. Morris
1917					
NHA	F. Nighbor	C. Benedict	S. Cleghorn	R. Crawford	J. Malone
PCHA	G. Roberts	H. Holmes	E. Johnson	J. Walker	G. Roberts
1918					
NHL	J. Malone	G. Vezina	H. Cameron	L. Berlanquette	J. Malone
PCHA	F. Taylor	H. Lehman	L. Cook	J. Walker	F. Taylor
1919					
NHL	E. Lalonde	C. Benedict	H. Cameron	F. Nighbor	O. Cleghorn
PCHA	F. Taylor	H. Holmes	A. Duncan	E. Johnson	F. Taylor
1920					
NHL	J. Malone	C. Benedict	S. Cleghorn	F. Nighbor	J. Malone
PCHA	F. Foyston	H. Holmes	B. Rowe	J. Walker	F. Foyston
1921					
NHL	B. Dye	C. Benedict	E. Gerard	L. Berlanquette	B. Dye
PCHA	F. Foyston	H. Holmes	L. Cook	M. MacKay	F. Foyston
1922					
NHL	F. Nighbor	C. Benedict	G. Boucher	F. Nighbor	H. Broadbent
PCHA	H. Holmes	H. Holmes	W. Loughlin	M. MacKay	J. Adams
WCHL	D. Keats	C. Reid	J. Simpson	R. Crawford	D. Keats
1923					
NHL	C. Benedict	C. Benedict	G. Boucher	F. Nighbor	B. Dye
PCHA	M. MacKay	N. Fowler	L. Cook	M. MacKay	F. Fredrickson
WCHL	E. Lalonde	H. Winkler	J. Simpson	D. Irvin	E. Lalonde
1924	–				
NHL	–	G. Vezina	G. Boucher	H. Broadbent	C. Denneny
PCHA	–	H. Lehman	A. Duncan	J. Walker	M. MacKay
WCHL	–	McCusker	R. Dutton	R. McVeigh	B. Cook
1925					
NHL	–	G. Vezina	S. Cleghorn	L. Berlanquette	B. Dye
WCHL	–	H. Holmes	H. Gardiner	J. Walker	M. MacKay
1926					
NHL	–	A. Connell	G. Boucher	F. Nighbor	N. Stewart
WHL	–	H. Holmes	R. Dutton	F. Boucher	B. Cook
1927	–	–	H. Gardiner	R. McVeigh	B. Cook
1928	–	–	E. Shore	F. Nighbor	H. Morenz
1929	–	–	E. Shore	F. Boucher	A. Bailey
1930	–	–	F. Clancy	F. Finnigan	C. Weiland
1931	–	–	E. Shore	P. Lepine	H. Morenz
1932	–	–	E. Shore	P. Lepine	B. Jackson
1933	–	–	E. Shore	F. Finnigan	B. Cook
1934	–	–	F. Clancy	F. Finnigan	C. Conacher
1935	–	–	E. Shore	H. Smith	C. Conacher
1936	–	–	E. Shore	F. Finnigan	S. Schriner
1937	–	–	B. Siebert	M. Murdoch	S. Schriner
1938	–	–	E. Shore	B. Northcott	G. Drillon
1939	–	–	D. Clapper	M. March	T. Blake
1940	–	–	E. Goodfellow	N. Metz	M. Schmidt
1941	–	–	D. Clapper	N. Colville	B. Cowley

Year	HART	VEZINA	NORRIS	SELKE	ART ROSS
1942	–	–	T. Anderson	N. Metz	B. Hextall
1943	–	–	E. Seibert	B. Davidson	D. Bentley
1944	–	–	E. Seibert	B. Davidson	H. Cain
1945	–	–	B. Hollett	N. Metz	E. Lach
1946	–	–	B. Bouchard	N. Metz	M. Bentley
1947	–	–	K. Reardon	N. Metz	M. Bentley
1948	–	–	J. Stewart	J. Klukay	–
1949	–	–	J. Stewart	T. Leswick	–
1950	–	–	K. Reardon	J. Klukay	–
1951	–	–	R. Kelly	J. Klukay	–
1952	–	–	R. Kelly	J. Klukay	–
1953	–	–	D. Harvey	M. Pavelich	–
1954	–	–	–	M. Pavelich	–
1955	–	–	–	M. Pavelich	–
1956	–	–	–	M. Pavelich	–
1957	–	–	–	M. Pavelich	–
1958	–	–	–	C. Provost	–
1959	–	–	–	D. Marshall	–
1960	–	–	–	D. Marshall	–
1961	–	–	–	G. Armstrong	–
1962	–	–	–	D. Keon	–
1963	–	–	–	D. Keon	–
1964	–	–	–	C. Provost	–
1965	–	–	–	C. Provost	–
1966	–	–	–	C. Provost	–
1967	–	–	–	D. Keon	–
1968	–	–	–	S. Mikita	–
1969	–	–	–	E. Westfall	–
1970	–	–	–	E. Westfall	–
1971	–	–	–	S. Mikita	–
1972	–	–	–	E. Westfall	–
1973	–	–	–	R. Ellis	–
1974	–	–	–	B. Clarke	–
1975	–	–	–	B. Clarke	–
1976	–	–	–	D. Marcotte	–
1977	–	–	–	B. Gainey	–

One Groovy Barn

Before 1900, hockey was played either on outdoor ponds with makeshift grandstands and promenades or in crude shinny barns. Both setups, quaint by today's standards, provided fans little or no respite from the howling winter winds.

On New Year's Eve 1898, a new arena opened in Montreal on the corner of Wood Avenue and St. Catherine Street. The facility, rather uncreatively christened "The Arena," was the first structure of its kind in Canada.

Advertisements for a triple-header opening night featuring Montreal's Victorias, Shamrocks, and MAAA promised a 30-piece band presentation. In place of today's between-periods hot dog and beer was the "finest buffet in recent memory": roast beef with all the trimmings. Twenty-five cents was worth a foot in the door, but it was between 35 and 50 cents for reserved seats and as much as five bucks for a six-seat box.

The Montreal Arena

For a dime, fans could rent a fur rug to shelter their legs from the biting cold. The rugs were said to be "generously large and big enough to protect two persons . . ."

Sportswriters called the Arena a "palatial residence of winter games." Some then-welcome features to the new rink were:

- Well-marked seating areas
- Well-heated lobby by the ticket office
- Steam-heated corridors, waiting rooms, retiring rooms, and buffets
- Wide promenades for those who enjoyed a good walk during intermission

The Arena could hold about 7,000 people — fantastically huge in an era when the average team was lucky to pack 3,000 persons into its roofed sardine can, but a far cry from the decadent 20,000-seat urban castles we call our hockey homes at the dawn of the twenty-first century.

The Curious Case of Fred Chittick

Fred Chittick was Ottawa's goalie from the mid to late 1890s. He was the Pete Peeters of his day — a goalie accustomed to the shield of a rock-solid defense. He led the AHAC in goals-against average in 1896 and 1897, but when Ottawa's defense sagged the next season, his average jumped to 5.25. Let's pick it up there:

It was early 1898. With Ottawa sputtering along at 1-3, Chittick pulled off an extremely bold stunt. Just before a mid-February engagement with the Montreal Victorias, he staged a one-man strike. Why? Because he had not been given his share of complimentary tickets to the game.

A goalie who had surrendered more goals in the first four games of the campaign than he had in the entire season previous would have had little or no leverage with which to pry free tickets from management's buckle. Indeed, who in their right mind would pay to see a goalie who the Montreal *Gazette*, in one of the understatements of the decade, said "had not been playing in championship form"?

Second-stringer Alex Cope was forced to make his debut under strained circumstances. The kid proved no match for the Victorias, who won 9–5. Somehow, the *Gazette*'s sportswriter mustered up the courage to call him a "star." Cope crawled to the season finish line sporting a ghastly 5.75 average. He was not seen again until 1904, when he appeared in two Federal Amateur Hockey League games for the also-ran Ottawa Capitals.

In 1899, Chittick once again found himself on the hot seat. After refereeing all but the last 12 minutes of the Quebec–MAAA game on January 21, he was accused by several MAAA members of being drunk. This understandably got his dander up and he protested that his character was being defamed. He was officially cut from Ottawa upon the appearance of the superb John Bower "Bouse" Hutton. The reasons for Chittick's removal are not well publicized, but it is generally believed that he entered into a dispute with Ottawa management regarding the then-wrongful payment of players. Apparently the fact that team brass "might" have been paying out had his knickers in a twist.

Sportswriters sided with Ottawa on the question of Chittick's expulsion, reasoning that he was a loose cannon. Although he returned to shut out the Quebeckers in the 1901 season finale, Chittick's career was kaput. Save for a bit of refereeing in 1904, he all but fell off the face of the hockey world.

Ticket demands? Money squabbles? Underachievement? From the sounds of it, Chittick was a century ahead of his time.

Flip Trihey: Live at the Ten-Spot

The year 1899 marked the debut of the Canadian Amateur Hockey League (CAHL). There was a new arena in Montreal, the debut of Russell Bowie, the continuing misadventures of Fred Chittick . . . and 10 goals in a game for Harry Trihey.

Ten goals in one game? Indeed. This future lieutenant colonel of Canada's 199th Battalion achieved this feat against Frank Stocking and his sad-sack Quebeckers on February 4. This is a regular-season record that, until now, has been buried under inches of dust.

Trihey, captain of the spiffy Montreal Shamrocks and one of the finer stick-handlers around, bagged a league-best 19 goals in only seven games, tying a four-year-old record. In his finest effort of the season, Trihey scored goals against Quebec in every conceivable way: on a breakaway, down the wing, tip-ins . . . 10 goals in all. Trihey blasted four goals in the first half of play, then began the second half with a natural hat trick. He rounded out a magical night by scoring three of the Shamrocks' last four goals.

As big a deal as 10 goals would be today, observers at the time did not seem overly impressed. The Montreal *Gazette* simply mentioned the "ease" with which he scored ". . . without turning one of his football-like hairs," whatever that was supposed to mean. Considering that star players often scored five or more goals in this era, a 10-goal effort would not have been that remarkable. Still, Trihey's performance has been eclipsed only by "One-Eye" Frank McGee's 14-goal outing for the Ottawa Silver Seven in 1905.

Trihey went on to score the winning goal in the championship-deciding game against Queen's University. After retiring in 1901 with a hand injury, he founded a successful law practice in Montreal.

All the Queen's Men

The 1887 Montreal Victorias finished with a league-best 5-3 record under the guidance of such luminaries as Jack Campbell and Arthur "Dolly" Swift. The V's maintained their winning ways until an 0-3 finish in 1890. After several fruitless campaigns, they attempted a comeback in 1893. They started out on the right foot by defeating the preseason favorite Ottawas 4–3 before playing Quebec to a 1–1 lock. This is when the wheels fell off the wagon. The Victorias dropped their final six decisions to end the campaign at 1-6-1, an effort earning them the keys to the AHAC basement.

Without question, a lack of offense was at the root of the Victorias' failure. They finished last in the league in goals scored and scored two goals or less in half of their outings. Although they played an up-tempo game, there was no teamwork. There was also a lack of experience — the team was a grab bag of boys barely old enough to shave. The newspapers thought it would be a few years before the team was competitive. But many of the players were of star quality: there was future Cup-winner Robert Jones between the pipes. Backing up team captain Edward Irwin on the blue-line were Roland Elliott and Jack Pullen. Norm Rankin starred on the front line as did Shirley Davidson, who in 1893 scored eight goals in six games. Graham Drinkwater also made good in three games. He would have a big hand in the Victorias' fortunes after he graduated from McGill University. In 1894, Bob McDougall and Gordon Lewis were added to the roster, as was defender extraordinaire Mike Grant.

Although it was not easy to replace Campbell on the blue-line, Mike Grant stood very tall. An outstanding skater who at age 11 had won speed skating titles in three different age groups, he subbed for an injured Davidson in a mid-January match against the MAAA. He made his first start on February 10 against the MAAA, an assignment in which he did anything but disappoint. One newspaper reporter spoke of a defender "impossible to get by." In his five starts in 1894, the Victorias went 4-1, allowing but eight goals. And four of these goals came in a February 24 loss to Quebec, a game in which Grant started at forward rather than at his usual cover-point position. The V's finished 5-3, in a four-way tie for the top spot. They ended up losing their playoff tussle 3–2 to the eventual champions, Montreal AAA. In this match, the Victorias were up 2–1 late in the second half when Grant was sent off for roughing. Triple-A scorer Archie Hodgson knotted the affair before Billy Barlow smashed home the winner in extra time. Yet, despite the V's elimination, they had seen remarkable progress.

The Victorias' combination play, or run-and-gun, came together in 1894. Solid forward play combined with Grant's consistent brilliance to provide a two-way punch. In 1895, they captured their first league title, yet they would need an opponent's help in order to capture the Stanley Cup. The Cup trustees had already accepted a challenge from Queen's University against the previous year's champs, Montreal AAA, setting up an interesting scenario: if the Triple-A beat the Golden Gaels of Queen's, the Victorias would be declared Cup champions. But if Queen's won, the Cup would have come to rest in Kingston, Ontario.

The MAAA won 5–1.

Graham Drinkwater climbed aboard the Good Ship Victoria full-time in 1895, and his presence would buttress the forward ranks considerably. The reliable Jones returned as the regular goalie, relieving Lewis. Harold Henderson also came on board, starting at the point in the final four games of the campaign. All things considered, the V's had become a formidable opponent, leading the AHAC in goals scored while allowing the least. Rankin led the team with 11 goals, McDougall and Drinkwater had 10 and 9 respectively, and Davidson added four to complete the forward scoring.

The Victorias took the title again in 1896, finishing the campaign with a 7-1 record. In the middle of the season, the Winnipeg Victorias made their first of many treks across Canada to play for the Cup. In mid-February 1896, they were described as the "greatest and most skillful team that ever played the game." Led by big Dan Bain up front and featuring Roddy Flett at point, Fred Higginbotham at cover, and G.B. "Whitey" Merritt between the pipes, Winnipeg was sure to give Montreal a run for its money.

In the big game, which Winnipeg took 2–0, Higginbotham was praised by observers for having controlled the play. Montreal's reachers were almost unable to get around him and when they did, he snatched the rubber and ran it out of harm's way. Grant, on the other hand, was reproached for lackadaisical play. Many felt that Montreal had been overconfident, perhaps in the belief that eastern hockey was superior to the western style. The Montreal *Gazette* concluded their article on the game by saying, "The Stanley Cup has gone west and it is quite likely to remain there for a considerable length of time." Despite the *Gazette* sportswriter's taste for melodrama, he'd be proven wrong as a prognosticator.

That December, Montreal traveled to Winnipeg in an attempt to reclaim the Cup. Many pundits gave the eastern V's little to no chance of defeating the hearty Pegs. Six of the seven players from the team that beat Montreal in February were back, but the death of Higginbotham had left a gaping hole in the team's defense.

Almost from the get-go, the hype surrounding Winnipeg was justified. They jumped to a 3–0 lead on goals by Bain, Howard, and C.J. "Tote" Campbell. Montreal struck back with goals by Davidson and Ernie McLea before Howard's second goal of the game put Winnipeg back in front by two. Montreal opened the second half like a house on fire, eager to silence their naysayers. Six minutes in, Davidson whizzed in his second of the night, followed shortly thereafter by McLea's equalizer.

At this point, Winnipeg was on its heels. As the prairie boys fell back, McDougall dashed coast to coast and shoveled one in to give the easterners their first lead of the night. In a panic, Winnipeg demanded an umpire switch similar to the one Grant had asked for in the first half. After a 20-minute delay, Bain rammed in his second of the game to knot things up again. The Winnipeg Rink erupted! Only minutes later, though, Davidson and McLea worked the puck beautifully into the Winnipeg zone, McLea finding the range for the final goal of the game. Montreal had regained the Cup!

In 1897, the champion Victorias steam-rolled the rest of the league en route to a 7-1 record. The feisty McDougall led the team with 11 goals while McLea backed up a fine Stanley Cup showing with eight in eight games. There were no serious challenges for the Cup in 1897, though. Only the also-ran Ottawa Capitals had the guts to lodge a formal challenge, and although they put up a good fight, they proved no match for the mighty V's. The final score was 15–2! Little wonder the Caps threw in the towel.

In 1898, the Victorias made it three in a row with a team some say was their most dominant. This time around, it was Frank Richardson between the pipes for five games, Hartland McDougall replacing Henderson at point, and Cam Davidson stepping in to replace Shirley Davidson up front. Fortunately for the Vics, this jumbling of the ranks did not hinder offensive production. Cam Davidson scored a league-best 14 times despite missing a game, while Bob McDougall and captain Drinkwater had 12 and 10 respectively. It comes as no surprise that no one came forward to challenge the V's for the Cup in 1898. The team that had butchered the Capitals in the previous season's playoff was even stronger now. Western teams saw little point in traipsing halfway across Canada for a buggy-whipping while teams from the smaller leagues were petrified. The Queen's Men were at their peak.

Although the AHAC folded before the 1899 season, the Victorias did not miss a beat. Their first year in the new CAHL yielded a 6-2 record, second only to the Montreal Shamrocks. In their last game of the year, with title and Cup at stake, the Victorias fell 1–0 to the Shamrocks on a Harry Trihey marker.

In the off-season, Drinkwater was moved to point to make room for Russell Bowie, who would team with Cam Davidson, McDougall, and McLea to form another strong forward unit. The 20-year-old Bowie scored 11 goals in seven games.

In the first game of Montreal's February 1899 defense of the Cup, Winnipeg rookie sensation Tony Gingras zipped in the opening goal. This lead lasted until only 90 seconds remained on the clock. Then, like a flash of lightning, Bob McDougall knotted the affair. With the crowd in a frenzy Drinkwater went coast to coast for a game-winner made to order for a Hollywood script. Montreal walked off with the 2–1 win.

Game two saw the unfolding of one of the biggest controversies in Cup history. With a 3–2 Montreal lead late in the second half, Bob McDougall savagely slashed Gingras on the leg. Referee Jack Findlay penalized McDougall for only two minutes

1895 Montreal Victorias

and the Winnipeg players were fit to be tied! After much bantering, Findlay left the building, refusing to explain himself. Officials were sent after Findlay and, in time, they were able to persuade him to return. Findlay gave Winnipeg 15 minutes to return to the ice. Without enough players to ice a team — most players were out carousing — Winnipeg was forced to forfeit the match. The Shamrocks took hold of the Cup by virtue of their regular-season title.

In 1900, the Victorias collapsed. They finished the schedule with a dismal 2-6 record. Only Bowie could escape blame, scoring 15 goals to take his place among the league's top guns. The departures of Lewis, Grant, Drinkwater, Davidson, and McLea were the very last nails on the coffin.

Every dynasty must come to an end, and some go more gracefully than others. The Victorias continued in the CAHL and its successor, the Eastern Canadian Amateur Hockey Association, until 1908. Perhaps the demands of professionalism were too much for the staunchly amateur Victorias. They finished at 4-6 in their last season, then folded, along with the 1-9 MAAA, who were similarly lost in the new professional game.

Snap!shots

DAN BAIN (The Masked Man, Big Dan)   Center
b. 2/14/1874, Belleville, Ontario
d. 8/15/1962, Winnipeg, Manitoba

Dan Bain

Canada's greatest athlete of the last half of the nineteenth century was Manitoba's roller-skating and cycling champ, Winnipeg's top gymnast, Canada's top trapshooter throughout the 1890s, and a champion figure skater and lacrosse player.

Dan Bain first skated for the Winnipeg Victorias in 1896 after answering an advertisement in the local newspaper. He made an almost immediate impact with club management and would assume a leadership role before long. He led Winnipeg to the Stanley Cup in 1896 and again in 1901, scoring a total of 10 goals in 11 Stanley Cup contests. In the 1901 Cup finals, he donned a crude wooden face mask to shield his broken nose. From then on, the media referred to him as the "Masked Man," a nickname that stuck even after his nose had healed.

Besides being a fabulous skater, the muscular, mustachioed Bain was a sure stickhandler who possessed a superb, heavy shot and a knack for setting up goals. He also excelled in the physical aspects of the game and was known throughout Canada as a brilliant all-around "hockeyist." The only quality he seemed to lack was patience with those unable to keep up with him in a game. In the early 1960s, he was interviewed at his country cottage, and he had a few choice words regarding the modern game of hockey: "They can't stick-handle or pass in today's game. I can't stand to watch it! When we passed in my day on the ice, the puck never left the ice and if a wing-man wasn't there to receive the pass, it was because he had a broken leg."

Bain was one of the 12 charter members of the Hockey Hall of Fame in 1945.

Peak Years   *1897–1901*
In a Word   *TREMENDOUS*

ALLAN CAMERON (Eagle-Eye) Defense
b. 1863
d. 1940

Allan Cameron entered organized hockey via the Montreal Crystals before 1885. He toiled with the C's until 1887, when the MAAA snapped him up. The mustachioed "toque bleu tromper" — loosely translated, "the rusher in the blue toque" — would flower into a top-flight cover-point, captaining the famous Winged Wheelers until his retirement in 1895.

Year after year, the MAAA iced players such as Tom Paton, Jack Findlay, "Bunnie" Lowe, and Archie McNaughton. Add to this list the defense pairing of Cameron and James Stewart and the MAAA were not to be taken lightly. While Stewart played a steady, stay-at-home style, Cameron was the very engine of the Wheeler attack. He was quite simply the most complete player of the 1880s. His genius for the two-way game was soon the talk of the circuit. According to newsmen, "nothing escaped Cameron's eyes." His defensive abilities were every bit as sharp as Stewart's and possibly the finest in the AHAC.

Cameron was an outstanding lacrosse player, starring on Montreal's superb Dominion of Canada teams of the 1880s. As a matter of fact, he was the only player to be on national championship hockey and lacrosse teams at the same time. After his playing days, he served as an executive in the MAAA organization.

Peak Years   *1888–92*
In a Word   *LINCHPIN*

JACK CAMPBELL Defense

Of the claims made as to who was the first rushing defender, Jack Campbell's is one of the more plausible. He was arguably the hockey star, headlining the Montreal Victorias from 1884 until 1891. With him on the blue-line, the Queen's Men finished first in 1887 and 1888.

Although solid defensively — and strong as a bull — Campbell's "old-time runs" drew the most applause. He was a marvelous skater, a smooth stick-handler, and among the best in the league at scoring goals, or "doing the needful." He was the first true "franchise player" and consequently the first star player to be consistently double- and triple-teamed by enemy checkers.

Matches between the Victorias and MAAA featured a fierce rivalry between Campbell and the great Allan Cameron. It must have been a treat to see these two quarterbacks trading rushes in a battle for hockey supremacy.

Campbell was granddaddy to a new breed of rushers including Mike Grant, Weldy Young, Magnus Flett, and Dickie Boon.

Peak Years   *1885–89*
In a Word   *ORIGINAL*

GRAHAM DRINKWATER Forward/Defense
5'11" 165
b. 2/22/1875, Montreal, Quebec
d. 9/27/1946

Graham Drinkwater

Time has all but buried the memory of Charles Graham Drinkwater, one of organized hockey's first true stars. The lanky forward first found success in hockey while attending McGill University, leading the MAAA Junior hockeyists to a championship in 1892–93. The following season, he won a championship with McGill's Junior football team and by 1895 he was a member of the Montreal Victorias. He would captain the club during his final two years, 1898 and 1899.

Drinkwater was a fine two-way talent, a star on defense beside Mike Grant as well as a standout center. Drinkwater skated with long, flowing strides and he combined polished all-around skills with uncanny battle sense. These tools enabled him to play a key role in four Stanley Cup victories. In 37 games, he scored 30 goals.

Drinkwater was inducted into the Hockey Hall of Fame in 1950.

Peak Years   *1895–99*
In a Word   *OUTSTANDING*

MIKE GRANT Defense
5'10" 170
b. 1/1874, Montreal, Quebec
d. 8/19/1955, Montreal, Quebec

Mike Grant

Mike Grant was one of hockey's first celebrities. From what is known, he literally packed arenas across eastern Canada from the mid 1890s onward. He was the first player about whom newspapermen consistently wrote and, although Jack

----

Campbell was probably the first of the pre-modern rushers, Grant was quite certainly the finest.

Grant showed great athletic ability early in life, winning speed skating titles in three different age categories. As a teen, he earned a solid reputation among Montreal's Junior hockey community. Several "seconds," or agents, for AHAC clubs approached the blacksmith's son, guaranteeing him a spot on their sides. He hung back, though, if only because he felt tied to his family's businesses. He was afraid his father would disapprove.

Then, just before the start of the 1892 hockey season, he was permitted to try out for the Young Crystals, the Montreal Crystals' Junior club. He made the team with ease and within a season was captain. Grant was snatched up by the Montreal Victorias in late 1893, and he would captain this club to Stanley Cup victories in 1895, 1896, and 1897. In 1901, he joined the Montreal Shamrocks before finishing his glorious career back with the Victorias.

After a refereeing stint, Grant became the first Canadian ambassador for the game of hockey in the United States. He embarked on many goodwill ventures to America, playing in exhibition games and "giving much good advice on skating and hockey to our neighbors across the border."

As a player, Grant did much to popularize the rush. His skating ability, both in terms of flat-out speed and overall power, was in a class of its own. He had a roguish air to him that served to fan the flames of fans' imaginations. It's easy to picture him tearing up the ice on one of his famous rushes, his trademark handlebar mustache twitching in the cool, heavy, night air.

As a side note, Grant's oldest son Donald, a wizard on Wall Street, became a top executive with major league baseball's New York Mets in 1962.

Mike Grant was elected to the Hockey Hall of Fame in 1950.

Peak Years   *1895–99*
In a Word   *SWASHBUCKLER*

CLARE McKERROW Center/Rover
b. 1877
d. 10/20/1959, Montreal, Quebec

Clarence McKerrow got his break with the MAAA in 1895 when he was called upon to replace an injured Billy Barlow in a Stanley Cup match against Queen's University. The young center/rover proved himself rather quickly, scoring a goal within minutes of being brought on.

McKerrow was a true gentleman, a honey of a skater, a natural goal scorer, and a diligent checker. Indeed, he was as determined on the lacrosse pitch as he was on the ice: he would captain the Canadian national lacrosse team in the 1908 Summer Olympics. Edouard "Newsy" Lalonde, often called the greatest lacrosse player of all time, said McKerrow gave him the most trouble on the lacrosse field.

McKerrow is said to have had the profoundest influence on the greatest hockey mind of the twentieth century, Lester Patrick. As a youngster, Patrick would go and watch the MAAA players practice. On one occasion, he mustered up the sass to ask the great McKerrow if he could carry his sticks and equipment bag. McKerrow took an almost immediate shine to the tall youth and the rest is, as they say, history. Later in his life, Patrick was quoted as saying that "it was Mr. McKerrow who taught me to carry myself with a certain air and act with class."

Peak Years   *1896–1900*
In a Word   *STYLISH*

TOM PATON Goal

Tom Paton was one of the founding members of the MAAA, an organization born when the Montreal Lacrosse and Snowshoe clubs merged. Paton, or "Tommy" as fans knew him, put in 12 seasons on the Montreal Lacrosse Club and was apparently one of the "trickiest" players in the Dominion. He was a stellar goalkeeper, putting together solid efforts from 1887 through the 1894 season. The short time he did spend playing for the MAAA was well spent indeed. He was, simply put, a gem.

In the 1889 final match, the Triple-A bashed the Montreal Victorias 6–1, thanks in large part to Paton's work between the pipes. According to records, he single-handedly kept the MAAA in the game long enough to ensure the victory.

Paton was one of the finest goalies of the pre-NHL era.

Peak Years   *1888–92*
In a Word   *WINNER*

HARVEY PULFORD (The Bytown Slugger)   Defense
6'1" 195
b. 4/22/1875, Toronto, Ontario
d. 10/31/1940, Ottawa, Ontario

Harvey Pulford

Few men in the annals of Canadian sport can touch Harvey Pulford's record of pure athleticism. Among his accomplishments are city, national, and international titles in hockey, football, lacrosse, rowing, paddling, boxing, and squash. He would place alongside Lionel Conacher as the top Canadian athlete of the first half of the twentieth century.

Pulford made his hockey debut in 1894 on the Ottawa Club, learning the tricks of the trade under the tutelage of the great Weldy Young. The raw-boned Pulford was seen to indulge in something rare in the league in those days: body-checking. Young taught Pulford the fine art of defending — when to hit, when to clear the puck away, when to carry. As he was not the nimblest afoot, he assumed a stay-at-home style.

Pulford also captained the Ottawa Rough Rider football team from 1894 to 1909 and starred for the Ottawa Capitals lacrosse club from 1896 to 1900. He was quite possibly the finest athlete ever to have come out of eastern Ontario.

The sight of big Pulford on defense struck waves of fear through the hearts of the enemy. He could take out a man with hits that "could have crippled even the Creator himself." All hyperbole aside, he was a bruiser, a battleship on blades. His immense talent was showcased in the 1905 Stanley Cup challenge series against the team from Rat Portage.

When the Thistles took game one, 9–3, Ottawa brass ordered Pulford to start throwing his weight around. The result was one of the most impressive displays of one-man ganging ever seen, and his teammates were sufficiently inspired to win the next two games, 4–2 and 5–4, and claim the Stanley Cup.

Pulford was Ottawa's captain from 1900 until 1906. He retired from hockey after the 1908 season as one of the hardest men in hockey.

Pulford was one of the first 12 men elected to the Hockey Hall of Fame in 1945.

Peak Years   *1899–1903*
In a Word   *STRAPPING*

HAVILAND ROUTH Forward
b. 1872, Montreal, Quebec
d. 1/1959

Sniper. Speedster. Shooter. These three words best describe the city of Montreal's first great goal-getter, Haviland Routh. The thickly-muscled, mustachioed MAAA winger was the blazing force behind Winged Wheeler Cup victories in 1893 and 1894. He was the AHAC's leading scorer in 1893 (12 goals in seven games) and again in 1895 (19 goals in eight games).

Although Routh was capable of skating or stick-handling his way through an enemy line, he was apparently one of the least conscientious defensive players of his time. He was always out for the goal, leaving the less glamorous pursuits to others. In modern terms, he was comparable in this sense to a young Brett Hull.

In 24 contests, Routh scored 39 times.

Peak Years   *1893–96*
In a Word   *THOROUGHBRED*

DOLLY SWIFT Rover/Defense

Arthur "Dolly" Swift played for the Montreal Victorias as far back as 1884. He had a most unnatural style — he carried the puck ahead of him, stick-handling with one hand — which was apparently quite distracting to play against. In any case, he was one of the more intelligent, innovative hockey players of hockey's pre-modern era.

Swift was one half of the first bona fide player rivalry in hockey, the other half being Weldy Young. Swift and Young clashed whenever Quebec and Ottawa met, their most famous get-together coming during a February 23, 1895, match in l'Ancien Capital. On this night the two men put on a most barbaric display that resulted in the Quebec club's suspension for the rest of the season and playoffs.

Although Swift would often be used on the defense, he was a natural rover. He hung up the skates after the 1899 season, seeing action in World War I as a Canadian Brigadier General.

Peak Years   *1892–96*
In a Word   *WILY*

HARRY TRIHEY (Flip) Rover/Center
b. 12/25/1877, Montreal, Quebec
d. 8/15/1942, Montreal, Quebec

Harry Trihey

Harry Judah Trihey also excelled in lacrosse and football, but it is his work in the game of hockey for which he is best remembered. This goal-scoring center captained the great Montreal Shamrocks around the turn of the twentieth century. With the help of fellow McGill University collegians Jack Brannen, Art Farrell, and Fred Scanlon, Trihey led the Irish to Stanley Cup glory in 1899 and 1900.

Trihey was an exceedingly fluid stick-handler. Although not of the run-and-gun persuasion, he had superior anticipation as well as a devastatingly hard shot. He called on these skills often, leading the CAHL in scoring in 1899 and 1900.

Trihey was the first to make use of a three-man forward line — today's center and two wingers — thus leaving his rover free to roam. He was also known for his "flip shot," with which he would lift the puck high into the air and try to land it behind the opposing goalie's shoulders. Montreal Canadiens defender Jean-Claude Tremblay tried his hand at something similar about 65 years later.

Trihey retired at the end of the 1901 season with a broken hand, and went on to become secretary-treasurer and ultimately president of the CAHL. He would also establish a successful law practice in Montreal and serve in World War I.

Trihey was inducted posthumously into the Hockey Hall of Fame in 1950. In 30 games, he scored 46 goals.

Peak Years   *1898–1901*
In a Word   *HOWITZER*

WELDY YOUNG (Chalk) Defense

Weldon Young was Ottawa's only world-caliber player at the beginning of the 1890s. Like the Montreal Victorias' Mike Grant, Young loved to rush. But it was his taste for the rough stuff that set him apart from the pack. Although the physical game was a passion of his, it was a very precise passion. Instead of hitting men willy-nilly, he would pick his spots, making the most of every situation.

Young was a hated man, even in Ottawa. He was a notoriously mean individual with a permanent scowl across his face. For a while, he was one half of a feared defensive partnership with big Pete Charlton; like Sprague Cleghorn and Billy Coutu some 30 years later, the Young-Charlton connection was feared and hated but highly respected around the horn.

Young was the de facto leader of the Ottawas through the 1890s, effecting a devilish streak in a team decidedly lacking in color. After retiring, he served in Ottawa's front office for about 20 years.

Peak Years   *1893–96*
In a Word   *WOLVERINE*

Statistics

The following is a preliminary piecing together of the statistical "black hole" of hockey history. A few of the seasons between 1887 and 1892 were fragmented and schedules as such were unheard of. Instead, over the course of a few months, the previous season's champion would accept challenges from other teams. If the challengers managed to defeat the champions, the title would change hands immediately. This procedure would continue until the season ended (meaning, the ice was no longer playable) in mid-March, at which time an official Dominion champion was declared. Of the six pre–Stanley Cup "seasons" in organized hockey, only the 1888 campaign stuck to something remotely resembling a formal schedule.

For various reasons, the period from 1887–92 in organized hockey has been overlooked. The following is merely an affirmation that, indeed, there was life before Lord Stanley.

1887 AMATEUR HOCKEY ASSOCIATION OF CANADA

Club	GP	W	L	T	Pts	WPct	GF	GA
Montreal Victorias	8	5	3	0	10	0.625	23	12
Montreal Amateur Athletic Association	4	3	1	0	6	0.750	8	5
Montreal Crystals	5	2	3	0	4	0.400	6	10
Ottawa Hockey Club	1	0	1	0	0	0.000	1	5
McGill University Hockey Club	2	0	2	0	0	0.000	2	8

Midway through the schedule, Montreal Crystals forward Frank Dowd won a speed skating race at the Crystal Ice Rink against fellow "hockeyists" Sam Lee, Desse Brown, William Drysdale, and Charles Gordon. The win cemented Dowd's reputation as the fastest bladesman in the Dominion of Canada.

Scoring

Player	Club	GP	G	A	Pts	PIM
Swift, Arthur	Victorias	4	7	-	7	-
Hodgson, Billy	MAAA	4	4	-	4	-
Craven, J.	Victorias	6	4	-	4	-
Campbell, Jack	Victorias	7	3	-	3	-
Dowd, Frank	Crystals	3	2	-	2	-
McQuisten, Sam	Crystals	3	2	-	2	-
Findlay, Jack	MAAA	4	2	-	2	-
Arnton, Jack	Victorias	5	2	-	2	-
Shearer, Andy	Victorias	7	2	-	2	-

Goaltending

Goalie	Club	GP	Mins	GAA	W	L	T	ShO	GA	SvPct
Arnton, Jack	Victorias	1	60	0.00	1	0	0	1	0	-
Norris, Jack	Crystals	2	120	1.00	-	-	-	0	2	-
Boon, G.	Crystals	1	60	1.00	-	-	-	0	1	-
Craven, J.	Victorias	1	60	1.00	-	-	-	0	1	-
Hutchinson, W.	MAAA	4	240	1.25	3	1	0	3	5	-
Arnton, Tom	Victorias	6	360	1.83	-	-	-	1	11	-
Norris, J.	Crystals	1	60	3.00	0	1	0	0	3	-
Shanks, A.	McGill/Crystals	2	120	3.50	-	-	-	0	7	-
Holden, D.	McGill	1	60	5.00	0	1	0	0	5	-

Although the Montreal Amateur Association won the Montreal Winter Carnival tournament, no champion was officially declared for the 1887 season.

1888 AMATEUR HOCKEY ASSOCIATION OF CANADA

Club	GP	W	L	T	Pts	WPct	GF	GA
Montreal Amateur Athletic Association	7	6	1	0	12	0.857	23	9
Montreal Victorias	7	5	2	0	10	0.714	25	11
Montreal Crystals	6	2	4	0	4	0.333	18	14
McGill University Hockey Club	6	0	6	0	0	0.000	6	38

Note: italics denote the national champion between 1888 and 1892, and the Stanley Cup champion from 1893 on.

Scoring

Player	Club	GP	G	A	Pts	PIM
Elliott, D.A.	Crystals	6	8	-	8	-
Campbell, Jack	Victorias	7	8	-	8	-
McNaughton, Archie	MAAA	2	6	-	6	-
Ashe, Fred	Victorias	5	5	-	5	-
Kinghorn, James	Victorias	7	5	-	5	-
Lee, Sam	Crystals	4	4	-	4	-
Hodgson, Archie	MAAA	5	4	-	4	-
Shearer, Andy	Victorias	7	4	-	4	-

Goaltending

Goalie	Club	GP	Mins	GAA	W	L	T	ShO	GA	SvPct
Scanlan, Robert	Crystals	1	60	1.00	1	0	0	0	1	-
Paton, Tom	MAAA	6	360	1.17	5	1	0	1	7	-
Crathern, J.C.	Victorias	5	300	1.20	-	-	-	1	6	-
Arnton, Tom	Victorias	2	120	2.00	-	-	-	0	4	-
Higginson, A.G.	MAAA	1	60	2.00	1	0	0	0	2	-
Virtue, William	Crystals	4	240	2.50	-	-	-	0	9	-
Norris, Jack	Crystals	1	60	4.00	0	1	0	0	4	-
Shanks, A.	McGill	5	300	5.80	0	5	0	0	29	-
McCaffrey, Ed	McGill	1	60	6.00	0	1	0	0	6	-

1889 AMATEUR HOCKEY ASSOCIATION OF CANADA

Club	GP	W	L	T	Pts	WPct	GF	GA
Montreal Amateur Athletic Association	5	4	1	0	8	0.800	21	7
Montreal Crystals	4	2	2	0	4	0.500	9	10
Montreal Victorias	2	1	1	0	2	0.500	4	8
Quebec Hockey Club	1	0	1	0	0	0.000	2	3
Halifax Chebuctos	2	0	2	0	0	0.000	2	10

Unseasonably mild weather in Montreal in January and February shortened the 1889 season to seven matches.

Scoring

Player	Club	GP	G	A	Pts	PIM
McNaughton, Archie	MAAA	5	7	-	7	-
Hodgson, Archie	MAAA	5	6	-	6	-
Lee, Sam	Crystals	4	5	-	5	-
Findlay, Jack	MAAA	5	5	-	5	-
Swift, Arthur	Quebec	1	2	-	2	-
Virtue, William	Victorias	2	2	-	2	-

Brown, Desse		Crystals	4	2	-	2	-
Lowe, George		MAAA	4	2	-	2	-

Goaltending

Goalie	Club	GP	Mins	GAA	W	L	T	ShO	GA	SvPct
Paton, Tom	MAAA	5	300	1.17	4	1	0	1	7	-
Norris, Jack	Crystals	3	180	2.00	2	1	0	0	6	-
Arnton, Tom	Victorias	1	60	2.00	1	0	0	0	2	-
Laurie, A.	Quebec	1	60	3.00	0	1	0	0	3	-
Scanlan, Robert	Crystals	1	60	4.00	0	1	0	0	4	-
Brown, J.	Chebuctos	2	120	5.00	0	2	0	0	10	-
Jones, Robert	Victorias	1	60	6.00	0	1	0	0	6	-

1890 AMATEUR HOCKEY ASSOCIATION OF CANADA

Club	GP	W	L	T	Pts	WPct	GF	GA
Montreal Amateur Athletic Association	*8*	*8*	*0*	*0*	*16*	*1.000*	*33*	*17*
Quebec Hockey Club	1	0	1	0	0	0.000	1	5
Montreal Dominions	3	0	3	0	0	0.000	8	15
Montreal Victorias	4	0	4	0	0	0.000	8	13

Scoring

Player	Club	GP	G	A	Pts	PIM
McNaughton, Archie	MAAA	7	14	-	14	-
Kingan, Sam	MAAA	3	6	-	6	-
Findlay, Jack	MAAA-Victorias	8	5	-	5	-
Brown, Desse	Dominions	3	4	-	4	-
Elliott, Roland	MAAA	8	4	-	4	-
Fairbanks, F.	Victorias	2	3	-	3	-

Goaltending

Goalie	Club	GP	Mins	GAA	W	L	T	ShO	GA	SvPct
Paton, Tom	MAAA	8	480	1.75	8	0	0	0	17	-
Jones, Robert	Victorias	3	180	2.67	0	3	0	0	8	-
Fyfe, Joe	Dominions	1	60	3.00	0	1	0	0	3	-
Laurie, A.	Quebec	1	60	5.00	0	1	0	0	5	-
Shaw	Victorias	1	60	5.00	0	1	0	0	5	-
Scanlan, Robert	Dominions	2	120	6.00	0	2	0	0	12	-

1891 AMATEUR HOCKEY ASSOCIATION OF CANADA

Club	GP	W	L	T	Pts	WPct	GF	GA
Montreal Amateur Athletic Association	*5*	*5*	*0*	*0*	*10*	*1.000*	*18*	*4*
Ottawa Hockey Club	2	1	1	0	2	0.500	1	3
Montreal Shamrocks	2	0	2	0	0	0.000	2	9
Montreal Victorias	3	0	3	0	0	0.000	2	7

Scoring

Player	Club	GP	G	A	Pts	PIM
Kingan, Sam	MAAA	5	6	-	6	-
Lowe, George	MAAA	4	4	-	4	-
Findlay, Jack	MAAA	3	3	-	3	-
McNaughton, Archie	MAAA	4	3	-	3	-

Goaltending

Goalie	Club	GP	Mins	GAA	W	L	T	ShO	GA	SvPct
Paton, Tom	MAAA	5	300	0.80	5	0	0	1	3	-
Morel, A.	Ottawa	2	120	1.50	1	1	0	1	3	-
Jones, Robert	Victorias	3	180	2.33	0	3	0	0	7	-
McKenna, Joe	Shamrocks	2	120	4.50	0	2	0	0	9	-

1892 AMATEUR HOCKEY ASSOCIATION OF CANADA

Club	GP	W	L	T	Pts	WPct	GF	GA
Ottawa Hockey Club	6	5	1	0	10	0.833	23	9
Montreal Amateur Athletic Association	*6*	*1*	*4*	*1*	*3*	*0.250*	*9*	*21*
Montreal Shamrocks	1	1	0	0	2	1.000	2	1
Britannias Hockey Club	1	0	0	1	1	0.500	2	2
Quebec Hockey Club	2	0	2	0	0	0.000	3	6

March 7, 1892
Montreal AAA 1 Ottawa Hockey Club 0

Almost everyone expected Ottawa to take this one. They were 10–8 betting favorites. The Montreal AAA, however, had different plans. "After the final whistle sounded, the Montrealers went wild with the excitement over the victory," wrote one journalist. "The members of the team had many compliments showered on them. They returned home at 11 o'clock [p.m.], one of the jolliest excursion parties that ever left the Capital."

An article in the Montreal Gazette *had many Ottawa fans "very sore" over the result, with not one good thing said about referee Jack Arnton. The AHAC official was being accused of allowing Montreal too many breaks over the course of the match. The fans said it was "a fixture" (a fix) for Arnton to allow the visitors breathers at their behest. One angry Ottawan sent this to the Gazette: "Our hockey team can lick yours any day on ice and at hockey; but in a lake and at breaking laces, to gain time and wind, we confess we are not in it."*

A number of fans wrote letters to the Gazette questioning the validity of the whole challenge system. Their question was short and sweet: How was it fair that the Ottawa Hockey Club, a team with a much better overall record on the season, could lose the championship to the 1-4-1 Montreal AAA? The Gazette 's response was that Ottawa had chosen the challenge system over the tournament and that "this is how they are getting back some of their own medicine." The newspaper would later jab: "Petulance is a characteristic of childhood. Ottawa is a little young yet and will know better when it reaches the age of reason."

Scoring

Player	Club	GP	G	A	Pts	PIM
Bradley, Robert	Ottawa	6	9	-	9	-
Kirby, Holder	Ottawa	5	4	-	4	-
Kerr, J.	Ottawa	6	4	-	4	-
Kirby, Chauncey	Ottawa	5	3	-	3	-
Russell, Herb	Ottawa	6	3	-	3	-
Lee, Sam	MAAA	4	2	-	2	-
Lowe, George	MAAA	6	2	-	2	-

Goaltending

Goalie	Club	GP	Mins	GAA	W	L	T	ShO	GA	SvPct
Fyfe, Joe	Shamrocks	1	60	1.00	1	0	0	0	1	-
Morel, A.	Ottawa	6	360	1.50	5	1	0	1	9	-
Cameron, W.	Britannias	1	60	2.00	0	0	1	0	2	-
Paton, Tom	MAAA	5	300	2.20	1	3	1	1	11	-
Patton, Bob	Quebec	2	120	3.00	0	2	0	0	6	-
Shaw	MAAA	1	60	10.00	0	1	0	0	10	-

The All-Stars

Position	Player	Season	GP	G		
P	Allan Cameron	1889	5	1		
CP	Mike Grant	1896	8	3		
R	Arthur Swift	1893	8	11		
LW	Dan Bain		STATS NOT AVAILABLE			
C	Harry Trihey	1899	7	19		
RW	Haviland Routh	1895	8	19		
					GAA	**ShO**
G	Tom Paton	1889	5		1.17	1

The
Oughts

In a Flash

COMPOSITE REGULAR-SEASON STANDINGS
(January 1, 1900–December 31, 1909)

Canadian Amateur Hockey League
Eastern Canadian Amateur Hockey Association

Club	GP	W	L	T	Pts	WPct	GF	GA
Ottawa HC/Silver Seven/Senators	82	59	22	1	119	0.726	544	305
Montreal Victorias	80	46	33	1	93	0.581	562	446
Quebec Hockey Club	91	38	53	0	76	0.418	516	595
Montreal Wanderers	42	36	6	0	72	0.857	324	190
Montreal AAA	79	35	44	0	70	0.443	383	449
Montreal Shamrocks	92	25	67	0	50	0.272	379	667
Westmount Hockey Club	10	3	7	0	6	0.300	55	75
Montreal Nationals	10	0	10	0	0	0.000	6	42

Federal Amateur Hockey League

Club	GP	W	L	T	Pts	WPct	GF	GA
Cornwall Hockey Club	31	13	17	1	27	0.435	112	133
Montreal Wanderers	14	12	2	0	24	0.857	82	45
Ottawa Victorias	19	10	8	1	21	0.553	91	96
Ottawa Montagnards	23	8	13	2	18	0.391	95	154
Smiths Falls Hockey Club	7	7	0	0	14	1.000	35	13
Ottawa Silver Seven	8	7	1	0	14	0.875	60	19
Brockville Hockey Club	15	7	8	0	14	0.467	89	62
Montreal Nationals	6	3	3	0	6	0.500	27	27
Ottawa Capitals	6	1	5	0	2	0.167	28	41
Morrisburg Hockey Club	11	0	11	0	0	0.000	25	54

Ontario Professional Hockey League

Club	GP	W	L	T	Pts	WPct	GF	GA
Berlin Dutchmen	27	16	11	0	32	0.593	153	121
Brantford Indians	27	15	11	1	31	0.574	188	179
Toronto Hockey Club	27	15	12	0	30	0.556	193	166
Galt Hockey Club	15	10	4	1	21	0.700	107	91
Guelph Hockey Club	18	3	15	0	6	0.167	61	116
St. Catharines Professionals	6	0	6	0	0	0.000	29	58

International Professional Hockey League

Club	GP	W	L	T	Pts	WPct	GF	GA
Houghton–Portage Lakes	72	50	20	2	102	0.708	305	253
Michigan Soo Indians	72	39	32	1	79	0.549	310	224
Pittsburgh Professional Hockey Club	73	35	36	2	72	0.493	297	280
Calumet-Larium Miners/Wanderers	73	33	38	2	68	0.466	275	307
Canadian Soo Hockey Club	72	20	51	1	41	0.285	277	400

HELLOS

Heinrich Himmler, *Nazi police chief*	November 7, 1900
Clark Gable *American film actor*	February 1, 1901
Howie Morenz *Canadiens legend*	June 21, 1902
Reginald "Hooley" Smith *Montreal Maroons star*	January 7, 1903
Frank "King" Clancy *Hall-of-Fame defenseman*	February 25, 1903
George Orwell *British writer and philosopher*	June 25, 1903
Robert Oppenheimer *American physicist*	April 22, 1904

GOODBYES

Friedrich Nietzsche *German philosopher*	August 25, 1900
Oscar Wilde *Irish poet*	November 30, 1900
Roy Bean *American judge*	March 16, 1903
Hod Stuart *Montreal Wanderers defenseman*	June 23, 1907
Geronimo *American Indian chief*	February 17, 1909

REGULAR SEASON

BEST RECORD
1907 Montreal Wanderers, 10-0

WORST RECORD
1906 Canadian Soo Hockey Club, 1-23

FAMOUS FIRSTS

GAME PLAYED, TWENTIETH CENTURY
Montreal Shamrocks 5, Ottawa Hockey Club 4, at Ottawa, January 6, 1900

GOAL SCORED, TWENTIETH CENTURY
William Duval, Ottawa Hockey Club, vs. Shamrocks, January 6, 1900

PLAYER TO REACH 200 CAREER GOALS
Russell Bowie, 1907

MISCELLANEOUS

MOST GOALS, SEASON
42   Ernie Russell, 1907

MOST GOALS, DECADE
223   Russell Bowie

BIGGEST PLAYER
Billy Nicholson, 5' 7" 275

SMALLEST PLAYER
Dickie Boon, 5' 4" 118

COOLEST HANDLES

William "Turkey" Bellingham
Frank "Pud" Glass
John "Bouse" Hutton
Alfred "Dubbie" Kerr
Percy "The Pieman" LeSueur
"One-Eyed" Frank McGee
Tom "Nibs" Phillips
Charles "Chubby" Power
Charles "Baldy" Spittal
Harry "Rat" Westwick

BEST SHOT
Harry Smith

BEST PASSER
Lester Patrick

BEST STICK-HANDLER
Russell Bowie kept the puck close to his body and was said to have had brilliant hand-eye coordination. Picture Wayne Gretzky before Wayne Gretzky.

BEST SKATER
Hod Stuart

WORST SKATER
Turkey Bellingham was about as fast as cold ketchup.

Fred "Cyclone" Taylor

FASTEST PLAYER

Fred "Cyclone" Taylor broke into the professional ranks in 1906 with Houghton of the IPHL and the hockey world was left breathless by his speed. He is said to have been able to skate as fast in reverse as forward.

BEST SNIPER

Russell Bowie was a pure scorer, averaging better than three goals a game over his 10-year amateur hockey career.

BEST PENALTY-KILLER

Rat Westwick had a unique, weaving skating style and used it to great effect. He is said to have been the first accomplished puck ragger in hockey. One source confirmed as much: "If ever Ottawa was a man short, the fans would usually give up a great cheer when the Rat got a hold of that rubber disk."

BEST BODY-CHECKER

Harvey Pulford was a brick wall on blades. In a 1905 Stanley Cup match against the speedy Rat Portage Thistles, he was given the green light to throw the body around. He was the major reason Ottawa scraped by to retain the Cup.

BEST POKE-CHECKER

Ernie Johnson would later earn the handle "India Rubber Man" because of his amazing 99-inch reach. It was said he could reach from wing to wing to break up a rush!

BEST SHOT-BLOCKER

Harvey Pulford

BEST GOALTENDER

Percy LeSueur

MOST UNUSUAL GOALTENDING STYLE

Billy Nicholson was probably the first goalie to drop to the ice to stop shots, predating Clint Benedict, who many believe was the first. Nicholson's considerable girth (5'7", anywhere between 250 and 300 pounds) had newspapermen wondering whether or not he would crack the ice when he flopped.

FINEST ATHLETE
Harvey Pulford

BEST DEFENSIVE FORWARD
Tom Phillips

WORST DEFENSIVE FORWARD
Jim Gillespie

BEST SHADOW
Blair Russell was a fine back-checker and an accomplished "marker" of opposing players.

BEST DEFENSIVE DEFENSEMAN
Hod Stuart

BEST OFFENSIVE DEFENSEMAN
Hod Stuart had top-notch skating ability, blazing speed, and a God-given genius for handling the puck. Like Doug Harvey and Bobby Orr, Stuart had the ability to control the tempo of a game.

BEST ALL-AROUND PLAYER
Tom Phillips

BEST UTILITY PLAYER
Jack Marshall was a true "Jack of all trades." He played every position except goal throughout his career, contributing to Cup wins in Winnipeg, Montreal, and Toronto along the way.

STRONGEST PLAYER
Harvey Pulford

TOUGHEST PLAYER
Alf Smith

BEST FIGHTER
Alf Smith

MOST ABLE INSTIGATOR
Alf Smith

DIRTIEST PLAYER

Baldy Spittal led a short, tumultuous career. In one 1904 match, he and goalie Bouse Hutton were the only Ottawa players left on the ice after the rest of the Silver Seven had been ejected on major penalties. Spittal skated up for the face-off and, just before the puck dropped, the referee issued this warning to him: "Behave yourself and you won't get the toss!" Spittal watched the puck drop before delivering a two-handed chop with his stick to the official's shins. The fans then went nuts and chased Spittal out of the rink.

CLEANEST PLAYER

Cecil Blachford was a quiet, unassuming star forward on the Montreal Wanderers dynasty. In 1907, he had his skull split open like a pumpkin when he was poleaxed by Baldy Spittal. Instead of lashing back, Blachford picked himself up, smiled at Spittal, and skated off to get his noggin stitched!

BEST CORNER-MAN
Alf Smith

BEST-LOOKING PLAYER

Tony Gingras was so handsome that he often received bouquets, pictures, and wet kisses from female fans before games.

UGLIEST PLAYER
Fred "Cyclone" Taylor

MOST UNDERRATED PLAYER

Pud Glass played alongside Ernie Russell, Hod Stuart, and Ernie Johnson, but is often forgotten. He was without a doubt the mighty Wanderers' hardest-working forward.

MOST CONSISTENT PLAYER
Pud Glass

MOST UNPREDICTABLE CAREER

Harry Smith was a rookie whiz kid, scoring a league-best 31 times in 1906. After that season, his love of the nightlife seemed to get the better of him. He would never regain his rookie form, but in 1910 he put in an excellent season, placing third in NHA scoring, even though he was considered out of shape. In 1911 he was fourth in the Ontario Professional league's scoring race.

SMARTEST PLAYER
Si Griffis

BEST INSTINCTS

Frank McGee was said by the Montreal *Herald*'s Elmer Ferguson to have "played with the instinct and the rhythm of an animal." McGee was said to be like a "steam engine with legs."

MOST HATED PLAYER
Alf Smith

MOST ADMIRED PLAYER
Hod Stuart

BEST LINES

Team:	Ottawa Silver Seven
LW:	Billy Gilmour
C:	Frank McGee
RW:	Alf Smith
R:	Rat Westwick

Team:	Montreal Wanderers
LW	Ernie Johnson
C:	Ernie Russell
RW:	Pud Glass
R:	Cecil Lachford

HIGHEST-PAID PLAYER

Tom Phillips signed to play with the Silver Seven for $1,800 in 1908. It was hockey's richest contract ever until two years later, when Cyclone Taylor signed with Renfrew for $5,250.

MOST TRAGIC CAREER
Owen "Bud" McCourt

PLAYER VERSUS TEAM

Pud Glass vs. Montreal Wanderers, 1907. In the thick of a "shamateurism" witchhunt, Glass was rumored to have signed as a pro with more than one club.

BEST HEAD COACH

Jimmy Gardner was a player/coach for years, mostly with the Wanderers. The old pro was said to have "known the game's angles like no other." Later on, he had a

hand in the birth of the Montreal
Canadiens.

BEST GENERAL MANAGER
Dickie Boon was the architect of the
Wanderers' dynasty.

OUTSTANDING SPORTSWRITER
Jimmie Hewitt, Vancouver *Province*

BEST STANLEY CUP FINAL
1905—Ottawa Silver Seven vs. Rat Portage
Thistles

IMPORTANT RULE CHANGES

1900
• Goal net introduced

1902
• Ten-dollar fine set for late game starts
• One-hundred-dollar fine set for defaulting
  on matches

1906
• Official "penalty timers" instituted
• Dual-referee system adopted
• Fine for late game starts raised to $25

1907
• After the puck strikes a goalie, members
  of his team may play the rebound without
  being called offside.
• Player injured in first half permitted to
  retire for ten minutes. The other side
  would drop a man to compensate.

The Net

I t is widely held that the first instance of the use of goal netting in Ontario hockey was in the little town of Beamsville in 1897. The story goes that Beamsville goalie William Fairbrother had local fishermen affix netting across his pipes. Newspaper reports indicate that most were "satisfied" with the netting.

Others feel netting made its debut in Southern Ontario Hockey Association (SOHA) play. Apparently, Hamilton was in a playoff with Paris, Ontario, in 1895 and many of the goals scored were disputed. This did not go unnoticed by the fishermen-laden Niagara team. Come next season, the Niagara squad is said to have affixed a fish net to the goal posts. This, they hoped, would help the goal judge separate sure goals from close calls.

Prior to the 1899 CAHL season, Quebec's Frank Stocking and Charlie Scott developed their own kind of netting. Critics felt the net interfered with play behind the goal, while others applauded the innovation. Stocking and Scott approached the rest of the league seeking support. It took a year but the CAHL decided to give the net a multi-game trial in exhibition play. The teams drew lots and it was determined that the Shamrocks and Victorias would use the nets on December 21, 1899. The league was sufficiently impressed and officially adopted the nets for the 1900 season. The Ontario Hockey Association followed the CAHL's lead.

Although it resolved many disputes, the net was not without its shortcomings. On more than one occasion, for example, the webbing was found to be attached too tightly. After shots, pucks would ricochet from the goal so quickly that officials were at a loss as to whether they had actually gone in. Other times, pucks could be shot through gaping holes in the netting, leaving the referee to scratch his head.

In 1912, Ottawa Senators goalie Percy LeSueur developed a new and improved netting. His design was novel in that it made included a crossbar, a crucial innovation. An account in the Montreal Gazette of an 1893 game detailed one instance in which the crossbar would have come in handy:

> The audience began to wonder when anybody was going to score when all of a sudden Watson lifted the puck from somewhere near center and that much sought-for disc of rubber went up among the rafters. Everybody looked up after it and wondered if it was lost. The players leaned on their sticks, apparently waiting for a new puck to be produced. Then, suddenly, Umpire Kelly put up his hand. He had discovered the puck in the region of his feet and he could not understand how it could have got there without coming through the poles

Percy LeSueur

and so he gave game. En passant, it might be just as well for an umpire to remember that they are not fifty feet high and that they are only six feet apart.

The crossbar was a definite plus and the National Hockey Association adopted the "LeSueur net" for the 1911–12 season.

Prior to the 1927–28 season, the NHL adopted the "Art Ross net," developed by the legendary player, coach, and manager. It featured an enclosed, semi-circular crease as well as a netting that trapped pucks shot from virtually all angles.

Hockey's First Fatality

In a Winnipeg bankers' league match just after the turn of the twentieth century, 23-year-old Dominion Bank clerk Fitz W. Barron was dinged by the puck on a clearing shot. He fell to the ice like a sack of doorknobs. His mates rushed him to nearest hospital but, although attempts were made by doctors to revive him, he lost consciousness and died. Later, it was learned that Barron had been playing hockey against doctor's orders. Apparently, he had a weak heart.

The Barron incident stands as the first fatality linked to hockey. In 1907, Owen "Bud" McCourt would become the first man to die in professional league play.

The Little Men of Iron

On February 26, 1902, the Montreal AAA defeated Russell Bowie and his Victorias to win the Dewar Shield and CAHL bragging rights. Without batting so much as an eyelash, the Triple-A issued a challenge to the Winnipeg Victorias, holders of the Stanley Cup since late January 1901.

The strapping Winnipeggers rallied behind a raw, thick pivot named Dan Bain. Big Dan, who was voted top Canadian athlete of the last half of the nineteenth century, could hit like a dump truck, shoot, pass, and put most men to shame on the face-off. To his right was the dazzling Tony Gingras, a honey of a skater with the finesse to match almost any man in hockey. He was also the heartthrob of dozens of female fans who, after the custom of the day, would drown the swarthy sweetheart in a sea of flowers for good luck before important matches. Back on the Winnipeg blue-line was Magnus Flett, who some, such as hockey contemporaries Graham Drinkwater and Harry Trihey, claimed was the first defenseman to rush the puck from end to end.

The Winnipeg–MAAA series would be a three-game set played on March 13, 15, and 17 at Winnipeg's Auditorium Rink. About 400 Montreal sportsmen gave their boys a send-off at the Canadian Pacific Railway station on March 9. During this two-day trip, the players busied themselves by running short sprints on railway platforms at each stop along the way. Upon their arrival in Winnipeg, they were greeted by about 800 people before being whisked away in "hacks," or horse-drawn sleighs, to the Clarendon Hotel. The Winnipeg *Tribune* proclaimed hockey to be on an equal footing with lacrosse as Canada's "national sport" and even dared suggest that one day American teams would be in the hunt for the Cup!

Few people gave the MAAA a snowball's chance of defeating the talented Pegs. The Manitoba *Free Press*, for example, asserted that the 1902 edition of the Victorias was "about the strongest that had ever represented the club."

The lineups for game one:

Winnipeg		MAAA
G. Brown	GOAL	Billy Nicholson
Rod Flett	POINT	Tom Hodge
Magnus Flett	COVER-POINT	Dickie Boon
Charles Johnstone	ROVER	Art Hooper
Fred Scanlan	LEFT WING	Jimmy Gardner
Dan Bain	CENTER	Jack Marshall
Tony Gingras	RIGHT WING	Charlie Liffiton

Montreal was also a machine with speed to burn. Rover Art Hooper had won the scoring championship — 17 goals in eight games — and was the club's go-to man. The club's slick pass-and-carry system was quarterbacked by whirling cover-point Dickie Boon. This puny fellow could skate like the wind and was a master of the rush. At center was 24-year-old Jack Marshall, the club's "Mr. Can-Do," while on his left was rookie Jimmy Gardner.

Coverage of the series in both Montreal and Winnipeg was extensive. Most of the major newspapers from Calgary to Montreal carried daily updates on the series — the Cup had finally become national news.

Many made the 1,500-mile trek to Winnipeg from Montreal to watch their boys perform. For the first game, some 4,500 people managed to elbow their way into the Auditorium, paying anywhere from 50 cents for general admission to $1.50 for reserve seats. Those in attendance were reported to be "mad with enthusiasm" even though conditions were poor. A recent spell of mild weather in Winnipeg had left an inch of water around the edges of the playing surface. As one reporter had it, "It was a common thing to see four men at one time sliding on their stomachs for a distance of fifteen yards over the water-covered ice."

Montreal fans were kept posted on the game's progress thanks to the Great North Western Telegraph Company. During the action, an operator sat at a little table located at ice-level, relaying game descriptions dictated to him by two or three so-called "experienced hockey men." Special receivers were installed at the downtown office of the Montreal *Star* at the corner of Peel and St. Catherine streets and at the newspaper's Point St. Charles office. Another receiver was set up in the MAAA gymnasium. Montrealers huddled by the hundreds around bulletin boards at these two locations to read excerpts from the game reports.

The following is taken from one of the telegraph commentaries:

Three minutes more to play. Face. Play in Victorias end . . . Flett is saving. Some warm ones. Scanlan and Flett take it up . . . offside. Face. Magnus Flett is on. Play on Montreal goal . . . Magnus Flett lifted one but it hit three Montrealers and went over the top . . . Gingras shoots wide. Scanlan shoots. Stopped. Offside in center.

1902 Montreal

Foster Hewitt, eat your heart out!

Betting odds ranged from even money to 5–4 in favor of Winnipeg, but little money was said to have changed hands in the first game. The Victorias won 1–0 on the strength of a goal by Bain.

Winnipeg boosters braved raging blizzard conditions to witness the second match. Because of the bitter cold, players on both sides took their pregame warm-ups wearing what looked like dressing gowns! Except for a few piles of snow, ice conditions were ideal and the arena was packed tighter than a can of sardines.

In downtown Montreal, record crowds huddled around the telegraphs. One Toronto *Star* sportswriter exclaimed: "It is doubtful if, even during the Dominion elections or during America's Cup races, that such a crowd has been seen . . . the roars and shouts were something tremendous and when it was all over, the surroundings of St. Catherine Street between Guy and St. Denis seemed to have gone wild with joy, and the noise and excitement was kept up long after the different hostelries, which did an unprecedented business, had been compelled to close according to law."

At the MAAA gymnasium, the cheering was so loud that the operator had trouble hearing the telegraph messages.

Winnipeg fans were stunned by the result of the match: MAAA 5, Winnipeg 0. The western press praised the "winged-wheel artists" and applauded the game as one of "brilliant rushes, quick passing, dead-on shots, skillful blocking, and speedy returns." Around this time the A-boys were dubbed "little men of iron" by the Winnipeg press. This nickname was given, said the Montreal press, as a tip of the hat to the pluck and determination of the smaller team from the east.

Prior to game two, "the betting was all Montreal, and as good as 10–7 could be had on the visiting team while 10–8 odds were freely offered and taken." The Montreal *Star* reported considerable betting on the outcome as a result of these odds.

On page 6 of the March 18 issue of the Montreal *Tribune*, a headline summarized the outcome of the final game: "Au Revoir! Sweet Stanley Cup." Indeed, the Montreal seven took the rubber match 2–1 after a "delirious evening" in the Auditorium. After scoring two goals in the first half, the AAA simply battened down the hatches and went into a defensive shell, trying merely to outlast the clock.

Pandemonium broke out in downtown Montreal once news of the victory was received. Streetcars were brought to a standstill as fans poured into the streets. Those at the MAAA gymnasium strained to catch every last word of the post-game reports coming over the wire.

A couple of days later, throngs of people turned out in Montreal to welcome their heroes home. The *Free Press* described the setting as one of crowds and "mucilaginous mud." In all, an estimated 30,000 people were on hand to cheer the team with "lungs of leather and throats of brass." Stores were decorated in the players' honor and the team was officially received at the Amateur Athletic Association after being borne from Windsor Station to the clubhouse in "human triumphal cars." The celebration lasted for several weeks as the victors made their way from banquet to tribute to reception to banquet.

From a financial standpoint, Stanley Cup hockey was not particularly lucrative. The MAAA received 25 percent of the net gate from the Winnipeg matches — only about $1,600. The Cup itself, though, had become a lodestone. In March 1903, for example, the Ottawa Silver Seven players, coach, and secretary were each given $100 diamond rings after their Cup win over the Montreal Victorias.

By 1903, hockey was making a move toward professionalism as semi-professionalism, or "shamateurism," infiltrated and changed the game of hockey forever. The MAAA win of 1902 stands out because it represents the beginning of the end of the purely amateur era, as well as the high-water mark of the city of Montreal's early dominance of the game. Indeed, the "Little Men of Iron" were the last of a special breed.

Cup Quarrels

In hockey's early years, there were many controversies as to how the Stanley Cup champion should be decided. Witness the 1894 season, when there was a four-way tie for first place in the AHAC. Just before the playoffs, Quebec withdrew, feeling they were getting the short end of the stick from the playoff format then in place. In 1899, a dubious decision by referee Jack Findlay led to the Winnipeg Victorias' forfeit of game and Cup against their Montreal counterparts.

In 1898 the AHAC was replaced by the Canadian Amateur Hockey League (CAHL). This new league held de facto control of the Stanley Cup, since one or another of its members almost invariably were defending champions. Rival leagues were understandably peeved with this arrangement and in 1904, officials from a number of Senior leagues moved that the Cup be replaced. The Cup survived the turmoil . . . .

In March 1903, the Silver Seven defeated the Montreal Victorias 9–1 in a two-game, total-goals series for possession of the Cup. The Seven went on to defend their trophy only days later, sweeping a two-game set from Rat Portage.

In a three-game set between December 30, 1903, and January 4, 1904, Ottawa successfully defended against the Winnipeg Rowing Club, a side that featured a young Joe Hall. Even though the games were played in sub-zero weather at Ottawa's Aberdeen Pavilion, fans were not deterred from coming out.

Game one belonged completely to Ottawa. The Seven really paddled the rowers, physically and on the scoreboard. The final score was 9–1. Game two was an entirely different situation, though. Eighteen-year-old Nick Bawlf scored twice, leading the westerners to a 6–2 victory. In a game the papers deemed the "greatest match ever played in Ottawa," the Silver Seven held on for a 2–0 victory in game three.

Ottawa found itself with but five days to prepare for its regular-season opener against the Montreal Victorias. Despite a slow start, the Silver Seven won its first four contests.

A Cup controversy took root prior to Ottawa's third meeting with the Victorias. Ottawa's train rolled into Montreal an hour and a half late for the match, much to the annoyance of 5,000 fans. The game was not finished by the midnight curfew, but Ottawa was credited with a 4–1 victory. Later that week, the Montreal Shamrocks came to Ottawa and had to wait an hour for their luggage. Delay of game, correct?

CAHL bigwigs were much displeased with the recent rash of late starts and called a meeting to deal with the issue. Ottawa and the Shamrocks were each fined 10 dollars for unsportsmanlike conduct. A motion was also raised ordering that the "unfinished" game of January 30 between Ottawa and the Victorias be replayed. Ottawa representative J.P. Dickson was understandably annoyed and threatened to withdraw the Silver Seven from the league. Since Ottawa held the Cup and Cup trustee Philip Ross backed their claim, it would be theirs to defend until the end of the CAHL campaign. A similar situation in 1898, when the Victorias jumped from the AHAC, had led to a decision by the Cup trustees that they, and not the AHAC champions, should be the ones to defend the Cup.

Ottawa officials offered a compromise. They said that if their game with the Victorias would have any bearing on the outcome of the championship, they would replay it. This compromise did not fly with the league, and the Silver Seven indeed ended up withdrawing, forfeiting the remainder of their games. They would still be accepting challenges for the Cup, though.

Mere weeks later, they took on the Ontario champion Toronto Marlboros, led by a young Tommy Phillips. The Seven had little trouble with Toronto, beating them 6–3 and 11–2. For the following season, 1904–05, Ottawa joined the Federal Amateur Hockey League, taking with them control of the Stanley Cup. Quebec went on to win the CAHL title but was denied the right to challenge the Silver Seven. This raw onion failed to amuse Quebec president Frank Stocking who, together with a number of media contacts, demanded that the trustees return the Cup to the CAHL. Trustee

Ross would not hear of it, though. Ottawa was called on to defend against the FAHL champions, the Montreal Wanderers, leaving Quebec out in the cold.

Ottawa and the Wanderers were slated to play a two-game series in Montreal, but the challenge failed to get past the first game. It was a rough game, as was often the case in those days when Ottawa was involved. The two sides stumbled to a 5–5 draw, but the W's refused to play extra time against the big, bad Ottawas. The Cup's trustees promptly scheduled another two-game series, this time, at the Silver Seven's behest, to be played in Ottawa. Needless to say, the Wanderers were not impressed with this arrangement but trustee Ross maintained that as Cup champions, Ottawa had the right to say where they wanted to defend their title. Ross, a prominent Ottawa sportsman, displayed a hometown bias that bordered on the disgraceful. The Ottawa–Montreal dispute was left unresolved and the series was abandoned, leaving the Cup in the hands of the Silver Seven. They went on to defend the silverware against Brandon, champions of the Manitoba and Northwestern leagues. A two-game series yielded Ottawa 6–3 and 9–3 victories.

Ottawa would win the Cup in 1905 and again in 1909, and the Silver Seven is remembered as "the" team of the pre-NHL era. The full story of their struggle to keep the Cup in 1904, though, is not as well documented. If the Cup trustees had been any kind of sportsmen, they would have set down some hard-and-fast rules for future challenges immediately after the 1904 debacle. Instead, the regulations governing Cup play were fluid and often skewed to suit the defending champions.

He Saves! He Scores!

Today a goalie would rarely, if ever, consider making a headlong dash up ice; in fact, the rules prevent him from crossing the center red-line. But in hockey's infancy it was not uncommon for goalies to corral the puck and take off with it, even though, with seven men a side, there was even less open ice than there is today.

The first documented case of a goalie turning himself into a puck carrier was during a January 1902 Stanley Cup challenge. H.G. "Dutch" Morrison of the Toronto Wellingtons "startled Winnipeg fans by darting from the net to check an opposing forward." The first recorded instance of a goalie scoring a goal was on February 18, 1905, when Montreal Westmounts goalie Fred Brophy skated the length of the ice to score on Quebec's Paddy Moran. The next season, Brophy proved his feat was no fluke. In a March 7, 1906, contest against the Montreal Victorias, he dashed the length of the ice to shovel one past goalie Nathan Frye. The newspapers did not look kindly upon this kind of hockey. The Montreal *Gazette* wrote, "At times, the game became farcical and the limit was reached when goalkeeper Brophy went down the ice and tallied . . ."

Big, blubbery Billy Nicholson made his own attempt at immortality in 1904. But, as Nicholson said, "I did go up the ice, got the puck, was in position to score, but I passed to Jack Marshall. That was the closest I ever got to scoring."

The rushing goalie craze settled down somewhat as hockey matured. This is not to say goalies stopped trying to score. In 1921, Hugh Lehman, then a member of the

Vancouver Millionaires, baffled the Ottawa Senators in a Cup contest with a fine display of passing. The Senators had never seen anything quite like it. Lehman would often stray 20 feet from his cage to make a pass. In game five, the *Gazette* noticed that he "skated out to the blue-line after a loose puck . . . sent in a shot which went as far as Benedict."

In a game against the Montreal Canadiens in 1947, the New York Rangers' Chuck Rayner grabbed the puck and skated up-ice. Upon meeting an enemy checker, though, "Bonnie Prince Charlie" passed off. Earlier that same year, with the Toronto Maple Leafs' Turk Broda pulled for an extra attacker, Rayner whizzed a hot shot that missed the empty net by a whisper.

Rayner did manage to score once, in an exhibition contest. During World War Two, he played with the Victoria Navy. In a pick-up game against a Canadian Army squad, Rayner picked up a rebound in a furious scramble in front of his net. Seeing nothing but open ice before him, Rayner took off. A renowned skater, he moved in on goalie Art Jones and slapped the puck home.

Although Rayner himself never mentioned it, some newspapers have suggested that he scored another one in 1951. A Toronto *Star* article held that, late in a game against a team of all-stars from the Maritimes, Rayner skated the length of the ice to score the final goal in a 15–5 victory.

In a 1966–67 game played before a national TV audience, journeyman Gary "Suitcase" Smith replaced Bruce Gamble in the Toronto Maple Leafs net early in the first period. Only minutes after entering the game, Smith was presented an opportunity to score. He grabbed a shoot-in and took off. Montreal defender J.C. Tremblay played Smith's trek cautiously. As Smith crossed the center red-line, he looked down to see if he still had the puck. Suddenly, Tremblay rocked him with a devastating check. This filled Smith's head with birds and stars, but no goals. Before Smith could attempt an encore, the league introduced a ban on such forays.

In 1970, Michel Plasse of the Central Hockey League's Kansas City Blues scored to ice a victory over the Oklahoma City Blazers. Thanks to a snowstorm in the area that night, only 850 people witnessed this historic event.

During a 1979 match between Billy Smith's New York Islanders and the Colorado Rockies, a delayed penalty was called against the Isles. A pass by Colorado's Rob Ramage squirted past everyone into the Colorado net and, since Smith was the last New Yorker to touch the puck before the penalty was called, he got credit for the goal.

When Ron Hextall reached the NHL in 1986, he developed a reputation throughout the circuit for everything from his maniacal tantrums to his stick-handling ability. Experts said it was only a matter of time before Hextall scored a goal and they were proven right on December 8, 1987. With a two-goal lead in the game, Hextall decided to let the puck fly at the empty net — Boston had pulled its goalie — scoring the first "true" goal by a modern goalie. He went on to add another in the 1988–89 playoffs against the Washington Capitals.

Chris Osgood scored a goal as a Junior with the Western Hockey League's Medicine Hat Tigers, in a January 3, 1991, game against the Swift Current Broncos. He repeated the trick on March 6, 1996, this time with the NHL's Detroit Red

Wings, against the lowly Hartford Whalers. Oddly enough, left winger Geoff Sanderson — who knows a thing or two about scoring goals, having netted more than 200 in the NHL — was on the ice for both Osgood scores!

In the first round of the 1997 playoffs, the New Jersey Devils' Martin Brodeur notched a goal against the Montreal Canadiens. Many observers felt Brodeur — whose marker came when the Devils were already up by two, and who proceeded to jump up and down like a madman once the puck crossed the goal-line — showed up the Habs in a bush-league manner. On January 2, 1999, Damian Rhodes of the Ottawa Senators joined the goal-scoring goalies' club in true Billy Smith fashion

Michel Plasse

when a New Jersey Devil put the puck in his own net on a delayed penalty. Rhodes had been the last Senator to touch the puck.

Goalie goals have become somewhat common, with a flurry having been scored over the past 10 years. Darcy Wakaluk, Robb Stauber, and Olaf Kolzig, among others, have scored, either in Junior or minor-league competition.

The Silver and the Gold

On January 11, 1905, the Dawson City Nuggets steamed into Ottawa's Union Station for a Stanley Cup challenge series with the mighty Silver Seven. A handful of Ottawa Silver Seven executives greeted nine weary young men and escorted them through the snowbound capital to the Russell Hotel. It was Wednesday afternoon and, despite pleadings via wire from Nuggets manager Joe Boyle to push it back, the first match would be in 48 hours.

So who were the Yukoners? Well, Randy McLennan was the sharp one with the mustache — the team captain. Next was George "Sureshot" Kennedy, Dawson's trigger man. On defense were Jim Johnstone and Lorne Hannay. Johnstone was a 190-pounder skilled in the body-bashing department, while Hannay was the hard-shooting cover-point out of Brandon, Manitoba. Up front with Kennedy were Hector Smith and Norman Watt, both of whom played a fine, no-nonsense brand of hockey. The former was a tricky little man, expert at setting up plays on the fly. Seventeen-year-old "Brother" Albert Forrest was Dawson's goalkeeper and, by most accounts, cat-quick.

After getting settled into the Russell, the Nuggets met for a drink. Almost out of nowhere came Mr. J.A. Acklin, a Yukon mining man in Ottawa on business. Before the Nuggets and several others, Acklin made this speech:

> If you boys succeed in defeating the Ottawa and Montreal clubs and win-
> ning the Stanley Cup, I will make you a present of $1,000. It's my desire to
> buy up the team for the purpose of winning the game. I simply want to see

1905 Dawson City Nuggets

the boys have a good time and I'm willing to put up the stuff. We all admire the grit of the boys in coming out after the silverware . . .

The Yukoners had come a long, long way to play for the Cup. They left Dawson City on December 19, 1904, dog-sledding 331 miles to Whitehorse. They then took the train to a speck in the wilderness called Skagway, Alaska, where they missed a steamboat connection — by two hours! They waited five days for the next steamer, which took them all the way to their train hookup in Seattle. Upon their arrival in Ottawa days later, the Nuggets had traveled more than 4,000 miles.

Despite appearing a little worse for wear, the boys were in decent shape. Even if they lacked grace, they took to their first practice in weeks with spirit. The Montreal *Gazette* said, "They are one and all fine big fellows, able to rough it up with the best of them, fast skaters and good stick-handlers."

The Dawson City *Daily News* was somewhat embittered by the Ottawa club's refusal to delay the first match. On January 13, the day of the game, the paper put this twist on the matter: "The Ottawas evidently are afraid of the Yukoners because they are allowing them only one day in which to practice for the match." Despite the fact that the Ottawa Silver Seven were working on their third Cup in a row, having amassed a 24-6-2 record over the past three years (season and challenges combined), most Dawson boosters were cock-sure. The *Daily News* continued: "Everywhere in Dawson today the hope is expressed that the Yukoners land the Cup and bring it to Klondike and keep it here forever. Should it once be landed here it is doubtful, some say, if enough talent could be massed in any one city to wrest it from the Yukoners."

The lineups:

Dawson City		**Ottawa**
Albert Forrest	GOAL	Dave Finnie
Jim Johnstone	POINT	"Bones" Allen
Lorne Hannay	COVER-POINT	Art Moore
Randy McLennan	ROVER	Harry Westwick
Norman Watt	LEFT WING	Frank White
Hector Smith	CENTER	Frank McGee
George Kennedy	RIGHT WING	Alf Smith

Dey's Arena was packed — with some 2,500 spectators, they say — and among the guests was Canada's esteemed governor general, Earl Grey, and a party from the

Government House. From the opening bell, the action was hard and chippy. The Nuggets had been warned of Ottawa's practice of knocking off challengers early, so they resolved to match the Silver Seven stride for stride. A foolish choice. The Watt-Smith-Kennedy combination soon proved no match for the Ottawa forwards, who dipsy-doodled the night away. The Silver Seven got four goals from "Dirty" Alf Smith and two apiece from Frank White and Harry "Rat" Westwick in a 9–2 laugher.

1905 Ottawa Silver Seven

The Manitoba *Free Press* wasted no time attacking the Nuggets: "It is true that the Dawson City men had only just arrived and that they had hardly had the time to get into proper shape, but the form they did show was of the most mediocre kind . . ." The Montreal *Gazette* was far more generous in its assessment of Dawson's effort: ". . . The team arrived with barely enough time to get ready to go on the ice . . . should not be judged on their play of tonight . . ."

While the Nuggets were spending almost a month traipsing through Canada's unforgiving winter, hopping steamers, trains, and dogsleds in the most bitter weather imaginable, the Ottawa Silver Seven were presumably skating together, eating three square meals a day, and sleeping in warm beds. The contrast is nothing short of blinding. While the *Free Press*'s assessment of the Nuggets' play was valid, the team should not have been dismissed as mediocre. Boyle, for one, was aware of this difference: "The assurance is given that the interval of Saturday and Sunday will give the boys the needed opportunity to stretch their legs . . . Monday's game will tell a different story."

That said, the Nuggets went out and lost game two by the gaudy score of 23–2. In this contest, White scored once, Smith twice, Westwick five times — and McGee an astounding 14 times! To quote the *Free Press*'s headline, Dawson was "terribly drubbed." While the first few minutes of the game were entertaining enough, the score was 10–1 for Ottawa at the half. In his finely crafted *Dawson City Seven*, current-day author Don Reddick wrote in the first person to transport us to the Nuggets' dressing room at halftime:

> The dressing room is a morbid scene. Our heads down or backs against the walls, our tongues out, and a rain of sweat across our faces. Joe Boyle is silent . . . Sureshot Kennedy makes a half-hearted attempt to rally the troops. There are no affirmations called in response, only the solid, sordid silence of embarrassment.

By halftime of the second game, Dawson knew its goose was cooked. In the second half, they merely went through the motions, and it showed. Ottawa's McGee ran wild, the Nuggets did little to stop him, and the final score was a sick joke.

In *Old Scores, New Goals*, Joan Finnigan left open the possibility that the "Ottawa ice-maker . . . slowed down the Dawson City team by flooding the ice with an inch of water, even though the temperature was well above freezing. Like race horses who do better on mud, the Silver Seven plodded through the slush to win the Stanley Cup . . ." This notion, by no means original, is rather silly. A team complaining that the ice had been tampered with after losing 2–1, or even 5–1 is one thing. But a team losing 23–2? On the night of January 16, 1905, there was precious little anyone or anything could have done for the Nuggets. McGee & Co. saw to that.

The press was surprisingly merciful toward the Nuggets. The Dawson City *Daily News* used terms like "broken up," "dead on its feet," and "lack of condition" to describe the buggy-whipped Yukoners. In what can only be described as horribly inaccurate, it was reported that "the Ottawas won today by a score of 23-2. Nevertheless, it was a good game." Even more outrageous was the *Gazette*'s take: "The only man on the Dawson team who played a really fine game of hockey was Forrest, who in goal gave as fine an exhibition as the most exacting could desire. But for him, Ottawa's figures might have been doubled." As good as the Silver Seven were, it strains the bounds of imagination to suggest even they could score 46 goals, against anyone.

The Ottawa–Dawson City Cup challenge of January 1905 has to be considered one of the saddest chapters ever written in the history of professional sport. It must be noted that, although no match for the Silver Seven under the best of conditions, the Nuggets were a decent enough side. After their Cup embarrassment, they embarked on a 23-game barnstorming tour of eastern Canada, designed as much to raise money for their trip home as to showcase their hockey skills. Their record was 13-9-1.

Perhaps the most poignant footnote to this saga is the story of the young goalie, Forrest, who walked, alone, the final 350 miles to Dawson City.

Bloodbath

One of the bloodiest matches in hockey history fell on January 12, 1907, when the Ottawa Silver Seven met the Montreal Wanderers in one of the first tilts of the 1907 ECAHA season. Even though play was barbaric and the stickwork was sickening, the game was expected to have been a classic. Newspapermen had screamed for weeks about how it would be "one for the ages." By the time the Silver Seven rolled out of Montreal, though, many were convinced they had been party to "as disgraceful an exhibition of rough and brutal play as has been seen in recent memory."

Before the Seven left for Montreal, there was a rumor going around that flashy Kenora Thistles cover-point "Tuffy" Bellefeuille would be joining them. Meanwhile in Montreal, the buzz centered around the scratching of star Wanderers sniper Ernie Russell from the lineup due to poor play. Apparently, he had skipped practice.

Hundreds of dollars in bets were wagered on the outcome of this contest . . . . Before the match, the Arena's betting pits must have looked like a McDonald's at lunchtime. Before long, a crowd of 7,000 had jammed into the Arena. Promenades above and below accommodated hundreds who had failed to secure seats, while the more desperate took to the rafters. The copious amount of pipe and cigarette smoke in the building caused a thick blue haze to envelop the rink. By game's end, the players moved like phantoms through the smoke. According to eyewitnesses, it was nearly impossible for someone at one end of the rink to make out what was going on at the other end.

The lineups:

Montreal		Ottawa
Riley Hern	GOAL	Percy LeSueur
Rod Kennedy	POINT	Charles "Baldy" Spittal
Hod Stuart	COVER-POINT	Harvey Pulford
Lester Patrick	ROVER	Harry Westwick
Ernie Johnson	LEFT WING	"Hamby" Shore
Frank "Pud" Glass	CENTER	Harry Smith
Cecil Blachford	RIGHT WING	Alf Smith

What had been promoted as a titanic struggle between two hockey superpowers turned out to be a bitter, grinding affair — low on finesse, and high on blood and sweat. As the sides took to the ice, the atmosphere in the rink intensified. Star Wanderers cover-point Hod Stuart skated up to the Ottawa boys and shook hands with none other than "Baldy" Spittal, one of hockey's crowned goons. Riley Hern did likewise. Just before the opening whistle, a large beaver hat showing off Ottawa's red, black, and white colors was thrown onto the ice. Ottawa forward Harry Smith skated over and picked it up, grinning from ear to ear, and went on to wear it in the first half! Montreal supporters got into to the act, tossing down a horseshoe decked with ribbons in the Wanderers' colors. Hern picked up the horseshoe and put it on the crossbar of his net for good luck.

The flow of play in the first minute or two was somewhat muddy. As the hometown cheers grew lustier, though, the Wanderers found their wind. Soon, they were skating like a house on fire — it looked as if the match would be an easy two points for the Redbands. Glass and Johnson combined for the game's first goal after breaking away at center. The pair looked like two kids on a playground playing keep-away as they passed it back and forth. Glass . . . over to Johnson . . . back to Glass . . . across to Johnson . . . on the tape to Glass . . . Montreal 1, Ottawa 0.

Glass's goal gave the Wanderers an enormous lift. As the forward line picked up speed, their defensemen rushed with increasing poise and confidence. It was at this point that Stuart and Ottawa's Alf Smith engaged in the rough stuff. First, Stuart sent Smith crashing into the boards. Only minutes later, Smith cross-checked Stuart from behind. As Smith belted Stuart around, the Silver Seven picked it up a notch. Suddenly, play was going end to end and the goalies were forced to stand on their heads. Then, at the 15-minute mark, it was Patrick . . . over to Blachford . . . Montreal 2, Ottawa 0.

Hod Stuart

Just after the resumption of play, Blachford was dinged on the head by a Kennedy shot. After a short delay, during which Harry Smith was punched in the face by a fan, the Ottawa center cut into the Wanderers zone — waiting, skating, over to Shore, shooting! Montreal 2, Ottawa 1.

Before long, on a Montreal power play — Harry Smith was off for tripping — Shore nailed his second goal of the game to tie the score at two. The red, black, and white seized the momentum with this goal and started to press the Wanderers goal. Then Pulford was sent off for boarding Stuart. On the Montreal power play, Johnson zipped in on the left side and let fly a 30-footer. LeSueur was equal to the blast but Blachford was in position to bat in the rebound. Montreal 3, Ottawa 2.

Blachford's second goal swung the pendulum back in favor of the W's. The Glass-Johnson combo once again proved expert at the tic-tac-toe passing game: Glass busted a move at center, passed over to big Johnson — Montreal 4, Ottawa 2.

Just after the second half began, Patrick was the recipient of a two-handed slash to the midsection from Pulford. Stuart and Alf Smith renewed their private battles before the latter was called off for slashing. It was then that the real butchery began. Shore and Westwick continued to hack Stuart until referee Quinn called them off as well.

Blachford, who was turning in a fine all-around effort, was the victim of an especially brutal Spittal high stick. Spittal must have mistaken his stick for an ax because he brought it down on Blachford's skull as if splitting a log. According to reporters, a sickening crack could be heard throughout the Arena and the crowd fell deadly silent as Blachford, his hands on his head, crumpled to the ice in a pool of blood. Unconscious and blood-soaked, he was carried off the ice. Dozens of stitches would be needed to close the wound. Spittal, he received a mere 10-minute penalty.

What had been a trickle of Ottawa penalties became a flood after the Spittal incident. Still, the Wanderers, who bombarded LeSueur with shots from all angles, failed to score, due in large part to some great penalty-killing by Westwick and Harry Smith.

Without warning, Johnson and Harry Smith got into a scuffle behind the Montreal net. When officials Emmett Quinn and Walter Cummings separated them, Johnson was lying facedown on the ice in a bloody, pulpy heap. Minutes later, Harry's brother Alf settled his score with Stuart. Stuart had just made a splendid rush on the right flank when Shore smacked him across the jaw. As the officials turned their attention to Shore, Stuart continued his rush, dodging Pulford as if he was three years old. Suddenly, out of nowhere, Alf Smith clobbered Stuart. The crowd immediately stormed to its feet, filling the rink with boos as Stuart was carried off. Ten minutes later, Stuart returned to action. Harry Smith continued the bloodletting, two-handing

Patrick across the chest as he attempted a shot. Westwick made matters worse when he took a wicked swing at Stuart. By this time, Stuart resembled a train wreck . . . his body a patchwork of bruises, his face a sorry mess of cuts, scrapes, and dried blood.

As the last minutes of the game ticked away, Pulford and Alf Smith got into an argument with referee Quinn. Before long, the two players had earned themselves three-minute penalties and game ejections. Finally, Spittal slashed judge-of-play Cummings across the shins.

After the closing bell, sportswriters called for league brass to suspend a number of players. Officials Quinn and Cummings promised to send a special report, detailing the actions of certain players, to the league's executive committee.

Ottawa fans thought their Seven would have won had they played it clean. Those in attendance were expecting to see a high-caliber game, the best against the best. A good many left the Arena disappointed before the final bell.

The Montreal *Gazette*'s game summary:

WANDERERS WON BRUTAL CONTEST
Champions cut down by Ottawa, stuck to task and downed assailants . . .
BUT LITTLE GOOD HOCKEY
Occasional skill shown in battle where strength was requisite quality

SCORING:

Half	Team	Scorer	Time
1	Montreal	Glass	2:00
1	Montreal	Blachford	13:00
1	Ottawa	Shore	17:00
1	Ottawa	Shore	22:00
1	Montreal	Blachford	25:00
1	Montreal	Johnson	27:30

On January 18, a special meeting of the ECAHA executive was held to examine the actions of Spittal and the Smith brothers. Motions to suspend the three, either for a week or a year, were rejected. According to committee members, Quinn and Cummings's reports were incomplete and seemed to have been influenced heavily by opinions expressed by the Montreal media after the match. Fred McRobie called the meeting a farce, then announced his resignation as league president.

When Ottawa rolled into Montreal via train on January 26 for a Saturday-nighter against the Victorias, city police met them at Windsor Station. The cops produced warrants for the arrest of Spittal and the Smiths and the trio was hauled off to the Guy–St. Catherine police station. An unidentified man bailed the players out.

At the January 31 trial, Quinn and Cummings's testimonies were found wanting; few of the details they described were confirmed by anyone else. When the dust settled, Spittal and Alf Smith were fined 20 dollars apiece and ordered by Judge Choquet to keep the peace for a year. Harry Smith was found not guilty.

An Ottawa-Montreal rematch took place on March 2 at Dey's Arena, and ticket scalpers commanded exorbitant prices. Stuart, Patrick, and Glass were greeted with a shower of lemons and a lusty chorus of boos from the crowd. There seemed little doubt what the outcome of the game would be. The smooth-skating Patrick and Johnson were all over the ice. Little Ernie Russell was his usual, spectacular self, scoring five goals, but Patrick, who had moved back to defense, was considered the sharpest man on the glass. The final score was 10–6 Wanderers as every Montrealer save Riley Hern figured in the scoring.

Casualties of War

Hockey players move at breakneck speeds, armed with splints of wood and razor-sharp blades on their feet. Injuries are a real, even an expected, part of the game; there's even the outside chance that death will rear its head during a hockey game. It's happened twice in the long history of major league hockey — to Owen "Bud" McCourt in 1907 and William "Bat" Masterton in 1968. Although the latter's death was an accident that could have been avoided, it was widely held in contemporary reports that someone was responsible for McCourt's death and should have been punished for it.

The McCourt tragedy took place in a make-up game on March 6, 1907, between the Cornwall Hockey Club and Ottawa Victorias. Early in the second half, the 21-year-old McCourt got into a skirmish with Ottawa's Art Throop and a number of players from both sides joined in. What happened next is not altogether clear, but it is known that Charles Masson struck McCourt over the head with his stick and the Cornwall forward began bleeding profusely. He was rushed to Cornwall's Hôtel Dieu hospital, where he later died.

Soon after McCourt's death, Masson was charged with murder; despite the Crown's strenuous objections, the charge was reduced to manslaughter. Masson was tried on April 10 in Cornwall. Eyewitnesses claimed to have seen McCourt being struck by other Ottawa players prior to Masson's blow, evidence that left Judge Magee no choice but to acquit Masson.

Without the aid of videotaped replays, Magee was forced to rely on the word of witnesses such as referee — and future NHA president — Emmett Quinn. Had such an incident occurred today, it may well have resulted in the sports trial of the century, and someone may well have been punished for McCourt's death.

Bill Masterton's case was much different. The big center might still be alive today had he been wearing protective headgear. In the first frame of a January 13, 1968, game between his Minnesota North Stars and the visiting Oakland Seals, Masterton carried the puck into the neutral zone and passed it off to a teammate. No sooner had he done so than he was sandwiched by Oakland's Larry Cahan and Ron Harris. Masterton fell and the back of his head hit the ice. He was rushed to Fairview Southdale Hospital, but the 29-year-old never regained consciousness.

Masterton had been an All-America at Denver University and was named most valuable player at the 1961 NCAA hockey tournament. After graduating he played for the Hull-Ottawa Canadiens of the Eastern Professional Hockey League, then joined the American Hockey League's Cleveland Barons. After just one year in Cleveland he retired and went back to Denver to earn his master's degree in finance. He ended up working for the Honeywell Corporation in Minneapolis and playing for the U.S. National Team.

In 1967 the National Hockey League doubled in size from six teams to 12, and suddenly players like Masterton, who'd been tagged as career minor leaguers, got a chance at cracking an NHL lineup. Minnesota purchased Masterton's NHL rights from Montreal and signed him in June 1967. The North Stars moved the erstwhile winger to center. He played 38 games in 1967–68, scoring four goals and eight assists.

Ironically, Bill Masterton had worn a helmet throughout his collegiate career, but elected not to wear one as a pro. A decade later the NHL heeded the lesson of the Bill Masterton case and made it mandatory for players to wear helmets. Those players who had signed an NHL contract prior to June 1, 1979, were exempted. The last of these helmetless heroes, Craig MacTavish, retired in 1997.

In 1992, the NHL allowed players the option of discarding their helmets if they first signed a waiver. A few, including the St. Louis Blues' Brett Hull and Pittsburgh Penguins goalie Ken Wregget, toyed with the idea, but quickly changed their tune when they found out they wouldn't be insured in the event of a head injury. So far no NHL player has elected to play bareheaded.

The World Series of Hockey

Just after the turn of the twentieth century, Pittsburgh was one of the biggest hockey markets in the United States. The Iron City had a team in the International Professional Hockey League from 1904 until 1907, and when that league failed, local promoters launched the Western Pennsylvania Hockey League.

The WPHL is said to have been the first semi-professional hockey league. The circuit featured four teams — the Bankers, Lyceum, Pirates, and Pittsburgh Athletic Club. Squads played a 15-game schedule, playing each opponent five times. At the end of the 1907 season the Bankers and Lyceum, both 11-4, faced off for a playoff. The Bankers, on the strength of Harry Smith's four goals, took home the Spalding Trophy with a 4–2 victory. Lyceum's two markers were credited to Harry's brother Tommy. Harry and Tommy Smith were not the only WPHL players familiar to Canadian hockey fans. Art Throop played for Lyceum while Fred Povey chased rubber for the Bankers. Other hockeyists who'd had "cups of coffee" in Canadian hockey also played in the WPHL.

At the end of their own schedule, the FAHL champion Montreal Wanderers traveled to Pittsburgh to play the Bankers for what was termed by the *Spalding Hockey Guide* as the "World's Championship Series."

The Montrealers had a very strong lineup. In goal was future Hall of Famer Riley Hern; playing in front of him were the likes of Ernie Russell, Art Ross, Ernie Johnson, and Frank "Pud" Glass. It came as no surprise, then, when the Bankers added Lyceum gunner Tommy Smith to their ranks. They needed the help, and badly.

There would be no "Miracle on Ice" in this series. Ross registered two goals en route to a 6–4 Wanderers victory in game one. In the second game, Montreal rolled to a leisurely 8–1 win, powered by Russell's hat trick and a pair by Johnson. The third game was meaningless, but the Bankers were able to claim a crumb of pride with a 6–3 win.

The *Real* First All-Star Game

In a discussion regarding the origins of today's annual All-Star Game, some hockey historians invariably point to the 1934 Ace Bailey benefit game between the Toronto Maple Leafs and stars from the rest of the NHL. Others trace the All-Star tradition back to the first "official" match in 1947, when the NHL's stars duked it out with the Stanley Cup champion Toronto Maple Leafs. But the first hockey game ever to follow an All-Star format pre-dates the NHL. On January 2, 1908, a benefit game was held in honor of the Montreal Wanderers' former star cover-point Hodgson "Hod" Stuart.

Stuart was one of the finer athletes ever to come out of Canada. He starred in hockey, lacrosse, football, and track and field. In hockey, he was a superlative defenseman. He skated, set up seemingly impossible plays, rushed, and was as hard as cold steel. Sadly, he drowned near Belleville, Ontario, in the summer of 1907, only months after leading the Montreal Wanderers to the Stanley Cup title. Before the beginning of the 1908 ECAHA season, Ed Sheppard and William Northey from the Westmount Arena came up with the idea of holding a benefit, with the proceeds going to Stuart's widow. The game would be played at the Arena, the former home of the Wanderers, and Montreal would play against stars selected from the rest of the league.

The lineups:

All-Stars		Wanderers
Percy LeSueur	GOAL	Riley Hern
Rod Kennedy	POINT	Art Ross
Frank Patrick	COVER-POINT	Walter Smaill
Grover Sargent	ROVER	Frank Glass
Jack Marshall	LEFT WING	Ernie Johnson
Joe Power	CENTER	Ernie Russell
Eddie Hogan	RIGHT WING	Cecil Blachford

Smaill was filling in at cover-point for the Wanderers' Bruce Stuart, who was banged up from a game out west. On the league side, Patrick stood in for Jack Laviolette. Patrick, the former McGill University team captain, was given a Montreal Victorias uniform to wear.

By game time, there were about 4,000 fans rocking the Westmount rafters. Proceeds from the game were expected to hit the $2,000 mark.

The first half belonged to the Wanderers. The stars looked out of sync, wholly unfamiliar with each other. Forwards got into tangles and many rushes which should have resulted in goals were broken up. On the other hand, Montreal's forward line was firing on all cylinders; their skating was strong and their attacks were ever so clever. Patrick opened the scoring five minutes in on a dazzling rush from deep in his own end. This goal seemed to set the tone and the Wanderers took a whopping 7–1 lead into the intermission. The only penalties handed out in the first half were to Patrick and Glass for their part in a bumping bee behind the Montreal goal. They'd be the only infractions in the entire game.

When the All-Stars lined up to start the second half, Grover Sargent switched places with Marshall on the front line, a move that seemed to work wonders. The league luminaries played hard, aggressive hockey, scrapping back as if they had a gun to their heads. Kennedy cashed in the first goal of the second half — the first of five in a row for the All-Stars — and the Wanderers fell back on their heels. Marshall's tally at the 26-minute mark made the score 7–6 and brought the crowd to its feet. At this point the Wanderers resolved to tighten the bolts and, in a four-minute span, Blachford bagged his second and third goals of the night. The W's came out on top by a 10–7 count.

Referees Bob Meldrum and Tom Melville had an easy time handling this match; offsides were infrequent and both teams played squeaky-clean hockey. Apart from the Glass-Patrick shoving match, there was no monkey business to speak of.

The Hod Stuart benefit raked in just over $2,100 for Stuart's widow. Warm wishes were extended to the players and to the Westmount Arena staff, who lent the rink for free, and to Ed Sheppard and William Northey for their "diligence in organizing and carrying out all of the details associated with the match."

The Late, Late, Late Show

One of the hottest beefs among fans and reporters in the early days of organized hockey had to do with games starting late. It was not uncommon for hockey to begin an hour late. One game in particular, in 1908 between the Montreal Shamrocks and Quebec Bulldogs, proved an extreme case — the puck was not dropped until 11:53 p.m.! This four hour delay was caused by a railway breakdown that delayed the arrival of the train carrying the game's officials — Blair Russell, Jack Marshall, and Pat Dunlap. When the game finally kicked off, the players took to a slushy ice surface. The Quebeckers won 7–3 thanks largely to a Herb Jordan hat trick. The final second ticked off the clock at precisely twenty minutes to two the next morning. Fans were not as tired as they were irked that they had to be up in a few hours for work.

The Professional-Amateur Debate

When Lord Stanley of Preston donated his now world-famous trophy to the Amateur Hockey Association of Canada, there was no such thing as a professional club. As time passed, though, competition for Stanley's mug compelled some owners to pay their more talented players as a means of ensuring success. The practice grew increasingly common, and purely amateur clubs began to struggle while the new "shamateur" clubs flourished.

The WPHL was likely the first semi-professional hockey league. It launched in 1907 and featured such Canadian stars as Hod Stuart and Art Sixsmith, as well as players who'd been barred from the Canadian amateurs after being accused of being pros. The identity of the first professional player isn't known, although the evidence suggests the 1902 Pittsburgh Hockey Club was the first team to openly pay its players.

The first truly professional hockey league was the International Professional Hockey League, formed in 1904 by Dr. Jack Gibson. Gibson was no stranger to professionalism: he'd been a member of a team in Berlin (now Kitchener), Ontario, that was banned from hockey in 1898 when it was revealed that the town's mayor had rewarded each player with a 10-dollar gold coin after a hard-fought win against nearby Waterloo. The IPHL proved to many owners that salaries were a powerful way to attract top players. The 1905 Houghton–Portage Lakes club featured Riley Hern, "Grindy" Forrester, Barney Holden, Bruce Stuart, Joe Hall, and Fred Lake. With this star-studded lineup, they still did not finish first that year. That honor belonged to the Calumet-Larium Miners.

The IPHL's example was proof enough for some that owners with enough passion — and, of course, enough dough — could build an exciting, and winning, club. The Kenora Thistles adopted this spend-to-win strategy to a successful end. In January 1907, the Thistles paid Art Ross $1,000 to play in their two Stanley Cup matches against the Montreal Wanderers. Montreal raised no objection to this arrangement, but maybe they should have: Kenora ended up defeating the Redbands to become the team from the smallest city, in terms of population, ever to win the Cup.

Since its formation, the CAHL had been the sole major league in Canada. That changed when the Federal Amateur Hockey League was launched in 1904. With the sudden increase in the number of teams came unprecedented demand for hockey talent. Team bigwigs found they had to work harder and harder to get their hands on the top dogs, which often meant they had to loosen their purse strings.

The Montreal Wanderers were frequently accused of paying out even though they maintained amateur status. James Strachan was the team's owner and when he founded the club in 1904, he'd convinced Cecil Blachford and Jack Marshall to jump from the MAAA to his team. Did Blachford and Marshall jump ship for the thrill of playing in a new league? Or was it just the money?

In 1905, Strachan tried to get his team into the CAHL by way of a merger with the Montreal Victorias. League president Fred McRobie immediately shot down this scheme, insisting that the CAHL was to "remain a purely amateur league," an indication he suspected the Wanderers of being "shamateurs." The Eastern Canada Amateur Hockey Association, the product of a merger between the CAHL and the FAHL, allowed for amateurs and professionals to play together, starting in 1907. The only string attached was that teams would have to provide signed declarations as to their players' status.

With new protocols in effect, hockey clubs began unabashedly courting professionals. The Wanderers proceeded to raid the IPHL, grabbing Riley Hern from Houghton–Portage Lakes and the great Hod Stuart from Pittsburgh. The dawn of the professional age caught many teams off guard, though. The Ottawa Silver Seven was forced to pay Harvey Pulford and Frank McGee to keep them from straying. The club also faced ongoing salary disputes with Alf Smith and Harry Westwick. The two eventually signed, as did Tom Phillips, Fred Taylor, and Marty Walsh.

The ECAHA had another problem on its hands when all-purpose forward Frank "Pud" Glass, who had spent the entire 1906 season with the Wanderers, apparently signed contracts for 1907 with both the Wanderers and MAAA. The Glass situation had many owners up in arms. And Wanderers' boss Strachan was not one of the league's favorite owners at this point. Representatives from all six clubs met to discuss the professional-amateur issue. The Montreal Victorias, for their purposes, wanted a return to full amateurism. They had built a very strong team in the late 1890s and saw amateurism as the way to go. Naturally, the Wanderers disagreed. After all, they had signed many players to contracts when the original decision to allow professionalism had been brought down. Despite the infighting, the league came to a decision, ruling in favor of the Wanderers and returning Glass to Strachan's stable.

The situation got out of hand soon thereafter as clubs like the MAAA, Victorias, and Quebec claimed not to have professionals on their rosters. Strachan enraged many with the claim that Blachford was still an amateur despite the common knowledge that the star forward was one of the first players he had signed in 1904.

Newsmen played up the fact that the 1907 championship race would come down to a battle between the professional Wanderers and amateur Victorias. The opening game did nothing to dampen this new, however short-lived, spirit of rivalry. The Victorias lost 6–5 in overtime, proving to the world that the amateurs could run with the money-boys.

The Wanderers blew away all comers in the 1907 regular season, finishing with a spotless 10-0 record. Then they challenged Kenora for the Cup in a series that spun yet more controversy. The Thistles, as previously mentioned, had employed ringer Art Ross in their January Cup series against the Wanderers. At the time, Montreal lodged no complaints. After losing, the Wanderers swore that Kenora would not catch them napping again. Without Ross, the Thistles tried to sneak Alf Smith and Harry Westwick, both of whom had played the regular season for the Ottawa Silver Seven, aboard. "No way," said acting Cup trustee William Foran. He told the two teams that only certified, bona fide players were to play in the series . . . no ringers, period. Despite Kenora's allegation that Montreal had imported Riley Hern and Hod Stuart, Foran stood firm in his belief that if ringers could be brought in at any time, then Cup competitions were senseless.

Meanwhile, the Thistles defeated Brandon for the Manitoba Professional Hockey League championship. Against trustee Foran's orders, Kenora met the Wanderers on March 23, 1907. Smith and Westwick were on the Thistles bench, but they weren't enough to beat the Wanderers, who bulled their way to a 7–2 win in the first match. Although Kenora took a good run at the Redbands in game two, winning 6–5, it was too little, too late. Montreal had won the series by an aggregate score of 12–8. Since the "simon-pure" team had emerged victorious, Foran gave in and awarded the Stanley Cup to the Wanderers.

In 1908 the MAAA and Montreal Victorias folded and, for obvious reasons, the ECAHA dropped the "Amateur" from its name. Part way through the 1909–10 season, the league folded and most of its teams hooked up with the new National Hockey Association. One of the teams in this new super-league was the Renfrew Creamery Kings, owned by wealthy mining magnate J. Ambrose O'Brien. Backed by a fat wallet, he lured Lester and Frank Patrick, Sprague and Odie Cleghorn, Bert Lindsay, and Fred "Cyclone" Taylor to Renfrew. It is believed Lester and Frank Patrick were paid $3,000 and $2,000, respectively, while Taylor scored $5,250.

Taylor's story is an interesting one, one that opponents of professionalism pointed to as one of the shortcomings of paying players. In late 1909, O'Brien was anxious to sign Taylor. Just the season before, the electrifying rover had helped lead the Ottawa Silver Seven to the Cup title. O'Brien's scouts approached Taylor with offers ranging from $2,500 to $3,000 for the upcoming season.

In mid December the young buck met with Ottawa representatives D.B. Mulligan and Weldy Bate and, by the end of the meeting, it looked as if Taylor was staying in the capital. Bate was heard to gush that "Taylor's word is as good or better than all the contracts ever signed." In truth, no contract was forged and, only days before the Senators' season opener, Taylor announced his intention to spend the season in Renfrew. Apparently, O'Brien and his cronies had made an offer that took Taylor's breath away.

Naturally, Ottawa brass and fans were livid! They wondered how their star could turn his back on them after assuring them otherwise. In the weeks that followed, verbal jabs flew back and forth. Taylor, for his part in the soap opera, did not seem to mind. He went on to pot 11 goals.

By 1910, most teams realized that to compete for the Cup they would have to sign players to professional contracts. Meanwhile amateur clubs watched as their stars abandoned them for the pros. In 1908 Sir Montague Allan donated the Allan Cup, which came to represent the national championship of Senior amateur hockey.

Although amateur teams could still challenge for the Stanley Cup, the chasm between them and the pros eventually became insurmountable, and in 1926 the National Hockey League took exclusive possession of the trophy.

The professional-amateur debate is interesting because it foreshadowed many of the problems that are apparent in today's hockey: players paid too much, owners with deep pockets "buying" championships, and the struggle among small markets to survive.

Blood and Iron

From 1904 until 1910, the Ottawa Silver Seven and the Montreal Wanderers waged some of the most hard-fought battles ever witnessed. Much blood was shed over the course of this rivalry, which was quite comparable to the Montreal Canadiens–Toronto Maple Leafs battle of the 1940s, '50s, and '60s.

The Silver Seven was the twentieth century's first true dynasty. Names like Harvey Pulford, "Dirty" Alf Smith, Harry "Rat" Westwick, and "One-Eye" Frank McGee took on mythic status throughout the Dominion of Canada. And the opposition? Well, few teams were foolish enough to take on the Seven lest they suffer an insufferable humiliation.

Before 1900, Ottawa had been a mediocre outfit. Throughout the 1890s, they toyed with success only to choke when all the marbles were on the line. Weldy "Chalk" Young, the dashing Mac Roger, Pulford, and a young Westwick were about the only stars in Ottawa back then. Almost immediately after the turn of the century, though, young bucks like Smith, McGee, John "Bouse" Hutton, and Art Moore walked into Bytown training camps and the rest, as they say, is history.

The Wanderers were formed in 1904 by James Strachan and were charter members in the new FAHL, which competed directly with the established CAHL. Strachan got the idea to apply for a Montreal franchise in the upstart league after being approached by four disgruntled MAAA players: Jack Marshall, Jimmy Gardner, Billy Nicholson, and Billy "Turkey" Bellingham. These four, members of the legendary "Little Men of Iron" Cup-winning squad of 1902, had grown tired of the MAAA's strict amateurism and thought a change was in order. Strachan snapped them up and built a team around them.

The Wanderers' inaugural season was a good one; they finished atop the FAHL with a 6-0 record. Marshall finished first in the league in scoring with 11 goals, while speedy Ken Mallen was second with 10. Their top-dog ranking earned the Wanderers a ticket to play the CAHL champion Silver Seven in a two-game, total-goals series, the winner to lay claim to the Stanley Cup.

Game one, the first-ever meeting between the clubs, was held before 6,000 fans at the Montreal Arena on a water-covered ice surface. The mighty Seven were without Pulford and Moore, both injured, so Smith and Frank McGee's brother Jim took over on the Ottawa blue-line. Meanwhile, Montreal's defense corps was at its bashing best. Bellingham, Billy Strachan, and hired gun "Pokey" Leahy put their weight and their sticks to good use, with the bristly Smith being their most frequent target. At one point in the match, Montreal goalie Nicholson found nobody in front of him and tore off on a solo rush! Within a few yards of Hutton, though, Nicholson passed off the puck. A fine match ended in a frustrating 5–5 tie when the W's refused to play overtime in a protest over referee Kearns's officiating.

A new series of two games was ordered to be played in Ottawa. Strachan wanted the tie game to be replayed in Montreal, but Ottawa nixed the idea. Cup trustee Phillip Ross affirmed Ottawa's right to defend their Cup wherever they wished. The series was called off and Ottawa ended up accepting a two-game challenge from the pride of Brandon, Manitoba.

Competition between the teams heated up when the Silver Seven broke away from the CAHL to join the FAHL in 1905. Both clubs dominated the circuit although Ottawa finished first overall at 7-1. They scored 60 goals in their eight games while allowing only 19! The Wanderers finished a close second at 6-2. Frank McGee ran away with the scoring race — 17 goals in only six games!

On February 11, 1905, the rivalry between Ottawa and Montreal was truly forged. The evening's match was billed as the "biggest match of the season." It was a terrific struggle between two sides willing to do almost anything to nail down first place. The play in this game was simply brutal — in fact, the next morning the game was described in one Montreal paper as "a saturnalia of butchery." The devilish Smith was up to his old tricks, baiting Marshall and Frank Glass, men who both played clean hockey. But the Redbands were no choirboys, either: Bert Strachan worked McGee over quite recklessly. At one point, the big defender poleaxed McGee with his stick, knocking him out cold. Minutes later, McGee was up and about, his head swaddled in bandages. He finished the night with three goals as Ottawa won 4–2.

Following is the aggregate record of games between the Wanderers and Silver Seven, regular-season and playoffs, between 1904 and 1910:

Club	GP	W	L	T	Pts	GF	GA
Ottawa Silver Seven	15	8	6	1	17	89	73
Montreal Wanderers	15	6	8	1	13	73	89

Based on the wins and losses, Ottawa holds the slight edge. The best sides put together by each team were the 1905 Silver Seven and the 1907 Wanderers. Here's how they stacked up, position by position:

Ottawa		Montreal
Dave Finnie	GOAL	Riley Hern
Harvey Pulford	POINT	Lester Patrick
Art Moore	COVER-POINT	Hod Stuart
Harry Westwick	ROVER	Cecil Blachford
Frank McGee	CENTER	Ernie Russell
Billy Gilmour	LEFT WING	Ernie Johnson
Alf Smith	RIGHT WING	Frank Glass

We rated each player on a scale from 1 to 10 in three different areas. Then we calculated a mean score to determine which team was stronger overall.

OOV	=	Overall Offensive Value
ODV	=	Overall Defensive Value
OLV	=	Overall Leadership Value
OV	=	Overall Value

1905 Ottawa Silver Seven

Player	Pos	OOV	ODV	OLV	OV
Alf Smith	RW	9.0	8.5	9.0	8.83
Harvey Pulford	P	7.0	9.5	9.5	8.67
Frank McGee	C	9.5	8.5	8.0	8.67
Harry Westwick	R	8.5	8.5	8.5	8.50
Dave Finnie	G	-	-	-	8.50
Art Moore	CP	6.0	9.0	9.0	8.00
Billy Gilmour	LW	7.0	7.5	7.5	7.33
Team Value					**8.357**

1907 Montreal Wanderers

Player	Pos	OOV	ODV	OLV	OV
Lester Patrick	P	8.5	8.5	9.0	8.67
Riley Hern	G	-	-	-	8.50
Hod Stuart	CP	7.5	9.0	8.5	8.33
Ernie Johnson	LW	8.5	8.5	8.0	8.33
Cecil Blachford	R	8.0	8.5	8.5	8.33
Ernie Russell	C	9.5	7.5	7.5	8.17
Frank Glass	RW	7.5	8.5	8.0	8.00
Team Value					**8.333**

TALE OF THE TAPE:

	Ottawa	Montreal
Goaltending	X	
Team Defense		X
Physical Game	X	X
Finesse Game	X	X
Forward Lines	X	
Edge	X	

Player for player, and skill for skill, Ottawa wins again, by the slightest of margins.

A detailed comparison could be a book in itself. The stories are there, the characters are there, and, with a little bit of digging, the statistics are there. Let us simply say that, although the difference between Montreal and Ottawa is remarkably small, in our opinion the feared Silver Seven were the greatest of their time.

*Snap!*shots

DICKIE BOON Defense
b. 1/10/1878, Belleville, Ontario
d. 5/3/1961, Montreal, Quebec

Dickie Boon

When a blond, wiry, 120-pounder by the name of Dickie Boon entered hockey's highest ranks, many assumed he would not last. But Boon made the naysayers eat crow. Boon combined blistering speed, superior hand-eye coordination, and a knowledge of the scientific aspects of the game to become one of hockey's first great rushing defenders.

Richard Boon opened his career with the Montreal Young Crystals in the early 1890s, helping them to a good measure of success. From there, he joined the MAAA defense, proving himself quickly. His skills and leadership inspired the MAAA "Little Men of Iron" of 1901–02, and he won Canadian speed skating competitions from 1901 to 1904.

It has been said that Boon, and not Mike Grant, was the first blue-liner to consistently rush the puck. Still others name the Winnipeg Victorias' Magnus Flett or Rat Portage's "Tuffy" Bellefeuille. In any case, Boon was one of the first to adopt "rusher" as his official role. Boon was also more than just a rusher: he used the poke-check to great effect long before Frank Nighbor and Jack Walker, the two usually credited with originating the maneuver. Montreal Shamrock forward Jack Brannen, himself a champion speed skater, thought Boon was the hardest defender in the league to stick-handle past because of his quickness, coordination, and anticipatory skills.

Boon retired at his peak and went on to become an architect of the great Montreal Wanderer clubs from 1906 until the late 1910s. He was named to the Hockey Hall of Fame in 1952.

Peak Years   *1901–05*
In a Word   *SPRITE*

RUSSELL BOWIE (Dubbie) Center/Rover
5'6" 122
b. 8/24/1880, Montreal, Quebec
d. 4/8/1959, Montreal, Quebec

Russell Bowie

Russell Bowie learned his hockey craft at Montreal's Tudor School, which turned out more than its share of prominent puck-chasers at the turn of the century (Ernie Johnson and Ernie Russell are other notables). In 1899, at the tender age of 18, Bowie made his hockey debut in an Ottawa–Montreal Victorias tilt. Montreal won the game, in which Bowie scored twice, 16–0.

Like Wayne Gretzky, Bowie was one of the most difficult players of his era to keep track of. Although he was invariably a "marked man," his agility usually kept him out of harm's way. A wizard with the wood, he used his skates to shield the rubber as he swung through the enemy line with a deftness that defied description.

Bowie was the top goal scorer in hockey from 1900 through 1908; in all, he counted an eye-popping 234 goals in 80 games. His career goals-per-game average of almost three will most definitely remain unbroken.

Bowie staunchly maintained his amateur status in the face of tantalizing professional offers from teams like the Montreal Wanderers. The Wanderers, aware of Bowie's love of music, even offered to buy him a grand piano in exchange for his signature on a pro contract. Bowie flatly refused. It was said that Bowie had accepted money from the Redbands, but a league investigation cleared him.

During a game in 1910, Bowie fell on the ice and broke his collarbone. Shortly thereafter, he retired. He would become one of the finest referees in eastern Canada and was a well-respected Montreal sportsman until his death in 1959 at the age of 78.

Bowie's scoring feats include 17 three-goal games, 9 four-goal games, 11 five-goal games, 5 six-goal games, 2 seven-goal games, and 1 eight-goal game. He was named to the Hockey Hall of Fame in 1945.

Peak Years   *1903–07*
In a Word   *PEERLESS*

PUD GLASS Right Wing
b. 1884
d. 3/2/1965

Frank "Pud" Glass was a chippy little guy who set up many a goal in his days as a Montreal Wanderer. He joined the club in 1905, its second year, and played alongside Jack Marshall and Cecil Blachford. Stanley Cups are won with solid, two-way play, a concern for goals being scored in both ends of the rink. Glass proved this truth time and time again. He was in perpetual motion; when he wasn't forechecking tirelessly to create room for scoring line-mate Ernie Russell, he was heading back to help his defenders with their chores.

Glass left the Wanderers to sign with the Montreal Canadiens in 1912, becoming the first ever English-speaking player of note to put on the uniform of the *bleu, blanc, et rouge*. After retiring, he refereed in the NHA.

Surprisingly, Glass is not in the Hockey Hall of Fame.

Peak Years   *1906–10*
In a Word   *COG*

BOUSE HUTTON Goal
b. 10/24/1877, Ottawa, Ontario
d. 10/27/1962

John "Bouse" Hutton stands as the only man to win the Stanley Cup, the Canadian football championship, and the Canadian lacrosse championship in the same year (1904). He is perhaps best known, though, as the "go-to" goalie of Ottawa's Silver Seven championship teams of 1903 and 1904.

Hutton was possibly the first acrobatic goalie, as he eschewed the rigid stand-up style so common in his day. It's said he sometimes resembled a jumping jack in the cage when the going was hot. A true entertainer.

Tommy Gorman, the prominent Ottawa sportsman and eventual manager of the Ottawa Senators, thought Hutton was the best goalie he ever saw, choosing him over the likes of Georges Vezina, Hugh Lehman, and Charlie Gardiner.

Hutton was made a member of the Hockey Hall of Fame in 1962.

Peak Years   *1900–1904*
In a Word   *ACROBAT*

ERNIE JOHNSON (Moose/The India Rubber Man)
Defense/Rover/Left Wing
6'1" 188
b. 2/26/1886, Montreal, Quebec
d. 3/25/1963 White Rock, British Columbia

Try to image the rinks of Montreal's Point St. Charles district around the turn of the twentieth century, where young boys, mostly of Irish descent, played hard and fought even harder. Here marks the beginning of the story of Ernie Johnson.

Ernie Johnson

The big, fair-haired Johnson entered Junior hockey in 1900 and by 1904 he was playing for the MAAA. "When I first started playing this game, I once played Junior on a Friday night, Intermediate the following Saturday afternoon, and then a Senior league game that Saturday night!" Johnson once said. "I played Senior ever since though." He turned professional with the Montreal Wanderers and played with them at left wing and cover-point on four Cup champions — 1906, 1907, 1908, and 1910.

Johnson left Montreal to join the New Westminster Royals of the Pacific Coast Hockey Association (PCHA) for the 1911–12 season. The Royals moved to Portland three years later, where they became the "Rosebuds." In 1916, Johnson contributed to a Portland league title and appearance in the Cup finals. During these finals, Johnson's return to Montreal triggered a major rhubarb among the locals. There had been hard feelings between Johnson and the Wanderers' management when he went west. Apparently the bitterness was dying hard because Montreal owner Sam Lichtenhein slapped his former star with a breach-of-contract suit.

Johnson earned the nickname "Moose" toward the end of his career. His big, muscular frame and 99-inch reach left many observers awestruck. "The year I quit, they buried my stick," Johnson later said. "It was the longest stick ever used. In those days, there were no size regulations and they couldn't take it from me because it was my means of livelihood."

And what a livelihood! Johnson used his stick to every advantage, even throwing it at the feet of opposing forwards, a practice that was outlawed in 1915.

Johnson was a powerful skater and one of the faster men of his day. Oddly, he played his entire career without any fingers on his right hand! In 1900, he lost the fingers after receiving a 2,300 volt electrical jolt.

Jack Marshall, who played point behind Johnson in Montreal, held the big blond in high regard: "By the time a forward got around Johnson on defense, the rest was easy for me," Marshall explained. "They were usually somewhere over by the boards."

Johnson was a regular First-Team All-Star on PCHA referee Mickey Ion's famous hand-picked squads and has been considered the finest all-around rearguard in hockey between 1900 and 1925. Regularly playing with broken jaws, fractured arms, even separated shoulders, Johnson was a gamer in the truest sense.

Johnson made the Hockey Hall of Fame in 1952.

Peak Years   *1907–11*
In a Word   *OCTOPUS*

JACK MARSHALL (The Human Locomotive) Forward/Defense
5'9" 160
b. 3/14/1877, Ste. Vallier, Quebec
d. 8/7/1965, Montreal, Quebec

Jack Marshall started out in 1901 as a center with the Winnipeg Victorias. The club went to Montreal in the spring of that year and defeated the Shamrocks for the Stanley

Cup. Marshall stayed on for a two-year stint with the MAAA, then he jumped to the Montreal Wanderers. After further gigs with the Ottawa Montagnards, the Wanderers again, the Shamrocks, the Wanderers yet again, and the Toronto Blueshirts, he ended his career in 1917 after one last go-round with the W's.

Marshall's robust skating style earned him the nickname the "Human Locomotive." He was a fine all-around player, a true jack-of-all-trades, who played the wings, at center, and at point. He was also a pioneer, being among the first players in eastern Canada to adopt the tube skate. In 16 seasons, Marshall appeared in 132 games, scoring 99 times. He picked up another 13 goals in 18 career Cup games. By career's end, he had captured the Cup a remarkable six times, a record that endured for some 50 years.

Marshall was elected to the Hockey Hall of Fame in 1965.

Peak Years   *1907–11*
In a Word   *HANDYMAN*

FRANK McGEE (One-Eye) Center/Rover
6'0" 191
b. 1879, Ottawa, Ontario
d. 9/16/1916, France

Frank McGee's name has been at the center of many a discussion regarding the greatest goal scorer in history. Although most of those who saw McGee play are not alive today to connect the dots for us, the records paint a vivid picture.

Frank McGee

McGee was a courageous, heavily muscled center and rover on the glorious Ottawa Silver Seven. Contemporary reports describe a man with scorching speed, one who exploded into the play. He was one of the top scorers of his era despite the fact he played his entire career with only one eye! During a 1902 exhibition game in Montreal, when McGee was a Junior, his left eye was scuffed by a high stick.

In the words of the Montreal *Herald*'s Elmer Ferguson, McGee "had a purely animal rhythm about him like no other player I've seen in this sport. It was that rhythm and beautiful instinct for this game that set him apart from the rest." Picture McGee tearing up the ice with a man on his back, his slick blond mane breaking through the arena's dimness. He stick-handles his way past his opponents, his genteel countenance contorted during battle. Just then, before a spectator can crack the next peanut, *BANG!* Ottawa goal, scored by McGee.

McGee's greatest scoring feat occurred during the Silver Seven's 1905 Cup defense against the Dawson City Nuggets. In a series the Nuggets trekked more than 4,000 miles to play, Ottawa took the Cup after 9–2 and 23–2 victories. McGee scored 14 of the 23 goals in game two, including eight in a row, a single-game output that will likely never be topped.

McGee played with the Silver Seven from 1903 until 1906, during which time he and his comrades repelled some of the best All-Star squads in Canada. When World War One broke out, he enlisted in the Canadian Armed Forces but was killed in action at the Battle of the Somme in 1916. He has since been remembered with the epitaph, "Here falls a mighty oak."

Montreal Wanderers' goalie Riley Hern once said of McGee, "If I had the choice of them all from which to pick a team, the first man I'd take would be McGee." In 45 regular-season and playoff encounters, McGee notched 134 goals.

McGee is a worthy member of the Hockey Hall of Fame.

Peak Years   *1903–06*
In a Word   *MYTHIC*

PADDY MORAN Goal

5'11" 180
b. 3/11/1877, Quebec City, Quebec
d. 1/15/1966, Quebec City, Quebec

Patrick "Paddy" Moran joined the Quebec Hockey Club in 1902 and played 15 of the next 16 seasons in the "Old Capital." After a one-year interlude with Haileybury in 1909–10, he returned to Quebec to backstop them to two Stanley Cup wins.

According to one source, "none ever played the game with so much zest and more loved to win and hated to lose." Indeed, Moran was a fireball in the cage. The husky netminder guarded his territory by attacking or even chasing enemy players down the ice. He once chased Newsy Lalonde the length of the rink. And although he was often named the top goalkeeper in the league, he tended nets for some poor Quebec sides over the years. Almost every night was a rubber rainstorm for the Irishman. Small wonder, then, that he had the local priest bless him before every match.

Moran was resourceful, too. To combat the drafty, sub-zero conditions common in the old arenas, he wore a big sweater-coat, which he would keep unbuttoned and use as a sail with which to trap shots on their way across the goalmouth.

Although there was no rule governing play around the net, skaters soon learned a healthy respect for Moran's personal space. Those who did not give way were hacked, slashed, and bodied by the big goalie as a reminder of who owned the cage.

Moran's 1958 election into the Hockey Hall of Fame came only after years of lobbying from peers, friends, and journalists.

Peak Years 1903–07
In a Word CRANKY

BILLY NICHOLSON Goal

5'7" 250

William Nicholson was one of the fattest men ever to play at the semi-professional or professional level. Originally the goalie for the MAAA "Little Men of Iron" — circa 1901 — he has been called the first true "butterfly" goalie. He was flopping to the ice to make saves at least 10 years before Clint Benedict, the goalie who has been generally credited with pioneering the style.

Throughout most of his career Nicholson was a solid, dependable goalkeeper. He played on some poor teams, such as the so-so 1907–08 Shamrocks and 1912–13 Toronto Tecumsehs. He rounded out his career with the Toronto Arenas in 1916–17.

The sight of Nicholson in full uniform, wearing his trademark toque and weighing anywhere from 250 to 275 pounds, must have been delicious. Apparently, whenever he crashed down onto the ice to make a save, everyone would hold their breath in fear that the ice would crack. He was surprisingly athletic, though, despite the constraints of his admittedly plus-sized frame. His career, while not of Hockey Hall of Fame caliber, compares favorably to the goaltending standard of his era.

Peak Years 1901–05
In a Word TANK

TOM PHILLIPS (Nibs) Left Wing/Right Wing
5'8" 150
b. 5/22/1883, Kenora, Ontario
d. 11/30/1923, Toronto, Ontario

Tom Phillips played shinny as a schoolboy before going east to play hockey for both McGill University (1902) and the MAAA. By 1905 he was back in Kenora, captaining the Rat Portage Thistles to two strong Stanley Cup challenges. He headlined a star-studded cast that included Eddie Giroux, "Tuffy" Bellefeuille, Si Griffis, Tom Hooper, and Billy McGimsie. Invading Ottawa in 1905, Rat Portage's best scored a sensational 9–3 upset in game one. Ottawa came back to take the second game, 4–2, and the third, 5–4, to retain the Cup.

Virtually overnight, Phillips was the talk of the hockey world. Stories were told of a speed-demon from out west, a hockeyist "game" to the core. This man had a vast repertoire of skills, each of them polished to a glimmer. He controlled the puck exceptionally well, possessed a deadly shot, and had a knack for defensive pursuits, especially the back-check.

In 1907, the Thistles journeyed to Montreal to lock horns with the Wanderers. In the opening tilt, Phillips scored all the goals for his side in a 4–2 triumph. When Kenora took the second game, 8–6, the Cup was finally theirs. Only two months later, though, the Wanderers regained the silverware from Kenora.

Phillips had a devastating shot. His blasts were often referred to as "cross fires." At a time when hockey fans argued on behalf of the Russell Bowies, Frank McGees, and Hod Stuarts as hockey's top player, "Nibs" was easily the all-around pick of the litter.

Phillips died at age 40 due to complications after the removal of a rotten tooth. He is a member of the Hockey Hall of Fame.

Peak Years   1903–07
In a Word   CROSS FIRE

ERNIE RUSSELL Center/Rover/Right Wing
5'8" 160
b. 10/21/1883, Montreal, Quebec
d. 2/23/1963, Montreal, Quebec

Ernie Russell played on all four Stanley Cup–winning Montreal Wanderer clubs and consistently figured among the leading scorers in the ECHA and later the NHA. In 1907, he scored an astounding 42 goals in nine games. Russell grew up in Montreal, excelling in all sports. He captained the Sterling Juniors hockey team when they won the Canadian title in 1903. That same year, he led the MAAA Junior football club to a title. He entered top-level hockey competition in 1905 with the MAAA and, a year later, he jumped to the spanking-new Montreal Wanderers where he made his mark.

Although Russell could pass, stick-handle, and skate, his scoring instinct was quickly shown to be his bread and butter. His genius around the net spurred the Redbands to Cup wins in 1906, 1907, 1908, and 1910. Many have said that the only reason the Wanderers failed to win in 1909 as well was that Russell had been expelled for the season by club brass, who'd been displeased that he played hockey for the Wanderers, but played other sports for the Montreal AAA. Upon his return in 1910, he and the Montreal Canadiens' Newsy Lalonde engaged in a furious race for the league scoring title, the likes of which had never before been seen. Lalonde won by a 38–31 count on the strength of a nine-goal performance in the last game of the season.

Russell operated at a frighteningly machine-like clip. For the first 50 years of the twentieth century, there were only a handful of men as deadly around the enemy net as he was. In 98 games, he scored 180 goals.

Russell was named to the Hockey Hall of Fame in 1965.

Peak Years   *1907–11*
In a Word   *POACHER*

ALF SMITH (Dirty Alf) Right Wing
5'7" 165
b. 6/3/1873, Ottawa, Ontario
d. 8/21/1953

Among the scores of hockey players over the years with the last name "Smith," none have proved as great as the one they called "Dirty Alf." Indeed, the roughneck play of Smith and longtime teammate Harvey Pulford earned the Silver Seven the sobriquet "dirty Ottawa."

Alfred Smith was possibly the meanest, most vicious hockey player of the early era. He was exceedingly expert with the stick, both for scoring and for head-cracking. He was an outstanding all-around player, a fortress of strength on the dynasty Silver Seven. The one-two offensive punch of Smith and "One-Eyed" Frank McGee was often lethal and capable of burying the enemy in a game's first 10 minutes.

Smith's first crack at hockey was with the Ottawa Electrics in 1890 and 1891. From there, he joined the Ottawa Capitals before joining the Pennsylvania league's Pittsburgh side. After spending a year in the States, he joined the Ottawa Hockey Club, co-captaining the Seven to Stanley Cup victories in 1903, 1904, and 1905.

At the end of the 1907 season, Smith and teammate Rat Westwick joined the Kenora Thistles for a Cup challenge series against the Montreal Wanderers. Without these two prized veterans, the Thistles would no doubt have been hard-pressed to compete, let alone win. A rematch between the clubs proved as much.

Smith went on to assume player/coach duties in Pittsburgh for a while, then he took to full-time bench duties with the Renfrew Millionaires.

In 65 games, Smith scored 90 goals. He is a worthy member of the Hockey Hall of Fame.

Peak Years   *1900–1904*
In a Word   *DIRTY*

HOD STUART Defense
6'1" 200
b. 1879, Ottawa, Ontario
d. 6/23/1907, Belleville, Ontario

Hodgson Stuart's story began in Ottawa's recreational hockey leagues, where he dazzled crowds with a complete mastery of the game. In 1904, he and his brother Bruce went to the States to join the IPHL. Stuart was a standout for the Houghton–Portage Lakes side in Michigan as well as for Pittsburgh. He also played with Calument of the IPHL.

The IPHL proved exceedingly rough. Lurid accounts of unprecedented savagery made their way into the newspapers at an alarming rate. Players of Stuart's talent attracted the most unpleasant of attention from the opposition. By 1907, he had had enough: "(Pittsburgh) could not offer me enough money here to go through what I went through last year in this league. Everybody had a slur for me and I could not lift my stick off the ice. That is a fact. I never lift my stick off the ice except in shooting and never check a man with the stick."

With the Montreal Wanderers, the team that went on to win the 1907 ECHA title, Stuart came through big-time. Instead of anchoring himself to the blue-line, he rushed the puck with remarkable ease and fluidity. With his help, the Redbands were able to regain the Cup from the Kenora Thistles. At the time, Stuart was being called the "greatest hockey player in the world," although he would not have long to savor the praise . . .

In the midday summer heat of June 23, 1907, Stuart went swimming with friends in the Bay of Quinte near Belleville, Ontario. As he dove into the water, he struck his head on a sub-surface rock. He died almost instantly. What may be considered hockey's first benefit game was held the following season to raise funds for Stuart's widow.

Stuart stands among a select group of hockey legends. He was capable of controlling a game's flow, much like Doug Harvey of the Montreal Canadiens some 50 years later. Stuart died in his late twenties. One can only imagine what his career would have been had he lived longer. In the eyes of Hall of Fame referee Chaucer Elliott, Stuart could, "skate, shoot, play-make, and play-break . . . and was a good fellow as well."

Stuart was one of the 12 charter members of the Hockey Hall of Fame, elected in 1945.

Peak Years   1903-07
In a Word   EFFORTLESS

RAT WESTWICK Rover
b. 4/23/1876, Ottawa, Ontario
d. 4/3/1957, Ottawa, Ontario

Harry Westwick

When people talk of the all-time great competitors in hockey, names like Bobby Clarke and Ted Lindsay often come to the fore. But many years back, a fierce competitor hit hockey's highest level and starred for well over a decade in Ottawa. His name was Harry Westwick.

Westwick was small, but he came to play every night. He was a key member of all three Cup-winning Ottawa Silver Seven teams – between 1903 and 1905 — and one of the best lacrosse players of his or any other era. Some say his famous nickname was born out of his agility on skates, his ability to be as "elusive as a rodent." Hockey historian Don Reddick, though, traces the moniker to the pen of a Quebec sportswriter who described Westwick as a "miserable, insignificant rat."

Westwick began his career as a goalie but, while playing a game for the Ottawa Juniors, he was pressed into action as a forward. His strange, weaving style of handling the puck caught the eye of the head coach and the rest is history.

Westwick's determination was exemplified in a game between the Montreal Victorias and Silver Seven in 1903. It was the end of the season and the two sides were embroiled in a battle for the Cup. In the first match, Westwick was forced to leave the ice three times because of injuries. Battered and bruised, he refused to quit. It was not until Bert Strachan broke a bone in Westwick's foot that he was forced to take himself out of the match. Even then, he insisted on skating off the ice, the bone of his right ankle protruding from his foot. Doctors worked on him for half an hour, at which time he begged them to permit him to see the end of the game. The final score was 2–2 and Ottawa went on to win the Cup in the next match. Westwick played the match on a broken ankle.

Westwick is a member of the Hockey Hall of Fame.

Peak Years   1900–1904
In a Word   SLIPPERY

The All-Stars

Position	Player	Season	GP	G	A
P	Harvey Pulford	1903	7	0	–
CP	Hod Stuart	1907	8	3	–
R	Russell Bowie	1907	10	38	–
C	Frank McGee	1906	6	17	–
LW	Tom Phillips	1908	10	26	–
RW	Alf Smith	1905	8	13	–
				GAA	ShO
G	Bouse Hutton	1903	8	3.25	0

The
Tens

In a Flash

COMPOSITE REGULAR-SEASON STANDINGS
(JANUARY 1, 1910–DECEMBER 31, 1919)

Canadian Hockey Association
National Hockey Association
National Hockey League

Club	GP	W	L	T	Pts	WPct	GF	GA
Ottawa Senators	194	118	76	0	236	.608	940	756
Toronto 228th Battalion	10	6	4	0	12	.600	70	57
Renfrew Millionaires	28	16	11	1	33	.589	187	155
Quebec Bulldogs	143	75	66	2	152	.531	671	674
Montreal Canadiens	193	96	96	1	193	.500	826	785
Montreal Wanderers	156	74	82	0	148	.474	782	810
Toronto Blueshirts/Arenas/St. Pats	137	64	72	1	129	.471	576	596
Montreal Shamrocks	15	5	9	1	11	.367	81	112
Cobalt Silver Kings	12	4	8	0	8	.333	79	104
Haileybury Hockey Club	12	4	8	0	8	.333	77	83
All-Montreal Hockey Club	3	1	2	0	2	.333	13	23
Toronto Tecumsehs/Onts/Ont-Shams	60	18	42	0	36	.300	196	302
Montreal Nationals	3	0	3	0	0	.000	23	43

Pacific Coast Hockey Association

Club	GP	W	L	T	Pts	WPct	GF	GA
Vancouver Millionaires	144	78	66	0	156	.542	731	651
Seattle Metropolitans	82	48	34	0	96	.585	330	262
Portland/New Westminster	124	60	64	0	120	.484	559	552
Victoria Aristocrats	103	44	59	0	88	.427	416	517
Spokane Canaries	23	8	15	0	16	.348	89	143

Ontario Professional Hockey League

Club	GP	W	L	T	Pts	WPct	GF	GA
Waterloo Professionals	34	21	13	0	42	.618	162	148
Berlin Dutchmen	35	21	14	0	42	.600	196	161
Galt Professionals	35	18	17	0	36	.514	197	201
Brantford Indians	32	8	24	0	16	.250	138	183

HELLOS

Marshall McLuhan *media theorist*	July 21, 1911
Bill Cowley *Boston Bruins center*	June 12, 1912
Milton Friedman *American economist*	July 31, 1912
Gene Kelly *American dancer and actor*	August 23, 1912
Elmer Lach *Punch Line member*	January 22, 1918
Richard Feynman *American physicist*	May 11, 1918
Terry Reardon	April 6, 1919

GOODBYES

Florence Nightingale *English nurse*   August 13, 1910
Leo Tolstoy *Russian writer*   November 20, 1910
Fanny Crosby *poet*   February 12, 1915
Frank McGee *Silver Seven scoring ace*   September 16, 1916
Joe Hall *Canadiens defenseman*   April 5, 1919
Sir Wilfrid Laurier *Canadian
  prime minister*   February 17, 1919

REGULAR SEASON

BEST RECORD
1910–11 Ottawa Senators 13-3-0

WORST RECORD
1911 Brantford Indians, 1-17-0

FAMOUS FIRSTS

GOAL SCORED, DECADE
Sibby Nichols

PENALTY, DECADE
Sibby Nichols

NHL GAME
December 19, 1917, Toronto Arenas 9,
Montreal Wanderers 10

NHL GOAL SCORED
Dave Ritchie

NHL SHUTOUT
February 18, 1918. Georges Vezina blanked
Toronto, 9–0.

AMERICAN TEAM TO COMPETE FOR STANLEY CUP
Portland Rosebuds, 1915

AMERICAN TEAM TO WIN STANLEY CUP
Seattle Metropolitans, 1917

ARTIFICIAL ICE RINK IN CANADA
The Victoria Arena was completed in time
for the PCHA's inaugural season in 1912.

PLAYER TO REACH 300 GOALS
Newsy Lalonde, February 20, 1918

MISCELLANEOUS

MOST GOALS, SEASON
44   Joe Malone, 1917–18

MOST GOALS, DECADE
245   Newsy Lalonde

BIGGEST PLAYER
Harry Mummery, 5' 11" 255

SMALLEST PLAYER
Tommy Smith, 5' 4" 140

COOLEST HANDLES
Edouard "Newsy" Lalonde
Hugh "Eagle Eye" Lehman
"Phantom" Joe Malone
Roy "Minnie" McGiffen
Archie "Sue" McLean
Howard McNamara, "The Dynamite Boy"
Frank "Dutch" Nighbor, "The Pembroke
  Peach"
Lester Patrick, "The Silver Fox"
Didier Pitre, "Old Folks"
George Poulin, "The Tabasco Kid"
Goldie Prodgers, "The Cinnamon Bearcat"
Fred "Cyclone" Taylor, "The Listowel
  Thunderbolt"
Georges Vezina, "The Chicoutimi
  Cucumber"

BEST SHOT
Didier Pitre was early hockey's Bobby Hull.
In 1914, chicken wire was installed in
Victoria's arena to protect fans from his shot.

BEST PASSER
Sam "Hamby" Shore

BEST STICK-HANDLER
Joe Malone

BEST SKATER
Jack Laviolette was the original Flying Frenchman.

WORST SKATER
Fred Lake was a sturdy defender for the Senators over six seasons but was said to have skated like an "eggbeater."

FASTEST PLAYER
Didier Pitre turned speed into a drawing-card feature. Today's practice of spitting up ice before stopping is said to have been started by Pitre!

BEST SNIPER
Newsy Lalonde

BEST PENALTY-KILLER
Russell "Rusty" Crawford went at the opposition "like a mad dog, always giving his best effort to beat them." Arf arf.

BEST BODY-CHECKER
Joe Hall

BEST POKE-CHECKER
Ernie Johnson

BEST SHOT-BLOCKER
Alex Irving may not have played professional hockey but his "Terry Turner Slide" was the stuff of, er, legend.

BEST GOALTENDER
Georges Vezina turned in some great performances behind teams not known for their defensive abilities.

MOST UNUSUAL GOALTENDING STYLE
Clint Benedict was one odd duck. His style was very similar to that of modern Czech import Dominik Hasek. Initially, whenever Benedict flopped to the ice, referees would penalize him. Fans in opposing rinks would scream "get a mattress!" After a while, though, his kinky style was accepted.

FINEST ATHLETE
Jack Laviolette

BEST DEFENSIVE FORWARD
Jack Walker was for many years the best defensive forward in the Pacific Coast Hockey Association, perhaps in all of hockey.

WORST DEFENSIVE FORWARD
Bruce Ridpath was what the old-timers called a loafer. His short and brilliant career was cut short when he was struck dead by a vehicle in 1911.

BEST SHADOW
Jack Walker shut down many a top gun with his jabbing poke-checks and sweeping hooks. Lalonde, Pitre, Morenz, Joliat . . . the "Old Fox" had their numbers.

BEST DEFENSIVE DEFENSEMAN
Ernie Johnson was for many years a fixture on PCHA All-Star teams. Because of his uncanny poke- and sweep-checking skills, he was often moved to rover, where his two-way skills could be best utilized.

BEST OFFENSIVE DEFENSEMAN
Harry Cameron was the first defenseman to shoot from the point in earnest and developed the so-called "curve-shot."

BEST UTILITY PLAYER
Ken Randall was a fine all-purpose player for the Toronto Blueshirts and Arenas, shining despite his fistic inclinations.

STRONGEST PLAYER
Harry Mummery

TOUGHEST PLAYER
Joe Hall

BEST FIGHTER
Frank Patrick was a master pugilist. After bashing a young Joe Hall in 1910, Patrick took his place in the upper echelon of hockey's Hard-as-Nails Club.

MOST ABLE INSTIGATOR
Ken Randall

DIRTIEST PLAYER
Carol "Cully" Wilson was the PCHA's answer to Joe Hall. Wilson was a mean, moon-faced man who specialized in running star players. His attack on Mickey

MacKay in 1919 stands as one of the ugliest incidents in the history of the game.

CLEANEST PLAYER
Frank Nighbor

BEST CORNER-MAN
Jack Marks

Louis Berlinquette

BEST-LOOKING PLAYER
Louis Berlinquette was a superb defensive forward for the Canadiens. He looked every bit the playboy with his steel-gray eyes, granite jaw, wavy salt-and-pepper hair, and bronze skin.

UGLIEST PLAYER
Cyclone Taylor became even more "beautiful" when his hair fell out. Among his more ghastly facial imperfections was a pair of Igor-type eyebrows.

BALDEST PLAYER
Cyclone Taylor was an early candidate for the Hair Club for Men. He gave new meaning to the word "egghead."

MOST UNDERRATED
Tommy Smith was overshadowed by better-known teammates for the better part of his career, most notably in Quebec, where he played alongside the likes of Joe Malone and Joe Hall. Smith quietly carved out a Hall of Fame career, scoring 240 goals in 159 games.

MOST CONSISTENT PLAYER
Bobby Rowe

MOST UNPREDICTABLE CAREER
Sprague Cleghorn

BEST INSTINCTS
Newsy Lalonde

MOST HATED PLAYER
Cully Wilson

MOST ADMIRED PLAYER
Cyclone Taylor was the jewel of the West Coast and a demigod in the city of Vancouver.

BEST LINES

Team:	Montreal Canadiens
LW:	Jack Laviolette
C:	Newsy Lalonde
RW:	Didier Pitre
R:	–
Team:	Vancouver Millionaires
LW:	Barney Stanley
C:	Mickey MacKay
RW:	Frank Nighbor
R:	Fred Taylor

HIGHEST-PAID PLAYER
Fred Taylor ate like a king in his puck-chasing days. His contract for the 1909–10 season with the Creamery Kings was worth $5,250, a fat salary in those days.

MOST TRAGIC CAREER
Joe Hall

PLAYER VERSUS TEAM
Newsy Lalonde vs. Montreal Canadiens (every season). Lalonde's stubborn holdouts with Canadiens manager George Kennedy were a preseason ritual throughout the decade.

BEST LAWS
Charlie Querrie was the head coach of the Toronto Blueshirts/ Arenas. His code of conduct is worth a peek:

Charles Querrie

- First and foremost, do not forget that I am running the club.
- You are being paid to give your best services to the club. Condition depends a lot on how you behave off the ice.
- It does not require bravery to hit another man over the head with a stick. If you want to fight, go over to France.

- You will not be fined for doing the best you can. You will be punished for indifferent work or carelessness.
- Do not think you are putting over something on the manager when you do anything you should not. You are being paid to play hockey, not to be a good fellow.
- I am an easy boss if you do your share. If you do not want to be on the square and play hockey, turn in your uniform to Dick Carroll and go at some other work.

BEST GENERAL MANAGER
George Kennedy, owner and manager of the Canadiens, was a shrewd businessman, especially skilled at getting players to sign for less money than they were worth.

OUTSTANDING SPORTSWRITER
Tommy Gorman, Ottawa *Citizen*

BEST STANLEY CUP FINAL
1918 — Toronto Arenas vs. Vancouver Millionaires
In this best-of-five series, Toronto's lunch-bucket style wore down the favorites from the West Coast. Vancouver's vastly superior skating and puck-handling abilities had been expected to confound Toronto. Instead, the Arenas pushed Vancouver to a winner-take-all fifth game, in which a dramatic third-period goal by Corb Denneny won the game, 2–1, and the series.

IMPORTANT RULE CHANGES

1911
- Games to consist of three 20-minute periods instead of 30-minute halves

1912
- Rover position is eliminated, reducing number of men on the ice from seven to six. However, the newly formed Pacific Coast Hockey Association keeps the seventh man.
- Teams to have no more than nine players on roster
- Player substitutions allowed
- Major fouls are accompanied by ejection from game and a $5 fine.

- Major fouls include:
    a) throwing the stick to prevent a goal from being scored;
    b) cross checking or striking an opponent;
    c) charging from behind;
    d) deliberate tripping or hooking;
    e) foul language.
- Each subsequent infraction after first one subject to $8 fine
- Minor fouls include:
    a) kicking, throwing, holding, or batting the puck with a hand;
    b) raising the stick above the shoulder except to lift the puck;
    c) loafing offside.
- Overtime introduced to break ties in regular-season games
- Percy LeSueur's goal-net model adopted by National Hockey Association

1913
- Holding, tripping, and loafing offside are defined as minor fouls.
- Throwing the stick, cross checking, charging from behind, kicking, and "collaring" (similar to today's roughing) defined as majors
- Match penalties issued for disabling or intentionally injuring opponent. Players are fined $25 for the first offense, and the offending party is sent off the ice until the injured party returns.
- Megaphone-coaching from sidelines disallowed

1914
- Referees to drop the puck for face-offs instead of placing it on the ice between two opponents
- Goalies who lie down to stop shots are fined $2. Second offense considered a major foul.
- Substituting "on the fly," i.e., while puck is in play, is allowed.
- Goalie sticks to be no wider than 3.5 inches at any point
- A dark line is painted between goal posts.

- Blue-lines introduced by Frank Patrick in the PCHA. Forward passing allowed only in neutral zone between the two blue-lines.

1915

- Offside no longer called when puck is played after goalie gives up a rebound.
- Charging an opponent into the boards is a major foul.
- Players assessed a match penalty sit off for 10 minutes and are fined $15. If the infraction is committed within 10 minutes of the end of the match, the player is fined $15 and a report detailing the foul is filed with league president's office.
- In PCHA, body-checking within 10 feet of boards is banned.

1917

- One-referee system is re-established.
- Goal awarded any time a stick thrown to prevent a goal

1918

- Goalies are permitted to drop to the ice to make a save.

This was a change made in the Clint Benedict era of goaltending, where flopping around like a fish out of water was a style on the rise. The rule change request was made by a number of referees and owners who said that the sport would become a farce with too many of these penalties being called against goalies.

1919

- Deferred penalty system adopted by PCHA.
- Forward passing permitted between the two blue-lines.

Baby Steps

The year was 1910. While America was moving warships to Nicaragua, a typical box lunch — two sandwiches, a slice of pie, and a banana — cost Joe Average 15 cents. The latest hit vaudeville production at Montreal's Princess Theatre was "The Little Terror," starring Cecil "The Dainty Comedienne" Spooner.

Hockey was coming off a successful run that saw the Ottawa Senators grab another Cup. Meanwhile, professionalism had become the soup of the day and, with the exception of a few staunch traditionalists, the players had gone pro.

Owners met in Montreal in November 1909 to decide the fate of their clubs in the wake of the ECHA's dissolution. This confab led to the creation of a new governing body for professional hockey: the Canadian Hockey Association (CHA). Ottawa delegates D.B. Mulligan and P.M. Butler returned home delighted with their club's connection to what was shaping up to be "the greatest professional hockey league in existence."

The Montreal Wanderers, unable to reach agreement with the CHA, were reportedly trying to form their own rival league, which was to include Renfrew, Cornwall, Cobalt, and a French-Canadian squad. Montreal player-coach Jimmy Gardner had just returned from Toronto, where he'd been signing some players, when the press was tipped off that there was "something doing." The imbroglio would soon come to a head.

When the Montreal *Star* pressed him about whether the Wanderers would be playing their home games at the Montreal Arena, the rink's manager mumbled, "The Wanderers hockey club will not play in the Arena, no matter what it will cost."

The National Hockey Association, or NHA, was formed on the evening of December 2, 1909, with the Wanderers, the Creamery Kings, and clubs from the mining towns of Cobalt and Haileybury as the initial entries. All four teams were required to put up a "good faith" bond of $1,000. Meanwhile, Cobalt representative Tommy Hare was on record as expecting the Montreal Shamrocks and Nationals to break away from the CHA to join the NHA. Popular opinion soon echoed the media's, with cries of "too much hockey" and "one big pro league is better than two" growing louder by the day.

Amid the buzz, star defender Frank Patrick was rumored to be joining the CHA's All-Montreal club, as was the high-flying Russell Bowie, despite the fact that both men were staunch amateurs. Fiery Quebec Bulldogs goalkeeper Paddy Moran was also said to be joining All-Montreal in spite of Quebec management's insistence that Moran was "cinched."

About this time, the Renfrew Creamery Kings started making shameless overtures for Ottawa hockeyists. Renfrew's "agents" were said to have approached Fred "Cyclone" Taylor, Fred Lake, Albert "Dubbie" Kerr, Marty Walsh, and Bruce Stuart with "luscious" contract offers. With the exceptions of Lake and Kerr, the players gave Renfrew's headhunters an emphatic "No." Shortly thereafter, agent George Martel paid a visit to Kerr's home in Brockville, Ontario, and tabled an $1,800 offer. Kerr countered with a $2,030 demand. Once Ottawa management got wind of the developing bidding war, they sent Bruce Stuart to convince Kerr to return to Ottawa. Kerr jilted Stuart and the Senators, saying he wanted to stay at home to await Martel's response. Ultimately Kerr and Walsh would re-sign with Ottawa for $2,700 each. Meanwhile Renfrew managed to land Frank Patrick and his brother Lester for $5,000.

Early in the season Kerr would be in an Ottawa hospital, in serious condition after taking a puck to the eye during a game. After he'd already undergone two operations to restore his sight, team vice president Bate ordered that no expense be spared in restoring Kerr's health: "Kerr's sight will be saved even if it takes all this year's receipts of the Ottawa Hockey Club to do it. He will not play hockey again until his eye is perfect."

Renfrew kept on raiding, making a most notable play for Bruce Ridpath, Ottawa's "$1,000 prized beauty" prospect. Renfrew and the Cobalt Silver Kings got into a bidding war for the young star, the former club fronting a $1,500 offer. Ridpath opted to stay with Ottawa.

Renfrew made an even bolder move when they pursued Cyclone Taylor, easily the finest cover-point in the game. The offer? Captaincy of the Creamery Kings and $2,000. After he met with Mulligan and L.N. Bate, the Senators felt confident enough to announce that Taylor would be staying in Ottawa for the upcoming season. "We did not have to sign him . . . Taylor's word is as good to us as all the contracts ever made," Bate gushed. "Taylor will play with Ottawa and he would not go to Renfrew for all the money up there." Taylor went to Renfrew.

As the preseason raiding went on, representatives from the two leagues came together at Montreal's Windsor Hotel to try to hammer out a merger. The proposed marriage fizzled on account of the CHA's reluctance to take on Cobalt and Haileybury, clubs it felt were too remote and "minor-league." As far as the Wanderers were concerned, if Cobalt and Haileybury were excluded, the CHA could count them out, too. Talks stalled. Later on, at a more private gathering, CHA president William Lunny made known to the owners a "secret schedule" for the upcoming season. There would be too much hockey in Montreal, he maintained, and the most sensible idea would be to have one big league with one big schedule.

Meanwhile the NHA announced it was adding a fifth club — a French-Canadian side that would share the Jubilee Rink with the Wanderers: *Les Canadiens*. Flashy Jack Laviolette was the first player "protected," or selected, by the new club. In short order the Canadiens added Didier Pitre, George "Skinner" Poulin, Edouard "Newsy" Lalonde, and Art Bernier. The CHA's French-Canadian team, the Montreal Nationals, made overtures to Laviolette, but the long-haired hockeyist turned them down.

Only a week before the dawn of the NHA regular season, a scandal broke. Pitre and Poulin were hauled into court on breach of contract charges. Apparently, Pitre had inked a deal with the Nationals before signing on with the Canadiens. Poulin was guilty of the same sin against the All-Montrealers.

The ill-starred CHA season was opened on December 30, 1909, as All-Montreal and the Nationals played before 1,800 Montreal Arena fanatics. Although both teams looked rusty and out of sync, the former took a 7–2 decision on the strength of a Jack Marks mortarboard trick (four goals).

The Ottawa-Renfrew soap opera continued into the early days of 1910. Cyclone Taylor was presented with a gift from his former coworkers at the Department of the Interior: a suitcase. This was by all accounts the Senators' way of inviting him to their

Newsy Lalonde

1910 Stanley Cup banquet: several months ahead of time. Without blinking, Taylor declared that the banquet would be held in Ambrose O'Brien's new hotel in Renfrew. Taylor expressed satisfaction with life in the creamery town and believed that ditching Ottawa was the wisest career move he could have made.

The Canadiens appealed Justice Bruneau's judgment that Didier Pitre's playing rights belonged to the Nationals. The chunky defenseman maintained that the Nationals had obtained his signature under false pretenses, and anyway there was nothing in his Nationals contract saying he could not play for another club at the same time. Justice Bruneau disagreed and declared the contract binding.

In front of a different judge, Justice Lavergne, Pitre was granted a suspension of the original decision. Thus, the young speedster was able to play for the Canadiens until the case was heard by the Court of Appeals.

Back on the ice, on January 5 the Senators grabbed the first game of a challenge series with the Galt Professionals, 12–3. It took Ottawa only five minutes to pour in four quickies. As Ken Mallen and Bruce Ridpath used their speed to drive Galt's defense to distraction, Marty Walsh punched home five goals. The headline a few days later after the second and, mercifully, final game of the series read: "CHAMPIONS TOOK IT EASY IN SECOND GAME OF TAME CUP SERIES." The Senators kept possession of Lord Stanley's mug by coasting to a 3–1 win. The match was played before a pathetic crowd of 800. Less than two weeks later the Senators defended their title yet again, setting down the Edmonton Eskimos 21–11 in a two-game, total-goals series.

With crowds becoming steadily skimpier, CHA president Lunny's point that, with six teams there was "too much hockey in Montreal," was being borne out. Officials from the two leagues again came together to discuss a merger. There was a greater sense of urgency this time, as many teams were lamentably weak, sadly incapable of "good show."

One of the prominent figures in bringing the two leagues together was Harry Trihey. The former Shamrocks' scoring star, now a lawyer, was no stranger to officiating at such a gathering. In 1906 he had mediated the dispute between the Canadian Amateur and Federal Amateur leagues. In the end the National Hockey Association added the Ottawa Senators and Montreal Shamrocks to its ranks, leaving the Quebec Bulldogs and two Montreal clubs — Nationals and All-Montreal — out in the cold.

Young Shamrocks buckaroo "Bad" Joe Hall had forged a nasty reputation out west and, in a match against the Creamery Kings, he showed why. Midway through the second half, Hall was cruising down the right wing with the puck when he ran into a Frank Patrick cross-check. A fight broke out immediately between the two, but it was put down. As Hall was being led to the penalty box, he attacked judge-of-play Rod Kennedy. Hall later explained that he was so enraged that, when he went to take

In February 1910, Emmett Quinn resigned as secretary of the now-defunct Canadian Hockey Association and handed over his records to All-Montreal secretary Gordon Shewan. Final balance of the CHA? Sixty-seven dollars in the black!

another run at Patrick, Kennedy had simply been in his way. At the beginning of the first overtime session, referee Hodge permitted Hall to return to action, even though he'd been given a game misconduct. Renfrew refused to play on.

At a special meeting of the NHA, Hall was reinstated but fined $100. Further, the bigwigs ordered a replay of the Shamrocks–Creamery Kings debacle. At a subsequent league meeting, Hall's $100 fine would be overruled.

STANDINGS (as of February 10, 1910)

Club	GP	W	L	T	Pts
Ottawa Senators	6	6	0	0	12
Montreal Wanderers	6	5	1	0	10
Renfrew Creamery Kings	5	3	1	1	7
Montreal Shamrocks	7	2	4	1	5
Cobalt Silver Kings	3	1	2	0	2
Montreal Canadiens	5	1	4	0	2
Haileybury Hockey Club	8	1	7	0	2

Renfrew's visit to Ottawa was one of the most anticipated matches of the season. Much of the buzz surrounded Cyclone Taylor, who had "betrayed" Ottawans by jumping ship.

During the first half, three whiskey bottles were thrown at the ice by fans, and one of them narrowly missed Taylor's head. At the end of 60 minutes, the game was locked at 5–5. In 1910, overtime was not a sudden-death affair. Teams played for two five-minute periods. In overtime, Renfrew's Hay Millar was called off for holding Gordie Roberts. When play resumed, Ridpath grabbed the puck and slapped it over to Marty Walsh, who blasted it past Renfrew goalie Bert Lindsay. A minute later, Stuart collided with Frank Patrick, and Patrick was penalized, putting the Senators two men up. Ottawa seized the moment, scoring twice in the next three minutes to make the final score 8–5. In a classic quote after the game, Patrick commented: "Luck was against us or we would have beaten Ottawa. Talk about the man with the horseshoe, I'll take off my hat to LeSueur any day."

When Ottawa went to Montreal to play the Wanderers, they found 150 policemen on hand at the Jubilee Rink for crowd control. The arena's management was mindful of a previous meeting between the teams that had resulted in windows and doors being smashed.

Ottawa had been hoping to include a young cover-point named Walter Smaill, formerly of Cobalt, in their lineup, although he'd never been released by the Silver Kings from his contract. Stepping onto a Montreal-bound train, Smaill told reporters he was walking out on the club after it had failed to honor its contract with him. He'd joined the Silver Kings for a modest salary, with the promise that the team would find him supplemental employment. Although they found him a position at the Kerr Lake

Majestic Hotel, the job proved too stressful for Smaill and he quit. Smaill said the team was four days late in paying him his salary, and were reneging on a promise to make up his lost non-hockey income. On the eve of the big game with the Wanderers, Smaill announced he would not be playing. Mallen stepped in to replace Smaill, while Sam "Hamby" Shore stayed back at cover-point.

Like children pouting over peas, Ottawa threatened the NHA with a split if their acquisition of Smaill was deemed invalid. A meeting was subsequently called and the NHA would declare Smaill and Lalonde eligible to play for Ottawa and Renfrew, respectively. Hockey's first great referee, Chaucer Elliott, was on hand to give his views on who would win the big match:

> I like the Wanderers. Every man on that forward line is a worker and a scorer . . . as things are now, I think the hockey brains are with the Wanderers . . . the defenses look pretty even up, although I would give the upper hand to the Wanderers. For one thing, there is the tremendous skating and speed of Ernie Johnson and the experience of Jack Marshall. Johnson can do more skating with less expenditure of energy than any player I know.

The game started with a thick mist of cigarette and cigar smoke hanging over the playing area. Like a scene from a ghost story, the players were seen gliding through the mist. The Wanderers spent most of the night in the Ottawa end. If not for the brilliant play of goalie Percy LeSueur, the Senators would have been buggy-whipped. Montreal featured some nifty tic-tac-toe passing and tireless skating and were rewarded with a 7–5 win. The only standouts for Ottawa were LeSueur and Lake, the point-man.

A crowd of 7,000 was said to have been orderly and subdued — uncommon traits for a Wanderers crowd — as the Wanderers delivered a 5–0 beating to Renfrew on February 25. Almost from the get-go, Renfrew was gagged by the Redbands' checking while Riley Hern was absolutely darling in nets, stoning Lester Patrick twice on breakaways. Gardner scored twice and Johnson "blocked many rushes, picking the disk away with unfailing accuracy."

Before a Renfrew–Ottawa match in March 1910, Taylor promised to score a goal while skating backwards. And, as the Montreal *Gazette* reported, he "not only starred against his former teammates but made good in the second half on his promise . . . got the goal on a pass from Lester Patrick, turning when going at full speed and hoisting a swift one into the corner of LeSueur's nets."

Newsy Lalonde, who'd been involved in a tight scoring race with the Wanderers' Ernie Russell, wrapped up the title with an eight-goal performance against Cobalt. Lalonde ended up with a remarkable 38 goals in just 11 games.

After polishing off a satisfying 11-1 regular season with a win against the Canadiens, the Wanderers found out they would be defending the Cup in a one-game, winner-take-all playoff against the Ontario Professional Hockey League champion Berlin Dutchmen. Berlin officials raised a stink when they learned how the gate receipts would be divided — 60 percent to Jubilee Rink management and 20 percent to each of the two contestants. Berlin had expected to take home more like 25 percent of the gate. The dispute wasn't resolved to Berlin's satisfaction, but they played anyway.

The Wanderers thrashed the Berliners, 7–3. Hyland scored three for Montreal while Seibert, Oren Frood, and Bert Corbeau counted for Berlin's goals. Only 1,200 fans paid to see what was a rather sloppy affair. Even when Berlin pressed, the local crowd fought off yawns and heavy eyelids. To make matters worse, ice conditions were exceedingly poor and "against good hockey."

TOP THREE, 1910:

Club	GP	W	L	T	Pts	GF	GA
Montreal Wanderers	12	11	1	0	22	91	41
Ottawa Senators	12	9	3	0	18	89	66
Renfrew Creamery Kings	12	8	3	1	17	96	54

The 1909–10 season was a horn of plenty: league discord and reorganization; bidding wars; colorful personalities and great men; the formation of the NHA; a three-way title race; a tight battle for the scoring title; all made this a special year in hockey's history.

Victory Verse

The following is an anonymous poem dedicated to the Quebec Bulldogs, the Stanley Cup champions of 1912:

You have heard of old King Nero, how his gladiators fought,
Of the hardy Spartan hero, and his manly forms of sport;
You must oft have read the story
of the battles red and gory,
Which were fought just for the glory
and the honor that they brought.

I would like to add my ditty to the songs they've written up,
How Quebec, the Rocky City, won the Stanley Hockey Cup;
They'd a team that worked like lightning, they'd a crowd that cheered them on,
You could see their faces brightening every time a game was won.

Captain Joe's the greatest blessing that the team could ever own,
He can keep the others guessing, and could tackle them alone;
Eddie Oatman is a dandy,
Eddie's heady and he's handy,
He is sure the real candy, as he more than once has shown.

Like the comet of friend Halley, Mac's a flyer on the wing,
He can shoot or pass or tally, or do any blooming thing;

1912 Quebec Bulldogs

On defense, a perfect wonder is our husky friend Joe Hall,
I'd as soon be struck by thunder as butt into Joe's stone wall.

Goldie Prodgers travels nearly twice as fast as light or sound,
You can only see him clearly when he stops to look around;
Then there's good old Paddy Moran,
Who can always close the door on,
Any team that tries to score on Paddy Moran, I'll be bound.

Jackie Marks is some good skater, though he hasn't had much show,
but he's sure an A-1 rater from the time he starts to go;
And in fact each one's a beauty
who will always do his duty,
And we're glad they've won the booty,
That's the Stanley Cup, you know.

The Terry Turner Slide

Before Wilfred "Bucko" McDonald and Bob Goldham perfected the shot-block, hockeyists had other unique ways of helping out their goalie. Take Alex Irving of the 1913 Cleveland Athletics, for example.

Around Cleveland, Irvy's shot-blocking method was known as the "Terry Turner Slide." As one newspaper account had it, "Irvy delighted in manufacturing hair-raisers on the ice and the fans enthused when he performed the stunts." Another source said, "It was a wonderful piece of work . . . fraught with danger."

As an opposing player sped down the ice, Irving would dash toward him. Once he was within 10 feet of the attacker, Irvy would dive headlong into the rusher's path, extending his stick to arm's length in order to foil the shot. According to one account, "The fans fairly went wild with excitement as everything depended on Irvy's success."

While blocking shots is important, seldom is it that "everything depends" on it. As for Terry Turner, he was a good-look, no-hit third-baseman and shortstop for the Cleveland Naps from the turn of the century until the early 1920s. Apparently, Cleveland hockey fans thought Irving's slide resembled Turner on the base paths.

Ross

In November 1909, the Eastern Canada Amateur Hockey Association, Canada's premier hockey league at the time, was voted out of existence. In its place sprouted the Canadian Hockey Association. Ross signed up to play for the All-Montreal club and gunned four goals in four games before the team folded. Left to his own devices, he immediately shopped himself around. Haileybury, a team propped up by mining barons, agreed to fork over $2,700 for Ross to be their player-manager. Despite the additions of Ross and goalkeeper Paddy Moran, the club finished a disappointing 4–8. At season's end, Haileybury was strapped for cash and, along with the Cobalt Silver Kings, withdrew from the league, leaving Ross once again a free agent.

Perhaps daunted by the gaudy salaries agreed to during the NHA–CHA bidding wars, the NHA owners set a salary cap for 1910–11 — $5,000 per team. As league president Emmett Quinn explained, each of a team's 10 players would receive $500. But because all players were not of equal value, those falling in the "star" category could make anywhere from $750 to $900.

The Ottawa Senators announced that its stars would be offered $600 apiece, meaning that Marty Walsh, Fred Lake, and Albert "Dubbie" Kerr would face pay cuts of better than 50 percent. Naturally, this league-wide cash freeze rankled Ross, who thought top-flight players should be paid top-flight salaries. Rumors that Ross would be forming his own league began to circulate.

Prior to the 1913–14 season, Ross held out for more money — $1,500 for the upcoming season. The Montreal Wanderers bigwigs were hardly prepared to pay, so Ross contacted Newsy Lalonde, Ernie Russell, Skene Ronan, and Didier Pitre in an effort to begin a player's fraternity league, something baseball's players had done in the summer of 1913. Ross's proposed league, though, failed to get off the ground and he begrudgingly re-signed with the Wanderers.

In late November 1914, the NHA suspended Ross for negotiating with players
under NHA contracts to play in a new league.
Wanderers owner Sam Lichtenhein, hockey's
answer to Ebenezer Scrooge, had declared that
none of his players would be paid more than
$600 for the 1914–15 season. Ross, whose
highest salary had been nearly five times that
amount, was after no less than $1,500 for his
services. To cover his bases, Ross hooked up
with a Montreal group headed by former
Montreal AAA luminary Clarence
McKerrow. On behalf of McKerrow's organization, Ross began seeking options on current
NHA players, primarily from the Canadien
and Wanderer camps, hoping to recruit them
for the proposed league. Among those report-

Art Ross

ed to be Ross targets were Harry Hyland, Sprague and Odie Cleghorn, Gordie
Roberts, Lalonde, Pitre, and Jack Laviolette. These options expired after 10 days,
with no sign of the new league. Still, Ross did not give up. He declared himself a free
agent, no longer subject to his Wanderers contract. League president Quinn did not
see it his way, and suspended him "from all organized hockey."

Such a ban would probably have had little effect on Ross's livelihood. McKerrow's
proposed league, if it ever got off the ground, would not likely have been considered part
of "organized hockey." And over in the new Pacific Coast Hockey Association, Frank
Patrick had little use for Quinn and it's doubtful he would have honored the NHA suspension. In any event, the suspension did not stick. A league meeting on December 18,
1914, cleared Ross to return to NHA play on January 7. He severed all ties with the

Percy and Millionaires' Row

During a match against the Montreal Wanderers, Ottawa Senators coach and goalkeeper Percy
LeSueur devoted himself to a new style of bench-bossing. At the beginning of the second period, the
Wanderers popped in a pair of goals. At this point, LeSueur is said to have made for the bleachers and
into the end-zone seats known as "Millionaires' Row." He goaded the fans into egging chubby Montreal
goalie Billy Nicholson on so as to put him off of his game. For the rest of the match, everything from programs to toe rubbers to half-smoked cigars and cigarettes were thrown at Nicholson's head.

The Montreal *Gazette* demanded an investigation into the incident. It was widely held that
LeSueur was not only responsible for his players' actions but for the fans' as well. LeSueur told the
press he went into the stands because he had been "asked by the officials to stop the blowing of a
whistle in the bleachers."

According to the Wanderers, the debris thrown at big Nicholson was no hallucination. But the
milquetoast president of the NHA, Emmett Quinn, ordered no investigation into the LeSueur matter.
"Mr. LeSueur has had a completely spotless record in this level of hockey for his entire career now
and I'm not about to start dragging his good name through the dirt," Quinn said.

Wanderers and, after skating with the Canadiens, joined the Ottawa Senators.

Ottawa and the Wanderers finished the 1914–15 season in a dead heat. In the first game of a two-game, total-goals playoff, Ross tallied once in the Senators' 4–0 win. In game two, the Wanderers could only manage a 1–0 advantage and Ottawa grabbed its ticket to the Stanley Cup finals.

Ross's battles with the NHA bigwigs were epic. How ironic it is, then, that this rebel not only went into management after his playing career ended, but he was successful as an authority figure. He managed the Boston Bruins from 1924 until 1954, coaching them for 16 of those years.

Art Ross did more for professional hockey than any other man in the early twentieth century. A staunch advocate of players' rights, Ross led a player revolt which ultimately enabled his hockey brethren to realize higher salaries. Indeed, he was a thorn in team barons' sides throughout his playing career. All the while, Ross was skating his way to the Hockey Hall of Fame. And although he competed in only three NHL games, the league annually awards the Art Ross Trophy to its leading scorer.

Uncle Sammy Is Watching!

Montreal Wanderers owner Sammy Lichtenhein was the George Steinbrenner of 1910s hockey owners. He was uncommonly outspoken, especially at the annual league meeting held prior to the start of each season, when he would voice a complaint or two, or seven, at what was otherwise essentially a gentlemen's club meeting.

He rode roughshod over his players with equal gusto. On February 19, 1915, with his Redbands in the thick of a championship race with the Ottawa Senators, Lichtenhein issued an ultimatum to his men: Shape up or you're benched for the rest of the season without pay. He announced he had hired a squad of private investigators to "keep an eye" on them between team practices and games to make sure they were not out carousing. Any player found to be frequenting bawdy houses or drinking to late hours would be benched without pay. Although the Montreal *Gazette* called Lichtenhein's a "novel idea in the way of handling hockey players," a few eyebrows were raised in the hockey community. Toronto owner Eddie Livingstone, for one, called Lichtenhein a "foolish man" if he reckoned these tactics would effect any change.

Despite his club's running a close second behind Ottawa in the league standings, Lichtenhein was dissatisfied. He promised that, if his boys did not defeat the Senators on February 20, and if those in his doghouse failed to show improvement, at least four of them would sit out the rest of the season without pay. The players thought Lichtenhein's latest tirade was either a joke or an empty threat.

Still, the Redbands came through, beating Ottawa 3–1.

God Bless the 228th

In the weeks preceding the 1916–17 season, there were fears that both the NHA and PCHA would suffer major talent losses as players enlisted to fight in World War One. Two top PCHA stars, Art Duncan and Eddie Oatman, had signed up, while the NHA coughed up Percy LeSueur, Howard and Harold McNamara, Samuel "Goldie" Prodgers, and Don Smith.

The 228th Battalion, also known as the Northern Fusiliers, became a magnet for athletes in armed service. Its lineup boasted Oatman, Prodgers, Duncan, the McNamaras, Amos Arbour, and Gordon Meeking. Howard McNamara was team captain, while Captain L.W. Reade acted as manager. There were already a number of military clubs playing at the Senior level in eastern Canada. Given the number of proven professionals on its roster, the 228th opted to apply for an NHA franchise, and was admitted on September 30, 1916. The Fusiliers thus became the first military outfit to compete in a major professional sports league.

Once admitted to the NHA, the 228th raised eyebrows when it began recruiting — some might say raiding — players from other teams. While not an unusual practice in 1916, it was certainly questionable behavior coming from a team whose primary role was to provide recreation for a military unit.

One sticky situation involved Gordon "Duke" Keats, who as a Toronto Blueshirts rookie in 1915–16 had scored 22 goals in 24 games. Toronto management was confident it could assemble a fine team around the 22-year-old center. But, even though he was under contract to play with the Blueshirts in 1916–17, Keats joined the Battalion. This move did not sit well at all with Toronto owner Eddie Livingstone, who had lost most of his team the year before to the PCHA's Seattle Metropolitans. Livingstone complained to NHA president Frank Robinson that the army had stolen Keats. After deliberating on the matter, Robinson ruled that if Keats played in the NHA, he should play for the team with whom he was under contract: Toronto. The 228th quickly appealed the ruling and Robinson was forced to meet with military authorities to come to a solution. In the end, he ruled it was "up to the army to decide." Eventually, Lieutenant Colonel Earchmann of the Battalion allowed Keats to play for Toronto, for whom he scored 15 goals in 13 games.

Eddie Oatman's presence in the 228th lineup was also controversial. Oatman had enlisted prior to the 1916–17 season, which displeased his PCHA team, the Portland Rosebuds, but they let him go on the assumption he was headed directly into overseas combat. When it started to look as if Oatman's real role in the 228th was as a ringer for the hockey team, PCHA president Frank Patrick's nose got out of joint. Of course, Patrick's indignation rings hollow when you consider that he'd led many raids of NHA rosters to stock his own fledgling league.

Oatman insisted he was a bona fide member of the 228th Battalion, pointing to the fact he had passed the military's physical examination. But it quickly became public knowledge that he had quietly been exempted from full duty because of "special circumstances."

Gordon Meeking, a diligent two-way forward who scored four goals for the 228th in 1916–17, also was granted a discharge that raised some eyebrows. Meeking had been deemed "medically unfit" to go overseas, which is interesting given that he was a professional athlete. Meeking actually was ashamed of his release. He did not go back to Toronto because he could not face his friends and relatives, who had given him a grand send-off to Germany. He would not reappear in hockey until 1921.

The 228th started the 1916–17 season with four wins in a row, establishing themselves early as the class of the league. The Fusiliers, decked out in distinctive khaki uniforms, were 6-4 after 10 games, and they were a high-scoring bunch — Oatman, Prodgers, and Arbour netted 17, 16, and 13 goals, respectively. In mid February the battalion was called overseas, and the NHA's governors convened on February 11 to decide how to handle the suspension of the 228th's franchise. The league cited a scheduling impasse as an excuse to drop the much-hated Eddie Livingstone's Toronto Blueshirts from the circuit as well. The season was split into two parts, with only Ottawa, Quebec, and the two Montreal teams playing the second half. During the off-season the NHA reorganized itself, becoming the National Hockey League, and once again excluded Eddie Livingstone's team.

Military teams were a tradition that would be resumed during World War Two, as many of the NHL's top players enlisted in armed service. Perhaps the best of these clubs, the Ottawa RCAF Flyers boasted the famed "Kraut Line" of Milt Schmidt, Woody Dumart, and Bobby Bauer up front. They won the 1942 Allan Cup, but even they could not match the 228th's unique claim of having competed in a major professional sports league.

Fight Night, Quebec-Style

The Toronto Blueshirts arrived late and hungry in Quebec City on the afternoon of February 3, 1917. Because the stove in their train's dining car had broken down en route from Toronto, the boys had missed their customary steak dinner. Consequently, they were in ill humor.

Referee Cooper Smeaton certainly had his work cut out for him. Quebec's lineup featured the league's bad boy, Joe Hall. In the first half, he delivered a savage cross-check across the face of Toronto forward Corb Denneny. So serious was the attack that the diminutive (5'8", 160) center was taken to hospital. In the second half, a Hall elbow knocked Reg Noble cold.

With only a couple of minutes left in the game, and the Bulldogs ahead 7–3, a rhubarb broke out near the Blueshirt net. Apparently, Toronto's Ken Randall was belted across the chops by a fan. Then, the rooters in that section of the rink started going wild. Randall was game, though. Climbing over the boards, he dropped his gloves and began whaling away on a man named Benoit Lelievre. By this point, the spectators needed little prompting to take leave of their senses: a handful poured out onto the ice to knuckle Toronto players, while many started throwing bottles and chairs. Smeaton called the game immediately, ushering the players from the ice.

With some difficulty, the Blueshirts made their way out of the arena, but they were waylaid on the railway platform by a group of furious Quebec supporters. Although the hockeyists generally "gave as good as they got," several were soundly thrashed.

The Predecessors

When the National Hockey League was founded in November 1917, few could have imagined it would become the most celebrated league in the history of the game. Over the previous 30 years or so there had been a number of important loops, each connected at least peripherally to the league we know today.

Amateur Hockey Association of Canada (1886–98)

Although hockey historians often point to 1893, the first time the Stanley Cup was awarded, as the game's Year Zero, organized hockey already existed, at least in a semi-formal sense. The Amateur Hockey Association of Canada was formed in December 1886, and its prime mission was to promote the game from sea to sea. Five teams competed in the winter of 1887, the league's debut season: the Montreal Amateur Athletic Association (MAAA), Montreal Crystals, McGill University, Montreal Victorias, and the Ottawa Hockey Club. All clubs except Ottawa were members of the Montreal city league. The winter of 1886–87 was unseasonably mild, which made scheduling matches a hit-and-miss proposition.

Until 1892, league membership was unstable, and there were no fixed schedules. Teams of that era played as many as eight games, or as few as one or two. For instance, the Victorias finished on top in 1887 with a 5-3 record, while the MAAA were second at 3-1. The Triple-A's "Winged Wheelers" were one of the few constants in those days. In 1887 they won the Montreal Winter Carnival tournament, arguably the first bona fide tournament ever played. The next year they rolled over the Victorias in a one-game playoff to grab the AHAC's first title. Between 1888 and 1894 the MAAA failed to post the league's best record only once — in 1892, and even then they defeated Ottawa in a one-game championship playoff.

The donation of the Stanley Cup in 1893 coincides with the introduction of stability to the AHAC. The league's five teams — Ottawa, Quebec, the MAAA, Victorias and Crystals — played an eight-game, home-and-home schedule. This lineup of teams would outlast the dissolution of the AHAC in 1899, sticking together until 1904. The only change along the way came in 1896, when the Crystals changed their name to the "Shamrocks."

The year 1894 was significant in two ways: there was a four-way tie for first place in the regular-season standings, and it marked the end of the Montreal AAA's domination of the league. The following year the Victorias, bolstered by the likes of Mike Grant, Graham Drinkwater, Shirley Davidson, and Major Gordie Lewis, won the first of four consecutive league titles.

Ironically, the Winged Wheelers were responsible for launching the Vics' four-year stranglehold of the Stanley Cup. The Victorias finished first in the 1895 AHAC standings, and as such would be expected to take on all comers for Lord Stanley's silverware. However, the Cup trustees had already accepted a challenge issued by the Queen's University Golden Gaels against the 1904 champions, Montreal AAA. Thinking quickly, the trustees ruled that if the Winged Wheelers beat Queen's, the Victorias would be awarded the Cup. The Montrealers won the one-game, winner-take-all match, 5–1, and the Cup was awarded to the V's. In February 1896, the Winnipeg Victorias mounted a successful Stanley Cup challenge, but their Montreal namesakes regained the title in December and held it until the end of the 1899 season, when it was the Shamrocks' turn to top the standings.

The beginnings of the AHAC's demise can be traced to December 1897, when the Ottawa Capitals, an Intermediate team, applied to join the AHAC. At the time, though, there was a rule on the books prohibiting Intermediate clubs from joining the Senior ranks until they had won the Intermediate league title. A year later the Caps' application was accepted, but the Victorias, Quebec, and the existing Ottawa club withdrew in disgust, followed quickly by Montreal AAA. These four clubs quickly formed a new league, the Canadian Amateur Hockey League.

Canadian Amateur Hockey League (1899–1905)

Looking to round out the numbers, the newborn CAHL added a team from McGill University. Before a game was played, however, the Montreal Shamrocks, the only one of the AHAC teams not already in the CAHL, applied for a franchise. McGill dropped out to let the talented Irish aboard.

The 1899 season saw the Shamrocks' Harry Trihey score 10 goals in a 13–4 victory over Quebec. This same Quebec squad, hockey's rogue franchise, defaulted its final two games after an 0-6 start had left them hopelessly out of the hunt. The Shamrocks, on the other hand, walked away with the Cup.

McGill applied for a franchise again in 1900, but was rejected. The Shamrocks, meanwhile, defended their league and Stanley Cup championships.

In 1901, Ottawa finished with an impressive 7-0-1 record despite having no scorers of any consequence. They made up for their lack of offense with a near-impenetrable defense and some rock-solid goaltending from John Bower "Bouse" Hutton. But the Winnipeg Victorias, a western hockey power led by strapping Dan Bain, challenged the Shamrocks for the silverware and beat them in two straight games. It was the Shamrocks' last hurrah: the next year, having lost Harry Trihey and his linemate, Art Farrell, they'd wind up in the CAHL basement with a 1-7 record. The Irish would fold in 1910, never having returned to the top.

The MAAA ended an eight-year drought in 1902, by winning the CAHL title and topping Winnipeg in three games for the Cup. Though their decline would not be as pronounced as the Shamrocks', the Winged Wheelers were tasting Cup victory for the last time.

With the rise of semi- and outright professional leagues in the United States, the CAHL began to suffer a serious talent drain. Key losses in 1903 included Hod Stuart and Charlie Liffiton.

Frank McGee made his Canadian league debut in 1903, finishing second in scoring with 14 goals. He would go on to score that many in a single game during a 1905 Cup challenge. Led by McGee, "Dirty" Alf Smith, and Harvey Pulford, Ottawa won its first Stanley Cup.

The CAHL, and its predecessor the AHAC, had been the predominant Senior amateur league in Canada, and until now had never been confronted by talent raids from

----

a rival league. But in 1904 the Montreal Wanderers, a founding member of the new Federal Amateur Hockey League, grabbed many of the MAAA's star players — Jack Marshall, Jimmy Gardner, Dickie Boon, and Billy Bellingham — and snagged Billy and Bert Strachan from the Montreal Victorias. Halfway through the season, Ottawa resigns from the league. Quebec was the best of the teams left in the CAHL, finishing 7-1, but they could not play for the Cup because it was controlled by the Ottawas.

Few were surprised when 1905 proved to be the league's swan song. The Montreal Westmounts and Nationals were admitted to make up for Ottawa's absence. Five of the league's six teams hailed from Montreal, making the CAHL little more than a city league. Groups hoping to join the loop — including Trois-Rivieres and the FAHL's Montreal Wanderers — applied to join the CAHL and were rejected. The Wanderers were no doubt turned away because their raiding of CAHL rosters the season before had done little to endear them to CAHL bigwigs. The on-ice highlight of 1905 took place on February 18 when Westmount goalkeeper Fred Brophy raced the length of the ice to score on Quebec's Paddy Moran, in the process becoming the first netminder ever to score a goal.

The Montreal Victorias were the league's best with a 9-1 record, but they did not get a chance to challenge for the Cup, which still belonged to Ottawa. The Victorias approached the Cup trustees about challenging the Silver Seven and were informed that they would have to wait until after the Silver Seven had played the Rat Portage Thistles. The challenge fell through when the trustees told the Victorias, who would have preferred to play a one-game, winner-take-all match or a two-game, total-goals series, that the challenge would have to be a best-of-three series.

Before the 1906 season, the CAHL approached the Ottawa Silver Seven and Montreal Wanderers to talk merger. After some back-and-forth, the merger was made, the Eastern Canada Amateur Hockey Association was born, and the CAHL, after seven years, was no more.

International Professional Hockey League (1904–07)

In 1903–04, Dr. Jack Gibson headed up the Houghton–Portage Lakes, one of the finest collections of ice talent assembled to that point: Gibson himself, Riley Hern, Hod and Bruce Stuart, and Ernie Westcott. The team went 24-2 that year, with a 273 goals for and only 48 against. It is widely held that Houghton–Portage Lakes was hockey's first true professional hockey team. Gibson realized that, if his team was to face a steady supply of decent competition, he'd have to attract the best players to his neck of the woods. And the only way to land the top stars would be to pay top salaries. Thus, he founded the IPHL the following year.

The IPHL featured many of the era's hockey greats — besides Hern and the Stuarts, there were Fred "Cyclone" Taylor, Jack Laviolette, Joe Hall, and Newsy Lalonde. The founding members were Pittsburgh, Houghton–Portage Lakes, Michigan Soo, Canadian Soo, and Calumet-Larium Miners. By 1907, rumors of favoritism by hometown referees were rampant, and on-ice violence was on the rise. At the end of the season, Pittsburgh decided to drop out, leaving the league with no "big city" to count on for large gate receipts. Calumet and Houghton–Portage Lakes announced that they too were folding, while attempts to attract clubs from Cleveland

and Duluth fell on deaf ears.

The IPHL folded after only three seasons.

Despite its short run, the impact of the IPHL on organized hockey should not be underestimated. When the league folded, dozens of star players returned to Canada and, having grown accustomed to playing for money, they started to demand salaries. The game of hockey has never been the same since.

Federal Amateur Hockey League (1904–07)

The FAHL was founded on December 5, 1903, in Montreal, in response to the Canadian Amateur Hockey League's refusal to add any new members. Among the charter members of the Federal league were the Ottawa Capitals and Cornwall, two teams that had been denied entry by the AHAC and the CAHL.

In the league's debut season, the Montreal Wanderers ran up a 6-0 record. They played the Ottawa Silver Seven, who'd withdrawn from the CAHL but weren't yet full-fledged FAHL members, for the Cup but the series was abandoned amid a storm of controversy after the teams played to a 5–5 draw. The Wanderers refused to play overtime in that game, because they were dissatisfied with the refereeing. When the Cup trustees tried to schedule a new series, the Wanderers objected because it was to be played in Ottawa.

In 1905, Brockville and the Ottawa Montagnards joined the Federal league, while the Montreal Nationals jumped to the CAHL. The Silver Seven and Wanderers placed one-two in the standings, then skipped during the off-season to a new league, the Eastern Canada Amateur Hockey Association, that also included four teams from the old CAHL — Quebec, the Montreal Victorias, Shamrocks, and AAA. The Federal league went bravely on, filling its vacancies with the Ottawa Victorias and Smiths Falls, who boasted the great Percy LeSueur between the pipes, and who swept their schedule with a 7-0 record. But by this point no one much cared anymore.

The Federal league came back for one last round in 1906–07, dropping Smiths Falls and Brockville, and adding Morrisburg. Mo'burg, as the locals called it, was not much of a club, finishing without a single victory.

Tragedy hit the FAHL during a game on March 6, 1907, between Cornwall and the Ottawa Victorias. During a skirmish, Owen McCourt was struck on the head by a Victorias player, and later died. McCourt was the first player in major-league hockey to die as a result of injuries sustained in a game.

The 1906–07 season, and the league's history, ended in an odd fashion. The Montagnards, who finished with the league's best record, withdrew in early March, as did second-place Cornwall. That left the third-place Ottawa Victorias, to claim the league title. The Victorias challenged the Montreal Wanderers for the Stanley Cup, and the Redbands drubbed them mercilessly, by 9–3 and 13–1 scores.

Eastern Canada Amateur Hockey Association (1906–09)

Formed on December 11, 1905, the ECAHA was the latest in a continuous string of leagues that started with the AHAC, continued through the CAHL, would be succeeded by the National Hockey Association, and would culminate in the birth of the National Hockey League.

The ECAHA was, in a sense, a hybrid, taking the Ottawa Senators and Montreal Wanderers from the Federal league, and Montreal's Victorias, Shamrocks, and AAA, and Quebec from the Canadian league. Ottawa and the Wanderers were the class of the league, finishing with identical 9-1 records, and setting the stage for a two-game, total-goals playoff between the rivals. The W's took game one on home ice, 9–1, and appeared to be home free. But Ottawa streaked out to a 9–1 lead in the second game, temporarily deadlocking the series. A pair of late goals by Lester Patrick thwarted the Senators' improbable comeback bid. Final score in game two was 9–3, giving the Wanderers a 12–10 aggregate score and the championship.

In 1907, league governors decided that professionals and amateurs would be allowed to compete together as long as their respective teams made each player's status public. The Wanderers signed pros Riley Hern and Hod Stuart, and announced they were paying salaries to Pud Glass, Moose Johnson, and Jack Marshall. The reinforcements let the Redbands blow through the ECAHA schedule like a hurricane, finishing 10-0.

The 1908–09 campaign saw the Montreal AAA and Victorias withdraw from the league under a cloud. This particular rhubarb surrounded a motion set forth by the Shamrocks and Wanderers that would effectively bar players from leaving the teams after playing out their contracts. This was an attempt to introduce a kind of reserve clause. The MAAA, who had signed Wanderers Riley Hern and Art Ross, and Didier Pitre from the Shamrocks, found such a motion unacceptable.

Only four clubs lined up for the 1908–09 season, all of them professional, so the league dropped the "Amateur" designation from its title, becoming simply the Eastern Canada Hockey Association. Ottawa's 10-2 record edged out the 9-3 Wanderers for the title.

The Wanderers changed hands before the 1909–10 season, but their new owner wasn't any easier to get along with. P.J. Doran also owned the Jubilee Rink, and he wanted to move his team there from the Montreal Arena. The trouble was, the Jubilee Rink was less than half the size, and the visitors' share of the gate would shrink proportionally. Doran's partners held a meeting on November 25, 1909, and decided to vote the ECHA out of existence, freezing out Doran and the Wanderers.

The remaining ECHA teams — Ottawa, Quebec, Shamrocks, and Nationals — reorganized under the banner of the Canadian Hockey Association, taking on a fifth club, All-Montreal, to replace the Wanderers. The Renfrew Creamery Kings, formerly of the Ottawa Valley league, applied for a CHA franchise and, like the Wanderers, were snubbed. The two orphans would band together to form their own league, the National Hockey Association.

Ontario Professional Hockey League (1908–11)

The OPHL, known as the "Trolley League" after the preferred method of transport between league cities, was Canada's first outright professional hockey league. Four franchises operated in the OPHL's debut campaign — the Berlin Dutchmen, Brantford Indians, Guelph Professionals, and Toronto Professionals. Edouard "Newsy" Lalonde and his 29 goals paced the Toronto side to the league title. They challenged the Montreal Wanderers for the Stanley Cup, but lost 6–4.

Galt (now part of Cambridge) and St. Catharines joined the league for its second season. Galt and Brantford topped the standings, with Galt challenging the Ottawa Senators for the Cup in January 1910. They lost a two-game, total-goals series, 15–4.

It was back to four teams for the 1909–10 season, with Waterloo replacing Toronto for the 1909–10 season while Guelph and St. Catharines — two teams with a combined record of 1-11 the year before — withdrew. Berlin (now Kitchener) won first place and the right to challenge for the Stanley Cup. The Dutchmen lost 7–3 to the Montreal Wanderers.

The OPHL's fourth season, 1910–11, was also its last. The Galt Professionals won their second title and went on to lose, 7–4, to Ottawa Senators in a Cup challenge match.

Canada's first professional league was no longer able to compete for talent with the previously amateur teams in the NHA, and the launch of the Pacific Coast Hockey Association — and the accompanying bidding wars — made sure the Trolley League was derailed for good.

National Hockey Association (1910–1917)

On the eve of the 1910 season, Canada boasted two elite leagues, composed of 10 teams in all, a whopping five of which were based in Montreal. Talent was spread thin, and that shortage led to bidding wars that sent player paychecks soaring. At the same time, the glut of teams took a bit out of gate receipts. On January 15, 1910, the CHA was dissolved, and two of its teams — the Ottawa Senators and Montreal Shamrocks — were taken in by the NHA. That left three teams — Quebec, the Montreal Nationals, and All-Montreal — without a league to play in.

The Renfrew Creamery Kings became the early favorite for the league title the second their well-heeled owner, Ambrose O'Brien, opened his change purse. In fact, the size of Renfrew's payroll led some wags to hang an alternate nickname on the club: the Renfrew "Millionaires." But the Montreal Wanderers, eager to take revenge on the clubs that had frozen them out of the ECHA, won the inaugural NHA title and, with it, the O'Brien Trophy.

The O'Brien family, one of the richest in Canada, owned the Renfrew side, and they also controlled three other teams — Cobalt, Haileybury, and the Montreal Canadiens. They lavished most of their attention, and resources, on the Creamery Kings, however, as was evidenced by the midseason transfer of Newsy Lalonde from the league doormat Canadiens to Renfrew. That they got away with the trade is a testimony to their clout within the league, but it did not bode well for the NHA's competitive balance.

Events during the 1910 off-season would greatly reduce the O'Briens' control over the league. Having lost a great deal of money, they withdrew their Cobalt and Haileybury teams, and the original Canadiens franchise was suspended when George Kennedy of the Club Athletique Canadien threatened to sue for trademark infringement. The Montreal Shamrocks also folded, while the Quebec Bulldogs and a new Canadiens team, owned by Kennedy, were admitted for 1911. The O'Briens would complete their exit from the NHA after the 1911 season, winding down the money-losing Renfrew franchise.

Seeking to bounce back from the losses, the NHA instituted a salary cap of just

----

$5,000 per team for the 1911 season. Players like Lester Patrick and Art Ross were making more than half that on their own the year before. Ross would try unsuccessfully to lead a player revolt and launch a rival league.

In 1912, the NHA switched from seven players a side to six, effectively dropping the rover position. It was done for economic reasons as much as anything. Meanwhile, almost out of nowhere, Lester and Frank Patrick launched the Pacific Coast Hockey Association. Many NHA players would jump to the coast in the years to come. In 1913 alone, Goldie Prodgers, Eddie Oatman, Jack McDonald, Ernie "Moose" Johnson, and Cyclone Taylor went west.

Ambrose O'Brien had sold the rights to his dormant Renfrew and Canadiens franchises to Toronto interests, and in 1912–13 the Blueshirts and Tecumsehs brought league membership back up to six teams. The following year the Tecumsehs were renamed the Ontarios, and during their last season, 1914–15, they were the Shamrocks. Prior to the 1915–16 season, Shamrocks owner Eddie Livingstone acquired the Blueshirts franchise. The NHA came down hard on Livingstone, insisting he could operate only one team. If this seems inconsistent with the O'Briens' ownership of several clubs a few years before, bear in mind the other NHA owners nursed an intense dislike for Livingstone. Undaunted, Livingstone merged his two teams and called them the Blueshirts.

As their 1915–16 seasons began, player raids between the NHA and PCHA escalated. The addition of a fourth PCHA team, the Seattle Metropolitans, left the league especially hungry for talent. The Mets zeroed in on Toronto's Blueshirts, luring Jack Walker, Cully Wilson, Frank Foyston, and Hap Holmes to the coast.

Back east there was a torrid three-way race for the NHA scoring crown between Newsy Lalonde (28 goals), Joe Malone (25), and Cy Denneny (24). The Montreal Canadiens took the league crown and defeated Portland to claim Lord Stanley's mug for the first time.

In 1916–17, the NHA made history when it admitted a team from the 228th Battalion, becoming the first major professional sports league ever to field a team from a military unit. The 228th played only 10 games, going 6-4, before it was called overseas.

The 228th's departure prompted the league to split the schedule into two 10-game halves. The owners also took the opportunity to rid themselves of Eddie Livingstone and his Toronto Blueshirts. The Canadiens led at the end of the first half, while Ottawa shone in the second. The clubs met in a playoff, with the Canadiens earning the right to play the PCHA champion for the Stanley Cup. The Habs went down as the first team ever to lose the Cup to an American team, as the Seattle Metropolitans cast them aside in four games.

A League to End All Leagues

T he seeds of the NHL were sown the very second Eddie Livingstone became an NHA owner. He purchased the Ontarios franchise prior to the 1914–15 season and immediately set out to fortify the roster. He grabbed the McNamara brothers (George, Howard, and Harold), Tommy Smith, Erskine Ronan, Alf Skinner, and the Dennenys, Cy and Corb. Despite this injection of talent, things did not pan out the way Livingstone had hoped. Halfway through the season, with the Ontarios struggling, he changed the team name to "Shamrocks" in an effort to change the team's luck. The Ontarios-Shamrocks finished in the second division again.

Prior to the 1915–16 season, Livingstone bought Toronto's other team, the Blueshirts, a move that displeased the NHA powers. They immediately forbade him from operating both franchises and gave him until November 20 to sell the Shamrocks. The ruling shows that the NHA was sometimes selective in enforcing its policies. Back in 1910 the O'Brien clan ran four of the league's seven clubs. Having been painted into a corner by the bigwigs, Livingstone responded by merging his two clubs in hopes of creating a Toronto powerhouse. His bid for revenge was blindsided when the PCHA granted a franchise to Seattle, named the Metropolitans. To stock their new club, Seattle brass swiped many of the better Blueshirts — Harry Holmes, Eddie Carpenter, Frank Foyston, Jack Walker, and Cully Wilson. As if that weren't enough, Livingstone got into a dispute with the owners of the Toronto Arenas, and threatened to move his team to Boston. He also threatened to sue the PCHA and its top man, Frank Patrick, claiming they had stolen his players. Livingstone settled with the rink owners in time for hockey season, and he was mollified, at least temporarily, when Holmes, Foyston, and Wilson returned to Toronto and played a few games for the Blueshirts after their PCHA season ended. Even with these reinforcements, Toronto's once-promising club finished in last place at 9-14-1.

During the off-season, Livingstone was at it again, this time with star player Cy Denneny. The plucky winger's family was in Ottawa, and he felt he couldn't afford to play for the $600 Livingstone was offering. He'd found a second job in the capital, and asked to be traded to Ottawa for the sake of convenience. The Senators offered Clint Benedict, the league's top goalie, but Livingstone refused. The mercurial Toronto owner also turned down a deal for goalie Sammy Hebert and $500 cash. Livingstone demanded either Frank Nighbor or $1,800 cash, but either price was too rich for Ottawa's blood.

Livingstone ended up trading Denneny for Hebert and $750 in what was reported to be the biggest deal in hockey history to that point. By this point, Livingstone had few if any friends in the hockey community. His handling of the Denneny affair had players around the league talking about forming a union, though this was never realized.

The NHA admitted the 228th Battalion, a military team based out of Toronto, for 1916–17, and their addition had Livingstone declaring war on his NHA partners on two occasions. One of his star players, "Duke" Keats, enlisted in the Battalion and hoped to play hockey for them as well. The Blueshirts' owner raised such a ruckus that the Battalion brass gave in and Keats played for the Blueshirts. Then, on February 10,

1917, only 10 games into the season, the 228th was called overseas to fight. At an emergency league meeting the next day, a disagreement arose as to how the rest of the season would be played. Livingstone suggested — "demanded" might be a more accurate word — that the league operate with five teams. The other clubs disagreed hotly and, after much fiery discussion, decided to drop Livingstone and his Toronto franchise from the league and disperse his players among the four remaining clubs.

But the NHA hadn't heard the last of Eddie Livingstone. He actually showed up at a league meeting on November 3, 1917, proclaiming to one and all that his players were available to the highest bidder. The other clubs were shocked at Livingstone's money-grubbing. A week later, they talked at length about forming a new league, one which would not include Livingstone, who had sold his Toronto franchise to the directors of the Toronto Arena.

At the November 17 NHA meeting, Quebec representative Mike Quinn announced that his Bulldogs were suspending operations indefinitely.

The 1917–18 version of the NHA would include Ottawa, Montreal Wanderers and Canadiens, and the Blueshirts who, having jettisoned Livingstone, had been permitted to rejoin the league as a replacement for Quebec. What remained unclear, however, was whether or not the Bulldogs had folded for good. When Quinn showed up at NHA meetings on November 22 and 26, it appeared Quebec was still kicking . . . for now.

The November 26 meeting at Montreal's Windsor Hotel made hockey history. At this get-together, the National Hockey League was officially formed, and franchises were granted to Ottawa, the Canadiens, Wanderers, and Toronto Arenas. The new league held a dispersal draft of the displaced Quebec players, and the Wanderers, who'd finished last in 1916–17, were given first choice. For some reason, they snagged Jack McDonald, leaving the Canadiens to grab Joe Malone, hockey's top gun. To this day it's not known why the Wanderers chose McDonald, a solid all-purpose player, but no match for Phantom Joe.

Even though he'd been frozen out of the new league, Eddie Livingstone continued to be a thorn in hockey's side. During the off-season he'd tried to put together his own league and taken out options on rinks such as Dey's Arena in Ottawa and Montreal's Jubilee Rink. In the days leading up to the 1917–18 NHL season, he filed injunctions, trying (unsuccessfully) to prevent the Senators and Canadiens from playing their home games. He and Quebec's Quinn also tried to bar players they'd lost in their respective dispersal drafts from joining their new teams. Livingstone even tried to claim he still owned the rights to Cy Denneny, whom he'd traded to Ottawa before the 1916–17 season!

The Wanderers would prove to be the new circuit's hard-luck team. Just before the season opened, Sprague Cleghorn broke his leg, while his teammate and brother Odie got news that his military exemption would be rescinded if he tried to play hockey. Next, George Carey, who'd come over from Quebec in the dispersal draft, took a full-time job in his hometown and decided not to join Montreal. But the last straw came when, only four games into the season, the Wanderers' arena burned to the ground. The NHL would finish its schedule as a three-team loop.

In Toronto, manager Charlie Querrie resigned, protesting that Livingstone continued to meddle in the team's affairs. The league stepped in very quickly, however, and Querrie was back within a week.

As significant as the formation of the NHL seems today, at the time the club owners had no idea they were creating what would become the world's dominant and longest-running pro hockey league. In their minds, the NHL was no more than a means of getting rid of the unpopular Livingstone. If not for Livingstone's petulance, the past 80 years of hockey history would have had a dramatically different face.

Two Men and a Jellyfish

Joe Hall. Newsy Lalonde. On the surface, polar opposites. One was a defender taking a special delight in the rough stuff; the other, although a scrapper, often the top scorer in the league. One thing they had in common, though, was a wicked temper. And although they would end up as teammates and roommates, they were at the center of some savage battles.

Born in England in 1882, Hall opened his Hall of Fame career in 1902 with the Brandon Regals of the Manitoba league. Two years later, Lalonde appeared in two matches with the Cornwall Victorias. Although Newsy has been remembered largely for his scoring prowess, he was one of the roughest men ever to play the game. Hall, however, was the most feared. A look at some of his more notable infractions tells the tale of his potential for brutality:

1913   Fined $150 and suspended for two weeks for striking referee Tom Melville.

1916   Assaulted Montreal Canadiens forward Amos Arbour, triggering a mini-riot on and off the ice. League president Emmett Quinn took no action.

1917   During a Quebec–Toronto match, bashed both Corb Denneny and Reg Noble. No disciplinary action taken.

1918   Got involved in a stick-swinging duel with Toronto's Alf Skinner. Both received match penalties and $15 fines as well as disorderly conduct charges.

Lalonde had his run-ins as well, his lowest hour coming during game two of the 1917 Stanley Cup finals. In the midst of his Canadiens' embarrassment at the hands of the Seattle Metropolitans, he butt-ended referee Del Irvine, who was only trying to calm a bumping bee between Jack Laviolette and Carol "Cully" Wilson. Miraculously, Lalonde escaped with a match penalty and a $25 fine.

Now, you may have noticed the name "Emmett Quinn" amongst Hall's misdeeds. Any discussion of the 1910s would be incomplete without a few words about Quinn and his feathery idea of justice. He was made NHA president prior to the 1910–11 season, having previously been a referee in several leagues. He was made secretary-treasurer of the ECHA in 1909, then became joint secretary of the NHA in 1910. His first season as league president was marred by wars between owners and players, a player revolt, and rumblings of a player strike and a rival league. In the midst of all this, he was notoriously inconsistent in doling out justice, beating down some like dogs while letting off others with a finger-wag. Examples of his leniency border on scandalous:

December 22, 1913	Lalonde smashed Odie Cleghorn into the boards. Sprague Cleghorn skated over and bashed Lalonde over the head with his stick, causing 12 stitches' worth of damage. Cleghorn was fined $50 in a Toronto court for assault. Quinn suspended Cleghorn for four weeks but reinstated him after only one game.
January 17, 1916	Gordie Roberts belted the goal judge in the face with his stick after a dispute over a goal. Quinn took no action despite the situation being brought to his attention by game officials Cooper Smeaton and Harvey Pulford.
February 16, 1916	Toronto's Ken Randall started a brawl with Ottawa. Quinn immediately fined and suspended Randall "indefinitely." Randall missed no games.

Combine these examples with his light treatment of Hall and it is easy to understand why Quinn had few friends among reporters of the day.

One of Hall's battle royals came against Frank Patrick of Renfrew. The Montreal *Gazette* said, "Patrick had pummeled Hall's face and nose into a mallowy pulp." With blood spattered across his brow, Hall lashed out at judge-of-play Rod Kennedy, apparently thinking it was Patrick. For this outburst, Hall was sent off but was allowed to return for overtime. Needless to say, Renfrew was furious. Hall was fined $100 and suspended for a week for his indiscretions. He refused to pay the fine, or the $27.50 cost of replacing Kennedy's suit, which had been torn and soiled in the melee.

The story of Hall and Lalonde's personal battles is both disturbing and entertaining. One night the two scrapped on the ice. When Hall found out Lalonde's wife had given birth that night, though, he went to the hospital and apologized for beating on her husband.

Another time, Hall slashed Lalonde across the throat with his stick, "practically severing his windpipe," according the Montreal *Gazette*. The next time Quebec played the Canadiens, the Westmount Arena was jam-packed. This time, Hall carved Lalonde for 18 stitches before the bloodied Frenchman smashed his stick over Hall's collarbone. Montreal bigwigs, far from being appalled, were thrilled as bloodthirsty fans were hooked on the feud.

During a contest on December 30, 1913, Hall and Lalonde were penalized for fighting. Lalonde got the last laugh this time, leaving an eight-stitch signature across Hall's face. But bad Joe had the memory of an elephant. In a subsequent match on January 14, 1914, he rammed Lalonde into the side fence, cutting the Frenchman so badly that two of his mates were required to carry him off the ice.

Joe Hall

Newsy Lalonde

Prior to the 1917–18 season, Hall joined Lalonde in Montreal. Someone with a well-developed sense of irony decided to pair these two "mortal enemies" as roommates. The setup, however ill-advised, worked out delightfully; the two men became friends, playing together and laughing together until Hall's premature death during the 1919 Spanish influenza epidemic.

The Adventures of Carol and Mickey

Every so often there comes a hockey player who combines a rowdy, rollicking style that sets the rest of the league on its heels with a considerable amount of skill. Consider John Ferguson, Eddie Shack, Wilf Paiement, and Bob Probert, just to name a few.

The archetype for this sort of player was a smallish forward for the Seattle Metropolitans during the 1910s: Carol "Cully" Wilson.

It was early 1919. At the box office, *Boston Blackie's Little Pal* and James Farnum's *Rainbow Rider* were the latest silent hits. At the same time, an uncommonly strong influenza bug was making the rounds of North America. In hockey, the PCHA title race was the talk of Vancouver, as was a nail-biter of a scoring race between Seattle's Bernie Morris and Vancouver's Fred Taylor.

On February 17, the league stacked up like this:

Club	GP	W	L	Pts	GF	GA
Vancouver Millionaires	13	7	6	14	36	29
Seattle Metropolitans	14	7	7	14	47	29
Victoria Aristocrats	13	6	7	12	19	44

The match that night between the Metropolitans and Millionaires was highly anticipated, drawing a league-record crowd of 8,000. The Vancouver seven won the contest easily, 6–1. Fred "Smokey" Harris and Fred Taylor led the Millionaires, who "showed wonderful stamina and skated at a terrific pace." Hugh "Eagle Eye" Lehman played well enough in goal to inspire one observer to comment, "Hughie's custodianship of the hempen was a pleasure to watch," while

Cully Wilson

superstar rover Mickey MacKay put in his usual fabulous effort, his hook-checks much in evidence. He was a marked man throughout the contest, though, especially by Wilson. The Seattle enforcer gave the "wee Scot" several bashings in the corners and more than a few hacks at center. Overall, the game was played at playoff intensity.

In the second meeting between Seattle and the Millionaires, Wilson ran wild. The Vancouver *Daily World* splashed the story across its sports section:

> In Bitterest Game of Season Millionaires Lower Colors of Seattle Squad — MacKay Injured
> ## WILSON FINED FIFTY DOLLARS
> President Patrick Punishes Seattle "Bad Man" for Assault on Mickey MacKay

For the better part of the game, Seattle used its high-powered attack to great effect. Lehman was bombarded with blasts "from every angle and at every possible speed." Rover Jack Walker was able to crack the Vancouver netminder's shell early in the third period. By this time, Wilson was wielding his stick like a baseball bat. The screwy Met was fuming over an apparent missed call earlier in the match when Barney Stanley cut him over the eye. Referee Mickey Ion would have nothing of it, throwing Wilson into the can and slapping him with a 10-minute misconduct. While he was off, Smokey Harris scored his second of the game. In time, Wilson's penalty ended and, after hopping over the boards, he ran every Millionaire in his sights.

Wilson was rumbling through center ice after MacKay, who was off on another pretty rush. Wilson made a bee-line for MacKay and smashed him across the mouth with his stick. The Vancouver dandy fell to the ice like a sack of rotten onions, the sight of steaming blood and scattered teeth both immediate and disturbing. The partisan Seattle crowd cheered like a gang of crazed hyenas, although, once preparations were made to transport MacKay off the ice, a deathly quiet choked the arena from basement to rafter. Hospital X rays revealed MacKay had suffered a fractured jaw and lost five teeth. Very upset by the loss of "their Mickey," the Millionaires "lost all science," playing a confused brand of hockey.

Seattle won the game 5–2, after Vancouver's top forward line combo — minus MacKay, of course — was "bungled miserably rush after rush." Wilson started off the match "behaving like a good little boy" but was razzed mercilessly throughout the first session by the fans. Seattle coach Muldoon ultimately yanked Wilson, replacing him with Muzz Murray.

Almost immediately after the match, Frank Patrick suspended Wilson indefinitely, but he would later reduce the penalty to a $50 fine. Wilson was charged with "willful assault" and came to be viewed widely as "the storm-center of the league and a player who tries to run everybody in it."

SEATTLE and CANADIENS
Stanley Cup Champions — 1916-17

Left to right—Seattle, Pacific Coast and Stanley Cup Champions, 1917: RALSTON (Referee) ROWE (Forward)
WILSON (Forward) WALKER (Forward) MORRIS (Forward) FOYSTON (Forward) RILEY (Forward) RICKEY (Defence)
CARPENTER (Defence) HOLMES (Goal)   Canadiens, N.H.L. and Stanley Cup Champions, 1916: VEZINA (Goal)
CORBEAU (Defence) COUTURE (Defence) NOBLE (Forward) LAVIOLETTE (Forward) SMITH (Forward)
LALONDE (Forward) BERLANQUETTE (Forward) McDONALD (Referee)

Seattle and Canadiens, 1917

The Wilson–MacKay incident had a profound impact on the course of the 1919 PCHA championships and Stanley Cup finals. The MacKay-less Vancouver squad was wiped out by Wilson and the Metropolitans in a two-game, total-goals playoff series, 8–5. Seattle went on to face the Montreal Canadiens in a series that would be canceled, because of the influenza epidemic, without a winner being decided.

Before long, Frank Patrick brought the hammer down on Wilson, banishing him from the PCHA for the entire 1919–20 season. The pariah joined the NHL's Toronto St. Patricks, moving on to the Canadiens, Hamilton Tigers, and Chicago Black Hawks before retiring for good in 1927.

Mickey MacKay

Fun with Mum

Harry Mummery, or "Big Mum" as he was known, played defense for the Quebec Bulldogs, Montreal Canadiens, Toronto Arenas, and Hamilton Tigers through parts of 11 seasons. He was likely the biggest player of his day, standing almost six feet tall and tipping the scales at anywhere from 220 to 260 pounds!

Longtime Toronto Maple Leaf trainer Tim Daly once described Mummery's strange eating habits during his stint with the Toronto Arenas. When he wasn't playing hockey, Harry was a fireman on the train that ran between Toronto and Stratford. He would sometimes get back to Toronto so late that he would have no time to order a meal and wait for it to be prepared. Instead he would go to a butcher's shop near the Mutual Street Arena and pick up a fat, juicy steak. After changing into his uniform at the rink, he would take a coal shovel, wash it off under a tap, put the steak on it, and shove it into the old potbellied stove in the dressing room! After wolfing down his dinner, he would have just enough time to lace on his skates and shuffle out onto the ice for the opening face-off.

When Mummery reported to the Montreal Canadiens in 1920, he brought his restaurant tabs with him, bounced into team owner George Kennedy's office, and plunked down the stack of receipts. Kennedy went through the list carefully, then cast a quizzical eye at Mummery. "Do you keep cats?" he asked.

Mummery replied that he didn't own a cat.

"Then who drank all of this cream?"

"Why, I did," was Mummery's answer. "I always drink a pint of cream after each meal. It's an antidote for ulcers. Besides, I like cream."

Harry Mummery

*Snap!*shots

HARRY CAMERON Defense
5'10" 155
b. 2/6/1890, Pembroke, Ontario
d. 10/20/1953, Vancouver, British Columbia

Harry Cameron

Harold Hugh Cameron was a loud, outspoken, essentially uncoachable player, hardly a dressing-room leader. Because of his temperament he did not stay with one team for more than four years in a row.

But as a player, Cameron was a dandy. He was one of the first, if not the first, to develop a curved shot — without benefit of a curved stick blade! He was a solid skater who possessed a sixth sense when on the attack. His scoring record is outstanding, especially considering the fact that he was a defenseman. He regularly topped NHL rearguards in scoring and placed fifth overall in the league twice.

Cameron teamed with Jack Marshall on the Toronto Blueshirts defense in 1914 and played a huge role in their defeat of the Montreal Canadiens in the playoffs, giving the city of Toronto its first Stanley Cup.

When Charlie Querrie assumed management of the Toronto Arenas in 1917, he and his star were on a collision course. Under Marshall's supervision, Cameron had been allowed to do whatever the hell he wanted, whenever the hell he wanted. Practices were optional and a training regimen was nonexistent. Querrie preferred to rule with an iron fist, but Cameron continued to break training and skip practices. Querrie fined his stubborn star time and time again, always in vain. It became a running joke in Toronto.

Querrie and Cameron coexisted, albeit uneasily, through the next two seasons. The Arenas even won a second Cup in 1918. But in the early days of 1919, Querrie had had his fill of Cameron, and sent him packing to Ottawa. There, the star blue-liner was teamed with fellow grouch Sprague Cleghorn.

Cameron was back in Toronto as the 1919–20 season began, but by January Querrie would blow his stack again and trade Cameron to the Montreal Canadiens. Traded back to Toronto in 1921, he seemed to mellow, scoring 36 goals in 48 games over the next two years. He closed out his major-league career with Newsy Lalonde's Saskatoon Crescents of the WHL in 1926, and hung on in the minors for another seven years.

In 315 games, split over several leagues, Cameron scored 173 goals and 264 points. He became a member of the Hockey Hall of Fame in 1962.

Peak Years   *1918–22*
In a Word   *GROUCH*

ODIE CLEGHORN Right Wing/Center
5'9" 195
b. 9/19/1891, Montreal, Quebec
d. 7/13/1956

Odie Cleghorn

Ogilvie James Cleghorn broke in with the Renfrew Creamery Kings for the 1910–11 season, signing, as did his brother Sprague, for a reported $1,000 for the season. When Renfrew dropped out of the league, Cleghorn went on to play six seasons with the Montreal Wanderers as a right winger and, after Ernie Russell retired, at center. Cleghorn's playmates included marksman Harry Hyland, power forward Gordie Roberts, silky-smooth Don Smith, and Russell's heir apparent, Alfred "Brownie" Baker.

Despite being rough and pudgy, Cleghorn was capable of threading his way through entire teams, cradling the puck in tight as he weaved his way to the net. The little fellow, known as "the game's premier puck wizard," used a short stick and was famous for a vast array of head feints and dekes. In his day, crowds delighted most in exhibitions of stick wizardry and in this regard he was the master showman. And although he was not as accomplished a pugilist as his brother Sprague, Odie was ready and able to mix things up.

Cleghorn missed the entire 1917–18 season due to a military exemption agreement — he could stay out of the military only if he didn't play hockey. He joined the cross-town Montreal Canadiens in 1918, putting up seven seasons there as a top-flight scorer. In 193 games in the NHA and NHL, he managed 214 goals and 267 points. He's also said to have invented the three-line system in the late 1920s. He died in 1956, on the day of his brother's funeral.

Peak Years   *1918–1922*
In a Word   *PEPPERY*

SPRAGUE CLEGHORN (Peg/The Big Train) Defense
5'10" 190
b. 3/11/1890, Montreal, Quebec
d. 7/11/1956, Montreal, Quebec

Despite a capacity for outright savagery, Sprague Cleghorn was one of the finest defenders the game of hockey has ever known. Fists, sticks, and swearing aside, he was the "Clark Gable of his day," able to make effortless transitions between the physical game and whirling rushes.

Cleghorn broke in as a forward with the Renfrew Creamery Kings before he was moved back to the blue-line. He learned his craft very well and his dashes would be a drawing card for many years. To Montreal Wanderer fans, the bruiser they called "Peg" was the apple their eyes between 1912 and 1917, as he successfully teamed with Art Ross, Goldie Prodgers, and Jack Marshall. In 17 years of major professional competition, he notched 169 regular-season goals and was for decades ranked second only to Harry Cameron in goals scored by a defenseman.

While Cleghorn was adept with the puck, he was possibly better without it. So harsh was his treatment of opposing forwards that many were scared to hang around the net. Despite what has been said about Cleghorn's unpredictability, his defensive ability compared quite favorably to contemporaries such as Eddie Gerard, Ching Johnson, or Buck Boucher. Cleghorn was by no means a dime-a-dozen goon.

The 1917–18 was a horrible one for Cleghorn. He broke his leg prior to training camp, then he was arrested for beating his wife with a crutch! That same year, the Wanderers folded and he signed with the Ottawa Senators.

After a couple of years in Ottawa, the NHL transferred Sprague's rights to the woeful Hamilton Tigers (formerly the Quebec Bulldogs). But Cleghorn refused to report, and the Tigers traded him to the Toronto St. Patricks. At the end of the regular season, he got his release from the St. Pats and rejoined the Senators for the playoffs. In April 1921 the league stepped in and assigned his rights to Hamilton a second time. Cleghorn was again a no-show in the Steel City and the Tigers dealt him to the Canadiens.

In a 1923 Montreal–Ottawa bloodfest, Cleghorn disabled three Senators as well as manager Tommy Gorman, who had leapt onto the ice. The rivalry was so overheated that, the next time the Canadiens played in Ottawa, Sprague had to be smuggled into

----

Ottawa's Aberdeen Pavilion arena via the furnace room so as to avoid the angry mob. He made up for this indignity by skating to center ice and thumbing his nose at the crowd!

In Montreal, Cleghorn paired with fellow archfiend Billy Coutu to form what was arguably the most frightening defensive duo ever seen. Cleghorn made history during the 1923 playoffs when Montreal owner Leo Dandurand suspended him for the remainder of the playoffs for his brutal attack on Ottawa defender Lionel Hitchman. This particular attack was described as "awful," "inexcusable," and "befitting an animal." On top of the ban, he was slapped with a $200 fine. Coutu had also been banished — again by his own manager — for similar behavior, and Montreal was knocked out of the Stanley Cup hunt.

Cleghorn was quite protective of his younger brother, Odie. On the night of hockey in front of a silk-hatted crowd at Toronto's Mutual Street Arena, the Cleghorn boys and their Montreal Wanderers were facing Newsy Lalonde and the Canadiens. During the game, Lalonde took out Odie rather harshly. Within seconds, Sprague had stormed across the ice and clouted Lalonde so severely the crowd thought the Frenchman was dead. Both Lalonde and Cleghorn were hauled into court but the charming Lalonde talked their way out of the jam. Cleghorn escaped with a $50 fine.

Despite his violent on-ice streak, Cleghorn had a reputation around the dressing room as a practical joker. The man whose favorite comedic prop was a joy buzzer would "keep the boys stitched with many a giggle and chuckle."

Cleghorn closed out his marvelous career with the Boston Bruins in 1928. He was a three-time Cup-winner and a warrior to the end.

Cleghorn was named to the Hockey Hall of Fame in 1958.

Peak Years   *1918–22*
Comparable Current Player   *Chris Chelios*
In a Word   *MONSTER*

JACK DARRAGH Right Wing
5'0" 168
b. 12/4/1890, Ottawa, Ontario
d. 6/25/1924, Ottawa, Ontario

For years, John Proctor Darragh was the spirit of the Ottawa Senators. He made his professional hockey debut on December 31, 1910, against Georges Vezina — also playing his first NHL match — and the Montreal Canadiens. Darragh scored a goal in a 5–3 Ottawa victory.

Though a left-handed shot, Darragh was used on the right wing to take full advantage of his wicked backhand shot — his was possibly the finest until Maurice Richard came along some 30 years later. Like Richard, Darragh was a clutch performer, scoring the Cup-clinching goal for Ottawa in 1920 and following up with another timely effort in another Ottawa Cup triumph in 1921. He was a blisteringly fast skater; he compared favorably to the two speed fiends of the day, Didier Pitre and Fred Taylor. It was said that Darragh "could match strides with anybody, no matter how big or small."

For years the combination of Darragh, Frank Nighbor, and Cy Denneny made fools of opposing defenses and goalies, thanks to Nighbor's silky smoothness, Denneny's bullet-shot and Darragh's breakneck speed.

Having contributed to Ottawa's Stanley Cup victories in 1910–11, 1919–20, and 1920–21, Darragh decided to hang up his skates. By all accounts he wanted to retire on top. After sitting out only a year, he returned, contributing to yet another Ottawa Cup win in 1923. Sadly, little more than a year later, he died of a stomach virus. He was only 33.

Jack Darragh entered the Hockey Hall of Fame in 1962.

Peak Years   *1917–21*
Comparable Current Player   *Jason Allison*
In a Word   *STERLING*

TOM DUNDERDALE Rover/Center
5'8" 160
b. 5/6/1887, Benella, Australia
d. 12/15/1960, Winnipeg, Manitoba

Thomas Dunderdale was a natural rover, a player with enough speed to attack and to get back in time to defend. He was a right-handed shot who was famous for his deft stick-handling. A summary of his career reads like a Rand McNally road atlas. Dunderdale played hockey at Waller Street Public School in Ottawa and later while attending business college in Winnipeg. He returned to Ottawa to play for the Cliffsides club in 1906 before going back to the Manitoba capital to put in time with the Senior Maple Leafs. He played one season and part of another before jumping to the Strathconas of the Northwestern Amateur league.

When the NHA was founded in late 1909, Dunderdale hitched a ride with the Montreal Shamrocks. Next he spent a season with the Quebec Bulldogs before jumping to the Victoria Aristocrats of the new Pacific Coast Hockey Association for more money. He played very well over the next four seasons, leading his team in scoring three times and taking home league honors in 1912–13. Victoria won the league title in 1912–13 and defeated the Stanley Cup champion Bulldogs in an exhibition series; Dunderdale scored three times in three games. In 1913–14, he scored in every one of Victoria's 15 matches and was named to the PCHA's First All-Star team as a center. He held out for more money in 1915 but was brought to terms by league president Frank Patrick.

Eventually, Dunderdale was dealt to the Portland Rosebuds, who would win the 1915–16 league championship. He played for two more seasons in Portland, returning to Victoria in 1919, before finishing up with the Edmonton Eskimos and Saskatoon Sheiks of the Western Canada Hockey League in 1924. He retired as the PCHA's top career goal-scorer.

In 290 games, Dunderdale scored 225 goals. He is a worthy member of the Hockey Hall of Fame.

Peak Years   *1912–16*
Comparable Current Player   *Dale Hawerchuk*
In a Word   *DANDY*

FRANK FOYSTON Center/Right Wing
5'9" 160
b. 2/2/1891, Minesing, Ontario
d. 1/19/1966, Seattle, Washington

Frank Foyston was a consistent, albeit underrated, star for many years with the PCHA's Seattle Metropolitans. He was usually among the top scorers in the league and was widely considered one of the best all-around hockeyists of the period from 1910 until 1930.

Foyston was often cited as the finest player in the PCHA. Bold and clever around the enemy net, his stick-handling wizardry and superior shooting enabled him to become one of the first men to hit the 200-goal mark. He was on the winning side in three Stanley Cup finals — with Toronto in 1914, Seattle in 1917, and Victoria in 1925.

After Foyston passed away in 1966, the Seattle *Post-Intelligencer* placed him in the sporting pantheon with these words: "You missed one of the all-time greats if you never saw Frank Foyston perform with a hockey stick. He wielded it like Fritz Kreisler his bow, Willie Mays his bat, and Arnold Palmer his two-iron."

In 361 games in several leagues, Foyston managed 240 goals and 319 points. He was named to the Hockey Hall of Fame in 1958.

Peak Years   *1917–21*
In a Word   *FORGOTTEN*

EDDIE GERARD Defense/Left Wing
5'9" 168
b. 2/22/1890, Ottawa, Ontario
d. 12/7/1937, Ottawa, Ontario

Eddie Gerard, a nearly forgotten hockey legend, was a sportsman to the core and one of the most effective defensemen the game has ever seen. This Scottish-Canadian was expert in hockey, football, and rowing, and would have been a star in any of these sports. Upon reaching the proper age, he joined the Ottawa City Amateur Senior hockey club and became an outstanding left winger. The Ottawa Senators were one of a crowd of football and hockey teams across Canada who, recognizing Gerard's incredible athleticism, clamored to sign him as early as 1910. In 1914, Ottawa reeled him in with a generous offer.

Gerard began on left wing in Ottawa but was moved to the defense. He had excellent speed, fine stick-handling ability, and amazing anticipation. While not the scorer that Cleghorn and Harry Cameron were, Gerard was exceptional in his own end. He was a hard, clean player with a go-go-go hockey philosophy.

In game three of the 1922 Stanley Cup finals, the Toronto St. Patricks lost Harry Cameron to injury, so they asked for and got permission to replace him with Gerard. Toronto shut out the Vancouver Millionaires, 6–0, and Gerard played so well that Vancouver vetoed his playing in game five. Even though Toronto went on to win the Cup, Gerard refused to accept payment for his part in the series.

Gerard was at his very best in his last year with the Senators. During the 1923 playoffs he was absolutely brilliant despite separating his shoulder and cutting his foot in the last game of the semifinals. His show of bravery sparked his fellow Ottawans to victory.

Shortly after his premature retirement, Gerard took over head coaching responsibilities for the Montreal Maroons, guiding this rough bunch to their first ever Cup win in 1926. He then accepted the coach/GM post with the New York Americans in 1931 but was back at the helm of the Maroons the next year.

A growth in his throat that had been a problem for some time steadily grew worse and in 1935, he was forced to retire from hockey once and for all. He died in 1937, presumably from throat cancer. In 202 games, he has 95 goals and 173 points to his credit.

Gerard was one of the 12 charter members of the Hockey Hall of Fame, inducted in 1945.

Peak Years   *1917–21*
In a Word   *COMPOSER*

SI GRIFFIS Defense
6'1" 195
b. 9/22/1883, Onaga, Kansas
d. 7/1950

Si Griffis

Silas Seth Griffis came to Canada with his parents. After a brief
stay in St. Catharines, Ontario, the Griffis clan moved on to Rat
Portage (now Kenora). It was in this rugged, tiny, northern
Canadian town that Griffis discovered the game of hockey.

A big man for his day, Griffis first played organized hockey
as a rover for the Rat Portage/Kenora Thistles. He turned pro in Kenora, and moved to
the cover-point position. In 1907, Kenora defeated the Montreal Wanderers for the
Stanley Cup but were quickly dethroned in a rematch. Griffis took this opportunity to
move to Vancouver, surprising everyone when he retired from hockey. The citizens of
Kenora gave him a large purse of gold and offered a home if he ever decided to move
back to the northern Ontario town.

After a four-year sabbatical, Griffis decided to try a comeback with Frank Patrick's
new Vancouver Millionaires. On opening night, Griffis played right defense for all 60
minutes, chalking up two goals and two assists. He captained Vancouver until his second and final retirement in 1919.

Griffis was a powerful skater, rated as one of the swiftest big men ever to play
hockey on the West Coast. His quiet leadership by example, coupled with a superlative
technical grasp of the game, made him one of the most effective blue-liners of his
time. He would have been an All-Star in any era.

Griffis made the Hockey Hall of Fame in 1950.

Peak Years   *1912–16*
In a Word   *WINGS*

JOE HALL (Bad Joe) Defense/Forward
5'10" 175
b. 5/3/1882, Staffordshire, England
d. 4/5/1919, Seattle, Washington

Although some of Joseph Henry Hall's former teammates maintained that his reputation as "Bad Joe" was blown out of proportion, he seemed to stir it up wherever he
played. He was a very physical defender and, despite what his supporters said about
him, he could be savage.

Hall played his first organized hockey in 1902 as a forward with the Brandon
Regals. The next year he hooked up with the Winnipeg outfit that unsuccessfully challenged the Ottawa Silver Seven for the Stanley Cup.

A year later, Hall was kicked out of the Manitoba Senior league for dangerously
rough play and he found work in the east with the Montreal Shamrocks. He skipped to
the Wanderers after one year, then rejoined the Shamrocks for 1910. Playing on a line
with Don Smith and Walter Bellamy, Hall fashioned a reputation for being a nutcase as
well as a brute.

An epic encounter between Hall and Frank Patrick made all of the papers. For days,
people raved over the "surprising fistic skills of Renfrew's Patrick" and were buzzing
about how Patrick smashed Hall's face to a pulp. Late in the match, Hall took out his
frustration on judge-of-play Rod Kennedy, breaking the official's nose in a flurry of
punches. For this, Hall was fined and suspended by NHA president Emmett Quinn.

After the Shamrocks folded, Hall signed on with the Quebec Bulldogs, joining a
powerhouse lineup that already boasted Joe Malone, Harry Mummery, and Russell

Crawford. With Quebec, Hall went on to become arguably the top defender in the NHA, and he certainly staked out his territory as hockey's baddest bad man. His blood feud with the Montreal Canadiens' Newsy Lalonde was quite possibly the most beastly ever witnessed in the history of organized sport.

With the formation of the NHL in 1917–18, Quebec folded and Hall joined the Canadiens. He and Lalonde not only called a cease-fire, but they actually agreed to be roommates! Hall's defense partner with the Habs was Bert Corbeau, who was just as unbalanced as Hall.

In 1919, Montreal made the finals against the Seattle Metropolitans. In the fifth game of a bitter series, Hall contracted Spanish influenza, which was sweeping the world that spring. Public health authorities in Seattle canceled the finals after several players succumbed to the flu. Hall died a few days later in a Seattle hospital.

Hall is a member of the Hockey Hall of Fame.

Peak Years   *1912–16*
In a Word   *BULLY*

HAP HOLMES Goal
5'10" 170
b. 2/21/1889, Aurora, Ontario
d. 1940, Florida

Harry "Hap" Holmes was a goalie of uncommon grit. Sportswriters called him "nerveless." He played in 409 top-level contests in his career with Toronto, Seattle, Detroit, and Victoria. If there had been a trophy for the league's top goalie in his day, he may very well have taken half a dozen. In all, he counted 40 shutouts, adding 7 more in 48 playoff contests, and he put up a career goals-against average of 2.81 and backstopped seven league championship squads and four Stanley Cup winners.

One of Holmes's most astonishing feats came when he was in the Seattle Metropolitan nets during the ill-starred 1919 finals against the Montreal Canadiens. After being shut out 7–0 in game one — which was played under the PCHA's seven-man rules — the Montrealers recovered to take the next game, 4–2. Seattle struck back in game three, winning 7–2. Then came game four.

After a grueling, scoreless 60 minutes, the teams summoned just enough energy in overtime to turn the game into an end-to-end affair. Holmes and Georges Vezina traded saves by the bushel, locking horns in one of the truly epic goaltending duels in hockey history. No substitutions were made for the first 15 minutes of overtime and, at the 20-minute mark, with both sides completely spent, referee Mickey Ion called the game a draw. Holmes had matched Vezina, save for save. The influenza epidemic of 1919 left the Cup series undecided, but Holmes would triumph over Vezina and the Canadiens six years later when he led the Victoria Cougars to a Cup title.

Holmes died in 1940 in southern Florida, but his name lives on in the Harry Holmes Memorial Trophy, an award presented every year since 1961 to the leading goaltender in the American Hockey League.

Holmes was named to the Hockey Hall of Fame in 1972.

Peak Years   *1918–22*
In a Word   *GAMER*

NEWSY LALONDE Center/Rover

5'9" 168
b. 10/31/1888, Cornwall, Ontario
d. 11/21/1971, Montreal, Quebec

Edouard Cyril "Newsy" Lalonde was, simply, the greatest hockey player of his time. This brilliant goal-scorer, who once potted nine in a single outing, earned his famous nickname as a cub reporter and printer's apprentice for the Cornwall *Free Press*. Drawing on a fine blend of grit and glitter, he went on to become hockey's brightest luminary.

Lalonde made his debut with the Cornwalls of the Federal league in 1904. What should have been a magical night for the young fellow was just short of disastrous when he fell onto an opponent's skate, severing one of his leg arteries. He continued to work at the *Free Press* for the next couple of years, dreaming of a career in hockey.

In 1906, the Canadian Soo team in the International Pro league sprung Lalonde from the print shop with a $35-a-week offer plus $16 to cover his traveling expenses. He immediately withdrew his last few dollars from the bank and boarded the train. The next night he was on the Soo bench, and he got his big chance when teammate Marty Walsh broke his leg. Lalonde later said of his debut: "I went all right for a while, and then I got jammed into the fence. It hurt and I didn't feel good." Famished and in pain, he took a deep, restorative swig from a bottle handed to him by boxer Jack Hammond. "It burned my mouth, my gums, and my throat. I thought I was a goner." As it turned out, Hammond had two bottles — one of whiskey and one of ammonia! In the heat of the moment, he handed Lalonde the wrong bottle. The youngster did recover, though, well enough to pot two goals.

Lalonde was the complete package: he could skate, shoot, stick handle, and pass expertly. He also was a skilled fighter with a volcanic temper. As a result, fans came out in droves to cheer him on or scream for his blood. Many of his "bad" contemporaries — Joe Hall, Ken Randall, Carol "Cully" Wilson, Sprague Cleghorn — bore long-lasting scars from their run-ins with Lalonde.

Lester Patrick, who was playing professional hockey when Lalonde first came up, commented on the Frenchman's ability: "Lalonde had an absolutely wicked knee-high shot that was almost impossible to keep out of the goal if he had a clear area in front. The only way to stop that man was have three or four players, or more if you could spare them, and skate him into the side boards."

The formation of the NHA in late 1909 brought Lalonde to Montreal, where he signed on with the Canadiens. In midseason he was traded to the Renfrew Millionaires, where he topped all goal-getters. He rejoined the Canadiens for the 1910–11 season, playing between Didier Pitre and Skinner Poulin, before heading west for a season with the Vancouver Millionaires, where he led the PCHA with 27 goals in 15 games. The next year it was back to the Canadiens, where he would be a mainstay for the next decade.

Lalonde was on his first and only Stanley Cup winner in 1916, when Montreal defeated Ernie Johnson and the Portland Rosebuds. Lalonde, of course, was the star of the series. They traveled west to play the Seattle Metropolitans for the Cup in the spring of 1919, and Lalonde was sensational, earning acclaim from the local press. But the outbreak of Spanish influenza hit Seattle, claiming the life of Canadiens star "Bad Joe" Hall, and the department of health canceled the finals in midseries.

Lalonde put in three more seasons in Montreal before running afoul of owner Leo Dandurand, who dealt Newsy to the WCHL's Saskatoon Sheiks in exchange for a youngster by the name of Aurel Joliat. Lalonde cheerfully assumed his new responsibilities as player-manager in Saskatoon, winning the league scoring derby at the ripe old age of 36. He played intermittently over the next three years in Saskatoon, at the same

----

time helping develop stars such as Bill and Bun Cook. It has been implied that Bill Cook, a deserving Hall of Famer, learned his craft from Lalonde.

On March 2, 1925, in a game against Vancouver, Lalonde scored the last goal of his career, pushing his mighty career total to 449. When the WHL was dissolved in 1926, Lalonde assumed head coaching duties with the New York Americans. He remained in hockey until the early 1930s when he took a job as branch manager of a government-run liquor store. Until his dying day in November 1971, he could often be found at the local rink watching a hockey game.

From one of the game's first superstars, the man who never made more than $4,500 a season, comes a lovely quote: "I can't go anywhere, on a train, a bus, or in a club without somebody who wants to talk to me. I tell you it's the most wonderful thing. It's worth more than any amount of money that I ever played for."

Lalonde made the Hockey Hall of Fame in 1950.

Peak Years   *1915–19*
In a Word   *WARRIOR*

JACK LAVIOLETTE (The Speed Merchant)   Defense/Right Wing
5'11" 170
b. 7/27/1879, Belleville, Ontario
d. 1/10/1960, Montreal, Quebec

Jack Laviolette

A product of Belleville, Ontario, Jean-Baptiste Laviolette began his hockey career in 1903 with the Montreal Nationals. After three seasons with the IPHL's Michigan Soo Indians, he joined the Montreal Shamrocks as a defenseman. In late 1909, he was asked to form and play for the first edition of the Montreal Canadiens. In this dual capacity would he gain recognition as the original Flying Frenchman.

After securing the necessary financial backing to start up the Canadiens, Laviolette found his sniper in Didier Pitre. When he added Newsy Lalonde and Ernie Dubeau, Laviolette had formed the nucleus of what has become the most successful sports franchise in history. He initially manned the Montreal point but later moved to the left wing to skate alongside Pitre and Lalonde. Laviolette's skating and great speed came to the fore on a line already blessed with top-flight skills.

The Montreal *Star* often featured Laviolette in its sports cartoons. He was one of the instantly recognizable players of his day, with his trademark coolie hat, long, jet-black hair whipping in the wind, powerful skating strides, and an assortment of fakes, dekes, pirouettes, and spin-a-ramas.

Laviolette was an avid race car enthusiast, which is a risky sport at the best of times. In the summer of 1919 he lost a foot in a crash when he was driving at Montreal's Delorimier Downs racetrack. Amazingly, he came back to do some refereeing in 1921 on an artificial right foot. His last hockey-related appearance was at the Montreal Forum in 1957, when a number of hockey veterans attended a charity old-timers game sponsored by the Quebec Oldtimers Hockey Association.

Laviolette was elected to the Hockey Hall of Fame in 1962.

Peak Years   *1910–1914*
Comparable Current Player   *Scott Niedermayer*
In a Word   *SHOWMAN*

JOE MALONE (Phantom) Center
5'10" 150
b. 2/28/1890, Sillery, Quebec
d. 5/15/1969

Joe Malone was one of the fine gentlemen of pre-modern hockey, a thoroughbred in an era of plow horses. He took no part in stick-swinging or fisticuffs, preferring to devote his energies almost exclusively to offensive pursuits.

Malone was born in the small town of Sillery, near Quebec City, playing his first organized hockey with the Junior Quebec Crescents in 1907–08. After one season with the Quebec Bulldogs, he did an 11-game stint with the Waterloo Professionals of the Ontario Professional league, rejoining the Bulldogs shortly thereafter.

While in Quebec, Malone posted impressive numbers — he scored nine goals against Sydney on March 8, 1913, eight goals in a game in 1917, and seven goals in an NHL game in 1920 — the latter a league record standing to this day. In 273 career games, he scored 343 goals.

A tall, handsome man, Malone favored a stand-up-straight skating style. He was deceptive on the blades and, although not a speedster, had a sixth sense around the net. His skill with the puck compared favorably to that of Odie Cleghorn. Both men were capable of stick-handling through entire teams. Because of this ability, as well as his shiftiness and ability to be in the right place at the right time, he became known as "The Phantom."

At the end of the 1916–17 season Quebec disbanded, leaving a number of star-caliber players up for grabs. Malone signed on with the Montreal Canadiens and he scored an incredible 44 goals in 20 games. After another season in Montreal, he was claimed by Quebec when they rejoined the league in 1919–20, and he scored a league-high 39 goals in 24 games. The Bulldogs moved to Hamilton the next season, and Malone coached, managed, and played two seasons for the Tigers. He refused to show up for Hamilton's 1922 training camp, and they dealt him back to Montreal, where he played out the string for two seasons.

Any discussion of the greatest goal scorers of all time would have to include Malone. He is a very worthy member of the Hockey Hall of Fame.

Peak Years   *1914–18*
Comparable Current Player   *Jaromir Jagr*
In a Word   *GHOSTLY*

HARRY MUMMERY (Mum) Defense
5'11" 258
b. 8/25/1889, Chicago, Illinois
d. 12/7/1945

This friendly giant broke into organized hockey in 1910 with the Manitoba league's Brandon club. After a year with the Moose Jaw Canadians, he joined the Quebec Bulldogs, for whom he played most of his career.

Mummery was huge, weighing about 220 pounds at the beginning of his career. By the time he retired in 1923, he was said to weigh as much as 265. Despite his size, he was a "one-man power play," moving with surprising speed. After gaining the puck, he would motor down the ice, brushing aside would-be checkers with his long, salami-roll arms. Then, if he got close enough, he would loft a heavy shot at the goalie.

In 213 top-level regular-season contests, Mummery scored 59 goals, a respectable total for a defenseman. He played on three league champions, and his name was inscribed on the Stanley Cup twice.

Mummery was one of the more colorful figures in pre-modern hockey. He was certainly one of the most prodigious eaters the sport has ever seen. His food bills (paid by his team) were enormous and, if the stories are to be believed, he could down a couple of five-pound steaks, quaff a huge mug of cream, scoff a whole apple pie . . . then go right out and play 60 strenuous minutes of hockey!

Peak Years   *1917–21*
Comparable Current Player   *Ed Jovanovski*
In a Word   *TRUCK*

FRANK PATRICK Defense
b. 12/21/1885, Ottawa, Ontario
d. 6/29/1960

Frank Patrick

The NHL rule book contains 22 pieces of legislation drawn up by Frank Patrick. He was one of the true innovators in hockey, having invented the blue-line, forward passing, and the penalty shot; he got the idea to keep track of assists; he also came up with the first standard playoff system.

In his earlier days, Patrick was a top-notch defender, a rugged, well-built man who never shied away from the rough stuff. He was also a strong skater whose stick-handling ability allowed him to indulge his fondness for the rush. Although not quite the offensive force his brother Lester was, Frank was a standout for teams such as the Montreal Victorias, Renfrew Creamery Kings, and Vancouver Millionaires.

The Patricks were true visionaries whose bold, bright ideas had lasting influence on the game of hockey. They saw the advantages presented by artificial ice, and built Canada's first artificial rinks in Vancouver and Victoria. To make the buildings pay, they formed a pro league, the Pacific Coast Hockey Association, in 1911. Not only did Frank play three seasons on defense for Vancouver, he also owned the team and acted as league president until its demise in the mid 1920s. At the start of the 1914–15 season, he decided to devote all his energy to executive matters. However, with his team headed for a championship, he could not stay off the ice. He played a pocketful of games that year and, when Si Griffis broke his leg, Patrick hopped over the boards yet again. He scored two goals as Vancouver swept the series from the Ottawa Senators in three straight contests.

In 1924 the Seattle Metropolitans folded, and the two remaining PCHA teams, Frank's Vancouver Maroons and Lester's Victoria Cougars, joined the Western Canada Hockey League. Two years later, that league also called it quits, and Frank Patrick engineered what was the biggest deal hockey had seen to date, selling the WHL's assets to the NHL. Frank served as managing director of the NHL in 1933–34, as coach of the Boston Bruins from 1934–36, and as assistant GM and business manager of the Montreal Canadiens on April 27, 1941.

Frank Patrick died of a heart attack in Vancouver on June 29, 1960, two years after he was elected to the Hockey Hall of Fame as a builder.

Peak Years   *1911–15*
In a Word   *BOSS*

LESTER PATRICK (The Praying Colonel, The Silver Fox) Defense
6'1" 180
b. 12/31/1883, Drummondville, Quebec
d. 6/1/1960, Victoria, British Columbia

Lester Patrick

Lester Patrick was one of the classier figures in hockey history, and he was one of the sport's most prolific builders. He was a perennial All-Star rover and defender for 21 seasons, and he just happened to have a penchant for team-building. And his ambitions did not end there: he and his brother Frank were behind the construction of rinks and operators of a league of their own.

As a tall, gawky-looking boy, Lester Patrick played shinny on the frozen ponds of Drummondville, Quebec. A move to Montreal in the early 1890s introduced him to the real game of hockey, and as a teenager he would haunt the old Victoria Rink. One evening, Montreal AAA forward Clare McKerrow met and took an immediate shine to Patrick, teaching him about hockey and about how to carry himself as a gentleman. McKerrow was a lasting influence in Patrick's long and eventful life.

Patrick got his first crack at hockey's top levels in 1903–04 in Brandon, Manitoba, where he played defense on a team that tried unsuccessfully to pry the Stanley Cup from the Ottawa Silver Seven. After a season at Westmount Academy, he joined the Montreal Wanderers in time for the 1905–06 season. It was with the mighty Redbands that he reached the peak of his considerable talent. Players like Ernie Russell, Frank Glass, and Cecil Blachford benefited enormously from Patrick's smooth passing.

In 1907, the Patrick brothers headed west to Nelson, British Columbia, to work for their father's lumber operation, and they played the next two years for a local Senior team. They were both drawn back east to play the 1909–10 season for the NHA's Renfrew Creamery Kings, then it was back to Nelson for one more year. In 1911, the brothers founded the PCHA, and Lester became owner and player-manager of the league's Victoria Aristocrats.

To stock their teams, the Patricks raided NHA rosters and managed to lure some top talent to the West Coast. To quote Lester later on in life: "We had a league of superstars on the coast from 1911 to 1925. In the early days there was Cyclone Taylor, Newsy Lalonde for a time, Harry Hyland, Ken Mallen, Eddie Oatman, and Tommy Dunderdale. They were among the biggest names of the day."

The PCHA folded in 1924, and the Victoria and Vancouver clubs joined the Western Canada league until it, too, faded from the scene in 1926. At the same time, the NHL was in the midst of a growth spurt, going from four to 10 teams between 1924 and 1926. One of those new teams was the New York Rangers, who had hired Conn Smythe as manager. Ranger brass were convinced, wrongly, that Smythe hadn't built a strong enough roster, so they called on Lester Patrick to manage and coach.

Lester Patrick was involved in one of the most unusual moments in hockey history when he put himself into the Ranger net during the 1928 Cup finals. New York had lost the first game of the best-of-five series, 2–0, to the Montreal Maroons, and in game two their situation looked desperate. Four minutes into the second period, star goalie Lorne Chabot was hit in the eye by a puck and had to be taken to hospital.

New York wanted to use Ottawa goalie Alex Connell, who was in the stands, but Maroons coach Eddie Gerard would have none of it. The rules said a replacement had to be someone already signed to a Ranger contract, and Gerard wouldn't give in on this point. The 44-year-old Patrick was left with no choice but to put on the pads and play. He would save 17 of 18 shots and hold the line for the Rangers, who won 2–1 in overtime. Joe Miller of the New York Americans was enlisted for game three, and he backstopped the Rangers to their first Cup title.

It wasn't the first time Patrick had come out of retirement. In 1925–26, Gordon Fraser and Harold "Slim" Halderson suffered major injuries, so Patrick, who at 42 hadn't played in the last three years, joined the blue-line corps, playing 23 games and leading his men to the Cup finals. Nor was he any stranger to pitching in between the pipes: he'd played 10 minutes of a game in goal for Victoria in 1921–22.

Patrick played in 205 top-level games during a career that spanned from 1904 to 1928. He captained eight clubs and was on the Cup-winning side as a player, coach, or GM six times. In all, he spent 33 seasons as general manager of clubs in Victoria and New York. He was the original "Mr. Hockey."

Lester Patrick was inducted into the Hockey Hall of Fame in 1947.

Peak Years   *1913–17*
In a Word   *NOBLE*

The Patricks: Hockey's Royal Family

```
                         Joe Patrick
          ┌─────────────────┼─────────────────┐
   Lester Patrick      Ted Patrick        Frank Patrick
          │                 │                 │
   Murray Patrick      Lynn Patrick        Joe Patrick
          │                 │
   Paul Patrick       Lester Patrick II
   Dick Patrick       Craig Patrick
                      Glenn Patrick
                          │
                      Dean Patrick
```

To borrow from a line from a hokey World War Two song, "There's always been a Patrick in organized professional hockey, and if there always is, hockey won't be any worse for it." Corny, yes, but true. Lester's sons, Lynn and Murray (better known as "Muzz"), both grew up to be NHL players, coaches, and managers. And Lynn's sons Glenn and Craig also played in the NHL, with Craig becoming a successful general manager with the Pittsburgh Penguins.

DIDIER PITRE (Cannonball/Bullet Shot/Pit/ Old Folks) Right Wing/Defense
5'11" 200
b. 9/1/1883, Valleyfield, Quebec
d. 7/29/1934, Sault Ste. Marie, Ontario

Didier Pitre was the "Bullet Shot" of pre-modern hockey and one of the very first French-Canadian hockey heroes. Weighing upwards of 200 pounds, he had huge legs able to support a thick, strong frame. Those legs drove him along at a smashing clip, giving him the momentum he needed to drive pucks with violent force. He could also stop on a dime, scraping a huge cloud of ice into the air as he dug his blades into the ice.

Pitre began his hockey career in 1903 as a defenseman on the ill-fated Montreal Nationals. After almost three seasons with the Michigan Soo Indians, he joined the Montreal Shamrocks. He also spent time with the Edmonton Eskimos and Renfrew

Creamery Kings before he settled with the new Montreal Canadiens in late 1909.

Pitre was the first man player-manager Jack Laviolette signed. It was Pitre and Laviolette's speed that inspired sportswriters to dub the Canadiens the "Flying Frenchmen." After being moved to right wing, Pitre's goal production jumped. His best year was 1914–15 when he notched 30 goals — almost half his team's total output! When Laviolette moved from defense to left wing alongside Pitre and Newsy Lalonde, the dynamite trio led the Habs to their first Cup win in 1916.

Pitre was one of hockey's first high-priced stars, a man not averse to holding out for ever-higher pay. One year, he signed for a whopping $3,000 at a time when the average salary was about $500. Ironically, Pitre shelled out most of his salary that year in fines for breaking training. Indeed, he was noted for deplorable training habits and missing practices. It has been said the burly Frenchman "trained on champagne," and that was not just hyperbole: Pitre would indeed reinforce himself between periods with a pint of ice-cold bubbly.

Pitre was a rugged individualist on whom team play was often lost, but who was highly valuable nonetheless. Picture the flame-red Canadiens uniform and his hair flying in the breeze . . . a man moving with a grace uncommon in a man of his size.

Pitre was also a gentleman. Montreal boss George Kennedy told a story of a game against the Montreal Wanderers, in which the star winger was being checked by Gordie Roberts. Roberts was tripping and butt-ending Pitre, sending him falling to the ice.

Kennedy screamed at Pitre, "Are you afraid of Roberts?"

"No, sure not," was Pitre's surprised response.

"Well, why don't you hit him back?" Kennedy snapped.

"How can I hit back?" Pitre asked. "Roberts, he is very polite, very nice. Each time I fall, he helps me get up and apologizes and says it is an accident . . . can I hit a man who is apologizing to me? No, never, it is not done."

In 339 games in several leagues, Pitre scored 313 times. He made the Hockey Hall of Fame in 1962.

Peak Years   *1912–16*
Comparable Current Player   *Peter Bondra*
In a Word   *DYNAMO*

GOLDIE PRODGERS Forward/Defense
5'10" 180
b. 10/18/1891, London, Ontario
d. 10/25/1935

After they lost their top forward line to the Quebec Bulldogs in 1911, the Waterloo Professionals faced a huge rebuilding job. They managed to secure players from Haileybury and the Cobalt Silver Kings, both of whom had dropped from the NHA, and added a new face who actually turned out to be the biggest prize of all.

Goldie Prodgers

Samuel George "Goldie" Prodgers was a big redhead fresh from a season with the London Wingers. He was a strong, fast skater with a special ability to use the body. Although he was a natural for the blue-line, the McNamaras — George, Hal, and Howard — were already there, so Prodgers was thrown onto a line with Edgar Dey and Harry Smith.

Prodgers' two-way skills impressed Quebec management and they signed him for the 1911–12 season. There he teamed with Joe Hall, helping Quebec to their first Stanley Cup championship. The next season, Prodgers jumped at an offer tabled by the

Victoria Aristocrats, who went on to win the PCHA title. Prodgers rejoined the Bulldogs in late 1913, spending a season there before jumping to the Montreal Wanderers. In 1915 he moved on to the Montreal Canadiens, the eventual Stanley Cup champions. He joined the army and played for Toronto's 228th Battalion, scoring 16 goals in 10 games before shipping out overseas. After missing two years due to military service, he came back with the Toronto St. Patricks, his sixth team in as many seasons. A 1920 trade took him to Hamilton, where he closed out his pro career in 1925.

Prodgers died prematurely of heart problems in late 1935. Lou Marsh, the former professional referee turned sportswriter, offered this tribute: "Goldie Prodgers was a game man, and his own worst enemy. He never spared himself anywhere, doing anything. He played the game very hard and clean, he gave and took his share of thumps with a smile that wasn't even a grin of delight at the damage he inflicted. He just loved the game."

Peak Years   *1916–20*
Comparable Current Player   *Trevor Linden*
In a Word   *BEEFY*

GORDON ROBERTS (Doc) Left Wing

5'11" 180
b. 9/5/1891, Ottawa, Ontario
d. 9/2/1966, Oakland, California

Gordon Roberts

Despite being one of the top wingers of his era, Dr. Gordon Roberts was never on a championship team. In January 1910, he and the Ottawa Senators defended the Stanley Cup against Edmonton. Ottawa's front line of Roberts, Marty Walsh, and Bruce Ridpath was outstanding, scoring 13 of their team's 21 goals in a two-game set.

Roberts joined the Wanderers for the 1910–11 season and entered McGill University at this time to study medicine. He remained with the Redbands for the next six seasons, during which they reached the playoffs only once. Roberts was one-third of a high-octane line, learning the tricks of the goal-poaching trade from the great Ernie Russell.

The horse-strong Roberts, one of the first legitimate power forwards, owned a hard, accurate shot. After Russell was put out to pasture, Roberts played alongside such luminaries as Harry Hyland, Odie Cleghorn, and Don Smith, putting up seasons of 30 and 29 goals in 1914 and 1915. In 1916 he earned his medical degree and opened a practice in Vancouver. At the same time he signed with the Millionaires of the PCHA, setting a league record with 43 goals.

After taking the 1918–19 season off, Roberts rejoined the Millionaires for one last year, dazzling fans from the left side of a line that also featured Barney Stanley, "Speed" Moynes, and Mickey MacKay. Roberts hung up his skates in style, scoring 15 goals.

About two years later, he headed back east to do some post-graduate work in Ottawa, and the Senators made a pitch for his services. Roberts politely declined, having decided once and for all that his medical career took precedence.

Roberts scored 203 times in 166 games. He is a member of the Hockey Hall of Fame.

Peak Years   *1914–18*
Comparable Current Player   *Keith Tkachuk*
In a Word   *FIGHTER*

ART ROSS Defense
5'11" 190
b. 1/13/1886, Naughton, Ontario
d. 8/5/1964, Boston, Massachusetts

Arthur Howie Ross was one of 13 children born to the boss of a Hudson's Bay Company fur-trading post in Northern Ontario. Ross, who spoke English and Ojibway growing up, learned to skate on Whitefish Bay using primitive clamp-on skates. His mother would swaddle him in layers of clothing, something he never forgot: "I must have become immune to body-checking in those days. I carried so much padding that an arrow couldn't pierce my armor." Deciding to make hockey a profession, he left home in 1904 to play hockey for Westmount of the CAHL. After a season there, he put in time with Brandon, the Montreal Wanderers, and Pembroke. Along the way the Kenora Thistles signed him as a ringer for their 1907 Stanley Cup challenge.

On November 25, 1909, the CHA was formed and Ross jumped to the All-Montreal club. After only eight games the league folded, freeing Ross to join the Haileybury Club for $2,700. In late 1910, he rejoined the Wanderers, putting up four seasons there before hopping aboard the Ottawa Senators. "Ross played like an eel," Harry Hyland once said. "He was one of the greatest stick-handlers I ever saw. He could spin on a dime, and he was so tricky there was no blocking him."

Ross invented the now-infamous "kitty-bar-the-door" strategy (today we call it the "trap") while traveling with his fellow Ottawans to Montreal for the 1915 NHA championship. In his mind, the speedy Wanderers could be stopped if he strung three defenders across the ice, 30 feet out from the goal. The Senators won the two-game, total-goals series 4–1. (The strategy didn't work against the Vancouver Millionaires in that year's Cup finals, however: the Senators lost 6–2, 8–3, and 12–3.)

Ross spent two seasons in Ottawa before closing out his career with the Wanderers. After refereeing and coaching stints in the NHA and NHL, he was "discovered" by Boston Bruins owner Charles F. Adams in 1924. As the story goes, Adams had been seeking a manager for his franchise. One night, while watching a Stanley Cup match in Montreal, Adams's fancy was caught by a referee who, in the face of much criticism, called a clean, honest, "no apologies" game. That referee was none other than Ross.

"Art Ross was a great player," Adams thought. "He knows the game and everybody in it. He's got courage, too. He's just the man to manage the Bruins."

Ross ran the Bruins, with great distinction, for the next 30 years. His teams won three Stanley Cups, racked up 10 first-place finishes, came in second six more times, and put up a record of 724-582-238 for a .546 winning percentage.

The B-shaped goal net he invented was used in the NHL through the 1980s, and he designed the bevel-edged puck still in use today. He also developed something called the "points system" — a precursor to the plus-minus statistic — introduced an Achilles tendon protector, and came up with an early helmet. He was a charter member of the Hockey Hall of Fame, inducted in 1945.

Peak Years 1908–12
In a Word PIONEER

TOMMY SMITH (Bulldog) Left Wing/Center
5'6" 150
b. 9/27/1886, Ottawa, Ontario
d. 8/1/1966, Quebec City, Quebec

Tommy Smith first got involved in hockey in high school, playing for St. Patrick's Lycaeum team in Ottawa. His first big-league break was with the Ottawa Victorias of the Federal league in 1905–06, and he tied for the league lead in goals with 12. He hooked up with the Ottawa Silver Seven at the end of the season, scoring six goals in three games and getting his name on the Stanley Cup. An offer from Pittsburgh of the International Pro league took him south of the border for the next three years, followed by tours of duty in Brantford, Cobalt, Galt, and Moncton.

By 1912, the Quebec Bulldogs were hot for the budding superstar, figuring he would be the ideal left winger for their superstar, Joe Malone. In his first season in Quebec, Smith scored 39 goals — just four less than league-leading Malone — and he drank from the Stanley Cup.

In 1913–14, Smith led the league with 39 goals in 20 games, including a 9-goal splurge against the Montreal Wanderers on January 21. Smith was eventually made team captain, only to be shuffled off to the Montreal Canadiens with Harry Mummery in 1916. He retired at the end of the 1916–17 season, but made a comeback with the Bulldogs in 1919–20 after coaching at the Senior level for a couple of years.

Because of his small stature, Smith was not inclined to rough it up the way his older brothers Alf and Harry did. On more than one occasion, though, Tommy surprised some of the more rugged types in the league when they tried to slap him around. Smith was also the top face-off man of his era.

After he retired from hockey, this shy and unassuming man carved out a fine career at the National Research Council in Ottawa. He passed away in 1966 after a failed kidney stone operation.

In 187 recorded games, Smith scored 314 goals. He is a member of the Hockey Hall of Fame.

Peak Years   *1910–1914*
Comparable Current Player   *Teemu Selanne*
In a Word   *SHARPSHOOTER*

CYCLONE TAYLOR (The Listowel Flash) Defense/Rover/Center
5'8" 165
b. 6/24/1883, Tara, Ontario
d. 6/9/1979, Vancouver, British Columbia

"The greatest player I ever saw" is how Frank Patrick described a young lad from the rough reaches of Southwestern Ontario who exploded onto the hockey scene only a few years into the twentieth century. Considered by many to be hockey's first bona fide superstar, Fred "Cyclone" Taylor was the very symbol of the new breed of hockey player — a professional, through and through. He was one of the fastest men of all time, could keep control of the puck as if it were glued to his stick, and was one of the early masters of the end-to-end rush. Later defensemen like Sprague Cleghorn, Harry Cameron, George Boucher, and Eddie Gerard attributed their rushing style to Taylor, whom they had tried to emulate.

Taylor began his long, brilliant hockey career at the age of 13, making his first appearance with the Listowel Mintos. Despite being much younger than his comrades, his speed and skill came to the fore immediately. At some point in his four years with the Mintos, he was tabbed the "Listowel Flash" as he led the way to a pair of Northern Hockey League championships.

Taylor's early success caused quite a stir in Toronto. But he turned down OHA boss William Hewitt's offer to join the Toronto Marlboros — Hewitt responded by banning him from the OHA — and signed on instead with the Houghton–Portage Lakes club in the International Pro league. There, he played alongside the likes of Bruce Stuart, Riley Hern, and Joe Hall. He put in two championship seasons with Houghton before the league folded. In 1908 he joined the Ottawa Senators for $500 and an off-season post in the Canadian Department of Immigration. In Ottawa he switched from forward to defense, and picked up his famous nickname from a very highly placed source.

It was after a match against the Montreal Wanderers, in which Taylor had notched four especially brilliant goals. One of the fans present was Canada's governor general, Earl Grey, who commented within earshot of an Ottawa *Free Press* reporter, "That new number four [Taylor] . . . he's a cyclone if I ever saw one." In a follow-up *Free Press* article, reporter Malcolm Brice wrote: "In Portage la Prairie they called him a tornado, in Houghton, Michigan, he was known as a whirlwind. From now on, he'll be known as Cyclone Taylor." The name stuck and a legend was born.

Taylor left Ottawa before the 1910 season under bitter circumstances. In the midst of the bidding war between the CHA and NHA, Taylor had assured Ottawa bigwigs that he would not be lured away by the astronomical salaries being thrown around by men like Renfrew owner Ambrose O'Brien. As it turns out, Taylor did indeed jump ship, signing with the Creamery Kings mere days before the season started.

It was with Renfrew that Taylor performed his most talked-about feat. On the night of March 9, 1910, so the legend goes, Taylor made good on a promise to score a goal against Ottawa while skating backwards. An incredible achievement, but did it really happen? The Renfrew *Journal*'s reporter certainly thought so:

> Taylor got the puck on a pass and, skating down in his usual fine fashion, he turned, and going backwards, he skated a piece and then sent the shot home to the Ottawa nets with skill and swiftness.

When the Patrick brothers started the Pacific Coast Hockey Association in 1911–12, they raided the eastern clubs for top talent. Taylor was one of the first blue-chip players to make the jump, lending credibility to the new circuit in much the same way Bobby Hull would do with his move to the World Hockey Association some 60 years later. Taylor was the cornerstone of the Vancouver Millionaires until 1921. Frank Patrick once said that Taylor was the "idol of the coast . . . [T]he fans would rise to their feet and roar as soon as he started up the ice with the puck."

Taylor was one of the main reasons the PCHA lasted as long as it did. He led the loop in scoring for five of seven seasons between 1912–13 and 1918–19. In 186 games in several leagues, he found the net 194 times. He was one of the brightest box office attractions ever seen in hockey and his drawing power would certainly rival Wayne Gretzky's if he were playing today.

Taylor was inducted into the Hockey Hall of Fame in 1947.

Peak Years   *1914–18*
Comparable Current Player   *Paul Coffey*
In a Word   *AWESOME*

GEORGES VEZINA (The Chicoutimi Cucumber, The Silent Habitant) Goal
5'6" 185
b. 1/21/1887, Chicoutimi, Quebec
d. 3/27/1926, Chicoutimi, Quebec

Georges Vezina

At the end of the 1910 hockey season, the Montreal Canadiens went on a barnstorming tour throughout the province of Quebec. One of their dates was in the logging town of Chicoutimi, which had no top-level hockey team to speak of. The Habs, led by the dynamic Newsy Lalonde, skated rings around the Chicoutimi Sagueneens. For all of this, the big-city boys failed to score on the tall youngster in the Chicoutimi nets, Georges Vezina, who wore winter boots instead of skates.

Joe Cattarinich, who was in goal for Montreal on this night, knew a goalkeeper when he saw one, and made a point of remembering his name. When George Kennedy bought the Canadiens during the off-season, Cattarinich recommended that he sign Vezina.

The man who would become a Montreal hockey legend started tending goal long before he learned how to skate. Up until the age of 18 he wore boots on the ice and, during practice, he had his mates throw rubber balls at him as a way of sharpening his reflexes.

Former Canadiens boss Leo Dandurand told the story of how, before one Canadiens–Maroons clash, Vezina told him: "It will be a close battle. I can hold them out at my end, Leo, but it will be tough to score against them. The best man is in the other goal, you know."

Vezina's modesty was just one of the marks of his greatness. He was a superb sportsman, neither boastful in victory nor bellyaching in defeat. Although his spoken English was poor and conversational skills were modest, his presence commanded respect. He was the spiritual leader of the original Flying Frenchmen.

Vezina's coolness on the ice earned him the handle "The Chicoutimi Cucumber." He stood erect in the cage, and he was blessed with lightning-quick reflexes and stick-handling skills uncommon among goalkeepers of his day. When the pressure around his net intensified, he often deflected the puck over the glass. And because he played on offensively oriented clubs, it was not uncommon to see him playing keep-away with an enemy checker until a teammate came to his aid.

Vezina backstopped the Habs to five NHA or NHL titles, and Stanley Cup wins in 1916 and 1924. He played in every one of Montreal's games between 1910 and November 28, 1925, a string of 367 consecutive regular-season and playoff games. Chest pains sidelined the great goalie for the balance of the 1925–26 season, and he died of tuberculosis on March 27, 1926. The Canadiens donated a trophy, the Georges Vezina Memorial Trophy, which is awarded each year to the NHL's best goaltender.

Vezina was one of the 12 charter members of the Hockey Hall of Fame, inducted in 1945.

Peak Years   *1912–16*
In a Word   *UNFLAPPABLE*

The All-Stars

Position	Player	Season	GP	G	A
D	Sprague Cleghorn	1916–17	19	16	3
D	Ernie Johnson	1916–17	18	6	–
R	Cyclone Taylor	1915–16	16	23	–
LW	Gordie Roberts	1917–18	23	43	–
C	Newsy Lalonde	1916–17	24	31	–
RW	Didier Pitre	1914–15	20	30	4
				GAA	ShO
G	Georges Vezina	1916–17	24	3.20	0

The
Twenties

In a Flash

COMPOSITE REGULAR SEASON STANDINGS
(JANUARY 1, 1920–DECEMBER 31, 1929)

National Hockey League

Club	GP	W	L	T	Pts	WPct	GF	GA
Ottawa Senators	333	186	108	39	411	**0.617**	906	687
Montreal Canadiens	332	175	123	34	384	**0.578**	965	776
Toronto St. Patricks/Maple Leafs	332	152	156	24	328	**0.494**	934	982
Hamilton Tigers/New York Americans	310	110	175	25	245	**0.395**	717	904
Boston Bruins	215	105	87	23	233	**0.542**	474	459
Montreal Maroons	215	98	90	27	223	**0.519**	435	394
New York Rangers	149	74	48	27	175	**0.587**	322	266
Pittsburgh Pirates	184	65	98	21	151	**0.410**	320	400
Detroit Cougars	149	56	73	20	132	**0.443**	289	311
Chicago Black Hawks	149	42	91	16	100	**0.336**	216	335
Quebec Bulldogs	22	4	18	0	8	**0.182**	82	158

Pacific Coast Hockey Association/Western Canadian Hockey League/Western Hockey League

Club	GP	W	L	T	Pts	WPct	GF	GA
Victoria Aristocrats/Cougars	186	88	91	7	183	**0.491**	508	529
Vancouver Millionaires/Maroons	186	87	95	4	178	**0.478**	590	565
Edmonton Eskimos	142	78	58	6	162	**0.570**	489	433
Calgary Tigers	142	71	67	4	146	**0.514**	416	400
Seattle Metropolitans	128	64	62	2	130	**0.507**	381	388
Saskatoon/Moose Jaw	142	62	73	7	131	**0.461**	444	474
Regina Capitals	112	55	55	2	112	**0.500**	352	365
Portland Rosebuds	30	12	16	2	**26**	0.433	84	110

HELLOS

Maurice Richard *Canadiens legend*	August 4, 1921
Tito Puente *Puerto Rican musician*	April 20, 1923
George Bush *American president*	June 12, 1924
Margaret Thatcher *British prime minister*	October 13, 1925
Gordie Howe *Wings/WHA legend*	March 31, 1928
Noam Chomsky *American theoretical linguist*	December 7, 1928

GOODBYES

Michael Collins *Irish revolutionary*	August 22, 1922
Pancho Villa *Mexican revolutionary*	July 23, 1923
Georges Vezina *Canadiens goaltender*	March 24, 1926
Harry Houdini *American escape artist/magician*	October 31, 1926
Wyatt Earp *American law officer*	January 13, 1929

REGULAR SEASON

BEST RECORD
1919–20 Ottawa Senators, 19-5-0

WORST RECORD
1927–28 Chicago Black Hawks, 7-34-3

BEST MINOR LEAGUE RECORD
1928–29 Vancouver Lions (Pacific Coast Hockey League), 25-8-3

FAMOUS FIRSTS

GAME OF DECADE
Ottawa Senators defeat the Quebec Bulldogs 3–2 (1/1/1920)

GOAL OF DECADE
Jack Darragh (1/1/1920)

PENALTY OF DECADE
Sprague Cleghorn (1/1/1920)

NHL GOALIE TO RECORD 10 SHUTOUTS IN SEASON
Alex Connell

MISCELLANEOUS

MOST GOALS, SEASON
39	Joe Malone, 1919–20
	Frank Frderickson, 1922–23 (PCHA)

MOST GOALS, DECADE
192	Cy Denneny

MOST ASSISTS, SEASON
18	Dick Irvin, 1926–27
	Howie Morenz, 1927–28

MOST ASSISTS, DECADE
90	Frank Boucher

MOST POINTS, SEASON
51	Howie Morenz, 1927–28

MOST POINTS, DECADE
261	Cy Denneny

COOLEST MIDDLE NAMES
Jack *Proctor* Darragh
Lionel *Pretoria* Conacher
Bill *Osser* Cook
Duke *Blanchard* Keats
Hal *Lang* Winkler

COOLEST HANDLES
Nels "Big Sam" Stewart
Harry "Go-Go" Oliver
John Ross Roach, "The Port Perry Woodpecker"
Jake "Jumping Jakie" Forbes
Ace Bailey, "Major Hoople of Bracebridge"
Roy "Shrimp" Worters
Jack Adams, "The Squire of Napanee"
Bert Corbeau, "Old Pig Iron"

BIGGEST PLAYER
Harold "Slim" Halderson, 6'3" 200

SMALLEST PLAYER
Roy Worters, 5'3" 135

BEST SHOT
Cecil "Babe" Dye had the hardest shot of his time. His was reportedly the first to smash the protective glass around the time-clock at Toronto's Mutual Street Arena.

BEST PASSER
Frank Nighbor

BEST ON-ICE INSTINCTS
Reg Noble was described by one *Toronto Daily Star* sportswriter as "an expert hound on the ice." He played any and every position with ease.

BEST STICKHANDLER
Mickey MacKay was a master at handling the wood and rubber. Some say that MacKay was the single largest hockey influence on Frank Nighbor. The "wee Scot" was also a fabulously frustrating poke-checker.

BEST SKATER
Howie Morenz

WORST SKATER
Clarence "Taffy" Abel was a savage body-checker but a poor bladesman.

FASTEST SKATER
Howie Morenz was like lightning. His skates left the ice in mid-stride, giving the illusion that he was airborne.

BEST SNIPER
Babe Dye

BEST BODY-CHECKER

Bert Corbeau was halfway between a rhinoceros and a junkyard dog. Young King Clancy told of how he was introduced to NHL body-belting after a run-in with the big bugger they called "Old Pig Iron."

BEST POKE-CHECKER

Frank Nighbor did not invent the poke-check. Men like Ernie Johnson and Jack Walker were poking before Nighbor. Nonetheless, he was the first to popularize the tactic.

BEST SHOT-BLOCKER

Taffy Abel

Clint Benedict

BEST GOAL-TENDER

Clint Benedict

MOST UNUSUAL GOALTENDING STYLE

Clint Benedict was forever flopping in his "bed."

FINEST ATHLETE

Dunc Munro was signed by the Montreal Maroons after he made a fine showing on the great 1924 Canadian Olympic team. He was a fine two-way defenseman and a world-class athlete who excelled at half a dozen sports while at university.

BEST DEFENSIVE FORWARD

Percy "Perk" Galbraith

WORST DEFENSIVE FORWARD

Babe Dye loved to score goals but was one of the most sluggish back-checkers around.

BEST SHADOW

Perk Galbraith

BEST PENALTY-KILLER

Perk Galbraith was like a coon hound in killing penalties. He chased the puck until he dropped and, if he gained possession, ragged it splendidly.

BEST DEFENSIVE DEFENSEMAN

Eddie Gerard was a talented performer on the rink, gridiron, diamond, and track. His ability to hold off the league's best was very much to the fore. He was one of the most important members of the Ottawa Senators dynasty of the early 1920s.

BEST OFFENSIVE DEFENSEMAN

George "Buck" Boucher was the offensive linchpin of the Ottawa Senators. He was famous for tip-tapping his stick on the ice while leading a rush.

BEST ALL-AROUND PLAYER

Frank Nighbor was similar to Jean Beliveau in that he skated and passed well, had a great shot, stick handled through entire teams, took face-offs with the best, and checked back.

BEST UTILITY PLAYER

Reg Noble

STRONGEST PLAYER

Ivan "Ching" Johnson was a giant and a master of the body-bash. Like Tim Horton some years later, Johnson possessed the strength of a silverback gorilla. They did not call him the "Holding Corporation" for nothing.

TOUGHEST PLAYER

Babe Siebert once thrashed the daylights out of the "Boston Strongboy," Eddie Shore.

BEST FIGHTER

Harry "Punch" Broadbent was feared by many. Not even Sprague Cleghorn, Bill Coutu, or Eddie Shore dared mess with Broadbent. As a rookie, he thrashed tough guy Ken Randall so brutally that few bothered him again.

MOST ABLE INSTIGATOR

Reginald "Hooley" Smith was brash and belligerent and vexing to play against. After a game in the 1927 Stanley Cup finals, Sprague Cleghorn chased him out of a downtown Ottawa diner brandishing a ketchup bottle.

DIRTIEST PLAYER

Billy Coutu was, well, cuckoo.

CLEANEST PLAYER
Frank Nighbor

BEST CORNER-MAN
Punch Broadbent was called "Mister Elbows." 'Nuff said.

BEST-LOOKING PLAYER
Clint Benedict

UGLIEST PLAYER
George Hainsworth looked like a 75-year-old man suffering from hemorrhoids.

BALDEST PLAYER
Ching Johnson was Humpty Dumpty in a Rangers jersey.

MOST UNDERRATED PLAYER
Reg Noble

MOST CONSISTENT PLAYER
Buck Boucher

SMARTEST PLAYER
Frank Nighbor

BIGGEST FLAKE
John Roach skated onto the ice before each game looking like he'd just quaffed 13 cups of coffee.

MOST HATED PLAYER
Sprague Cleghorn was no teddy bear. His team once had to sneak him into an opposing team's rink via the basement furnace room. Even old ladies hated this guy.

MOST ADMIRED PLAYER
Frank Nighbor

BEST LINES
Team: New York Rangers
LW: Bun Cook
C: Frank Boucher
RW: Bill Cook

Team: Montreal Maroons
LW: Babe Siebert
C: Nels Stewart
RW: Hooley Smith

Team: Montreal Canadiens
LW: Aurel Joliat
C: Howie Morenz
RW: Billy Boucher

Team: Ottawa Senators
LW: Cy Denneny
C: Frank Nighbor
RW: Punch Broadbent

The best line of the bunch was the mighty Cook-Boucher-Cook connection. Warmest regards go to the pure, unadulterated power of Montreal's "S-Line" and the blinding speed of the Joliat-Morenz-Boucher unit.

HIGHEST PAID PLAYER
Dunc Munro, captain of the Montreal Maroons, didn't starve during his hockey-playing days. He was paid $7,500 per season by the late 1920s.

MOST TRAGIC CAREER
Jack Darragh died suddenly in 1924 of peritonitis, an untimely tragedy cutting short a fantastic career.

PLAYER VERSUS LEAGUE
Sprague Cleghorn vs. the National Hockey League
From his days in Ottawa in the late 1910s, it seemed wherever Cleghorn went he was hated, even by his teammates.

MOST LOPSIDED TRADE
On September 18, 1922, Canadiens boss Leo Dandurand made one of the smartest trades in hockey history when he dealt an aging Newsy Lalonde to the Saskatoon Crescents for the rights to some kid by the name of Joliat.

BIGGEST FLOPS
Harry Watson was not so much a flop as he was a disappointment. The man Conn Smythe named to his all-time hockey team did not play a single game in the NHL. Sad. This 1924 Olympian was a force.

BEST HEAD COACH
Art Ross

BEST GENERAL MANAGER
Leo Dandurand

BEST SPORTSWRITER
Doug Vaughan of the *Windsor Star* and his references to "bumping bees" and

"beef-trusters" are the stuff of journalistic legend. He was the old-time version of Dick Beddoes — a colorful writer whose work was a treat to read.

BEST MINOR-LEAGUE PLAYER
Harry Watson

BEST STANLEY CUP FINAL
1925, Montreal Canadiens vs. Victoria Cougars
This series boiled down to Howie Morenz of the Canadiens vs. Jack Walker of the Cougars. The latter prevailed.

IMPORTANT RULE CHANGES

1921–22
- goalies allowed to pass puck forward to own blue-line
- overtime limited to 20 minutes
- minor penalties changed from three to two minutes

1923–24
- match penalties further defined as actions deliberately injuring or disabling an opposing player; for such actions, game ejection and a $50 fine assessed; match penalty recipients to meet with league president to receive additional punishment

1925–26
- delayed penalty rules introduced
- each team must have minimum four players on ice at all times
- no more than two defensemen permitted to remain inside team's own blue-line after puck passed out of the defensive zone
- only team captains permitted to speak with referees
- goalie pads limited to 12" in width
- teams permitted to dress 12 players per game

1926–27
- blue-lines repositioned to 60 feet from goal-line, thereby enlarging the neutral zone
- nets standardized, with posts securely fastened to ice

1927–28
- passing permitted in defending and neutral zones
- goalie pads reduced in width from 12" to 10"
- game standardized at three 20-minute periods separated by 10-minute intermissions
- teams to change ends after each period
- ten-minute overtime to be played if score still tied after regulation time
- minor penalty assessed for deliberately picking up puck while it's in play
- minor penalty assessed for deliberately shooting puck out of play
- maximum length of hockey sticks limited to 53" from heel of blade to end of handle; no minimum length stipulated
- home team given choice of which goal to defend at start of game

1928–29
- forward passing permitted in attacking zone if receiver in neutral zone when pass made; no forward passing permitted in attacking zone
- minor penalty assessed for passing puck back into defensive zone
- teams permitted to dress no more than 12 skaters per game (not including goalies)
- full ten-minute overtime (not sudden death) to be played if score still tied after regulation time

Sprague and the Senators

Ahhh, Sprague and the Senators. No, not a 1950s rock band, but the feud Sprague Cleghorn had with the Ottawa Senators in the early 1920s. It may also refer to the big fellow's jazz band, but that's another story.

After a winter stint with Ambrose O'Brien's Renfrew Creamery Kings in 1910–11, Cleghorn joined his brother Odie of the Montreal Wanderers. Sprague Cleghorn anchored the Redband defense corps through 1916–17 (he led the NHA in assists in 1914–15 with 12). Then came a season of change for the older Cleghorn brother.

On January 2, 1918, the Montreal Arena, the Wanderers' home rink, burned to the ground. No arena meant no club, and no club meant the Wanderers' players went into a dispersal draft. On January 4, the Ottawa Senators of the NHL snapped up Sprague Cleghorn. Odie was selected by the Montreal Canadiens.

The very next day the bruising defenseman was in the news. He was arrested on a charge of assault; his wife had called the police after he had walloped her with his crutch (a broken leg kept Sprague Cleghorn on the sidelines for the entire 1917–18 season). The charges were dropped two weeks later, but this incident (and rumored others) would follow him around like a bad smell.

The 1918–19 season was Cleghorn's first in the NHL. At the time, the league featured only three clubs: the Senators, the Canadiens, and the Toronto Arenas. The Arenas ran into financial problems in the second half of the season and were forced to withdraw from the league. This forced the NHL to alter its post-season plans. A best-of-seven series was played between the NHL's two remaining squads, the Senators and Canadiens. Without the services of the injured Frank Nighbor, however, Ottawa was no match for Montreal. Cleghorn made good, scoring two goals and four points in the series. Brother Odie had seven markers for the Canadiens, who won in five games.

The 1919–20 season would be much kinder to Cleghorn and the Senators. Losing star defender Harry Cameron to the Toronto St. Patricks proved to be a matter of addition by subtraction, as it allowed Ottawa coach Pete Green to throw Eddie Gerard back on the blue-line with Cleghorn. The duo anchored the Senators — they swept both halves of the season. The Senators defeated the Seattle Metropolitans for the Cup in a hard-fought five-game series.

The 1920–21 season saw the rose quickly come off the bloom of the Cleghorn–Senators relationship. Rumors began flying around that the big lug was in his teammates' doghouse, presumably due to his arrest for spousal abuse and his more-than-occasional dirty play on the ice, which threatened to tarnish his team's on-ice reputation. Soon, the Senators would be free of their troubled defenseman.

Three games into the campaign, the NHL claimed that all former Montreal Wanderers were league property and could be dispersed as the NHL brass saw fit. Cleghorn and Harry "Punch" Broadbent were ordered to report to the fledgling Hamilton Tigers. To no one's surprise, Canadiens' manager George Kennedy defended the NHL's move in a statement to the press: "Cleghorn is not the property of the

Sprague Cleghorn

Ottawas. Instead, he belongs to the NHL to which he reverted when the Wanderers went out of business. The league, as it was, would have resulted in a farcical race. How many times would Ottawa people have paid to see one-sided games? They're too monotonous. People want excitement. We've got to help out the weaker clubs or we cannot continue."

Cleghorn was not pleased. He went on record as saying that he would "play for Ottawa or not play at all." Apparently, he had a solid second job at Ottawa's Hud and Co. and was in no hurry to leave the capital city.

NHL president Frank Calder suspended Cleghorn and Broadbent, who was also holding out, resolving that neither would play in the NHL until they were reinstated. Cleghorn's sit-down did not seem to set off any alarms in the Hamilton camp. They held out hope that he would eventually suit up for them. Soon enough, though, it was apparent that the big man's threat was genuine. Hamilton caved in and dealt him to nearby Toronto for that oft-dealt player: future considerations.

Cleghorn would play 13 regular-season games for the St. Patricks in 1920–21, scoring three goals and eight points. Toronto then came up against the Senators in the playoffs. After a 5–0 Ottawa victory in game one, Cleghorn was dropped from the St. Patricks roster. Toronto coach Dick Carroll was dissatisfied with the big fellow's effort.

Cleghorn took all of his gear and placed it in the Senators dressing room. "The Senators are the only club that ever treated me [sic] white and I'm never going to play hockey except for Ottawa. It wasn't human to compel me to play against them." The *Toronto Daily Star* backed Carroll, saying, "Cleghorn came against his own inclination. He was strongly entrenched in Ottawa and that may be the explanation of his indifferent game against his old teammates last week when Ottawa won 5–0."

The Senators finished off the St. Patricks 2–0 in the return match to earn the right to defend the Stanley Cup against the Pacific Coast Hockey Association (PCHA) champions, the Vancouver Millionaires.

Ottawa wasted no time in snagging Cleghorn to fortify an already dominant blue-line corps. He would play an integral role in the Senators' successful Cup win against the Millionaires. Only two days after the Cup win, however, Ottawa secretary Tommy Gorman transferred his rights once more to Hamilton. After he again refused to report, Hamilton shipped him off to Montreal in exchange for Harry Mummery and Amos Arbour.

Cleghorn was insulted. He dropped his Senators-only stance and set about plans to exact revenge on the Senators organization. Cleghorn, still smarting from being shuffled around the league, reported to Montreal, his hometown.

The Ottawa–Montreal rivalry was probably hockey's biggest of the early years. Games between teams from these two cities were generally hard-fought and drew capacity crowds. The rivalry began with battles between the Ottawa Silver Seven and the Montreal Wanderers. In the new era, the Senators and Canadiens took up the gauntlet.

The first installment of "Cleghorn versus Ottawa" took place December 24, 1921. The Senators routed Montreal 10–0. Cleghorn appeared sluggish and out of shape. He was certainly not the megaforce he had been in the past.

Four days later, though, the fireworks began when Ottawa again faced Montreal, winning 2–1 in overtime. Cleghorn started putting the hurt on his new enemies. He administered a severe beating on gentle Frank Boucher in the second period, an atrocity that earned him a paragraph in the following day's *Ottawa Citizen*: "It was rough hockey and Sprague Cleghorn led in the attacks on his former teammates. He got Boucher and injured him painfully and also made attempts to land Nighbor and Broadbent."

Cleghorn was just getting warmed up, though. In the next meeting, the bruising bull ran goalie Clint Benedict. And as bad a boy as Cleghorn had become, few were prepared for the hurricane that would rock the Canadian capital on February 1, 1922.

Midway through the first period of the tilt, Cleghorn broke Frank Nighbor's left arm with a slash. Early in the second stanza, Cleghorn high sticked Gerard over the eye for four stitches. Then, in the third, he cross-checked Cy Denneny into the boards from behind, busting up the Ottawa winger's face. Referee Lou Marsh made attempts to curb Cleghorn's violence, to no avail. The February 2 *Citizen* headline read: "Nighbor suffers injured arm, Gerard is stitched, and Clancy and Denneny carried off as a result of disgraceful work by Canadien defenceman."

In a report to the league office after the game, Marsh suggested that both Sprague Cleghorn and brother Odie receive fines for their use of foul language in objecting to calls. The *Citizen* did not mince words in its game summary, calling Sprague Cleghorn the "present-day disgrace of the National winter game" and saying that he "led the attack on the Champions and accounted for the casualties reported above."

The teams met again two weeks later in a hotly anticipated rematch. Crowds lined up hours beforehand, seeking entry into the Mount Royal Arena. The two teams scored 12 goals in a wide-open 6–6 draw. Although plenty of penalties were called, the play was generally clean.

A week later, the teams met once again in an important match for the Canadiens, who needed a win to retain any hope of making the post-season. This was easier said than done, since Montreal had not beaten the Senators in their previous six encounters. Ottawa's finest notified both clubs that a "repetition of the rough play which marred the last appearance of the Canadiens here would result in the immediate arrests of the offenders." As with many over-hyped sequels, the match was a dud. Only one penalty was called in a 4–3 Ottawa victory. Cleghorn, suddenly the Senator fans' whipping boy, was soundly razzed by the famed "Millionaires" section. He was forced to enter the arena via the furnace room to avoid the rabble. During the game, a fan threw a boot rubber at Cleghorn. Another tossed down an apple, which ended up plunking Senators defenseman Eddie Gerard on the head.

The next two seasons saw Cleghorn continue his hostility toward the Bytowners. In the final Ottawa–Montreal encounter of 1921–22 on December 23, he scored the opening goal in leading the Canadiens to a 2–1 victory. But he was in anything but the Christmas spirit. As the *Citizen* pointed out, he "marred his brilliant game by making a dead set for Gerard while the Cap'n was on the ice." Montreal fans were treated to another roughneck affair, though referee Marsh managed to keep the festivities under some control. Cleghorn proved unmanageable; he turned King Clancy into a chopping block, forcing the little fellow to retire for the night.

In the 1922–23 season, Montreal caught up to the Senators, who had been the class of the league for years. The Canadiens had acquired Aurel Joliat (from the Saskatoon Sheiks in exchange for Newsy Lalonde) and Joe Malone prior to the season. Little Joliat scored 13 goals in 24 games that season.

As Montreal powered up, Cleghorn seemed to cool down. In fact, there was only one major incident involving Cleghorn in the regular-season meetings between the two clubs. But the 1923 playoffs would prove to be far different.

In game one of the Ottawa–Montreal semifinals in Montreal, Cleghorn and fellow hothead Billy Coutu started with the rough stuff from the word go. In the second session, Cy Denneny scored. Following the goal, Coutu chased down Denneny and smashed him over the head with his stick. Near the end of the game, Cleghorn began bashing Lionel Hitchman, perhaps to avenge an earlier attack on Odie. Sprague smashed Hitchman across the face repeatedly. The fans went bananas, showering the ice with debris. Leo Dandurand could not believe his eyes. Embarrassed at the actions of his players, he immediately suspended and fined both Cleghorn and Coutu, rendering them ineligible for the return match in Ottawa. The Senators would take the series in five games, 3-2 on aggregate.

In 1923–24, Cleghorn played some of the most inspired hockey of his career, especially against Ottawa. Montreal and the Senators had each played two games the season before a December 26 date in Ottawa. The teams were billed "the greatest of hockey rivals." This game marked the first meeting between the teams since the infamous 1923 final. Ticket requests came from all over the Ottawa Valley: Pembroke, Renfrew, Arnprior — even fans from Almonte wanted to be part of the action. Although it was an exciting tilt, a bloodbath it was not. Ottawa eked out a 3–2 victory in overtime. The *Citizen* proclaimed that "Sprague Cleghorn played one of his best games." In the next series of games against the Senators, Cleghorn was on his very best behavior. The Senators, meanwhile, fired up the Ottawa–Cleghorn feud anew. Tommy Gorman filed a complaint with Frank Calder, claiming that the Canadiens, chiefly Cleghorn, were deliberately fouling his boys. After some deliberation, the NHL threw out Gorman's grievance. Although in past years Gorman may have had a point, Cleghorn had of late been a very good boy. But this would soon change.

The big defenseman had been looking forward to the February 2 Ottawa–Montreal match ever since Gorman made the allegations against him. Lord and Lady Byng were in the house for the game and they had brought Prince Eric of Denmark to watch Canada's sport of choice. The Canadiens won 1–0 on this night. Cleghorn, meanwhile, returned to form by taking out George "Buck" Boucher knee to knee before butt ending his old buddy Lionel Hitchman in the eye.

The 1924–25 campaign was Cleghorn's last as a member of the Canadiens. Despite nearing the end of his career at 34 years of age, he had one last stone to cast at the Senators organization.

The Canadiens faced the Senators on January 24, 1925. Both teams were in the thick of the race for the regular-season championship. In the span of 60 minutes in a game won 3–2 by Montreal, Cleghorn and Buck Boucher of the Senators collided. As they fell to the ice in a heap, one of Cleghorn's skates cut Boucher near the mouth, a wounding Boucher felt was intentional. As Cleghorn attempted to help the bleeding Boucher back to his feet, the big Ottawan began throwing punches. Both benches emptied. Even spare Ottawa goaltender Joe Ironstone got into the act, brandishing his stick like a scimitar. The bloody battle was Cleghorn's grand hurrah in the Ottawa–Montreal feud.

Despite his reputation, Big Sprague was one of the era's greatest defensemen and would have copped many a Norris Trophy had the award been up for grabs during his salad days. Unfortunately, many remember him as a wife-abusing madman whose sole desire was to decapitate his opponents.

Perhaps we should look at Cleghorn as a product of his era and not judge him by today's kinder, gentler standards.

Just a Sec

Horrors! The Ottawa Hockey Club is in danger of losing Frank Nighbor, its brilliant centre man. Nighbor has not accepted another offer from Eddie Livingstone, nor has he jumped to the Western Outlaws. Frank has gone on the stage. He and other Pembroke residents launched an amateur performance and 'Dutch' is said to have gone so big that Klaw and Erlanger have flashed him an offer. Nighbor's hit, in fact, is said to have been almost as sensational as he scored on the night he sang "Sweet Adeline" in the Barron Hotel, Vancouver. The Ottawas intend to send a deputation up to Pembroke shortly to attend Nighbor's debut. Clint Benedict will supply the vegetables.

— *Ottawa Citizen*, October 1, 1921

King of All Trades

In this final game of the final series, Frank "King" Clancy became the first player to play all six positions in a Stanley Cup match. He had already played the five skating positions when Benedict was sent off in the second period for a match penalty. In stepped King, who held down the fort until his goalie's return.

   Clancy asked if he could take the Cup home to present to his father, who was a fine sportsman in his day. The Senators granted his wish. Nearly a year later, league president Frank Calder contacted the Senators looking for the Cup. The team in turn called King, who was forced to take it off his mantel and return it.

Quote of the Decade

"[Jake] Forbes stuck to his nets like a burr and he made the hardest shots from [Babe] Dye, [Reg] Noble, and [Jack] Adams look like a shower of cotton-wadding snow balls at an Xmas festival in a home for the paralyzed." — Lou E. Marsh, sportswriter

Snowbound!

O n February 20, 1924, much of eastern Ontario and western Quebec was clobbered by a winter storm. By nightfall, reports held it to be the most brutal snowstorm in 19 years. The situation did little to blanket the enthusiasm of Montreal hockey fans, though. By 8:30 p.m. sharp, the Mount Royal Arena was packed, as usual, with 6,000 fans. You see, Ottawa's champion Super Six were in town to face their Canadiens. Or so they thought.

   As the storm approached Ottawa, Senators coach Pete Green herded his boys onto a Canadian National express train. The party left the capital shortly after noon and, although it was late arriving in Pembroke, the train pulled out of Union Station in Pembroke

King Clancy

at 1:30, right on schedule. It would not go much further, though.

Only seven miles east of Hawkesbury, in Cushing Junction, the train was snow-bound. There would be no game.

Back at the Arena, would-be spectators waited . . . and waited . . . and waited. Shortly after ten o'clock, the match was called off. At first, the fans did not know why the game was cancelled. The fans were understandably peeved. Dozens lined up to cash in their ticket stubs. Some panicked fans were seen frantically searching rows of seats for their stubs.

Meanwhile back at Cushing Pass, some of the Senators tried to shovel the train of its snow-shackles. King Clancy and Cy Denneny were a rescue party, plowing through at least a mile of snow to get milk for a baby on board the train. While on the mission, however, Denneny tumbled down a well. Fortunately, his injuries were not severe.

The Senators were snowbound all night. The train did not reach Montreal until eight-thirty the next morning. Upon arrival, Green immediately checked them into the Windsor Hotel. Faster than you can say "snowstorm," the Senators were in bed.

Taming the Tiger Ten

When the 1924–25 campaign crashed to a close, the keys to the NHL penthouse were in the paws of the 19-10-1 Hamilton Tigers, who only the year before had sucked dirt in the league cellar.

The Yellow and Black were a motley crew, indeed. Led by American-born Billy Burch, the ever-ready Green brothers, Wilfred and Redvers, and veteran trench-mutt Ken Randall, the Tigers were hardly the league's poster boys. They were a rowdy collection, a muscle brigade.

The Tigers' contracts covered their services for only 24 of the 30 regular-season contests held that season, and did not include the playoffs. On a train ride from Montreal to Hamilton, the Tigers, represented by fiery captain Wilfred "Shorty" Green, informed GM Percy Thompson that unless each Tiger was paid a $200 play-off bonus, they would be skipping the post-season completely.

As soon as the Hamilton party reached the Steel City, Thompson got a hold of NHL president Frank Calder, and let him in on what Green had told him. Needless to say, the big cheese was livid. He considered the strike a "hold-up" and gave the Hams until eleven o'clock on the morning of Friday, March 13, to abandon their folly. The players thumbed their collective noses at Calder.

As Toronto and the Canadiens began their playoff to see who would meet the Tigers for the right to wagon westward to battle for the Stanley Cup, Calder readied the fourth-place Ottawa Senators as Hamilton's post-season replacement. The Tigers had been declawed!

Reports out of Toronto and Montreal began to circulate that players in those cities were being paid extra for the playoffs. Surely, reasoned Green and his boys, a $200 bonus was not asking too much. Surely, a Tiger deserved the same rewards as a St. Pat or a Canadien.

Frank Calder

On Saturday, March 14, the Tigers met with team directors to hammer out a deal. The two sides were miles apart in their thinking. After Green squelched representative Dr. Leeming Carr's offer of a $100 bonus per player, Calder suspended the Tiger Ten and slapped $200 fines to their hides.

The players argued on, claiming that they were often forced to pay their own expenses during the regular season. The Montreal *Gazette* rang in, pointing out that the Tiger contracts called for their services until the end of March.

The Hamilton *Spectator*'s sports editor got in on the act. In a piece entitled "The Public Be Damned," he proclaimed, "The dear old public is the goat again." Amid a storm of controversy, and threats of lawsuits from the league, Green found the composure to pen this communiqué:

To the Public of Hamilton:

Speaking on behalf of the Hamilton National Hockey League Club, and having been duly appointed by these players to act in this capacity, I wish to make the following facts known to the Hamilton sports-loving public prior to leaving your city:

In the first place, we went into this strike thoroughly and before making our decision we discussed the subject from all angles, wishing only to act in a really gentlemanly and businesslike manner. The boys, to a man, are unanimous in what they consider their just dues . . . we regret the fact that you who so earnestly supported us throughout the regular playing season must be denied a chance to see us in the finals. We have enjoyed being here with you and, to a man, would rather play to a Hamilton crowd than to any other on the circuit . . . [S]upport was sadly lacking from the executive end of our club . . . [W]e desire to thank the supporting public of Hamilton and trust that the unbiased fans will see our side of the argument.

— Members of the Hamilton Professional Hockey Club. W. Green, Captain.

Offers to purchase the troubled Tigers began coming in and, according to the *Gazette*'s Vern DeGeer, "Percy Thompson breathed a sigh of relief, for Hamilton had gone through a poor financial season and it was apparent on all sides that the Mountain City wasn't big enough to support NHL competition."

The Hamilton Tigers were ultimately sold for about $75,000 to Tex Rickard, who would bring major league hockey to New York City for the first time. A new team — the Americans — made plans to move into Madison Square Garden.

About 30 years after the strike, Shorty Green told reporter Milt Dunnell, "I never regretted my part in the strike, even though it cost me a chance at the Stanley Cup. We realized hockey was becoming big. All we asked was the players be given some share of revenue. I'd do the same thing tomorrow."

Go West, Young Cup!

After disposing of the Toronto St. Patricks 3–2 and 2–0 in the 1925 playoffs, the Montreal Canadiens motored west to meet the WCHL champion Victoria Cougars. Both teams had finished third in their respective leagues, and had managed to beat out all comers for a ticket to the Big Show.

Game One

Montreal Canadiens 2, Victoria Cougars 5

The first game of the finals was played under western rules, which at the time were almost identical to those of the NHL.

Period	Team	Scorer	Assists
1	Victoria	Jack Walker	
1	Victoria	Harold Halderson	Frank Frederickson

By the first bell, the Cougars were out in front by two. Manager Lester Patrick was quick with the brash predictions: "I thought we could do it, and I'm sure of it now. Victoria will take the world's championship if the boys continue to play as they have started."

2	Victoria	Jack Walker	

Jack Walker, at 36, proved himself an effective two-way force for Victoria. His second goal of the contest turned out to be the winner.

3	Victoria	Gordon Fraser	Frank Frederickson
3	Montreal	Billy Coutu	Howie Morenz
3	Victoria	Gordon Fraser	Harold Hart
3	Montreal	Howie Morenz	

Victoria skated circles around the Frenchmen in the final session. Despite a strong showing from Morenz throughout the match, Montreal just could not do it. Georges Vezina, usually a wall in nets, stunk up the place, allowing five goals on 21 shots.

Game Two

Montreal Canadiens 1, Victoria Cougars 3

Game two was played in Vancouver before a crowd of 11,000. Back in Montreal, crowds swarmed to the corner of Peel and St. Catherine streets to hear telegraphic reports of the contest.

Period	Team	Scorer	Assists
1	Victoria	Jack Walker	
1	Victoria	Frank Frederickson	Harold Halderson

Again, Montreal came out as flat as week-old ginger ale. Walker set the tone early with a highlight-reel goal. Before the first buzzer, Frederickson added another for the Cougars on a pass from Harold "Slim" Halderson. Montreal was floundering . . .

| 2 | Montreal | Aurel Joliat | Sprague Cleghorn |

An early Montreal goal by little Joliat made it 2–1. This was as close as the Canadiens would get.

| 3 | Victoria | Jack Walker | |

On a power play, Walker sealed the deal for Victoria. Between his masterful poke-checking, Gordon Fraser's solid defending, and Hap Holmes's 27 saves, Montreal had no chance. They were outshot 35–28.

Game Three

Montreal Canadiens 4, Victoria Cougars 2

It was back to basics in game three, in which the Frenchmen, behind a Morenz hat trick, finally returned to life.

Period	Team	Scorer	Assists
1	Montreal	Howie Morenz	Aurel Joliat
1	Victoria	Jocko Anderson	

The two sides played it even through the end of the second period. A duel between Vezina and Holmes, however, quickly became a lopsided shooting gallery.

3	Victoria	Harold Hart	
3	Montreal	Aurel Joliat	Billy Boucher
3	Montreal	Howie Morenz	
3	Montreal	Howie Morenz	

After Harold "Gizzy" Hart stuffed a quick one in behind Vezina, the Frenchmen woke up. A Joliat marker put matters even before Morenz broke the tie with a gutsy one-man effort. The "Stratford Streak" followed up at 11:02 and the Cougars were cooked.

Game Four

Montreal Canadiens 1, Victoria Cougars 6

Period	Team	Scorer	Assists
1	Victoria	Frank Frederickson	Jack Walker

The "Pride of Victoria" took an early lead when Frederickson scored a nifty one. The big Norseman's second goal of the finals set the tone of the game.

2	Victoria	Harold Hart	
2	Montreal	Billy Boucher	
2	Victoria	Harold Halderson	
2	Victoria	Frank Foyston	Harry Meeking

The Cougars pulled away in the middle frame.

| 3 | Victoria | Frank Frederickson | Jack Walker |
| 3 | Victoria | Clem Loughlin | Gordon Fraser |

Victoria outshot the Frenchmen 21–6 in the final frame. After another Frederickson marker at 7:05, Loughlin tallied, completing Montreal's humiliation. As in the three previous games, Walker's two-way work was sparkling.

Montreal was shut down wholesale. The western boys short-circuited not only Joliat and Boucher but also the fabulous Morenz. Though Morenz, also known as the "Mitchell Meteor," notched four brilliant goals in the series, his play was weak at crucial points in the four-game set. This had much to do with the work of Walker and Frederickson. Walker had a poke-check equal to that of Senators' star Frank Nighbor, while the big center, like modern Swedish NHL ace Mats Sundin, was a master puck-controller. Up against these two men and Hap Holmes's hot goaltending, the Montreal Canadiens had their work cut out for them. Maybe they should have brought sharper knives.

Chew on This

The *New York Times* ran a complete statistical record of the 1927–28 NHL season at the end of the regular season. Under close scrutiny their statistics are found to contain many mistakes. However, there are some truly interesting, thrilling even, statistical gems among their numbers.

For example, a sophomore Eddie Shore played an average of just over 53 minutes per game, a remarkable amount of time. The most proficient goaltender proved to be George Hainsworth, who stopped 1,371 of 1,419 shots for a remarkable .966 save percentage. And the top goal-getter? Why, none other than Howie Morenz, who bagged 33 in 43 games.

In the 1927–28 campaign, there was an average of 3.67 goals and 1.81 assists in a 60-minute game. Seventy years later, in the 1997–98 season, the average NHL contest featured 5.2 goals and 8.81 assists. This shows a 42 percent jump in goal scoring since 1927–28; however, it demonstrates a 400 percent increase in the number of assists! Of course, these numbers have fluctuated over the years.

That Was Then, This Is Now

Hockey is still largely untapped, statistically. In 1998, *Total Hockey* proved for the first time that hockey was as much a numbers game as it was one of yarns and yuk-yuks. With well over 1,000 pages of statistics, there was for the first time the sense that hockey had come of age, had joined baseball and football. Fine and dandy. One question looms ever large, though, despite the best efforts of *Total Hockey*, Stan Fischler's *Encyclopedia*, and the legendary Charles L. Coleman's *Trail of the Stanley Cup* series. Is the comparison of hockey players from different eras possible? Would Maurice Richard's 50 in 50 be worth as much today? Would Joe Malone have scored 44 goals in 20 games today? How about George Hainsworth's 22 shutouts in 44 games in 1928–29? Would the little guy shut out his opponents so masterfully in today's game? These kinds of questions can be answered. It's simply a matter of taking a closer look at the numbers. Sure, there are factors to consider in any cross-era discussion, factors such as league talent level, diet and exercise regimens, equipment quality, and the "no forward passing" rule still in effect in 1927–28. For simplicity's

---

sake, though, let's assume that these factors struck a balance along the way. After all, although an old-time skater had duller skates, a straight stick, and crude gear, the goalie in front of him had a smaller blocker, no throat protector, and no face mask to hide behind. For every little advantage the shooter has taken in the last 70 years, the goalie has also taken one.

Meet Nels Stewart, the Montreal Maroons' top stud in 1927–28:

	GP	G	A	Pts	Time
Nels Stewart	41	27	7	34	38.07317

The fellow they called "Old Poison" was a scoring machine and a beast of a competitor who spent five seasons with the USAHA Cleveland Indians before making the jump to the NHL by way of the rowdy Montreal Maroons, English Montreal's answer to the Flying Frenchmen. In Stewart's first full season with the big boys, he scored a league-tops 34 goals in 36 games, leading his team to their first ever Stanley Cup championship. In 650 NHL games in Montreal, Boston, and New York, Stewart managed 324 goals. He scored 27 of those goals in 1927–28, playing alongside the likes of man-mountain Babe Siebert, and Hooley Smith.

But how would Stewart have fared in the comparatively watered-down NHL of 1997–98? Well, first we compute NHL goals and assists per 60-minute game in both 1927–28 and 1997–98. Because Stewart did not compete against himself, we leave his numbers out of the computation. When we add up total minutes, goals, and assists, we find

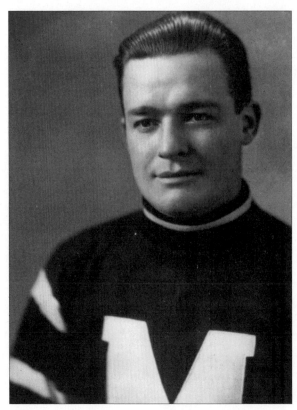

Nels Stewart

that in 1927–28 there were 3.667 goals scored and 1.807 assists awarded per 60-minute game. In 1997–98, these numbers are 5.196 and 8.807. Obviously, the numbers from 1997–98 are considerably higher.

Next, we figure out Stewart's numbers. Because he played 41 of 44 games in 1927–28, we calculate his 27 goals to get a 76-game representation of just over 50 goals ($41/44 = x$, $(27/x) = y$, $y \times 82 = z$). We then divide the figure into the 1927–28 goals-per-game average (minus Stewart's influence on the overall average of 3.667) and multiply it by the 1997–98 average. We are left with 72.221722 goals.

Is that it? Is 72 goals what the 1927–28 version of Nels Stewart would have scored 70 years later? No. We know he played, unofficially, 38.07317 minutes (38 minutes and four seconds) per game, and that no first-line forward in the modern-day gets anywhere near this much ice-time. So, we cut him down to size. We divide 72.221722 into his 1927–28 ice-time and multiply that number by 23.833333, the exact time Pittsburgh Penguin hotshot Jaromir Jagr was on the ice in each of his 77 games in 1997–98. Our figure now shows that Stewart would have scored about 45 goals, an impressive number of goals in an NHL where the top guns scored 52.

Next, we apply this simple formula to assists as well, arriving at these scoring totals:

	GP	G	A	Pts	Time
Nels Stewart	76	45	40	85	23:50

Stewart's 1927–28 season is worth about 45 goals and 40 assists in 76 games at 23.833333 minutes played per game. And where might he have squeezed into the 1997–98 NHL scoring race? Dig this:

Player	GP	G	A	Pts	Time
Jaromir Jagr	77	35	67	102	23:50
Peter Forsberg	72	25	66	91	23:07
Pavel Bure	82	51	39	90	23:43
Wayne Gretzky	82	23	67	90	21:35
John LeClair	82	51	36	87	21:38
Ziggy Palffy	82	45	42	87	22:28
Ron Francis	81	25	62	87	23:04
Teemu Selanne	73	52	34	86	23:38
Nels Stewart	76	45	40	85	23:50
Jason Allison	81	33	50	83	19:41

So, Stewart would have finished ninth in NHL scoring in 1997–98 based on the numbers he put up 70 years earlier. Not bad, but not becoming of a player many have said is one of the greatest scorers in hockey history.

Fine, but 1927–28 was hardly Stewart's finest year overall, either. Only two years earlier, in his rookie season, Stewart bagged 34 goals in 36 games. In 1929–30, he was worth 39 goals and 55 points. But, unfortunately, we don't have the minutes-per-game figures for those seasons. With no way of knowing for sure if in his rookie season he scored 34 goals playing 25, 35, or 45 minutes per game, transferring his achievements to 1997–98 equivalents would be a hack job, to say the least. And to simply "adjust" a player's numbers is misleading. We have already established that Stewart would not have gotten the chance to score 72 goals in 1997–98. He wouldn't be taking 50 shifts a game. The game has changed.

Look at these kinds of statistical exercises as numbers games. Enjoy the stats presented here, but take them with a grain of salt.

The Hawks Stunk

The fluctuations in hockey's goals-per-game (GPG) and baseball's runs-per-game through the years are fascinating. Today, with goal scoring at near-drought levels, baseball fans are watching balls go over the fence at an almost unprecedented rate. While Dominik Hasek acts as a brick wall in the cage for the Buffalo Sabres, Mark McGwire and Sammy Sosa are sending horsehide into oblivion at rates that would have made Babe Ruth perspire.

But this is by no means a new phenomenon. In the late 1920s, baseball experienced an Industrial Revolution of sorts, manufacturing runs at unprecedented rates, while in hockey, the goals-per-game rate sunk to record lows. Despite a mass influx of talent from the doomed Western Hockey League, the NHL was as dry as the Sahara.

In 1927, the NHL saw its GPG decline from about 4.5 to under 4 goals scored per game. Come next year, the GPG dropped to just over 3.5, and by 1929, following the rhythm of the failing stock market, it hit an all-time low of 3.0. Most pitiful of all were the 1928–29 Chicago Black Hawks, quite possibly the worst offensive team in hockey history. The 1927–28 Hawks had scored 68 goals in 44 games and finished last with a 7-34-3 record. While their record improved in 1928–29, it was in no part due to a sudden spurt of offense. These Hawks were impotent — *33 goals scored in 44 games*. Read that again — 33 goals in 44 games!

Why were they so pathetic? Where do we start? Well, to begin with, the Hawks had lost personnel from the previous season. Charles "Rabbit" McVeigh and Babe Dye were sold to the New York Americans, while Mickey MacKay was sent to Boston. At approximately the same time, Corb Denneny, Amby Moran, and Bob Trapp retired. But these losses don't explain 33 goals in 44 games. Or do they?

Looking at the final statistics for the 1928–29 Hawks, we see Vic Ripley leading the team in scoring with 11 goals and 13 points. And just who the heck was Vic Ripley? Turns out he wasn't that bad, a solid player with enough talent to collect an NHL paycheck for seven years. He was the only Hawk to score over 10 points in 1928–29. Here were the top five scorers on the team:

Player	GP	G	A	Pts	Time
Vic Ripley	34	11	2	13	31
Johnny Gottselig	44	5	3	8	26
Dick Irvin	39	6	1	7	30
Ty Arbour	44	3	4	7	32
Mush March	35	3	3	6	6

Not exactly a group that strikes fear in the heart of goalies.

Then there was the off-ice problem. The Hawks had played throughout the 1920s in the Chicago Coliseum, and were set to move into Chicago Stadium for the 1928–29 season. As a result, they let their lease at the Coliseum run out. So what? You guessed it . . . Chicago Stadium wasn't ready in time. The suddenly homeless Hawks played most of their "home" season out of Fort Erie.

Chicago had believed that Chuck Gardiner in nets and Herb Gardiner and Clem Loughlin on the blue-line would serve them well. They were right. They just forgot to acquire some offense along the way. The Hawks played a record eight straight games without scoring a goal. They scored more than two goals in a game only once in 44 games. They scored more than one goal only eight times. They were shut out an embarrassing 20 times! And to top it off, they had a 15-game winless streak tucked in there somewhere. Absolutely dreadful! Needless to say, Chicago didn't draw very well. After all, who wanted to go see a team that got shut out almost half the time they went out?

To be fair, no one in the NHL was scoring much in 1929. And no one was going to see games, or at least not as many as had in previous years. Thankfully, NHL bigwigs made changes for the 1929–30 season, allowing forward passing anywhere on the ice, and wiping out the offside rule for the first month of the season. In 1929–30 the GPG doubled from the previous season to about 5.7.

Some interesting stories arise from this team's history, however. Irvin finished third in team scoring in his last year as a player, and went on to a marvelous coaching career. Player/coach Herb Gardiner was also in his last year as a player. Chicago's goalie was the Chuck Gardiner, certainly one of the finest goalies of all time. He had the league's worst goals-against average — an absolutely abysmal 1.93!

NHL scoring has never suffered an ebb similar to the one in the late 1920s since. And the NHL has been spared an abomination like the 1928–29 Chicago Black Hawks.

Clancy-ese

Introducing the English language according to Francis "King" Clancy. Toronto's all-time favorite sports hero was a butcher of l'Anglais, as evidenced by snippets of his conversations with Brian McFarlane, found in his book *Clancy*.

<Warning: The following material may not be suitable for young readers!>

ENGLISH	CLANCY-ESE
brawl	hullabaloo or hey-rube
wow!	by Jiminy!
fighting ability	bob-and-weave
scolding	what-ho
big guy	gazaboo
taunt	use the blarney
beaten/defeated	boomed
dirty players	cuties
He was fast.	He could start on a dime and leave you with a nickel change.
I don't like you.	I think you're a big stuffed so-and-so and a couple of horse's kisses as well.
Hockey was fun.	The days when I played hockey were gay and carefree and rollicking.

The Battle of Montreal

The city of Montreal knows very well the term "rivalry." In the mid-1970s, it was the Canadiens against the Philadelphia Flyers. Throughout the 1960s, it was the Canadiens and Toronto Maple Leafs duking it out for hockey supremacy. Back around the turn of the twentieth century, the Montreal Victorias seemed to be in an eternal struggle with the powerhouse Winnipeg Victorias for Stanley Cup glory. While these rivalries were nothing to be sneezed at, these teams weren't battling for a single town's affections. The Maroons and Canadiens did just this between 1924 and 1938.

From the get-go, culture remained a major difference. While the Maroons drew a largely English following, the Canadiens enjoyed the approval of French Canada. And both sides were well aware of which side their bread was buttered on. By late 1926, the Stanley Cup champion Maroons were without a single French Canadian on their roster. The same season's edition of the Canadiens, who finished a ghastly 11-24-1, had five. Of course, the gulf between the clubs in the standings would not usually be this wide.

Brian McFarlane describes the new feud as an intense, at times hateful, one in his book:

> It was explosive. When the English-backed Maroons met the French-supported Canadiens, the on-ice battles were often overshadowed by skirmishes in the stands. Emotions became so feverish that a missed goal or an "undeserved" penalty would trigger a rash of pushes and punches, with police and ushers rushing in to keep English and French fans apart. The damage was usually minimal: a torn jacket, a hat yanked off and thrown away, the occasional black eye, and enough '20s-style "trash talk" (in two languages) to shock fans ten rows away.

As McFarlane notes, Dandurand created the rivalry between the Maroons and Canadiens. After all, he was the one who gave rise to the Maroons in the first place. The Battle of Montreal would never have occurred had he not taken action.

The first ever game between the Maroons and Canadiens took place on December 10, 1924, with the Flying Frenchmen coming up with a 5–0 victory. The Maroons, featuring former Ottawa Senator Punch Broadbent, star Olympic defender Dunc Munro, and crack goalie Clint Benedict, came out flat against their neighbors. Canadiens speed boy Aurel Joliat counted four times.

By the halfway point of 1924–25 the Maroons were 7-6-2 and only two points behind the second-place Canadiens, but they would experience a substantial drop-off, finishing in fifth place at 9-19-2, out of the playoff picture.

The 1925–26 season was much kinder to the Maroons. After signing bruising Babe Siebert in March and nasty Nels Stewart in June 1925, the M's sailed through the season. They met the Canadiens six times in 36 games, beating them all but once. Stewart, a rookie, ended with 34 goals in 36 games, good enough to win the Hart Trophy. In a complete twist on the previous campaign's second half, the Canadiens went 2-15-1 in the home stretch. In the playoffs, the Maroons got by the Pittsburgh Pirates and Senators before dismantling the Victoria Cougars for the Stanley Cup.

In the 1926–27 playoffs Clint Benedict, the NHL's top goalie, went up against the top 1-2 scoring punch around in Joliat and Howie Morenz. The first match between the M's and Canadiens ended 1–1. According to reports, the Maroon rough boys took Morenz for a ride and the little fellow's usually electrifying play was marred by rough work when he was goaded into dirty play. In game two he got revenge, tallying the series-winning goal after bursting around the Maroons defense. Stewart had a great deal of trouble keeping up with the Mitchell Meteor.

In the 1928 playoffs, the Maroons came within a win of their second Cup in as many years. The following season, however, they fell to last place in the Canadian Division with a 15-20-9 record. The Canadiens, meanwhile, owned the NHL and cruised to an outstanding 22-7-15. In total, they allowed only 43 goals in their 44 games. Goaltender George Hainsworth easily won his third-straight Vezina Trophy with a 0.98 goals-against average and 22 shutouts! Despite reaching these lofty heights, the Canadiens were obliterated by the Bruins in the first round of the playoffs.

In 1929–30, Maroons manager Eddie Gerard threw Stewart, Siebert, and former Olympic hockey star Hooley Smith together on a line. This trio, known henceforth as the "S-Line," would tear up the NHL with a flurry of elbows, fists, and goals. Stewart finished with 39 goals and 55 points in 44 games. The Canadiens, meanwhile, were making a little noise of their own. Morenz led the Frenchmen with 40 goals, third in the league behind Boston Bruins Dit Clapper and Cooney Weiland. Both the M's and Canadiens reached the finish line with 51 points atop the Canadian Division. The dreaded Bruins (American Division) had 77 points, but the Canadiens captured the Cup.

In October 1932, Stewart was shipped off to the rival Boston Bruins. Around the same time, Siebert was sold to the New York Rangers. Why would any wheeler-dealer in his right mind sell two-thirds of the magnificent "S-Line"? Simple. Young bucks like Baldy Northcott, Jimmy Ward, and soon-to-be rookie of the year Russ Blinco had come of age. While each "S-Line" member was contemplating life at 30, the oldest of the new kids on the block was only 26. Besides, the "S-Line" really hadn't accomplished much. Apart from running roughshod over the league during the regular season, the man-mountains were empty-handed. No parades. No bubbly. No Cup rings. Still, the city of Montreal was sad to see Stewart and Siebert go. They had scored a collective 268 goals in seven seasons.

The rivalry between the Maroons and Canadiens faded in the 1930s. As teams in Toronto and New York grew to maturity, the aging Canadiens and the disemboweled Maroons lost a step or two. In 1932–33, Stewart notched 18 goals in 47 games on a 25-15-8 Bruins club. Siebert, meanwhile, helped the Rangers reach Cup glory, contributing a goal and a thousand bone-crunching body-checks in eight playoff games. The only bright spot on the Maroons was their top line — Smith, Northcott, and Paul Haynes. The trio finished among the top five in scoring, all three outpacing Joliat and Morenz.

In October 1934, the Canadiens dealt the great Morenz, along with Lorne Chabot and Marty Burke, to Chicago for Roger Jenkins, Lionel Conacher, and Leroy Goldsworthy. Morenz put in a season and a half with the Black Hawks before being shuffled off to the Rangers. He returned to the Canadiens for the 1936–37 season, where he played well until he suffered a broken leg during a game late in the season. He deteriorated in hospital, and died only months later, on March 8, 1937.

After another Maroons Cup win in early 1935, which represented the last stand of Lionel Conacher and Alex Connell, the dream was over. While the 1935–36 season yielded yet another first-place finish, the party was definitely over. The Great Depression, which had already claimed the hockey life of the Ottawa Senators/St. Louis Eagles franchise, began to set its icy gaze on the M's. In the face of the economic pinch, Hooley Smith was dealt to Boston. Another strong finish in 1936–37 did little to thicken an ever-thinning crowd of Maroon supporters. Then Conacher and Connell retired, which was probably the final nail in the franchise's coffin

The Maroons staggered to the finish line in 1937–38 at a frightful 12-30-6. On August 25, 1938, the club brass successfully petitioned the NHL for permission to suspend operations for a year. On May 13, 1939, the Maroons advised the league that they were finished.

In a matter of months, the Canadian Arena Company snapped up all stock and assets of the Canadiens. Donat Raymond, builder of the Forum, promised to protect the struggling Canadiens from the same fate as the Maroons, and remained true to his word. In 1943–44, the Canadiens began a string of four straight first-place finishes.

So who won the Battle of Montreal? There are many factors to consider. First, how well did each team do? For starters:

Club	1st Place	2nd Place	3rd Place	Cups	Points
Montreal Canadiens	5	3	4	2	45
Montreal Maroons	2	5	4	2	40

In assigning one point for a third-place finish, two points for a second, three for a first, and ten for a Stanley Cup championship, we find that the Canadiens won the Battle of Montreal 45–40. Although we assign these points arbitrarily, it simply doesn't matter: the Canadiens of Howie Morenz, Aurel Joliat, and George Hainsworth accomplished more than the Maroons.

How did the Canadiens fare in head-to-head battle with the mighty, rumbling Maroon machine? The proof is in the numbers:

Season	GP	W	L	T	Pts
1924–25	6	4	0	2	10
1925–26	6	1	5	0	2
1926–27	6	5	1	0	10
1927–28	6	2	2	2	6
1928–29	6	4	0	2	10
1929–30	6	1	4	1	3
1930–31	6	3	1	2	8
1931–32	7	5	1	1	11
1932–33	7	3	3	1	7
1933–34	6	2	3	1	5
1934–35	6	4	1	1	9
1935–36	8	1	6	1	3
1936–37	8	2	3	3	7
1937–38	8	4	4	0	8
	92	41	34	17	99

Against the Maroons, the Canadiens racked up 41 wins and 99 points in 92 regular-season contests. Their 41-34-17 record translates into a .538 winning percentage — not great, but just enough to put them over the hump.

Perhaps a positional analysis will put some creative flesh on the bones of such a dry statistical overview. The following is a tale of the tape between the starters on the 1929–30 edition of these teams:

Montreal Canadiens				Montreal Maroons
George Hainsworth	X	G		Flat Walsh
Battleship Leduc		D	X	Red Dutton
Sylvio Mantha	X	D		Dunc Munro
Aurel Joliat	X	L		Babe Siebert
Howie Morenz	X	C		Nels Stewart
Nick Wasnie		R	X	Hooley Smith

The players with X's beside their name performed at a higher level at the peak of the Maroons–Canadiens rivalry in the late 1920s and early 1930s — we are not saying that these were better players overall.

With the exception of big Nick Wasnie, who shared his ice-time with a man by the outlandish name of Wildor Larochelle, the Canadiens were an all-star lineup from head to toe. Hainsworth was among the very best goalies in the league with a 20-13-9 record and a 2.42 goals-against average. As for Walsh, he played 30 games in what was his first full NHL season. While his regular-season statistics are good, his playoff performance was clearly inferior to that of Hainsworth, who was 5-0-1 with three shutouts and a microscopic 0.75 average in the post-season. Who can argue with that?

The Canadiens forwards were, with the exception of the right wing, superior. While Stewart and Siebert were top-notch warriors, the Canadiens forwards were true champions. Maroons Stewart and Siebert, at around 6 feet, 190 pounds, were birds of a bashing feather. But Morenz and Joliat were the most feared 1-2 punch in the NHL by 1930, possibly the finest in hockey history. Although much smaller and finer-boned than the Maroon man-mountains, the Morenz–Joliat connection was without peer. Morenz's skills were legendary, but he not only wanted to win, he *had* to win.

The Canadiens held a definite advantage over the Maroons: they had a captive audience. Since the birth of Les Canadiens in 1910, Quebeckers could finally cheer for their team. Whereas the Maroons had to vie for English Montreal's affection with every other team in the league — especially Ottawa and Toronto — the Bleu, Blanc, et Rouge could always count on the majority of French Canadians for support.

Poet Wilson Macdonald articulates the pride of the French Canadian for the Canadiens:

Wen I am tire of travail-trop
I put on coat of coon
And go to see Canadiens
Mak' meence-meat of Maroon.

Snap!shots

JACK ADAMS (Jawn/Jolly Jack/The Squire of Napanee) Center
5'9" 175
b. 6/14/1895, Fort William, Ontario
d. 5/1/1968, Detroit, Michigan

John James Adams was a raw, talented center who played top-level hockey in Toronto, Vancouver, and Ottawa over 10 years. He was known as a great digger and a fiery leader. One game in 1919 speaks volumes about his burning desire to win. In the late stages of the tilt, many of his Toronto Arena mates had been battered and bruised. Mighty oaks like Harry Mummery, Ken Randall, and Rusty Crawford were in particularly rough shape. Mummery was the first one sent hobbling from the ice, followed quickly by Randall, who was taken away on a stretcher. As for big Crawford, he was whacked across the forehead by Canadiens star Newsy Lalonde. Arenas goalie Hap Holmes lost a handful of teeth. Adams' head was cut up in a flurry of body-checks, cross-checks, and high sticks. Despite it all, the pudgy pivot played till the end, dashing up and down the boards with blood dripping over his eyes and ears.

Adams' career in hockey began in 1911, when at age 16 he made the senior team that won the Thunder Bay, Ontario, hockey title. Michigan's copper town of Calumet found Adams a spot on their team in 1915, and he spent his final amateur year in Sarnia, Ontario. He turned professional with the Arenas in 1918 as a right winger. In his rookie season, the Arenas defeated the Vancouver Millionaires for the Stanley Cup. After an unspectacular season in Toronto, he headed west and signed on with Vancouver in time for the 1919–20 season. Over the next couple of years, he blossomed into a top scoring threat and in 1921–22 led the PCHA with 26 goals and 30 points. That same season, Vancouver again made it to the Cup finals. Although he made good with six goals in five games, the silverware was taken by Babe Dye and the Toronto St. Patricks.

The next season, it was back to Toronto and to the St. Patricks for Adams. He put up four productive seasons there before being sold to the Ottawa Senators in the summer of the 1926. His last year as an NHL player was 1926–27 and although he wasn't used on the top line, he was lauded for his guts, brains, and leadership skills. The Senators took the Cup and Adams took early retirement.

After hanging up his blades for good, Adams accepted the manager–coach post with the Detroit Cougars. He would hold on to this job for the next 35 years, raking in 12 regular-season championships and seven Stanley Cup victories along the way.

The man they called "Jolly Jack" was inducted into the Hockey Hall of Fame in 1959 and remained with the Red Wings until after the 1961–62 NHL season. Adams was named its first recipient of the Lester Patrick Trophy in 1966 for his outstanding contribution to American hockey. He died of a massive coronary on May 1, 1968, while at his desk as the president of the Central Hockey League.

Peak Years   *1921–25*
In a Word   *SCORPION*

CLINT BENEDICT (Prayin' Benny) Goal
b. 9/26/1892, Ottawa, Ontario
d. 11/12/1976, Ottawa, Ontario

During a January 7, 1930, game between the Montreal Maroons and Canadiens, Howie Morenz caught a break and skated in on Clint Benedict, the Maroons' 37-year-old goalie. Forward Jimmy Ward lunged at Morenz in an effort to impede the Canadiens superstar. Far from helping matters, Morenz used Ward as a screen as he drove the puck. Benedict, who couldn't see through the traffic, met the puck face-first. He would wake up in the hospital with a cut forehead and a broken nose, deciding then and there to make his next game appearance wearing a protective mask.

Benedict had a Boston design firm come up with a mask for him, but it was awkward and he soon discarded it. He then auditioned a catcher-style face mask in practice only to find it similarly bulky and impractical. Finally, he donned a prototype mask made of leather and constructed like a football face-piece. After losing to the Chicago Black Hawks 2–0 wearing the kooky-looking mask, he abandoned it, saying, "the nosepiece protrudes too far and obscures my vision on low shots." He retired shortly thereafter.

Clint Benedict had signed with the Ottawa Senators for the 1912–13 NHA season. He would go on to all-world status in the Dominion capital. His list of feats as a top-level goalie are eye-catching, to say the very least:

• member of four Stanley Cup teams — three with Ottawa and one with the Montreal Maroons
• NHL goals-against average leader 1918–19, 1919–20, 1920–21, 1921–22, 1922–23, and 1926–27
• NHL shutout leader for seven consecutive seasons (1917–18 to 1923–24)

Any talk of the greatest goalie of the NHL's formative years will invariably come around to Benedict and Georges Vezina. Stylistically, Benedict was the antithesis of Vezina, the goalie hockey purists derided for spending more time on his knees in net than on his feet — the original Dominik Hasek. Benedict's habit of dropping to make a save and flopping around in goal-mouth scrambles infuriated the opposition so much that the NHL was compelled to officially outlaw such behavior.

Benedict was inducted into the Hockey Hall of Fame in 1965.

Peak Years   *1919–23*
In a Word   *FLOPPER*

FRANK BOUCHER (Raffles) Center
5'9" 185
b. 10/7/1901, Ottawa, Ontario
d. 12/12/1977, Kemptville, Ontario

Frank Boucher

The Patrick brothers (of PCHA fame) were blind to young Frank Boucher's ability until he played for Tommy Gorman after he was signed to play for the Ottawa Senators in 1921. Boucher was ultimately stolen back by Frank Patrick to play for the Vancouver Maroons. Around this time, sportswriter Andy Lytle dubbed Boucher "Raffles" after a famous fictional safe-cracker (a tribute to his puck-stealing ability). Frank built his reputation as an apprentice of the great Mickey MacKay. With the death of the WHL in 1926, Ottawa grew anxious to reclaim Boucher. Ranger GM Conn Smythe had different ideas, steering the youngster to Lester Patrick's fledgling New York Rangers. Boucher was immediately assigned to the top line between Bun and Bill Cook. The Cook-Boucher-Cook unit went on to become one of the sharpest, most deadly combinations in hockey history.

The Lady Byng Trophy was donated in 1925, to be awarded to the player judged to have shown the highest degree of sportsmanship combined with a high standard of playing ability. An inspection of Boucher's record reveals why this remarkable center won the Lady Byng seven times in eight seasons. In 557 NHL contests, Boucher earned

----

but 119 penalty minutes! After winning his seventh Lady Byng, he was given the trophy to keep, and Lady Byng donated another trophy to replace it.

Two-time Cup-winner Frank Boucher was among the scoring elite in two professional leagues, racking up a combined total of 217 goals and 513 points over an 18-year playing career. Boucher and the Cook brothers perfected the tic-tac-toe passing play. Boucher was the Wayne Gretzky of his day — that is, an offensive genius, a computer on skates. In 1936, two Stanley Cups later, the Cook-Boucher-Cook line was broken up. Coach Patrick threw his aging star onto a line between Lynn Patrick and Ceece Dillon. Boucher would call it quits at the end of 1937–38. In 1939, with 55-year-old Lester Patrick wanting less responsibility within the Rangers organization, Boucher was appointed head coach and, subsequently, manager.

As chairman of the NHL Rules Committee in the 1940s, Boucher first hit upon the idea of the red-line as a means of ending the five-man "ganging" attacks that kept defending teams locked in their own zone for minutes at a time. In 1943–44, with the pathetic Rangers hard-pressed for personnel due to the war, he penciled himself into the starting lineup. The 42-year-old played quite well in 15 games.

Boucher was inducted into the Hockey Hall of Fame in 1958.

Peak Years   *1926–30*
Comparable Recent Player   *Wayne Gretzky*
In a Word   *PRECISE*

BUCK BOUCHER Defense
5'10" 169
b. 8/19/1896, Ottawa, Ontario
d. 10/17/1960, Ottawa, Ontario

Before turning to professional hockey as a career, George "Buck" Boucher played football with the Ottawa Rough Riders and was considered a star halfback. His puck-chasing career began in the Ottawa City League, where he played with the New Edinburghs. By the time he cracked the NHL in 1915, he was one of

George "Buck" Boucher

Canada's top athletes. Although the Ottawa Senators would boast such talents as Eddie Gerard, Sprague Cleghorn, King Clancy, and Lionel Hitchman on the blue-line, the man they called Buck was the linchpin.

In 1919, Boucher was moved back to the defense from forward. Although he wasn't a particularly fast skater, his puck-control was otherworldly. According to reports, opposing players could hear the curious tap-tap of his stick on the ice as he navigated his way through opposing teams. In all, he figured in four Stanley Cups in Ottawa and during his prime was considered one of the league's elite talents. It's often said that King Clancy was the first of the modern rushers, but Boucher, a stick-handling wizard, started the proverbial puck rolling. In the latter part of the 1928–29 campaign, Ottawa began to falter. Boucher, whose star was beginning to wane, was more often than not the target of the fans' ire, which he was very sensitive to. Team owner Frank Ahearn, a kind and sentimental man, took pity on Boucher. Ahearn wanted his boy to wind up his career on a club where he could be of help, on which the Cup would be more than a fantasy. In addition, Ahearn wanted him to receive the same salary on another team, and moving expenses. Montreal Maroons head coach Eddie Gerard was contacted about obtaining Boucher and the M's skipper jumped at the chance. Boucher was shipped to Montreal for forward Joe Lamb. Though past his prime, he was a solid addition to the team.

After his playing days, Boucher coached in Ottawa, Montreal (Maroons), Boston, and St. Louis. He would lead a team to the Allan Cup championship and help select and train the Ottawa RCAF (Royal Canadian Air Force) side that won the Olympic championship for Canada in 1948.

Buck Boucher was inducted into the Hockey Hall of Fame in 1960.

Peak Years 1921–25
In a Word GALLOPING

PUNCH BROADBENT (Old Elbows) Right Wing

5'7" 183
b. 7/13/1892, Ottawa, Ontario
d. 3/6/1971, Ottawa, Ontario

Harry "Punch" Broadbent played amateur hockey with the Ottawa New Edinburghs and the Ottawa Cliffsides from 1909–12. He made the leap to the Ottawa Senators in 1912–13, scoring 20 goals in 20 games. After two seasons, just as he was reaching his peak, he left to serve with the RCAF in World War One. He earned the Military Medal for heroism in combat.

Harry "Punch" Broadbent

"It's an unfortunate thing," sportswriter Baz O'Meara later reminisced, "but Punch might have left an even greater record if it hadn't been for the war. He lost four of his best seasons in his career because of service in World War One, and it was tribute to his ability that he came back and still did so well in hockey."

After the war, Broadbent rejoined Ottawa. As one of the vital cogs in a dynasty, he figured in Stanley Cup wins in 1920, 1921, and 1923. He was a true power forward and an all-around hockey talent.

Only weeks before the start of the 1924–25 NHL season, Broadbent was sold with Clint Benedict to the Montreal Maroons in an apparent effort to balance the league. Though considered past his prime by this point, the squat and muscular winger scored five goals in a game on January 7, 1925, en route to a 15-goal season, while Benedict played a huge role in bringing the Cup to Montreal in 1926.

During the 1921–22 season, Broadbent's name was etched in the NHL record books after he scored one or more goals in 16 consecutive games, breaking Joe Malone's 1918 streak (14 games).

Broadbent was returned to Ottawa for the 1927–28 season in exchange for Hooley Smith and cash. A year later, he was sent to the New York Americans, putting in a full season before quitting hockey to rejoin the air force. In 11 NHL seasons, the man they called Punch scored a total of 122 goals and contributed to four Cup wins. He was deadly with both the puck and the elbow, as much at home in the slot as in the trenches. But he was more than just an elbow-happy scorer. Punch Broadbent was among the very finest back-checkers of his day and a big reason the Senators' defensive style was so difficult to crack. He was so feared throughout the league for his fistic abilities that even psychopath Sprague Cleghorn steered clear.

Harry Broadbent was inducted into the Hockey Hall of Fame in 1962.

Peak Years 1920–24
Comparable Recent Player Brendan Shanahan
In a Word ELBOWS

BILLY BURCH Center
6'0" 200
b. 11/20/1900, Yonkers, N.Y.
d. 11/30/1950

Bill Burch

William Burch was born in Yonkers, New York, but moved to Canada as a boy and learned his hockey knocks in the Toronto area. He would ply his trade with the OHA's Toronto Canoe Club Paddlers and Toronto Aura Lees. The tall, fit youth turned professional with the Hamilton Tigers in 1923 and centered a crackerjack line between Wilf and Redvers Green.

In 1924–25, the Tigers finished in first place. Burch ended up notching 20 goals and 24 points in 27 games and was awarded the Hart Trophy as the NHL's most valuable player. In the midst of a labor dispute, the Tigers folded. Burch and his team moved to New York in 1925 to become the Americans. In an effort to drum up ticket sales, Burch was crowned the "Babe Ruth of hockey," a billing that was nearly impossible to live up to. In addition to the sudden pressure of star status, Burch was made team captain. While in New York, the young, good-looking center grew fond of the party life, which may explain the sudden drop in his offensive production.

Burch was a big, strong man blessed with all-around offensive abilities. Although not an overly rough player, he played a hard, clean game. His specialty was the puck-control game, using his superior hand-eye coordination and long reach to set up sparkling offensive plays. This gift combined with a hard, accurate shot and a defensive conscience made Burch everything a coach could possibly want in a player.

In 1927, Burch won the Lady Byng Trophy. He missed a healthy chunk of the 1927–28 season with a serious knee injury but returned to form the next season, when his Americans made the playoffs and gave the cross-town Rangers a scare. Burch remained in New York until 1932, when he was sold to the Bruins. After a short spell in Chicago, he broke a leg and decided to call it a career.

In 390 games, Burch scored 137 goals and 190 points. He became a member of the Hockey Hall of Fame in 1974.

Peak Years   1924–28
In a Word   POSER

BILL COOK Right Wing
5'10" 175
b. 10/9/1896, Brantford, Ontario
d. 4/6/1986, Kingston, Ontario

William Osser Cook was born in the same town as Wayne Gretzky and raised in Kingston, Ontario. He broke in with the OHA's Kingston Frontenacs. After a stint in the Canadian army, he returned to Kingston but soon decided that hockey was his destiny. He packed up his mother and younger siblings and headed west, where he homesteaded while playing hockey in Sault Ste. Marie, Ontario, for the Greyhounds. He and his younger brother Fred (nicknamed "Bun") played together on the WCHL Saskatoon Crescents. When New York Rangers manager Conn Smythe spotted the older Cook, he knew he had to have him. Smythe's replacement, Lester Patrick, signed Cook and named him team captain.

Bill Cook was put on a line to the right of former Pacific Coast star Frank Boucher, and his brother Bun. Under Patrick's guidance, this trio dominated the NHL. Smooth and precise pattern passing became their trademark and the foundation of the team's winning system. Bill was the line's trigger man. He made an instant splash in the league in 1926–27 with 33 goals and 37 points in 44 games. In the Rangers' sophomore season, they won the Stanley Cup.

Bill Cook was a remarkable blend of brains, beauty, and brawn. He was an outstanding stick-handler, a hard and fast skater, and had an incredible shot. He was a huge physical presence with a mean streak. The big winger went on to tie Charlie Conacher in 1931–32 for the league lead in goals with 34 and would win his second scoring title in 1932–33 before captaining his Broadway men to their second Cup.

In 1935–36, Patrick broke up the Cook-Boucher-Cook line when Bun was forced out of the lineup with arthritic pain. Bill remained the Rangers' team captain until retiring midway through the 1936–37 NHL campaign.

Ranger boss Lester Patrick praised his star winger. "I need the Bill Cooks. The other players, when it comes right down to it, will follow the Bill Cooks."

In 591 games in two leagues, Cook scored 317 goals and 508 points. He entered the Hockey Hall of Fame in 1952.

Peak Years   *1925–29*
In a Word   *CAPTAIN*

CY DENNENY (The Cornwall Colt) Left Wing
5'7" 168
b. 12/23/1891, Farran's Point, Ontario
d. 10/12/1970, Cornwall, Ontario

Cy Denneny

Cyril "Cy" Denneny's professional hockey story begins in 1914 when he joined the NHA's Toronto Ontarios-Shamrocks. In January 1917, he was traded by the Toronto Blueshirts to the Ottawa Senators, where he went on to become a prolific winger. After joining the Senators in 1917, Denneny made protecting Frank Nighbor and Jack Darragh, his sweet-natured linemates, job one. Later, Denneny played with Punch Broadbent. The two were referred to as the "Gold Dust Twins" on account of their ability to keep opposition bad boys honest.

Denneny's 12-game consecutive goal-scoring streak and league-leading 36 markers in 1917–18 convinced Ottawa brass they had a stallion on their hands. The chunky winger stayed with the Senators until 1928, firing in more goals than any other Ottawa hockeyist in history and never dropping below fourth in NHL scoring in 11 seasons. He won five Stanley Cups in his career and potted the winning goal in overtime of the 1923 finals against the mighty Edmonton Eskimos.

Short and stocky, Denneny looked more like a bulldog than a goal-scorer. Not an exceptionally fast skater, he possessed one of the more accurate shots of his day and was one of the first players to use opposing defensemen as screens. He retired in 1929 as the top-scoring left winger of his time.

Fresh from his fifth Cup win with the Boston Bruins in 1929, Denneny tried his hand at refereeing before turning to coaching in the Upper and Lower Ottawa Valley leagues. Before long, he was called back to the NHL to manage and coach the 1932–33 Senators. This gig would fall through after only one year.

Denneny, a career 279 goal-scorer, became a member of the Hockey Hall of Fame in 1959.

Peak Years   *1920–24*
In a Word   *BULLDOG*

RED DUTTON Defense
6'0" 185
b. 7/23/1898, Russell, Manitoba
d. 3/15/1987, Calgary, Alberta

"Get that man!" and "Keep punching!" were two of Mervyn Dutton's favorite expressions. At age 16, the young man whose own mother nicknamed him "Red" began lusting for glory on the battlefields in Europe. The rusty-haired teen left his private boarding school dormitory, lied about his age, and joined the Princess Pats Light Infantry Regiment for immediate service overseas in World War One.

Dutton was hit by shrapnel at Vimy Ridge. For a while, it was thought his gangrenous leg would have to be sawed off. Although in great pain, Dutton begged the Canadian Army surgeons to leave it alone. The physicians ultimately relented, leaving him to work his limb seven hours a day for the next 18 months. His leg eventually returned to health.

In Winnipeg after the war, Dutton played hockey in local leagues from morning until past midnight. This kind of dedication would soon pay off. He was signed by the WCHL Calgary Tigers in 1921, and played with them through 1925–26. When the Patrick brothers sold the WCHL in 1926, Dutton signed on with the Montreal Maroons, where he starred on defense beside the likes of Dunc Munro, Reg Noble, and Toots Holway. Baz O'Meara of the Montreal *Star* once wrote of Dutton's body-crunching: "Dutton bashed all comers with fine disregard for reputations. He loved nothing better than to leave an opponent lying on the ice gasping for breath."

Dutton was a strong-skating defenseman with all-around ability. Although his roughness was a perfect fit on the rugged Maroons, he was by no means a cheap-shot artist. He was a stay-at-home defender, although his 13 assists in 43 games in 1929–30 suggests he was capable of leading a rush. On May 14, 1930, he was packaged with three other players and sent to the New York Americans for $35,000. He stayed with the tough-luck Amerks as a player through the end of the 1935–36 season, when he decided to hang up his skates in favor of coaching. As coach–general manager, he led the Americans to the playoffs for the first time in six seasons, and remained with the organization until its collapse in 1942. When NHL president Frank Calder died in 1943, Dutton stepped in. He remained the league's biggest wig until he appointed Clarence Campbell to take over three years later.

Despite being one of the most penalized players of his day, Dutton was the very model of class and decorum as league president, carrying this approach into his successful business dealings.

Dutton was inducted into the Hockey Hall of Fame in 1958.

Peak Years   *1925–29*
In a Word   *THUNDERING*

BABE DYE Right Wing
5'8" 150
b. 5/13/1898, Hamilton, Ontario
d. 1/2/1962, Chicago, Illinois

Cecil "Babe" Dye played many sports as a youth and was a top athlete at the Jesse Ketchum School in Toronto. Despite Dye's smallish frame, he was a superb football player and would become a star halfback for the CFL's Toronto Argonauts before turning professional with the green and white livery of the

Babe Dye

Toronto St. Patricks hockey club in late 1919. Connie Mack offered Dye a $25,000 bonus to sign with the Philadelphia Athletics baseball club, but Dye's first love was hockey.

Although the arrogant and cocky Dye had difficulty breaking into the St. Patricks lineup in 1919–20, he managed to score 11 goals in 23 games. He began the following season with the Hamilton Tigers but was back in Toronto lickety-split.

In 1920–21, he turned it around and led the NHL in scoring with 35 goals in 24 games. The following year, he scored 11 goals in seven playoff matches to lead the St. Patricks to the Stanley Cup. In all, Dye scored 202 times in 271 games. He topped the league in goal-getting three times and in points twice. Between 1921 and 1925 he twice scored five goals in a game, and on two occasions he had 11-game scoring streaks.

Dye was a slow skater but could thread a needle with his bullet-like shot. Charlie Querrie, who coached and managed Dye in Toronto, claimed he knew Dye would score a goal as soon as the puck hit the winger's stick. Once, at the tail-end of a practice at the old Mutual Street Arena in Toronto, he proved it. Showing off for a group of young rink rats who were hanging around, he lined up three pucks on the ice and took dead-aim at a clock off at one end of the ice. He missed with his first shot, and hit it with his second and third shots, smashing the clock to pieces!

Dye's days in Toronto ended in October 1926 when Querrie sold him to the Chicago Black Hawks, where he continued his goal-scoring ways, potting 25 goals in 41 games. At 1927 training camp in Winnipeg he sustained a compound leg fracture. Although he would appear in 10 games in 1927–28, he was clearly out of form. After failed comeback attempts in New York and Toronto, he retired with the NHL's highest goals-per-game average up to that point.

Dye had brief minor-league coaching stints in St. Louis and Chicago before joining a large Chicago paving contract firm as a foreman. He worked steadily until his death in January 1962.

In 1970 Dye became a worthy member of the Hockey Hall of Fame.

Peak Years   *1921–25*
Comparable Recent Player   *Brett Hull*
In a Word   *BAZOOKA*

FRANK FINNIGAN (The Shawville Express/The Slumbering Romeo) Right Wing
5'9" 165
b. 7/9/1903, Shawville, Quebec
d. 12/25/1991, Ottawa, Ontario

Prior to becoming a professional hockey player, Frank Finnigan worked as a Bell Canada lineman in Pontiac County, Quebec. The young buck was up a telephone pole working when a long-distance call from Ottawa was made to him at a Chinese restaurant on Main Street. Senators owner Frank Ahearn wanted to talk terms. Someone ran out of the restaurant to tell Finnigan the news. The lineman signed an $1,800 contract in February 1924, a figure that grew to $3,400 with bonuses.

Finnigan made his debut with Ottawa as a substitute, which in those days meant bench-warming duty. Only when oldsters Frank Nighbor and Cy Denneny reached the end of the road in 1927 did Finnigan begin to see any ice-time. That year, "Finny" starred for the highly favored Senators as they defeated the Boston Bruins for the Stanley Cup after a bloody playoff.

Finnigan was as talented as he was tough. "Ah, Frankie," King Clancy once sighed. "He used to come in well before every game and unwind the tape from around his hockey stick. Then he would take the skate-sharpener and sharpen the edges of his stick carefully, put the tape back on, and go out and play. He never used more than one stick a year!" Finnigan was an ox-strong skater who strode in a low crouch. He was hard to knock off his feet. He became one of the finest defensive forwards of his generation, a master shadower. Later on in Finnigan's career, Leafs coach Dick Irvin commented that if he had a team of Finnigans, he'd never lose.

By 1927–28, Finnigan was a regular on a line with Nighbor and Hec Kilrea. In 1931, Finnigan was claimed by the Toronto Maple Leafs in the dispersal draft held after the cash-strapped Senators organization shut down. In 1931–32, the hard-drinking Irishman contributed to another Cup victory. After only one season in Toronto, he was returned to Ottawa. He battled on with his beloved Senators until the franchise was moved to St. Louis in 1934; his contract was then transferred to the Eagles. He landed back in Toronto in February 1935, where he rounded out his career.

Finnigan spent the rest of days at the same McLeod Street dwelling in downtown Ottawa. Just before his death on Christmas Day 1991, Finnigan lent his support and inspiration to the NHL resurrection of the Ottawa Senators. After he passed away, the franchise was reborn and his old jersey number was immediately retired.

Peak Years   *1927–31*
Comparable Recent Player   *Mike Peca*
In a Word   *SPARK*

JAKE FORBES (Jumping Jakie) Goal
5'6" 140
b. 7/4/1897, Toronto, Ontario
d. Deceased

Verner "Jake" Forbes opened his junior amateur-level hockey career in 1916 with the OHA's Toronto Aura Lees before graduating to the senior amateur Toronto Goodyears. Forbes turned professional in time for the 1919–20 campaign with the Toronto St. Patricks. Backing this young franchise were the likes of Reg Noble, Babe Dye, and Corb Denneny. Forbes and this edition of the St. Patricks made it as far as the semifinals in 1921 before being ousted by the Ottawa Senators.

Forbes was a participant in one of the most bitter contract disputes in NHL history. The acrobatic little goalie engaged in hostilities with Toronto brass just before the 1921–22 season. Contract talks grew so desperate that management finally threw up their hands and went to "Plan B" — they suspended Forbes and replaced him with John Roach (the St. Patricks went on to win the Stanley Cup). With compromise an impossibility, Toronto traded Forbes to the Hamilton Tigers. The little fellow put in two miserable seasons in the Steel City before posting a 19-10-1 record with six shutouts and a 1.96 goals-against average in 1924–25. The effort was wasted, though, as the Hamilton players moved to strike before the playoffs. League president Frank Calder suspended the whole team and, inside of a few months, the franchise was moved to New York and renamed the Americans.

Forbes played often and well for crime boss Bill Dwyer's Americans. Roy Worters took over the starting position in 1928–29. Forbes would spend the next few years between the majors and minors, making stops in New Haven, Providence, and Springfield. He played 11 games for the IAHL Syracuse club in 1935–36 before deciding to call it a career.

Forbes is a forgotten star. Granted, he wasn't the top goalie in the game, but he certainly was colorful. The little fellow played on some interesting teams and lit the imaginations of the fans with his acrobatics between the pipes.

Peak Years   *1924–28*
Comparable Recent Player   *Mike Richter*
In a Word   *ZESTY*

FRANK FREDERICKSON Center
5'11" 180
b. 6/11/1895, Selkirk, Manitoba
d. 4/28/1979, Toronto, Ontario

Big Frank Frederickson received his first pair of skates at age five. One winter his father flooded their Winnipeg backyard to encourage the neighborhood children to play hockey.

At first, young Frank could speak only Icelandic. He learned *Frank Frederickson* English well enough to earn entry into the University of Manitoba, where he played center on the varsity ice hockey team and violin in a dance band. Then World War One interrupted his life. The fearless young man joined the Royal Flying Corps and became a fighter pilot. On the way back to England from Egypt, his transport ship was torpedoed by a German submarine. The future hockey star was left floating on a life-raft in the Mediterranean for 12 hours wearing pajamas and clutching his cherished violin. He was saved by a rescue boat, surviving to learn the game of hockey.

After a star performance with Canada's gold medal–winning Winnipeg Falcons at the 1920 Olympic Games in Antwerp, Frederickson returned to Winnipeg to play violin in a band at the Fort Garry Hotel. But Lester Patrick had other plans for the budding musician. One night, the PCHA bigwig parked himself in the hotel ballroom, wooing and cajoling the big fellow to no avail. It was only when Patrick requested "Ain't We Got Fun" that Frederickson reluctantly agreed to skate for the Victoria Cougars.

Frederickson twinkled in Victoria. In 1922–23, he led the Cougars to the playoffs for the first time in nine years. Frank finished first overall in league scoring with a record 55 points in 30 games. The tall Icelander continued to be one of the top stars in Canada until the collapse of the WHL in 1926, when he was snapped up by the NHL's Detroit Cougars. After only 16 games in the Motor City, he was shipped to the Boston Bruins with Harry Meeking in exchange for Duke Keats and Archie Briden. After a stint in Pittsburgh, Frederickson returned to Detroit, where he closed out his career.

In 324 professional games, Frederickson scored 168 goals and 266 points. He was elected to the Hockey Hall of Fame in 1958.

Peak Years *1921–25*
In a Word *ACE*

LIONEL HITCHMAN (Hitch) Defense
6'0" 167
b. 11/3/1901, Toronto, Ontario
d. 1/12/1969

Lionel Hitchman, a former RCMP officer, joined the Ottawa Senators toward the end of the 1923 season, in which he helped his team win a Stanley Cup. He became a regular on the Senators defense the following season after the premature retirement of Eddie Gerard due to a bout with throat cancer. Art Ross purchased Hitchman in early 1925 to bolster the Boston Bruins' inaugural roster, which was quite weak on all sides. That first year in Boston, the big defenseman teamed with Red Stuart. Prior to the 1926–27 campaign, Hitchman was joined by the great Eddie Shore, who would be his defense partner until after the 1933–34 season.

Hitchman and Shore formed the backbone of mighty Boston teams from the late 1920s to early 1930s. They became one of the more formidable defense pairings ever. While Shore was leading bulldog rushes and bashing opponents around, Hitchman was the reliable, responsible defender. While not incapable of leading the odd rush, he knew his role and played it well.

One of Hitchman's old teammates, Dit Clapper, thought Hitchman to be one of the most unusual hockey players he ever laid eyes on. Opponents carved Hitchman's face up so frequently that it came to resemble a relief map of Alberta. But Hitchman rarely retaliated. Clapper laughed at how Hitchman would get cut "accidentally" and cluck-cluck to himself later about his carelessness in leaving his face in the path of an opponent's stick. Once during a playoff game against the Maroons, Hooley Smith broke Hitchman's jaw. At the start of the next period, the big guy skated out onto the ice wearing a jaw-brace and a football helmet. This did little to stop nasty Nels Stewart from clubbing poor Lionel over the head so hard he split his head open. Hitchman commented from the hospital bed after the game: "It was just an accident. I got my head in the road of Stewart's stick."

Hitchman was a durable warrior and one of the game's steadiest defensive forces. The Boston mainstay was a top-notch hitter who always played it clean.

Peak Years   *1926–30*
In a Word   *LUG*

DICK IRVIN (Dead-Eye Dick) Center
5'9" 162
b. 7/19/1892, Hamilton, Ontario
d. 5/16/1957, Montreal, Quebec

James Dickenson Irvin was born in a small village about a mile and a half south of Hamilton, Ontario, in the summer of 1892. The Irvins moved to Winnipeg in 1899, settling in the north end of the city. A young Irvin skated with his friends on the Red River and before long was the top hockeyist of Winnipeg's corner rinks. Junior amateur hockey wasn't organized in western Canada at that time, so the boys formed teams and challenged clubs from other parts of the city. Irvin first attracted the attention of the hockey world in 1908 as a center with the McDougall Lion Methodist church. A year later, he was starring for Machray School, showing himself to be a wizard with the puck.

Irvin's first team in major competitive hockey was the Winnipeg Strathcona junior amateurs, which had no league to play in but which took on challenges from all comers. In 1913, he moved to the senior amateur level with the Winnipeg Monarchs, contributing brilliantly to an Allan Cup victory in 1915. He stayed with the powerhouse Monarchs for another season before turning professional with the PCHA's Portland Rosebuds. The 24-year-old was an immediate sensation in the majors, notching 35 goals and 45 points in finishing fourth overall in league scoring. After a year of military service and a two-season stint with Regina's SSHL club, he re-entered the pro ranks with the WCHL Regina Capitals. The Caps took the title in 1921–22 but by 1925–26 the team had relocated to Portland as the Rosebuds. In 1925 Irvin tied Saskatoon's Bill Cook for the newly named WCHL lead in goal with 31.

After the WHL closed up shop in 1926, Irvin joined the Chicago Black Hawks. That first season, he was given the captaincy of the young Hawks and responded by finishing second overall in league scoring with 18 goals and 36 points. Not long after the beginning of the 1927–28 campaign, he suffered a fractured skull at the hands of Red Dutton. He came back for the 1928–29 season, but hung up his skates at the end of the season, saying he'd "had enough of the playing end of things."

Irvin began his long and storied coaching career in Chicago in 1930. His revolutionary approach of revolving three fresh forward units in a game attracted the attention of Conn Smythe. The Leafs boss had just finished building a new rink and wanted to make a fresh start. Irvin was just the man for the job, and Smythe wasted no time in snapping him up. Irvin cut his coaching teeth with the Maple Leafs of the 1930s. He won a Stanley Cup in 1932. Frequent verbal clashes with Smythe over team direction would take its toll on the fiery skipper. After the 1940 Cup finals, he tendered his resignation, but he wasn't out of work for long.

Irvin joined Montreal, guiding a blend of young and old players to a level of success the franchise hadn't seen for quite some time. Players like Maurice Richard, Elmer Lach, Toe Blake, and Bill Durnan worked hard for Irvin as the Canadiens took the Cup in 1944 and again in 1946. The wily old bird had returned the Flying Frenchmen to their perch atop the NHL heap. He coached the Habs to a Cup win in 1953, then turned the coaching reins over to Blake. Irvin then coached Chicago again in 1955–56, and retired for good due to illness in 1956. He passed away the following spring.

In 249 professional hockey games, Dick Irvin managed 153 goals and 215 points. He became a member of the Hockey Hall of Fame in 1958.

Peak Years *1922–26*
Comparable Recent Player   *Joe Nieuwendyk*
In a Word   *SLITHERING*

AUREL JOLIAT (Mighty Mite/The Mighty Atom/The Little Giant) Left Wing
5'7" 138
b. 8/29/1901, Ottawa, Ontario
d. 6/2/1986, Ottawa, Ontario

Aurel Joliat proved that a small man can hold his own in hockey by becoming one of the finest left wingers ever to play. For 16 seasons, the little man soared up and down left wing with the Montreal Canadiens. Though one of the greatest of the Flying Frenchmen, Joliat wasn't a French Canadian but the son of a Swiss Protestant who immigrated to Ottawa at the turn of the century.

Joliat embarked on an NHL career in 1922–23 beside Billy Boucher and the inimitable Howie Morenz. Although some have considered Joliat lucky to have had Morenz as his center for 11 years, others have seen Joliat as the catalyst. Morenz himself praised his winger: "If it wasn't for Joliat, you wouldn't be writing about me so much."

Joliat was an exceedingly tricky and agile skater, a winger so fast and so small he was difficult to hit. He didn't have a hard shot (Tiny Thompson once said Joliat couldn't break a pane of glass with it) but it was accurate. Joliat scored 284 goals in 708 regular-season and playoff contests. This master stick-handler could fade away from checkers like a wraith. But he was best known for his bullet-like speed. Babe Dye of the Toronto St. Patricks once skated over to the Montreal bench and screamed at owner Leo Dandurand: "I'm tired of chasing that shadow of yours, that Frenchman, Joliat. Move him to center, Leo, hold a mirror to each side of him, and you'll have the fastest line in hockey."

Joliat always wore a peaked black cap on the ice and beware to the fool who ever knocked it off his head! One of the most important bits of advice veteran skaters gave NHL rookies was "Whatever you do, don't touch Joliat's cap!"

Joliat's approach to the game attracted a good deal of attention, much of it negative. Montreal Maroons star Hooley Smith carried on a feud with the little Canadien for years. Once, having had enough of Smith, Joliat said: "Just as I was chasing Smith over the boards this chief of police, who had a seat along the edge, grabbed me by the shoulders. I reached over and dragged him right out on the ice, and tore his coon coat right off his back. Only fight I ever won."

Joliat, a three-time Stanley Cup winner, was selected to the First All-Star Team in

1931 and to the Second Team in 1932, 1934, and 1935. In 1934, he took home the Hart Trophy. A big night was held for him in 1935 for his 500th career NHL game. Two seasons later, the return of Morenz and the resurrection of the Joliat-Morenz-Johnny Gagnon combination was cheered vigorously. After Morenz died, Montreal replaced him with Paul Haynes, but Joliat had begun to lose his legs. After a season of short, sluggish shifts, he retired. Years later, however, he angrily charged that the Canadiens had "fired" him, forcing him out of uniform before he was ready to go.

Joliat took a head coaching stint with senior amateur teams in Verdun and Valleyfield and served as an NHL linesman for two years before quitting due to arthritis. From there, he opened up and ran a grocery store in Montreal's west end before closing up shop and taking a job as a license inspector for the Quebec Liquor Commission. He returned home to Ottawa in the late 1940s, where he took a job as a ticket agent for the Canadian National Railway, where he worked until his death in 1986.

In 654 games, Joliat scored 270 goals and 460 points. He was inducted into the Hockey Hall of Fame in 1947.

Peak Years *1924–28*
In a Word *VIM*

DUKE KEATS Center
5'11" 195
b. 3/1/1895, Montreal, Quebec
d. 1/16/1971

Duke Keats

The late Frank Patrick once said that Keats was "the brainiest pivot that ever strapped on a skate because he could organize plays and make passes every time he start[ed] up ice." Keats uncannily could figure out how a play was going to work before it even happened (a gift that has often been attributed to Wayne Gretzky).

By age 14, Gordon Keats was tearing up the Cobalt Mining League on the O'Brien Mines team. In the wake of his storied stints in Haileybury and Peterborough, the professional teams started to remember his name. After a while, people were coming from all over to sneak a peek at hockey's newest wunderkind. Keats received offers from every professional hockey town in the country. He signed in the fall of 1915 with the Toronto Blueshirts. In 1915–16, his rookie season, the tall and muscular lad was stuffed in between Corb and Cy Denneny, a unit that would become the highest scoring in the NHA that season. Keats lived up to his billing, scoring 22 goals and 29 points in 24 games.

Before the start of the next season, Keats and several other pro players enlisted for military duty with the famous 228th Battalion. The big center was slated to play with the Battalion in the NHA in 1916–17, but Blueshirts' owner Eddie Livingstone had other ideas. He successfully appealed, and Keats played with his club until the 228th went overseas, in February of 1917.

After returning from military service, Keats played amateur hockey in Edmonton, remaining with the Eskimos through the club's entry into the new Western Canada Hockey League in 1921–22. The big fellow shredded opposing WCHL defenses that season to the tune of 31 goals and 55 points in 25 games.

Keats hit his peak in Edmonton. The "Iron Duke," hailed on all sides as one of the most dominating forces ever seen, was the best player in the league. Throngs of people clamored to see this big, strong center perform miracles with the puck. He shot as well as anyone anywhere, combining unparalleled offensive ability with a hard, clean style to become the greatest player to play in Edmonton before Gretzky.

Keats played a big role in bringing the title to Edmonton in 1922–23, though his team was bested by the mighty Ottawa Senators in the Stanley Cup finals, during which Punch Broadbent shadowed Keats like a wet horse blanket. Keats carried on in Edmonton until the collapse of the WHL in 1926, upon which his rights were sold to the Boston Bruins. Over the next few years, he played in Boston, Detroit, and Chicago. Early in the 1928–29 campaign, Keats entered into a dispute with Black Hawks owner Frederic McLaughlin and left the team. He flew south and agreed to a fat contract with the Tulsa Oilers of the American Hockey Association.

Keats returned to Edmonton in 1932–33 intent on starting a new professional hockey league out west. He retired as a player after two seasons.

In 256 games in two leagues, the Iron Duke scored 184 goals and 279 points. He was inducted into the Hockey Hall of Fame in 1958. He remained a hockey icon across western Canada until his death in 1971.

Peak Years *1921–25*
Comparable Recent Player   *Keith Primeau*
In a Word   *IRON*

MICKEY MacKAY (the Wee Scot) Center/Right Wing
5'9" 162
b. 5/25/1894, Chesley, Ontario
d. 5/21/1940, Nelson, B.C.

When discussing the best stick-handlers of all time, many names spring to mind — Mario Lemieux, Denis Savard, Jean Beliveau, Gilbert Perreault. But don't forget Mickey MacKay. Duncan McMillan "Mickey" MacKay was an expert handler of the disc during his 16-year career. He still tops the PCHA's all-time scoring list with 290 points in 247 games. And although he rivaled the great Cyclone Taylor as the best in the West, MacKay has drifted into obscurity.

A product of Chesley, Ontario, MacKay got a flying start with the Chesley Colts before moving up to senior amateur hockey in Edmonton and Grand Forks, British Columbia. While playing with Grand Forks in 1913, young MacKay had an idea there were better things in store for him. MacKay wrote Frank Patrick, telling the PCHA bigwig he wanted to turn professional with the Vancouver Millionaires. Patrick, who often received such letters, wrote MacKay back, suggesting he try hooking up with Toronto or some other club closer to home. He advised MacKay get in touch with Jimmy Murphy, who was handling Toronto at the time. But fortune was with the young man.

"I don't know what made me change my mind," Patrick later said, "but I sent a following letter with [money for?] transportation and told him to report to Vancouver. It was one of those sixth sense hunches." MacKay put on an exhibition of his soon-to-be trademark skating and fancy stick-to-puck skills in practice that morning, after which the young whiz kid signed on the dotted line.

In 1914–15, his first professional campaign, MacKay took the league by storm, potting 33 goals and 44 points in 17 games. The rookie finished second behind Taylor for the scoring crown. MacKay played 11 of his first 12 seasons in Vancouver. In that span, through 1925–26, he was the league's top goal-getter three times, an impressive feat considering his competition — Taylor, Bernie Morris, Tom Dunderdale, Frank Foyston, and Frank Frederickson. An offensive genius, MacKay was a clean and gentlemanly player and a fine defensive forward, who was often asked to play rover so he could poke check to frustration.

In 1926, MacKay traveled east to join the NHL with the Chicago Black Hawks. In true form, the aging superstar was his club's leading scorer the following year. After a handful of games in Pittsburgh, MacKay moved on to Boston, where he would close out his marvellous career.

The "Wee Scot" died in a car accident near Nelson, British Columbia, at age 45. Said Frank Patrick afterwards: "MacKay was perhaps the greatest center we ever had on the coast."

MacKay became a member of the Hockey Hall of Fame in 1952.

Peak Years *1919–23*
Comparable Recent Player *Alexander Mogilny*
In a Word *MICHELANGELO*

HOWIE MORENZ (The Stratford Streak/The Mitchell
   Meteor) Center
5'9" 165
b. 6/21/1902, Mitchell, Ontario
d. 3/8/1937, Montreal, Quebec

Howie Morenz

Within a year of buying the Montreal Canadiens in 1921, Leo Dandurand got to work rebuilding his club. First, he dealt an aging Newsy Lalonde to the Saskatoon Crescents in exchange for Aurel Joliat. A year later, Dandurand signed a shy boy from southwestern Ontario to fill Lalonde's enormous shoes. The young prospect's name was Howarth Morenz.

The boy who would be voted Canada's outstanding hockey player of the first half-century in 1950 got his start on the frozen lakes around his hometown. Dandurand heard about "this Morenz kid" from some of his scouts and decided to take a closer look. The Canadiens boss couldn't believe his eyes! Morenz started with the Flying Frenchmen in 1923–24, making an immediate impact in a Stanley Cup win. Morenz made a breakthrough in his sophomore season, scoring 27 times in 30 games and finishing second on the team in scoring.

Morenz's incredible speed and incendiary offensive skills whipped crowds everywhere into chaotic joy. His incredible skating ability gave him the illusion of gliding on air. Although players like King Clancy accelerated faster than Morenz, no one could outpace him once he got going. His bullish play led to a string of minor injuries and the premature wear on his once-iron skating legs.

In 1927–28, Morenz won the first of his three Hart trophies with 33 goals and 51 points in 43 games. By then, his star had helped sell the sport in America, where he was titled the "Babe Ruth of Hockey." In 1931, he won his second Hart.

Over the years, the list of Morenz's injuries grew. In 1933–34, he missed a month's action with a badly sprained ankle, and when he returned he was used sparingly. In the playoffs that year, he broke his thumb and hurt his wrist. It was the beginning of the end. Dandurand sent Morenz to the Chicago Black Hawks.

In early 1936, Morenz was shipped to the New York Rangers. He was still a very spirited player for the team, despite being past his prime. He would round out the 1935–36 campaign on Broadway before being returned to his beloved Canadiens.

On the night of January 28, 1937, the old magic had returned. Morenz was flying around the rink, a half-smile on the face as he charged to and fro. On a rush into the Chicago zone, he was knocked off-balance by defenseman Earl Seibert and flew hard into the boards. The sound of Morenz's leg snapping could be heard high up into the stands.

In St. Luke's Hospital in Montreal, he put on a clown face for the fans while privately despairing that his hockey-playing days were over. He told his linemate and friend Aurel Joliat that he would never play again and, pointing upwards, that he would watch his Canadiens "from up there." Morenz died on March 8, 1937, from a coronary embolism, though many have said he died of a broken heart. The turnout at the funeral the following week was tremendous. The casket was placed at center ice in the Montreal Forum. Tens of thousands came to pay their final respects to their beloved "Stratford Streak," hockey's most electrifying performer.

In 550 games, Morenz scored 270 goals and 467 points. He deservedly became a member of the Hockey Hall of Fame in 1945.

Peak Years   *1926–30*
Comparable Recent Player   *Pavel Bure*
In a Word   *STARBURST*

FRANK NIGHBOR (Dutch/The Pembroke Peach) Center
5'9" 160
b. 1/26/1893, Pembroke, Ontario
d. 4/13/1966, Pembroke, Ontario

Frank Nighbor

No one was as much admired as the jewel of a team's hockey crown as Frank Nighbor was with the Ottawa Senators.

Nighbor was an effortless skater, a master of setting up smooth combination plays with his wingers. Ottawa fans cheered when they saw their "Pembroke Peach" skating back-wards and waving his stick like a magic wand just before he thwarted the opposition with a sweet, perfectly precise poke- or hook-check. He was the first-ever recipient of the Lady Byng trophy in 1925. A year earlier, he bagged the first-ever Hart Trophy. This eminently stylish center was a crafty goal-scorer and a phenomenal play-maker. He was one of the original and best stick-check artists. Nighbor played hockey in his home-town of Pembroke, Ontario, and in Port Arthur before turning professional with the Toronto Blueshirts in 1912. He made an immediate impact in his rookie season, scor-ing 25 goals in 19 games. The following year, he joined the PCHA's Vancouver Millionaires, and in 1914–15 was thrown beside Mickey MacKay and Cyclone Taylor. This treacherous trio would lead Vancouver to a Stanley Cup romp over the Senators. Nighbor signed with Ottawa in 1915 and became a hockey icon.

A flawless play-maker and defensive factor, Nighbor was also a talented and prolif-ic goal-scorer. He twice scored six goals in a game, and five in a game twice. In 1917 Nighbor dented the twine in 11 consecutive games. He tied sniper Joe Malone for the scoring lead with 41 goals in 1916–17 before finishing among the new NHL's scoring leaders in each of the next few seasons.

Nighbor's Senators blossomed into the NHL's best team of the 1920s, a powerhouse that would win the Cup in 1920, 1921, 1923, and 1927. Despite this success, the Senators organization was losing money. In early 1930, Nighbor was traded to the Toronto Maple Leafs. It would be the old smoothie's last year in the NHL.

"I roomed with Frank in Ottawa, who was then regarded as the greatest hockey player in the world," teammate King Clancy gushed. "What a great thrill it was for me to be with a player of that stature. It was enough to be playing on the same team with him, but rooming with him — that was something else! Nobody could handle a hockey stick like Frank Nighbor."

In 438 games in two leagues, Nighbor scored 255 goals and 366 points. He was elected to the Hockey Hall of Fame in 1947.

Peak Years   *1918–22*
In a Word   *CRAFTSMAN*

REG NOBLE (Old Sarge) Center/Left Wing/Defense
5'8" 180
b. 6/23/1896, Collingwood, Ontario
d. 1/19/1962, Alliston, Ontario

Reg Noble

Championships seemed to follow Reg Noble wherever he went. His hockey career opened at Collingwood Business College in the early 1910s. He moved on to the town's junior amateur club, helping it win the OHA title in 1914–15. He spent the following season with the Toronto Riversides, who themselves took the OHA senior-level championship. He made the jump to the pros with the Toronto Blueshirts in 1916 but the team disbanded partway through the 1916–17 season. The hard-skating, hard-drinking left winger was claimed by the Montreal Canadiens, but it was ruled that he had arrived too late to play for them in the Cup playoffs that year.

The NHL was organized in the fall of 1917. Noble was dressed in the Toronto Arenas colors. With the NHA reorganizing, the Canadiens had chosen not to retain Noble's playing rights. Toronto snapped him up in December 1917. Noble scored 30 times in 20 games that year and was a major factor in the team's Cup win the following spring.

Noble was a difficult player to handle. He was a free spirit who preferred to do things his own way on and off the ice. Noble received many fines and suspensions for breaking training and other indiscretions, but the scrappy hard rock carried on in Toronto. Noble, who toiled alongside the likes of stars such as Babe Dye, Corb Denneny, Jack Adams, and Duke Keats, helped the St. Patricks (formerly the Arenas) win another Cup in 1922.

After playing only three games for the St. Patricks in 1924–25, Noble was sold to the fledgling Montreal Maroons for $8,000. Maroons' owner James Strachan had always admired Noble and was convinced the veteran could provide the kind of leadership his young team needed. Taking advantage of Noble's fine stick-handling skills and positional hockey instincts, coach Eddie Gerard moved the fan favorite to defense with Dunc Munro. Noble helped the Maroons win their first-ever Stanley Cup in 1925–26.

After another season in Montreal, Noble was sold to Detroit for $7,500. The thick, grizzled 37-year-old would lead a young Cougars/Falcons defense for the next five seasons. In December 1932, he was traded back to the Maroons, where he finished his NHL career the following April.

Reg Noble was inducted into the Hockey Hall of Fame in 1962.

Peak Years   *1921–25*
Comparable Recent Player   *Rick Tocchet*
In a Word   *SALTY*

HARRY OLIVER (Pee Wee/Go-Go) Right Wing/Center
5'8" 155
b. 10/26/1898, Selkirk, Manitoba
d. 6/16/1985, Winnipeg, Manitoba

Harry Oliver was introduced to the game of hockey on the ponds near Selkirk, Manitoba. "When I was a kid, there was no organized hockey," he said just before his death. "We just went out and played, sometimes on an outdoor rink, but mostly on the river."

In an era when a small man could finesse his way to professional hockey, Oliver was considered to be in a class by himself. He moved with the speed and grace of a greyhound. Always the perfect gentleman on and off the ice, Oliver never smoked or drank and was always dressed to the nines. As a skills player, he let the likes of Red Dutton, Eddie Shore, Billy Coutu, and Sprague Cleghorn do the fighting for him, amassing only 215 minutes in penalties over 16 seasons in the NHL and the WCHL.

In 1926–27, his first in the NHL, Oliver led the Boston Bruins in scoring. In the 1927 playoffs, he starred on a line with former western-league ace Frank Frederickson and hard-working Perk Galbraith. Boston made it all the way to the finals, only to lose to the Ottawa Senators in a bloody series. Oliver experienced Cup glory in 1929.

Oliver, with linemates Marry Barry and Galbraith, softened up the opposition for the Dynamite Line, Dit Clapper, Cooney Weiland, and Dutch Gainor. In November 1934, a 34-year-old Oliver was auctioned off to the New York Americans for an undisclosed amount of cash. After spending three relatively uneventful seasons in New York, he called it a career.

Oliver became a member of the Hockey Hall of Fame in 1967.

Peak Years   1924–28
In a Word   DAINTY

KEN RANDALL Right Wing/Defense
5'10" 180
b. Kingston, Ontario
d. DECEASED

Among the most rough and uncut characters to grace the pages of hockey history was Ken Randall. He played in three different leagues in his first three seasons before trying out unsuccessfully with the NHA Toronto Blueshirts, who sent him to Sydney, Nova Scotia, to play in the Maritime League in the 1912–13 season. He returned to the NHA with Toronto in 1915 and moved on to the Wanderers in 1917. The tomato-faced Irishman signed on with Toronto in time for the 1917–18 season, in which he scored 12 goals in 19 games. In the spring of 1918, the Arenas took the Stanley Cup. Randall collected a whopping 33 minutes in penalties in seven games.

Randall was frequently in trouble with NHL brass. One incident, in February 1918, occurred after he finished serving a one-week suspension for quarreling with officials. Just before the start of a Toronto–Ottawa match on February 23, Arenas boss Charlie Querrie was told that Randall's suspension had been lightened to a $15 fine and that he would be permitted to play, provided he settled back fines totaling $35. Of course, Randall forked over the dough — $32 in bills and the remaining three bucks in pennies. The officials turned their noses up at the copper. Randall then filled a bag with the pennies and threw it out to center ice. An Ottawa player smashed open the bag with his stick. Players from both teams had to gather up every one of the pennies, which were scattered from net to net, and Randall was forced to produce the three dollars in bills.

In 1922, Randall was on another Cup-winner, splitting his time between the blueline and right wing on a line with Reg Noble and Babe Dye. Randall was a chunky, barrel-chested pug, prone to weight fluctuations. But for a big man, he could hustle. He handled the puck well and had a good shot. His best offensive season in the NHL came in 1918–19, when he scored nine goals and 15 points in 15 games for the Arenas.

Randall was shuffled off to Hamilton in late 1923, where he was slated to be the Tigers' player-coach. Early on, though, he showed himself to be unsuited to the coaching life and was soon replaced by Percy LeSueur. Randall was on another title-winner in 1924–25 but a failed player strike killed his shot at Lord Stanley's Cup.

Randall was a colorful slam-bang hockeyist, the kind of bulldog every coach wants in the dressing room. Although he has not been enshrined in the Hockey Hall of Fame, he was nonetheless one of the top hockey players in the new NHL.

Peak Years *1918–22*
Comparable Recent Player *Kevin Stevens*
In a Word *HOOLIGAN*

JOHN ROSS ROACH (The Port Perry Woodpecker/Little Napoleon) Goal
5'5" 130
b. 6/23/1900, Port Perry, Ontario
d. 7/9/1973, Detroit, Michigan

Small, skittish John Ross Roach opened his NHL career with the Toronto St. Patricks in 1921 and was on a Stanley Cup winner in his rookie season. After seven uneventful seasons in Toronto, Roach and Butch Keeling were shipped off to the New York Rangers in exchange for Lorne Chabot, Alex Gray, and $10,000.

In Roach's first season in New York, he posted a 21-13-10 record, with a 1.41 goals-against average and 13 shutouts. In the 1929 playoffs, he put up three consecutive shutouts before the Blueshirts were vanquished in the finals by the Boston Bruins. With the institution of new forward passing rules in 1929–30, his goals-against average, like that of most other goaltenders, skyrocketed. After leading the league in shutouts in 1931–32 with nine, he was sold to the Detroit Red Wings. In his first year in Motown, Roach was 25-15-8, with a 1.88 GAA and 10 shutouts. Despite being edged out in the Vezina Trophy sweepstakes by Boston's Tiny Thompson, Roach managed to grab a First Team All-Star selection.

"He was one of the real good ones," teammate Ebbie Goodfellow recalled. "He was on the small side, but he was all there. He was awfully good and he had some really good years."

Roach sustained a broken jaw in a car accident during his thirteenth season and coach Jack Adams benched him in favor of a little Welshman by the name of Wilf Cude. Roach's injury was slow in healing and he spent most of the season in the minors. The next season, he suffered two serious facial cuts and retired. He spent the rest of his days working and living in the Detroit area.

Peak Years *1924–28*
Comparable Recent Player *Mike Vernon*
In a Word *WEE*

JACK WALKER (Hookcheck/The Old Fox) Left
    Wing/Right Wing
5'8" 153
b. 11/28/1888, Silver Mountain, Ontario
d. 2/16/1950, Seattle, Washington

Jack Walker

When an unknown hockey team from Port Arthur, Ontario, took a 13–4 drubbing from the Ottawa Senators in a 1911 Stanley Cup challenge, people talked about the outstanding hook-checking of Port Arthur forward Jack Walker. The neat little guy eventually cracked the professional ranks, playing 16 seasons as a world-class hockeyist. Walker played most of his hockey in leagues that pre-dated or rivaled the NHL.

After shuffling between Toronto and Moncton for a season, the slick forward landed in the bigs to stay in time for the 1913–14 NHA season. The old Torontos went on to Cup glory that year, with Walker scoring 20 goals and 36 points in 20 games. He would spend another season in Toronto before flying for the sunnier skies of the PCHA and a new team, the Seattle Metropolitans.

In Seattle, Walker was part of another Cup victory in 1917. Walker spent nine seasons in Seattle as the finest all-around talent on the West Coast. He helped win three league titles, and twice won the Muldoon Trophy as the western circuit's most valuable player.

Walker joined the Victoria Cougars for 1924–25 and figured in yet another Cup win, scoring four goals and two assists in four contests against the Montreal Canadiens. In that series, he shut down superstar Howie Morenz.

When the WCHL folded in 1926, Walker's rights were transferred to the Detroit Cougars. He would play a leadership role in Detroit through 1927–28 before returning to Seattle to play minor-league hockey. After a couple of seasons of hockey in California, he returned to Seattle to manage, coach, and referee games in the Seattle City Hockey League. He made his last public appearance on the ice in 1937 in an old-timers exhibition match in Vancouver.

During his playing days and later as a coach, Walker spent hours helping the rookies, teaching them the art of the hook-check. Walker was as good at poke-checking as Frank Nighbor was.

In 349 professional games, Walker scored 147 goals and 243 points. He became a member of the Hockey Hall of Fame in 1960.

Peak Years   *1917–21*
In a Word   *CLEVER*

The All-Stars

Position	Player	Season	GP	G	A	Pts
D	George Boucher	1921–22	23	13	12	25
D	Red Dutton	1927–28	42	7	6	13
LW	Aurel Joliat	1927–28	44	28	11	39
C	Howie Morenz	1927–28	43	33	18	51
RW	Babe Dye	1924–25	29	38	6	44
				GAA	**Sho**	
G	Clint Benedict	1923–24	24	2.18	4	

The Thirties

In a Flash

COMPOSITE REGULAR-SEASON STANDINGS
(JANUARY 1, 1930–DECEMBER 31, 1939)

National Hockey League

Club	GP	W	L	T	Pts	WPct	GF	GA
Boston Bruins	476	259	154	63	581	.610	1,353	1,014
Toronto Maple Leafs	477	237	168	72	546	.572	1,367	1,124
New York Rangers	475	217	171	87	521	.548	1,270	1,082
Montreal Maroons	407	173	170	64	410	.504	1,039	1,011
Montreal Canadiens	474	198	198	78	474	.500	1,126	1,189
Detroit Cougars/Falcons/Red Wings	475	194	197	84	472	.497	1,104	1,110
Chicago Black Hawks	474	184	212	78	446	.470	968	1,078
New York Americans	477	159	232	86	404	.423	1,046	1,310
Ottawa/St. Louis	215	60	125	30	150	.349	460	623
Philadelphia/Pittsburgh	72	6	60	6	18	.125	132	303

HELLOS

Steve McQueen *American actor*	April 24, 1930
Jean Beliveau *Canadiens legend*	August 31, 1931
Glenn Gould *Canadian pianist*	September 25, 1932
Michael Landon *American actor/director*	October 31, 1936
Bill Cosby *American comedian*	July 12, 1937
Bobby Hull *Chicago Black Hawk sniper*	January 3, 1939

GOODBYES

Ernst Rohm *Nazi S.A. chief*	July 1934
Didier Pitre *original "Flying Frenchman"*	July 29, 1934
Oliver Wendell Holmes *U.S. Supreme Court judge*	March 6, 1935
Goldie Prodgers *1910s hockey star*	October 25, 1935
Eddie Gerard *original Hockey Hall of Famer*	December 8, 1937
Sigmund Freud *Austrian psychoanalyst*	September 23, 1939

REGULAR SEASON

BEST RECORD
1929–30 Boston Bruins, 38-5-1

WORST RECORD
1930–31 Philadelphia Quakers, 4-36-4

BEST MINOR-LEAGUE RECORDS
1935–36 St. Paul Saints (American Hockey Association), 32-13-3
1936–37 St. Louis Flyers (American Hockey Association), 32-13-3

FAMOUS FIRSTS

PLAYER TO SCORE
250 NHL CAREER GOALS
Howie Morenz, December 28, 1933

PLAYER CREDITED WITH 250 NHL CAREER ASSISTS
Frank Boucher, March 9, 1937

PLAYER TO SCORE
300 NHL CAREER GOALS
Nels Stewart, March 17, 1938

COAST-TO-COAST RADIO BROADCAST OF AN NHL GAME
January 7, 1933, the Detroit Red Wings 6, Toronto Maple Leafs, 7.

NHL GOALTENDER TO REGISTER 75 CAREER SHUTOUTS
George Hainsworth, March 18, 1933

NHL GOALTENDER TO REGISTER 200 CAREER WINS
John Ross Roach, March 9, 1933

NHL ALL-STAR GAME
The Ace Bailey benefit game, held on February 14, 1934

PENALTY SHOT
Taken by Armand Mondou of the Montreal Canadiens, vs. Toronto's George Hainsworth, on November 10, 1934 (Hainsworth stopped him.)

NHL GOALTENDER CREDITED WITH AN ASSIST
Tiny Thompson, Boston, January 14, 1936

MISCELLANEOUS

MOST GOALS, SEASON
43   Cooney Weiland, Boston, 1929–30

MOST GOALS, DECADE
203   Nels Stewart

MOST ASSISTS, SEASON
37   Joe Primeau, Toronto, 1931–32

MOST ASSISTS, DECADE
194   Frank Boucher

MOST POINTS, SEASON
73   Cooney Weiland, Boston, 1929–30

MOST POINTS, DECADE
359   Nels Stewart

COOLEST MIDDLE NAMES
Gus *Solberg* Marker
Russ *Percival* Blinco
Red *Geatrex* Heron
Marty *Alphonsus* Burke

COOLEST HANDLES
Jimmy Fowler, "The Blonde Bouncer"
Bill Carson, "The Stratford Teeth-Puller"
Murray "Mudhooks" Murdoch
Harry "Yip" Foster
Butch Keeling, "The Oil Man of Owen Sound"
Herb "Monkey" Drury
Cecil Dillon, "The Thornbury Teaser"
Ken "Peanut" Doraty
Harold "Baldy" Cotton, "The Cork Screw"
Alex "Mine Boy" Levinsky
Lorne "Sad Eyes" Chabot

BIGGEST PLAYER
Harry "Yip" Foster, 6'6" 198

SMALLEST PLAYER
Roy "Shrimp" Worters, 5'3" 135

BEST SHOT
Charlie Conacher put a few opposing goalies out of commission with his hot, heavy blasts.

BEST PASSER
Joe Primeau

Harvey "Busher" Jackson

BEST STICK-HANDLERS
Johnny Gottselig and Harvey "Busher" Jackson

BEST SKATER
Johnny Sorrell, a speedster as well as an accomplished checker, was Detroit's most valuable player throughout much of the 1930s.

WORST SKATER
Nels Stewart had the flat-out speed of a rusty barge.

FASTEST SKATER
Hec Kilrea was a third-year winger with the Ottawa Senators when he shattered the NHL speed skating record at the Montreal Forum with a time of 16.4 seconds. He hauled in a purse of $400 for his efforts.

BEST SNIPER
Nels Stewart was the original Phil Esposito.

BEST ON-ICE INSTINCTS
Eddie Shore

BEST PENALTY-KILLER
Frank Finnigan. "I'd give anything to have a team of Finnys," Dick Irvin, Sr., said.

BEST BODY-CHECKER
Reginald "Red" Horner made his splash onto the NHL scene in 1929. The former supermarket delivery boy was one of the first true policemen in hockey.

BEST POKE-CHECKER
Frank Boucher had a devastating poke-check, which he learned from Frank Nighbor while the two were teammates in Ottawa.

BEST SHOT-BLOCKER
Lionel Conacher

BEST GOALTENDER
Charlie Gardiner was the first goalie who truly made an art of puck-stopping. He was a risk-taker who made highlight-reel stops. The excitable Scot's frequent sorties away from his crease whipped an already boisterous Chicago crowd into a frenzy, while his on-ice exhortations inspired his teammates to work harder.

BEST GLOVE-HAND (GOALIE)
Charlie Gardiner

FINEST ATHLETE
In 1950, Lionel Conacher would be voted Canada's top athlete of the first half of the twentieth century. He was a standout running back for the Toronto Argonauts as well as a star lacrosse player.

BEST DEFENSIVE FORWARD
Frank Finnigan

WORST DEFENSIVE FORWARD
Nels Stewart

BEST SHADOW
Alfred "Pit" Lepine would have been a first-liner on any NHL team other than the Canadiens. Despite his great all-around ability, he languished in the shadow of a character by the name of Morenz.

BEST DEFENSIVE DEFENSEMAN
Marvin "Cy" Wentworth played for Chicago and the Montreal Maroons and Canadiens, and he was known as one of the finest positional defenders around. He was expert at checking with his stick as well as his body, and he was never known to take a stupid penalty.

BEST OFFENSIVE DEFENSEMAN
Dick Irvin, Sr., said Eddie Shore was the best offensive defenseman he ever saw, although he was never keen on the big bruiser's defensive abilities. Shore was a colossal force in hockey in the 1930s, having as great an effect on the game as Bobby Orr would have some 40 years later.

BEST ALL-AROUND PLAYER
Aubrey "Dit" Clapper was the right wing on Boston's "Dynamite Line" in the early 1930s before switching to defense.

BEST UTILITY PLAYER
Murray Murdoch

STRONGEST PLAYER
Art Coulter was one tough-as-nails SOB, playing hard-nosed hockey despite countless injuries during an 11-year NHL career.

TOUGHEST PLAYER
Eddie Shore

BEST FIGHTER
Murray "Muzz" Patrick was at one time heavyweight boxing champion of the Canadian Armed Forces. One story has him taking apart Boston strong boy Eddie Shore piece by piece.

MOST ABLE INSTIGATOR
Frank "King" Clancy

DIRTIEST PLAYER
Dave Trottier was master of kicking the skates out from under his opponents. This rambunctious Montreal Maroon enjoyed administering the "slewfoot" as much as he delighted in carving up enemy defenders.

CLEANEST PLAYER
Joe Primeau

BEST CORNER-MAN
Lawrence "Baldy" Northcott was one of the league's more eager muckers in his day. Standing six feet tall and weighing over 180 pounds, he was well equipped to do battle with the league's hard-rocks near the fence.

BEST-LOOKING PLAYER
Busher Jackson was one of pro hockey's original playboys. His swagger, athleticism, and good looks served him well in a life of wine, women, and song.

UGLIEST PLAYER
Joe Jerwa

BALDEST PLAYER
Ivan "Ching" Johnson. Ladies and gentlemen, hats off to the baldest player in NHL history!

MOST UNDERRATED PLAYER
Syd Howe was one of the greatest Red Wings ever. This multitalented player, who could play just about any position, was the NHL's all-time scoring leader for a spell.

MOST CONSISTENT PLAYER
Dit Clapper

MOST UNPREDICTABLE CAREER
Lorne Chabot was notorious for his volcanic temper. The towering, beetle-browed netminder was traded so frequently, it seemed (with the exception of a five-year stint in Toronto) as if the former Allan Cup star was on a different NHL club each season.

SMARTEST PLAYER
Frank Boucher

BIGGEST FLAKE
Eddie Shore was equally strange on or off the ice. Once, as a player, he drove from Boston to Montreal through a blizzard, arriving exhausted and half-frostbitten a day later. Miraculously, he made it to the Forum in time to put in a standout performance. When Shore bought the AHL's Springfield Indians, he was the owner, general manager, head coach, equipment manager, trainer, and popcorn vendor. His strict discipline and outlandish training regimens made Springfield a hockey Siberia. He was the NHL's answer to Ty Cobb.

MOST HATED PLAYER
When Eddie Shore dealt a career-ending injury to Ace Bailey in 1933, it abruptly ended any goodwill the Boston defenseman may have enjoyed in the hockey world. Even though Bailey and Shore shook hands some months after the incident, few forgot Shore's brutality and many harbored a grudge against him to the grave.

MOST ADMIRED PLAYER

Charlie Conacher was lionized by young boys across Canada thanks to Foster Hewitt's radio broadcasts.

BEST LINES

Team: Toronto Maple Leafs
LW: Busher Jackson
C: Joe Primeau
RW: Charlie Conacher

Team: New York Rangers
LW: Bun Cook
C: Frank Boucher
RW: Bill Cook

Team: Boston Bruins
LW: Dutch Gainor
C: Cooney Weiland
RW: Dit Clapper

HIGHEST PAID PLAYER

Eddie Shore, $14,000 per season

MOST TRAGIC CAREER

Charlie Gardiner was the game's top goalie in the first half of the 1930s (the Vezina Trophy winner in 1932 and 1934) and had just single-handedly won the Stanley Cup for his Chicago Black Hawks when he died, apparently of a brain tumor, in June 1934.

BIGGEST DISAPPOINTMENT

After graduating from McGill University, **Nels Crutchfield** was traded for the rights to Lionel Conacher and Herbie Cain in 1934. He'd been talked up as being Howie Morenz, Frank Nighbor, and Nels Stewart rolled into one. He sustained career-ending injuries in a September 1935 car accident.

BEST HEAD COACH

Jack Adams. Before the onset of morbid obesity and heart problems, "Jolly Jawn" was a superb bench boss in Detroit. One of his favorite motivational techniques was to walk around the dressing room before a game, with train tickets to Omaha, Nebraska, conspicuously sticking out of his jacket pocket.

BEST GENERAL MANAGER

Tommy Gorman. For years, "Tay Pay" was a top sportswriter in Ottawa before turning his attentions to the Senators' front office. After he built the Bytown powerhouses of the 1920s, Gorman molded the Maroons into a Cup-winner in the mid 1930s and the Hawks in '34.

BEST SPORTSWRITER

D.A.L. McDonald's features in the Montreal *Gazette* about hockey stars at the turn of the century and before were works of art and one of the last remaining links to hockey's infancy.

BEST BROADCASTER

Foster Hewitt. Who else?

BEST MINOR LEAGUE PLAYER

For years, **Hubert "Hub" Nelson** was the top goalie in the minor leagues, starring between the pipes for the St. Louis Flyers and Minneapolis Millers of the American Hockey Association. The New York Rangers and Chicago made several efforts to buy him but the Flyers' front office opted to keep him. He never did play a game in the NHL; the closest he came was backing up Frank Brimsek on the powerful Coast Guard Cutters during World War Two.

BEST STANLEY CUP FINAL

1934 — Chicago Black Hawks vs. Detroit Red Wings
Charlie Gardiner was fabulous in capturing the Cup for a .500 Hawk team.

IMPORTANT RULE CHANGES

1929–30

- Ice divided into three zones: defending, neutral and attacking
- If a player was caught throwing his stick in his own zone, his team was charged with a goal against. Otherwise, the player was assessed a major penalty.
- Teams allowed to dress no more than 15 players for a game

1930–31

- A player who has lost or broken his stick during play is forbidden from taking part in the action until he recovers his lost stick or gets a new one.
- Puck must be shot or carried into attacking zone before another attacker can enter.

1931–32

- "Cherry-picking," — loitering near the opposing net without the puck — is outlawed.
- Defending skaters are not allowed to fall on the puck within 10 feet of their own net.

1932–33

- Each team is required to have a captain on the ice at all times.
- If a goalie is removed from the ice to serve a penalty, the team's coach would appoint a substitute.

1933–34

- No more than two skaters, plus the goalie, are allowed to stand in the defensive zone.
- NHL rinks are required to have a time clock.
- Two referees on the ice, replacing the old complement of one referee and one linesman

1934–35

- Penalty shot introduced

1937–38

- Penalty shot awarded when a player other than the goalie falls on the puck within 10 feet of the net.
- Rules dealing with icing are introduced.

1938–39

- Player taking a penalty shot is permitted to skate before shooting.
- League reverts from two-referee system to one referee and one linesman.

Being for the Benefit of . . .

In recent years, the NHL's All-Star game has degenerated into a TV-friendly goalfest showcasing the league's tremendous offensive talents. But things weren't always thus: the first NHL All-Star game was held in 1947 at Toronto's Maple Leaf Gardens and over the next 20 years, with few exceptions, the events were hard-fought matches between the reigning Stanley Cup champions and the rest of the league's luminaries.

Prior to 1947 hockey had staged a number of All-Star events. Coincidentally, each of these games was set up to raise funds. The first such occasion was in 1908, to benefit the widow of Hodgson "Hod" Stuart, a Hall of Fame defenseman who had died in a swimming accident. In 1915, a team of NHA stars played a team drawn from the Grenadier Guards, and the proceeds aided soldiers heading overseas for World War One. The PCHA held a similar match in 1917. The NHL mounted three such events, all of them in the 1930s.

Ace Bailey Benefit Game, Maple Leaf Gardens, Toronto, February 14, 1934

Irvine "Ace" Bailey was a 5'11", 160-pound right winger who'd won the NHL scoring title in 1928–29. The night of December 12, 1933, would be a fateful one for the "Major Hoople of Bracebridge." During the second period at Boston Garden, Bruin defenseman Eddie Shore was separated from the puck, and none too politely, by King Clancy. Regaining his feet, Shore made a bee-line for Bailey, the first blue sweater he saw, and ran him from behind, sending the Leaf headfirst to the ice.

Bailey was rushed to hospital, where he walked a fine line between life and death for the next few days. He pulled through, after two major operations on his brain, but he would never play hockey again. With his livelihood gone, the NHL and its players moved quickly to help. A game was scheduled between Bailey's former Leaf teammates and an All-Star club, stocked with two players from each of the league's other eight teams. The Leafs wore special blue-and-white uniforms with "ACE" stitched across the front, while the All-Stars wore orange and black jerseys emblazoned with "NHL."

Prior to the game, Bailey made his way to center ice to drop the puck for the ceremonial face-off and he received a standing ovation. In order of their jersey numbers, each of the All-Stars skated over to greet Bailey. The first to do so was Chicago's fabulous netminder, Charlie Gardiner. After he rejoined his teammates, a stony silence fell over the Gardens. Then, No. 2, Eddie Shore, dropped his gloves and stick on the ice and approached Bailey. As the two shook hands — Bailey beaming, Shore with a sheepish smile — the sound of applause and cheering filled the air.

Ace Bailey, Babe Siebert, and Howie Morenz

The game itself saw both teams playing a wide-open, offensive style. By the final buzzer, the Leafs had outshot the All-Stars 52–41. Not unexpectedly, there was also very little hitting — today's hockey fan would have trouble distinguishing this game from a modern All-Star match.

The game started off with Toronto's Baldy Cotton, Bailey's best friend, finishing off a three-man rush with mustachioed Andy Blair and little Ken Doraty. Three minutes later, Busher Jackson took a nifty cross-ice pass from speedy Hec Kilrea and deked Gardiner to make it 2–0 for the Ace-men. Late in the first, the combination of Nels Stewart and Jimmy Ward got the stars back in the game, as Stewart beat Leaf goalie George Hainsworth.

Early in the middle frame, Toronto regained the momentum. Jackson picked up his second of the contest on a long shot from the side. But the All-Stars would not quit. Two quick goals by Howie Morenz and Frank Finnigan knotted the game at three. Only 30 seconds after the score was tied, though, the Leafs' Hap Day rushed down the wing and beat Gardiner to make it 4–3. Four minutes into the third, Jackson jetted up the ice and let fly a shot . . . stopped by Gardiner! Kilrea pounced on the rebound and put it in. Late in the period, Blair picked Ward's pocket in the All-Stars' zone and moved in on goal. Although Gardiner came out to cut down the angle, Blair managed to spot a streaking Doraty, who made it 6–3 for Toronto. With only seconds to play, Blair broke in alone and beat Gardiner for the game's final score.

Besides raising $20,000 for its beneficiary, the Ace Bailey benefit game was met with such enthusiasm in hockey circles that the Toronto *Mail and Empire* reported that "it is likely that it will be the first of a series of annual games." In fact, after the game, Leaf owner Conn Smythe had presented his Leafs with the Ace Bailey Cup. The Toronto boss hoped the trophy would be given to the winner of an annual All-Star game, in which the league's brightest lights would face off against the leader, in alternating years, of each of the league's divisions — American and Canadian. This idea failed to get off the ground, and it would be more than a decade before the All-Star game became an annual event.

Howie Morenz Memorial Game, The Forum, Montreal, November 3, 1937

In his prime, Howarth Morenz, the "Stratford Streak," had no equal in hockey. The ebullient center led the Montreal Canadiens in goals every season between 1924–25 and 1931–32. After slipping during the next two campaigns, he was unexpectedly dealt to the Chicago Black Hawks, where he spent the 1934–35 season. He started 1935–36 with Chicago but was soon dealt to the Rangers for Glen Brydson.

Without Morenz, the Canadiens seemed lost. They brought back their "Mitchell Meteor" in 1936, a move that revitalized the aging speedster's career. Playing between old linemate Aurel Joliat and Johnny "Black Cat" Gagnon, Morenz felt like he was 20 again. But there would be no Hollywood happy ending to this comeback tale. During a game against the Black Hawks on January 28, 1937, Morenz was chasing a loose puck near the boards, pursued by big Earl Seibert. As if struck by lightning, Morenz fell to the ice clutching his leg. It turned out that the point of his skate got stuck in

Frank Finnigan

the boards and he lost his balance, breaking his leg. He was rushed to hospital, where he would remain until his death on March 8 from a heart attack.

Apparently, investments Morenz had made during his player career hadn't panned out, and he left little money for his wife and three children. Again the NHL stepped in. On November 2, 1937, the Howie Morenz memorial game was played at the Montreal Forum. Players from the two Montreal teams, the Canadiens and Maroons, joined forces against stars from the rest of the league. A crowd of nearly 9,000 turned out, raising more than $20,000 for the Morenz clan.

Johnny Gagnon opened the scoring two minutes into the first period on a pass from bespectacled Bishop's University alumnus Russell Blinco. The lead held up for most of the first period until Dit Clapper knotted things up. Minutes later, Johnny Gottselig put the All-Stars ahead to stay. The second period saw only one goal, when Cecil Dillon completed a three-way passing play with Gottselig and big Marty Barry. Early in the third, Pit Lepine brought Montreal back to within one, but a pair of quick goals by Charlie Conacher and Sweeney Schriner spelled the beginning of the end. Barry made it 6–2 at the 15-minute mark. Most teams would have thrown in the towel, but not Montreal. They cut the deficit to three on a Babe Siebert marker. Just 33 seconds later, Siebert set up the next goal, finding Gagnon for his second of the night. With 45 seconds left on the clock, Paul Haynes cut the All-Stars' lead to one with an unassisted effort but the Morenz-men would run out of time, losing 6–5.

Babe Siebert Memorial Game, The Forum, Montreal, October 29, 1939

Albert "Babe" Siebert, the big defender who'd played for the Maroons, Rangers, Bruins, and Habs, was slated to become the head coach of the Canadiens for the 1939–40 season. But the 35-year-old family man drowned in Lake Huron during the summer of '39 while trying to retrieve an inflated inner tube for his daughter. Just a few days before the season opened, a memorial game was held at the Montreal Forum.

The All-Stars flew out of the gate, pressuring Siebert's Canadiens relentlessly. The game quickly became the Syl Apps Show, as the multitalented Toronto pivot scored a goal and assisted on three others to lead the All-Stars to a 5–2 victory over the Frenchmen. Buzzing Bobby Bauer opened the scoring, finishing off a three-way passing play launched by Apps and Johnny Gottselig. Ninety seconds later, Eddie Shore converted an Apps pass to make it 2–0. Apps tipped in a Bauer shot to make it 3–0 early in the second stanza before Earl Robinson got one back for Montreal. Two more goals by the All-Stars made it a 5–1 game. Late in the second, Montreal's Louis Trudel rounded out the scoring.

At the beginning of the final frame, the normally cantankerous Shore began dancing excitedly to the Forum's orchestral music. Urged on by the crowd, Shore "cut a rug" for several minutes, amusing onlookers to no end.

Just a Sec . . .

"The league-leading Philadelphia Arrows plastered a 4–0 defeat tonight on the New Haven Eagles in the last Canadian-American hockey contest for the local sextet. After a tough first period, during which nine penalties were imposed, one a major, the game settled down to a quiet affair. In the third frame Wilf Cude, the Arrows' goaler, left his nets long enough to nail a mouse that scampered across the ice. His 'feat' was applauded boisterously by the women spectators." (Associated Press report, March 28, 1933)

The King of Carlton Street

Special "nights" are no longer all that special, it seems. We have everything from "Retro Night" to "Toga Night" to "Fight Night" to "Shooter Night." On March 17, 1934, though, the Toronto Maple Leafs set a new trend. They resisted the togas, thought nothing of disco balls, and threw something called "Clancy Night."

Francis "King" Clancy was in his 13th season in the NHL, his fourth as a Toronto defender. Leaf management decided it was time to honor Clancy with a special night. Posters advertising the event showed the star's moon-face dominating a rural Irish setting. "The King!" blushes a bonnie lass. "The world's best!" announces a gentleman in a carriage.

Cheesy, yes, but it sold tickets: Maple Leaf Gardens was packed to the rafters. Clancy's father Tom was among those in the stands at 8:30 p.m., waiting for the guest of honor to skate out. The rink was decked out in green and gold, with a large shamrock at center ice. Leaf defenseman Alex Levinsky made his way onto the ice pulling a huge sleigh, upon which sat the King himself! Always the ham, Clancy wore a crown and carried a scepter. His dismount from the royal carriage was greeted with a deafening standing ovation.

The Knights of Columbus presented Clancy with a lovely tea service. The Leaf directors gave him a silver chest. His teammates showed their appreciation by giving him a grandfather clock, while a car dealership plunked a car radio on his lap. Clancy, apparently not wanting the celebration to end, played the entire first period in a green uniform with a white shamrock on the back.

The game itself was a lively one:

King Clancy

Period	Team	Scorer	Assists	Time
1	New York	Earl Seibert	Vic Ripley	5:11
2	Toronto	Red Horner	Buzz Boll, Joe Primeau	4:35
2	Toronto	Buzz Boll	Red Horner, Joe Primeau	5:05
2	New York	Ceece Dillon	Murray Murdoch	13:45
3	Toronto	Ken Doraty	Joe Primeau	12:18

Although the hometowners managed a 3–2 victory over the razzle-dazzle Rangers, it was a battle all the way. Until tiny Ken Doraty's marker at 12:18 of the third session, it was anyone's game.

Spring and Winter —
The Story of the Ottawa Senators

On March 15, 1934, the star-spangled New York Americans edged the Ottawa Senators before 6,500 capital-area fans. Late in the first period, Ottawa winger Nick Wasnie caught Roy Worters over the eye with his stick, and the New York goalie was forced to leave the game. Ottawa had no choice but to lend Alex Connell to the Amerks. Connell was brilliant, and Ottawa lost the game and their NHL franchise, which folded after the 1933–34 season. The red, white, and black would not be seen again in the major league for nearly 60 years.

The Senators had been one of the five founding members of the National Hockey League in 1917, and they were one of the league's powerhouses during the 1920s, winning Stanley Cups in 1920, '21, '23, and '27. Between 1920 and 1927, Ottawa ran up a record of 148-70-12, good for a remarkable .670 winning percentage (which would translate to 107 points over an 80-game schedule).

The club's early days in the NHL weren't quite so illustrious. Coached by Eddie Gerard and managed by former Ottawa *Citizen* sports editor Tommy Gorman, in 1917–18 the Senators posted a 9-13 record, good for third in a three-team league. Despite the poor showing, Ottawa boasted a strong, young core of players: dependable Jack Darragh, two-way ace Eddie Gerard, flashy Frank Nighbor, "Buck" Boucher, and 36-goal scorer Cy Denneny. After a mediocre 5-5 placing in the first half of 1918–19, the Ottawas shifted gears, winning seven of eight to finish 12-6 on the season. Nighbor and Denneny placed third and fourth respectively in league scoring. The playoffs saw Newsy Lalonde and the Canadiens punch out Ottawa in five games.

In 1919–20 the Senators truly made their presence felt around the NHL, posting a 9-3 record in the first half and going 10-2 in the second, earning the right to meet the PCHA's Seattle Metropolitans, the defending Stanley Cup champions, in the Cup finals. Ottawa won two of the first three games — 3–2, 3–0, and 1–3 — on home ice at Dey's Arena before slushy ice dictated a move to Toronto's Mutual Street Arena. The Senators followed up a 5–2 loss with a 6–1 win in the fifth and deciding match, enabling the boys to return to a hero's welcome. The Cup was in the Canadian capital after a nine-year absence.

Ottawa won the first half in 1920–21, led by Denneny's 34 goals — only Babe Dye of Toronto, with 35, scored more. In the NHL playoff the Senators blanked Dye's St. Patricks, 5–0 and 2–0, earning the right to travel west to play Vancouver. In game one, the mighty Millionaires eked out a 2–1 win over the boys in the barber-pole jerseys. All five games in the series would be decided by one goal. Ottawa took the next two, 4–3 and 3–2, while Vancouver grabbed game four by a 3–2 margin. Denman Arena was packed for the deciding game — in fact, fans were being turned away — as the Senators triumphed, 2–1, winning the Cup for the second year in a row.

By late 1922, Ottawa was good to go. Although newcomer Aurel Joliat was making a lot of noise in Montreal, the Senators managed to take the title with 14 wins in 24 games. Denneny was again second in the scoring race with 21 goals and 10 assists for 31 points, while George Boucher was seventh with 24 points. In the playoffs, Ottawa defeated the Frenchmen in a two-game, total-goals series by an aggregate score of 3–2, and it was off to Vancouver again. There had been some changes in the west since Ottawa's last visit two years previous: the Millionaires were now called the Maroons, and there were two leagues, the PCHA and the new Western Canada Hockey League. After eliminating the Maroons, two games to one, Ottawa swept the Edmonton Eskimos in a best-of-three series. Vancouver boss Frank Patrick admitted that this edition of the Senators was the greatest team he had ever seen. In Ottawa, Rideau and Sussex streets were filled with sunny-faced onlookers waiting for the Senators' train to arrive.

Shortly after the 1922–23 season, Tommy Gorman and E.P. Dey sold the Senators to a local group led by Frank Ahearn, son of the owner of Ottawa Electric. The new owners erected a new 10,000-seat arena — equipped with artificial ice — along Argyle Street. The world champions had almost all their players return for the 1923–24 campaign. A notable no-show was captain Eddie Gerard, who had been forced to retire because of a growth in his throat. The Super Six came out of the gate with both guns blazing, winning seven of their first eight games. By season's end on March 5, 1924, Ottawa was at 16-8, six points better than the Canadiens. Cy Denneny had finally broken through and won the scoring title. But Montreal had the hot hand in the playoffs, winning both ends of the two-game, total-goals series by scores of 1–0 and 4–2 — Habs rookie Howie Morenz was the star of the series.

The Senators, minus Jack Darragh, who died in June, dropped to fourth in 1924–25, finishing behind everyone except the expansion Montreal Maroons and Boston Bruins. They returned to the NHL penthouse a year later with a 24-8-4 record. Even though the Maroons would go on to win the Cup, Ottawa's new blood — Hooley Smith, King Clancy, Alex Connell, Frank Finnigan, and Hec Kilrea — had proven its mettle.

In 1926–27, Ottawa's youth movement paid off. Even though they placed no players in the top 10 scorers, the Senators roared to a 30-10-4 finish, good for first place in the league's new Canadian Division. Connell tended goal in all 44 games, racking up 13 shutouts and a remarkable 1.49 goals-against average. The Super Six made it all the way to the Cup finals, where they won an unusual best-of-five series: the series was

1927 Ottawa Senators

called off after the Senators had won two and tied two of the first four games. This particular Cup victory was celebrated all over the city of Ottawa. A civic banquet was held and local dignitaries applauded this, the Senators' ninth Cup triumph.

The 1927 Stanley Cup championship would be the storied franchise's high-water mark. After more than 30 years of excellence, Ottawa hockey began an irrevocable slide. Rumors of financial problems began to surface as the team was dismantled. Hooley Smith and Ed Gorman were the first to be let go, and Jack Adams retired.

The onset of the Great Depression in 1929 did little to ease the Ahearns' financial burdens. And NHL expansion to U.S. centers such as New York, Boston, and Chicago had made Ottawa the smallest market in the league. In 1929, Cy Denneny was sent to Boston, and in October 1930, King Clancy was shipped to Toronto for Art Smith and Eric Pettinger and, more importantly, $35,000 cash.

In his autobiography *Clancy*, the King describes his shock at being shuffled to Hogtown so abruptly:

> To this day, I'm surprised at the amount of money involved in the deal that brought me to the Leafs. I was dumbfounded at the time. I figured I was worth about four cents a pound. When I heard how much money Mr. Smythe handed over to Ottawa, I must confess I thought he was a foolish man. But Mr. Ahearn was a hard man at the bargain counter and he needed the money badly. He'd had several bids for my services. When the deal was completed, he took me aside and said, 'King, we're

sorry to lose you. But we had a bad year last season. We lost $32,000 and this is the only way we're able to get it back.' And so I was sold to the Leafs in 1930.

In 1930–31, the Stinking Six posted a 10-30-4 record, easily the worst in the Canadian Division. Joan Finnigan remarked in *Old Scores, New Goals* that "My father [Frank Finnigan] always claimed that Frank Ahearn was under pressure from Thomas Ahearn, his father, to get out of the risky business of backing an enterprise like a hockey team where profit was always at the mercy of the whims of the crowd … father and son were in direct conflict."

The league gave Ahearn permission to suspend operations for the 1931–32 season, but when the Senators were reinstated for 1932–33, they were clearly no longer able to compete. Even though the likes of Finnigan, Earl Roche, and Allen Shields were in their lineup, Ottawa put up records of 11-27-10 and 13-29-6 before the franchise was transferred to St. Louis for the 1934–35 season.

Which brings us back to March 15, 1934, the last game the Ottawa Senators would play in their original incarnation. As Brian McFarlane wrote in *Total Hockey*, "Over 6,500 fans applauded . . . then left the arena with solemn faces, knowing it was the end of a memorable era in Canadian hockey."

Shore Scores More

If Howie Morenz was hockey's Babe Ruth, Shore was surely hockey's Ty Cobb. He was a stunning talent with a short fuse whose finesse was often overshadowed by his temper, which was about as hot as they came. Where Eddie Shore was concerned, you either loved the guy, or, more likely, you hated him. As one of hockey's all-time greatest defenders, he was a greater pest than Claude Lemieux, and he had a penchant for delivering hard, often questionable, hits — comparable to Ulf Samuelsson today. Despite, or perhaps because of, his rough edges, Boston fans lionized him. Fans in other NHL rinks could generally be heard screaming for his blood.

Off the ice, Shore was a constant headache to Bruins management. A stickler for getting what he figured he was worth — and more — he held out a number of times throughout his career, occasionally forcing NHL president Frank Calder to intervene for the sake of keeping the league's top drawing card on the ice.

In 1933, Art "The Brain" Ross sought to trim the B's payroll. Not surprisingly, the "Edmonton Express" disagreed with Ross's "wage warfare" and headed back to his Alberta home. Calder suspended Shore immediately — a punishment Ross, certain that his team would "get along fine without their defector," went along with. But when Boston was thrashed 6–1 by the Leafs in the 1933–34 opener, Shore was soon welcomed back at full salary.

Shore's contrariness reached its zenith in 1939. The Bruins had blitzed their way through the 1938–39 schedule en route to a five-game Stanley Cup victory over Toronto. The aging Shore was at his best in the playoffs, earning First All-Star Team honors for the seventh time in his stunning career. Although he was nearly 37, Boston thought he was still capable of anchoring the Bruins' blue-line. But the big defender had different ideas; planning to wind down his career, Shore had purchased the AHL's Springfield Indians for $42,000 with an eye toward operating the club as a player/owner. The business move was also a canny bargaining ploy, because Shore knew Ross wanted to keep his living legend in a Bruins uniform. With a team of his own, Shore needed the Bruins a lot less than Boston needed Eddie Shore. Although Ross did not necessarily applaud Shore's business move, he did his best to keep his living legend in a Bruins uniform. Shore, for his part, was all ears. He knew he had the upper hand in any and all negotiations and was curious to see what his boss would propose.

Ross presented a novel proposal, one to which the defenseman seemed agreeable: Shore would play in Boston's home games, but when the Bruins went on the road, he would stay behind and look after the Indians. The arrangement would take effect on December 15, 1939, unless the Bruins encountered an emergency. According to a joint statement, the Boston club would "give Shore every assistance in planning his new organization."

It wouldn't take long for an "emergency" to befall the Bruins. Jack Crawford, one of Boston's biggest and best, was injured in a November 10 exhibition tilt in Owen Sound and Ross was suddenly short a defender. Enter Shore. Though he was not bound to play until December 15, Eddie offered his services to the B's and suited up for the next few home games. There was no trouble until November 28, when Boston was scheduled to play at home against the Leafs. That same night, Springfield was entertaining the Philadelphia Ramblers. Although Ross expected Shore to play, there was no reaching the blue-liner — he was too busy leading his Indians to a 4–2 victory. Ross was furious, but it was wholly in character for Shore. Just a couple of days earlier, Shore had remarked to a reporter, "I wish I did not have to make those trips to Boston to play for the Bruins in their home games." And, strictly speaking, Shore did not have to play in any games prior to December 15.

A few weeks later, Red Dutton of the New York Americans inquired about securing Shore's services. Ross had clearly had enough of Shore at that moment because he told Dutton, "I'll give him to you for $5,000 if you can get me the money within an hour." Dutton rushed out, acquired the necessary cash, and hurried back to Ross with minutes to spare. The Boston boss had cooled his jets in the interim, though, and he backed out of the deal.

As the new year dawned, Shore was getting restless. He was forbidden to play with the Indians because he was tied to his Bruins contract. But Ross wasn't calling upon him to suit up for the B's anytime soon, either. Finally, when it became apparent that Shore would not play a

Eddie Shore

major part in the NHL campaign, Ross relented

and loaned him to Springfield — on the condition that Shore could be called up by Boston in case of — you guessed it! — an "emergency." Ross explained his change of heart by saying, "Shore has made a heavy investment in the Springfield club and we want to give him a hand."

Then on January 24, 1940, Ross dealt Shore to the Amerks for Eddie "Pee Wee" Wiseman and $5,000, the same amount discussed a month earlier. New York management welcomed Shore with open arms, and gave him an unusual degree of latitude. He was free to play in any games he wished, whether it was for the Americans or for Springfield.

Shore was supposed to report to the Americans for their February 1 game against Chicago. Yet, in his excitement to return to the NHL, he showed up a few days early and made his Amerks debut on January 30 against the Canadiens. Shore was a sub in his first few games with New York, gradually making his way into the starting lineup.

The trade did improve the Americans, enabling them to slip past the pathetic Habs into sixth place and the final playoff berth. (Incidentally, the playoff structure in 1939–40 was completely asinine. For one thing, six of seven teams made the tournament! And in the first round, the first-place team played second-place, third versus fourth, and fifth versus sixth. That meant one of the league's top two teams was eliminated after just one round, while a fifth- or sixth-place bottom feeder was guaranteed to advance!)

New York Americans	GP	W	L	T	Pts	WPct	GF	GA
Pre-trade	32	9	21	2	20	.313	64	94
Post-trade	16	6	8	2	14	.438	42	46

Oddly enough, the Bruins also improved markedly after they jettisoned their malcontent defenseman:

Boston Bruins	GP	W	L	T	Pts	WPct	GF	GA
Pre-trade	31	19	8	4	42	.677	98	66
Post-trade	17	12	4	1	25	.735	72	32

Shore played but 13 games (including regular season and playoffs) with the Amerks in 1939–40, then announced his retirement from the NHL. He went on to play 91 games over the next two years in Springfield, before hanging them up for good . . . although he answered the call for one more game, with the Buffalo Bisons, during the 1943–44 season, announcing his retirement from the NHL at season's end. He went on to play parts of the next two seasons in Springfield before taking his full retirement, give or take a game of course. Upon hanging up the skates, he turned to the business side of the sport.

He held a stake in the Springfield Indians until the late 1970s. During that time he acted as the team's coach, general manager, janitor, peanut vendor — you name it. Although he'd been a frequent salary holdout during his playing career, he pulled a 180-degree turn as an owner, developing a reputation as hockey's greatest penny-pincher. The 1966–67 team was so infuriated with Shore that they went out on strike.

The Eagles Had Landed

At a September 22, 1934, meeting, directors of the Ottawa Senators petitioned NHL brass to approve a transfer of their team to St. Louis. The governors approved the move, which came as a surprise since they'd rejected a St. Louis franchise application only two years before — travel costs would be too high, they'd said. But now, for the first time in its history, the NHL was going west of the Mississippi.

A Toronto *Globe* sportswriter asserted in October 1934 that "St. Louis fans will support the major league team if the Eagles are in the running. They will not countenance a loser." Since the Eagles' roster would be made up largely of the woeful 1933–34 Senators, fans in the Show Me state of Missouri would be a hard sell indeed.

The move quickly caused an uproar from the city's existing hockey club, the St. Louis Flyers of the American Hockey Association. Flyers owner Doc Wainwright claimed the AHA and NHL had an agreement that banned the big league from moving west of the Mississippi, and he threatened to sue for $200,000 if the Eagles tried to play a game in St. Louis. The NHL, for its part, claimed that an agreement had existed with the AHA, but it had expired a few years earlier.

Wainwright never followed through on his threat, and the Eagles opened their season on November 8, 1934, against the defending Stanley Cup champions, the Chicago Black Hawks. Before 12,600 fans, including St. Louis Mayor Bernie Dickman, who dropped the ceremonial first puck, St. Louis got down to business. Earl Roche scored the Eagles' first ever goal at 14:35 of the middle frame of a 3–1 loss.

With the excitement generated by the opener, St. Louis was expecting a good crowd for their second home game, two days later against the New York Rangers. But only 6,000 fans showed up to see Bill Beveridge kick out 44 Ranger shots in a 4–2 Eagles win. It was downhill from there, both on the ice and at the box office. St. Louis would drop their next eight decisions, scoring but eight goals in that span. They grabbed the keys to the basement and remained there to the end. Their lack of depth was most evident in a December 15 dance with the Montreal Canadiens, when Scotty Bowman and Irv Frew patrolled the blue-line for the entire 70 minutes of a 1–1 draw.

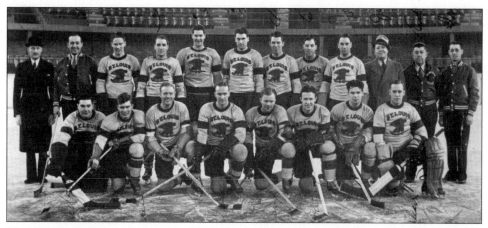

The St. Louis Eagles

After 13 games and a 2-11-0 record, St. Louis brass replaced Eddie Gerard behind the bench with Buck Boucher. The Eagles would go 9-20-6 under his hand, a clear improvement. What Boucher could not do, though, was put fans in the seats. Even the league-leading Toronto Maple Leafs, featuring the likes of Busher Jackson, Charlie Conacher, and George Hainsworth, drew a crowd of only 3,000. By late December, talk abounded that the Eagles were going to fold.

Syd Howe, with 27 points in 36 games, was probably the best the Eagles had to offer. He had come over from Ottawa in the transfer to score 27 points in 36 games. Great as he was, St. Louis shipped him to the Detroit Red Wings with Bowman for journeyman defenseman Ted Graham and $50,000 in February 1935. Two days later the team's last "name" player, Frank Finnigan, was sold to Toronto. The "Shawville Express" had been a living legend in Ottawa, and it looks like management was paying him one last favor by sending him to a contender.

Around this time, reports appeared saying that the Eagles would play the remainder of their home dates in Ottawa — not impossible to believe, since the team was still the property of the Ottawa Hockey Association. But club brass denied the rumors, and no such move materialized. The Eagles staggered across the 1934–35 finish line at 11-31-6, dead last in the NHL, scoring a league-low 86 goals.

During the off-season, the Ottawa Hockey Association asked the NHL for permission to suspend operations for a year, as had been done in Ottawa in 1931–32. The league turned thumbs down, however, and on October 15, 1935, the St. Louis Eagles franchise was revoked and its players were distributed via a draft to the other clubs.

The draft went thus:

First Round

New York Americans	Pete Kelly
Montreal Canadiens	Bill Beveridge
Detroit Red Wings	Carl Voss
New York Rangers	Glenn Brydson
Montreal Maroons	Joe Lamb
Boston Bruins	Bill Cowley
Toronto Maple Leafs	Gerry Shannon

Second Round

New York Americans	Eddie Finnigan
Montreal Canadiens	Irv Frew
Detroit Red Wings	M. Peterkin
New York Rangers	Vern Ayres
Montreal Maroons	W. Taugher
Boston Bruins	Ted Graham
Toronto Maple Leafs	Cliff Purpur

Third Round

Montreal Canadiens	Paul-Emile Drouin
Montreal Maroons	Henri Lauzon
Toronto Maple Leafs	Jimmy Dewey

Fourth Round

Toronto Maple Leafs	Mickey Blake

The Chicago Black Hawks did not participate in the draft.

With that, the St. Louis Eagles joined the ranks of the NHL's forgotten franchises, taking their place alongside the Pittsburgh Pirates, Philadelphia Quakers, Montreal Maroons, and New York Americans. Big-league hockey would return to the Missouri metropolis 30 years later, when the NHL added the Blues in its Great Expansion of 1967.

Meandering Mascot

News item taken from the June 4, 1936, edition of the Toronto *Globe & Mail*:

"Last year, the Americans got into the NHL playoffs for the first time in history and now they've lost their mascot. It's Carl Voss's one-year-old fox terrier which strayed from his residence, 179 Walmer Road, yesterday. Carl tells us that the dog was quite a favorite with the players last winter in New York and his picture was carried in a number of New York papers. Naturally, he's endeavoring to locate him."

Zero Heroes

O ver the past few years, goaltending aficionados have enjoyed an embarrassment of riches. But the exploits of the Dominik Haseks and Patrick Roys of the present day threaten to overshadow two of the greatest examples of goaltending over an extended period: Ottawa's Alex Connell in 1927–28 and Boston's Frank Brimsek in 1938–39. Their displays of goaltending genius demand further study.

Alex Connell

The 1927–28 Ottawa Senators ran into money problems and were forced to peddle Hooley Smith and Ed Gorman. Meanwhile, Jack "Jolly Jawn" Adams chose to retire. A lineup split between aging greats like Cy Denneny and Frank Nighbor and up-and-comers King Clancy and Frank Finnigan was no longer a match for the league's best. By midseason, Ottawa sat in fourth place in the Canadian Division with a record of 8-8-4. They were 14 points behind the pace-setting Montreal Canadiens. Enter Alex Connell.

Connell shut out the New York Americans, then stood firm in a 9–6 win over the Chicago Black Hawks. At 14:21 of the second period of a 2–1 win over the Canadiens, Sylvio Mantha directed a Howie Morenz feed past the black-capped Ottawa netminder. It would be the last goal scored on Connell for almost a month. Three days later, Connell shut out the Toronto Maple Leafs, 4–0. Then came the Montreal Maroons; he stuffed them, 1–0. People started to take notice: so far, Connell hadn't allowed a goal in 154 minutes and 59 seconds.

On February 7, 1928, Ottawa took the train to New York to face the Rangers. This one ended after a 10-minute overtime period in a scoreless draw, and Connell's shutout streak jumped to 224 minutes, 59 seconds. New York made the return trip two days later only to battle the Senators to another scoreless draw. At 5:27 of the second period, Connell broke his own record for the longest shutout sequence (250:59, set in 1925–26).

About a week later, Ottawa hosted the Pittsburgh Pirates. Once again, neither team could find the net and Connell's streak reached 364:59. Two days later, the Canadiens came to Ottawa, Connell stood on his head yet again, and the Canadiens were 1–0 losers.

Alex Connell

The Senators went to Chicago on February 22 and big Duke Keats slipped one past the secretary of the Ottawa Fire Department at 15:50 of the second. After 460 minutes and 49 seconds, someone finally beat Alex Connell. In the 70 years since, no one has even approached this mark.

Until 1967, the NHL's official records listed Connell's streak at 446 minutes and nine seconds. That year, Minnesota goalie Cesare Maniago made a shutout run of his own, and the press went scurrying to their record books. It was discovered that league record keepers had missed 14 minutes of Connell's streak. Case closed? Well, not exactly. The NHL lists Connell's streak at 461 minutes and 29 seconds, a full 40 seconds more than the actual time. So where did this extra 40 seconds come from? Probably from Ottawa's February 1 overtime win over the Maroons; the Senators scored with 40 seconds left in OT. The league may be erroneously crediting Connell with 40 seconds that weren't played.

An interesting footnote to Connell's streak: immediately after the string was broken, the Ottawa backstop went on to post shutouts in each of his next two games. His efforts gave the Senators a 12-game unbeaten streak, during which Connell racked up nine shutouts.

Frank Brimsek

The Boston Bruins went into the 1938–39 season with Cecil "Tiny" Thompson between the pipes. Thompson had been a Beantown favorite for the past decade and was coming off a Vezina Trophy–winning season. Even though he was 33 and manager Art Ross had been making allusions all summer to "secret plans" regarding his team's goaltending situation, no one really believed anyone other than Thompson would be backstopping the Bruins in 1938–39.

Thompson missed the first two games of the season with a gashed forehead, and rookie Frank Brimsek filled in. Tiny would start the next five games, going 3-1-1 with a 1.55 goals-against average. His last game for Boston was an 8–2 win over the New York Americans on November 27, 1938. Almost immediately thereafter he was traded to the Detroit Red Wings for goalie Normie Smith and $15,000. The trade touched off rumors that Thompson and Eddie Shore had never gotten along, and that Shore, who'd recently re-signed after a lengthy holdout, wouldn't return unless Thompson was moved out of Boston. Ross of course refuted these claims, saying that "If Thompson remained with us, I fear it would be only two years before we would have been forced to replace him with Brimsek." Ross softened the blow to Tiny somewhat by giving him $1,000 as a parting gift.

Brimsek took over as the Bruins' starter on December 1 at the Montreal Forum. Although the Canadiens took the match 2–0, the Eveleth, Minnesota, native was determined to succeed. The eccentric goalie, who had a habit of constantly checking his pad straps, let his play do the talking.

Brimsek began his legendary streak in Chicago before a crowd of 17,894. Coincidentally, tending the Hawk goal was Mike Karakas, Brimsek's predecessor in the Eveleth High School nets. It was a close game from the start but Milt Schmidt managed a marker in the second period to give the B's a 1–0 lead. Early in the third session, Dit Clapper, who had earlier said that he would rather quit hockey than play in front of any goalie but Tiny Thompson, added an insurance marker. Clapper's goal seemed to rattle Karakas, who would go on to allow three goals in the final period. Brimsek, on the other hand, overcame his initial jitters and was unbeatable.

Two days later, the Hawks came to Boston to complete the home-and-home. Playing in front of the home crowd would be a major test for the rookie, who skated out to take his place and received a cool reception from the Garden crowd. Brimsek went on to record another shutout, this one by a score of 2–0 on goals by Bobby Bauer and Gord Pettinger. The fans were convinced, and they gave their new hero a standing ovation at game's end.

On December 11, Brimsek met the powerhouse New York Rangers at Madison Square Garden. Led by the Colvilles — Neil and Mac — Bryan Hextall, and Babe Pratt, and backstopped by Davey Kerr, Broadway's Blueshirts were going to be no picnic. The Rangers pestered and peppered the Boston rookie all night, but he repelled every siege on his cage. Final count: 3–0, Boston.

The Bruins went home to face the Canadiens, and Brimsek's shutout streak came to a crashing at the hands of Herbie Cain. Toe Blake added a goal in the third period of the game to cut the Bruins' lead to 3–2, which would be the final score. Although he'd allowed two goals, Brimsek had won for the fourth straight time. More importantly, he had won over the Bruin faithful. Some even went as far as to dub him "Mr. Zero" for his string of shutouts.

Frank Brimsek

No sooner had his first shutout streak ended than "Mr. Zero" started a new one. In the December 15 rematch with the Habs, Cooney Weiland potted the game's only goal in a 1–0 Bruin victory. Three days later, Brimsek and the Bruins traveled to the Motor City to meet Tiny Thompson and his Red Wings. The two goaltending wizards matched zeros for the first two periods, but in the end the night belonged to Brimsek. The Bruins netted two goals in the third period to prevail 2–0. Brimsek now had put up back-to-back shutouts.

Two days later in Boston, it was the New York Americans' turn. Although not a powerful force in the NHL, the Amerks featured high-scoring Sweeney Schriner, "Cowboy" Tom Anderson, Lorne Carr, and a 36-year-old Nels Stewart. The star-spangled warriors fired 23 blanks at Brimsek as Boston took the match 3–0. Three shutouts in a row, for the second time in seven games!

Boston hosted the Rangers on Christmas Day, and Santa Claus must have decided that Brimsek was on his "naughty" list, because he gave the Bruins a lump of coal. In the second period, the Rangers' Dutch Hiller flew into the Bruin zone and spotted Bryan Hextall in the slot. The big winger zipped the puck to a streaking Phil Watson, who would make no mistake. Brimsek's streak was over.

Brimsek continued to play great hockey for the Bruins but would never again revisit his early "glory days." In his first shutout streak, he went 231 minutes and 54 seconds before allowing two goals on December 13 against the Canadiens. His second scoreless run lasted 220:24.

Photographers found it nearly impossible to get dressing-room shots of Brimsek. Any time a photographer expressed a desire to take a picture of him, he would cover his eyes with a towel. Apparently, he thought the flash would ruin his eyes.

The rest of the 1938–39 season was a dream for Brimsek. He continued to play brilliantly, capturing the Vezina and Calder trophies, and he was named to the First All-Star Team. His stellar play continued into the playoffs, where he posted a 1.25 average as the Bruins rolled to their first Stanley Cup win in a decade.

Connell vs. Brimsek

Which streak was more impressive, Connell's or Brimsek's? On one hand, Connell's streak was uninterrupted while Brimsek's was broken halfway through. It could also be argued that Brimsek had a better supporting cast, making the feat of the Ottawa Fireman harder to accomplish. Compare the two years in which the streaks took place:

Goalie	Season	Games	Goals/Game	ShO	ShO%
Alex Connell	1927–28	220	3.67	99	45.0
Frank Brimsek	1938–39	168	4.91	40	23.8

Note: Shutout column refers to games played by all NHL teams during the season being studied in which a goalie posted a shutout.

The game was more wide-open in Brimsek's era, making shutouts nearly twice as hard to come by. And in Connell's season, forward passing wasn't allowed in the offensive zone, naturally contributing to lower scores.

In 1927–28 Connell was in his fourth NHL season. On the other hand, Brimsek's streak was accomplished in the first 10 games of his NHL career. He'd been thrown directly into the mouth of the lion, having been tapped to replace a fan favorite in Tiny Thompson. And Brimsek was no Patrick Lalime or Blaine Lacher, who rose out of relative obscurity to turn the league on its ear for a spell. In fact, Brimsek had been touted as "the next big thing" and not only did he live up to the billing, he went on to spin a Hall of Fame career in Beantown.

Brimsek's string gets our nod for the most impressive display of goaltending in NHL history.

Stars and Stripes Were Second Fiddles

Pause for a moment to consider the "second fiddle." Always the afterthought, never hitting the big time, toiling in the shadow of the more famous, the more successful, or the more industrious sibling. Ed McMahon to Johnny Carson. Scottie Pippen to Michael Jordan. Burger King to McDonald's. And in the NHL, the Americans to the Rangers.

Ironically, the New York Americans were the league's first entry in the Big Apple. The Amerks, as they were often called, made their debut for 1925–26 and they stuck around for 17 undistinguished seasons, making the playoffs only five times.

The Americans were the NHL's second U.S.–based franchise, trailing the Boston Bruins by one year. They were born out of labor unrest north of the border. In 1924–25 the Hamilton Tigers had finished on top of the standings with a 19-10-1 record. But the players were miffed because the regular season had been extended from 24 games to 30, without any corresponding pay raises. On the eve of the 1925 playoffs, the entire team refused to play unless they were given more money — $200 per man, to be precise. NHL president Frank Calder responded by disqualifying the Tigers from the playoffs and suspending every last player indefinitely. On April 17, 1925 — at the same meeting that saw the Hamilton players suspended — the NHL governors announced that New York entrepreneur Bill Dwyer had purchased the Tigers for $75,000, and would shift the franchise out of the southern Ontario city and into the brand-new Madison Square Garden.

Dwyer knew little about hockey. He'd been encouraged to get into the game by Bill McBeth, a Canadian who wrote for the New York *Herald-Tribune*. A bootlegger and an eccentric who hung out with some shady characters, Dwyer would inject plenty of color and verve into the Americans.

Given the Tigers' 1924–25 success, big things were expected from the Americans, who were to be managed by Tommy Gorman, who'd steered the Ottawa Senators to three Stanley Cups in four years. The lineup boasted top-line center Billy Burch, who was hyped to Manhattanites as the "Babe Ruth of hockey." He was even a hometown boy, hailing from nearby Yonkers, New York. Burch would score 22 times, while Redvers "Red" Green chipped in 13 goals. Beyond that, the Amerks were dreadfully short of offense, scoring only 68 goals in all, and they ended up fifth in the seven-team NHL with a 12-20-4 record.

The Americans drew big enough crowds to the corner of Eighth and 50th that Madison Square Garden management decided to horn in on the action. In 1926 the NHL welcomed the New York Rangers, along with the Chicago Black Hawks and Detroit Cougars. Now up to 10 teams, the league split into two divisions, "Canadian" and "American." Someone at the NHL office must have had a sense of irony since they put the New York Americans into the Canadian Division with Toronto, Ottawa, and the Montreal Maroons and Canadiens. The Amerks made few major roster changes, despite the availability of numerous top players from the defunct Western Canada Hockey League.

Americans jersey

Midway through the second month of the 1926–27 season, the Stars & Stripes acquired Lionel "Big Train" Conacher from Pittsburgh for Charlie Langlois and cash. The Amerks won five of their next seven contests and were third in their division at the season's midway point. But this success would prove to be fleeting. They stumbled through the second half to finish fourth in their division.

The Americans, particularly Burch and Conacher, liked to "hit the town," and they were abetted by Boss Dwyer, who owned some of New York's hottest night spots. After a March 15 loss to Detroit, the two rascals were suspended one game for breaking training. One yarn has them getting into a scuffle with one another late one night. Burch had raised Conacher's dander somehow and the "Big Train" chased him down a hallway, vowing to put him out of commission. Burch ducked into an open door and slammed it shut behind him. Conacher, moving like a runaway freight train (naturally), missed the door completely and smashed through the adjacent wall. This little incident caused $700 in damages.

Off the ice, Dwyer provided the New York media with plenty of copy. In June 1927, he was sent off to Atlanta Penitentiary on a bootlegging rap; he'd spend the next two years behind bars. Lacking strong guidance, the Americans settled into second-rate status. Whatever talent they did stumble across usually ended up going on to star elsewhere. Consider Marty Barry. He played in nine games in 1927–28 before being dispatched to the minors. In 1929, the Boston Bruins grabbed him in the intra-league draft, and the big center went on to enjoy a Hall of Fame career.

In 1927–28 the Amerks had mediocre Joe Miller in net, and only Chicago allowed more goals. Ironically, the only time Miller displayed any competence that year, he was in a Ranger jersey. Lorne Chabot had been felled by a shot in game two of the Stanley Cup finals, and the Americans loaned Miller to the Blueshirts. Over the balance of the series, the pride of Morrisburg, Ontario, played three games, allowing just three goals.

Amerks management decided to go after a top goalie for 1928–29, and their search led them to Roy "Shrimp" Worters, the Pittsburgh goalie who was a contract holdout. They also acquired aging veterans Punch Broadbent and Babe Dye. Worters was still under suspension for his holdout, and NHL president Calder was in no hurry to lift the ban. James "Flat" Walsh was borrowed from the Maroons to tend net in the meantime, and he allowed only one goal in four games. When Worters finally arrived, he stood on his head game in and game out, so that even though the Amerks weren't scoring, they reached the halfway mark atop the Canadian Division with a record of 11-6-5. Worters' incredible play carried over to the second half and the Amerks got their first taste of playoff hockey. For his extraordinary season, in which he posted 13 shutouts and an eye-popping 1.15 goals-against average, the "Shrimp" was awarded the Hart Trophy as the league's most valuable player.

As luck would have it, the Amerks drew their crosstown rivals, the Rangers, as their first ever playoff opponents. The teams met in a two-game, total-goals series, and in the first game Worters and Ranger puck-stopper John Ross Roach were unbeatable. They traded save after sensational save in a scoreless draw. Ranger Butch Keeling converted a Paul Thompson feed for the only goal of the second match, and the Amerks were through.

As well as the Americans had played, they were an old bunch. Broadbent, Dye, and Eddie Bouchard were finished. George Massecar and Bill Brydge were acquired to spruce up the blue-line while George Patterson, Bill Boyd, Bill Holmes, and Roy Burmeister also made their way in. Not exactly a group that would strike fear into the hearts of men. The Americans won only two of their first 14 games in 1929–30 and they sunk into the league cellar. As usual, they boasted one of the weakest offenses in the league, and they ended the season at 14-25-5. Worters stumbled through the campaign, finishing ahead of only Pittsburgh's Joe Miller in goals-against average. Their lone bright spot was Normie Himes, who paced the team with a respectable 50 points, good for eighth in the scoring race.

Things would not get much better over the next few years. The team sold Conacher to the Maroons prior to the 1930–31 season. By all accounts the affable Conacher didn't seem to want to leave New York — in a game between the Amerks and Maroons, he came off the Maroons bench during a break and lined up on the Americans blue-line! The Amerks fought hard throughout the 1930–31 season, finishing at 18-16-10, good for 46 points. Despite their respectable record, the Maroons, who also had 46 points, edged New York out of the playoffs by virtue of having won two more games.

After winning the Vezina Trophy, Worters struggled through 1931–32. Meanwhile, team scoring was low as usual. It all added up to a 16-24-8 record and no playoff berth. During the off-season the Amerks sold Billy Burch to Boston.

The Amerks didn't scare too many opponents heading into the 1932–33 season, but with six games to go they were neck-and-neck with the Canadiens for the final playoff spot. They went 2-3-1 over their last six games, and although they ended up tied with the Habs with 41 points, Montreal had won three more games and they went to the playoffs instead. To add insult to injury, the Rangers brought home their second Cup that year.

In 1933–34, Worters was superb. When he was between the pipes, the Americans were 12-13-10. Unfortunately, they were 3-10-0 without him and the playoffs were out of reach once again. But during the season they picked up crafty play-maker Art Chapman who was acquired from Boston along with Bob Gracie.

Lorne Carr and Dave "Sweeney" Schriner were acquired in separate deals from the IAHL's Syracuse Stars, and they were major additions. In Chapman, Carr, and Schriner, the Amerks finally had some bona fide scoring punch. They opened the 1934–35 campaign like a house on fire, winning four of their first six games. But the wheels quickly fell off and they staggered to the midpoint with a 7-12-4 record. Then the fun started. The New York *Daily News* reported the players were on the verge of revolting. They were owed money (some as much as $1,000), the dressing rooms were deemed inadequate, and injured players were not receiving proper treatment. There had been rumblings for years that Dwyer was in dire financial straits. Now it looked as if the stories were being borne out. It was a fall from grace for someone who typically threw $50,000 house parties. In the face of such distraction, the Amerks did well to finish above the lowly St. Louis Eagles, who brought up the NHL rear in their only year of existence.

In 1935–36, two more important pieces of the puzzle were added: Tommy "Cowboy" Anderson and Eddie "Pee Wee" Wiseman. With these additions and a solid returning nucleus, many were calling this the strongest Americans team ever. Red Dutton was named player/manager. At the break, the Americans were 9-12-3. More importantly, they boasted the league's second-best offense. They finished with 39 points, 11 behind the American Division–trailing Rangers, but good enough for third in the Canadian Division and their first playoff spot in seven years.

The Amerks drew Chicago in the first round and stunned everyone by clipping the Hawks 3–0 in the opener behind splendid efforts from Worters and Schriner. It was a two-game, total-goals series, so even though New York lost game two in Chicago, 5–4, they were propelled into the second round of the playoffs for the first time in club history. Their opponents in the semifinals would be the Toronto Maple Leafs, who took game one 3–1. A 1–0 Americans victory in the second game set up a winner-take-all rubber match in Toronto. Although the Americans fought valiantly, two late Leaf goals sealed their doom.

Despite their on-ice success, dark clouds continued to hover over the franchise. The team ran out of money at the end of the year, forcing the league to pay the players' salaries. That was only the beginning. Dwyer was broke, so on October 19, 1936, NHL governors took back the Americans franchise, claiming that the club had "failed to comply with a formal demand for payment of the club's indebtedness to the league." The team would continue to operate under league control. Dwyer did not take this lying down; he tried to file an injunction against the NHL but the move was quickly thwarted. The league convened in early November and came up with what seemed like a workable solution but Dwyer would have no part of it. Art Ross and Conn Smythe were appointed to confer with Dwyer and they quickly reached a meeting of the minds: Dwyer was given an option to buy back his share of Americans stock, subject to certain conditions being met. The option was never exercised.

On the ice, the Americans continued to score goals at a respectable rate. But their defense, it seemed, wanted to rest. After shooting out of the gate faster than Carl Lewis, going 4-1-2 in their first seven starts, the Amerks went into their inevitable swoon. Despite the addition of veteran Nels Stewart in late December, the Amerks sputtered to a 6-15-3 record at the half. Worters suffered a hernia on January 5, ending his NHL career. Things improved somewhat in the second half, but not enough for the Americans to escape their destiny. They would finish the season at 15-29-4 with the highest goals-against total in the league. One bright spot was the continued impressive play by Schriner, who copped his second consecutive scoring title.

The main concern for the Americans during the spring of 1937 was to find a permanent replacement for Roy Worters. They found him in Earl Robertson, whom they acquired from Detroit for defenseman Red Doran. Early in the 1937–38 season the Amerks bolstered their blue-line, adding veterans Hap Day and Ching Johnson. The offensive genius of Schriner and Stewart created leads the new and improved defense could protect.

The Amerks finished with a record of 19-18-11, good for second place and a playoff spot. In game one of their first-round dance with the Rangers, speedy winger Johnny Sorrell scored in double overtime. The Rangers took the second game on the strength of two Clint Smith goals. The deciding game was an epic. Alex Shibicky and Bryan Hextall gave the Rangers a quick two-goal lead before Lorne Carr and Nels Stewart knotted matters. At the end of 60 minutes the score was tied at two, and three extra periods failed to break the deadlock. Then, 40 seconds into the fourth overtime period, Carr snapped a loose puck past Davey Kerr to secure victory. The giant had finally been slain! To the semifinals the Americans marched, to face the Black Hawks.

The Amerks took the first game 3–1 before falling 1–0 in game two. Game three was in New York, and the home team came out flying. When Carr opened the scoring, the Broadway crowd was abuzz with talk of Cup finals for the Amerks. But Earl Seibert scored late in the second period and Alex "Mine Boy" Levinsky and Elwyn "Doc" Romnes scored in the third for a 3–1 Chicago lead. A late Red Beattie goal failed to bail out the Amerks, who bowed out of the playoffs.

George Hainsworth and Roy Worters

Day and Johnson announced their retirements, which spelled trouble for the defense corps, but the run-and-gun offense was still strong, which meant the fans were in for some exciting games. The league reverted to a single-division format with the demise of the Montreal Maroons in 1938. Midway through 1938–39, the Americans were sitting comfortably in third place. Their weak defense was beginning to crack, but Robertson in goal could still steal the odd game. Heading into the playoffs, the fourth-place Americans' luck went from

Nels Stewart made NHL history on March 17, 1938, when he scored his 300th career goal against the Rangers, becoming the first to reach this magical plateau.

bad to worse when Robertson injured his leg in the last game of the season. Enter Alfie Moore, who'd put up some decent numbers in Hershey but in two games with the Amerks had surrendered 14 goals. Only a year before, during game one of the Cup finals, the Toronto native had been plucked from a tavern near Maple Leaf Gardens and pressed into service in the Chicago nets when Mike Karakas was injured. Moore shut down the Leafs 3–1, setting the stage for one of the grandest upsets in Cup history. Would he duplicate his heroics of the previous year? In a word, no. The final tally in the two-game, total-goals series was Toronto 6, Americans 0.

By late 1939, the Americans' financial wounds were critical. To staunch the bleeding, they were forced to deal Schriner. Lacking a drawing card, they dug into the game's past and acquired Busher Jackson, Charlie Conacher, and Eddie Shore. These aging veterans were unable to halt the slide. The Amerks finished sixth place at 15-29-4. Incredibly, this was good enough for a playoff berth. The NHL had decided to allow the top six (of seven) teams into the post-season. Despite this good fortune, the Amerks would be kicked out early, dropping two of three to Detroit.

The Americans franchise was on its last legs in 1940–41. Quite simply, there was little talent left due to the war. The team was woeful offensively and even worse defensively. Red Dutton tried everything to jump-start his team, but nothing worked. In late January 1941, he announced he was handing the starting goaltender's job to 20-year-old Chuck Rayner. Although the future Hall of Famer showed promise, he couldn't lift the Americans out of their hole. The final numbers were frightening: 8-29-11, their worst record ever. To top it off, the Amerks were dead last in goals scored and goals allowed (nearly four per game).

The 1941 off-season saw the Americans in desperate straits. They dealt off Carr and Jackson. Dutton decided to change the team's name to the *Brooklyn* Americans in a fruitless attempt to differentiate themselves from the wealthy Rangers. Although they continued to play home games at Madison Square Garden, they decided to practice in Brooklyn and adopt it as their "home town."

Wherever they called home, the outlook for 1941–42 was bleak. But someone forgot to tell Tommy Anderson. The 31-year-old Scot had been a solid contributor to the Americans since 1935 but he'd played in the shadows of Schriner, Carr, and Stewart. With all three departed, Anderson stepped up into the spotlight, scoring career-high points, even though he'd been moved from left wing to defense. Although they remained in the basement, the Americans managed to confound the experts by doubling their previous season's win total. Anderson, who finished 10th in the scoring race, was named to the First All-Star Team and awarded the Hart Trophy as the league's most valuable player. It would be his last NHL season.

Madison Square Garden decided not to renew the Amerks' lease and the team was forced to suspend operations. They would never play another game.

The New York Americans have been compared to baseball's St. Louis Browns, who lived in the shadow of the more established, and wealthier Cardinals. Like the

Americans, the Browns were often a bumbling crew. On the ice, the Americans never amounted to much, but their history closely parallels that of the NHL during the period, from the boundless optimism during the Roaring Twenties, when the league grew by leaps and bounds, through the bust years of the Depression. And they did survive 17 NHL seasons, outlasting teams in Pittsburgh, Philadelphia, St. Louis — even the Montreal Maroons lasted only 14 years. Along the way the club produced some solid NHL players, their owner is one of the biggest characters in hockey history, and manager Red Dutton would serve a few years as NHL president.

Hardcore Hainsworth

Did you ever wonder how it was physically possible for George Hainsworth to play 3,008 minutes in 1929-30? In his day, games were 40 minutes long. Hainsworth appeared in 42 of Montreal's 44 games that year. Even if all 42 games went the full 40 minutes, the maximum number of minutes that the "Human Icicle" could have played is 2,940. Needless to say, the 3,008 statistic piqued our curiosity. After researching this discrepancy, here's what we found:

	GP	MINS	GA	GAA
Previously Published Stats				
1929-30	42	3,008	108	2.15
Career	465	29,415	937	1.91
The Real Stats				
1929-30	42	2,680	108	2.42
Career	465	29,087	937	1.93

Snap!shots

LARRY AURIE (The Little Rag Man, Little Dempsey) Right Wing
5'6" 148
b. 2/8/1905, Sudbury, Ontario
d. 12/12/1952, Detroit, Michigan

Larry Aurie was the "pint-sized guy with the big fighting heart." Adjectives such as "peppery," "gutsy," and "plucky" all suited this little red-haired buzz bomb. When he landed in Detroit in 1927 — the same year as team boss Jack Adams — the team was known as the Cougars.

In the era of chunky Ching Johnson, nasty Nels Stewart, and bumping Babe Siebert, the smallish Aurie was at a clear disadvantage. Even so, he gave way to nobody and the Motown fans loved him for it. The feisty little winger, a master at ragging the puck, was an important part of Detroit's top line. Although his playing weight ranged from only 139 to 148 pounds, Aurie was one of the terrors of the NHL.

When Aurie left the Wings in 1938, his number, 6, was retired on the orders of Detroit owner Jim Norris. An emotional Adams was quoted as saying, "Larry Aurie was the most courageous player, pound for pound, that I have ever seen in hockey." In 489 games, "Little Dempsey" scored 147 goals and 276 points.

After retiring from the NHL, Aurie coached the Wings' farm team in Pittsburgh. In 1944, he left this post to take a regular 9-to-5 job in Detroit. Nine years later, on December 12, 1952, he suffered a stroke at the wheel of his car and died in Detroit's Mount Carmel Hospital. He was only 47.

Peak Years *1932–36*
In a Word *PUNCHY*

ACE BAILEY Right Wing/Center
5'10" 160
b. 7/3/1903, Bracebridge, Ontario
d. 4/7/1992, Toronto, Ontario

Irvine Bailey's signing to a Toronto contract in 1926 was meant to make the Hogtown faithful forget all about scoring whiz Babe Dye, who had recently moved on to Chicago. That autumn, Conn Smythe purchased the St. Patricks, renamed them the Maple Leafs, and made Bailey and Hap Day the cornerstones of his "new" franchise. Bailey quickly became the Leafs' top scoring threat, leading the NHL in both goals and points in 1928–29. With the emergence of the legendary "Kid Line" of Charlie Conacher, Joe Primeau, and Busher Jackson in 1930–31, Bailey faithfully accepted the role of defensive specialist. He utilized his natural two-way talent to become one of the top penalty-killers in the game.

Brutal tragedy struck on December 12, 1933. In the thick of a Leafs–Bruins tilt in Boston, the Leafs were short two men and Bailey was practicing his renowned puck-ragging skills. Down the ice, a groggy Eddie Shore was picking himself up after suffering a fierce King Clancy body-check. Shore charged at the first man he saw — it happened to be Bailey, who was trying to catch his breath. Shore shouldered Bailey in the kidneys, catapulting him into the air. Players on the ice reported hearing the sickening crack of Bailey's skull hitting the ice and fracturing.

As dark luck would have it, two of America's more talented brain surgeons were in Boston that night attending a medical conference. Over the next three days, they performed two desperate operations on Bailey. Finally, the fevered physicians gave up, informing reporters and Conn Smythe that the fallen hockey star was dying. As the death watch continued outside the Leaf star's room, the voices of one Nurse Ahn and a colleague could be heard from within. Observers found the nurses trying to revive Bailey by softly slapping him, begging him to get back on the ice. Many who heard of the two Nightingales were moved to tears. Later that day, a haggard Nurse Ahn emerged to inform the assembled that they could leave . . . Bailey would live!

A benefit game — the NHL's first All-Star contest — was held in Bailey's honor at Maple Leaf Gardens on February 14, 1934. Each player skated out in his own uniform to receive a special All-Star sweater from the Ace himself. When it was Shore's turn, a bandaged Bailey extended his right hand to the man who had nearly killed him and the house erupted into cheers.

Although Bailey made a full recovery, he was never able to play professional hockey again. He became a member of the Hockey Hall of Fame in 1975.

Peak Years *1928–32*
In a Word *UNLUCKY*

MARTY BARRY Center
6'0" 175
b. 12/8/1905, St. Gabriel, Quebec
d. 8/20/1969, Halifax, Nova Scotia

Certain sportswriters of the day hailed Martin James Barry as the "greatest passer the game has ever known" and "one of the cleanest players in hockey . . . a great playmaker and offensive threat at center ice."

Marty Barry

Barry, a product of Montreal's amateur hockey system, agreed to his first professional contract with the New York Americans in 1927. He split his first season between the Amerks and the Philadelphia Arrows of the Canadian–American Hockey League. The New Haven Eagles of the CAHL purchased his contract prior to the 1928–29 season, and he rewarded them by leading the league with 19 goals and 29 points.

In 1929–30, Barry put together his first successful season in the NHL in Beantown. Although Art Ross knew he was taking a chance on Barry (he only had nine games of NHL experience), the big fellow did not disappoint. He established himself as a major scoring threat, leading the club in goals for three years in a row. In 1930–31 he ignited a string of six consecutive 20-goal seasons. And although he failed to lead the Bruins to a Stanley Cup championship during his time there, he did help them capture three regular-season titles.

In the summer of 1935, Detroit boss Jack Adams dealt Cooney Weiland to Boston for Barry and slotted him between Larry Aurie and Herbie Lewis to give the Wings one of the most feared front units of the decade. Barry had a big hand in Detroit's 1936 Cup win, and he was the hero of their follow-up triumph in 1937. In these playoffs, he was tops in assists and points and tied for the lead in goals. He especially shone against the New York Rangers in the finals.

Barry earned the Lady Byng Trophy and a First All-Star Team nod in 1936–37. Despite his genial disposition, he was one of the league's top "policemen." As a big man, he was found to be remarkably handy with his dukes from early on, a reputation that followed him throughout his career.

After closing his NHL career with the Canadiens, Barry suited up with the Pittsburgh Hornets, before taking a job as player/coach of the American Hockey Association's Minneapolis Millers. He coached army teams in Montreal during World

War Two and in 1946–47 began an 11-year career as head coach of the St. Mary's College Juniors in Halifax.

In 509 games, Barry scored 195 goals and 387 points. He was elected to the Hockey Hall of Fame in 1965.

Peak Years *1932–36*
Comparable Recent Player *John LeClair*
In a Word *BIG*

KING CLANCY Defense
5'7" 155
b. 2/25/1903, Ottawa, Ontario
d. 11/10/1986, Toronto, Ontario

With shamrocks in his eyes and a Maple Leaf emblazoned on his chest, Francis Michael Clancy was truly the "King" of hockey in his day. Actually, the cheery little imp inherited his nickname at an early age from his father, Tom, a star football player at the turn of the twentieth century.

King Clancy played his amateur hockey with St. Brigid's Athletic Club of the Ottawa City league. It was here that he realized just how much smaller he was than the other lads. One of his teachers, a Mr. Moriarity, once asked the puny Irishman what his hockey stick was used for. Clancy, ever the smart-ass, replied, "Why sir, you can . . . handle the puck with it, you can shoot with it, and you can pass . . ."

"Very good, Clancy!" was the old man's response. "What else can you do with it?"

"Gosh, Mr. Moriarity, I guess that's just about all you can do with it."

"No, Frankie," Moriarity said, "it's not all you can do with it." Smiling, he approached Clancy with a stick and jabbed him with it. "You're just a little fellow, so I want you to remember this. In order to take care of yourself when you're on the ice, this thing is always the equalizer. The hockey stick is always the equalizer."

The Ottawa Senators signed Clancy in late 1921 to a three-year contract for $800 a season plus a $100 signing bonus. In his biography, Clancy spoke of his tryout with the Senators: "My first time out, they tried to knock me around quite a bit. Every rookie has to go through this. They knew all the tricks and could make it rough on a kid coming in trying to catch a place on the club. Especially if the kid was only five foot six and weighed about as much as a sack of potatoes."

In only Clancy's second season, he helped the Senators capture the Stanley Cup. By this time, he was feeling his oats. According to one source, he "electrified the spectators with his speed, stick-handling, aggressiveness, and demon-like back-checking." As Ottawa's old guard came to the end of their candle, it was he who emerged as one of the leaders. By 1927, after another Cup win, he was one of the top defenders in the NHL. One man in particular took notice of the King: Toronto Maple Leafs owner Conn Smythe. In October 1930, in the biggest deal in hockey up to that point, Smythe secured Clancy in exchange for Eric Pettinger, Art Smith, and $35,000 cash.

Although Hap Day was de facto captain of the Leafs, Clancy was to become the spirit of a team that won its first Cup in 1932. Despite his small stature, he was unafraid to take on the big boys. Legend has it he once challenged an unruly Boston fan to a post-game scrap, only to be told that he had picked a fight with the heavyweight boxing champion of the world, Jack Sharkey. On top of his indomitable spirit, Clancy had world-class skills. One of the top rushers of hockey's pre-modern age, he had one of the fastest acceleration rates in the league. He also owned a potent shot, and he could pass and stick-handle with the best.

Clancy was honored on "King Clancy Night" at Maple Leaf Gardens on March 17, 1934. "I was amazed at the work they went to just for me. I wasn't a native son; you might even say I was a stranger from another city. Yet they gave me the greatest tribute an individual could ever hope to get."

After retiring in November 1936, Clancy went on to coach the Montreal Maroons for the first half of the 1937–38 season. After a poor start, and amid rumblings of the franchise's imminent death, he quit. From there, he became one of the NHL's top referees, working over the next 10 years among the likes of Bill Chadwick, Mickey Ion, and George Hayes. In 1950, he returned to the Leaf organization, serving as head coach from 1953 to 1956. After Howie Meeker took over behind the bench, Clancy was given the title of assistant general manager.

With his own inimitable Gaelic charm, Clancy became the most effective goodwill ambassador the Maple Leafs had ever seen. Harold Ballard's only close friend died of a heart attack at age 83, leaving behind a grateful world.

The King is a very worthy member of the Hockey Hall of Fame, to which he was inducted in 1958.

Peak Years   *1928–32*
In a Word   *LEPRECHAUN*

DIT CLAPPER Defense/Right Wing
6'2" 195
b. 2/9/1907, Newmarket, Ontario
d. 1/21/1978, Peterborough, Ontario

Aubrey Victor Clapper was the first man ever to play 20 years in the NHL. Great athleticism and an amazing physique allowed him to become not only the best all-around player of his generation but one of hockey's most respected. He got his nickname when his younger brother lisped his name, "Vic," as "Dit."

Dit Clapper

Clapper quickly made his splash in Boston, playing on the famous "Dynamite Line" with Cooney Weiland and Dutch Gainor. The Bruins took the Stanley Cup in his sophomore year, 1928–29. Next season the Dynamite trio helped Boston rewrite the NHL record books as the B's steamrollered to an astounding 38-5-1 record. Clapper scored 41 goals and 61 points that season.

As Clapper's legend grew, he became a prime target for opposing checkers. Before a game in 1932, the bruising Leaf defenseman Red Horner announced, "I'm going to stop this Clapper tonight!"

"Well Red," King Clancy chirped back, "you'd better be very careful because this fellow hits pretty good and knows how to fight."

"Well, I'm going to try him anyways," Red responded.

Before Horner knew it, Boston's big Number 5 had him on his knees with a couple of punches. Clancy knelt beside his teammate on the ice to ask him if he was hurt. Horner's response: "Gee, that fellow can hit!"

But unlike his colleague Eddie Shore, Clapper was noted more for his peacekeeping than his brawling. He had but one real nemesis in the league: the eminently dirty Dave Trottier of the Montreal Maroons. In a 1937 playoff match, Trottier made the mistake of butt-ending a Boston rookie. Clapper, normally one of the most even-tempered players around, blew his stack and took Trottier down. Clapper was busy pummeling Trottier when the referee yanked the big Bruin up by his hair and hurled a few insults at him. An astonished Clapper asked the official to repeat his curse, which he did twice. Clapper promptly decked the referee. As a result, he was ejected from the game.

The next day, the battered referee walked up to him and said, "I want to apologize for saying the things I did to you which caused you to lose your head." The referee then wrote in his report to then NHL president Frank Calder: "I was talking loud when I should have been throwing them into the penalty box." Clapper received a $100 fine for striking the referee — a Rhodes scholar by the name of Clarence Campbell.

During the 1937 season, Boston was retooling after a few sub-par seasons and were putting the finishing touches on a new dynasty. Youngsters Milt Schmidt, Bobby Bauer, Woody Dumart, and Bill Cowley would soon be tearing up NHL rinks. There was still a hole on defense, and Art Ross knew just the man to fill it. The combination of the volatile Shore and the classy Clapper on the blue-line was an instant success. After another guzzle from the Cup in 1939, both Shore and Clapper were selected as the league's top defenders. That same season, they both made the First All-Star Team.

In his 17th season, 1943–44, Clapper began suffering from nagging injuries but his great leadership and hockey brains were still very much in evidence, as he was selected to the Second All-Star Team. In his last three years in Boston, he served as captain and player/coach. Under his tutelage, players like Jack Crawford, Pat "Boxcar" Egan, and Murray Henderson developed. On February 12, 1947, Clapper capped his glorious hockey career with induction into the Hockey Hall of Fame. He continued to act as head coach of the Bruins through the 1948–49 campaign.

Peak Years   *1936–1940*
In a Word   *BRICK*

CHARLIE CONACHER ("The Big Bomber") Right Wing
6'1" 202
b. 12/20/1910, Toronto, Ontario
d. 12/30/1967, Toronto, Ontario

Charlie Conacher

Of all the members of Canada's foremost athletic family, Charlie Conacher was the best hockey player. He started playing at Toronto's Jesse Ketchum School for Boys, the same school attended by former Toronto great Cecil "Babe" Dye. From there, Conacher joined the North Toronto Juniors, very quickly graduating to the outfit's Senior side, and in 1927 he signed on with the Toronto Marlboros. After winning the 1929 Memorial Cup with the Marlies, Charlie moved up to the Toronto Maple Leafs.

By this time, Charlie's sporting idol, his brother Lionel, was carving out a name for himself with Pittsburgh and New York in the big leagues — and making excellent money. This, of course, appealed to the younger Conacher. Years later he would comment: "The National Hockey League represented money. We didn't have a pretzel growing up. We didn't even have enough money to buy toothpaste."

Conn Smythe struck gold in 1930 when he called up Conacher and Harvey "Busher" Jackson and plunked them on either side of puck wizard Joe Primeau. Here marked the birth of the famed "Kid Line" and the blossoming of one of the finest scoring wingers hockey has ever known.

Conacher was a major factor in Toronto's Cup win in 1932, scoring six goals in seven playoff games. He won a pair of scoring titles in the mid 1930s and he made All-Star teams every year from 1932 to 1936. In his nine seasons with Toronto, the Leafs won four Canadian Division titles and reached the Cup finals five times.

"I never had a finer friend in Toronto than Charlie," King Clancy said years later. "He was my protection as a Maple Leaf. I wasn't too big and not too good with my mitts, although I tried to win many a battle. If you got a punch in the chin, you either

----

went down or stood up, shook your head, and took it. But Conacher was Toronto's policeman for many years and a great one. He didn't go looking for trouble, but if it came along he would clear it up."

Known as the "Big Bomber," Conacher was as adept at making shifty moves around the net as he was letting fly with the most powerful shot of the 1930s. Thanks in part to Foster Hewitt's dedicated radio ramblings, young boys across Canada dreamt of the day when their shot would be as deadly as the Big Bomber's.

Conacher's physical style would catch up to him. In 1936–37 and '37–38, he missed nearly two-thirds of his team's games. After he scored his 200th career goal in 1938, Smythe traded him to Detroit. In the fall of 1939 he landed with the New York Americans, where he did a two-year stint before retiring in 1941. He turned to coaching, guiding the Oshawa Generals to a Memorial Cup win in 1944. He returned to the NHL as head coach of the Chicago Black Hawks in 1948, but after a couple of years he entered the business world, where he managed hotels.

One of the most exciting Leafs of all time died of cancer in a Toronto hospital at the end of 1967. He became a member of the Hockey Hall of Fame in 1961.

Peak Years   *1932–36*
In a Word   *POWER*

LIONEL CONACHER (Big Train, Connie the Clutch)
Defense
6'2" 195
b. 5/24/1901, Toronto, Ontario
d. 5/26/1954, Ottawa, Ontario

Lionel Conacher

Lionel Conacher was the oldest of 11 children born to a working-class family in a district his kid brother Charlie called "one of Toronto's higher class slums." Lionel began his astonishing pursuit of sports at school and continued long after the family's poverty forced him to abandon his education. The guy they called the "Big Train" was a true sports legend, excelling in just about any game he tried. In 1920 he won the Canadian light heavyweight boxing championship. The same year, he hit a home run that gave his team the Toronto semi-pro baseball title, then hopped a cab across town and scored four goals and an assist for his lacrosse team, who were down 3–0 when he arrived. In 1921, he led the Toronto Argonauts to the Grey Cup, scoring two touchdowns, two converts, and a field goal. That night, he laced on the skates to play in a Senior hockey game and scored a goal.

Conacher considered hockey to be his weakest sport, but it also paid the best, so he set his sights on the NHL.

By late 1922, Conacher had turned down contract offers from both the Toronto St. Patricks and Montreal Canadiens. An athletic scholarship to Bellefonte Academy in Pittsburgh drew him south of the border. He would go on to captain the Pittsburgh Yellow Jackets to two Fellowes Cups and the United States Amateur Hockey Association title. The highly regarded defender chose to turn professional on November 11, 1925. Some say it was for his sake that the Yellow Jackets were reassembled in the NHL as the Pittsburgh Pirates. In his second pro season in the Iron City, he was traded to the New York Americans for Charlie Langlois and $2,000.

Conacher honed his defensive skills in New York under the guidance of old Western Canada league star "Bullet Joe" Simpson, and he would become an integral part of a stone-wall defense corps that included hard-nosed veteran Leo Reise and the short, squat Bill Brydge. Conacher also established himself as one of the NHL's wildest party boys, enjoying many of Broadway's nighttime offerings.

In 1929–30, Conacher served as player/coach but gave up that role when he was traded to the Maroons prior to the 1930–31 NHL campaign. In Montreal, he enjoyed some of his best years, scoring a career-high 28 points in 1932–33. In 1933, Colonel McLaughlin's Chicago Black Hawks negotiated with the cash-strapped Maroons for Conacher's services, and it was in the Windy City that the strapping defenseman won his first Stanley Cup. The following year, he returned to the Maroons in a three-way deal. Conacher played his last three NHL seasons in Montreal, adding a second Cup win to his unrivaled sporting resume in 1935. He was runner-up for league MVP honors in 1934 and 1937, made the First All-Star Team in 1934 and the Second Team in 1933 and 1937, his last NHL season.

Conacher devoted the rest of his life to public service, first as a member of the Ontario Legislature from 1937 and then as a federal MP from 1949. In the spring of 1954, while playing a game between the MPs' baseball team and the Ottawa Press Gallery, the "Big Train" was finally derailed, suffering a massive heart attack.

Conacher was inducted into the Hockey Hall of Fame in 1994, and he is a member of the Canadian Sports Hall of Fame as well as the Canadian football and lacrosse halls of fame. The Big Train was also named Canada's male athlete of the half century in 1950.

Peak Years   1928–32
In a Word   UNSINKABLE

HAP DAY Defense/Left Wing
5'11" 175
b. 6/14/1901, Owen Sound, Ontario
d. 2/17/1990, St. Thomas, Ontario

It was old Charlie Querrie, the erstwhile Toronto owner, who talked young Clarence Day into a professional hockey career. The sharp youth would do so on one condition — that he would not be forced to quit his studies toward a career as a pharmacist. He signed with the Toronto St. Patricks in 1924 and made his NHL debut against the Montreal Maroons on December 15 of that year, playing on a line with Jack Adams and Babe Dye. Seasons of 10 and 14 goals put Day "on the map," so to speak.

In February 1927, Conn Smythe and his associates bought the St. Patricks and changed their name to the Maple Leafs. Before long, Smythe brought Day, who'd been a superb defensive forward, back to the blue-line. In 1930, Smythe made one of the biggest deals in NHL history when he obtained King Clancy from Ottawa, and the Day–Clancy pairing proved to be pure magic from the very first. Clancy's vim was the perfect complement to Day's heady, steady, and ready style.

Day was a prankster, to be sure. Apparently, he was the leader of what the Toronto media referred to as the "Three Musketeers of Mirth and Mayhem" — Day, Clancy, and Charlie Conacher. Mild-mannered Joe Primeau was the unwitting victim of one of the funniest of the trio's gags. The Leafs had been invited to a Halloween party and everyone but Primeau, who was ill, attended. Hours later, the revelers returned to their hotel rooms to discover that every bed sheet in every room had been twisted in knots! Primeau naturally became the prime suspect, since everyone knew he was the only one who'd stayed behind. The other players pulled the emergency fire hose from the wall, stuck the nozzle through the transom of Primeau's room, and turned on the faucet full force! Awakened by the watery deluge, Primeau opened his door and demanded to know what was going on. Years later the true culprit's identity was still up for grabs. Hap Day would recall, "The rest of the guys figured it must have been Clancy, so the next day they threw him in the showers with all of his clothes on." Clancy, for his part, claimed that "Day was the guy who suggested we slip away from the party and tie up the bed clothes."

Day played the 1937–38 season as a New York American, then retired. After a couple of years as a referee, he was appointed head coach of the Maple Leafs, leading Toronto to five Stanley Cups in 10 seasons, and eventually became the club's general manager.

Day was called the "perfect professional athlete" by his peers. And although Smythe had many stars play for him during his lengthy involvement with the Leafs, it is doubtful another player stood higher in his estimation than the man who once owned and operated a pharmacy at Maple Leaf Gardens — Clarence Henry "Hap" Day.

Day became a member of the Hockey Hall Fame in 1961.

Peak Years   1928–32
In a Word   CEREBRAL

CHARLIE GARDINER Goal
b. 12/31/1904, Edinburgh, Scotland
d. 6/13/1934, Winnipeg, Manitoba

Charlie Gardiner

When he died suddenly in the summer of 1934, Chuck Gardiner was lauded as the greatest goalkeeper in hockey history. And for good reason, too. The curly-haired Scot was one of the few European players of his time who had made good in the NHL. He had come to Canada at age seven and learned how to skate on the corner lots around frosty Winnipeg. Because he was such a poor skater, he was often left to tend the nets. In later years, he admitted he'd learned to use his hands and feet so skillfully and quickly because they would have frozen had he not kept them busy in the sub-zero weather!

The young Scotsman was a natural athlete who proved to be a first-class rugby, baseball, and hockey player. He gave up rugby at his mother's behest after he was injured in a local Junior match, and he quit baseball because it cut in on his work. But he stuck with hockey. Playing every chance he got, he worked himself up through the Midget, Juvenile, and Junior ranks. When he let in a dozen goals during an Intermediate game at Portage la Prairie, he stayed home the next day and cried; when he was playing for the Selkirk Fishermen in 1925, he walked down back alleys to avoid fans after a loss in a big playoff game.

In 1926, Barney Stanley of the Chicago Black Hawks organization gave Gardiner his big chance and assigned him to the AHA's Winnipeg Maroons. A year later, he was skating with the big team.

As a rookie in Chicago, Gardiner had the benefit of playing under the tutelage of Hugh Lehman who, Gardiner later said, taught him all he knew about tending goal. The legendary Duke Keats taught Gardiner to outguess enemy forwards, and gave the young Scot the encouragement he needed.

Gardiner took over Lehman's post in 1927, and his skillful hands and lightning-fast feet combined with an uncommon intelligence to make him one of the finest net-minders ever seen. His on-ice daring — he would not hesitate to dive in among sharp skate blades for the puck, or skate far from his net to break up a play — made him a fan favorite. But he was also a keen thinker, a leader, and a champion of the first order.

Gardiner's finest hour came during the 1934 Stanley Cup finals, which he almost single-handedly won for Chicago. Although he was a very sick man before and during the series, he refused to give in. His greatness was proven in the fourth and deciding match against the pesky Detroit Red Wings, when he repelled each and every attack for a 1–0 Hawks victory. Two months later he would die of a brain hemorrhage.

According to coach Tommy Gorman, "Never before in the history of hockey had a better exhibition of goal-keeping been given than that which Gardiner put up against

Detroit in that championship final." Gorman would also later gush: "He was one of the finest fellows on and off the ice I have ever met." And Duke Keats called Gardiner "one of the finest boys in hockey, a clean-living sportsman, and a man you could always depend on."

Marvin McCarthy, sportswriter for the Chicago *Herald-American*, remembered Gardiner this way:

> Another valiant warrior lies at eternal ease in the shadow of professional ice hockey's symbol of courage, the Georges Vezina Trophy, for keepers of the goals. Chuck Gardiner is dead. Curly-haired Chuck, holy terror of the ice, young Blind Fury personified, who times galore has startled and thrilled us with headlong rushes into the very thing that I'm afraid, played a part in his death — the hurtling puck.
>
> No onslaught that stout Chuck ever faced was so sudden or stunning as Death's swift charge that laid him low. The last red light has flashed for Charles Gardiner.

Gardiner won the Vezina Trophy in 1932 and 1934 and made the First All-Star Team in 1931, 1932, and 1934. He was inducted into the Hockey Hall of Fame in 1945.

Peak Years   *1930–34*
In a Word   *CATLIKE*

EBBIE GOODFELLOW   Defense/Center
6'0" 185
b. 4/9/1907, North Gower, Ontario
d. 9/10/1985, Sarasota, Florida

By the age of 20, Ebenezer Goodfellow was playing for the Ottawa city Senior league's Ottawa Montagnards and had been scouted by the Senators. Early reports said the tall, skinny kid was a frail commodity, and so the Senators took a pass.

Jack Adams, who'd just retired as a Senators player and taken the job of manager of the brand-new Detroit Cougars, had several top-notch scouts combing the land for talent. One of them, Nate Nelson, spotted Goodfellow in action for the Montagnards and immediately signed him.

Goodfellow turned pro with the Detroit Olympics of the Canadian Professional Hockey League in the fall of 1928 and was sensational. Not only did he lead the circuit in scoring, but his brilliant play was a major factor in his team's first-place finish. He moved up the next year to the Cougars and he continued to tear up the ice, scoring 17 goals and 34 points in 44 games. He followed that up with 25 goals and 48 points, good for second in league scoring.

Goodfellow played his entire 14-year career in Detroit, contributing to four league championships and three Stanley Cup wins. In 1936, after years of centering Herbie Lewis and Larry Aurie, Goodfellow was moved back to the blue-line. After the shift, he became a three-time All-Star (1936, '37, and '40), and he won the Hart Trophy in 1940.

Goodfellow served as team captain for several years, becoming player/coach in 1941. He was assistant coach to Adams in 1942, filling in for his boss during the 1942 Cup finals.

"He was a good one," Sid Abel said of Goodfellow. "One of the real stars of the league. He was known at that time as one of the defensemen who could shoot a heavy puck and was one of the hardest shots in the league. He was a hard-nosed player, but a real nice fellow."

After his playing days, Goodfellow coached the St. Louis Flyers. When he took the reins in 1947, the team was deep in the cellar of the AHL's Western Division. He was given two years to remedy the situation, and not only led St. Louis out of the basement, he took them to first place in the division in his second season as coach. The Chicago Black Hawks tapped him for coaching duties in 1950, and he lasted through the 1951–52 season.

After he left hockey, Goodfellow worked as a manufacturer's representative for International Tools in Windsor, Ontario, and he retired to Florida in the mid 1970s. He was active in the Red Wings alumni association, an organization he helped found. While recovering from spinal surgery, the original leader of the Detroit Red Wings succumbed to cancer at his home. He was 78.

Goodfellow became a member of the Hockey Hall of Fame in 1963.

Peak Years   *1932–36*
In a Word   *LEATHER*

JOHNNY GOTTSELIG Left Wing
5'11" 158
b. 6/24/1905, Odessa, Russia
d. 5/15/1986

Although Johnny Gottselig was born in the Ukraine, he grew up on the semi-tundra near Winnipeg, Manitoba. He developed his hockey skills from an early age, working his way up to the Memorial Cup–winning Regina Pats in 1924–25. After a one-season stint in his adopted hometown of Winnipeg, he was claimed by the Chicago Black Hawks.

This tall, skinny sophomore led the Hawks with 21 goals in 1929–30 and topped his mates in both goals and points in each of the next two seasons. Although Ranger import Paul Thompson would become the club's main offensive threat, Gottselig played a key role in Chicago's first ever Stanley Cup win in early 1934.

Among other things, Gottselig was a flashy stick-handler, always quite prominent with his dexterous work in close, and respected around the league as a "fellow who could make a fool of you if you didn't watch him closely." In 1934–35 he again led Chicago in goals while playing on a line with an over-the-hill Howie Morenz and Mush "The Mighty Midget" March. The oil-slick Gottselig helped Chicago win another Cup in 1938 and made the Second All-Star Team in 1939.

Gottselig remained with Chicago until late 1940, when he was named player/coach of the team's AHA satellite club in Kansas City. With the manpower shortage during World War Two, he was called back to the Windy City in 1942. His last NHL game came in 1944–45. March of 1945 saw him replace Paul Thompson as head coach of the Hawks, and he served in this capacity until late 1947, when he was replaced by Charlie Conacher and named assistant to team president/general manager Bill Tobin.

In 589 games, Gottselig scored 176 goals and 371 points. He played in the memorial games for Howie Morenz in 1937, and Babe Siebert in 1939.

Peak Years   *1931–35*
In a Word   *NIFTY*

GEORGE HAINSWORTH Goal
5'6" 150
b. 6/26/1895, Toronto, Ontario
d. 10/9/1950, Gravenhurst, Ontario

George Hainsworth played the better part of his amateur hockey in Berlin, Ontario (now Kitchener), where his skill and composure under fire attracted the attention of the local Juniors in 1913. The smallish goalie went on to play on championship teams at the Junior, Intermediate, and Senior levels before turning professional with the WCHL Saskatoon Crescents in 1923–24.

He hooked up with the Montreal Canadiens in 1926 after Newsy Lalonde touted him to team bigwig Leo Dandurand as a replacement for the late, great Georges Vezina. Montreal's new boy proved an immediate success, winning the Vezina Trophy in each of his first three seasons and posting goals-against averages of 1.47, 1.06, and 0.92! In 1928–29, Hainsworth left an indelible mark on the NHL record books by registering 22 shutouts in 44 games.

Forward passing rules were revolutionized after 1928–29, making it impossible for Hainsworth to post such stratospheric numbers again. Still, he helped the Canadiens win back-to-back Stanley Cups in 1930 and 1931 behind such stars as Howie Morenz, Aurel Joliat, Pit Lepine, and Sylvio and Georges Mantha.

In October 1933, Hainsworth was traded to Toronto for Lorne Chabot. Hainsworth went on to backstop the Leafs to two Canadian Division titles as the team reached the finals twice over the next three years. As age crept up on this homely little man, Conn Smythe brought in Walter "Turk" Broda. After a short spell back with the Canadiens, the 41-year-old Hainsworth decided to call it a career.

Hainsworth's record of 94 career shutouts stood more than 25 years, until Terry Sawchuk topped it in 1963–64. If you factor in Hainsworth's 10 shutouts in Saskatoon, his major-league total comes to 104, one better than "Ukie."

Like the great Vezina before him, Hainsworth was cool as ice between the pipes, performing with an almost complete lack of what we today call "showmanship." Expressionless, unexcited, he faced storms of rubber and blocked the heaviest drives from some of the finest snipers ever seen without so much as batting an eyelash. Once, after being complimented by Montreal *Herald* scribe Elmer Ferguson on one of his many shutouts, the little guy was heard to remark, "I'm sorry I can't put on a show like some of the other goalers. But I just can't do it. I can't look excited because I'm not. I can't shout at other players because that's not my style. I can't dive on easy shots and make then look hard. I guess all I can do is stop pucks."

Hainsworth died tragically in a car accident on October 9, 1950, and, despite calls for his immediate enshrinement in the Hockey Hall of Fame, he did not gain entrance until 1961.

Peak Years 1928–32
In a Word ROBOT

RED HORNER Defense
6'0" 198
b. 5/28/1909, Lynden, Ontario

In 1926, Reginald "Red" Horner decided to try out for a spot on Frank Selke's Toronto Marlboros. Selke, who would go on to greatness as a dynasty builder in the NHL, studied all 72 Marlboro candidates digging into the ice at the old Mutual Street Arena. At the time, Senior hockey luminary Allister "Shrimp" MacPherson was slated to be captain. Big Horner, who was Selke's grocery delivery boy, did little to distinguish himself from the crowd. In the next workout camp, MacPherson told Selke, "I hope you don't have any serious thoughts of giving that big redhead in the North Toronto sweater a chance to play with the team." Selke asked MacPherson why he thought this. The young star replied: "Oh, he'll get you a lot of penalties. He always has his elbow in your kisser or his fanny in your tummy all the time he's on the ice." Selke thought for a minute, then figured that any Bantam who could bother MacPherson was worthy of a place on the team. Selke immediately signed the rough-and-tumble Horner.

Immediately upon his arrival in the NHL in 1928, Horner's extremely robust play ruffled feathers around the league. In his second career game on Christmas Night 1928, the Maroons' Nels Stewart broke Horner's hand. Smythe assigned veteran teammate Hap Day to give the kid some pointers — to "show him the ropes," as it were. Horner would later say that his being teamed with Day on defense gave him the confidence he needed to make it in the NHL and the "inside dope to get the job done in the end."

In 1932, Horner won his first Stanley Cup. Although he'd missed a mess of regular-season dates and wasn't 100 percent for the playoffs, he managed to steam ahead and help Toronto finish off the Rangers.

In 1932–33, Horner started an eight-year run of leading the league in penalty minutes, establishing himself as one of the all-time "bad boys" of the game. Despite this dubious achievement, Horner was a true professional, a player with rather a graceful air about him. According to Selke, "Lou Fontinato, John Ferguson, Howie Young and others are rough, but none of them had the poise which established Red Horner as the bad man supreme and the idol of all the gals in the arenas."

Smythe and Selke felt there was "no better team player in the league" than Horner. Although not a graceful skater, he was apparently able to accelerate from a standstill as quickly as anyone in the league, except perhaps Howie Morenz and King Clancy. Although Horner could pass the puck adequately, his strength clearly lay in the physical game.

The fact that Horner was intensely hated by opponents actually worked to Toronto's advantage. On a rush, the big brute would draw the attention of two or three checkers. He would then zip the puck over to Joe Primeau, Busher Jackson, or Charlie Conacher, who were by this time well in the clear. Selke called Horner the "sacrificial lamb of the Maple Leafs during the 1930s and a good man for selling tickets." Fans across Canada wanted to see him play . . . not because they liked him, but because they'd love to have given him a "brick house — letting him have the bricks one by one!"

Horner's greatest honor in hockey came at the beginning of the 1938–39 season, when the Leafs named him team captain. He wore the "C" with pride until his retirement after the 1940 Cup finals. He became a member of the Hockey Hall of Fame in 1965.

Peak Years   *1933–37*
In a Word   *HORNET*

BUSHER JACKSON Left Wing
5'11" 195
b. 1/19/1911, Toronto, Ontario
d. 6/25/1966, Toronto, Ontario

Big Harvey Jackson was an intensely handsome man with almost pretty features, wavy hair, and a winning smile. He was one of the most graceful skaters of his time and possessed a hard, accurate shot from either the forehand or backhand. The man that Leaf trainer Tim Daly first nicknamed "Busher" was probably the most complete offensive package in the 1930s. Frank Selke rated Jackson as one of the finest left wingers he'd ever seen, calling him the "Lindbergh of the ice lanes."

"Joliat and Lindsay may have been better all-around players, but Jackson was the classiest," Selke gushed. "He did everything with a flourish."

Distractions got in the way of Jackson's genius, though. Booze, women, and bad investments became the norm for him. He never really had much control over his private life and seemed to live day-to-day. In 1931–32, the young superstar finally realized his huge potential when he led the league in points. To that date he was the youngest ever to do so.

After Joe Primeau retired prematurely in 1936, and Charlie Conacher went down with an assortment of injuries, the famous "Kid Line" was dissolved and Jackson was teamed up with Syl Apps and Gordie Drillon. Together, these three formed a potent combination. Despite his continued great play, Jackson's lurid social habits put him at odds with the straitlaced Conn Smythe, who couldn't abide Jackson's lackadaisical approach to the game and overall lack of self-discipline. After Jackson dislocated his shoulder in the 1939 finals, Smythe sent him packing. He was dealt, along with Buzz Boll, Doc Romnes, Jim Fowler, and Murray Armstrong, to the New York Americans for Sweeney Schriner.

Jackson played on a line with Armstrong and Lorne Carr for two seasons, but his production tailed off considerably. Unable to negotiate a satisfactory contract with Amerks boss Red Dutton, Jackson was sold to Boston in 1942.

Busher's three years in Boston were characterized by sporadic bursts of production. He was at his best when he played with his brother Art and pass-master Bill Cowley. Jackson regained much of his old form in 1942–43, potting 19 goals, including a hat-trick in a game against the Canadiens. He was in top form during the playoffs that year, scoring the winning goal in an overtime struggle against the Canadiens. He closed out his NHL career a year later. Truly a great star, he scored 241 goals and 475 points in 633 games. One can only image how much greater he could have been had he been able to discipline himself properly.

Jackson's life after hockey wasn't as successful as those enjoyed by his old line-mates Primeau and Conacher. His appetites and a string of bad business deals kept Jackson securely in the red for the rest of his life.

His last years seemed to be filled with black luck. He broke his neck and lost partial use of his right hand after tumbling down a flight of stairs in 1958. Eight months later, he was back in the hospital with a bad case of jaundice that left his nervous system in tatters. Jackson was now broke and without a family. The NHL tried to help him out but there wasn't much they could do for him. Hockey people would lower their heads in shame and glance furtively at Jackson when he would walk into a room — why did it have to end this way? The dazzling smile was gone and he now looked eternally unhappy. It was a sad end for a hockey legend. He died of a rotten liver in 1966.

After 20 years of being passed over, Jackson's name was finally enshrined in the Hockey Hall of Fame in 1971.

Peak Years   *1931–35*
Comparable Recent Player   *Sergei Fedorov*
In a Word   *GORGEOUS*

CHING JOHNSON (The Holding Corporation, The Great
   Wall of China) Defense
5'11" 210
b. 12/7/1897, Winnipeg, Manitoba
d. 6/19/1979, Takoma Park, Maryland

Ching Johnson

Ivan Wilfred "Ching" Johnson was one of the most genial
defenders to ever clutch an opposing player's sweater. As an all-star
blue-liner with the New York Rangers, he was expert at wheeling forwards out of position with his famous clutch-and-grab technique.

Johnson was born in Winnipeg, and was active in lacrosse and football until he
went overseas with the Canadian Army in World War One. He first broke into organized hockey with Winnipeg's Senior Monarchs in 1919, then hooked up with the
Eveleth, Minnesota, side in the United States Amateur Association. In 1923 he joined
the Minneapolis Millers, where he was paired up with the lumbering Clarence "Taffy" Abel.

When Conn Smythe was organizing the New York Rangers in 1926, he purchased
both Johnson and Abel, and the two became one of the most effective defense duos of
their day. Despite their obvious lack of speed, few were the goals scored whenever
these bruisers were on the ice. Legendary sportswriter Damon Runyon once said of
Johnson's ever-present grin, "He's got a true castor oil smile." Loosely translated, the
big man's smirk masked his brutal intentions.

Johnson took First-team All-Star honors in 1931–32, and 1932–33, and he played a
huge role in Ranger Cup wins in 1928 and 1933. Slow as molasses in January, the big
lug had a pure love for the game of hockey and showed it by giving his all every night.

After 11 seasons with the Rangers, management felt Johnson was too old and too
slow. Lester Patrick handed the burly boy his unconditional release in late 1937, and it
wasn't long before he got a phone call from Red Dutton, the Americans manager, offering him a contract. Johnson rounded out his career as a part-time player and coach
and was released at season's end. He spent two more years with his old club in
Minneapolis as a playing coach.

In 1958, Johnson was inducted into the Hockey Hall of Fame.

Peak Years   *1929–33*
In a Word   *HUMPTY*

PIT LEPINE Center
6'0" 168
b. 7/30/1901, Ste. Anne de Bellevue, Quebec
d. 8/2/1955

This tall, gangly veteran of the Montreal city Senior league joined the Montreal
Canadiens in 1925–26. Alongside his brother Hector, Pit tore up the minor leagues
and, early on, sportswriters were comparing his style to that of former Ottawa Senators
great Frank Nighbor.

Sporting a mop of prematurely gray hair, Pit soon became a French Canadian icon.
His superb all-around abilities wooed Canadiens fans almost from the first moment he
stepped on the ice. According to legendary news hound Baz O'Meara, Lepine was a
"wonderful player, smooth, gifted with a great shot . . . a marvelous two-way poke-
check . . . the embodiment of grace on the ice, a man whose skill and dexterity only
really became tremendously apparent after Morenz had left." A honey-smooth skater
and play-maker, Lepine was the head coach's go-to guy when it came to shadowing or
penalty-killing. The great Frank Finnigan — himself a superhuman defensive player for
Ottawa and Toronto — rated Lepine one of the greatest defensive forwards of his time.

It was Lepine's "misfortune" to play on the same team as the meteoric Morenz. As is often the case when a good player plays beside a great player, Lepine was overshadowed. With Morenz playing as much as 40 minutes per game, it was next to impossible for Lepine to shine. Still, in 526 games, he managed 143 goals and 241 points.

Peak Years   *1930–1934*
In a Word   *ALMOST*

SYLVIO MANTHA Defense
5'10" 178
b. 4/14/1902, Montreal, Quebec
d. 8/7/1974, Montreal, Quebec

By 1923, Montreal Canadiens boss Leo Dandurand had a club laden with aging, over-the-hill veterans. The looming reconstruction job would be a formidable task. The first step was to secure a solid, young defenseman to replace Sprague Cleghorn and Billy Coutu, both of whom were getting long in the tooth. This is where Sylvio Mantha came in. Dandurand signed the Montreal boy almost as soon as he discovered him.

Another prize rookie that year was the legendary Howie Morenz. Mantha and the "Stratford Streak" were a factor in the Canadiens' winning the 1924 Stanley Cup even though the former didn't see a lot of ice-time in sets against the Calgary Tigers and Vancouver Maroons.

Mantha started to see more ice-time after Cleghorn was traded in 1925, and he gained valuable experience when the Habs paired him with WHL veteran Herb Gardiner. By the time of Montreal's next Cup win in 1930, Mantha ranked among the best defensive defensemen in hockey. He earned a Second All-Star Team selection in 1930–31 and 1931–32.

After a season as the Canadiens' player/coach, Mantha moved on to Boston for 1936–37, his final campaign. For the next two years, he served as an NHL linesman and as a referee in the AHL. Tired of the travel, he returned to Montreal to coach Junior and Senior hockey.

Mantha was one of those players everyone seems to forget. His contribution to the champion Canadiens from the mid 1920s to early 1930s was great. It was he who anchored the Morenzes, Aurel Joliats, and Billy Bouchers as an ever present defensive conscience.

Mantha became a member of the Hockey Hall of Fame in 1960.

Peak Years   *1928–33*
In a Word   *STALWART*

MUSH MARCH (The Mighty Midget) Right Wing
5'5" 154
b. 10/18/1908, Silton, Saskatchewan

Harold "Mush" March was one of the Black Hawks' original stars, putting in an admirable 17 years of NHL service in Chicago. All told, he scored 153 goals and 383 points and was thought of as one of the top clutch players during the 1930s.

A native of Silton, Saskatchewan, March played his Junior hockey with the Regina Monarchs, with whom he won a Memorial Cup in 1927–28. He made his NHL debut in 1928–29 and before long had assumed a regular place in the Hawks' lineup.

The little winger would score many a big goal for Chicago over the years. Perhaps the hugest of these came in overtime of the deciding game of the 1934 Cup finals, when he slammed one by Detroit's Wilf Cude.

March was a dandy skater with a plucky spirit, good play-making sense, and fair-to-good goal-scoring ability. He was always among the fastest on the ice at any given time, and his quickness enabled him to become a top-notch penalty-killer.

A consistent performer, March reached double figures in goals eight times and topped the 30-point mark five times. He retired following the 1944–45 season to make room for the whiz-bang Bentley brothers. He later returned to the game and served 11 years as a linesman.

Peak Years   *1933–37*
Comparable Recent Player   *Sami Kapanen*
In a Word   *PEP*

BALDY NORTHCOTT Left Wing
6'0" 184
b. 9/7/1908, Calgary, Alberta
d. 11/7/1986, Winnipeg, Manitoba

Lawrence "Baldy" Northcott was a big and scrappy player with no affinity for the enemy whatsoever. He loved to hit, was a speedy player for his size, and was probably the most effective man in the corners in his day.

Lawrence Northcott

The Montreal Maroon everyone called "Baldy" — an ironic handle, as he had ample hair — was a star left winger for the North Bay Trappers of the Northern Ontario Hockey Association in 1929. A few of James Strachan's men discovered the rough-and-tumble Northcott and signed him to a deal.

In five appearances with the M's in 1928–29, he toiled alongside a curly-haired speed artist named Jimmy Ward and ex-Olympic luminary Dave Trottier. This unit remained intact for three seasons. In 1933, Northcott was selected to the NHL's First All-Star Team. By then, the Maroons' big gun was on a line with Ward and the fabulous Hooley Smith. Northcott played an important role in the Maroons' Cup win in 1935, scoring a trio of playoff game–winning goals.

When Smith was sold to the Boston Bruins, Northcott played a couple of seasons on a line with Russ "Beaver" Blinco and Earl Robinson. When the Maroons folded, Northcott moved to Chicago, but after scoring only five goals in 46 games in 1938–39, Northcott decided to call it quits.

In 446 games, he scored 133 goals and 245 points.

Peak Years   *1932–36*
Comparable Recent Player   *Shayne Corson*
In a Word   *BULL*

JOE PRIMEAU (Da Preem, Gentleman Joe) Center
5'11" 160
b. 1/29/1906, Lindsay, Ontario
d. 5/14/1989

Although Joe Primeau didn't start skating until the age of 12, he developed into a crackerjack hockeyist. His skills attracted the attention of St. Michael's College in Toronto in 1923, and he moved up to the Senior Marlboros in 1926–27, scoring 11 goals in 10 games.

Meanwhile, in Manhattan, Conn Smythe was putting together the Rangers, and he recommended signing Primeau. Smythe's associates felt the center was too small and frail, and they turned thumbs down. Smythe remembered Primeau, however, and as soon as he took over the Toronto St. Patricks (soon to be renamed the Maple Leafs), he snapped up the Lindsay native.

Primeau made a handful of appearances with the Leafs in 1927–28 and 1928–29 before grabbing a permanent spot on the blue and white. When Smythe teamed Primeau with a pair of other rookies — Harvey "Busher" Jackson and Charlie Conacher — the legendary "Kid Line," perhaps the most dominant forward unit in hockey history, was conceived. In the middle of it all was the slightly built Primeau, as cool and calm an ice-general as there ever was.

Primeau's finest season came in 1931–32, when he finished only three points behind Jackson in the NHL scoring race. That same season, the Leafs took the Stanley Cup. In the finals against the Rangers, Primeau was exceptional, assisting on six goals in seven games.

By this time, Primeau was one of the top centers around. His genius for the pass, his slipperiness, enabled him to rack up record assist totals. For good measure, he was a superb defensive forward and penalty-killer.

In 1933–34, Primeau finished second again in the scoring race, this time to Conacher. Primeau ended up scoring an All-Star nod that year. In an exhibition game prior to the start of the 1934–35 regular season, he broke his thumb and missed 11 games. This marked the end of the "Kid Line." He retired at the end of the next season at the relatively young age of 30 so he could dedicate more time to his construction business. He also went on to become the first and only coach to guide his teams to a Memorial Cup, an Allan Cup, and a Stanley Cup championship.

In 310 games over nine years, Primeau scored 66 goals and 243 points. He became a very worthy member of the Hockey Hall of Fame in 1963.

Peak Years   1930–35
Comparable Recent Player   Adam Oates
In a Word   WIZARD

EARL SEIBERT Defense
6'2" 198
b. 12/7/1911, Kitchener, Ontario
d. 5/12/1990, Agawam, Massachusetts

Earl Seibert, today a forgotten man, was a brilliant defenseman who played 15 years in the NHL. During his career he was named to NHL All-Star teams an eye-popping 10 years in a row — four times to the First Team and six times on the Second.

Earl Seibert

The big rearguard started out on the frozen lakes and streams surrounding his hometown of Kitchener, Ontario, then called Berlin. He played hockey in the mid to late 1920s, starring for the OHA's Kitchener Greenshirts. His fine blend of strength, size, and skill drew the attention of many scouts, and in 1931, the solemn-faced youngster inked a deal with the New York Rangers.

Playing alongside the likes of Ott Heller and Ching Johnson, burly Earl blossomed into a star and helped the Broadway Blueshirts to a Stanley Cup in 1933. Before the start of the 1935–36 campaign, he became embroiled in contract talks with Lester Patrick. The boss grew so incensed when Seibert showed up with his father, who was to "represent" him, that he traded the star blue-liner to the Chicago Black Hawks straight-up for Art Coulter.

Seibert was a strong, fast skater, an intimidating force with his stick and his body. He was also one of the better shot-blockers around. Family friend Joe Pompei later said of Seibert, "He had an acceleration with his second step no one could match and he was probably the best skater of the 1930s." Earl also owned excellent puck-handling skills and he was almost impossible to knock off his skates. There were many who thought he would have done equally well as a forward.

One night in 1937, something happened that would affect the rest of Seibert's life. In a game between Chicago and the Canadiens, he slammed Howie Morenz into the boards. In an attempt to wiggle free, Morenz caught his skate in a rut on the ice and fell, breaking his leg badly. Six weeks later, hockey's premier superstar died in hospital, rocking the sports world. For years, Montreal fans would boo big Seibert mercilessly. "My father never got over that until the day he died," Earl's son Oliver said a few hours after laying his father to rest.

Seibert was the biggest factor in Chicago's Cinderella Stanley Cup victory in 1938 and, according to his son, was given a piece of the team by owner Major McLaughlin. When McLaughlin died, though, manager Bill Tobin wouldn't recognize the deal and swiftly dealt Seibert to the Detroit Red Wings, where he closed out his big-league career in 1946.

After retiring, he teamed up with Eddie Shore in Springfield to coach the Indians of the AHL. In 1951, sick of Shore's reign of tyranny, Seibert cut himself loose. Shore later said of the only man he was ever afraid to fight: "It's lucky he was a calm boy, because if he ever got mad, he'd have killed us all."

After washing his hands of hockey for good, Seibert settled down in Agawam, Massachusetts, as owner of the Stateline Package Store, a retail liquor outlet.

Seibert's father was Oliver Seibert, an early star of the old Ontario Professional league. In 1961, the senior Seibert was elected to the Hockey Hall of Fame, and two years later Earl followed him in. It was the first ever father-and-son combination voted into the Hall.

Only a handful of others have equaled or bettered Seibert's 10 consecutive All-Star selections. He certainly belongs in the same category as Eddie Shore and Dit Clapper, whose play he could generally match.

Peak Years   1938–42
In a Word   STRONG

EDDIE SHORE (Old Blood & Guts, The Boston Strongboy) Defense
5'11" 190
b. 11/25/1902, Ford Qu'Appelle, Saskatchewan
d. 3/17/1985 Agawam, Massachusetts

Though he'll be remembered forever as the original "Big Bad Bruin," Eddie Shore actually began his pro career in 1924 with the WCHL Regina Capitals — as a forward! He joined the Boston Bruins in August 1926, making his NHL debut on November 16 at the old Boston Arena. He earned an assist.

"Eddie Shore caught the fancy of the fans. The new defense man is tall, yet sturdily built. His speed is exceptional and he handles his body and stick well." So wrote A. Linde Fowler in the old Boston *Transcript*. By season's end, he had fought Nels Stewart and Frank Foyston, been fined $40, and thrice suspended for major infractions.

After a game in 1928, Shore was said to have tramped the streets of Boston looking for a doctor to sew up an ear he'd had severed. Although team doctors thought the ear couldn't be saved, he found a physician willing to try. Against the doc's orders, Shore refused the anesthetic: "Just give me a mirror. I want to be sure you sew it on right."

In a bloody game between Boston and the Maroons in 1929, Nels Stewart, Hooley Smith, and Babe Siebert worked Shore over as if he were a stockyard steer. The "'S' Line" broke his nose, slashed his face to ribbons, and knocked out several of his teeth. Amazingly, the big Bruin kept playing despite being scarcely able to see out of his blackened peepers. As one report had it: "Shore, already acknowledged as the greatest hockey player in the game, set the seal on his courage by playing the last period with blood streaming down his face from a deep gash over the left eye, carrying on until he was at last literally smashed down when the brawny Babe Siebert high-sticked him across the face in the final minute." Shore was unconscious for 15 minutes. The damage? A broken nose, four shattered teeth, two black eyes, a gash or two on his cheekbone, and a two-inch cut over his left eye! Oddly, Siebert was not penalized. After the game, Bruins owner Charles F. Adams handed Shore a check for $500.

Shore embodied the rough-and-tumble game of hockey of the late 1920s and 1930s. He was a high-octane performer with a temper to match. Although he could rush like a storm, he would knock down anyone who stood in his way. Despite the fact that All-Star teams were not created until 1931, he managed to secure nominations eight times in nine seasons. Seven of those nods were to the First Team. He still stands as the only defenseman to be awarded the Hart Trophy four times.

Shore scored his last goal as a Bruin in 1939–40. He was traded later that season to the New York Americans for Eddie Wiseman and $5,000. In New York he ended his NHL playing career, then took on the ownership reins with the AHL's Springfield Indians.

Shore was named to the Hall of Fame in 1947.

Peak Years   *1929–33*
In a Word   *DEVIL*

BABE SIEBERT Left Wing/Defense
5'10" 200
b. 1/14/1904, Plattsville, Ontario
d. 8/25/1939, St. Joseph, Ontario

Albert "Babe" Siebert made his jump to the NHL in time for the 1925–26 season, debuting with the Montreal Maroons on a line with Bill Phillips and Punch Broadbent. Big Siebert soon proved himself a fierce competitor, a star who combined tireless back-checking with speed and play-making ability. Early on, though, coach Eddie Gerard explored his potential as a defender. In 1929, Siebert was thrown onto a line with Nels Stewart and Hooley Smith. With big Stewart pouring in the goals, Siebert and Smith forechecked like fiends. The combination gained fame as the "'S' Line."

During the 1929–30 season, Siebert got into a war with Boston's Eddie Shore. During a game between the M's and B's, Siebert and a throng of his mates gang-tackled the Bruins defender. With Shore pinned to the ice, Siebert administered him a savage beating. Shore never forgot this incident, going so far as to ignore Siebert when Babe was dealt to the Bruins a few years later.

The fabulous "Triple S," which had become the terror of the NHL, was broken up dramatically in 1932. Stewart was dealt to Boston and Siebert to the Rangers. During Babe's early years with Montreal, coach Eddie Gerard had had him perform spot duty on the blue-line, and in New York Lester Patrick moved him permanently to defense. Boston's Art Ross needed a defenseman when Eddie Shore was suspended for his attack on Ace Bailey, so Siebert moved to the Bruins.

He was on the move again in 1936, this time to the Montreal Canadiens with Roger Jenkins in exchange for Leroy Goldsworthy, Sammy McManus, and $10,000. Although Siebert's speed had waned, he had become one of the better blue-liners around. The new Canadiens captain shored up the defense and led his boys to a Canadian Division title. This, after Montreal had finished dead-last the year before.

Siebert was awarded the Hart Trophy in 1937, garnering his second of three con-secutive First All-Star Team nods. He was slated to take over as head coach of the Canadiens in 1939–40, but he drowned in August 1939. The NHL held an All-Star

----

game — only the third in NHL history — to benefit the Siebert family on October 29.

Sportswriter Elmer Ferguson painted the following picture of the man who drowned trying to retrieve an old, inflated inner tube for his beloved daughter:

> Mrs. Siebert, pretty blonde sweetheart of the Babe, was an invalid for most of their marriage together. But always when his team was playing in Montreal, she had a rink-side seat at the Forum, from which adoringly she would watch her husband whirl through the game, balancing his team on defence, hurling his power into attacks.
>
> Perhaps in these games, the Babe would become embroiled in fistic battle. Perhaps he would suffer penalties, earn the disfavor of the crowd by his bruising style of play. Perhaps the game would make him seem like a crude and uncouth person, rough and brutal. From the dressing room, the Babe would stride along the promenade until he reached the chair where his fragile bit of an invalid wife sat. Bending down, he would kiss her, then he would gather her up into his great muscular arms, stride out of the rink, and deposit her carefully in a waiting car that would take her home to the kiddies that he adored so much.

In 592 games, Siebert scored 140 goals and 296 points. He was elected to the Hockey Hall of Fame in 1964.

Peak Years   *1929–33*
Comparable Current Player   *Bobby Holik*
In a Word   *BASHING*

HOOLEY SMITH Center/Right Wing
5'10" 167
b. 1/7/1903, Toronto, Ontario
d. 8/24/1963, Montreal, Quebec

Hooley Smith

Looking back on his long career, Dit Clapper said he never saw a meaner hockey threesome than Nels Stewart, Babe Siebert, and Hooley Smith — the Montreal Maroons' feared "'S' Line." "They had a butcher's touch, those three," Clapper said. "When they went to work on you with a stick, it was 'Goodnight, Irene.'"

Reginald Smith got his start in hockey with the Toronto Parkdale Canoe Club in 1921. He gained a measure of notoriety with the Toronto Granites, developing into one of the top prospects of his time and leading the powerful Granites to Allan Cup wins in 1922 and '23. The Granites were chosen to represent Canada at the first Winter Olympics in Chamonix, France, and they dominated the tournament. In only five Olympic matches, Smith scored 17 goals and added 16 assists. Harry Watson led the team with 36 goals!

When the gold medal–winning Granites returned from Europe, there was a frantic scramble among all NHL teams for the services of Dunc Munro, Harry Watson, and Smith, the "hockey genius." After a great deal of haggling, the Ottawa Senators finally managed to sign the dazzling young speedster. Smith joined the Senators in time for the 1924–25 season and was put on right wing alongside Frank Nighbor and Cy Denneny. It was a perfect fit! Smith's soon-to-be trademark hook-check combined with Nighbor's legendary poke-check to form an impenetrable wall against enemy rushes.

Despite Smith's obvious genius for the game of hockey, his early years in the NHL were marred by a tendency to incur too many penalties. Most came in response to being baited by opponents.

In 1927, Ottawa made it to the Stanley Cup finals against the Bruins. It was in this series that Smith attacked quiet Harry Oliver, touching off perhaps the bloodiest brawl in NHL playoff history. Smith was almost immediately slapped with a one-month suspension effective at the start of the following season.

Although Ottawa won the Cup in '27, they began to suffer financially. The next season the highly prized, but troublesome, Smith was one of the first gems to be auctioned off. He joined Munro on the Maroons in exchange for Punch Broadbent and an undisclosed amount of cash.

Maroons head coach Eddie Gerard teamed his cocky star with fan favorite Jimmy Ward and Nels Stewart. Eventually Ward was replaced with big Babe Siebert, and the storied "'S' Line" was born. The new unit was a veritable wrecking crew. Stewart's goal-scoring genius combined remarkably well with Siebert's brute strength and body-checking, and Smith's passing, speed, and defensive abilities.

With the departure of Siebert and Stewart in 1932, Smith was moved to center on a line with Ward and Baldy Northcott. The ever-mellowing Smith captained the M's to a Cup in 1935 and got a First All-Star Team nod in 1936.

The Maroons, by then struggling under an ever-increasing financial strain, sold Smith to Boston, where he played a season before joining the New York Americans. With the Amerks, he teamed with Red Beattie and Johnny Sorrell before coach Red Dutton thought to use him back on defense with Joe Jerwa and an aging Charlie Conacher. Smith was one of the biggest thorns in Dutton's side, though. In his last NHL season, Smith was suspended for insubordination. After he scored his 200th career goal, though, all was forgiven.

Smith was nasty with a capital "N," a devil with flair. He was a whizzer on the blades, a player you hated playing against but one who ultimately commanded your admiration. In 715 games, the Hall-of-Famer scored 200 goals and 415 points.

Peak Years 1928–33
Comparable Current Player Jeremy Roenick
In a Word COCKY

NELS STEWART (Old Poison, Big Sam) Center
6'1" 200
b. 12/29/1902, Montreal, Quebec
d. 8/21/1957, Wasaga Beach, Ontario

This burly 200-pounder was an awkward skater with short, choppy strides. He was at the same time one of the meanest men ever to take the ice, and one of the game's most prolific goal scorers. What he couldn't do with his fists (which was almost nothing), he did with his stick. The deadly accuracy of his shot would earn him the nickname "Old Poison."

Stewart was born in Montreal but raised in Toronto's Balmy Beach district. He grew up with future linemate Reginald "Hooley" Smith. Stewart played with the OHA's Parkdale Canoe Club before joining the Cleveland Indians of the USAHA in 1920. He and bruising winger Albert "Babe" Siebert were ultimately signed by the Montreal Maroons in a youth movement that would play a large role in the club's winning of the Stanley Cup in the spring of 1926.

The additions of Stewart and Siebert went a long way in turning the Maroons into a rollicking, kick-ass contender. With the two young bucks anchored by hard-rock defenders Dunc Munro and Reg Noble, "Dunc's Army" was capable of leaving opponents black, blue, battered, and usually beaten. Stewart led the NHL in scoring during his rookie season with 34 goals, and he was handed the Hart Trophy as league MVP. He performed marvelously in the playoffs that year, leading the Maroons with six goals

----

and nine points in eight games.

Stewart, Siebert, and Smith — brought in from the Ottawa Senators — were thrown onto a line for the 1929–30 season to form one of the scariest forward lines around: the "'S' Line," also known as the "Triple-S Line." This trio could smash you into the ice, undress you with their speed and stick-handling, or beat you in the corners. Their blend of beauty and bash saw the Maroons to the top of the NHL's Canadian Division with a 23-16-5 record. Big Stewart finished the season with 39 goals and copped his second Hart Trophy.

For the 1932–33 campaign, Steward joined Boston. The big fellow continued to rank among the league's top scorers over the next few seasons. In the waning days of his career, he was dealt to the New York Americans, where many NHL veterans went to die in the late 1930s. He remained there until his retirement at the end of the 1939–40 season. After hanging up those big skates of his, "Big Sam" joined the O'Keefe Brewing Company, carving out a career for himself as a sales representative in the Niagara Peninsula district. He died at his summer home near Toronto in August of 1957, aged 54.

Nels Stewart's 324 career NHL goals would stand as a hockey benchmark until Maurice Richard broke the record with his 325th in November 1952. In 650 games, the Hall of Fame (1962) center added 191 assists for a total of 515 points.

Peak Years   *1927–31*
Comparable Current Player   *Cam Neely*
In a Word   *POISON*

TINY THOMPSON Goal
5'10" 160
b. 5/31/1905, Sandon, British Columbia
d. 2/9/1981, Calgary, Alberta

Cecil "Tiny" Thompson's rookie season in 1928–29 was possibly the greatest ever for a netminder: an incredible 1.15 goals-against average, 12 shutouts, and 26 wins in 44 games. At a time when most goalies were small in stature, "Tiny" stood tall. Actually, his famous nickname came about because of the "tiny" size of his goals-against average, not from his build.

Although Thompson had ability, the cold, hard fact is that he played behind a very powerful defense, one that included such names as Eddie Shore and Lionel Hitchman. This definitely had a lot to do with his success. Take a look at one of his peers — Davey Kerr of the New York Rangers. Kerr routinely faced more shots per game yet he still managed to post averages close to the league's best — a sign he was doing a lot more goaltending. Although Thompson deserves all he has received, he is by no means to be considered one of the greatest goalies of all time.

With the advent of new forward passing rules in 1929–30, Thompson's average rose to 2.19. He won the Vezina Trophy that season — and deservedly so — and would do so again in 1933, 1936, and 1938. He was named to the First All-Star Team in 1936 and 1938 after claiming Second-Team berths in 1931 and 1935.

Thompson was a serious-minded man, perhaps much too serious for his own good. His teammates often swore he would one day suffer a nervous breakdown, although he never succumbed completely to the pressure. Still, like peers John Ross Roach and Jake Forbes, Thompson was a chronic worry-wart, and dreaded the thought that his play might slip and his place might be taken. During the 1931–32 season, he missed four games and was replaced in nets by backup Percy Jackson. His wife became so fed up with his antics that she left Boston, never to return. Tiny was also obsessive about protecting his vision. Like Hall of Fame second baseman Rogers Hornsby, Thompson very rarely read and watched few movies. "After all," he said, "the only thing a goaltender has is his eyes."

In 1938, Art Ross replaced Thompson with rookie Frank Brimsek and shipped the veteran cage-man to Detroit. Thompson would close out his playing career with the AHL Buffalo Bisons in 1940–41.

Thompson became a member of the Hockey Hall of Fame in 1959.

Peak Years 1930–1934
In a Word MELODRAMATIC

The All-Stars

Position	Player	Season	GP	G	A	Pts
D	Eddie Shore	1932–33	48	8	27	35
D	Earl Seibert	1937–38	48	8	13	21
LW	Busher Jackson	1931–32	48	28	25	53
C	Nels Stewart	1929–30	44	39	16	55
RW	Bill Cook	1931–32	48	34	14	48
				GAA	**Sho**	
G	Charlie Gardiner	1933–34	48	1.63	10	

The Forties

In a Flash

COMPOSITE REGULAR-SEASON STANDINGS
(JANUARY 1, 1940–DECEMBER 31, 1949)

National Hockey League

Club	GP	W	L	T	Pts	WPct	GF	GA
Detroit Red Wings	535	259	192	84	602	.563	1,734	1,495
Montreal Canadiens	538	256	203	79	591	.549	1,680	1,485
Toronto Maple Leafs	536	251	207	78	580	.541	1,759	1,558
Boston Bruins	537	241	209	87	569	.530	1,827	1,712
Chicago Black Hawks	539	199	267	73	471	.437	1,685	1,905
New York Rangers	536	183	271	82	448	.418	1,568	1,949
New York/Brooklyn Americans	123	33	73	17	83	.337	294	443

HELLOS

Cassius Clay *boxer*	January 17, 1942
Paul Henderson *Canadian hockey hero*	January 28, 1943
Freddie Mercury *British rocker*	September 8, 1946
Bobby Orr *Incomparable defenseman*	March 20, 1948
Twiggy *British model*	September 19, 1949
Burton Cummings *Canadian rocker*	December 31, 1949

GOODBYES

Leon Trotsky *Russian writer*	August 20, 1940
Harvey Pulford *Ottawa hockey legend*	October 31, 1940
Harry Trihey *Montreal hockeyist*	August 15, 1942
Adolf Hitler *German dictator*	April 30, 1945
Milton Hershey *American chocolatier*	October 13, 1945
Mahatma Gandhi *Indian social thinker*	January 30, 1948
Babe Ruth *American baseball legend*	August 16, 1948

REGULAR SEASON

BEST RECORD
1943–44 Montreal Canadiens, 38-5-7

WORST RECORD
1943–44 New York Rangers, 6-39-5
Team GM Lester Patrick grew so despondent with his team that he considered suspending franchise operations until the end of World War Two. So desperate had the situation become that 42-year-old head coach Frank Boucher suited up for 15 games.

BEST NON-NHL RECORD
1943–44 Boston Olympics (Eastern Amateur Hockey League), 39-4-2

FAMOUS FIRSTS

NHL GOAL OF THE DECADE
Frank "Buzz" Boll (1/1/1940)

NHL PENALTY OF THE DECADE
Earl Robinson (1/1/1940)

NHL PLAYER TO SCORE 50 GOALS IN A SEASON
Maurice Richard, 1944–45

NHL PLAYER TO NOTCH 50+ ASSISTS IN A SEASON
Elmer Lach, 1944–45

NHL DEFENSEMAN TO SCORE 20 GOALS IN A SEASON

Flash Hollett, 1944–45

NHL PLAYER TO BE SUSPENDED OUTRIGHT FROM FURTHER LEAGUE PLAY

Babe Pratt was nailed by league president Red Dutton for "conduct prejudicial to the welfare of hockey." In plain English, the big defenseman from Stony Mountain had been caught gambling on the outcome of NHL hockey games, although never against his own team.

NHL PLAYER TO RAISE STICK IN CELEBRATION AFTER A GOAL

Billy Reay started the now-commonplace practice of raising one's stick into the air after scoring. He did it after scoring for Montreal in a 5–2 victory against the Chicago Black Hawks.

NHL GOALIE TO COME STRAIGHT OUT OF A CANADIAN UNIVERSITY

Jack Gelineau, a standout netminder at McGill University, played for the Boston Bruins and the Chicago Black Hawks.

PRESIDENT OF THE NHL OTHER THAN FRANK CALDER

Mervyn "Red" Dutton assumed NHL presidential duties on February 5, 1943, one day after the death of Frank Calder.

HOCKEY STICK NOT MADE OUT OF WOOD

The aluminum hockey stick. Art Ross came up with the idea of a metal-handled stick with a replaceable wooden blade. The innovation was tested briefly at the beginning of the 1939–40 season, though no one knows how successful it was.

MISCELLANEOUS

MOST GOALS, SEASON

50   Maurice Richard, 1944–45

MOST ASSISTS, SEASON

54   Elmer Lach, 1944–45

MOST POINTS, SEASON

82   Herb Cain

COOLEST MIDDLE NAMES

Vivan *Mariner* Allen
John *Linthwaite* Bend
Frederick *Tennyson* Hunt
Bryan *Aldwyn* Hextall

COOLEST HANDLES

More so than any other decade in history, the 1940s was a gold mine of nicks and handles. Our personal favorite was a moniker worn by either a very bad or a very unlucky goalie who appeared in nine games for the New York Rangers in 1942–43, Steve Buzinski.

Steve "The Puck Goes Inski" Buzinski
Sid Abel, "Old Bootnose"
Vivan "Squee" Allen
Max Bentley, "Dipsy Doodle Dandy"
Emile Bouchard, "The Big Beekeeper"
Frank Brimsek, "Mr. Zero"
Bob "Killer" Dill
Pat "Boxcar" Egan
Leo Gravelle, "The Gazelle"
Don Grosso, "The Count"
Mel "Sudden Death" Hill
Rudolph Kampman, "My Old Dutch"
Gil Mayer, "The Needle"
Frank "Ulcers" McCool
Pete Langelle, "The Automatic Man"
Harry Lumley, "Apple Cheeks"
Alf Pike, "The Embalmer"
Chuck Rayner, "Bonnie Prince Charlie"
Wally Stanowski, "The Child Comet"

BIGGEST PLAYER

Babe Pratt, 6'3" 212

SMALLEST PLAYER

Cliff Purpur, at 5'5" 145, was nicknamed "Fido." He was the New York Yankees' Yogi Berra's favorite hockey player.

BEST SHOT

Kenny Reardon was a bull in a china shop kind of defenseman with a violent slapshot. At first, his shot was inaccurate, but he honed his blaster into a feared weapon on the Montreal power play.

BEST PASSERS

Elmer Lach and **Bill Cowley** were masters

of finding the open man. Lach was a physical player, setting up many of his plays while digging in the corner, while Cowley's style was much more polished.

BEST INSTINCTS
Maurice "The Rocket" Richard was like a bloodhound, always sniffing out goals. From a young age, he showed uncanny on-ice instincts similar to those of a Mario Lemieux or a Wayne Gretzky.

BEST STICK-HANDLER
Max Bentley was one of the greatest stick-handlers ever to play hockey. He had a showy, exciting style similar to that of Sabre great Gilbert Perreault. According to eyewitnesses, Bentley "attacked" the puck with a fervor.

BEST SKATER
Syl Apps was often referred to as "Nijinsky of the Ice."

Syl Apps

WORST SKATER
Kenny Reardon was a unique player. Not only was his hard-charging playing style a problem for opposing players but his teammates often found it difficult to follow his unorthodox lead. He looked like a sugar-crazed eight-year-old running on skates.

FASTEST SKATER
Leo Gravelle was called "Gazelle" for good reason. Honorable mention as fastest skater: Bill Mosienko, Syl Apps, Bryan Hextall, and Tommy Anderson.

BEST SNIPER
Maurice Richard. No arguments, please.

BEST PENALTY-KILLER
Nick Metz

BEST BODY-CHECKER
Black Jack Stewart performed the teeth-rattling body-check better than anyone in the history of the NHL. Although there were bigger men than this 5'11", 190-pounder, no one hit with as much shattering force. Jack Adams, Stewart's coach for many years, said his star defenseman was one of the strongest players he'd ever seen.

BEST POKE-CHECKER
Leo Lamoureux

BEST SHOT-BLOCKER
Wilfred "Bucko" McDonald was likely the first blueliner to master the art of the shot-block. "Rollicking Bucko" handed down his shot-blocking secrets to Bob Goldham in Goldham's rookie season.

BEST GOALTENDER
Bill Durnan

BEST GLOVE-HAND
Frank Brimsek had a glove-hand often described as "Brimmy's Lightning."

MOST UNUSUAL GOALTENDING STYLE
Bill Durnan was a freak of nature, probably the only ambidextrous goalie in hockey history. He often switched hands as an opposing player broke in just to psyche him out.

FINEST ATHLETE
Syl Apps was, in addition to being a superb hockey player, an Olympic pole-vaulter, and participated at the Olympics in Berlin in 1936. He was also one of the greatest track and field, hockey, and football stars ever to come out of McMaster University. The Toronto media called him the "Commissioner of Athletics."

BEST DEFENSIVE FORWARD
Nick Metz

WORST DEFENSIVE FORWARD
Gordie Drillon was only tolerated by Toronto Maple Leaf boss Hap Day because he clicked offensively beside Syl Apps on the top line. Drillon, a lazy player who didn't much care for back-checking, was eventually shipped to Montreal.

BEST SHADOW
Nick Metz

BEST DEFENSIVE DEFENSEMAN
Jack Stewart

BEST OFFENSIVE DEFENSEMAN
Bill "Flash" Hollett pinched aggressively in the enemy zone knowing he had the blazing speed to recover in time.

BEST ALL-AROUND PLAYER
Milt Schmidt

BEST UTILITY PLAYER
Nick Metz was the older of two brothers (his brother was Don Metz) who spent the late 1930s and most of the 1940s with the Toronto Maple Leafs. His nickname, "Handyman," was fitting as he was the Leafs' master plumber — a responsible defensive forward, a clutch scorer, and one of the best penalty-killers in NHL history.

STRONGEST PLAYER
Butch Bouchard

TOUGHEST PLAYER
Johnny Mariucci was the Chicago Black Hawk "protector" and one of the fathers of hockey in the state of Minnesota. This former American collegiate football player earned 23 stitches in his first week in the NHL alone! Apparently, he thought he was still on the gridiron.

BEST FIGHTER
Edwin "Murph" Chamberlain was one tough customer. A well-worn NHL anecdote summarizes Chamberlain's career: an unnamed Montreal rookie showed up in training camp with a swagger in his step and defiantly glaring at the veterans. The second the puck dropped in the team's first practice, Chamberlain was standing over the prone body of the cocky rookie, whom he just laid a lightning-quick beating on. Apparently, no one blinked. Business as usual.

MOST ABLE INSTIGATOR
Bill Ezinicki

DIRTIEST PLAYER
Bill Ezinicki

CLEANEST PLAYER
Clint Smith

BEST CORNER-MAN
Ray Getliffe was Montreal's premier "holler guy" of the 1940s. He was a fierce forechecker, one of the league's top diggers.

BEST-LOOKING PLAYERS
Syl Apps and Grant "Nobby" Warwick. Apps was the healthy, happy all-Canadian boy, raised on Heinz beans, Swift sausages, and whole milk. Warwick had Hollywood looks and a model's chin, though he would have stood nose to nose with Danny DeVito.

Johnny Mowers

UGLIEST PLAYER
Johnny Mowers' horse teeth would have put Mister Ed to shame.

BALDEST PLAYER
Boston's Jack Crawford wore a make-shift leather helmet for years. It wasn't to protect his noodle, though, but rather to cover up his baldness. Picture a fuzzy egg with a beanie strapped on top.

MOST UNDERRATED PLAYER
Nick Metz

MOST CONSISTENT PLAYER
Neil Colville. Not much has been said about the tall, prematurely gray center and later defenseman who wore Ranger blue for many seasons. He was one of the finest all-around players of the time.

MOST UNPREDICTABLE CAREER

Wally Stanowski was a colorful player. He would wind himself up like a corkscrew in his own end just before taking off on a rush. But his career, like his beautiful skating, was like a roller-coaster ride, thanks in large part to a bum ankle.

SMARTEST PLAYER

Sid Abel had poise and savvy beyond his years, qualities that would help him become one of the greatest Red Wing captains of all time.

MOST HATED PLAYERS

Bill Ezinicki and **Maurice Richard.** Both players were enemies on the ice and were rabidly hated by fans outside of their home cities. "Ezzy" was disliked for his savage play while Richard was hated and respected at the same time for his scoring theatrics. Richard was great, but unless he was on your team, you had to hate him.

MOST ADMIRED PLAYER

Syl Apps

BEST LINES

Team: New York Rangers
LW: Patrick Lynn
C: Phil Watson
RW: Bryan Hextall

Team: Chicago Black Hawks
LW: Doug Bentley
C: Max Bentley
RW: Bill Mosienko

Team: Montreal Canadiens
LW: Toe Blake
C: Elmer Lach
RW: Maurice Richard

Team: Boston Bruins
LW: Woody Dumart
C: Milt Schmidt
RW: Bobby Bauer

PLAYER VERSUS TEAM

Harvey "Busher" Jackson vs. New York Americans. Jackson's long, bitter contract holdout with the New York Americans in 1941 left the cash-strapped club no alternative but to deal him to Boston.

MOST LOPSIDED TRADE

Chicago dealt Max Bentley and utility forward Cy Thomas to Toronto in exchange for Gaye Stewart, Gus Bodnar, Bob Goldham, Bud Poile, and Ernie Dickens. Any Hawk fan of sound mind would agree that Chicago bigwig Bill Tobin was a fool to part with the dazzling Bentley.

Honorable mention goes to Conn Smythe's outfoxing of Lester Patrick in 1942 in shipping Dudley "Red" Garrett and Hank Goldup to New York in exchange for Babe Pratt. Pratt, a superstar defenseman, went on to win a Hart Trophy and helped the Leafs win the Cup in 1945. Garrett and Goldup played a combined 225 career NHL games.

BIGGEST FLOPS

Hank Goldup was a star left winger and back-to-back scoring champ with the Kingston Dunlop Forts, and starred with the Toronto Marlboros. A highly touted prospect in 1939, he was snapped up by Leaf scout "Squib" Walker. Unfortunately, Goldup failed to live up to his advanced billing scoring 143 points in 202 games.

BEST HEAD COACH

Toe Blake played under **Dick Irvin Sr.** for years; Blake coached Scotty Bowman in Montreal Junior hockey. See a pattern?

BEST GENERAL MANAGER

Tommy Gorman was assigned the gargantuan task of resurrecting a Montreal Canadiens organization at death's door at the beginning of the 1940s. They were two Cups richer by the time he turned over the GM reins to Frank Selke Sr. in 1946.

BEST SPORTSWRITERS

Elmer Ferguson and **Andy O'Brien.** Ferguson was for many years Montreal's resident sportswriting guru, while the bespectacled O'Brien wrote perhaps the "tastiest" copy.

BEST BROADCASTER

Foster Hewitt was almost as popular as the great names he spoke over the air. Although he sometimes showed a pro-Toronto bias, he had a classic hockey broadcasting voice.

BEST MINOR-LEAGUE PLAYERS

Danny Lewicki
Bucky Buchanan
Phil Hergesheimer
Andy Barbe
Roger Leger
Andre Corriveau
Ray Powell
Fred Robertson

Lewicki was one of the most publicized young star players of the late 1940s. After a 1949 holdout with Leaf boss Conn Smythe (an early version of Eric Lindros's rejection of the Quebec Nordiques in 1991), Lewicki was forced to languish in the minors. He was signed by the Maple Leafs in time for the 1950–51 season.

BEST SEASON

In **1941–42** the NHL featured a down-to-the-wire title race between New York, Toronto, and Boston, and a thrilling scoring race.

BEST STANLEY CUP FINAL

1942, Toronto vs. Detroit. It was the greatest playoff comeback in hockey history. Hap Day versus Jack Adams. Syl Apps versus Jack Stewart. Toronto won in seven.

IMPORTANT RULE CHANGES

1940–41

• NHL mandates use of between-periods ice flooding to improve quality of the league's ice surfaces.

1942–43

• overtime suspended

1943–44

• One of the major rule changes in the twentieth century is made with the introduction of the center red line.

1945–46

• synchronized goal lights introduced

1946–47

• system of hand signals by officials designed to "keep fans better informed on rule infractions"

1948–49

• The number of players teams are allowed to dress for a game increases from 15 to 16, not including goalies.

The War off the Ice

On September 3, 1939, Great Britain declared war on Nazi Germany. Canada rallied to Britain's aid the very next week, albeit hesitantly. It was clear almost immediately to those operating hockey clubs that many of their boys would be leaving. At a September 20, 1939, meeting, NHL governors determined that hockey operations should continue as normal. The panic button was not to be pushed — yet.

In the first year of the war, it was business as usual in the NHL. Attendance was on the rise in most centers, and the game's entertainment value remained favorable. Bear in mind, however, that players had not yet been called overseas en masse. Those who were serving, even those called into action under the National Resources Mobilization Act, could opt to do their duty at any time of the year. In a July 1940 letter to his players, Leaf boss Conn Smythe was confident "there will be hockey in the National Hockey League unless we are stopped by our own Government or Hitler . . ."

On December 7, 1941, the Japanese bombed Pearl Harbor, and the Americans, who up to this point had been maintaining an isolationist policy regarding foreign matters, almost immediately declared war on the Japanese. The Germans and Italians, in turn, declared war on the Americans.

The Americans were now fully involved in the war, and they needed able bodies. NHL clubs knew their duty. After the annual NHL meeting on May 15, 1942, the league issued a press release, stating: "The National Hockey League expects to operate in the season 1942–43 and, like any other business, will do whatever the governments of Canada and the United States request it to do." Many clubs, though, particularly the New York Rangers, called for a halt to NHL operations for the duration of the war. (The Rangers had sustained the loss of several key players and would ice some of the worst teams in their history.)

At a September 28, 1942, meeting, NHL president Frank Calder stated that "with the institution of the National Selective Service it at first seemed that suspension of operations for 1942–43 must follow." The war threatened the very existence of organized hockey in North America.

With North America's role in the war increasing by 1942, it seemed increasingly unlikely that the NHL would continue as it was. But the governments of both Canada and the States realized how important hockey was to the public and declared, "in the interest of public morale" the NHL should carry on. The NHL had to follow certain regulations, however. The most difficult rule to swallow was the one that forbade the

---

In World War Two, fighting-aged men were at a premium. Athletes were particularly attractive to the draft board because of their youth and blue-ribbon health. A good many budding hockey careers were either interrupted or ended outright. Syl Apps, Walter "Turk" Broda, Frank Brimsek, and Boston's Kraut Line of Milt Schmidt, Woody Dumart, and Bob Bauer lost significant chunks of their careers to the war. But hockey was not the only professional sport affected. Athletes from other sports lost playing time in their prime, and their stats suffered. What would Boston Red Sox legend Ted Williams' career statistics have been had he not missed four of his prime years to the war? His 521 career home runs were a tremendous feat, but he might have had 700 but for the interruption.

league from employing any person actively serving in the military in Canada or the States. This condition ensured that players would honor their service obligations and that there would be no reincarnation of the 228th Battalion, which during World War One was at the center of much controversy.

The 1942–43 season was the NHL's first real wartime campaign. More than 80 players, some of them stars, signed up for military service. As a result, the level of play in organized hockey suffered. Boston lost Schmidt, Dumart, and Bauer, and the Rangers were left with only one of their regular defensemen in Ott Heller. Meanwhile, Montreal lost only Kenny Reardon, which gave them a significant advantage over the other teams. More on that later.

The NHL introduced a number of rule changes because of the war effort. For one, overtime was eliminated in all regular-season games as a result of wartime restrictions on train scheduling. Also, the number of players allowed per team was cut from 15 to 14. With the war draining hockey's talent pool, the NHL was forced to make such drastic changes.

The rule that disallowed hockey clubs to employ men enrolled in the military caused controversy prior to the fifth game of the 1942–43 semifinal between Montreal and Boston. The Canadiens, down three games to one and desperate to get back into the hunt, tried to dress Terry Reardon, who had joined his brother in the military earlier that season. League president Red Dutton stepped in and quashed Montreal's request, citing the government regulation. Montreal GM Tommy Gorman tried to convince Dutton that Boston's Jack Shewchuk was also involved with the military, but the big cheese wouldn't bite.

Goal-scoring in the NHL increased dramatically during World War Two. Consider the case of Montreal's Maurice Richard and his 50 goals in 50 games in 1944–45. The NHL goals-per-game average was just over seven that season, among the highest figures of the entire forward passing era. Have a look at a list of five of the league's starting goalies:

Boston Bruins	Paul Bibeault
Chicago Black Hawks	Mike Karakas
Detroit Red Wings	Harry Lumley
New York Rangers	Ken McAuley
Toronto Maple Leafs	Frank McCool

There was the first player to wear #0 in an NHL game in Bibeault. Karakas was hardly a Vezina Trophy threat. Lumley was a future Hall of Famer. McAuley was one of the least effective goalies in NHL history. McCool was a one-year wonder. With the exception of Lumley, this is a weak collection of goalies, easy pickings for a talent like Richard.

The talent in front of these goalies was equally sub-par. Consider the "notables" who saw wartime action — Fido Purpur, Aldo Palazzari, Marcel Dheere, Ralph Wycherley. Leaf boss Conn Smythe, in a letter to scout Squib Walker, said, "You have to admit that one NHL player is worth two wartime NHLers." It's easy to see just how Richard was able to score 50 goals in 50 games. In all fairness, though, his feat is no less impressive than Wayne Gretzky's 50 goalies in 39 games in 1981–82, a season in which over eight goals a game were scored, the highest average since the NHL's earliest years.

1945–46 Montreal Canadiens

In 1943–44, even more hockey players answered their countries' call to duty. Boston lost ace goalie Frank Brimsek, while the Wings were hit with the loss of Jack Stewart and Sid Abel, among others. The Maple Leafs lost stars Turk Broda, Syl Apps, and Sweeney Schriner. Meanwhile, the purging of the Broadway Blueshirts continued. They suffered the departures of Lynn Patrick, Phil Watson, and Alf Pike. They also lost Red Garrett, who had been filling in admirably on the blue-line. The situation became so desperate in the Big Apple that manager Lester Patrick put forth the idea that the Rangers suspend operations. The New York Americans folder after the 1941–42 season.

The effects of the war ended with the 1944–45 season. The struggling Rangers again went into the season with porous Ken McAuley as their top goalie. While McAuley significantly improved his goals-against average from the season before, he still reminded the Gotham faithful of Steve "The Puck Goes Inski" Buzinski.

Toronto was in similar straits, and was forced to reach in deep to find a passable starting keeper. The Canadiens would not let the Buds keep Paul Bibeault, whom they had loaned to the Leafs. Toronto grabbed Frank McCool as a free agent. The skittish goaltender would put up a superb playoff effort in leading Hogtown to the Cup.

Without doubt, Montreal was the top wartime club. Despite winning the Cup only once from 1943–45, they were the team to beat. In 1943–44 they erupted, winning 38 of 50 games. The following season, they ran up a 38-8-4 record. With a developing nucleus of stars in Richard, Elmer Lach, Toe Blake, Butch Bouchard, and Bill Durnan, the Canadiens were afraid of no one. They were, however, lucky enough to retain much of their roster while other clubs lost their men to military service.

And just how did the Canadiens manage to escape the wartime player drain? Richard, like many of his fellow francophones, saw no point in participating in what he perceived to be an "English" war. Although as able-bodied as a man could be, Richard thumbed his nose at the war, a gesture no doubt backed by then–Montreal mayor Camilien Houde. But what of Durnan, Lach, and Blake? Chances are they simply preferred a life of hockey to a life of blood and honor on the battlefield. The wartime Canadiens are not always mentioned in discussions of hockey's greatest teams, and with good reason. They dominated the talent-poor wartime NHL.

The boys who served in the military should be applauded. They sacrificed their careers, their identities, and their place in hockey history for us. While it may not have been a budding hockey star's preference to leave his livelihood behind for the battlefield, he sucked it up and fought nonetheless. We do well to remember not only the players who starred in the NHL, but also those who starred in World War Two.

Hogtown Toe

Toe Blake as a Leaf? The thought of the "Old Lamplighter" in blue and white is enough to nauseate any Montreal fan, but it almost happened in 1940.

After a 1938–39 season in which he won the Art Ross Trophy, Blake felt compelled to demand a pay raise. Of course, Montreal's bigwigs thought otherwise. Blake held out until the eve of the season, signing a contract that club president Ernie Savard termed "a significant increase."

In late 1939, the Canadiens were nowhere close to being the top NHL team, while the Leafs were one of the teams to beat. By the new year, the Leafs were trying to gain on a New York Rangers squad in the midst of a record-breaking unbeaten streak. Just when things were getting interesting, high-flying Syl Apps of the Leafs broke his collarbone. Toronto was all but written off for the season. Smythe, however, disagreed. He felt that if he could plug the hole left by Apps' absence, life would be good again. With this in mind, he went after the disgruntled Blake.

Toe Blake was not exactly in Montreal management's good books at this time. Smythe seized this opportunity and offered Montreal Nick and Don Metz, "Murph" Chamberlain, Reg Hamilton, and "Bucko" McDonald for Blake. At age 28, McDonald was the oldest of the players on the table. The Canadiens gave Smythe's generous offer the thumbs-down.

Imagine the damage Toronto could have done in the 1940s if they had acquired Blake. Often, the best deals are the ones that are never made.

Keep Punching!

Coach Mervyn "Red" Dutton and his Brooklyn Americans finished the 1941–42 season without a playoff spot, closing out a miserable year in an 8–3 drubbing by the mighty Boston Bruins. In usual form, "Keep Punching" Dutton was throwing a hissy-fit long after attendants had turned out the Boston Garden lights. He stormed into his team's dressing room, screaming "You were lousy!"

Red Dutton

among other things. He then jabbed his finger at protégé defenseman Wilf Field, adding, "I'm fining you $100!"

"Why don't you make it $250?" Field shot back. "Then you'll have that bonus of mine!"

"Okay, I'll make it $250, you — !"

The two men got into a fight — Field against big Dutton himself, the "roaringest of roaring managers." A handful of punches later, other players rushed in to break it up. And who won? Well, on the train ride back to New York, the combatants had a little talk.

"I've fined a lot of players in my time," Dutton eyed Field, "but did I ever make one stick?"

"I never heard of you doing it, Red."

"Well, you'll get your $250 bonus as I promised you, but don't start swinging at your boss again or I'll have to knock your fresh ears off."

"Okay Red, it's a deal."

Eskimo in the Cupboard

Rookie initiation has been a training camp tradition for decades. In the early 1940s, the Chicago Black Hawks decided to have some fun with a rookie reporter. This particular greenhorn, who worked for a wire service, came to camp eager to make a good first impression.

Knowing an easy target when he saw one, Hawks publicity man Joe Farrell hatched the idea for a delicious practical joke. He posed as team boss Bill Tobin and had an accomplice play the part of coach Johnny Gottselig. A veteran sportswriter was let in on the prank. The writer approached the rookie and told him that Chicago had signed a "real Eskimo" by the name of Johnny Ooglenook. To convince the cub of the story's authenticity, the writer translated "Ooglenook" as "Great Whale Hunter." He then told of how Ooglenook skated like greased lightning and of how he handled the puck as if it were glued to his stick. Furthermore, Ooglenook was said to have been given his first pair of skates by a "Hudson's Bay factor," who then taught him how to play the game.

The rookie was so ecstatic he could barely control himself. His first day on the job and he'd already sniffed out a major scoop. As he furiously scribbled down notes, he imagined what the headline might be. Farrell felt sorry for the young man and, after stealing a few more giggles, filled him in on the prank. The rookie reporter, although clearly dejected, took it in stride. He would go on to a enjoy a long and successful writing career.

One for the Book

By March 1942, World War Two was in full swing. The Japanese navy had just lost 26 ships at Java, Victory war bonds were selling like hot-cakes (from $50 on up), and tickets for a hockey game at the Montreal Forum ranged from 60 cents for standing room to $2.50 for rink-side. Hockey fans were in for a crackerjack finish to the 1941–42 regular season as well as one of the more scintillating post-seasons in memory.

The word "goal" was on everyone's lips by the middle of the 1941–42 season. The New York Rangers, more specifically the Lynn Patrick-Phil Watson-Bryan Hextall unit, took their high-octane game to another level. As of late February 1942, the Rangers were on pace to break the NHL team scoring record.

In Boston, star defenseman Dit Clapper sat out most of the season with injuries, and the Kraut Line left in February to join the war effort. The Beantowners were sitting ducks. But thanks to the play of Bill "Flash" Hollett, Eddie Wiseman, and goalie Frank Brimsek, the B's buzzed on.

Chicago, meanwhile, was still mired in the muck of mediocrity. Their luck would change, though. Young wizards Max and Doug Bentley combined with rookie speed-artist Bill Mosienko to breathe new life into the dying Hawks. The team would soon be feeling its oats.

In Montreal, Tommy Gorman and skipper Dick Irvin resurrected the Canadiens, who had been pronounced dead only a couple of seasons before. A hot core of young talent was beginning to gel. Kenny Reardon was already drawing comparisons to Toronto legend King Clancy, while his brother Terry skated on the top line alongside Toe Blake. Meanwhile, scouts were going gaga over a young French player named Maurice Richard.

Here's a rundown of what happened from March 1, 1942, until the end of the Stanley Cup finals.

On March 1, the Royal Canadian Air Force (RCAF) Flyers defeated the Hull Volants 6–4. Starring for the Flyers were Boston's Milt Schmidt, Woody Dumart, and Bob Bauer. Dumart had two goals and an assist, Schmidt earned two helpers, and Bauer added one of each.

On March 4, Marc T. McNeil of the Montreal *Gazette* deemed Toe Blake the "most conscientious workman in the National Hockey League," and saw him as the catalyst for the Canadiens securing a playoff spot.

On March 5, with a handful of games left in the regular season, only six points separated the NHL's top three scorers:

Player	Team	G	A	Pts
Bryan Hextall	Rangers	22	29	51
Lynn Patrick	Rangers	27	21	48
Phil Watson	Rangers	14	34	48

On March 10 NHL president Frank Calder named Syl Apps as the winner of the Lady Byng Trophy. Here's how the voting went:

Player	Team	Votes
Syl Apps	Leafs	100
Gordie Drillon	Leafs	66
Bill Thoms	Hawks	64

Marc T. McNeil compared King Clancy and Montreal's Kenny Reardon. When Dick Irvin heard that McNeil said that Reardon had a long way to go, he replied: "Of course he makes mistakes. Any young player does. But I'll tell you something . . . Clancy wasn't the perfect defenseman by any means . . . he made mistakes, plenty of them . . . but he could afford to make those mistakes because he could get away with them. Clancy could make two or three mistakes a game . . . Before you could take advantage of them, he was doing something else to make up for them . . . I only hope Kenny Reardon fulfills the promise that he has shown of being called the second Clancy."

On March 12 Toronto *Globe & Mail* sports editor Vern DeGeer gave Montreal's Terry Reardon a fair shot at winning the Hart Trophy. "Dick Irvin showed local hockey fans one of the niftiest forward lines to operate against the Leafs this season. The leader of that line was Terry Reardon, flanked by Toe Blake and Joe Benoit. With all of the evidence, it isn't difficult to conceive of Reardon as a strong contender for the Hart this April in a field that must include Apps, Lynn Patrick, Tommy Anderson, Bill Thoms, Sid Abel, and Flash Hollett."

In a crucial weekend match on March 14 described as "blood and thunder" hockey, Montreal topped the Wings 4–3. Terry Reardon scored the game winner. With seven minutes left in the final session, Johnny Quilty and Sid Abel began throwing punches and a brawl soon erupted. The main event had Ray Getliffe pairing off with big Eddie Bush. The little Montrealer surprised many by slapping Bush around before the officials stepped in. In other mini-wars, Jack Portland took on Jack Stewart, Charlie Sands knuckled up to Syd Howe, and Kenny Reardon squared off with Eddie Wares. Detroit bad boy Jimmy Orlando could not leave the bench for fear of a $25 fine but he did manage to crack a fan or two over the head with his stick. This particular sin earned him a match misconduct penalty and an automatic game ejection.

On March 15 the New York Rangers trounced the Black Hawks 5–1 to clinch the league title. In this game, New York, with 177 goals, broke the single-season team goal-scoring record of 174 goals set by the Leafs in 1933–34.

In the first round of the playoffs, the top two teams met up in a seven-game series. The Leafs, backstopped by Turk Broda, knocked off the regular-season champion New York Rangers in six games. While the two top dogs of the league battled it out in the NHL's crazy playoff format of the time, the other four playoff teams strove for second season excellency. In one series, Boston tripped up Chicago in three games, while the Red Wings disposed of the Canadiens, also in three games.

In this first installment of the semifinals, Boston got a "going-over" on home ice, losing 6–4 to the Red Wings. Jack McGill counted three times in a losing cause.

Game two, played in front of over 13,000 screaming fans at the Olympia, saw the Red Wings stuff the Bruins 3–1. Joe Carveth scored two of Detroit's three goals. Again, Brimsek was awesome despite being bombarded with 43 shots. Mowers faced only 17 from the belly-up B's.

The bookies had Toronto as 8–5 favorites over the Wings.

Hap Day

With lines like Apps-Metz-Drillon, Taylor-Schriner-Carr, and Langelle-Davidson-McCreedy, the Leafs were clearly the deeper of the two teams. On defense, Toronto had a healthy foursome in McDonald, Stanowksi, Kampmann, and 19-year-old Bob Goldham. At the last line of defense, it was Broda versus Mowers.

"We may not have the greatest hockey club in the world," Jack Adams allowed, "but it's a club that's loaded with fighting heart. If there's anything that wins hockey championships, it's just that."

In game one at Maple Leaf Gardens, David stoned Goliath before a crowd of 14,185. Detroit slapped the Leafs around in the first two minutes of play. Grosso, then one of hockey's forgotten center-ice stars, directed a Motown surge, twice ramming the puck home, and setting up Abel for the other in pacing the visitors to a 3–2 win.

Immediately after the game, self-proclaimed "number one fan" Harry Jacobson raced into the Detroit dressing room and spread around $115. Not far behind him was Dave "number two fan" Ferguson, who handed out $75. This money was raised by a group of fans who thought their boys deserved a little reward for their efforts.

"There's nothing wrong with our club physically," Day sighed after the game. "It's a question whether or not we've got the stuff that champions are made of. That wasn't hockey out there, it was a fair display of hoodlumism . . . Detroit's stock in trade. But we've got to adjust ourselves to the kitty-bar-the-door tactics if we're going to win the Cup."

Meanwhile, Jack Adams was delighted with the game's result. "Full of fight, that's our team. Johnny Mowers played one of his best games for us. We had good defense patrolling and our forwards did a great job on that line of Apps, Drillon, and Metz. We fore-checked them right into the ice, that's what we did. Remember what I told you about Grosso and Abel? Two of the best forwards in hockey today . . . they can keep up with the best that Toronto has to offer."

Fine words indeed from a man who told sportswriter Vern DeGeer at the beginning of the season that he had a team of "just ordinary hockey players."

In game two, Grosso continued in his role as Leaf-killer, bagging two more goals in a 4–2 Detroit triumph. With Grosso and Mowers leading the way, Detroit was awesome in what was another lead-pants effort from the Hogtowners. Grosso's eighth goal of the playoffs tied an NHL post-season record.

"We're still in the league, I guess," Adams jiggled. "We outfought them, out-hustled them, and should have beat them 7–3."

A daring statement from Detroit's head talent scout, Carson Cooper, pricked up more than a few ears in the enemy camp. The Detroit *Times'* Lew Walter had the "crinkly-haired Coop" on record as saying: "Just let Sid Abel, Grosso, Syd Howe, and all the rest keep this up and the Leafs will go down in four straight. They're so disorganized they don't know what they're doing. Look at them now, they played streamlined hockey in the first game and we pinned their ears back 4–2! Now what?"

Apps, for one, was looking for a comeback from his Leafs. "This is the year of the comeback. We start our drive tomorrow night in Detroit."

Day, suffering from a wretched case of the flu, told the media: "We're down, but don't count us out. This team likes Olympia ice and I think we can make our moves count."

The Motor City boys ran over Toronto again in game three, 5–2, despite spotting them two early goals. A capacity crowd of 13,354 was described as "stark, raving mad with unbounded enthusiasm" as Detroit "came one step closer to a sweep and one of the biggest upsets in recent hockey history."

Toronto started out strong. Lorne Carr popped in a pair in the opening canto. But by the end of the frame, the game was knotted at two. Big Eddie Bush potted the final goal at 7:11 of the third. The husky defender figured in all five of his team's goals.

"They're unbeatable," Broda cowered after the game. "They're too hot and they can't seem to do anything wrong."

The knell of the 1941–42 Toronto Maple Leafs had sounded.

In game four Abel and Bruneteau started the red raiders on what appeared to be the road to victory by scoring early in the second canto. Toronto struck back when war-dog Bob Davidson slapped the puck home in 13:54. Liscombe's 35-footer sent Detroit ahead 3–2 five minutes into the third frame before Apps counted to knot the game once again. Suddenly, Nick Metz proved himself the hero once again, counting the winner in 12:45.

Jack Adams

With less than two minutes left on the clock and Toronto ahead 4–3, Wares was given a 10-minute misconduct penalty for directing profanities at referee Mel Harwood. The rugged boy skated over to the bench, grabbed a hot water bottle, and handed it to Harwood. The referee immediately slapped Wares with a $50 fine. Shortly thereafter, Harwood nailed Detroit with a bench minor for having too many men on the ice. Grosso was chosen to serve the infraction. He skated over to the penalty box, took one step in, and skated back to Harwood, drop-

Vern DeGeer of the *Globe and Mail* polled 100 NHL players on who they thought should be on the 1941–42 First and Second All-Star Teams:

First Team		Second Team
Frank Brimsek	GOAL	Turk Broda
Earl Seibert	DEFENSE	Dit Clapper
Tommy Anderson	DEFENSE	Jack Crawford
Lynn Patrick	LEFT WING	Sid Abel
Syl Apps	CENTER	Phil Watson
Bryan Hextall	RIGHT WING	Bob Bauer

Compare that to the official teams:

First Team		Second Team
Frank Brimsek	GOAL	Turk Broda
Earl Seibert	DEFENSE	Pat Egan
Tommy Anderson	DEFENSE	Bucko McDonald
Lynn Patrick	LEFT WING	Sid Abel
Syl Apps	CENTER	Phil Watson
Bryan Hextall	RIGHT WING	Gordie Drillon

Can you say "Nostradamus"?

ping his stick and gloves at the arbiter's feet in disgust. Without hesitation, Harwood slapped "The Count" with a $25 fine for unsportsmanlike misconduct. As the final whistle sounded, Jack Adams vaulted over the boards and made a bee-line for the penalty box. The porky, red-faced lunatic lunged over the railing and attacked Harwood. Unholy bedlam broke loose as Adams and Harwood traded dukes, both men holding their own. Linesmen Sammy Babcock and Don McFayden got into a mix-up with some fans near the Detroit bench. In the midst of the pandemonium, a group of Detroit fans happened upon NHL president Frank Calder. A mob closed in on the elderly hockey statesman with the intention of making a run at him but, fortunately, a group of policemen dispersed the crowd and escorted Calder to safety.

Adams was suspended indefinitely by Calder and the league meted out over $300 in fines to Detroit. Adams later commented to the press that he got a "lousy deal" from Calder, adding, "they can't keep me out of Maple Leaf Gardens, I'll buy my way into the place."

Ebbie Goodfellow took over behind the Detroit bench after Adams' suspension was confirmed. "Sure, we're worried," Detroit scout Carson Cooper joked. "Why, the Leafs only have to win three games, and we need to win one. Boy, are we worried!"

Toronto began their victory march in game five while Orlando and Bush rode the penalty bench. Nick Metz scored on a play with Apps and Stanowski. The hard-skating Stanowski followed with one on his own in a "ganging attack" (power play).

"We'd rather win from [the Leafs] more than any one else because they gloat so much."
— *Syd Howe*

"Those Leafs will know they've had their hides blistered when they get through this series."
— *Sid Abel*

"The Toronto Maple Leafs are whipped."
— *Lew Walter,* Detroit Times

"Toronto has conceded the Stanley Cup to the Red Wings."
— *Mark Beltaire,* Detroit News

"The Wings will win their third Stanley Cup in seven years."
— *John Sabo,* Detroit Free Press

*"The Red Wings did throw the first punch and it landed precisely where
Smythe had suspected it would. Flush on the too-comfortable, too-indolent,
too-don't-give-a-damnish chins of their opponents. But they haven't thrown
a damn thing more fierce that an expostulation. All our boys have done is catch.
We've been plugging a flock of bums all season long. "*
— *Andy Lytle,* Toronto Star

Midway through the third period, Grosso ran Don Metz into the boards. Goldham then smashed Grosso into the fence. The pair were separated after a short scuffle and sent to the box, where Grosso then attacked Goldham. A mob scene followed, with fans joining the players in an old-fashioned punch-up. As soon as referee King Clancy restored order, two fans entered into a slugfest at the southeast corner of the Gardens. The bout was renewed a second time before police stepped in to quell the disturbance.

Detroit's roughhouse tactics proved to be their downfall. They were outskated, out-hustled, and outpassed in a 9–3 Toronto victory.

"What I can say," Day beamed, "is that the boys did all the talking for me on the ice. We still have two big games to go and that's what we've got to concentrate on."

Toronto accomplished the unlikely in game six in tying the series at three games apiece. Broda, one of hockey history's true clutch performers, stopped all 32 Wing shots. The game was uncharacteristically clean.

Nobody was happier with the game result than Day. "I'm no mastermind. My team just went out and played . . . I thought we were lucky."

"We got the breaks in the first three games, now they're getting them," Goodfellow whined. "Since they changed their lineup, the Leafs have a great club. But we're going to give them a battle . . . it won't be any setup."

The Little Idea That Couldn't

Walter Brown felt the Bruins were in need of protection from the oft-rowdy Garden minions. Brown planned to install Plexiglas dugouts over the player benches. These transparent shells would serve to shelter the players from fan attacks. Ever the salesman, Brown pitched the idea to team management, to no avail. President Weston Adams saw a major flaw in the idea in that "it would deprive the fans of the personal contact to which they are accustomed, through their closeness to the players."

Before a record Gardens crowd of 16,218 in game seven, the Leafs etched their names into the history books with a 3–1 triumph. Speedy Syd Howe put Detroit in front in the first two minutes of the middle session, a goal that held up until the third. Toronto answered the call, scoring three straight goals to secure a comeback as thrilling as anything out of the dripping pages of hockey history.

Game seven was the least exciting game of the finals. Both sides came out flat. There were a few anxious moments after the Wings scored and, at times, it looked as if Toronto was tired out. The Gardens, wall-to-wall with fans, sounded like a tomb by the start of the third session. The building remained quiet until Schriner

Syd Howe

tipped home a delayed blast from Carr. "It was a blind shot," Schriner panted after the game. "I didn't know I had scored until I heard the crowd shouting and then saw the light go on. The biggest light I ever saw in my life."

The game winner came about three minutes later after Davidson blocked a Detroit attempt to clear the puck out of their end. He knocked the puck over to Goldham, who whizzed it over to McCreedy. Mowers was about 20 feet out of his net in anticipation of McCreedy's shot. Suddenly, the puck landed at Langelle's feet. Toronto's "Automatic Man" drove the rubber smack-dab into an unguarded net as Jack Stewart vainly attempted to block the shot. Toronto hammered the last nail into the Wings' coffin in 16:13 of the third when Schriner scored again on a pass from Carr.

"Hap did a great job!" said Jack Adams in the dying seconds of the match. "Toronto deserved to win, I guess . . . but I think they were a little bit lucky."

Goodfellow said, "Any team that can come back and win four straight deserves all of the credit."

With Smythe, Maple Leaf Gardens president G.R. Cottrelle, and the rest of his Leaf cronies in tow, Day shouted, "Well, we did it the hard way, fellows!"

At the center of the comeback stood two men — Jack Adams and Clarence "Hap" Day. On one side stood a raging, tomato-faced dictator, a beast of a competitor. On the other stood the quiet, thoughtful pilot of the Good Ship Maple Leaf. Both men,

---

Hockey used to be a beautifully simple animal. The relationship between player and fan seemed much more intimate. The rapport between coach and player seemed more functional. And the sport itself had an intimate, even naïve, beauty. Fans felt like members of the team when they attended a match. As we look back, all the while distracted by the clink of coin and the rustle of dollar bills, we cannot help but be saddened. Was hockey of 40 and 50 years ago a cooler game? It all depends on who you ask. However, as the haunting sound of Foster Hewitt's voice skips from coast to coast through a battered, old radio on a blizzardy Saturday night, we can well imagine a time some say couldn't be beat.

former playing greats themselves, were the spirit behind the tooth-and-nails 1942 finals. Without Adams' antics and subsequent suspension at the end of game four, there may not have been a Toronto comeback, as Goodfellow was far from ready to lead the Wings. Without Day's cool leadership, though, the Leafs would have been sucking dirt long before the finals.

Clubhouse Capone

Antonio "Tony" Demers spent parts of five seasons with Montreal between 1937–38 and 1942–43. His finest season came in 1940–41 when he scored 13 times and added 10 helpers. Before making the NHL, this native of Chambly Basin, Quebec, played in England of all places, netting 20 goals in 1936–37 with the Southampton Kings of the British National Ice Hockey League.

Despite sustaining a broken leg early in late 1942, Demers enlisted in the Canadian Armed Forces, staying on until being discharged in early 1944. Then he joined the Rangers to complete an earlier trade involving Phil Watson. Unfortunately, Demers played only one game in the Big Apple. He kicked around lower circuits for several years, winning the Most Valuable Player award in the Quebec Senior League in 1948–49 before running afoul of the law.

In 1948–49 Demers was convicted of beating his girlfriend to death and was slapped with a 15-year prison term. He served eight of those years at St. Vincent de Paul Penitentiary before making parole. Needless to say, the rap ended Tony's hockey career. Demers earned more notoriety off the ice than on it.

Kenny Loves Cal

Kenny Reardon and Cal Gardner endured one of the hottest feuds in hockey history. In a game between New York and Montreal in March 1946, a bench-clearing brawl broke out. The Habs' Reardon had six teeth knocked out in the melee but hadn't the foggiest idea who did it. After the game, he mistakenly pointed to Bryan Hextall as the culprit.

In another New York–Montreal tilt, Reardon and Gardner clashed at center ice. Reardon was fined $200 by league president Clarence Campbell while Gardner was hit with a $250 slap on the wrist. Afterwards, Reardon was happy that Gardner was nailed for $50 more.

In September 1949, a sports writer interviewed Reardon — an interview that would come back to haunt him. During the interview, Reardon stated that he would "see to it that Cal Gardner got 14 stitches in the mouth" and even if he had to wait until his last game in this league, he assured that "Gardner would get it good and plenty."

Kenny Reardon

Cal Gardner

On New Year's Eve 1949, Toronto and Montreal faced off for the last game of 1949. Midway through the game, both Reardon and Gardner met at center ice, Reardon sending Gardner crashing to the ice. Some say Reardon elbowed the scoring Leaf center in the mouth while others saw Reardon's hit as a legitimate shoulder check. Gardner was rushed to hospital where it was discovered he had a badly broken jaw. When Reardon learned of the injury, he said, "It couldn't have happened to a nicer guy."

In March 1950 NHL president Clarence Campbell imposed a $1,000 fine on Reardon for his threats made during the interview in 1949. The fine was a peace bond that assured league powers that Reardon was not going to touch Gardner.

At a press conference, Reardon said: "I've been a bad boy. Gardner is a good kid and I'm sorry that there may have been occasions on which I referred to him as a baboon, ape, or troglodyte. Those were rash and impulsive words on my part and I propose to wash out my mouth with soap and water. I can't imagine why I ever said those things!"

Gardner had a few words of his own. "Ain't that sweet of him. There's only one thing that still dirties our beautiful friendship — I still happen to hate his guts."

Ulcers

The NHL career of Frank McCool, while not a long one, was particularly interesting. As a 26-year-old rookie, he won the Calder Trophy. However, before his second professional season had closed, he was out of the league, never to play again. But this does not begin to tell the story of the man they called "Ulcers."

Consider McCool's journey to the NHL. He played his first real hockey at Gonzaga University in Washington. Back then, Gonzaga would enter into tournaments with the likes of noted college hockey powers UCLA and USC.

The University of Toronto hockey team, coached by Irvine "Ace" Bailey, trekked to California one year in the late 1930s to play against the best California team. McCool was exceptional, playing well enough to earn a tip of the hat from Bailey. McCool moved on to Calgary in the Alberta Active Services League. He received a tryout with the New York Rangers prior to the 1943–44 season, but was forced to quit due to ulcers.

Fast-forward to 1944–45. With many players involved overseas in the final push to topple Nazi Germany, the search was on across the NHL for talent to fill the rosters. The Maple Leafs had trudged through the previous season with Benny Grant and Paul Bibeault between the pipes. The team suffered a first-round playoff defeat at the hands of Montreal, the eventual champions. Toronto had tried to retain Bibeault but were denied this liberty by the Canadiens, who owned his rights. Montreal wanted him back. After he surrendered five goals to Maurice Richard in the second game of the 1944 playoffs, one must wonder why. Keeping Bibeault would have cost Toronto Gaye Stewart and Bob Goldham, a price far too steep.

Enter McCool. His ulcers had proven to be his ticket out of the military and Toronto immediately signed him, not knowing exactly how good the kid was but trusting the opinion of Lorne Carr, a veteran Leaf forward whose opinion held weight.

Toronto started the 1944–45 season like a hay-stuffed barn on fire, winning their first six games. McCool won the Calder and the Leafs finished the season in third place, earning them the right to take on Montreal in the playoffs. The Canadiens had dominated all season long, botching only 8 of their 50 games. Toronto was the heavy underdog — on paper.

The McCool-led Leafs stunned the critics by taking the first two games at the Forum, where the Canadiens had lost only twice all year. Montreal rebounded to grab game three in Toronto but the Leafs, on the strength of a Gus Bodnar overtime winner, took the fourth tilt for a 3-1 series lead. Montreal, no doubt angry and humiliated, exploded in game five. Richard was on fire, scoring four times in a 10–3 Montreal triumph. The Leafs knew they didn't want to return to Montreal for game seven. With this in mind, McCool returned to form in game six, shutting down the Canadiens. Just like that, the upset was complete — the Flying Frenchmen were grounded!

The finals proved to be McCool's coming-out party. Despite having won the Calder and his solid performance in the semifinals, few were expecting what McCool would do in the first three games of the finals. McCool posted three straight shutouts, giving Toronto a commanding 3-0 series lead. His post-season shutout streak reached 193 minutes before hard-skating "Flash" Hollett solved him in the fourth game. The Leafs were home-free. Or were they?

Detroit had not forgotten about the spring of 1942 when the Maple Leafs crawled back from a 3-0 deficit to win the Cup. As if playing a game of tit-for-tat, Detroit clawed its way through McCool to tie the series at three games apiece. The Leafs were given little to no chance of winning the Cup at this point. In fact, only two Toronto sportswriters made their way to Detroit to cover game seven! However, McCool came through. With Toronto up 2–1 with eight minutes left to play, McCool's ulcers began flaring up. He pleaded with referee Bill Chadwick for permission to get some milk at the bench to settle his tumultuous tummy. Chadwick agreed and McCool rushed to the dressing room. He returned 10 minutes later, ulcers in pocket, ready to take on the world.

As McCool rejoined the battle, Detroit pushed unsuccessfully for the equalizer. The Maple Leafs had their first Cup in three years.

McCool vanished as quickly as he had burst upon the hockey scene. Prior to the

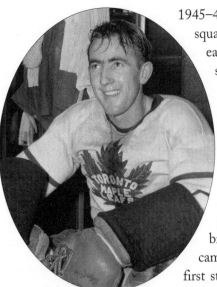

Frank McCool

1945–46 season, he and team overlord Conn Smythe squabbled over salary. McCool, who had been earning $4,500, wanted a $500 raise but Smythe stood firm. The city's press and fans almost immediately came down on Smythe. How could McCool be denied a $500 raise after almost single-handedly winning the Cup?

The critics shouted louder after Toronto's 0-4-1 start to 1945–46. In time, Baz Bastien was replaced in net. This was not McCool's cue, though. Navy recruit Gordie Bell took over. The Leafs left McCool to swing in the breeze until November 22, when they finally came to terms. McCool got his raise. He made his first start on December 1, 1945, against the Hawks and was blasted 8–2. Then, after a February 3 start in which the cellar-dwelling Rangers put six goals past him, McCool was finished. Toronto decided that Turk Broda, fresh from a stint in the military, was their man.

The Leafs finished the season out of the playoffs and McCool never again appeared in the NHL. He returned to Calgary, where he worked for the Calgary *Albertan* until his death in 1973. While his NHL career was a short one, his glittering performance in the 1945 playoffs will forever represent the possibility of a nobody setting the hockey universe on its ear.

Yogi on Ice

Who knew New York Yankee great Yogi Berra was such a hockey fan? Berra had up-close experience in hockey. He was an ardent supporter of the St. Louis Flyers of the United States Hockey League. He even had season tickets to Flyer games behind the team bench. He was good friends with Don "The Count" Grosso and Hec Pozzo, two fellow Italians on the team.

Berra once got it into his head that he should skate with the Flyers as a way of rounding into form for New York Yankees spring training. He discussed his idea with Grosso and Pozzo and they got, as the *Hockey News* put it, "the chunky Italian" on the ice.

The Flyers found Berra's ice antics quite amusing. He took some ribbing gracefully. He challenged the boys to take their cuts at major league pitching. No Flyers took Berra up on his dare and the chunky Italian's hockey career came to a close as he waddled south to join the Yankees for spring training.

They Called Him Baz

It was extremely difficult for goalies to break into the NHL during the Original Six era. Even the great Johnny Bower failed to break in at first. The "China Wall" was given his first opportunity in 1953–54, and played well for the New York Rangers at the age of 29. But he would not see regular NHL action again until 1958–59.

Aldege "Baz" Bastien had a similar problem. He could not find a team to play with. In the mid-1940s, he was the Toronto Maple Leafs' top goaltending prospect, but was stuck behind Turk Broda. Not much room for promotion there.

Bastien's only NHL opportunity came in 1945–46. Broda was temporarily retired from hockey, while the previous season's hero, Frank McCool, was holding out. Bastien, signed by Toronto as McCool's emergency replacement, was thrust headlong into the fire. He was a disaster! In his first five starts, none of them wins, he surrendered 20 goals. Bastien was promptly dispatched to the Pittsburgh Hornets.

Aldege "Baz" Bastien

In Pittsburgh, Bastien worked hard to make it back to the big-time. In 1948 and 1949, he earned the Hap Holmes Trophy, the AHL's answer to the Vezina. With Broda approaching 35 years of age, Toronto was grooming Baz for the starting role. With an AHL record of 116-64-34 under his belt, Bastien went to training camp in the fall of 1949 expecting a phone call from Toronto. The call never came.

In a routine camp scrimmage, a wild shot struck Bastien on the right eye. He would never see out of that eye again. The Leafs and Hornets played a benefit game for him on October 17, 1949, raising over $5,000 for the washed-up goalie from Timmins, Ontario.

The NHL had a bylaw in place that, for insurance reasons, prohibited partially blind players from playing. It was known as the Trushinski bylaw, named after Frank "Snoozer" Trushinski, a Kitchener Greenshirts defenseman who had lost his eye in a game in 1921.

Bastien embarked on a life in hockey management. He worked with the Hornets for the next two decades before moving on to the NHL. He worked with numerous top-level clubs, returning to Pittsburgh to become manager of the Penguins until his death from injuries suffered in a March 1983 car accident.

Bastien was one of the AHL's top goalies in the 1940s. Had he played 20 years later, he would have seen more than five NHL games. He would have been wearing a mask.

No More Bets

Hockey has been tied to gambling for nearly one hundred years. In 1915, defenseman Harry Mummery of the Quebec Bulldogs of the NHA claimed to have been approached by gamblers with offers to throw games for quick cash. Seven years later, the PCHA was shaken by rumors of several players conspiring to throw contests.

In the early 1930s, newspapers reported that gamblers had attempted to bribe goalie Lorne Chabot. NHL president Frank Calder acknowledged that gamblers were around the NHL and warned everyone who cared about the game to watch out for "gambling cliques who are out to try and fix games."

The New York *American* said that "some sports may be strong enough to get by successfully in spite of contact with the so-called 'wise money' and the sure-thing element, but it is safe to assume that the hockey followers will prefer to take their game straight."

In the latter half of the 1940s, hockey gambling reared its head once more. But this time it was the players, not the gamblers, who had the NHL suits in a flutter. Babe Pratt was suspended in early 1946 by Red Dutton for what was termed "conduct prejudicial to the welfare of hockey." And what was Pratt's crime? Gambling on his Maple Leafs to win. And although no games were actually fixed, he was barred from organized hockey.

Apparently, Pratt got his start in gambling when he wagered with a noted flim-flam man that he would score in an upcoming game. Dutton felt that even if Pratt had only bet on his own team to win, the gamblers could garner valuable information for use in fixing other matches.

Dutton had already warned Pratt and several others that anyone caught gambling would be dealt with harshly. Still, Pratt was readmitted to the NHL after serving only sixteen days of what could have been a life suspension. When grilled by the media about his shady dealings, he fired back that he had bet on his team to win and was doing no harm to anyone. The NHL Board of Governors, perhaps blinded by his star status, allowed him to play out the rest of the season.

The gambling bug flared up again in 1947–48 with the Billy Taylor–Don Gallinger incident. Taylor was a crafty pivot specializing in setting up the nifty scoring play. Don was another of the league's talented centers who, although not as skilled as Taylor, had been an important part of the Bruins since 1942.

Taylor and Gallinger were teammates for only half of the 1947–48 campaign, but they caused themselves and the game considerable damage in that short time. League president Clarence Campbell uncovered evidence of players wagering on matches, although there was no proof of games being fixed. Using a wire-tap, and with the assistance of the Detroit Police Department, the NHL was able to nab the guilty parties.

Taylor and Gallinger had been in contact with James Tamer, a Detroit gambler and paroled bank robber.

Taylor, Gallinger, and Tamer were incriminated over a February 18, 1948, game between Boston and the Hawks. At the time Chicago was one of the league's weakest squads. Gallinger told Tamer that Boston's Clare Martin had sustained a head injury in a previous game and that Jack Crawford's daughter was gravely ill. The Bruins would not be anywhere near full power. Gallinger bet $1,000 on Chicago. Tamer managed to entice Taylor into plunking down $500 on Chicago. The Bruins won 4–2.

Billy Taylor

When the evidence surfaced, both Taylor and Gallinger were immediately suspended for what Campbell termed "conduct detrimental to hockey and for associating with a known gambler." At the same time, he was adamant that "nobody fixed anything, anywhere."

Gallinger tried out with baseball's Philadelphia Phillies in early 1950. The pariah hockeyist also had tryouts with the Philadelphia Athletics, Boston Red Sox, and Boston Braves and had even been offered a contract by A's manager Connie Mack, which Gallinger turned down in favor of entering the armed forces. Rumors that Gallinger was going to play in Philadelphia were shot down by Phillies brass (likely to avoid a media circus).

Trouble followed Gallinger for years after his suspension from the NHL. In 1953, the Ontario Hockey Association awarded a Senior game to Sarnia after Gallinger had been spotted entering the Kitchener dressing-room before a game.

Billy Taylor popped up in industrial leagues across Ontario, starring on teams such as Billy Taylor's Sporting Goods, a team in the Oshawa Commercial League.

Taylor and Gallinger were not reinstated by the NHL until 1970, with hockey following baseball's lead in reinstating Detroit Tigers ace hurler Denny McLain from a suspension for his involvement with a bookmaking operation. Gallinger had applied for reinstatement in 1949, 1955, and 1962, while Taylor, according to NHL sources, had chosen to pay his debt in silence. After being readmitted to the league, Taylor signed on in coaching or scouting positions for several teams. Gallinger, however, never returned to hockey.

A 1971 *Toronto Star* piece sounded the gambling alarm once again. NHL security head Frank Torpey stated that "in talking to people who should know, I've found they feel that as the popularity of hockey increases, gambling will increase." Torpey might have added "As gambling in hockey increases, hockey's popularity will increase."

Don Gallinger

Why did Babe Pratt get off with a 16-day suspension while Billy Taylor and Don Gallinger were expelled for life? Was this disparity due to Pratt's all-world status, that he was one of the finer defensemen of his time? If Taylor was Hall-of-Fame-bound, would he have been punished so harshly? Pratt bet on his teams only to win while both Taylor and Gallinger wagered against their own team. Pratt should have served more than 16 days, but his crime was not near as odious as Taylor and Gallinger's.

Un Chapeau pour Madame B.

If you do something nice for someone, you will be paid back tenfold. If this is the case, Butch Bouchard must have had quite the night with his wife on November 6, 1948.

Bouchard's defensive partner, Glen Harmon, owned a hat boutique in Montreal. It turns out that Bouchard's wife was a frequent visitor to the Harmon hat emporium. On one of those visits, Mrs. Bouchard took a fancy to a particular bonnet which big Butch had already been eyeing prior to that night's game against the Red Wings. He was all set to purchase the hat for his wife until he noticed the high price.

Harmon noticed the despair on Bouchard's face and proposed a wager: If the big defenseman were to pot two goals against Detroit's Harry Lumley — not an easy task — Harmon would give Bouchard the hat. This seemed like a safe bet to Harmon as Bouchard had scored but four goals the season before and only one in the first seven games of 1947–48. Harmon, however, underestimated a woman's influence.

Buoyed by the thought of pleasing his wife, Bouchard scored both goals in a 2–0 Montreal victory. As the Montreal *Gazette* reported the next day, "Bouchard 2, Detroit 0, Harmon Broke."

Dirty Ol' Mariucci

Throughout much of the 1940s, Chicago was a high-flying outfit. The speedy Max and Doug Bentley, Bill Mosienko, and Bill Thoms injected some much-needed excitement into a previously flat hockey culture. The new and improved Black Hawks were adept at scoring goals, and beautiful ones, using a fine blend of speed and instinct. About the only rap against them was their lack of size and physical play. Chicago needed a player to protect their small, fragile stars.

Enter Johnny Mariucci. Mister Elbows. Dirty Ol' Mariucci.

This tough American Midwest-bred hombre came in willing to do anything. Ah yes, just the man for the job. Born in Contina, Italy, John Mariucci came to the States as a lad. A top-flight football player in high school, he didn't put on a pair of skates until he was 17. After graduating from the University of Minnesota, where he played on the 1939–40 hockey team, he was signed by Chicago.

Mariucci earned 44 stitches in his first 22 professional hockey games. Coach Johnny Gottselig put Mariucci to work immediately, making use of the rough player's fistic ability. Whenever Chicago's fancy boys were getting

John Mariucci

hammered, Gottselig would sidle over to Mariucci and whisper, "Better put that bum in his place . . ." The bruising Mariucci never disappointed.

Even after his NHL career ended in 1948, Mariucci's life made for fine copy. In an exhibition game against the AHL Springfield Indians when Mariucci was with the St. Louis Flyers, a rookie player slapped Mariucci across the face. The old fighter issued a warning. When the rookie repeated his stunt, Mariucci dropped his stick and clobbered him. Springfield goalkeeper Jim Henry opened the gate to let the frightened boy escape Mariucci, who chased him all the way to the dressing room. The next day, Mariucci had a talk with Springfield coach Earl Seibert, telling him, "Do me a favor . . . don't play that kid against us again or you'll have a dead pigeon on your hands."

Later that day, there was a knock on Mariucci's hotel room door. It was none other than the rookie, who said, "I want to apologize Mr. Mariucci, and can I please play against your club tonight?"

The War on Fat

In late 1949, hockey hopes in Toronto were running high. Only months earlier, the Leafs had taken home their third Stanley Cup in a row. Many Blue and White boosters had their sights set on a four-peat.

Fat chance.

By September, Jim Thomson and young Bill Barilko were inked to contracts. In camp, youngsters George Armstrong, Tim Horton, and Danny Lewicki showed themselves well. Yet despite the wide-eyed exuberance of the youngsters, the Leafs as a whole were in poor physical condition. In the team's first exhibition match on September 12, goalie Turk Broda was rocked for five goals in a shutout loss to the St. Catharines, Ontario, minor-leaguers. Right after the game, Broda was cursed and belittled by the crowd.

Toronto impresario Conn Smythe bit his lip until November. The Leafs had a good November overall, but in the last two weeks of the month, they were drowning. Some thought the boys had lost their burning passion to win. The defensive corps stopped hitting, the forward lines were dry as a bone, and Broda looked like a beached whale. Skipper Hap Day was concerned, and for good reason. "Whenever we get a lead, we can't seem to hold it," Day moaned. "It seems like the guys relax after we get ahead and you can't relax for a second in this sport."

Smythe and Day pinpointed two bugbears: the rapidly improving Red Wings and complacency, which sneaks up on many championship teams. Smythe was concerned that the Leafs were becoming fat, both mentally and physically. So, on November 29, he initiated what hockey historian Brian McFarlane termed the "Battle of the Bulge." Smythe read the riot act to the Maple Leafs that evening, replacing the porky Broda with Gil Mayer, a younger, slimmer player from Toronto's satellite club in Pittsburgh. When asked about his eating habits, Mayer confessed: "I eat everything . . . but my weight never changes. Milkshakes are my favorite and I drink them all the time to gain weight."

Smythe issued a "reduce or produce" ultimatum to Broda, Garth Boesch, Vic

Lynn, Harry Watson, and Sid Smith. Watson was the heaviest on the team, tipping the scales at 205. He was ordered to shed 5 pounds. Broda, a plump 197, was told to lose 7. Boesch, at 195, was to sweat off 3. Lynn, at 189 pounds, was ordered to lose 9, and Smith, weighing 183, was to shed 3. All players in Smythe's new "Lard League" were given until the afternoon of Saturday, December 3 — only four days — to lose the excess jiggle.

Although Smythe singled out five men, his primary target was Broda. "If the Turk doesn't devalue his pounds and sharpen his play, he'll wind up in a Pittsburgh Hornets' jersey or on the sidelines," Smythe blustered. "The honeymoon is over. I'm taking Broda out of the nets and he's not coming back until he shows some common sense. I'm running a fat man's team, apparently. Two seasons ago Broda weighed 185 pounds. Last season he went up to 190 — and now this. A goalie has to have fast reflexes and you can't move fast when you're overweight. We'll let them try buying their own roast beef for a change."

Broda, who had missed only four games in his first 11 seasons for the Leafs, was deeply hurt. *Toronto Star* columnist Red Burnett contacted Mrs. Broda, finding her to be quite puzzled. Apparently, her chubby hubby had been on a diet for months and his appetite had dwindled down to nothing. "I don't know what I can cut off Turk," she cried. "He hardly eats a darn thing now and has the smallest appetite in the house. Why, the girls and I eat more than he does." Lady Broda said she would allow Broda only skimmed milk, and his after-dinner nap would be replaced by a brisk walk. Apparently, "all this weight-watching was affecting the family budgie, who was no longer allowed his favorite dish of mashed spuds."

By the end of November 29, Broda was down to 193 pounds, thanks to a grueling session at Toronto's west end YMCA. "I had a three-hour workout at the gym and I've had nothing but two glasses of grapefruit juice and three soft-boiled eggs all day," he sighed. "For dinner I had only a dash of grapefruit. I'm going straight home to bed and I'm not having anything, except a pinch of fruit juice before the practice tomorrow." A well-known nutritionist advised that the way to lose weight was through will-power. "Being overweight is caused solely by eating more food than is needed," he told Broda.

Smythe dropped a bombshell when he sent four players and cash to the AHL Cleveland Barons for 23-year-old goalie "Angular" Al Rollins. The lean, mean newcomer was an immediate challenge to Broda.

Broda's fellow dieters were well on their way to meeting Smythe's

Turk Broda

demands. Boesch had dipped down to 189, Watson was at 200, Lynn was only 2 pounds shy of his goal, and Smith had half a pound yet to sweat off.

Big Watson came in for quite a heckling in a December 1 game against the Red Wings. Many of the 14,015 fans in attendance were heard to bellow "go back to the gym!" and "get some more fat off!"

The climax of this week-long calorie crusade came on Saturday afternoon when, one-by-one, the players stepped on the scales as Smythe watched on. Watson, Boesch, Lynn, and Smith weighed in under their set limits. Finally, it was Broda's turn. He waddled forward sheepishly and stepped onto the cold metal of the scale platform. After bobbing up and down for a few seconds, the needle settled at a hair under 190! Broda had made the cut. Ecstatic, he bounded off the scales and gobbled, "I'm going to have a small steak after the game tonight," after asking the boss's permission, of course.

"There may be better goalies around somewhere, but there's no greater sportsman than the Turkey," Smythe chuckled. "If the Rangers score on him tonight, I should go out and buy him a malted milk just to show I'm not trying to starve him to death."

Around the NHL, the opinions were mixed regarding Smythe's war on fat. While Montreal Canadiens skipper Dick Irvin praised Smythe for establishing order and discipline, Boston's Art Ross was somewhat less impressed: "Tell Connie Smythe to fatten any of his players as high as they can go and we'll buy them at $100 per pound on the skate."

The tale of the tape-measure:

Date	Broda	Watson	Boesch	Lynn	Smith
November 29	197	205	195	187	183
Smythe's limit	190	200	192	182	180
December 3	187.5	196	189	181	179

Broda skated out to his usual post between the pipes to face the Rangers as a regimental band played "Good Times Are Here Again" and "She's Too Fat for Me." Toronto won 2–0 and Turk was in fine form. He went on to enjoy his best season in years, posting a career-best nine shutouts and the third lowest goals-against average in the league.

Toronto is a happy burg, the cheers are loud and long,
The streets are lined with people and the avenues lilt with song.
On every side, both near and far, the air is filled with tunes,
The air is also filled with kites, rockets and balloons.
The King and Queen are flying to Toronto in a plane,
The hotel dining rooms are serving nothing but champagne.
The Maple Leaf directors, led by Connie, are a sight,
They're garbed in silk and satins, holy Nellie, what a sight.
Why, why this joyous revelry, why do they celebrate?
Why don't you know, you small-town boob, that Broda's down to weight!
— Toronto Star

A Bad Day for Teeder

Late 1949 was not very kind to Toronto center Ted Kennedy. On Saturday, November 19, he was on his way to Maple Leaf Gardens from his home in Whitby for an encounter with the Red Wings. According to police reports, driving visibility was quite poor. Driving along Eglinton Avenue in Scarborough, Kennedy made a quick move to pass a truck and struck two young boys. He immediately rushed the two boys to a local hospital. One of them, 10-year-old Robert Armstrong, was pronounced dead on arrival.

This incident visibly shook Kennedy, who missed the two weekend games against Detroit. No charges were laid, though, as the police deemed the mishap purely "accidental."

Connie vs. the World

Constantine Falkland Smythe, who was no stranger to conflict and disagreement, knew he couldn't please everyone. He was a very hard-headed individual, set in his ways. As such, he often rubbed other people the wrong way. And he didn't pick and choose who would suffer his wrath. He was an all-star agitator, a renowned rankler. It was "Mess with the Leafs and deal with Smythe" in the Toronto Maple Leafs' golden era. The old bird's battles with Jack Adams and the Detroit Red Wings are proof of his pugnacity, as are his views on military conscription. But he saved perhaps his grandest tirades for the Bruins, specifically Art Ross.

Before life in the NHL, Conn Smythe was on the University of Toronto Varsity Blues coaching staff. In 1924, the Blues went on a road trip, a barnstorming tour of New England. At the time, Boston was struggling through their inaugural NHL campaign, winning only one of their first 12 games before Smythe's visit. Always the agitator, Smythe mentioned to the Boston media that his Blues could defeat the Bruins. Ross, of course, took exception to Smythe's comments. Thus began what Smythe called "a lifelong feud" with Ross.

Bruins' owner Charles Adams had given Smythe his start in the NHL. In 1926, when Smythe was managing the Blues, the infant Rangers were searching for a hockey man to head up their team-building process. Adams recommended Smythe to Ranger boss Colonel John Hammond. Adams even helped Smythe load up the Rangers with talent. This purchase gave the league's American franchises the talent they needed to compete with the Montreal and Toronto outfits. Boston snagged Eddie Shore, Harry Oliver, Duke Keats, and Archie Briden, while Smythe's Rangers grabbed Bill and Bun Cook and Frank Boucher. This trio would form the nucleus of the Rangers for the next decade or so.

So, if Smythe had a good history with the Bruins, why the feud?

According to Smythe, Ross held a grudge about the run-in with the Varsity Blues in 1924. Ross exacted his revenge four years later. Smythe was looking to further stock his flourishing Maple Leafs franchise. He approached Ross, who recommended Jimmy "Sailor" Herberts, at the time Boston property. Smythe took the bait and paid Ross a low five-figure sum for Herberts. But the sailor's ship had already sailed. The 30-year-old

Herberts had a measly eight points in 31 games. The shrewd Smythe had been taken.

Ross continued going after Smythe, attempting to right the "wrong" of 1924. Ross allegedly hired two thugs to goad Smythe into a fight, which would land Smythe in jail. After a Toronto–Boston game, the goons stepped up to Smythe and tried to start something. Ross, meanwhile, waited patiently in the background, ready to pounce should punches be thrown. Smythe yelled at the two toughs, and Ross charged at Smythe. Frank Selke, Smythe's assistant at the time, noticed Ross and dove at him, hitting him with a vicious cross-body block. Smythe and Selke then high-tailed it for the Toronto dressing room.

In March 1931, tensions between Smythe and Ross flared up again after their teams played to a 3–3 draw. After the match, Smythe and Ross entered into an argument. Ross threw a punch. Smythe easily sidestepped the jab and bystanders immediately separated the pair.

At the time, Benny Grant, a Toronto-owned goalie, was on loan to a Boston farm club. After this disagreement, Smythe recalled Grant. Eddie Gerard, who managed the farm club, instructed Grant to stay put as it was Gerard's contention that Smythe could only recall Grant should something have happened to Lorne Chabot, Toronto's regular goalie. Grant stayed put.

The defining moment in the Smythe–Ross rivalry occurred on December 12, 1933, in the middle of the now-famous Eddie Shore–Ace Bailey incident. Shore, mad with rage after being flattened by Leaf tough guy Red Horner, hammered Bailey from behind, causing the star Leaf to fall headfirst onto the ice. Smythe was in the thick of the melee that ensued. He slugged a fan, after which Ross tried to persuade the police to press charges. The charges were withdrawn only when the severity of Bailey's injury was determined, when Smythe was under great stress. He was at death's door.

An irked Charles Adams charged that Smythe was guilty of "conduct prejudicial to the best interests of the NHL" and demanded that Frank Calder take immediate disciplinary action. In a letter to Calder, Adams claimed that in getting involved in the December 12 brawl, Smythe didn't "warrant the respect" of the fans. Under section 3(a) of the NHL constitution, Calder had the power to "fine, suspend, or expel." Calder didn't take any action against Smythe.

The most publicized incident in the Smythe–Ross feud occurred in 1940. Boston was in a slump. Looking for a little sport, Smythe took out an ad in the Boston papers that read, "If you're tired of seeing the kind of hockey the Boston Bruins are playing, come to the Boston Garden tonight and see a real hockey club, the Toronto Maple Leafs." Ross was hopping mad. Smythe, however, was positively glowing. The Garden was a sellout and, even though his Leafs lost, Smythe had a smile on his face. Ross demanded that Calder fine Smythe $1,000. The Leaf boss planted his tongue firmly in his cheek and yelped, "I put money in their pockets and they want to fine me for it."

After Smythe returned from the war, he went to Ross and made peace. Ross had raised two sons who had served in the war, and Smythe figured that "anybody who could rear two boys like that must be all right!"

Weston Adams, however, continued to pick on Smythe whenever he had the chance. Early in 1947–48, before a game between the Leafs and Bruins, Adams confronted league president Clarence Campbell with a charge that Toronto was guilty of illegal player substitution. Once Smythe got wind of these allegations, he launched into a tirade, screaming that his Leafs preferred to settle their problems on the ice rather than squealing like school-children.

Conn Smythe

The two teams met in the first round of the playoffs that season and tempers flared once again. After game three, Beantown fans jumped Leaf coach Hap Day and defenseman Garth Boesch. It took a number of players and officials to break up the brouhaha. Smythe was incensed at the lack of protection offered his Leafs. Adams came to the Toronto dressing room, presumably to apologize, but Smythe had him tossed out. Seems the Major was in no mood for small talk.

One day in February 1950, Smythe held court with Boston media types and derided the Bruins for their inability to sell out the Boston Garden. Adams trashed Smythe at an impromptu press conference, branding the Leaf boss as a "skunk." The quick-witted Smythe shot back, "no person ever won anything in this league by crying."

Another time, Ross complained, with reason, that Toronto took all of the favorable home dates (Saturday nights), leaving the B's with something of a rough schedule. Only six times in 1949–50 did Boston have three home games in a week. Conversely, the Leafs played the majority of their home games on Wednesdays and Saturdays.

Throughout the feud, Smythe's aim was to promote the game, to stir up the controversy and sell tickets. Smythe would ride into town a few days before the game, talk shop with the media, and throw in a subtle, or not so subtle, dig at the home team. This kind of showboating fired up the troops and filled arenas. For all of his short-comings, he wanted a strong NHL. He helped promote other teams, figuring that having six strong teams was good business. Ross and Weston Adams were certain that Smythe would go to bat for them if Boston was in financial trouble.

In the 1950s, Smythe and Ross saw their roles in their respective organizations diminish. The Toronto–Boston rivalry lost some of its punch.

Now, with a realigning NHL preparing for the 21st century, the two teams are in the same division again. We hope the rivalry can be rekindled, but there is no Connie Smythe or Art Ross to light the flame.

Yeah, But Could They Score off the Ice?

A quick glance at back-issues of *Hockey News* from the 1949–50 season reveals this interesting tid-bit: Detroit led the NHL in the number of bachelors per team. In all, only seven of Jack Adams' 18 Wings, or 39 percent, were hitched.

Detroit's "scoring percentage" fell far short of the NHL average. Of the NHL's 108 players in 1949–50, 66 were married, with an average of two kids.

On the ice that year, the Red Wings scored 229 times, just five goals short of the NHL record. Apparently, Detroit was saving its scoring for the games.

----

*Snap!*shots

SID ABEL (Old Bootnose) Center/Left Wing
5'11" 170
b. 2/22/1918, Melville, Saskatchewan

Someone once said that "Sid Abel has filled every job in the sport of hockey except for ticket printer." While this is not entirely true, it's not far off either. In five decades, Abel played, coached, scouted, and managed, collecting a few trophies and rings along the way.

Abel was signed by Detroit before the 1938–39 season. He split the season between the Wings and the Pittsburgh Hornets, playing in 15 games in the Motor City. By 1940, Abel was on a line with Don "The Count" Grosso and Eddie Wares. In the semi-finals with Toronto that year, Abel and Gus Marker initiated a brawl after which 17 players were fined $25 each.

It was not until 1940–41, though, that Abel put in his first full professional season. By 1941, the Abel-Grosso-Wares connection, known as the "Liniment Line," was firing on all cylinders. With 11 goals and 33 points in 47 games, it looked like the boy from Melville, Saskatchewan, was going places.

Abel was prominent in Detroit's 1943 Cup win, scoring five goals and 13 points in 10 playoff contests. He spent the next two years at war, and returned for seven games in 1945–46. In 1947, he was teamed with Ted Lindsay and a young Gordie Howe to form what was arguably the greatest line in hockey history. The trio was christened the "Production Line." They wreaked havoc on the NHL. In 1948–49, Abel and Lindsay tied for third in league scoring. The next season, Lindsay, Abel, and Howe finished 1, 2, 3.

Abel was tagged with the nickname "Old Bootnose" after a game in which Howe punched Maurice Richard in the face, knocking him to the ice. Abel looked down at Richard and yelped, "How do you like that, you Frenchman?" Richard then got up like a shot and decked Abel, breaking his nose in two places, hence the nickname.

Abel was a superb two-way talent. Not only was he a top-notch offensive producer but he was also one of the finest defensive centers of his time. His had keen instincts and he was natural on-ice leader. He was named Detroit captain in 1946 at the age of 28. He left the game as a Hawk in 1953, a member of three Stanley Cup–winning teams.

Abel took on managerial duties in Detroit in 1962–63 and proved himself to be a shrewd dealer. He was lauded for his ability to judge talent and for his pulling a stagnant Detroit franchise out of the mud with timely trades and signings. For example, he acquired All-Star goalie Roger Crozier in exchange for troubled Howie Young.

After stopovers in St. Louis and Kansas City, Abel returned to Detroit in 1977. He went to work in the Wings publicity department in corporate season-ticket sales renewals. Some years later, he became a Detroit hockey color commentator.

Sid Abel became a member of the Hockey Hall of Fame in 1969.

Peak Years *1946–50*
Comparable Recent Player *Saku Koivu*
In a Word *IGNITION*

SYL APPS (Nijinsky of the Ice/The Commissioner of Athletics) Center
6'0" 185
b. 1/18/1915, Paris, Ontario
d. 12/24/1998, Kingston, Ontario

Syl Apps first came to the attention of Conn Smythe after one of the Major's friends saw Apps play hockey for McMaster University in 1934. Smythe chuckled when he heard the name of the young phenomenon was Sylvanus Apps. Nevertheless, Smythe himself went to watch Apps and was so impressed that he offered the tall, good-looking center a contract with the Leafs.

But Smythe would have to wait. After winning the British Empire pole-vaulting crown in London in 1934, Apps was off to the 1936 Berlin Olympics. He would recall his London triumph as one of the two most thrilling episodes in his sporting life, the other being when he led the Leafs to a miraculous Cup win over Detroit in 1942.

Apps joined Toronto in late 1936. In his November 5, 1936, debut he centered a line with Harvey "Busher" Jackson and big Bob Davidson. The Toronto *Telegram* had nothing but good things to say about the 21-year-old rookie from McMaster University: "Apps made the best impression of the newcomers. It was thought he might display nervousness, but instead he acted like an old-timer. Some of his passes were beauties and he played his position to the king's taste."

Apps would star in Toronto for 10 years. He sipped club soda from Lord Stanley's mug in 1942, 1947, and 1948. He made the First All-Star Team twice, the second team three times, and won the Lady Byng Trophy once. In 1943, Apps enlisted in the Canadian Armed Forces and saw action in World War Two. After returning from duty, he maintained his high standards in leading the Leafs to two more Cups.

Though a big man for his time, Apps moved with speed and grace and possessed one of the most accurate shots around. As a boy, his father would flood a narrow lane behind the family home. An eager Apps would nail a garbage can lid to the garage door and shoot pucks at it.

Apps was a role model for all young Canadian boys. He was a clean-living man, someone who never drank, smoked, or swore. The worst curse he was capable of was "By hum!" And as for the greed that is often attributed to professional athletes, he tried to give back a portion of his salary to a shocked Conn Smythe in 1943 when he missed half the season with a broken leg. By hum!

After hanging up his skates, Apps entered provincial politics and became a Conservative MPP for 12 years. He served as Ontario's Minister of Correctional Services. In the summer of 1983, he acted as official mediator in an attempt to unify Ontario's three amateur hockey bodies. He lived in Kingston, Ontario, until his death on Christmas Eve, 1998.

In 423 games, Apps scored 201 goals and 432 points. He was enshrined in the Hockey Hall of Fame in 1961.

Peak Years   *1939–43*
Comparable Recent Player   *Joe Sakic*
In a Word   *CANADIAN*

BOBBY BAUER Right Wing
5'6" 160
b. 2/16/1915, Waterloo, Ontario
d. 9/16/1964, Kitchener, Ontario

Bobby Bauer

In 1935, Boston assigned Bobby Bauer, a hot prospect out of the St. Michael's Majors, to the Boston Cubs of the Can-Am League where the B's could monitor his development. Even though he was a skater, stick-handler, and play-maker par excellence, critics saw him as being a tad small for upper-level play. He responded by scoring 15 goals and 28 points in 48 games with the Cubs.

He would eventually get an offer from the Providence Reds, a semi-professional Boston affiliate. In Providence, he was teamed with Milt Schmidt, a huge, strong center, and Woody Dumart, a beefy, hard-working left-flanker. Head coach Albert Leduc called this trio "The Sauerkraut Line." The "sauerkraut" would of course be shortened to "Kraut," leaving us with the "Kraut Line," one of the greatest lines ever assembled.

Art Ross summoned Bauer during the 1936–37 season in an emergency situation. The little guy played quite well in his NHL debut, scoring a goal and earning himself a spot on the roster for next season. He went on to score 20 times in his rookie season playing alongside Schmidt and Dumart, who had followed him to Boston. The Kraut Line contributed greatly to Boston's first-place finish, with Bobby earning the first of three consecutive selections to the NHL's Second All-Star Team. In each of the following three seasons, Boston finished first in the NHL and won the Stanley Cup in 1939 and again in 1941.

In 1939–40, the Krauts finished 1, 2, 3 in scoring, with Bauer winning his first of three Lady Byng trophies. Toward the end of 1941–42, Bauer was among the first players to be sent off to war. He would return for the 1945–46 season, showing himself very well in the playoffs. Next season, he enjoyed a career-high 30 goals and again won the Lady Byng. At season's end, though, he retired with a nagging shoulder injury suffered at the hands — and shoulders — of Jack Stewart. After a one-year stint as head coach of the Guelph Biltmores, Bauer joined the Kitchener Dutchmen as an amateur player, leading them to the OHA finals in 1948, 1949, and 1950.

To commemorate the March 18, 1952, "Kraut Night" Boston fans were holding, Bauer signed a one-game NHL contract. He rejuvenated his old linemates and helped make history. Milt Schmidt scoring his 200th career goal in a 4–0, playoff spot–winning triumph over Chicago. Bauer, Schmidt, and Woody Dumart were showered with gifts, individual checks for $4,500, glistening silverware, and assorted manna ranging from $1,500 juke boxes to cases of peanut butter. After 327 NHL regular-season games and 260 points, Bauer hung up his skates for good.

In late 1952, Bauer accepted a position as president, manager, and head coach of the Dutchmen and under his tutelage the club won two OHA Senior championships and two Allan Cups. The second Allan Cup team was chosen as Canada's representatives at the 1956 Winter Olympics in Cortina, Italy, where they went on to snatch the bronze medal. Upon returning to Canada, Bauer retired from coaching. Four years later, though, he was convinced to take the helm for the Dutchmen once again at the 1960 Winter Olympics in Squaw Valley, California, and his boys took the silver. Following the Olympics, Bauer began to pass along the secrets of his coaching wizardry in countless information sessions with his younger brother, Father David Bauer, who would become a coaching legend at St. Michael's School for Boys. Through David, Bobby helped solidify the concept of national team hockey as we know it today.

In 1996, Bauer was inducted into the Hockey Hall of Fame.

Peak Years   1939–43
Comparable Recent Player   Robert Reichel
In a Word   JACKRABBIT

DOUG BENTLEY Left Wing
5'8" 145
b. 9/3/1916, Delisle, Saskatchewan
d. 11/24/1972, Saskatoon, Saskatchewan

Doug Bentley joined the Hawks in 1939, scoring 12 goals in 39 games for Chicago in his rookie campaign. He was the NHL's top point-getter in 1942–43 with 73 and led the league in goals scored the following season. After the war, he and his brother Max were teamed up with young Bill Mosienko, a speed demon from the left side. Thus, the "Pony Line" was born, a unit that stands as possibly the speediest, slickest line combination ever seen.

Although Doug took more shots than Max, he wasn't nearly as dazzling a stick-handler. Still, he racked up the most points of any NHL player in the 1940s.

In 1950, Doug Bentley was named the top player in Hawks history. It was a lofty honor to be chosen over such past Windy City luminaries as Mush March, Johnny Gottselig, Dick Irvin, and his kid brother Max.

By the 1951–52 season, Doug was slowing down. He appeared in only eight games in Chicago that year, finishing in Saskatoon. In 1953–54, he had one last hurrah with the Rangers alongside Max before retiring from the NHL. Doug remained in hockey as a player, coach, and scout, last suiting up with the Los Angeles club of the Western Hockey League in 1961–62.

While most of us never saw the Bentley boys play, we can imagine them swooping up and down the ice during practice, their slick, black hair glistening under the old lights, their sallow faces belying colossal hockey talents.

Bentley's accomplishments in the NHL were recognized when he was elected to the Hockey Hall of Fame in 1964.

Peak Years   1943–47
In a Word   HYPNOTIC

MAX BENTLEY (The Dipsy-Doodle Dandy) Center
5'9" 155
b. 3/1/1920, Delisle, Saskatchewan
d. 1/19/1984, Delisle, Saskatchewan

As a youth, Max Bentley was diagnosed as having an abnormally weak heart. The family doctor told the scrawny-looking young lad he would be dead within a year if he didn't avoid overexertion. Thank God he didn't listen to that quack.

Bentley got his big break in hockey in 1940 when Chicago head coach Paul Thompson finally relented to Max's older brother Doug, who had been screaming, "If you think I'm good, you should see my kid brother Max!" The first time team owner Bill Tobin set eyes on the pale, sallow, and frail-looking Bentley, he thought he'd been taken for a rube. Yet, although Max weighed only about 146 pounds soaking-wet with change in his pockets, he possessed dazzling hockey skills, not the least of which was breathtaking stick-handling ability and speed.

Bentley was sent down to the Kansas City Americans for seasoning, but his career almost ended before it even started due to his lack of self-confidence. Kansas head coach Johnny Gottselig talked Bentley into sticking with hockey and took the young

----

star-to-be under his wing, reviving Bentley's flagging spirits. Eventually, he was called up to the big leagues. The Bentleys quickly became the darlings of action-starved Chicago.

After the war, speedball Bill Mosienko joined the Bentleys to form the "Pony Line," possibly the fastest combination in the history of hockey. Max was just hitting his peak when he was called into the Canadian Armed Forces in 1943. He would return in time for the 1945–46 season. He won that year's scoring race, was picked for the First All-Star Team, and was took home the Hart Trophy. In 1946–47, Max again won the scoring title, edging out Maurice Richard in the final game of the schedule.

At the very peak of his powers, Bentley was traded to Toronto with Cy Thomas for Gus Bodnar, Bud Poile, Gaye Stewart, Ernie Dickens, and Bob Goldham. This deal, which ignited hostilities in Chicago, was a coup for Conn Smythe, a way of putting the finishing touch on his Maple Leafs, who would win the Stanley Cup in three of the next four years. Bentley was to become the greatest second or third-line center ever seen. Remember that Toronto already had Syl Apps and Ted Kennedy. The acquisition of Bentley gave them possibly the greatest depth at this position of all time.

In 1952–53, bothered by a back ailment, Bentley (an extreme hypochondriac) drove home to Delisle, Saskatchewan, without telling anyone. He would later tell a Toronto sportswriter that he was through with hockey. Smythe, however, talked Bentley into finishing out the season.

On August 11, 1953, Toronto sold Bentley to the Rangers, where he scored 14 goals and 32 points before quitting the NHL for good.

In Smythe's eyes, Bentley did more to round off the powerhouse Maple Leafs than anyone else. The crusty Toronto boss recalled years later Bentley's famous hypochondria:

> One time, Max asked to see me in my office and when he showed up, he told me had a really bad illness. He claimed he had cancer in a rather critical part of his male anatomy. I said that it was his lucky day because I had read in the paper that morning of a doctor in Scotland who had perfected a cure for Max's problem and I would make travel arrangements for him to go to Glasgow imme-diately. But I told Max that there was one problem: the cure involved cutting off the diseased parts. Funny, but I never heard again about Max's cancer.

Goalie Chuck Rayner called Bentley "easily the most accurate shooter" of his era. He was the first forward ever to drop back to the point on the power play, during his Toronto days. He is best remembered, though, for his ability to feather the puck through whole teams while skating at top speed. He was a little magician.

After retiring from the NHL, Bentley moved back home and played minor hockey in Saskatchewan for a couple of years before settling down to the full-time job of farm-ing with his brother Doug.

In 646 games, Max Bentley scored 245 goals and 544 points. He was inducted into the Hockey Hall of Fame in 1966.

Peak Years   *1943–47*
Comparable Recent Player   *Denis Savard*
In a Word   *DAZZLING*

TOE BLAKE Left Wing
5'10" 180
b. 8/21/1912, Victoria Mines, Ontario
d. 5/17/1995, Montreal, Quebec

Hector "Toe" Blake was signed by the Montreal Maroons on February 21, 1935. He spent most of the season bouncing back and forth between the Maroons and the OHA Hamilton Tigers. He began 1935–36 in Providence but by mid-February had been traded with Bill Miller and Ken Gravel to the cross-town Canadiens in exchange for star goalie Lorne Chabot.

Blake truly found himself with the Canadiens. In 1938–39, he scored 24 goals and 47 points for the NHL scoring crown. That season, he took home the Hart Trophy and was a First Team All-Star selection. He was, at this point, one of the only bright sparks on the foundering Canadiens.

Blake was a well-rounded athlete. Although he was not the greatest in any one area, he was a force to be reckoned with. He skated hard, shot hard, checked hard, and played every game as if it were game seven of the Stanley Cup finals. In a league where dedication was sometimes spread a little thin, he was loyal to his cause to the end. He saw the Canadiens through one of the darkest periods in their history — the one between Howie Morenz and Maurice Richard — and fit in well on Cup-winners in 1944 and 1946. He was a tireless back-checker as well as a skilled passer. With Blake on left flank, it's little wonder the "Punch Line" of Blake, Elmer Lach, and Maurice Richard flourished.

Blake left the NHL in January 1948 with a broken leg. After a few years in the minors, he hung up the skates for good. A coaching post in Buffalo eventually led to a return to Montreal and to the head coaching position with the Canadiens. Under Blake, "Le Bleu, Blanc, et Rouge" won 500 of 914 regular-season games between 1955 and 1968.

Blake had intensity and a hair-trigger temper. Both qualities served him well but also got him into hot water now and again. His most serious run-in came in game three of the 1961 Cup semifinals against the Black Hawks. Chicago led the match 1–0 until, with seconds to go, Henri Richard scored. After about 52 minutes of overtime, Murray Balfour scored the winning goal for Chicago while Dickie Moore was serving a penalty. After the game, Blake reportedly walked across the ice and decked referee Dalton McArthur. The next day he was fined $2,000 by NHL brass. The one thing Blake hated, above all else, was losing.

In 1968, after guiding Montreal to its eighth Cup in 13 seasons, Blake announced his retirement. "This is my last year," he said. "The tension is too much. It gets tougher every year. I'm quitting for good. With me, it has to be a combination of things. My nerves. My health. The players, I grant you, are part of it too. The game's gotten so big now, it's harder to control."

After retiring, Blake ran his tavern at the Forum full-time while acting as Canadiens GM Sam Pollock's part-time advisor. He turned down the opportunity to act as head coach of the 1972 Team Canada squad because his nerves were still ragged. In 1979, he accepted a post as team vice-president and stayed there until 1982, when he quit to look after his tavern full-time.

A touching excerpt from a Red Fisher tribute tells of Blake's last days in a Montreal hospital. Longtime friend and ex-teammate Floyd Curry stopped in for a visit. "Blake stared at an empty plate," Curry said. "Then he lifted it with both hands, tilted it towards him and let the crumbs fall into his open mouth.

'Good, eh Toe? Very good. Remember me, Toe?'"

Red Fisher said, "It is that time of year — a time for breathing in deeply and reflecting on what really counts. A time for remembering the good times. Remember Toe."

Blake died after an eight-year battle with Alzheimer's disease. He was enshrined in the Hockey Hall of Fame in 1966.

Peak Years   *1941–45*
In a Word   *PROUD*

BUTCH BOUCHARD (The Big Beekeeper) Defense
6'2" 205
b. 9/11/1920, Montreal, Quebec

Butch Bouchard

Emile "Butch" Bouchard first came to the Canadiens training camp as a gangling 185-pounder who had just ridden 50 miles on a bicycle to compete at the team's tryouts. As he was the biggest player in camp, he had little problem bodying the veterans around during scrimmages. The powers-that-be were impressed enough to offer him a contract. He would spend 15 years with Les Glorieux during which the team took home four Stanley Cups.

Bouchard was so strong he could break up fights simply by grabbing hold of the combatants with his big, meaty hands. But though he was a powerhouse, he never bullied an opponent. He was robust and played the game cleanly. Still, he was a fearsome opponent.

Bouchard was the rock-hard complement to the more mobile, offense-minded Doug Harvey and acted as Montreal's policeman for years. Bouchard enjoyed his most productive season in 1944–45, scoring 11 goals and 34 points in 50 games.

Always the entrepreneur, Bouchard established and operated his own restaurant in downtown Montreal, Chez Butch. He would later start a beef farm outside of Montreal. He still operates the farm today with his son Pierre, who himself played in 595 NHL games between 1970 and 1982.

Butch Bouchard became a member of the Hockey Hall of Fame in 1966.

Peak Years   *1945–49*
Comparable Recent Player   *Scott Stevens*
In a Word   *POLICEMAN*

FRANK BRIMSEK (Mister Zero/The Minnesota Icicle/Frigid Frankie) Goal
5'9" 170
b. 9/26/1915, Eveleth, Minnesota
d. 11/11/1998, Virginia, Minnesota

While playing for the EAHL Pittsburgh Yellow Jackets, Frank Brimsek first attracted the attention of NHL scouts. After signing with the Boston Bruins, he was sent to Providence for seasoning. In 1937–38, he went 25-16-7 with the Reds, recording a 1.75 goals-against average and five shutouts. Only seven games into the next season, he was called up to Boston. The Bruins already had star netminder Tiny Thompson but he was getting a little long in the tooth and team brass was out for new blood. Enter Brimsek, the man they would call "Mister Zero."

Boston manager Art Ross tested Thompson and Brimsek before deciding who would be the top dog. Ross donned skates, grabbed a stick and puck, and motioned for the two goalies to join him. He tried Thompson first, firing 25 pucks at him from 10 feet out. Ross scored six times. He then fired 25 at young Brimsek, who kicked them all out!

Brimsek suffered a 2–0 loss to the Canadiens in his debut as the Bruins' number one keeper. "I'll never forget that first game in the Garden and how the fans reacted," he recalled. "Usually, when the Bruins hit the ice there was a lot of cheering, but when I hit the ice, things were so quiet that I could honestly hear the people breathing. It was a very cool reception to say the least." Immediately following this opening loss, he began weaving his magic in an almost unbelievable rookie season. He posted three consecutive shutouts and held the Canadiens at bay until one minute into the second period of the fourth game. By the time Montreal scored, Brimsek had already broken Thompson's team record mark of 224 minutes and 47 seconds of shutout goaltending with a new mark of 231 minutes and 54 seconds. Brimsek then recorded three consecutive shutouts to give him a mind-blowing total of six blankings in his first 10 NHL games. He won the Vezina Trophy in 1938–39 with a 1.56 goals-against and 10 shutouts, and picked up the Calder as well.

After missing two seasons to the war, Brimsek returned in 1945. However, two-and-a-half years of standing on a steel ship deck had apparently damaged his legs and he was never really the same goalie again.

Prior to the 1949–50 season, Brimsek asked for a trade. The Bruins sold him to the Hawks for cash in a transaction said to have been the richest since Conn Smythe's $35,000 King Clancy purchase of 1930. Brimsek played the full 70 games in 1949–50 and put up decent numbers for a mediocre club. He retired at season's end.

Hap Day called Brimsek the "greatest goalie [he had] ever seen." Frank Selke and Art Ross also thought Brimsek to have been the best goalie of their time. The greatest American goalie ever, the man with one of the fastest glove-hands in the history of the game, ended his career with two Stanley Cup rings, two Vezina trophies, and eight All-Star Team nominations.

Brimsek was inducted into the Hockey Hall of Fame in 1966. He is also a member of the U.S. Hockey Hall of Fame.

Peak Years　　1939–43
Comparable Recent Player　　*Grant Fuhr*
In a Word　　*LIGHTNING*

TURK BRODA (The Fat Man/Turkey Eggs/Slip) Goal
5'9" 180
b. 5/15/1914, Brandon, Manitoba
d. 10/17/1972, Weston, Ontario

Walter Broda earned the nickname "Turk" not long after the first time he laced on a pair of ice skates. As a youngster in Manitoba, the back of his neck would turn beet red whenever he was irked. One day, an onlooker, noting his crimson neckline, shouted: "Look at the turkey!"

Toronto boss Conn Smythe first noticed Broda during the 1935–36 season. Smythe was originally interested in Earl Robertson of the Windsor Bulldogs but after watching a Bulldogs–Detroit Olympics game in which Broda shone, Connie's choice was clear. His regular goalie, 41-year-old George Hainsworth, was getting long in the tooth. Smythe knew he had to sign Broda, and he did.

Early on in his career, Broda had a penchant for letting in long shots. According to coach Hap Day, "Turk [had] been known to boot the odd soft one, miss a two-foot putt, trump a partner's ace, but never to make a fumble in the knife-and-fork league." Day worked Broda's hand speed by having him practice without a stick while teammates fired pucks at him from 20 and 30 feet out.

Broda was a true money goalie, posting post-season goals-against averages of less than 2.00 six times. All told, he was a career 1.98 second-season netminder, with 13 shutouts in 101 playoff matches. He had two First All-Star Team selections, won two Vezina trophies, and five Stanley Cup rings. Gary Lautens, late *Toronto Star* humorist, once said of Broda, "When the playoff bucks were on the line, the Turk could catch a line in a hurricane."

Broda was recruited for active military duty in October 1943, and returned on February 6, 1946. After playing a mediocre 15 games in 1945–46, the $10,000 goalie was back to form the following season, posting a 31-19-10 record and leading the Leafs to their first of four Cups in the next five seasons.

A great prank was played on Broda during a press and radio dinner before a game at Maple Leaf Gardens. Dave Price, who was doing a gag broadcast with Leaf trainer Tim Daly, was interrupted by an urgent message. According to the message, a six-day-old infant had been abandoned in its birthday suit. A hall-wide call was made for financial aid with which to tend to the infant's needs. A collection plate was passed around as Price continued reading aloud further details of the tragedy. At one point, he made the suggestion that any person wishing to take the infant permanently into his home should stand up. Broda, whose chair had been wired to a series of storage batteries and was charged, stood up in a shot, and was the first and only man to rise. Just then, a Gardens attendant rushed in and placed the infant in question in the Toronto goalie's arms — a six-day-old baby pig.

Broda went on to become a successful Junior hockey coach, twice guiding his boys to the Memorial Cup before stepping aside for a spell. After further coaching stints with the Marlboros and Quebec Aces, he had come to the end of the line. He died of a massive heart attack on October 17, 1972, at the age of 58.

Jack Adams said, "Turk Broda didn't have one nerve in his whole body. He could tend goal in a tornado and never blink an eye."

Broda is a very worthy member of the Hockey Hall of Fame, inducted in 1967.

Peak Years   *1939–43*
In a Word   *HAMSTEAK*

NEIL COLVILLE Center/Defense
5'11" 185
b. 8/4/1914, Edmonton, Alberta
d. 12/26/1987, Vancouver, British Columbia

Neil Colville

Before World War Two, the Rangers were looking to form a line to replace the legendary combination of Bill and Bun Cook and Frank Boucher. They found the right stuff in Neil Colville, who was signed on October 18, 1935, his 19-year-old brother Mac, and another youngster, Alex Shibicky. The trio, all right-hand shots, were an instant hit and Depression-era New York writers dubbed them the "Bread Line." The prematurely grey Neil, at center, was the backbone of the line. He was a fancy stick-handler and play-maker who employed a deceptive body motion. The line was patterned after the Cooks-Boucher trio, noted for precision passing and razzle-dazzle play.

In 1942, New York lost the Shibicky-Colville-Colville line to the war effort. While posted in Ottawa, Neil performed for the Ottawa Commandos of the Quebec Senior League, scoring 12 goals and 42 points in only 22 games. The Commandos, combining the collective talent of Colville and a number of NHL stars, won the Allan Cup in 1943.

Colville returned to the NHL for four games in early 1945 and was full-time again for the 1945–46 season. Colville played defense for the next three seasons.

Colville was one of the smarter players of his day. By the mid to late-1940s, he was considered a "master at the Rangers' style of precision passing." He served as team captain for a number of years, during which time he was named to the Second All-Star Team three times.

Late in the 1948–49 season, Colville sustained a serious groin injury and retired. He went on to coach the Blueshirts.

Colville was elected to the Hockey Hall of Fame in 1967.

Peak Years   *1939–43*
Comparable Recent Player   *Ron Francis*
In a Word   *VETERAN*

ROY CONACHER Left Wing
6'2" 175
b. 10/5/1916, Toronto, Ontario
d. 12/29/1984, Victoria, British Columbia

While not as well-known as his two older brothers, Lionel and Charlie, Roy Gordon Conacher was an excellent hockey player in his own right. Roy and his twin brother Bert were the youngest of five boys. Oddly, Roy's favorite sport growing up was baseball and only after Lionel handed him a discarded stick and threatened to knock his teeth in if he didn't play did the kid take up hockey.

Roy started out at Toronto's Jesse Ketchum School, after which he put in a few seasons in the OHA and one in a Senior hockey loop in Northern Ontario. In 1938, he was invited to Boston training camp. Because he was a Conacher, expectations ran high. He made a good impression on the Bruins. After a tremendous rookie camp, he shot out of the blocks, scoring at a terrific pace. By season's end, he had taken the goal-scoring crown with 26 in 47 games and finished second to teammate Frank Brimsek for the Calder Trophy. His hell-blazing pace continued into the playoffs, when he potted six more goals, among them the Cup-clinching marker against Toronto in the finals.

The next season, he was again up among the scoring leaders until a broken wrist sidelined him for 16 games. He would play two more years before joining the RCAF in 1942 for war. He missed the next four NHL campaigns and the bulk of his prime.

Like the other Conacher boys, Roy was a big man, though slimmer than his brothers. He was a sure stick-handler with a sharp, heavy shot, the trademark of the hockey-playing Conachers.

After being honorably discharged from the RCAF, Conacher returned to Boston. Manager Art Ross, however, thought it impossible for a man to return to the NHL after a four-year absence and resume his previous pace. The boss traded Conacher to the Detroit Red Wings. Conacher took it all in stride and scored 30 goals. The following season, Jack Adams was unable to sign Conacher to a contract and the big winger announced his retirement. Two weeks later, though, Adams wrapped up a deal that sent Conacher to Chicago. Six weeks later brother Charlie took the head coaching job in the Windy City. Roy went on to top the NHL in scoring in the 1948–49 season with 68 points. He made it to the First All-Star Team despite playing for a second-division club.

Conacher would play three more seasons before retiring due to numerous injuries in 1951–52. He finished his career with 226 goals, one more than brother Charlie. Not bad for the "forgotten Conacher." He was inducted into the Hall in 1998.

Peak Years   *1939–43*
Comparable Recent Player   *Brian Bellows*
In a Word   *SHOOTER*

BILL COWLEY Center
5'10" 165
b. 6/12/1912, Bristol, Quebec
d. 12/31/1993, Ottawa, Ontario

William Cowley played his first hockey at Ottawa's Plouffe Park, as a goalie no less. He soon switched to center, a move that would change the course of his life forever.

Cowley first drew notice as a member of the Primrose Juniors. Three seasons later, he was with the Halifax Wolverines of the Maritime Big Four, turning professional in 1934–35 with the NHL St. Louis Eagles. Only a year after that, he was acquired by the Bruins, where he went on to hockey stardom.

Cowley played in 13 NHL seasons, 12 with Boston. Although never a prolific goal-scorer, he had an uncanny ability to deliver the puck "on a dime to either wing." In the 1940–41 season, he racked up 62 points, 45 for assists. He was runner-up in scoring in 1943 and finished in the top 10 eight times in his career. His most impressive season was 1943–44, when he amassed 71 points in only 36 games when he suffered an injury. "I was so far ahead when I got hurt . . . I never thought anyone would catch me," he said, "but Herbie Cain did."

According to Cowley's teammates, he was about as fast as an anchored rowboat. Nevertheless, the crafty pivot always found a way to set up his wingers. He quietly became the NHL's all-time career scoring leader on February 12, 1947, erasing a mark of 528 points put up by the great Syd Howe.

The guy they called "Cowboy" earned an impressive total of awards and accomplishments. He played on three title-winners — 1939, 1940, and 1941 — and on two Stanley Cup champions. He bagged the Hart Trophy as league MVP in 1941 and 1943 and the Art Ross as top scorer in 1941. He was named the league's First All-Star center four times (1938, 1941, 1943, 1944) and Second All-Star center in 1945.

Cowley went on to coach hockey teams in Renfrew and Vancouver before going into the hotel business. He became a member of the Hockey Hall of Fame in 1968.

Peak Years   *1939–43*
In a Word   *VELVET*

JACK CRAWFORD (The Round Squire of Grasmere)
   Defense
5'11" 200
b. 10/26/1916, Dublin, Ontario
d. 1/18/1973, Boston, Massachusetts

Jack Crawford

Jack Crawford was a great high school football player at St. Michael's School for Boys in Toronto. Crawford began losing his hair on the gridiron at St. Mike's. "When I played football as a teenager for St. Mike's, the paint would peel off inside of my helmet and the doctors say that some chemical in the paint triggered the skin infection that caused all of my hair to fall out over the years."

Yeah, nice story, Jack.

Crawford blossomed into a top-notch defenseman in Boston, a First All-Star in 1946. He was remarkably consistent, rarely made a mistake in handling the puck, and was often the NHL players' choice as the league's steadiest, most effective defender.

The big Irish boy went on to contribute to Bruin Cup victories in 1939 and 1941 as one of Beantown's favorite players. He was a sunny guy with a penchant for dressing-room joke-swapping.

After the NHL, Crawford ran his wholesale grocery business in the Greater Boston area. He died in Boston in 1973.

Peak Years   *1941–45*
Comparable Recent Player   *Larry Murphy*
In a Word   *KOJAK*

WOODY DUMART (Porky) Left Wing
6'1" 200
b. 12/23/1916, Kitchener, Ontario

Woody Dumart played Junior hockey in his hometown, Kitchener, before being called up to Boston for good in 1937–38. He and friends Milt Schmidt and Bobby Bauer formed the Bruins' big line, the "Kraut Line." This unit was one of the most feared of all time.

Dumart was the least publicized of the Krauts. Still, with his clean, hard checking and shot off of the wing, he was a valuable member of the Boston Bruins throughout his career. Milt Schmidt had this to say about his bulky winger: "I've known few men who exceeded Woody in his talent, both ways on the ice. The only comparison that comes readily to mind is Bob Davidson. Opponents always hated to play against him because he was so strong and checked them so closely. But they never resented him, because he played the game so cleanly."

You'd think a player of Dumart's size would have racked up more penalty minutes. Not so. He was an honest player who played heads-up hockey. He was especially reliable in important games, collecting 23 penalty minutes in 88 career playoff matches.

The guy they called "Porky" enlisted in the RCAF with his linemates in 1942. The trio served the free world well before returning to the B's for the 1945–46 season. That season, Dumart scored 22 goals and 34 points in 50 games, a respectable total.

Dumart, as one of the finer two-way talents of his time, was often called upon to cover some of the game's greatest players. Just as the Canadiens' Claude Provost would do to Bobby Hull years later, Dumart shut down Gordie Howe in the 1953 playoffs. Big Howe scored only twice in six games. Dumart's linemate at the time, Joe Klukay, did a fine job in silencing Ted Lindsay in that series. Dumart and Klukay were the reason Boston upset the powerhouse Red Wings.

Toward the end of his career, Dumart became the elder statesman of the Bruins dressing room. He always put on his game jersey at 8:00 p.m. sharp. When the rest of the team saw him suiting up, they knew what time it was.

Dumart earned three All-Star nominations and two Stanley Cup rings. After retiring in 1954, he opened up a sporting goods business in Needham, Massachusetts. He stayed in touch with the team through old-timers hockey, and gave back to the greater Boston area through his devotion to youth hockey.

Dumart became a member of the Hockey Hall of Fame in 1992.

Peak Years   *1940–44*
In a Word   *STOUT*

BILL DURNAN Goal
6'0"
b. 1/22/1916, Toronto, Ontario
d. 10/31/1972, Toronto, Ontario

Durnan was ambidextrous, able to catch, block, and hold his stick with either hand. He learned this skill as a 13-year-old church league goalie under the tutelage of coach

Steve Faulkner. The skipper told Durnan that because he was not quick and didn't have good lateral movement, he should learn to do things with both hands. Durnan spent a lot of time over the next while practicing his goaltending trick. It would serve him well over the course of his career.

Assistant Toronto GM Frank Selke Sr. wanted Bill Durnan. He signed Durnan to a professional contract, and it looked like the goalie was going places. Then, one weekend, Durnan and a buddy were wrestling in the sand on Wasaga Beach when he suddenly wrenched his knee, tearing all the ligaments and displacing cartilage. The Leafs ultimately tired of waiting for their prospect to regain his wheel and cut him loose.

Durnan put in four seasons with the Kirkland Lake Blue Devils, the last of which led to the Allan Cup. Durnan's brilliance caught the attention of Canadiens scouts, who persuaded him to sign with the Montreal Royals, a Canadiens farm club. At the time, Durnan was working for a Montreal steel company, and the plant boss was Len Peto, a Montreal hockey club director. Peto applied leverage to his puck-stopping employee to get him to sign with the Canadiens. By 1943, he was in the NHL.

Durnan was an immediate sensation in Montreal. In his first season, 1943–44, he posted a 2.18 goals-against average to grab the Vezina Trophy and the First All-Star nod. He was the first Canadiens cage-guard since George Hainsworth to haul in the Vezina. In the next six seasons, Durnan won five more Vezinas, beaten out only once, by the Leafs' Turk Broda. In all, Durnan backstopped four title winners and two Cup-winners. In 1948–49, he put in an amazing 309 minutes and 21 seconds of consecutive shutout hockey, still a modern goaltending record.

The team always came first with Durnan. He was what the old-timers called a "holler guy," directing his teammates with his deep, penetrating voice. Unlike the happy-go-lucky Broda, Durnan was deadly serious, an uptight and nervous athlete. And hockey wasn't the only sport he excelled at. He was a fantastic softball pitcher who was a draw everywhere he went, once recording an astounding 24 strikeouts in a nine-inning game.

On March 2, 1950, after sustaining a severe skate cut to the head, Durnan decided to call it a career. On April 4, prior to the fourth game of the semifinals against the Rangers, he went to coach Irvin and quit.

Durnan was inducted into the Hockey Hall of Fame in 1963.

Peak Years   *1944–48*
Comparable Recent Player   *Ed Belfour*
In a Word   *ODD*

OTT HELLER Defense
6'0" 195
b. 6/2/1910, Kitchener, Ontario
d. DECEASED

Erhardt "Ott" Heller was the pillar of the Rangers defense corps for 15 years. He was a big, strapping German lad from Berlin, Ontario (now Kitchener), who skated with the speed of a greyhound and the strength of a Clydesdale.

Ott Heller

Heller had a brilliant Junior stint with the Kitchener Greenshirts in the late 1920s before the Rangers discovered him. He was promoted to the Springfield Indians in 1929 and then brought up to the NHL. He and Earl Seibert came aboard the Rangers for the 1931–32 campaign. Both horses made an immediate impact in helping the Broadways get to the Cup finals against Toronto.

In the 1933 playoffs, the Rangers won the whole ball of wax. Heller, who scored three times in the post-season, was lauded by coach Lester Patrick as the "perfect hockey player."

Heller went on to play 15 consecutive seasons in the NHL. Heller was the model of consistency on the blue-line, a master of guarding the fort. His breathtaking speed and skating, however, also allowed him the option of leading the odd rush. He was the definition of an all-around talent.

After the NHL, Heller had stints with several teams. In the early 1950s, he was player-coach of Jim Hendy's Cleveland Barons.

Peak Years   *1937–41*
In a Word   *STALLION*

BRYAN HEXTALL Right Wing
5'10" 183
b. 7/31/1913, Grenfell, Saskatchewan
d. 7/25/1984, Portage la Prairie, Manitoba

With the breakup of the Rangers' Bun Cook-Frank Boucher-Bill Cook line around 1936, Lester Patrick was forced to look to the future. He found a diamond in the rough in a young, strong lad from the prairies by the name of Bryan Hextall, who was 180 pounds of pure, corn-fed muscle.

Bryan Hextall

Hextall found his stride in 1938–39, scoring 20 goals and 35 points in 48 games. The 1939 playoffs were tough on the boy, though, who recorded only one assist in seven games. His breakthrough season came in 1939–40, with 28 goals and 46 points in 60 games. He led New York to the Stanley Cup. He earned his first of four straight All-Star Team nominations.

Hextall was a swift man for his size. What made him different from many shooters was his ability to stick handle through heavy traffic to a good shooting position. And if anyone got in his way, he had a pair of raw dukes and wasn't afraid to use them.

Hextall led the league in scoring in 1941–42. From 1938–39 through 1943–44, he scored 20+ goals in six straight seasons, counting 142 times in 292 regular-season games. He led the NHL in goals in 1939–40 and 1940–41.

Hextall performed admirably and always gave his best, though he never won another Cup. With the departure of fiery Phil Watson in late 1943, the Rangers took a nose-dive in the standings. Hextall carried his Blueshirts through a 6-39-5 campaign. He spent a year with the OHA St. Catharines Saints, and played 106 more games with the Rangers before deciding to call it a career in 1948. He retired from hockey with 187 goals and 362 points in 449 games.

Two of Bryan's sons, Bryan Jr. and Dennis, also played in the NHL, while grandson Ron became a standout goalie for the Philadelphia Flyers in the 1980s. As for Bryan Sr., he owned and operated a lumber yard until his death of a massive coronary in 1984. He was inducted into the Hall of Fame in 1969.

Peak Years   *1939–43*
Comparable Recent Player   *Wendel Clark*
In a Word   *TOUGH*

- -

ELMER LACH (The Nokomis Flash/Elmer the Great/Evergreen Elmer) Center
5'10" 170
b. 1/22/1918, Nokomis, Saskatchewan

Elmer Lach had a rare combination of speed, courage, brains, and determination. He was the glue that held together the Punch Line, a unit he centered between Toe Blake and Maurice Richard. Lach played through frequent injuries.

Toronto scout Squib Walker originally discovered Lach. Walker pressed Conn Smythe to sign the skinny kid from Nokomis, but the Major didn't think he had NHL stuff.

Lach turned pro in 1940 with the Canadiens, going on to score seven goals and 21 points in 43 games in his rookie campaign. He steadily improved and, with the formation of the Punch Line, he realized his full potential as a play-maker. With the emergence of Richard in the 1944 playoffs, Lach took his place on one of the most deadly lines of all time. He earned five All-Star Team selections, a Hart Trophy, an Art Ross Trophy, two scoring championships, and three Stanley Cups.

"When it comes to giving sly butt-ends and using his elbows, that Elmer Lach is in a class by himself," said Chicago tough guy Johnny Mariucci. "Then, too, he never flinched when on the receiving end."

Lach was a passer extraordinaire, an offensive force, but Dick Irvin Sr. lauded his defensive abilities: "Lach was the only player I knew who could check four ways — forecheck, backcheck, and both sides of the rink as well." In 664 games, Lach scored 215 goals and 623 points.

After retiring in 1954, Lach worked in public relations for a Montreal shipping firm. He was elected into the Hockey Hall of Fame in 1966.

Peak Years   *1942–46*
In a Word   *CATALYST*

NICK METZ (Handy Andy/Handyman/Old Mr. Eternity) Left Wing
5'11" 165
b. 2/16/1914, Wilcox, Saskatchewan
d. 8/25/1990, Wilcox, Saskatchewan

Red-haired prairie farm boy Nick Metz starred in Junior with the St. Michael's Majors from 1932 to 1934. He played on a line with Art Jackson and Regis "Pep" Kelly that led the Majors to a Memorial Cup win in 1933–34.

Metz was easily one of the best defensive forwards ever and was a fantastic utility player as well, able to excel at any skating position. He was an underrated commodity on a team with names like Conacher, Primeau, Apps, and Broda. Over the years, Metz's poise and manner had a calming, even sobering effect on rookies.

Metz's finest season was 1940–41, when he scored 14 goals and 35 points in 47 games. Although not known for his offensive capabilities, he was certainly no slouch. Conn Smythe thought a lot of the Saskatchewan farmer: "That Metz is the best all-around player in the league. He can play anywhere, and good. In any kind of going, you can use him at center, on the wings, or at defense and he'll give you all he's got." In 1946–47, he played alongside Joe Klukay on the Maple Leafs to form possibly the greatest one-two penalty-killing punch in NHL history.

Metz retired in 1948 and returned to tending to his wheat farm in Wilcox, Saskatchewan.

Peak Years   *1940–44*
Comparable Recent Player   *Mike Keane*
In a Word   *PLUMBER*

BILL MOSIENKO (Mosi/Wee Willie) Right Wing
5'8" 160
b. 11/2/1921, Winnipeg, Manitoba
d. 7/9/1994, Winnipeg, Manitoba

Bill Mosienko opened his hockey career in Winnipeg in 1939–40. He scored his first NHL goals on February 9, 1942, on fellow Winnipegger Jim Henry of the Rangers. Mosienko's two goals came in a span of 21 seconds (a unit of time that would become more famous for Mosienko later on in his career).

Mosienko put in his first full season in 1943–44, scoring 32 goals and 70 points in 50 games. He went through the entire 1944–45 season without accruing a single penalty. Not surprisingly, he was awarded the Lady Byng Trophy. Mosienko soon took the left wing on Chicago's Pony Line, a crack scoring unit featuring Max and Doug Bentley.

In 1950, Mosienko won an NHL speed skating contest at the Montreal Forum. No one was surprised when "Wee Willie" breezed his way past representatives from the five other teams. Three years later, he was named the NHL's fastest skater in a poll of sportswriters and sportscasters held in all six NHL cities. He was possibly the speediest man on skates in his day. He was also one of the few capable of stick handling at top speed.

On the night of March 23, 1952, with Chicago trailing the Rangers 6–2 in the third period, Mosienko was sent on with Gus Bodnar and George Gee. Bodnar won the face-off in the Rangers zone and fed the puck to Mosienko, who swooped in on goal and beat rookie Lorne Anderson with a low shot to the glove side. Bodnar won the next draw and snapped the puck again to Mosienko. Like lightning, the little Pony was away to the races, scoring another goal on the fast break. The next face-off was again won by Bodnar, who zipped it over to a streaking Mosienko. He faked Anderson low and went upstairs for his third goal in only 21 seconds! Only minutes later, he narrowly missed his fourth goal. Mosienko's record of three goals in 21 seconds has withstood the test of time.

After retiring from the NHL in 1955, Mosienko went on to play for the Winnipeg Warriors of the WHL, leading them to the league title in 1956. Amazingly enough, his trademark speed never left him and in his final year with the Warriors, he established career highs for goals (42), assists (46), and points (88). After hanging up his skates for good in 1959, he remained active with the Manitoba Oldtimers and the Hockey Players Foundation, playing in annual golf tournaments around Canada.

Bill Mosienko passed away in the summer of 1994, one of Winnipeg's most cherished sons. He became a member of the Hockey Hall of Fame in 1965.

Peak Years   *1943–47*
In a Word   *BUZZBOMB*

BABE PRATT Defense
6'3" 212
b. 1/7/1916, Stony Mountain, Manitoba
d. 12/16/1988, Vancouver, British Columbia

Babe Pratt

Towering Walter Pratt was promoted to the Rangers in January 1936, and played 17 games in his rookie campaign. He joined a defense crew that included aging great Ivan "Ching" Johnson, whom Pratt replaced as a regular in the 1937 playoffs.

The happy-go-lucky Pratt played for eight seasons with New York, helping the team win the Stanley Cup in 1940 and finish first in the 1941–42 campaign. On November 27, 1942, he was dealt to Toronto, where he enjoyed the most productive seasons of his career. In 1943–44, he scored 17 goals and 57 points in 50 games, good for 13th in league scoring, the Hart Trophy, and a spot on the First All-Star Team. In the 1945 finals, he was brilliant, scoring the series-clinching goal for the Leafs in game seven.

On January 30, 1946, Pratt found himself at the center of one of the biggest controversies in sports history when he was expelled from the NHL by president Red Dutton for gambling. At the appeal, he admitted to gambling and promised not to do it again. Miraculously, he was reinstated after missing only five games. Conn Smythe traded him to Boston six months later, where he would spend his final season in the NHL.

After a year in the AHL, Pratt spend another three seasons with New Westminster, British Columbia, and one with Tacoma, Washington, of the PCHL before retiring. His son, Tracy, played in the NHL from 1968 until 1977. One of the more well-loved sports figures on Canada's West Coast, Babe Pratt was elected into the Hockey Hall of Fame in 1966.

Peak Years   *1941–45*
Comparable Recent Player   *Kevin Hatcher*
In a Word   *STUD*

CHUCK RAYNER (Bonnie Prince Charlie) Goal
5'11" 205
b. 8/11/1920, Sutherland, Saskatchewan

Chuck Rayner entered the NHL in 1940, posting a 2-7-3 record in 12 games for the foundering Americans franchise. He was one of the few stars in the lineup of the old Brooklyn Americans when they played their last season of professional hockey in 1941–42. He joined the Canadian Navy in the summer of 1942, and, upon his return to hockey in 1945, he was told he was now property of the Rangers (the Amerks had folded, and the Rangers signed Rayner as a free agent in 1945.

Rayner liked to yap during games, directing his team like a sergeant directing a military offensive. He was a roving goaltender with the skating and stick-handling abilities of a forward. On delayed penalties or in the last minute of a close game, he often left the net.

Rayner became a part of one of the first goalie platoon situations in 1945–46 when Rangers' coach Frank Boucher alternated him with Jim Henry. Boucher sometimes alternated his goalies every three minutes!

Near the end of a game against the Canadiens in late January 1947, Rayner did the unthinkable and carried the puck up the ice to man the point position on the power play. Rayner scored the only goal of his career in an exhibition game against a Canadian Army team during the war. According to reports, he picked up a loose puck and took off. The brilliant-skating Navy goalie outdistanced his pursuers, moved in on goalie Art Jones, and fired one into the mesh!

"When I played defense in front of Charlie," Fred Shero remembered, "there was a defenseman on the Canadiens named Kenny Reardon, one of the toughest players in hockey. In this game, Reardon checked Rayner as he went through the crease. Well, you should have seen Charlie go after him. He chased Reardon to center ice and kicked the shit out of him. Charlie was one of the toughest players I ever saw play the game."

Rayner's finest season was 1949–50, when he became only the second goalie ever to win the Hart Trophy. The balloting: Rayner 36, Kennedy 23, Richard 18, Abel 10, Durnan 6, Schmidt 6, Laprade 3, Lindsay 3, Broda 2, Kelly 1.

Rayner was awarded the Westside Trophy as Rangers MVP for three of the eight season he played with them. He left the NHL in 1953 as one of the greatest goalies never to win a Stanley Cup. He was inducted into the Hockey Hall of Fame in 1973.

Peak Years   1947–51
Comparable Recent Player   Ron Hextall
In a Word   ORNERY

KENNY REARDON (Horseface) Defense
5'10" 187
b. 4/1/1921, Winnipeg, Manitoba

Kenny Reardon was signed by the Canadiens on October 26, 1940, after having spent three years with hockey clubs in Winnipeg and Edmonton. He was originally Ranger property under an "Option 'B'" contract, but Montreal snapped him up when his name was left off the "B" list.

After putting in two solid seasons, Reardon went to war. He was back in time for the Canadiens' Cup-winning 1945–46 season. He provided muscle from the blue-line, proving especially effective in the playoffs.

Reardon oozed color. His odd movements threw off not only his opponents but also his teammates. His peculiar skating style made him look more a crashing footballer than a polished ice-flyer. He played a hard-charging, pit-bull style and played every game as if it was his last. He was a fan favorite in Montreal in the 1940s.

However, Reardon was hated in the other NHL centers. Fans called him "Big Ox," "Butcher," and "Horseface." Reardon took this abuse in stride. Once, before a game at Madison Square Garden, he posed for a picture in the visitor's dressing room on all fours with a plug of hay in his mouth.

After calling it a career in 1950, Reardon accepted a post in the Canadiens front office as assistant GM. He stayed on until the mid 1960s. He took a managerial position with the Atlantic Salmon Association in March 1973.

Reardon was elected into the Hockey Hall of Fame in 1966.

Peak Years   1945–49
In a Word   COWBOY

MILT SCHMIDT (The Count of Sauerkraut/Uncle Miltie) Center
6'0" 190
b. 3/5/1918, Kitchener, Ontario

Hall of Fame referee Red Storey was asked to pick his all-time NHL all-star team: Bill Durnan in goal, King Clancy and Eddie Shore on defense, Howie Morenz at center, with Gordie Howe and Ted Lindsay on the wings. "Now I'll pick you another team that'd knock the socks off of that one," Storey continued. "Give me five Milt Schmidts up front and put your grandmother in goal and we'd never lose."

One day, Frank Selke Sr. pleaded with Leaf boss Conn Smythe to take two promising kids from Kitchener — Woody Dumart and Milt Schmidt. Smythe made a rare scouting mistake in not signing the German boys, who were snapped up by Boston to form two-thirds of a dynamite unit known as the "Kraut Line." In the fall of 1935, Schmidt came to Bruins training camp at Quebec City. The gangling 17-year-old was given a pair of new skates and boots and sent to London, Ontario, for another year of seasoning.

Schmidt played his first full season in 1937–38, scoring 13 goals and 27 points in 44 games. Only a year later, he played an integral role in the Bruins' 36-10-2 Cup-winning season. In 1939–40, the "Kraut Line" placed 1-2-3 in NHL scoring, Schmidt followed by Dumart and Bauer.

The "oaken-hearted" Schmidt was a superb play-maker, known for creating brilliant scoring plays at breakneck speeds.

Despite being one of the more aggressive players in the NHL, he played the game clean and hard. This battler waded through broken jaws, torn rib cartilage, groin pulls, severed tendons in his ankles, and bum knees, injuries that might have driven any normal athlete to retire. Not Milt. In the thick of Boston's drive for a playoff spot in 1950–51, he hurt his left elbow so severely he couldn't even raise it above his head. So what did he do? He went out and collected seven goals in six key games down the stretch. With a performance like that, is it any wonder he won the Hart Trophy that year?

In early December 1948, fellow Bruin Jack Crawford suggested Schmidt move back to defense to avoid many of the injuries his devil-may-care style brought about. Although he gave it a try for a spell, manager Art Ross moved him back to the front line as "he wasn't the same Milt back on the blue."

Bad knees forced Schmidt to retire from hockey in 1954–55 and immediately took over the Bruins head coaching job, leading them to the finals in two of the next three years. In 1967, he succeeded Hap Emms as an oft-second guessed general manager. He managed a Boston Cup-winner in 1970 and would see one more championship two years later before accepting the GM position with the Washington Capitals.

Schmidt was given the Lester Patrick award in 1996 for career contributions to Boston Bruins hockey. In 776 games, Schmidt scored 229 goals and 575 points. He is one of the most revered figures in B's history, and was inducted into the Hockey Hall of Fame in 1961.

Peak Years   *1939–43*
Comparable Recent Player   *Mark Messier*
In a Word   *LION*

JACK STEWART (Black Jack) Defense
5'10" 190
b. 5/6/1917, Pilot Mound, Manitoba
d. 5/25/1983, Detroit, Michigan

Jack Stewart signed his first professional contract in 1937 and played his first semi-pro game with the Pittsburgh Hornets, a Detroit affiliate. He was quick to establish himself as a defenseman par excellence and was called up to the NHL for Detroit's final 32 games of 1938–39.

Although Stewart missed Detroit's two Cups in 1936 and 1937, he played a huge role in a 1943 championship, when the Wings took out Boston in four straight. Although he scored but one goal in 10 playoff contests that year, he was a thunderous physical force, a body-checking menace. Stewart was a punishing hitter, easily the most feared of his time. His impeccable timing gave him the power behind his hits. According to teammate Sid Abel, "he had an arm like a cement wall." Defensively, he was among the finest in the NHL and a strong, hard skater with deceptive speed and rushing ability.

Much can be said about Stewart's differences with Bruin legend Milt Schmidt. Although most hockey feuds are overblown and forgotten by the battling parties by season's end, Stewart and Schmidt truly disliked each other. The feud began in November 1945 when Bobby Bauer, just out of military service, was assailed by Stewart during a game. The smallish Bauer ended up with his arm in a sling. "Stewart went out of his way to get me when I wasn't looking," he spat. "It was a dirty play." From that point on, Schmidt, who was one of Boston's policemen, made a point of going after Stewart. For three full seasons the feud endured until, at the 1948 All-Star game, they shook hands. This gesture of goodwill did not, however, cultivate any affection between the two men. "They still hated each other's guts," someone told Jerry Nason of the Boston *Globe*, "even if they have stopped skating down each other's throats!"

Stewart was traded to Chicago on July 13, 1950, where he played with commendable spirit for a pathetic team. He retired after the 1951–52 season with a slipped spinal disc.

Over the course of Stewart's career, peers frequently referred to him as the toughest defender in the NHL. At a B'nai B'rith dinner in Boston one year, Syl Apps, Sweeney Schriner, Maurice Richard, Milt Schmidt, Hap Day, and others rated Stewart as the best at his position in the 1940s.

He would later coach the Kitchener Juniors, the Chatham and Windsor seniors of the OHA, and Pittsburgh Hornets. He retired from hockey for good in 1963 and spent the rest of his days working as a field judge at a Detroit horse track. Stewart became a member of the Hockey Hall of Fame in 1964.

Peak Years   *1941–45*
In a Word   *ANVIL*

The All-Stars

Position	Player	Season	GP	G	A	PTS
D	Jack Stewart	1947–48	60	5	14	19
D	Dit Clapper	1940–41	48	8	18	26
LW	Toe Blake	1944–45	49	29	38	67
C	Syl Apps	1940–41	41	20	24	44
RW	Maurice Richard	1944–45	50	50	23	73

Position	Player	Season	GP	GAA	ShO
G	Bill Durnan	1948–49	60	2.10	10

The Fifties

In a Flash

COMPOSITE REGULAR-SEASON STANDINGS
(JANUARY 1, 1950–DECEMBER 31, 1959)

National Hockey League

Club	GP	W	L	T	Pts	WPct	GF	GA
Montreal Canadiens	701	363	210	128	854	.609	2,110	1,556
Detroit Red Wings	702	357	212	133	847	.603	2,001	1,579
Toronto Maple Leafs	700	275	283	142	692	.494	1,714	1,695
Boston Bruins	702	271	291	140	682	.486	1,787	1,911
New York Rangers	703	249	314	140	638	.454	1,803	2,073
Chicago Black Hawks	702	194	391	117	505	.360	1,679	2,274

HELLOS

Karen Carpenter *American pop singer*	March 2, 1950
Darryl Sittler *future Leaf superstar*	September 18, 1950
Guy Lafleur *future Hab legend*	September 20, 1951
David Berkowitz *American psychopath*	June 1, 1953
Mark David Chapman *American psychopath*	May 10, 1955
Bo Derek *American actress and a "10"*	November 20, 1956
Terry Fox *Canadian cancer activist*	July 28, 1958

GOODBYES

Albert Einstein *American physicist*	April 18, 1955
Sprague Cleghorn *Ottawa great*	July 11, 1956
Odie Cleghorn *hockey great*	July 13, 1956
Bela Lugosi *American actor*	September 16, 1956
Laura Ingalls Wilder *American writer*	January 10, 1957
Frank Lloyd Wright *American architect*	April 9, 1959

REGULAR SEASON

BEST RECORD
1950–51 **Detroit Red Wings**, 44-13-13

WORST RECORD
1953–54 **Chicago Black Hawks**, 12-51-7

BEST MINOR LEAGUE RECORD
1956–57 **Cincinnati Mohawks**
(International Hockey League), 50-9-1

FAMOUS FIRSTS

PLAYER TO REACH 500 CAREER GOALS
Maurice Richard, 1957–58

PLAYER WITH 200+ PENALTY MINUTE SEASON
Lou Fontinato, 1955–56

TEAM WITH 100-POINT SEASON
Detroit Red Wings, 1950–51

HOCKEY NIGHT IN CANADA GAME (FRENCH)
Detroit Red Wings vs. Montreal Canadiens (10/11/52)

HOCKEY NIGHT IN CANADA GAME (ENGLISH)
Boston Bruins vs. Toronto Maple Leafs (11/01/52)

GAME TELEVISED COAST-TO-COAST IN U.S.
Chicago Black Hawks vs. New York Rangers (01/05/57)

TELEVISED NHL ALL-STAR GAME
10/08/1950
Detroit defeated the NHL All-Stars 7–1.

ALL-STAR GAME HAT-TRICK
Ted Lindsay, 1950

BLACK PLAYER
Willie O'Ree, 1957–58

GOALTENDER TO WIN FIVE STRAIGHT VEZINA TROPHIES
Jacques Plante, 1955–56 to 1959–60

NORRIS TROPHY WINNER
Leonard Kelly, 1953–54

STANLEY CUP WON IN GAME SEVEN OVERTIME
Detroit Red Wings, 1949–50 finals

TEAM TO WIN CUP IN EIGHT STRAIGHT
Detroit Red Wings, 1951–52

MISCELLANEOUS

MOST GOALS, SEASON
49   Gordie Howe, 1952–53

MOST GOALS, DECADE
385   Gordie Howe

MOST ASSISTS, SEASON
56   Bert Olmstead, 1955–56

MOST POINTS, SEASON
96   Dickie Moore, 1958–59

COOLEST MIDDLE NAMES
Billy *Tulip* Reay
Cal *Pearly* Gardner

COOLEST HANDLES
Bob Bailey, "Bashin' Bob"
Hy Buller, "The Blue-line Blaster"
Jim "Pencil" Conacher
Ray Gariepy, "Rockabye Ray"
Andy "Spuds" Hebenton
Jacques Plante, "Jake the Snake"
Jim Thomson, "Jeems"

BIGGEST PLAYER
Bud MacPherson, 6'4" 200

SMALLEST PLAYER
Guy Rousseau, 5'5" 140

BEST SHOT
Bernie "Boom-Boom" Geoffrion. A teenager who lived in the Laurentians north of Montreal would wake up every Saturday morning in the summer to a loud banging outside. Further investigation showed that the maker of the racket had constructed a rink with boards that was apparently up year-long. The owner was none other than Geoffrion, and the ruckus was him practicing his feared slapshot.

BEST PASSER
Doug Harvey was, like Bobby Orr, a master of setting up the pretty goal. Harvey would start in his own end, shuffling the puck back and forth on his stick as he stood behind the net. When he saw an opening, he would zip a tape-to-tape pass to center ice, hitting one of his forwards on the fly. If that forward was Maurice Richard or Jean Beliveau, Harvey could often count on earning an assist.

BEST STICK-HANDLER
Jean Beliveau was by many accounts the Golden Era equivalent of Mario Lemieux, a big, smooth center with a grab-bag of dekes, flicks, and tricks at his disposal. And at 6'3", Beliveau was not the easiest man to knock off the puck. He was like a moving fridge.

BEST SKATER
Red Kelly

WORST SKATER
Ted Kennedy looked like a king crab on blades.

FASTEST SKATER
Andre Pronovost

BEST SNIPER
Maurice Richard takes the nod in this category in both the 1940s and 1950s, despite the emergence of Gordie Howe. While big Howe could beat you more ways, Richard

was possibly the greatest player of all time from the enemy blue-line in.

BEST PENALTY-KILLER
Joe Klukay

BEST BODY-CHECKER
Leo Boivin looked like a dump truck. His flying hip-checks made you feel as if you were hit by one.

BEST POKE-CHECKER
Bill Quackenbush

BEST SHOT-BLOCKER
Bob Goldham was a slow, plodding kind of player but a fast, uncanny shot-blocker. He learned his craft from Wilf "Bucko" McDonald, possibly the greatest shot-stopper in the history of the game.

BEST GLOVE-HAND (GOALIE)
Jacques Plante

MOST UNUSUAL GOALTENDING STYLE
Terry Sawchuk tended nets in a "gorilla crouch," his back hunched over, blocker and glove hands dragging on the ice, and his head down at his knees. Like Patrick Roy, Sawchuk was an odd, at times unnerving, goalie to watch, let alone play against.

FINEST ATHLETE
Doug Harvey was heavyweight boxing champion of the Canadian Navy in the late 1940s. He was offered professional baseball and football contracts before finally settling on a career in hockey.

BEST DEFENSIVE FORWARD
Marty Pavelich was the man Gordie Howe said was the heart and soul of the dynasty Red Wings of the early 1950s.

WORST DEFENSIVE FORWARD
Bronco Horvath

BEST SHADOW
Tony Leswick

BEST DEFENSIVE DEFENSEMAN
Doug Harvey played a game of anticipation. Rarely was the master outfoxed.

BEST OFFENSIVE DEFENSEMAN
Red Kelly consistently scored 15 to 20 goals in an era when (for defensemen) scoring 10 goals was considered excellent.

BEST ALL-AROUND PLAYER
Red Kelly

BEST UTILITY PLAYER
Don Marshall has rarely received the credit he deserves. He was the glue holding Montreal together from the mid-1950s through the early 1960s. The original Mr. Everything.

STRONGEST PLAYER
Tim Horton is famous for everything from Stanley Cups to donuts and coffee. He is remembered by former players for his "Horton Bear Hug," which could crush most men.

TOUGHEST PLAYER
Ted Lindsay didn't care how he got the job done. If he had to bite you, kick you, or belt you across the mouth, he would do it if it would help his team win.

BEST FIGHTER
Gordie Howe established himself as a player you don't mess around with after humiliating NHL bad man Lou Fontinato. Howe broke Fontinato's nose in several places, putting him in the hospital.

MOST ABLE INSTIGATOR
Tony Leswick was the biggest thorn in Maurice Richard's side. During many games, just before a face-off, Leswick would skate up to the Rocket and, putting on a poor French-Canadien accent, chirp, "Bonjour Maurice, ça va bien?"

DIRTIEST PLAYER
Ted Lindsay

CLEANEST PLAYER
Bill Quackenbush earned only 95 penalty minutes in 774 NHL games as a defenseman. 'Nuff said.

BEST CORNER-MAN
Marcel Bonin once wrestled a bear in a

traveling circus. "I ressle duh bear buh duh bear ee beat me," he later said.

BEST-LOOKING PLAYER
Andy Bathgate

UGLIEST PLAYER
Marcel Pronovost

BALDEST PLAYER
Bob Armstrong was King Onion-Head, outshining New York's follically challenged Ivan Irwin.

MUST UNDERRATED PLAYER
Harry Lumley was Terry Sawchuk's perennial bridesmaid.

MOST CONSISTENT PLAYER
Tom Johnson

MOST UNPREDICTABLE CAREER
Elwin Ira "Al" Rollins started his career like a house on fire in Toronto, posting goals-against averages of 1.77 and 2.20 in his first two seasons. Toronto sportswriters were chirping loudly about the find the Leafs had in the man they called "Angular Al." In 1952, Rollins was traded to the sinking Black Hawks and his GAA rose steadily over the next few years — 2.50, 3.23, 3.41, 3.00, 3.21. In 1960, he was loaned to New York, where he posted a 3.10 GAA in 10 games before jumping to the WHL Portland Buckaroos. Who could have known his career would take such a nose-dive?

SMARTEST PLAYER
Doug Harvey

BIGGEST FLAKE
Jacques Plante knit toques in his spare time.

MOST HATED PLAYER
Ted Lindsay

MOST ADMIRED PLAYER
Jean Beliveau

BEST LINES
Team: Detroit Red Wings
LW: Ted Lindsay
C: Sid Abel
RW: Gordie Howe

Team: Boston Bruins
LW: John Bucyk
C: Bronco Horvath
RW: Vic Stasiuk

HIGHEST-PAID PLAYER
Jean Beliveau

MOST TRAGIC CAREER
Herbie Dickinson was an extremely promising Ranger prospect until he suffered a career-ending eye injury after being struck with a puck prior to a game on November 5, 1952.

PLAYER VERSUS TEAM
Sawchuk vs. Boston Bruins, 1956–57

MOST LOPSIDED TRADE
Detroit's Glenn Hall and Ted Lindsay to Chicago for Johnny Wilson, Forbes Kennedy, Hank Bassen, and Bill Preston

BIGGEST FLOPS
Eric Nesterenko. Nesterenko was no slouch in the NHL, scoring 250 goals in 1,219 top-level games. He was a far cry, though, from the "next Jean Beliveau" label Toronto media types tagged him with in the early 1950s.

BEST HEAD COACH
Hector "Toe" Blake

BEST GENERAL MANAGER
Frank Selke Sr.

BEST SPORTSWRITER
Milt Dunnell, *Toronto Star*

BEST BROADCASTER
Rene Lecavalier was the early hockey voice of French Canada, and what a voice he had.

BEST MINOR LEAGUE PLAYER
Guyle Fielder. This little guy scored almost 600 goals in a minor league career spent with such clubs as the Lethbridge Native Sons,

Seattle Totems, and Salt Lake Golden Eagles.
He was held pointless in nine NHL games.

BEST STANLEY CUP FINAL
In 1951, Toronto defeated the Canadiens in
five games, all of which were decided in
overtime. The series was solved by the
famous Bill Barilko marker in game five.

IMPORTANT RULE CHANGES
1950–51
- Each team required to have emergency
  goalie at games for use by either side in
  case of illness or injury

1951–52
- Goal crease enlarged from 3′ x 7′
  to 4′ x 8′
- Face-off circle enlarged from 10′ to 15′
  radius

1956–57
- Any player serving minor penalty allowed
  to return after goal scored by opposition

Those Hard-Luck Barons

Remember the Cleveland Barons? They were the club born when the California Seals moved to Ohio in 1976. Preceding them was an AHL squad of the same name that almost ended the NHL's six-team era over a decade before the Great Expansion of 1967.

In the early 1950s, the city of Cleveland was the premier minor league hockey city in North America. Not content being a bridesmaid, though, Cleveland, under the leadership of local mover/shaker Jim Hendy, fixed its gaze on the NHL. This is not to say Cleveland was the only American city interested in bringing the pro game to town. On the contrary. Philadelphia and Los Angeles were two of expansion's major players while St. Louis, San Francisco, and Buffalo were also showing keen interest.

In May 1952, Cleveland officially applied for a professional hockey franchise. Critics were up in arms almost immediately; what the NHL did not need was another doormat. Cleveland boosters, however, were confident their Barons would not be a doormat. After all, the team owned its own rink and was financially secure. Further, they controlled as many players as were on NHL clubs and had their own farm system. In the past two years, they had sent Tod Sloan, Al Rollins, and Wally Hergesheimer to the NHL.

Dink Carroll of the *Montreal Gazette* posted the Cleveland Barons' possible NHL opening day lineup:

Goal

Johnny Bower

Forward

Doc Couture, Steve Wochy, Ed Hildebrand, Eddie Olson, Jack Gordon, Bob Bailey, Cal Stearns, Vic Lynn, Glen Sonmor, Ken Schultz

Defense

Phil Samis, Bob Chrystal, Red Williams, Fred Shero, Ed Reigle

At a May 14 NHL governors' meeting, Cleveland's application was considered with great interest. Indeed, the Barons looked to be on their way to the big time and many newspapermen had Cleveland as a lock for the NHL. According to Carroll, "there is a very good chance that the Cleveland Barons will be included in the NHL next season." The league's decision to delay the creation of the 1952–53 schedule until a final decision on the bid was made did little to dampen Cleveland's enthusiasm. After examining the Barons' financial statements, though, NHL bigwigs opted to reject Cleveland. There were fears that the bidders did not have the necessary capital to run a team. Further, they failed to observe a stipulation stating that fully 60 percent of the Cleveland Arena's voting stock be owned by local residents. And the arena sat only 10,000, which was far short of Mr. Campbell's 15,000-seat minimum. This sudden turn of events startled Hendy and the city of Cleveland. Critics charged that the

NHL's assessment of the Barons was unfair. Conn Smythe was not one of those crit-ics, though. When asked about Cleveland's chances, he had replied: "I wouldn't bet on it." Asked again in 1953, he commented: "This is the greatest game in the world and these are the greatest teams. Only a moron would want to change it."

The decision to bar the Barons from the NHL went deeper than money. Quite simply, the league doubted Cleveland was of major-league caliber. This, despite sever-al attempts on the part of Hendy and his Cleveland group to prove otherwise. In 1952–53, Hendy challenged the Stanley Cup champion Detroit Red Wings to a best-of-five series against his Barons if they were to take the AHL championship. He even offered gate guarantees as an incentive. The NHL turned down Hendy's challenge on two counts. First, Cleveland was not at the time the AHL champions therefore had no right to speak for the AHL. More importantly, the NHL claimed that the Stanley Cup was "for competition between teams of major-league caliber, whereas the Barons were "operating in a league of acknowledged lower standing." Despite stepping on Cleveland's franchise bid, Campbell promised that the city would be given "first crack at an NHL franchise." The Barons were passed over in the next four expansion rounds.

Had all franchise applicants received expansion teams, who knows how many career minor-leaguers would have played and starred in the National League? A big-ger NHL would have required more players and, thus, we would have seen Guyle Fielder, Willie Marshall, Kelly Burnett, and Herb Carnegie cutting up big-time ice.

Despite their initial failures, the Cleveland, Los Angeles, and Philadelphia fran-chise bids set the NHL on a course toward the Great Expansion. It showed the other six NHL owners, long stuck in the mud of complacency, that many American cities had big-league aspirations.

Dick and the Sticks

In January 1950, Montreal Canadiens' coach Dick Irvin hatched the nutty idea of having his play-ers apply bright red tape to their stick blades. Before a game in Toronto, Irvin justified his scheme: "It makes it easier for players to spot their teammates in power-plays, scrambles, and passing."

The Canadiens generally approved of the "new" blades, with only one mild complaint com-ing from defenseman Butch Bouchard: "I get a little dizzy looking at them."

The tape was slippery and was easily worn, so the Frenchmen went back to black. GM Frank Selke had a special tape chemist work on not only a new red tape but also on a wear-resistant paint to grace the players' sticks with Hab red, white, and blue.

Teeder's Leafs and the Legend of Bashing Bill

It was early 1951. The Pontiac Silver Streak had just rolled off the assembly line, boasting a dial-cluster dash and a swell ventilating system. Gosh and golly, it was the "most beautiful thing on wheels" and "at the lowest price for a straight-eight in Canada."

And hockey . . . well, it was pretty swell, too.

In March, the lowly Chicago Black Hawks lost Doug Bentley for the remainder of the season due to a pulled groin. Dandy Doug, as he was known, was the quarterback of Chicago's offense.

A New York–area hockey fan served temperamental Detroit netminder Terry Sawchuk with a court summons for Sawchuk's involvement in an apparent stick attack on the fan in a February 25 match at Madison Square Garden.

Montreal's Maurice Richard earned a misconduct from referee Hugh McLean for his part in game-time battles with Detroit's Ted Lindsay and Gordie Howe. The Rocket locked horns with big Leo Reise in the sin bin before lashing out at linesman Eddie Mepham. Later, Richard met up with McLean in the lobby of New York's Picadilly Hotel. The two nearly came to fisticuffs. NHL boss Clarence Campbell fined Richard $500 for the incident at the Picadilly.

New York Telegram columnist Jim Burchard was certain Campbell's lynching of the Rocket would inspire a public fund-raiser: "He'll probably make several hundred dollars out of the deal. That's what happened a couple of years ago when Richard was fined following an altercation with Vic Lynn and Bill Ezinicki."

League governors met in New York and agreed on a refereeing rotation of Bill Chadwick, George Gravel, Hugh McLean, and Red Storey for the 1951 playoffs. The four men were the most able zebras in the league, in that order.

Gordie Howe tallied three goals and added an assist in a game against Chicago, setting a new single-season scoring record. The big Saskatchewan farm boy hit the 83-point mark, overcoming former Boston Bruin winger Herbie Cain's 1943–44 mark by a tick.

A column by Toronto sportswriter Hal Walker pondered one of the hotter questions of the day: "Does the team of the goaltender win the Vezina?" Put another way, "Is the Vezina Trophy doomed to be an award for the team and, by association only, the team goalie?" Walker presented a letter that was sent in by a Toronto-area hockey fan:

> The publicity given to the Vezina Trophy gripes this hockey fan . . . how can anyone talk of Mr. Terry Sawchuk as being any kind of trophy winner when he stands in the nets for one hour while the opposition throws a measly ten shots at him . . . Harry Lumley stands in the nets for the same length of time . . . and has 51 shots at him . . . A goalkeeper does not win the Vezina Trophy; the team in front of him wins it for him . . . it should be publicized as a team trophy, or the method of awarding the trophy should be changed . . . Why not keep track of the total number of shots on goal and compare these with the

number of goals scored against the individual?. . . Use a system similar to that of an earned-run average in baseball. This method would also [solve] the argument over who should play goal in Toronto.

An encounter between Montreal and Toronto was the stage for a test-run of the new medium of the time: television. This test was a success and the CBC announced tentative plans to start broadcasting a regular Wednesday night game. Two cameras — one with a five-inch lens, the other a twelve-incher — were set up in Maple Leaf Gardens' gondola. Reg Horton, CBC's technical director, said that although there were technical difficulties, the "images were sharp while the ability of the cameramen to follow the play was surprising."

Imperial Oil expressed interest in becoming the prime sponsor of televised hockey or, as it was fast becoming known, *Hockey Night in Canada.*

Detroit took home regular-season honors with a record of 44-13-13 for 101 points. The Leafs were a close second, only six points off the pace.

Boston skipper Lynn Patrick was feeling up about his team's chances in the playoffs: "I feel right now we are at our peak. We have a good chance . . . breaks may decide it." Soon after, defenseman Murray Henderson went out and cracked a few ribs.

Now for the playoffs. The *Globe and Mail* headline read, "The Rocket Explodes!" after the Canadiens edged the Wings 3–2 in game one of their first-round series. With the Rocket's winning tally at 1:09 of fourth overtime, the Frenchmen took a 1-0 lead in a series in which they were the underdog. Montreal skipper Dick Irvin thought the game was won on "legs, hustle, desire, and ambition."

Maurice Richard came through for Les Habs again in game two. This time, at the 2:20 mark of third overtime, he zapped a shot past Terry Sawchuk to put Montreal up two games to none. Little Gerry McNeil made 42 saves against the Wings, robbing Gordie Howe and Ted Lindsay a number of times.

Before a packed Forum crowd, Detroit stuffed the Canadiens 2–0 in game three to cut Montreal's series lead to 2-1. Gordie Howe celebrated his 23rd birthday by scoring the game-winning goal. Young Sawchuk was especially expert in the Detroit cage, stoning the Rocket, Elmer Lach, and Paul Meger in a third period full of scoring opportunities.

The Detroiters, hot off a victory in game three, stunned the Canadiens 4–1 in front of 14,428 Forum fans to square the series at two games apiece. A game five crowd of 14,221 saw Les Canadiens pick themselves up off the floor, scoring five unanswered goals in the second and third frames. Young Bernie Geoffrion sizzled a mighty 55-footer past Terry Sawchuk for the win. Montreal would go on to finish off the Wings at the Forum.

The Toronto Maple Leafs bowed to the Boston Bruins in the first installment of their series 2–1. Milt Schmidt and Bill Quackenbush turned in particularly strong efforts while ex–McGill University star goalie Jack Gelineau played the finest game of his career. Leaf-turned-Bruin "Wild Bill" Ezinicki was at his best, knocking down several of his old teammates, including Bill Barilko and Cal Gardner. Al Rollins sustained strained knee ligaments in a collision with Boston winger Pete Horeck.

Joe Primeau announced that the injured Rollins would not play again until the beginning of the following season. Turk Broda — that "slippery ol' Turkey" — was brought in to tend the Toronto nets for the length of the Cup chase. When asked about the goaltending change, Broda was heard to gobble: "Well, I'm just going to go out and do my best for the boys between these pipes."

In game three at the Boston Garden, the Torontos phased out the faltering Bostons by a 3–0 count. According to *Globe and Mail* sports editor Jim Vipond, Broda was superb in turning back 16 shots. The game itself was very rough, with referee Bill Chadwick dishing out 54 minutes in penalties. Ezinicki was the naughtiest boy on the night, spending a total of 20 minutes in the can.

Schmidt's sudden knee injury would cripple the Bruins' chances of besting Toronto. Schmidt limped to practice and team doctors found his to be a case of "wrenched knee ligaments." Bruins coach Lynn Patrick said, "Our chances of beating the Leafs rest with the fact of whether Milt is healthy or not."

In game four, Toronto bombed the Bruins 3–1 in a wide-open affair. Sid Smith, Max Bentley, and "Bashing" Bill Barilko tallied for the Leafs while Dunc Fisher dented the twine for the only Bruin score.

Toronto took the fourth match by a 4–1 mark, thanks to a weak Bruin defense. The Leafs would go on to butcher the punchless Bruins 6–0 for a ticket to the finals.

On April 11 the *Hockey News* posted their NHL All-Star Team selections for the 1950–51 season:

Player	Position
Terry Sawchuk	GOAL
Jim Thomson	DEFENSE
Red Kelly	DEFENSE
Ted Lindsay	LEFT WING
Milt Schmidt	CENTER
Gordie Howe	RIGHT WING

Reports out of the Canadiens' Laurentian training camp had injured Doug Harvey skating regular shifts in practice. He was expected to suit up for game one of the Stanley Cup finals with the aid of a leather knee brace.

"[My guys] have lots of spirit," Dick Irvin gushed after a team practice. "When they're so relaxed and enjoy a practice the way they just did, you have to feel pleased."

Montreal was riding high coming into the finals after shutting down the mighty Wings. Despite this fire and grit, the Canadiens had won only 2 of their previous 14 games against Toronto. Dick Irvin, that wily old bird, was playing possum in stating that Doug Harvey and Bernie Geoffrion would be sidelined for at least the first game of the finals. Irvin went on to add that his boys considered it an honor to be playing against "the great Maple Leafs."

In Toronto, Harry Watson was back from his shoulder injury, and Al Rollins was also ready.

In game one, Toronto's Sid Smith opened the scoring only 15 seconds into the first frame, converting a Tod Sloan feed. Maurice Richard squared the affair 15 minutes later. After a Sloan tally early in the second, speedy Montreal rookie Paul Masnick back-handed a Richard rebound past Turk Broda. Late in the third session, referee Bill Chadwick disallowed a Gus Mortson tally because Cal Gardner was in Gerry McNeil's crease. This gave the Habs a chance to ice the game. Broda, however, outreached Elmer Lach in deflecting a Bud MacPherson shot. Bill Barilko then blocked a Richard sizzler from the slot. At the other end, Mortson bounced a hard shot off McNeil's pads while Howie Meeker did everything but score in a goalmouth scramble. Smith eventually poked home the game-winner for the blue and white at 5:51 of extra time.

Dick Irvin charged that Toronto boss Connie Smythe intentionally had the Leaf Gardens' ice softened and the rink's temperature set higher in the opening game to slow down the Canadiens, who, of late, were feeling worn out by a hectic travel schedule. And what was Smythe's response? How about: "Any water on the ice during the game was Irvin's tears."

Game two was a fantastic display of passing, stick-handling, and hitting. Both sides worked like demons. It was a costly loss for the Leafs, however, who ended up losing blue-liner Fern Flaman to injury. Montreal goalie Gerry McNeil starred, stopping 32 shots. The pivotal goal came at 8:16 of the third session, and it was a strange one. With Maurice Richard in the penalty box, Ted Kennedy grabbed the puck and scuttled down the wing. He then fired a pass to Tod Sloan, whose shot rebounded off McNeil's pads, off Kennedy, and into the net. Sloan was initially credited with the goal but the scorekeeper gave it to Kennedy. The goal stood despite loud complaints from Dick Irvin that Kennedy was in McNeil's crease.

In overtime, the Canadiens adopted a high-pressure style and, as a result, got most of the scoring chances. At about the three-minute mark, Doug Harvey led a rush up the ice and, moseying over the red-line, zipped a clean pass over to a streaking Richard, who uncorked a mighty blast for the clincher.

Maurice Richard also scored the first goal game three, sending a Bert Olmstead rebound past "Angular Al" Rollins. Toronto's Gus Mortson could have been a tad quicker on the rebound but there was little anyone could have done to stop Richard in his feeding frenzy. At 5:58 of the second session, Sid Smith, taking a drop-pass from Max Bentley, whizzed the puck knee-high past Gerry McNeil to knot the affair. McNeil whined to referee Bill Chadwick that Smith was offside, but the little goaler's complaints fell on deaf ears. Happy birthday, Gerry!

Play was very tight until 4:47 of the first overtime frame, when Kennedy drove home the winning spike from a sharp angle. Dick Irvin took it badly: "It was just one of those games where we were outlucked . . . when Rollins looks three times in his net, that's a tough break for the team trying to score." Irvin also had words for Conn Smythe: "Smythe talked about what motion pictures showed on other goals in the series. I wonder if he would want to see pictures of Kennedy's goal. You know, the play happened right over where Smythe was sitting. I guess he just hollered 'Don't blow it' and the whistle didn't blow."

Toronto gun Sid Smith opened the scoring only 38 seconds into game four, but

the Rocket tied the affair late in the first period on one of his trademark back-handers
from the slot. The Leafs battled in the second
period like hellcats. After much frantic
action, Howie Meeker managed to bat one in
from the corner. The Buds carried this 2–1
lead deep into the third, when Primeau pulled
his troops into a defensive shell. Montreal's
Olmstead-Lach-Richard unit, however, combined for the tying goal at 13:49. Richard, a
threat all night, did most of the heavy work.
Al Rollins stopped a Richard shot, but Elmer
Lach gobbled up a fat rebound.

Bill Barilko

The scoring of this goal ushered in "ten
o'clock galoshes" at the Forum. Fans threw old
galoshes, or "rubbers," onto the ice along with
newspapers and game programs. The ensuing delay seemed to enliven the Leafs. Five
minutes into overtime, Max Bentley stripped Bernie Geoffrion of the puck at the blue-
line. The little dandy from Delisle dished it off to speeding freight train Harry Watson.
The hefty Leaf crashed home the winner at 5:15, silencing 14,552 Montrealers.

Irvin seemed down on his Canadiens' chances, almost consigned to the fact that
his men had run out of gas. The Leafs' Joe Primeau, however, was playing it cool: "We
have to go out there and give everything we have and a little more in the next game. .
. we have to be ready because it's a cinch that the Canadiens are going to throw us their
best shot, and we don't want to return to Montreal."

The only Maple Leaf scratched for game five was Fern Flaman. Doug Harvey,
Bernie Geoffrion (sore knees), and winger Calum MacKay were out for Montreal.

In game five, the Leafs racked up 16 shots in the first session alone. If not for the
acrobatics of goalie Gerry McNeil, Maison d'Habitant would have folded like a deck
of cards. At 8:56 of the second period, Maurice Richard hit the first mark, carrying
defender Jim Thomson on his back only to bull the puck past Rollins with one hand!

Journeyman Hab center Bob Dawes was assigned the gargantuan task of shadowing Ted Kennedy. Early in the second frame, Dawes, in an attempt to body the Leaf
captain, went crashing into the boards. He sustained a compound fracture of his right
leg. Those in attendance were horrified at the sight of Dawes' leg dangling from his
stretcher. At 12:00 of the second session, Tod Sloan tied the score on a typical
"Slinker" goal, on a quick, tidy conversion of a Kennedy feed. Early in the third, Paul
Meger potted the go-ahead goal for Montreal, using Klukay as a screen to fire a bullet past Rollins. The minutes peeled away.

With 39 seconds left, play was whistled down, meaning a face-off in the Montreal
zone. Irvin put the Olmstead-Lach-Richard power trio out with Bouchard and Doug
Harvey. Primeau countered with Kennedy, Smith, Thomson, Morton, Sloan, and
Bentley. Kennedy, the best face-off man in the biz, outdrew Lach and zipped the puck
back to Max Bentley, who dipsy-doodled his way through a maze of red sweaters and

fired on the net. Rebound! Smith was there, and put it off the post. Rebound to Sloan — goal! The Leafs had tied it up at 19:28.

In extra time, the action was frantic. Cal Gardner's line hopped over the boards and worked the puck into the Montreal end. Watson fired the puck behind the net. Meeker beat Tom Johnson to the puck and threw it out to a streaking Bill Barilko, who slammed home the game- and Cup-winning marker! Time of the goal: 2:53. Although Bouchard went over to congratulate the Leafs, most of the Canadiens made a bee-line for the dressing room.

"We just out-Irished them!" Smythe puffed in the dressing room afterwards. In the press room, Primeau looked exhausted: "It will take a few days to realize we're the Stanley Cup champions."

After the speeches, Smythe piped up: "You know who's going to retire? Not Primeau!"

On April 28, the NHL released their 1950–51 First and Second Team All-Star selections:

First Team		Second Team
Terry Sawchuk	GOAL	Chuck Rayner
Bill Quackenbush	DEFENSE	Jim Thomson
Red Kelly	DEFENSE	Leo Reise
Ted Lindsay	LEFT WING	Sid Smith
Milt Schmidt	CENTER	Sid Abel/Ted Kennedy
Gordie Howe	RIGHT WING	Maurice Richard

Smythe was livid about the unanimous selection of Schmidt over Kennedy for first-team center. "What does a hometown boy have to do to gain recognition in this city?" the King of the Maple Leafs blew. "Ted Kennedy was the champion player of the National Hockey League. They can have the all-stars, we'll take the champions."

On August 26, young Leaf defender Bill Barilko boarded a plane on Friday, August 24, with his friend, Dr. Henry Hudson. They were headed to Seal River, about 500 miles north of South Porcupine, for a fishing holiday. After refueling at four o'clock on the afternoon of Sunday the 26th, Barilko and Hudson vanished. Authorities launched air and land searches over the next month, all in vain.

On September 23, as training camp opened, the Barilko mystery — that is, whether or not Barilko and Hudson were still alive — was the buzz of the hockey universe. Almost all of Barilko's teammates resigned themselves to the fact that he was dead. Gus Mortson, though, held out hope that his friend was still alive somewhere in the wild. Mortson said he had a hunch that Barilko and Hudson landed on Abitibi Lake, that their plane may have sunk and that they swam to a nearby island. Unfortunately, Mortson was wrong.

Bill Barilko had indeed lost his life, and the way people feared he had. The plane carrying Barilko and Hudson had gone down in the middle of nowhere. It took authorities 11 years to recover the remains of Toronto's once-promising blue-liner. As if Barilko's disappearance cursed the Leafs, they didn't win another cup until the same year his remains were discovered, 1962. The lunch-bucket Leafs went on to win four of the next six Cups.

Cranky Old Men

In early 1952, Maurice Richard began complaining of stomach pains. New York GM Frank Boucher got wind of this and was soon painting the Montrealers, especially their head coach Dick Irvin, as a bunch of cry babies. Irvin was understandably irked by the charge, replying that if Rangers skipper Bill Cook would lace up the skates in a January 13 contest, he would take Richard's place in the Canadiens lineup. On behalf of Cook, Boucher accepted the challenge. "I guarantee that if Irvin takes the ice, Cook will skate out and make him look sick — just as he always made Irvin look sick when they played against each other," Boucher puffed.

As it turns out, the "Great Nursing Home Challenge" fizzled out. The Rocket returned on January 12, scoring three goals against the dead-end Chicago Black Hawks.

The Barilko death remains one of the most dramatic incidents in the history of professional hockey. The 24-year-old defender, on the threshold of stardom, had killed the Canadiens, scoring one of the most important goals in Leafs' history.

WILLIAM BARILKO (1927–1951)

Maxie Loses It

In early March 1953, the Toronto's Max Bentley picked up and left. Period. Plagued by injuries real and imagined, the sallow-faced superstar checked out of his Toronto hotel and simply disappeared. Leaf officials had no idea where he might be and it was not until a record check was run at the Canada–U.S. border that his whereabouts were determined. Apparently, he had registered at the Port Huron, Michigan, customs office and was on his way back to the family farm in Delisle, Saskatchewan. The little wizard had only recently returned to game action after being out for two weeks with a nagging back injury. Seems the pain was just too much for him.

In late February, Bentley's wife, Betty, had suggested he retire from hockey. He took her advice, and how! His disappearing act was of great concern to Conn Smythe and team management, whose team was clawing for a playoff spot. "Bentley was not on any orders to play or skate until he himself felt he was ready," Hap Day insisted.

"How do I know how sick Bentley really was?" coach Joe Primeau stammered. "I know that he was getting awfully depressed. I don't know what the club will do. As far

Everyone Loves Alice

Mrs. Alice Richard, who hid her face when either of her two hockey star sons got into fights, was honored at Boston Garden on February 12, 1956. The gray-haired mother of Maurice and Henri was chosen in — of all places — Boston as hockey's Mother of the Year.

At the game, Mama Richard was presented with a plaque at center ice by Beantown mayor J.B. Hynes. Later she told the press that in the 21 years she had been watching her son Maurice play, she had missed only two home games! When asked which of her two famous sons was her favorite, she replied, "No, they are just two of my sons, I have five altogether you know."

Max Bentley

as I know, this has never happened before in the history of the Leafs."

According to Max's father, Bill, Max was on his way home by car. Bill talked with Day and Smythe about his son's status but would not spill the details of these telephone conversations to the media.

"I think Max Bentley will do the right thing," Smythe said upon returning from a Florida vacation. "I expect to hear from him some day . . . right now he's mentally down."

When he got home, Bentley made it clear he would only be taking calls from Smythe. The little guy ended up telling Smythe he would be resting on the farm for a week or so, at least until he was feeling well enough to return to Toronto. "The Leafs have always been good to me," he said. "I most certainly will do my best to get well and be of help to them in the playoffs." Unfortunately, the Leafs finished out of the playoff race.

Russia, Anyone?

In early February 1956, Jack Adams issued a press release stating that he would be taking his mighty Wings over to Russia. There, he planned to pit the boys against Russia's best at Moscow's Dynamo Stadium. "If the state department can make the proper arrangements, we'll go . . . just like that," Adams promised.

Adams was not surprised at the United States hockey team's defeat of Canada at the 1956 Winter Olympics. He was, however, floored when the Russians beat Canada's Kitchener-Waterloo Dutchmen. He saw an opportunity to even things out in taking his reigning NHL champions overseas, with a possible tour of the Soviet Union to boot.

Unfortunately, the U.S. State Department turned down the request. Jolly Jawn's dream was never realized.

A Tale of Two Teams

In the 1950s, only three teams got to sip from the Stanley Cup. Nine of these Cups were won by either the Detroit's machine-like Red Wings or Montreal's firewagon Canadiens. The only other team to strike silver in the decade was the Toronto Maple Leafs. The decade belonged to the Wings and the Habs. From January 1, 1950, to December 31, 1959, the Habs struck for five Cups and made nine final appearances (they would win their fifth-straight Stanley Cup at the end of the 1959–60 season). As for the Red Wings, they scratched their way to four Cups and five final appearances. The Wings dominated from 1950 to 1955 while Les Canadiens closed out the decade as kings of the NHL.

Two Wings and a Loonie

What is it between the Wings and Maple Leafs? Seems every time the two sides battle, someone's life was in danger. In 1950, Gordie Howe almost died during a game with Toronto and the 1956 Cup semifinal series between the clubs was no church picnic.

The first two games of the 1956 series were taken by Detroit. In the second game, Leaf sniper Tod Sloan, a 37-goal scorer on the season, collided with Howe and sustained a serious injury. Prognosis? A fractured shoulder, gone for the rest of the playoffs.

On the day of game three, Detroit's real problems began. The *Toronto Star* received telephone calls from an anonymous source threatening the lives of Howe and Ted Lindsay should they take part in the evening's contest. Extra security was assigned for the game to ensure that no threats were carried out. The *Star* reported the threats on the front page of their late edition: "Will Shoot Howe, Lindsay to Avenge."

While most papers dismissed the calls as cranks, Howe and Lindsay were a tad concerned. Teammate Bob Goldham suggested they give rookie Cummy Burton a jersey sporting Howe's #9 on the back and Lindsay's #7 on the front, and have him skate up and down the rink to see what would happen. For some strange reason, Burton refused.

The game itself proved anti-climactic. Lindsay scored twice and Howe struck for another. Lindsay's overtime clincher would give the Detroiters a 3-0 series lead. After notching the big goal, Lindsay took his stick and made like a rifleman, firing imaginary shots into the crowd.

Which of the two dynasties was greater? How were these dynasties built? Why did the Wings decline in the second half of the decade? Read on.

The Big Red Machine

Detroit's run began in the 1948–49 season. They collected 75 points in 60 games, good for the first of seven consecutive Prince of Wales trophies. The seeds of this dynasty, however, were sown much earlier. Ted Lindsay joined in 1944–45 and Gordie Howe came aboard two years later. Veteran Sid Abel, a Motowner since 1938, hooked up with the two youngsters to form the "Production Line." Defenseman Red Kelly joined in 1947 and the brilliant but volatile Terry Sawchuk was brought in to replace an injured Harry Lumley in early 1950. Four men — Lindsay, Howe, Kelly, and Sawchuk — would form the nucleus of a dynasty.

In 1947–48, Detroit finished only five points back of the Maple Leafs. From the get-go, defense was key to Detroit's success. Kelly, Leo Reise, Bill Quackenbush, and Jack Stewart patrolled the Wing blue-line with authority while Lumley held down the bottom line. Lindsay led the league with 33 goals while little Jimmy McFadden, a surprise 24-goal scorer, took home the Calder as the NHL's top rookie. Despite this kind of team success, the Wings were rubbed out in four games by Toronto in the finals.

Though they lost Howe for 20 games and Lindsay for 10 in 1948–49, Detroit managed to cop the Prince of Wales Trophy by nine points over the Boston Bruins. Abel led the loop with 28 goals while Quackenbush became the first ever blue-liner to bag the Lady Byng Trophy. In the playoffs, Detroit survived Gerry Plamondon's 5 goals to beat the Canadiens in seven before being swept once again by Toronto in the final round.

Detroit Red Wings, World Hockey Champions and Stanley Cup winners in the 1951–52 season, commenced operations in the N.H.L. in the 1926-27 season. They were known then as the Cougars, became the Falcons in 1930 and the Red Wings in 1933.

Members of last year's championship team, shown here, left to right are:
Front Row: Terry Sawchuk, Ted Lindsay, Captain Sid Abel, Gordie Howe, Glen Skov, Coach Tommy Ivan, Bill Tibbs and Trainer Carl Mattson.
Second Row: General Manager Jack Adams, Tony Leswick, Metro Prystai, Marty Pavelich, Leo Reise, Red Kelly, Benny Woit.
Back Row: Marcel Pronovost, Bob Goldham, Fred Glover, Vic Stasiuk, Alex Delvecchio and Assistant-Trainer Ross Wilson.

1951–52 Red Wings

In 1949–50, Detroit finished with 88 points, 11 more than Montreal. Lindsay emerged as the top line's play-maker with a league-best 55 assists. Lumley was his usual rock-solid self in goal. He succumbed to an injury in an early January charity game, forcing the team to call Sawchuk up from Indianapolis for seven games. After salting away the Leafs in the semifinals, Detroit met the New York Rangers in the finals. With a 3-2 series lead and a 3–1 lead in game six, New York could not put the Wings away. Pete Babando scored at 8:31 of double-overtime in game seven to give Detroit their first Cup in seven years.

Just prior to the 1950–51 season, Wings GM Jack Adams dealt Lumley, Stewart, Al Dewsbury, Don Morrison, and Babando to the Chicago Black Hawks for Jim Henry, Bob Goldham, Gaye Stewart, and Metro Prystai. Adams felt free to trade Lumley with the emergence of Sawchuk while the addition of Goldham would serve to solidify the defensive corps. By mid-season, Toronto and Detroit were the class of the NHL, clearly itching for a playoff rematch. Detroit wound up with a record 101 points and their third-straight Prince of Wales. Sawchuk grabbed the Calder and a spot on the First All-Star Team while Howe achieved Triple Crown status, leading the NHL in goals (43), assists (43), and points (86). As it turns out, the big rematch did not materialize. The Motowners met up with Montreal in the semifinals only to be banged out in six.

Detroit aimed higher for 1951–52. Alex Delvecchio was added to the mix as were Benny Woit, Johnny Wilson, Larry Zeidel, and Tony Leswick. With a brick-solid defense, Howe's league-leading 47 goals, and a healthy Sawchuk, Detroit rolled to its fourth title in a row. In the playoffs, they caught fire. After sweeping Toronto, they squashed the Canadiens in four. Detroit became the first team ever to sweep the playoffs in eight straight games. Sawchuk was as sharp as a razor during these playoffs with four shutouts, less than one goal allowed per game, and an astounding .978 save percentage!

Before the 1952–53 season opened, Leo Reise was shipped off to the Rangers for winger Reggie Sinclair in an attempt to add depth up front. Howe would again be the NHL's leading goal-getter with 49 while Sawchuk reeled in another Vezina. All told, it was a smooth ride for Detroit en route to their fifth straight Prince of Wales. The playoffs, though, were not such a cakewalk. The Wings destroyed Boston 7–0 in game one of the first round but after that it was all Bruins. Detroit lost the next three contests, hoisting the white flag.

The 1953–54 season saw Detroit cruise to yet another Prince of Wales over the up-and-coming Canadiens. Detroit grabbed a couple of goodies in Earl "Dutch" Reibel and Bill Dineen. Reibel stepped in between Lindsay and Howe to notch 48 points. Howe won the Art Ross Trophy while 49-pointer Kelly grabbed both the Lady Byng and Norris prizes. In the playoffs, Detroit solved the Leafs in five before meeting Montreal. The Big Red Machine jumped out to a 3-1 series lead but were forced to a seventh game before Leswick drove home the final spike.

Jimmy Skinner replaced Tommy Ivan behind the bench just before the 1954–55 campaign and Larry Hillman was brought in to bolster the blue-line. Detroit squeaked by the Canadiens — 95 points to 93 — for another Prince of Wales championship. The title may not have been theirs had Maurice Richard avoided suspension in mid-March. In the playoffs, Detroit trashed the Leafs in four straight. Next up was Montreal and it took the Wings the full seven games to lay them to waste for the Stanley Cup.

The 1955–56 season marked the beginning of Detroit's decline. Sawchuk, Vic Stasiuk, and Marcel Bonin were dealt to the Bruins for Warren Godfrey, Ed Sandford, and Real Chevrefils. As in 1950, "Trader Jack" moved his top goalie to make room for a young stud, in this case Glenn Hall. Adams dealt Leswick, Woit, Johnny Wilson, and Glen Skov to the Hawks for Bucky Hollingworth and Jerry Toppazzini. Detroit was left with only nine regulars from the year before. In an attempt to plug the leaks, Adams dipped his pudgy fingers into the farm, grabbing John Bucyk and Norm Ullman. Detroit finished a distant second behind the now-mighty Canadiens. Detroit beat the Leafs in round one of the playoffs before being dismantled by Montreal.

In 1956–57, Detroit returned to its familiar post atop the standings. Howe cleaned up at the awards table, scoring both the Art Ross and Hart awards. In the playoffs, Boston took the Wings in five games on the strength of a Simmons goaltending clinic.

Adams became hell-bent on cleaning house. He sent Hall and labor troublemaker Lindsay to Chicago for four clearly inferior players — Forbes Kennedy, Johnny Wilson, Hank Bassen, and Bill Preston. Adams later reacquired Sawchuk from the Bruins in exchange for Hillman and Bucyk. While not a bad team on paper, Detroit finished only third in 1957–58. In the playoffs, they were no match for the Frenchmen, who cut them to ribbons.

In 1958–59, Detroit earned all of 58 points. Bye-bye, Red Wings.

Detroit vs. Montreal

How did the Detroit and Montreal teams of the 1950s compare position by position? Let's take a look.

Center
Montreal A+
Detroit   A-

Down the middle, Montreal had a huge talent in Beliveau, who was the Mario Lemieux of his day. Detroit, on the other hand, had Sid Abel and Alex Delvecchio. Although both Abel and Delvecchio were stars in their own right, they were complementary players who supported the Howes, Kellys, and Lindsays. They were simply not on the same level. Behind Beliveau there was Henri Richard, Ralph Backstrom, Ken Mosdell, and Phil Goyette, all star-quality players. Detroit just wasn't as deep. Edge: *Canadiens*.

Left Wing
Detroit   A+
Montreal A

Ted Lindsay was Detroit's star portsider. A smallish player, he nevertheless had the killer instinct, giving 101 percent game in, game out. While Henri Richard was often referred to as the "French-Canadian Lindsay," he was not a huge physical presence, nor was he a true winger. Moore and Olmstead were Montreal's main left-siders during the dynasty years. Both were Lindsay's equal in most areas, except for leadership skills.

Back up the great Lindsay with the likes of Tony Leswick, John Wilson, and Vic Stasiuk and this was one solid left side. Wings by a whisper. Edge: *Detroit*.

Right Wing
Montreal A+
Detroit   A

Detroit had Howe while the Canadiens had Maurice Richard. Who was greater? Some have likened the Howe–Richard comparison to the Ruth–Aaron and Russell–Chamberlain comparisons in baseball and basketball, respectively. Richard was colorful and explosive, much like the Babe, while Howe was "Aaronesque" in manner — modest but consistently productive. Both wingers were raw, ox-strong brutes, the top wingers of their era. Richard was more of a one-way player, deadly from the opposition blue-line in, while Howe was an all-around talent. Voters have traditionally preferred Howe, giving him seven First All-Star Team nominations between 1950 and 1960. The Rocket, however, was the go-to man, the quintessential assassin. After Howe, the Wings suffered on the right flank. Montreal, on the other hand, could sit the Rocket in favor of Geoffrion or Claude Provost. Again, the Wings lacked depth. Edge: *Canadiens by a hair*.

Defense
Detroit   A
Montreal A

On the blue-line, the two dynasties were more than solid. Montreal had quarterback Doug Harvey while the Wings iced the brilliant and efficient Red Kelly. Calm beyond his years, Harvey seemed immune to panic. He would wait as long as it took for a play to develop before zinging a tape-to-tape pass to a streaking teammate. An all-around athlete, he saved his best hockey for the big games and was known to coast if the game was in the bag. Kelly has been seen as the poor man's Harvey. So deft a stick-handler and so dangerous an attacker was Kelly that he was often moved to center during games. He actually played out his career as a pivot with Toronto. After Kelly and Harvey, Detroit faced off Marcel Pronovost, Bob Goldham, and Leo Reise against Tom Johnson, Butch Bouchard, and Jean-Guy Talbot. Pretty close. Edge: *Tie*.

Goal

Montreal   A+

Detroit   A

There has been much debate as to which of Jacques Plante and Terry Sawchuk was the greater goalie. The question is difficult to answer because of the stark contrast in the two Hall of Fame net-keepers' styles. Plante was an eccentric, reclusive toque-knitter. He was a roving goalie, often booed by the Forum faithful for his out-of-the-crease ventures. An unorthodox goaltender, he nevertheless got the job done, and how! Sawchuk was one of the best angles goalies hockey has ever seen. Despite lacking the consistency and stability of Plante, Sawchuk was, at his peak, certainly worth the price of admission. Stability was key, however. Edge: *Canadiens*.

All told, the Detroit and Montreal dynasties were both marvels of management. Let's tally up those grades:

	C	LW	RW	D	G	Overall
1950–1955 Detroit Red Wings	A	A+	A	A	A	A
1956–1960 Montreal Canadiens	A+	A	A+	A	A+	A+

The difference: Depth.

The years Howe and Beliveau came into their own were the years their respective teams won their first Cups. Detroit's "Mister Hockey" erupted for 35 goals in 1949–50, the year the Wings downed New York for the Cup. Beliveau had a very good year in 1954–55 but truly emerged the following season, posting 47 goals and 88 points. Not surprisingly, Montreal began their streak of five consecutive Cups that very year.

Detroit, while a strong, exciting club, lacked Montreal's forward depth. This fact was never played out in greater detail than during the 1953 playoffs against the Bruins. As Milt Schmidt, Woody Dumart, and Joe Klukay combined to shut down the "Production Line," Detroit had no one else to pick up the slack. The Wings were banished in six games. Montreal, on the other hand, had Geoffrion, Moore, Olmstead, and Backstrom — depth Detroit could only have dreamed of.

Now let's look at the regular-season records that put Detroit just out in front, on paper:

	GP	W	L	T	Pts	WPct
1950–55 Detroit Red Wings	387	219	90	78	516	.709
1956–60 Montreal Canadiens	315	184	79	52	420	.700

During Montreal's five-year NHL reign, the Leafs were in and out of contention (they were still in the embryonic stage) and Chicago was ever-improving, at best. As for Detroit, they were in serious decline while the Rangers and Bruins were average at the best of times. Montreal's dynasty had to face the Rangers and Bruins in the 1957 playoffs, not exactly a rocky road to the Cup. Detroit, on the other hand, was forever locking horns with powerful clubs in Toronto and Montreal. Montreal had less competition than did the Red Wings, a fact that unfortunately means little on paper.

Shifting gears, we see statistics that reveal that, while Detroit played a tighter defensive game, the Canadiens played it wide-open without shirking their defensive responsibilities:

	PLAYOFFS					
	GF/GP	GA/GP	Dif	W	L	WPct
1950–55 Detroit Red Wings	3.09	1.98	+1.1	36	21	.632
1956–60 Montreal Canadiens	3.40	2.16	+1.2	40	9	.816

Granted, Montreal was not as tight as the Red Wings defensively, but their Dif (goals for/goals against differential) was higher. This leaves us with the possibility that however well Detroit played, the Canadiens were a touch more dominant. And the playoffs? Again, Montreal comes out just ahead of the Wings. Although Detroit was the first team to sweep the playoffs in eight games — a feat the Montrealers matched in 1960 — the Canadiens never went to a seventh game in a Stanley

Cup final that they won. Only once, in fact, did they have to go to a sixth game! Also consider that Montreal's dynasty did not crash after life at the top. Unlike the Wings, who began a steady descent after 1955, the Canadiens took the Prince of Wales Trophy in three of the four years following their 1956 to 1960 reign. There is something to be said about a power that steps down gracefully.

Why exactly did Detroit crash and burn after 1955? Several theories abound on the issue. One is that Sawchuk was overworked, although the statistics indicate nothing of the kind. In 1953, Tommy Gorman said of Sawchuk, "Next year, he'll be 34!" Sawchuk was 24 at the time. Gorman was referring to the fact that although Sawchuk was a great angles goaltender, since every shot hit him straight on, he suffered much bodily wear and tear. Indeed, there was a tremendous strain on goalies in the 1950s. Although these brave men faced harder shots from men bigger and stronger than ever before, he was rarely given a night off. Between 1950–51 and 1954–55, Sawchuk missed only 12 of 350 regular-season games. This combined with the number of shots he faced and the fact that he drank heavily leaves little wonder he lost it. His alarming weight gain — from 165 pounds in 1950 to 205 by 1955 — was one reason Jack Adams shipped him off to Boston. Bad trades were another factor in Detroit's decline. Most of these trades occurred after Bruce Norris, a notorious party boy, acquired control of the team from Marguerite Norris. Adams was given more power and, moving Sawchuk to make room for young Hall, received little in return. "Trader Jack" defended the swap by claiming he "didn't want complacency to set in." He then dealt Hall and Lindsay to the Hawks in the most lopsided deal of the decade. Then, suddenly needing a top goalie, Adams surrendered Bucyk to reacquire Sawchuk. Lunacy? How about the destruction of a dynasty? Come playoff time, Adams was forever tinkering with his roster. This lack of consistency affected the Wings. In the words of Ted Lindsay, "If Adams hadn't jerked around with the roster, I'm convinced we would have won six or seven Stanley Cups instead of four."

The 1956–60 Montreal teams are remembered as perhaps the most dominant in hockey history. Had Jack Adams not messed with Detroit line up and made so many stinky trades, things might have been different.

The Flying Frenchmen

In 1950, Montreal embarked on an ambitious rebuilding project. Doug Harvey and Maurice Richard were already in camp, but most of the seeds of dynasty had yet to be planted. At the start of the 1950–51 season, the Canadiens found themselves without stars Bill Durnan and Kenny Reardon. The remedy? Well, management hoped Gerry McNeil would step into Durnan's shoes in goal while Johnson's presence on the blueline would make up for the loss of Kenny Reardon. Jean Beliveau and Bernie Geoffrion popped in for short visits from the farm team and Bert Olmstead came over from Detroit. Montreal finished third, inspiring hope for the future. In the playoffs, they ran up against the heavily favored Red Wings and beat them in six before being blanketed by Toronto in five games.

In 1951–52, Montreal stepped up to the mike. Veteran defender Glen Harmon left, but Dollard St. Laurent was there to fill the gap. Dickie Moore and Dick Gamble were also brought aboard. The Habs wound up in second with a solid 78 points and might have been closer to the 100-point Wings had they not lost Richard to a groin injury for six weeks. Geoffrion took home the Calder Trophy on the strength of a 30-goal effort while Elmer Lach led the league with 50 assists. Montreal met the Bruins in the first round of the playoffs, winning the first two games. The pesky Bruins took the series to a seventh game before Les Glorieux sealed the deal. That is as far as they would go — the Wings blew them away in four straight in the finals.

Montreal continued their winning ways in 1952–53, finishing only 15 points behind the Wings in the Prince of Wales race. Jacques Plante saw action in mid-season when McNeil went down with a fractured cheek bone. Management did not want Plante to turn professional, though, so he was used in only three games. (At the time, a player could appear in only three NHL games until the team had to sign him to a contract. The Habs weren't ready to do that just yet.) In the semifinals, Montreal rolled over the Hawks in seven. With Boston having taken out the Wings, it was a fairly smooth road for the Frenchmen to their first Cup victory in seven years.

Montreal made good again in 1953–54, recording 81 points. Beliveau finally signed on, inking a contract on the day of the All-Star game. The Habs had to buy the entire QSHL to get him! He ended up missing 26 games with a rash of injuries. A lowlight to the season came on December 20 when Geoffrion got involved in a stick-swinging duel with New York's Ron Murphy. Clarence Campbell suspended the high-flying Hab for the remaining eight games between the two clubs. Richard returned to his sniping ways, bulging the twine a league-tops 37 times. Montreal swept the Bruins in the first round to advance to the finals against Detroit. Tony Leswick scored the winner in overtime of game seven to return the Cup to the Motor City.

Before the 1954–55 season, Elmer Lach and Gerry McNeil retired, meaning Plante was now top dog of the Montreal nets. Don Marshall was brought in to help out and Jean-Guy Talbot, a strapping blue-liner from Cap de la Madeleine, Quebec, also make his Montreal debut. The Canadiens were locked in a first-place neck-and-neck duel with Detroit when they hit Boston on March 13. In the third frame of this match, Richard and the Bruins' Hal Laycoe entered into a bumping bee, one linesman Cliff Thompson did his damnedest to break up. Mistaking Thompson for a Bruin, Richard struck him twice. This earned the big Frenchman a suspension for the remainder of the season, including the playoffs. The sentence led to a riot in downtown Montreal. The playoffs were a foregone conclusion with the Rocket sitting up in the press-box. Although Montreal managed to dismantle the Bruins in five, they were ultimately snuffed out by the Wings.

Before the start of the 1955–56 season, Montreal brought in Toe Blake to take over the coaching reins from Dick Irvin. (After the previous season, general manager Selke had demanded that Irvin resign for supposedly mishandling the Rocket.) The team Blake walked into has been called the most impressive collection of hockey talent ever assembled. The 1955–56 Canadiens allowed a paltry 131 goals, tied with the 1953–54 Maple Leafs for the least goals allowed in a 70-game season. There were 10 future Hall-of-Famer players (plus Blake and Selke) on the job that year, a good reason the juggernaut finished with 100 points and a .714 winning percentage. Beliveau took the Art Ross and Hart prizes, Plante nabbed the Vezina, and Harvey made off with the Norris. Beliveau's 47 goals led the loop while Olmstead's 56 helpers were tops. In the playoffs, Montreal dumped the Rangers before whipping Detroit back in five games.

Next came the addition of speedy Andre Pronovost and slick Phil Goyette to the Montreal ranks. Despite injuries to a few key players — Geoffrion missed 29 games and Plante 9 — the Canadiens finished second to Detroit with 82 points. Plante nabbed another Vezina while Harvey copped his third straight Norris Trophy. In the playoffs, Geoffrion stormed back with a vengeance, blasting seven goals in a five-game semifinal against New York. Montreal then went on to best the Bruins for the Cup despite the heroics of Boston goalie Don Simmons.

In 1957–58, Charlie Hodge put on Montreal's big "C-H" to help out Plante and bear-wrestling Marcel Bonin hopped over from Boston. Injuries continued to plague the Canadiens, however. Despite notching his 500th career goal on October 19, 1957, against Chicago, Richard missed 42 games with a severed Achilles tendon. Beliveau, Plante, and Geoffrion missed significant chunks of the season as well. Undaunted, the Frenchmen ran away with the title. Dickie Moore's 84 points earned him an Art Ross Trophy, Plante again took the Vezina, and Harvey grabbed yet another Norris. In the playoffs, Montreal started off on the right foot by punching out the Red Wings in four straight. They went on to erase the pesky Bruins in six, hoisting their third Cup in as many years.

With the players at their healthiest in years, Montreal ran roughshod over the league in 1958–59, earning 91 points for a first-place finish. Plante took the Vezina once more, Moore repeated as the league's top scorer, and Johnson took home the Norris. Ralph Backstrom rounded out Montreal's list of trophy-takers by scooping the Calder. The playoffs were the same old story for the Canadiens. They blotted out Chicago in six before cuffing the upstart Leafs in five for the Cup.

In 1959–60, Montreal was on top of the pack once again. Plante grabbed his fifth straight Vezina while Harvey regained the Norris Trophy. In the playoffs, Montreal made the final championship of their five-year run an unforgettable one by sweeping to the Cup in eight straight games.

Just For Kicks

Much has been made of the amazing numbers Dominik Hasek has put up in the second half of the 1990s. Without question, he is one of the top puck-stoppers in hockey history. But how does he stack up against the likes of Harry "Apple Cheeks" Lumley, Patrick Roy, and Curtis Joseph? Let's take a look at the numbers:

Club	Goalie	Season	GP	Mins	GAA	AGAA	W	L	T	ShO	GA	SVPct	ASVPct
Leafs	Lumley	1954–55	69	4140	1.94	1.97	23	24	22	8	136	.930	.928
Habs	Roy	1989–90	54	3173	2.53	1.78	31	16	5	3	134	.912	.938
Blues	Joseph	1992–93	68	3890	3.02	2.22	29	28	9	1	196	.911	.935
Sabres	Hasek	1998–99	64	3817	1.87	1.87	30	18	14	9	119	.937	.937

KEY: GP (games played); Mins (minutes); GAA (goals-against average); AGAA (adjusted goals-against average); W-L-T (won-loss-tied); GA (goals against); SVPct (save percentage); ASVPct (adjusted save percentage).

We've adjusted the stats to put everyone on a level playing field. The 1989–90 numbers for Patrick Roy were a 2.53 GAA and a .912 save percentage. Was Roy tops in the league that season in these categories? Yes. But wait! If Roy had such a great season, why does his NHL-best 1989–90 performance pale beside Harry Lumley's best? Lumley barely gets more than a passing mention in most discussions about the greatest goalies of all time, yet Roy is often discussed. The answer lies in the even playing field.

In 1954–55, defense was job one in hockey. In this climate, goals came at a premium – at the rate of 5.04 per 60-minute contest! Compare this to the over seven goals-per-game climate both Roy and Curtis Joseph suffered through. The difference is like night and day. While in the 1950s a player's primary concern was playing solid defense, the game in the late 1980s and early '90s was like a shooting gallery, with players scoring 50 and 60 goals everywhere you turned. Remember that up until the 1954–55, the 50-goal plateau had been reached only once.

In order to level the field, we must first determine the exact scoring climate in a given NHL season, which is largely determined by the goals-per-game average. From here, we transfer a player's statistics from their era to another. We've transferred Lumley's, Roy's, and Joseph's stats to the 1998–99 season, when the Dominator ruled. While the adjusted numbers for Roy should come as no surprise, those of Joseph and Lumley are startling. Cujo falls right behind Hasek, and Apple Cheeks isn't far behind. Who knows how Lumley would have played as a Maple Leaf in 1998–99.

Lumley should be considered in every discussion regarding the top goalies in NHL history. Unfortunately, this is just not the case. Roy, Sawchuk, Dryden, and Hasek come up most often, but no one thinks of Lumley. The next time you and your friends rank the top five goalies of all time, be sure to put in a good word for old Apple Cheeks.

*Snap!*shots

ANDY BATHGATE (Handy Andy) Right Wing
6'0" 180
b. 8/28/1932, Winnipeg, Manitoba

Andrew James Bathgate was signed by the New York Rangers in 1952 after two years with the OHA Guelph Biltmores. He joined the Rangers to stay in 1954–55, chalking up 20 goals playing alongside Larry Popein and Dean Prentice.

Bathgate was tricky, much the weaving type on his blades. He was a wizard with the puck and his slapshot was one of the hardest ever seen. He was a very clean player, not at all a fan of the rough stuff. Despite showing a distaste for back-checking, he was an effective, even dangerous, penalty-killer. From 1956 through 1963, he led his team in scoring, averaging almost 30 goals a season in an era when 20 was considered excellent. Rangers GM Muzz Patrick considered Bathgate the finest player to hit Broadway since Bill Cook.

In 1959–60, Bathgate got into some hot water. He ghosted an article for *True* magazine, wherein he lamented the rising level of violence in the NHL. His rebuke was aimed at specific players and teams. Clarence Campbell fined Bathgate and Patrick on the grounds that the article was damaging, to the NHL and to the game itself.

Bathgate's chance to be on a Stanley Cup winner came in February 1964 when the Toronto Maple Leafs acquired him and Don McKenney in exchange for Dick Duff, Bob Nevin, Arnie Brown, Bill Collins, and the rights to Rod Seiling. Bathgate was an instant success in Hogtown, playing alongside Red Kelly and Frank Mahovlich. Toronto won the Cup that year. A year later, Bathgate was shipped off to the Detroit Red Wings. He spent one season in the Motor City before closing out his NHL career with the Pittsburgh Penguins.

Although Bathgate had a certain untouchable, Did-I-mess-my-hair? way about him, he was a true legend of hockey. In 1,069 games, he scored 349 goals and 973 points. He was inducted into the Hockey Hall of Fame in 1978.

Peak Years   1958–62
Comparable Recent Player   Steve Yzerman
In a Word   GRACE

JEAN BELIVEAU (Le Gros Bill) Center
6'3" 210
b. 8/31/1931, Trois Rivieres, Quebec

Jean Beliveau dazzled many when he first came up in 1951 but the Quebec Citadels (his Junior team) would not part with him. Two years later, he played three games for the Montreal Canadiens, notching an impressive five goals. The Quebec Aces, though, like the Citadels before them, refused to release their big center so Canadiens GM Frank Selke bought the entire Quebec Junior league. The media picked up on the story of the "Man Who Stayed Away." The *Toronto Star* printed a wanted poster:

Jean Beliveau. Age 20. 6'2" 195 lb. Wanted by Canadiens to play NHL hockey. Reward $15,000 a season . . . and he turns it down. There's a reason. Jean Beliveau, star of the Quebec Aces, is hockey's highest paid "amateur." In addition, he picks up a few odd thousand a year as a public relations man and doing a daily radio broadcast.

Selke eventually signed Beliveau before the 1953–54 season for $20,000 a shot. The big guy spent his entire career in Montreal, winning 10 Stanley Cups, 10 All-Star selections, an Art Ross, two Harts, and the first ever Conn Smythe Trophy in 1965. He led his team in scoring five times, retiring with more goals than any other center in NHL history to that point. A born leader, he was captain of Les Glorieux from 1961–62 through 1970–71. He was a big, strong, good-looking player whose height and bearing gave him an almost kingly quality. He was a gorgeous skater with long, sweeping strides that cloaked his excellent speed. He used his incredible reach to good effect in stick-checking and possessed arguably the smoothest puck-handling skills of all time. The similarities between Beliveau and Mario Lemieux, another French-Canadian superstar, are eerie.

Beliveau had a defective heart and this affected his on-ice performance. He was unable to take long shifts, to rack up ice-time like the other big stars of his era. The Canadiens, though, always had other blue-chip centers to spell him, fellows like Henri Richard and Ralph Backstrom. One can only imagine how many records Beliveau might have smashed without the heart problem.

Beliveau retired in 1971 in grand style, helping bring the Stanley Cup back to Montreal. Since retiring, he has worked in the Canadiens' front office and put out a book titled — what else? — *Jean Beliveau*.

Beliveau was elected to the Hockey Hall of Fame in 1972. In 1,125 games, he scored 507 goals and 1,219 points. Lofty personal achievements, to be sure. But he was first and foremost a "team man." As he wrote in his autobiography in 1994, "If they say anything about me when I'm gone, let them say that I was a team man. To me, there is no higher compliment."

Peak Years   *1957–61*
Comparable Recent Player   *Mario Lemieux*
In a Word   **ELEGANT**

LEO BOIVIN Defense
5'7" 190
b. 8/2/1932, Prescott, Ontario

Leo Boivin made the NHL for good in 1952 after a stint with the AHL Pittsburgh Hornets. Leaf boss Conn Smythe wanted a replacement for Bill Juzda, who had retired at the end of the previous season. After two disappointing years in Hogtown, Boivin was dealt to the Boston Bruins.

Boivin was a short and squat player, part bulldog, part Sherman tank. He made straight-up rushes and dished out fierce, open-ice hip-checks. He had a low center of gravity, which made him very difficult to knock down or pass by on the outside lane. Tim Horton, also a stupendous body-checker, considered Boivin the hardest defenseman in the NHL to beat one on one.

Boivin appeared in two Stanley Cup finals with the Bruins in 1957 and 1958 but tasted defeat at the hands of the mighty Montreal Canadiens both years. He was made team captain in 1963 and, despite being on some poor teams, he worked like a dog. He was good enough to play in the All-Star game three times in his career (1961, 1962, and 1964).

On February 18, 1966, Boivin was traded to the Detroit Red Wings for Bill Lesuk, Gary Doak, and future considerations. He later made stops in Pittsburgh and Minnesota before retiring at the end of the 1969–70 season. Over 1,204 regular-season and playoff NHL games, he scored 75 goals and 335 points. He served as coach of the St. Louis Blues in 1975–76 and 1977–78.

Leo Boivin became a worthy member of the Hockey Hall of Fame in 1986.

Peak Years   *1959–63*
Comparable Recent Player   *Lyle Odelein*
In a Word   *JACKHAMMER*

FERN FLAMAN Defense
5'10" 190
b. 1/25/1927, Dysart, Saskatchewan

The Boston Bruins brought up Fern Flaman from the Hershey Bears in time for
the 1946–47 season. In 23 games, coach Dit Clapper saw Flaman's crude talent and
admired the youngster's willingness to use his fists and body. Although not the
prettiest of rushers, he was a huge physical presence in front of his net and along
the boards. In the early going, though, he received little playing time. Clapper already
had experienced veterans in Jack Crawford, Murray Henderson, Pat Egan, and Terry
Reardon, so he had little need for an extra body.

Flaman's break came in 1950 when he was dished to the Toronto Maple Leafs,
where he was paired with Bill Barilko and, along with Jim Thomson and Gus Mortson,
helped the Buds win the Stanley Cup at season's end. Flaman spent three more seasons
in Toronto before being returned to Boston for Dave Creighton in 1954. Conn Smythe
did not think much of Flaman as a fighter.

Flaman served as captain of the B's from 1955–56 until his retirement at the end of
the 1960–61 season. Under his leadership, Boston went to the finals twice and carved
out a measure of respectability at a time when the Montreal Canadiens were taking the
world by storm.

Flaman became the player-coach of the AHL Providence Reds and led his team to
the best record in the Eastern Division in 1962–63. The following season, he took on
managing duties before hanging up his skates for good. He went on to coach and manage the Los Angeles Blades of the Western Hockey League. After a two-year stint as
coach of the Fort Worth Wings, he went on to build Northeastern University's hockey
team into a powerhouse. From 1991 to 1995, he was a scout with the New Jersey
Devils, who won the Stanley Cup in his final year.

Flaman was elected into the Hockey Hall of Fame in 1990.

Peak Years   *1955–59*
Comparable Recent Player   *Mark Tinordi*
In a Word   *GORILLA*

BILL GADSBY Defense
6'0" 185
b. 8/8/1927, Calgary, Alberta

In 1946, the Chicago Black Hawks made an important move in bringing up William
Gadsby from Edmonton. He would be the one and only real blue-chipper in Chicago
in an eight-year run during which the team finished last six times. Despite being tied
to a losing franchise, Gadsby managed two All-Star selections. He really was the only
blue-chipper in the Windy City during the first half of the 1950s. In his last season in
Chicago, he was second in team scoring with an impressive 41 points.

Gadsby was a powerful, raw-boned man with a rugged style. Although numerous
injuries forced him to play in great pain, he managed to last 20 years in the big league.
He was one of the better play-making defenders of his day, with a heavy shot from the
point. Such qualities made him indispensable on the Chicago, and later New York

Ranger, power play. He excelled on the defensive side of the game as well, especially adept at blocking shots and using his thickly muscled frame to move would-be scorers out of harm's way. While his size permitted him to play an intimidating physical game, he was a clean player.

Just into the 1954–55 season, Gadsby was dealt to the Rangers for Allan Stanley. Gadsby played seven seasons on Broadway, and enjoyed his peak years there. He was a big reason the Rangers made the playoffs three times toward the end of the 1950s. With the big guard in their lineup, the Blueshirts were a force to be reckoned with. Their power play was especially dangerous, with Gadsby and Andy Bathgate on the points, Red Sullivan in front, and Dean Prentice and Camille Henry on the wings.

At the end of the 1959–60 campaign, Detroit GM Jack Adams showed great interest in obtaining Gadsby. Adams tried to negotiate a deal that would see Red Kelly and Billy McNeil go to New York for Gadsby and Eddie Shack. Kelly refused to report to New York, but Adams did eventually secure Gadsby's services in June 1961. The star blue-liner finished his NHL playing career in Detroit. "I could have played a couple of more years," said Gadsby later, "but the body was talking back to me. When the body starts talking back to you and you can hardly get the legs out of bed next morning, it's time to quit."

Gadsby was elected to the Hockey Hall of Fame in 1970.

Peak Years   *1956–60*
Comparable Recent Player   *Chris Pronger*
In a Word   *RAW*

BERNIE GEOFFRION (Boom Boom) Right Wing
5'11" 185
b. 2/16/1931, Montreal, Quebec

Bernard Geoffrion made the jump from the Nationales, where he was a huge star, to the Montreal Canadiens during the 1950–51 season. In his first full stint with the Canadiens the following season, he led his team in scoring with 30 goals en route to winning the Calder Trophy. Montreal coach Dick Irvin was understandably excited: "When Maurice Richard hangs up his skates, [Geoffrion] will take over as the greatest player in the NHL."

One thing young Geoffrion had was a temper. During the 1953–54 season, he was involved in a vicious stick-swinging incident with the New York Rangers' Ron Murphy. Murphy was seriously injured in the altercation and Geoffrion was cuffed with an eight-game suspension by NHL president Clarence Campbell.

Geoffrion manned the point on the power play alongside Doug Harvey, where his blistering slapshot stood as the centerpiece of perhaps the most deadly power play unit of all time. In 1960–61, he did the impossible, tying Maurice Richard's record of 50 goals in a season, snatching the Art Ross and Hart trophies at season's end.

Geoffrion retired at the end of the 1963–64 season, but came back in 1966, signing on with the Rangers, where he headed an impressive playoff run. That season, the Blueshirts were especially effective against his former teammates.

Boom Boom was one of the deadliest snipers of his time. He played with a burning passion for the game and, although not the smoothest skater, was quite the hustler. He was a fine stick-handler and, of course, is famous for having one of the hardest slap-shots the NHL has ever seen.

In 883 games, Geoffrion scored 393 goals and 822 points. He made the Hockey Hall of Fame in 1972.

Peak Years   *1958–62*
Comparable Recent Player   *Al MacInnis*
In a Word   *BOOMING*

DOUG HARVEY (Dallying Doug) Defense
5'11" 180
b. 12/19/1924, Montreal, Quebec
d. 12/26/1989

Douglas Norman Harvey starred for the Montreal Royals before being called up to the Montreal Canadiens halfway through the 1947–48 season. Under the tutelage of defensive mutts like Kenny Reardon, Butch Bouchard, and Glen Harmon, Harvey developed his game and before long had few, if any, peers.

In 1952, he was voted to the NHL's First All-Star Team, an honor that was his for 9 of the next 10 years. He had the right stuff in all aspects of his game — checking, rushing, stick-handling. He had Napoleonic control of the play. He had a unique style. Whenever he got a hold of the puck, he would not give it up with a quick, careless pass. Rather, he would wait patiently until his forwards were high before zipping a bullet pass to one of them on the fly. Often he would take the puck behind his own net and then would freeze, gently shuffling it back and forth on his stick. If Montreal was trying to protect a lead and the other team was pressing, he would slow the game down. If the Canadiens were gunning for a goal, though, he would change gears and quarterback a storm against the enemy. Rarely was he caught napping or panicking during a game. "I never liked to give the puck away too much," he once said. "I used to get hell for it the first few years, cutting in front of my own net and playing in my own end with it. I had a few arguments with [coach] Dick Irvin, but he was the boss. So I tried to change but I couldn't."

In 1961, Canadiens GM Frank Selke, still peeved at Harvey for having taken part in the 1957 players' uprising, traded him to the New York Rangers. Selke might have traded the troublesome Harvey sooner but probably feared being chased down St. Catherine Street by fans and hung from a flagpole.

Harvey toiled in New York until his outright release in 1963. He filled in nicely in Detroit and in St. Louis before retiring in 1969.

Harvey stands to this day as possibly the greatest defender of all time. Smarter than Shore. Smoother than Clancy. Sturdier than Orr. He meant so much to his team that he was thought by some to be more vital to Montreal's success than Jean Beliveau, Jacques Plante, or Maurice Richard. Without him, there may not have been a dynasty at all. The Detroit Red Wings' Ted Lindsay said that if his team had Harvey, they would have won nine Cups instead of "only" four. Enough said.

Harvey was elected to the Hockey Hall of Fame in 1973.

Peak Years   *1954–58*
Comparable Recent Player   *Ray Bourque*
In a Word   *QUARTERBACK*

GORDIE HOWE (Mr. Hockey/The Big Guy) Right Wing
6'0" 205
b. 3/31/1928, Floral, Saskatchewan

Gordon Howe is generally considered the greatest right winger of all time, arguably the greatest player — period. Although not the flashy, showboating kind, he was a smooth skater with a superb sense of balance. His easy skating style made him look lazy but he could turn on the jets in the blink of an eye. He was called the best "two-handed stick-handler" since the Chicago Black Hawks'

Gordie Howe

Johnny Gottselig. An ambidextrous player, Howe would often switch hands on a break-away just to throw the opposing goalie into a dither. So good was the Big Guy that Maurice Richard, his arch-rival, once said: "Gordie could do everything." Not exactly an eloquent statement, but the truth nonetheless. In his unparalleled career in hockey, there seemed nothing the great Howe could not do.

The greater part of Howe's game, however, was physical. He was always one of the strongest players in the NHL and made use of that strength. "His shoulders were thick and rounded," said Jean Beliveau, "and sloped into a huge chest that was all knotted muscle."

As a fighter, he had few equals. Once, after clobbering the New York Rangers' Eddie Shack, he flattened heavyweight Lou Fontinato! Nobody really bothered Howe after that game. He was the most dangerous corner-man in the NHL for most of his career, using heavy elbow- and stick-work to get his way. Many a brash, young rookie had his clock cleaned by a Howe elbow down near the chicken-wire.

Howe won the Hart and Art Ross trophies six times. He earned an incredible 21 NHL All-Star Team nominations and played on nine first-place teams, four of which took home the Stanley Cup.

After a two-year break in the early 1970s, Howe signed with the Houston Aeros of the upstart World Hockey Association. Although he was by then well over 40 years of age, he didn't miss a beat. In 1973–74, he was good for 100 points in 70 games. After making a favorable appearance at the Summit Series in 1974, he continued to batter WHA goaltenders. Then approaching 50, Howe put up point totals of 99, 102, and 68 before signing with the New England Whalers as a free agent. After seasons of 96 and 43 points, the 51-year-old wonder moved with the Whalers to the NHL for the 1979–80 season. His first season in the NHL in nine years was a good one — he scored 15 goals and 41 points. At the end of the season, he decided to call it a career. A magnificent career.

During the 1997–98 season, Howe appeared in an IHL game with the Detroit Vipers. In doing so, the 69-year-old became the first and only hockey player to play in six decades. And he conducted himself rather well against the whippersnappers.

Off the ice, he was mild and soft-spoken, the opposite of his on-ice manner. This softness of manner, this "golly-gee" country-boy way, would serve to limit the force of his overall leadership. Otherwise, Gordon Howe was the definition of the term "hockey player."

In 2,186 games in two professional hockey leagues, he scored 975 goals and 2,358 points. He was elected to the NHL All-Star Team a record 21 times and has four Stanley Cup rings. Howe became a very worthy member of the Hockey Hall of Fame in 1972.

Peak Years   *1950–1954*
Comparable Recent Player   *Eric Lindros*
In a Word   *GRANITE*

TOM JOHNSON (Bow Tie) Defense
6'0" 180
b. 2/18/1928, Baldur, Manitoba

Sometimes a team needs that steady, nondescript player, that guy who seems to never smile or frown. He is the ultimate leveler. On bad days he's playing cards while on good days he's . . . playing cards again. Thomas Christian Johnson was just such a player. On a team filled with egos and the potential for those egos to break down team chemistry, Johnson acted as a kind of Polident. He helped hold all the teeth in one mouth.

Johnson got his break with the Montreal Canadiens in the fall of 1950. Like many rookies, he was too aggressive, drawing many bone-headed penalties. In his first season, he racked up 128 minutes in penalties. He soon settled down to become one of the main ingredients in the cement that held together the Canadiens defense. He was certainly a steady contributor on six Stanley Cup–winning teams.

Although an average skater and not the quickest afoot, Johnson was a sure stick-handler and passer, and rarely coughed up the puck in his own end. He liked the rough stuff from time to time, even in his later years, but it was not unusual to see him flying off on a rush. Many people who saw him play insist he was overrated, that he rode on the back of Doug Harvey. Game footage proves such statements to be true, but only to a limited degree. Yes, Johnson benefited greatly from playing alongside a talent like Harvey but he held his own and was one of the most consistent defenders of the decade. "I was classified by some as a defensive defenseman. I stayed back and minded the store. With the high-powered scoring teams I was with, I just had to get them the puck and let them do the rest."

In all, Johnson played 978 games in his career. He was good enough to win the Norris Trophy in 1959 and to secure a spot in the Hockey Hall of Fame in 1970.

Peak Years *1956–60*
Comparable Recent Player *Adam Foote*
In a Word *SOLID*

RED KELLY Defense/Center
6'0" 195
b. 7/9/1927, Simcoe, Ontario

Leonard "Red" Kelly came from the St. Michael's Majors to join the Detroit Red Wings for the 1947–48 season. He played 13 seasons in all in Detroit and in that time was on four championship squads. In eight seasons with the Toronto Maple Leafs, he would be a part of four more Cups.

He was one of the first true rushing defensemen, playing his position with the touch of a forward. Occasionally, he would play left wing and completed his career as a two-way center with the Toronto Maple Leafs. He skated in a semi-crouch style similar to Wayne Gretzky's, only much more powerfully. Kelly was fast on the break and a fine play-maker. Because his skills demanded so much attention from opposing checkers, his presence on the ice created room for his teammates. Gordie Howe and Ted Lindsay were often left to free-wheel.

During his first couple of seasons in Detroit, Kelly was paired with Bill Quackenbush, whose clean, efficient style was similar to his own. This style of play would bring Kelly the Lady Byng Trophy four times in his career.

In early 1960, Detroit manager Jack Adams, in his godly wisdom, decided to trade Kelly. Initially, a deal with the New York Rangers was hammered out but, because Kelly refused to report, the deal was called off. Adams then got a call from King Clancy, who was acting on behalf of Leaf coach and manager Punch Imlach. In his anger, Adams threw Kelly away for Marc Reaume in what stands as one of the silliest deals in hockey history.

In 1962, Kelly was elected to the Canadian House of Commons and for the next three years did double-duty as a hockey player and legislator! Immediately recognizing Kelly's two-way potential, Imlach turned him into a center. Kelly rounded out his career in Toronto as one of the first players in the NHL to regularly wear a helmet.

After retiring as a player, he went on to coach the Pittsburgh Penguins, the L.A. Kings, and the Leafs. He made the Hockey Hall of Fame in 1969.

Peak Years   *1952–56*
Comparable Recent Player   *Brian Leetch*
In a Word   *ATHLETE*

TED KENNEDY (Teeder) Center
5'11" 180
b. 12/12/1925, Humberstone, Ontario

Theodore Kennedy was the farthest thing from a good skater, probably one of the shabbiest of his time. Despite this limitation, he played extremely well for his Toronto Maple Leafs. During a shift Kennedy would scuttle around the ice like a crab, coming back to the bench huffing and puffing, only to return to the ice a short time later fresher than ever. This kind of perseverance endeared him to teammates and fans alike. "I had to work hard at my skating," he said. "I relied heavily on my wings and I always had good, fast wingmen with me. Whenever anyone was chasing me, I don't remember anyone ever catching me. Whether it was out of fear, I don't know."

Theodore Kennedy was an exceptional play-maker, and always seemed to know where and when to set up his man. Howie Meeker called Kennedy a "thoroughbred plow-horse," which testifies to his all-around ability. As well as being an excellent defensive center, he was thought by many sportswriters of the day to have been the best face-off man in the NHL, the best on the draw since legendary Montreal Maroon Nels Stewart.

Although Kennedy was not the most dominant "skills" player in the league, he consistently ranked near the top of the scoring race. He was always one of Toronto's biggest producers in the post-season, his finest effort coming in the 1947–48 playoffs when he scored eight goals and 14 points in nine games. In all, the Humberstone, Ontario, native played in six All-Star games and took home a Hart Trophy in 1955. When Syl Apps retired in 1948, Kennedy was made captain of the Leafs. He would sport the big "C" proudly until the end of the 1956–57 season (except for 1955–56, when he temporarily retired).

Kennedy retired as not only one of the greatest Leafs in club history but also as one of the gutsiest captains in NHL history. In 696 games, he scored 231 goals and 560 points. He was inducted into the Hockey Hall of Fame in 1966.

Peak Years   *1948–52*
Comparable Recent Player   *Doug Gilmour*
In a Word   *CHAMPION*

JOE KLUKAY (The Duke of Paducah/Kluke) Left Wing
6'0" 175
b. 11/6/1922, Sault Ste. Marie, Ontario

Any serious Stanley Cup contender needs a crasher, a big intimidating forward who can turn a game's flow around with one huge hit. The Toronto Maple Leafs were fortunate in 1946 to have found their crasher in Joe Klukay.

In the mid-1940s, Klukay was one of Leaf boss Conn Smythe's prized scoring prospects down on the farm. But Klukay soon found that the Leafs already had enough offense. He adjusted to become one of the top penalty-killers–defensive forwards ever to step on the ice.

He showed himself to be a strong skater, one who prided himself on his mental toughness, his cool under fire. He never appeared to be out of place, playing an amazingly sound, technical brand of hockey. As a rookie, he learned the defensive craft alongside Nick Metz, a legendary penalty-killer for the Leafs. "We just concocted a system," said Klukay of his time with Metz, "It had to be the easiest, the most effective way to go about killing a penalty. You had one guy going in and we'd try to contain them in their own end. It worked for ten years, so we couldn't knock it."

Klukay was traded to the Boston Bruins at the beginning of the 1952–53 season. There, he would prove quite valuable. His efforts were much to the fore during the 1953 Stanley Cup semifinals against the heavily favored Detroit Red Wings. Acting as shadow, he held Gordie Howe to only two goals in six games! Klukay was sent back to Toronto in late 1954. After a season and bit back in Hogtown, he decided to call it a career.

Were you protecting a one-goal lead with two minutes remaining? Klukay was your man! Using one part technique and one part barbarism, the big lad from Sault Ste. Marie, Ontario, helped drive the Leafs to Cups in 1947, 1948, 1949, and 1951.

Peak Years   *1949–53*
In a Word   *THUMP*

EDGAR LAPRADE Center
5'8" 157
b. 10/10/1919, Port Arthur, Ontario

Edgar Laprade was one of the New York Rangers' best players during one of the franchise's darker periods. He was a play-maker whose effortless skating style enabled him to rag the puck like a little wizard. He back-checked tirelessly and was a stellar face-off man, making him quite valuable to the Rangers in short-handed situations. And Laprade was as clean as he was effective. In fact, there were three seasons where he was not penalized at all!

Laprade spent the better part of a decade playing hockey in his hometown of Port Arthur, Ontario. Between the ages of 16 and 23, he played for the Port Arthur Juniors, Seniors, and Bearcats. From there it was on to a pocketful of games with the Winnipeg Army, followed by a season with the Barriefield Bears. In mid-October of 1945, the little center signed as a free agent with the New York Rangers.

In 1950, Laprade came close to being on a championship team when his Broadways took the Detroit Red Wings to the seventh game of the Stanley Cup finals. The Rangers lost in OT.

Going on the evidence of old game reels, Laprade was timid, soft, even. He could easily be thrashed about by opposing players. In 1948, he suffered a serious concussion after a terrific check from Toronto Maple Leafs nut bar Bill Ezinicki.

At the beginning of the 1953–54 season, the Rangers obtained Max Bentley and managed to coax Laprade out of retirement to star on a line with Bentley. This set-up lasted until Laprade pulled a groin the following season. He decided to retire once and for all as one of the best Rangers of all time.

In 501 games, Laprade managed 108 goals and 280 points. He became a proud member of the Hockey Hall of Fame in 1993.

Peak Years   *1947–51*
Comparable Recent Player   *Craig Janney*
In a Word   *BUTTER*

TONY LESWICK (Tough Tony/Mighty Mouse) Left Wing/Right Wing
5'6" 160
b. 3/17/1923, Humboldt, Saskatchewan

Anthony Leswick proved himself as one of the best defensive forwards in the NHL throughout his career. Although a natural left-flanker, he could play both sides and was a bullish penalty-killer — that is, if he wasn't in the box himself. He was a swift, strong skater who always hustled. He had a knack for getting his team going with a big hit on an opposing player. And although his shot couldn't break a pane of glass, he was a decent stick-handler as well as a heads-up passer. Pound-for-pound, little #8 was one of the best fighters in the league and was not one to shy away from a punching bee. "I did a little bit of fighting," he once confessed. "I could take care of myself. I wasn't afraid."

It was in shadowing the league's star players, however, that Leswick earned his stripes — why Detroit Red Wings' manager Jack Adams dealt for him in the early 1950s. Some say Adams made the deal so his boy, Gordie Howe, would not have to put up with the little New York Ranger pest anymore.

Leswick's favorite target was Maurice Richard. Leswick would be all over the Rocket for an entire game, mixing a shower of anti-French insults with a flurry of butt-ends and slashes. Leswick was especially skilled at goading his targets into penalties. Referee Bill Chadwick was once quoted as saying that Leswick "could bring the worst out in a saint!"

Despite the apparent nastiness of his game, though, Leswick was a winner. He has three Stanley Cup rings to prove it.

Peak Years   *1949–53*
Comparable Recent Player   *Martin Lapointe*
In a Word   *PEST*

TED LINDSAY (Terrible Ted) Left Wing
5'8" 160
b. 7/29/1925, Renfrew, Ontario

Robert Blake Theodore Lindsay starred with the St. Michael's Majors before signing on with the Detroit Red Wings in 1944. A few years later, Detroit skipper Tommy Ivan formed the "Production Line," plunking Sid Abel between Lindsay and Gordie Howe. In 1951, Lindsay and one of his most hated foes, Bill Ezinicki, were each banished for three games and fined $300 for their part in an ugly stick-battle. About four years later, Lindsay slugged a mouthy spectator during a game, good for a 10-game suspension from the desk of NHL president Clarence Campbell.

Indeed, Lindsay packed a lot of punch into his 160-pound frame. He seemed to be in a state of perpetual motion. In every aspect of the game the saucy little fellow seemed supernaturally charged. If Howe was the muscle behind the dynasty Wings, Lindsay was surely the spirit.

Despite finishing second in league scoring in 1956–57, Detroit manager Jack Adams dealt Lindsay to the Chicago Black Hawks. Lindsay never forgave Adams for this although some say the real reason for the trade was Lindsay's leading involvement in the new NHL Players' Association. "Clarence Campbell was a joke," sneered Lindsay. "He talked about the greatest pension plan in the world, in professional sport. That was a farce."

Lindsay was on four Cup-winners and nine first-place teams while in Detroit. He copped nine All-Star selections and captained the Motowners from 1952–53 through 1955–56. He played out three fairly productive seasons with the Hawks before retiring at the end of the 1959–60 season. In 1964, Detroit lured him out of retirement. He gave it everything he had but knew he had come to the end of the road. Upon retiring for good later in 1965, Lindsay owned more goals than any other left-flanker and more penalty minutes than any other player in NHL history.

Lindsay was inducted into the Hockey Hall of Fame in 1966. In 1,068 games, he managed 379 goals and 851 points.

Peak Years   *1950–1954*
Comparable Recent Player   *Mark Recchi*
In a Word   *DEMONIC*

ED LITZENBERGER Right Wing/Center
6'3" 194
b. 7/15/1932, Neudorf, Saskatchewan

Edward Litzenberger was a tall, gawky center from the Montreal Canadiens' farm system. In his first full NHL season in 1954–55, he was sold to the cellar-dwelling Chicago Black Hawks as part of a league-wide effort to boost the weak sister club. He blossomed in the Windy City. He remains the only player in NHL history to win the Calder Trophy after being traded in the middle of his rookie season. Because he played with both teams, he managed to play in a record 73 games that season.

Although he avoided back-checking as if it were the plague, he was a smooth skater, a highly skilled dipsy-doodle artist, and the owner of a heavy, hard shot. In 1956–57, he racked up 32 goals, his first of three consecutive 30+ goal seasons. He hit a personal high in 1958–59 with 33 goals and 77 points. Hockey historian Charles L. Coleman says, "Litzenberger was more of an offensive than defensive player . . . He was somewhat temperamental and did not always display his full talent."

Litzenberger's life hit rock-bottom in early 1960 when his wife died in a car accident. He was never the same player again. In 1960–61, he was made captain of the Hawks, leading his crew to their first Stanley Cup since 1938. He was shuffled off to the Detroit Red Wings in 1961 but did not please manager Jack Adams who, in midseason, released the big forward on waivers. Litzenberger would play a minor role in three Toronto Cup wins, closing out his career after stints in Toronto farm teams in Rochester and Victoria.

In 618 games, Litzenberger scored 178 goals and 416 points.

Peak Years   *1955–59*
Comparable Recent Player   *Dave Andreychuk*
In a Word   *GANGLY*

HARRY LUMLEY (Apple Cheeks) Goalie
6'0" 195
b. 11/11/1926, Owen Sound, Ontario
d. 9/13/1998, Owen Sound, Ontario

In the game of hockey, one or two players will invariably steal most of the headlines at their position. In the 1980s, centers like Bernie Federko and Dale Hawerchuk suffered from "Gretzky-itis," a condition brought about by the presence of hockey's new savior and golden boy, Wayne Gretzky. In situations like these, perfectly super players will be overlooked as "the one" grabs most of the glory. Such was the case with Harry "Apple Cheeks" Lumley, who for years played in the shadows of Jacques Plante and Terry Sawchuk.

Lumley played two games with the Detroit Red Wings in 1943–44 before returning to Indianapolis for seasoning. The following year, he was called up and would soon become the regular goalie for the Detroiters. In 1950, he back-stopped the Wings to the Stanley Cup. His reward? He was traded to the weak Chicago Black Hawks. Through the next two seasons, he faced a maelstrom of rubber. Despite having a Keystone Kops defensive corps in front of him, he managed to put up respectable goals-against averages. In 1952, he was dealt to the Toronto Maple Leafs for Cal Gardner, Gus Mortson, and Al Rollins. With a much better back-line in front of him, Lumley posted two straight seasons of at least 10 shutouts, and won the 1953–54 Vezina Trophy. The next season, he bested Detroit's Terry Sawchuk in goals-against average and in save percentage but was denied his second-straight Vezina, as Sawchuk allowed fewer goals.

Lumley was underrated. He was unceremoniously dumped by Detroit in the early 1950s, left to shoulder some awful Hawk squads. Yet, he continued to put up numbers comparable to those of the NHL's goaltending elite. Although not as quick a goalie as Jacques Plante and not as flashy as Terry Sawchuk, big Lumley was nonetheless effective. At 6 feet 200 lb., he could certainly cover a lot of the net. A lifetime goals-against average of under 3.00 with a winning percentage of over .500 makes him one of the all-time overachievers in NHL history.

Lumley remains as one of the most underrated players ever. Only when he was inducted into the Hockey Hall of Fame in 1980 did the big man from Owen Sound get the recognition he deserved.

Peak Years   1952–56
In a Word   BRIDESMAID

FLEMING MACKELL Center
5'8" 167
b. 4/30/1929, Montreal, Quebec

Fleming Mackell came out of the St. Mike's Majors to join the Toronto Maple Leafs in 1948. He was a tough, chippy little center whose father, Jack, did spot-defense duties on the Ottawa Senator dynasty teams of the early 1920s.

Like a lot of small players, Mackell was a maddening guy to play against. He was a tricky skater who would dart from point to point on the ice. He had superb acceleration, was a nifty stick-handler, and had a star-quality shot. And the boy had heart. It was almost comical to see this little firefly trying to take on guys twice his size, looking like some banty rooster sticking his chest out. "There was a lot of intimidation if you weren't big," he said. "If you weren't a rough, tough player, you could never show that you didn't like the rough stuff or they would run you out of the league."

While never in the top echelon of NHL scorers, Mackell was nonetheless a gifted offensive player. His finest season came in 1957–58, when he followed up a 20-goal,

60-point regular season with five goals and 19 points in 12 playoff games. In 665 games across 13 NHL seasons, the spirited center scored 149 goals and 369 points.

He turned in fine performances in both the 1949 and 1951 playoffs, his Toronto Maple Leafs copping the Stanley Cup both years. In 1952, however, Toronto big boss Conn Smythe, tired of waiting for Mackell to reach his potential, dealt him mid-season to the Boston Bruins. The smallish center didn't fare too well in the last half of the year with the B's but showed up just in time to make the playoffs interesting. He had solid seasons with the Bruins in 1952–53 and 1956–57 through 1958–59. Regularly among the tops in voting for the Most Outstanding Bruin, he was a key player on some of Boston's stronger teams in the late 1950s.

Peak Years   1953–57
Comparable Recent Player   Theoren Fleury
In a Word   ROOSTER

DICKIE MOORE Left Wing
5'10" 185
b. 1/6/1931, Montreal, Quebec

Richard Winston Moore cracked the Montreal Canadiens during the 1951–52 season on a line with Elmer Lach and Maurice Richard. His hard-nosed play earned him 18 goals by season's end. Coach Dick Irvin was impressed. The young man's blood seemed to run red, white, and blue.

Moore was out for most of the 1952–53 season with a knee injury but was back for the last quarter of the schedule, skating alongside Billy Reay and Bernie Geoffrion. The following season, Moore broke his collarbone and was not back until the end of February. He made a nice comeback, however, leading all players in playoff scoring. Moore's breakthrough year came in 1957–58, when he became an integral part of Montreal's dynasty.

If not for the sad state of Moore's knees, he would have enjoyed a longer career. "Every time he put his equipment on we held our collective breath, willing those shaky pins to carry this consummate pro through one more game," said teammate Jean Beliveau.

Moore played through a great amount of pain to win scoring races in 1958 and 1959, never straying from his no-nonsense approach to the game. In 1959–60, his rickety knees caught up with him, causing him to miss eight games. For the next three seasons, he continued to play well but in 1963, called it a career. When claimed by the Toronto Maple Leafs in 1964, Moore decided to come out of retirement, playing in 38 games with the Buds before retiring once more. He came out of retirement for a third time in 1967 to play for the St. Louis Blues, but retired to his construction supplies business for good after tasting defeat at the hands of the Canadiens in the 1968 finals.

Moore had passion, could hit, could fight, was a solid skater and a sure stick-handler, and had a beautiful way of making touch-passes on the fly.

Moore made the Hockey Hall of Fame in 1974. In 719 games, he scored 261 goals and 608 points.

Peak Years   1957–61
In a Word   GUTS

GUS MORTSON Defense
5'11" 190
b. 1/24/1925, New Liskeard, Ontario

Gus Mortson was one of those players you just loved to hate — unless he was one of your own! In a manner not unlike that of Ulf Samuelsson or Darius Kasparaitis in the 1990s, Mortson earned his corn smashing, crashing, and bashing opponents of all shapes and sizes. The big man from New Liskeard, Ontario, put in his first season with the Toronto Maple Leafs in 1946–47. In all, he spent six seasons in Toronto, during which he was on one regular-season championship team and four Stanley Cup–winners.

From the late 1940s through the early 1950s, he made up one half of the infamous "Gold Dust Twins," a nickname given to the rugged defender and his partner Jim Thomson. They both enjoyed the physical game and, as a result, often set the tone of Leaf games. "Thomson and I, we kept track of all the goals against because that was your only arguing point when you had to go see [Conn] Smythe for a contract," said Mortson. "All the years we played in Toronto, we [Thomson and Mortson] had less than a one goals-against average."

The physical game was easily Mortson's strongest suit. A fine skater and rusher, he loved nothing more than crashing some poor opponent into the corner chicken-wire. It was this lust for the rough stuff that often got Mortson in trouble, as his penalty record indicates. In 1950–51 and 1951–52, he was issued major suspensions. In both cases, he had reportedly tried to hurt another player. He led the NHL with 133 penalty minutes in his rookie season of 1946–47 and topped the category three more times in his career.

Before the 1951–52 season, Mortson was traded to the Chicago Black Hawks in a deal that saw goalie Harry Lumley shipped to Toronto. Mortson would put in six uneventful years as a Hawk, five of those years on a team that missed the playoffs. After stints in Detroit and in the amateur ranks, he hung up his skates for good.

Peak Years   *1950–1954*
Comparable Recent Player   *Ulf Samuelsson*
In a Word   *MALEVOLENT*

BERT OLMSTEAD (Dirty Bertie) Left Wing
6'2" 183
b. 9/4/1926, Scepter, Saskatchewan

Bert Olmstead came up through the arid Chicago Black Hawks farm system in 1948–49, playing a few games in the Windy City. In December 1950, he was shipped to the Detroit Red Wings who, in turn, dealt him to the Montreal Canadiens for Leo Gravelle and a bag of cash. Olmstead found his niche with the Canadiens.

Olmstead was a bashing kind of player who dove into the corners with zing. But he was also a perfectionist. As teammate Jean Beliveau would later comment, "[Olmstead] could hammer an opponent senseless, and seconds later chew you out on the bench because you were three inches out of position." You could expect a war if you were to follow Olmstead into the corners . . . in the form of a butt-end, an elbow, or a swat in the mouth. Although lacking the finesse of the Beliveaus and Bathgates, Olmstead was a pass-master and had excellent scoring instincts. Montreal coach Dick Irvin found in Olmstead a replacement for Toe Blake on what was the "Punch Line." Olmstead was on the 100-point championship team of 1955–56. Playing with Jean Beliveau and Bernie Geoffrion, Olmstead racked up four goals and 10 assists in the 1956 playoffs and was voted to the NHL's Second All-Star Team. He would play on two more Cup-winners in Montreal before being claimed by the Toronto Maple Leafs after the 1957–58 season in the intraleague draft.

Without Olmstead, Toronto may not have won their first of three successive Cups in 1961–62. He provided great leadership and, for a time, acted as assistant coach to Punch Imlach. Olmstead commanded so much respect in the Toronto dressing room that even crazy Eddie Shack listened up. Before the beginning of the 1962–63 season, Imlach reckoned Old Man Time had caught up with Olmstead and left the big winger unprotected in the intraleague draft. The New York Rangers were quick to snatch him up. Olmstead refused to bite the Big Apple, and retired.

In 848 games, Olmstead scored 181 goals and 602 points. He was elected to the Hockey Hall of Fame in 1985.

Peak Years   *1953–57*
Comparable Recent Player   *Kirk Muller*
In a Word   *CRUSTY*

MARTY PAVELICH Left Wing/Center
5′10″ 170
b. 11/6/1927, Sault Ste. Marie, Ontario

Every great team needs stars. It needs its Eric Lindroses, those who can take a game into the palm of their hands and turn its tide with a big goal. The team needs a top-notch goalie, a man with that special genius for claiming a game's momentum for his side with a snake-fast save. Players such as these win games. But, as Don Cherry once said, while the Wayne Gretzkys of the hockey world win games for you, players like Marty Pavelich bring you home Stanley Cups.

Pavelich was one of the best defensive forwards of all time and a major reason for the rise of a dynasty in Detroit. A slim winger equally as comfortable at center, Pavelich was a slithering leech of a checker who killed penalties and shadowed the opposition's big guns.

Although Pavelich was never a great scorer, point totals of 29, 36, 33, 29, and 30 in Detroit's dynasty years attest to his ability. The checking winger made appearances in the All-Star game in 1950, 1952, 1954, and 1955.

Although not the speed-burning type, he was able to keep up with the league's reachers, popping in the odd goal or two. For years, he played on a line with Glen Skov and Tony Leswick, the second line on those great Detroit Red Wing teams. According to Detroit manager Jack Adams, this line was the real reason his Stanley Cup–winning teams were so successful. The trio was given the job of blanketing the opposition's top lines.

In 1957, at the age of 29, Pavelich decided to call it a career. "You're kind of hero-worshipped," he would say later of life as a professional hockey player. "You get kind of a false feeling about yourself. Once you get out of the game, you've got to think of yourself as a human being like everyone else."

Peak Years   *1951–55*
In a Word   *LEECH*

JACQUES PLANTE (Jake the Snake) Goal
6'0" 175
b. 1/17/1929, Mont Carmel, Quebec
d. 2/26/1986

When Gerry McNeil went down to injury in the 1952–53 season, Montreal Canadiens' skipper Dick Irvin called up a young Jacques Plante from Buffalo. Irvin was impressed with the rookie, who gave up only four goals in three games. Consequently, Irvin showed no hesitation in bringing up Plante from the Montreal Royals to spell McNeil during the playoffs. The following season, Plante was called up again and in 17 games racked up five shutouts! He would become Montreal's full-time goalie in 1954–55 and in the next nine years was on five Cup-winners, copping the Vezina six times. In 1962, he even managed to pinch the Hart Trophy.

The Snake was a paradox. He was an extrovert on the ice, tending his nets with panache. Off the ice, though, he was an oddball. He was moody, rarely associating with his teammates on any level. He knitted his own toques to relax. Back on the ice, he was a reflex goalie with a lightning-quick glove-hand. He was also an exceptional skater — the best skater on the Canadiens, in fact. Such speed allowed him to roam out of his nets to stop errant passes or to fire the puck up-ice to a forward. Although a common practice among goalies today, roaming was almost unheard of in Plante's era. His nickname, according to Jean Beliveau, was a tribute to his way of striking out at shooters.

Not long after the start of the 1959–60 season, he was struck in the face by a wicked Andy Bathgate backhand. Plante was seriously cut from the shot and, after being sewn up, he returned to the game wearing a face mask. He was the first NHL goalie to adopt it permanently. The mask would soon be standard issue for all net-minders, thanks to this first so-called "Masked Marvel." Montreal fans were tiring of Plante's eccentricities. Spectators began mixing in jeers with their cheers. The press worsened the situation by magnifying his strange off-ice habits. He was traded to the New York Rangers at the end of the 1962–63 season. He retired in 1965, after two so-so years on Broadway. Four years later, "Jake the Snake" came out of retirement to play for the St. Louis Blues, helping them to two Stanley Cup final appearances. He rounded out his career in the early 1970s with the Toronto Maple Leafs, mentoring a young Bernie Parent.

Plante was inducted into the Hockey Hall of Fame in 1978.

Peak Years   1956–60
Comparable Recent Player   *Patrick Roy*
In a Word   *NUTTY*

MARCEL PRONOVOST Defense
6'0" 190
b. 6/15/1930, Lac la Tortue, Quebec

Marcel Pronovost started the 1950–51 season in Indianapolis but came up for the last 37 games of the Detroit Red Wings' season. He was a powerful skater and a fine puck-carrier but was somewhat reckless. At the end of a rush, he often crashed into the corner-boards, opposing players, or the opposing team's net. This kind of abandon resulted in many injuries and to his being named the NHL's MIP — Most Injured Player. In addition to broken noses, Pronovost suffered a fractured vertebra, cracked cheekbones, and several broken limbs. Though not a hard-rock defenseman, he seemed to wish he were. He would try to hit everything in sight, often coming up with nothing more than a handful of air. He was, however, one of the NHL's most skillful stick- and poke-checkers.

After 16 standout seasons in Detroit — including a place on four Cup-winning squads — Pronovost was traded to the Toronto Maple Leafs, where he closed out his career.

In all, Pronovost played 21 years in the big leagues with Detroit and the Toronto Maple Leafs. Along the trail, he managed five Stanley Cup rings, four All-Star nominations, and 11 appearances in the All-Star game. He was only the seventh player in NHL history to play 1,000 games.

Despite the often perilous nature of his game, Pronovost stood tall and brave. "Making a dangerous play on the ice didn't make me any more nervous than crossing the street might make someone else," he later said. "He doesn't worry about getting hit by a car and I don't worry about getting hurt on the ice. If I did, I'd probably go crazy."

He was elected to the Hockey Hall of Fame in 1978.

Peak Years   1955–59
In a Word   KAMIKAZE

BILL QUACKENBUSH Defense
5'11" 180
b. 3/2/1922, Toronto, Ontario

Hubert George Quackenbush got his start with the Detroit Red Wings in 1942. By the end of the 1945–46 season, he was one of the top blue-liners in the NHL, controlling the puck in a way not unlike the Montreal Canadiens' Doug Harvey.

Quackenbush was a unique specimen, especially for his time. Not a body-thumper, he liked to poke- and stick-check enemy rushers. He was the single biggest influence in the development of Red Kelly's style of play. "I wasn't a body-checker," said Quackenbush. "I was a poke-checker. I had to play a certain style. I found that if I did a lot of body-checking, I got tired very easily. I was on the ice an awful lot because I didn't get penalties."

As an indication of his clean play, Quackenbush accumulated only 22 minor penalties and 1 major over the course of six complete NHL seasons — playoffs included! During the 1948–49 season, he played in the full 60-game schedule without spending a single minute in the sin bin.

At the end of the 1948–49 season, the Boston Bruins' Art Ross expressed great interest in obtaining Quackenbush from Detroit. Quackenbush was dealt to the B's with Pete Horeck for Pete Babando, Jimmy Peters, and Clare Martin. Quackenbush went on to lead Beantown's backing corps for the next seven years. When Quackenbush retired at the end of the 1955–56 season, Red Kelly was the only NHL defenseman with more assists. After 14 years of play, the gentlemanly Quackenbush had served only 95 minutes in penalties for an average of 0.12 minutes per game. This remains an unchallenged record for a defenseman.

Quackenbush made the Hockey Hall of Fame in 1976.

Peak Years   1948–52
In a Word   GENTLEMAN

MAURICE RICHARD (The Rocket) Right Wing
5'10" 195
b. 8/4/1921, Montreal, Quebec

Maurice Richard joined the Montreal Canadiens when the club was at the brink of folding, having finished deep in the second division for three straight years. His arrival may have been the very salvation of Les Glorieux. Here was a man who was bred for stardom in French Canada — dark, strong, angry, the very personification of Gallic fire.

He quickly captured the hearts and minds of a generation of French Quebecers.

Jean Beliveau once described Richard as a "highly tuned, highly specialized hockey instrument." His famous nickname, "The Rocket," was given on account of his mad, whirling-dervish rushes, his edge-of-your-seat charges into enemy territory. He was an excellent stick-handler and could often be seen carrying a player on his back on break-aways. "I didn't even know myself what I was going to do coming in past the blue-line," he once confessed. "I tried never to make the same move twice in a row. I always tried to make a different play." His tricky dekes attracted a lot of holding, tripping, and slashing from checkers. He had an amazingly accurate shot and could score from just about any angle. From 10 feet inside the opposition's blue-line, he was the most deadly assassin of all time. Legendary referee Red Storey said, "When God created the perfect goal-scorer, it came in the form of The Rocket!"

Although he never led the league in scoring, Richard was the leading goal-getter five times. In his third year he set a record, potting 50 goals in 50 games. That 50-in-50 mark stood for over thirty years. In 1952–53, he broke Nels Stewart's career goal-scoring record and ended up with 544, a mark that would stand until Gordie Howe broke it in the mid-1960s.

Unfortunately, Richard also had a volcanic temper and would duke out any player who rubbed him the wrong way. Consequently, he was a regular occupant in NHL president Clarence Campbell's doghouse. The most significant of Richard's many run-ins with the NHL was his assault of linesman Cliff Thompson in a game late in the 1954–55 season. For his part in the incident, Richard was suspended for the balance of the season through the playoffs. This set off the storied "Richard Riot," which saw the whole of Montreal's downtown come under the control of hooters, looters, and other assorted rowdies.

Richard was part of eight Stanley Cup–winning teams. He was voted to the NHL's All-Star Team 14 times. He retired in 1960, arguably the most exciting player in hockey history, and made the Hockey Hall of Fame in 1961.

Peak Years   1947–51
In a Word   ASSASSIN

TERRY SAWCHUK (Ukey) Goal
6'0" 195
b. 12/28/1929, Winnipeg, Manitoba

Terrence Gordon Sawchuk was called up by the Detroit Red Wings in 1950 to replace an injured Harry Lumley. Sawchuk became Detroit's regular goalie in 1950–51, finishing the season with the Calder Trophy and a First All-Star Team nod. In the next four years, he back-stopped the Red Wings to four championships and three Stanley Cups, picking up All-Star ratings every year and snagging three Vezinas. At the end of five-plus years in Detroit, he racked up 57 shutouts while posting an overall goals-against average of below 2.00.

Sawchuk was a big man with exceptional reflexes. He chose to work from a bizarre "gorilla-crouch" style, with his head hung low and his arms sweeping the ice. This style allowed him to defend his goal against goal-mouth scrambles and screened shots. He was a fiery competitor and it was not rare to see him with his nose pressed to the glass bawling out the goal judge on an iffy goal. Montreal Canadiens' center Jean Beliveau said, "[Sawchuk] was an angles goalie who wanted you to shoot. But, if you preferred to put a move on him, he was happy to oblige."

At the end of the 1954–55 season, Detroit GM Jack Adams dealt Sawchuk to the Boston Bruins. Sawchuk continued his winning ways in Beantown, chalking up nine shutouts in 1955–56. In December 1956, he was hospitalized with severe mononucleosis. He was back in action two weeks later but was clearly not well. Succumbing to stress, fatigue, and depression, he quit the game outright to recuperate.

His reputation took quite a beating during his recess and, after Don Simmons finished out the season for the Bruins, Sawchuk was air-mailed back to Detroit.

He started drinking heavily, becoming increasingly moody and distant. He would never again reach the top of his profession, although his star would still shine on occasion. He played for his beloved Red Wings until his release at the end of the 1963–64 season. The Toronto Maple Leafs snapped him up in the draft.

He and oldster Johnny Bower tended the Toronto nets under head coach Punch Imlach's platoon system. In 1967, Sawchuk played an important role in bringing the Cup back to Hogtown. In 1970, Sawchuk was seriously injured in a senseless dispute with house- and teammate Ron Stewart. Sawchuk died a few weeks later of liver complications.

Sawchuk remains one of the greatest goalies of all time. He was elected to the Hockey Hall of Fame in 1971.

Peak Years   *1952–56*
Comparable Recent Player   *Dominik Hasek*
In a Word   *SEETHING*

TOD SLOAN (Slinker) Center/Right Wing
5'10" 175
b. 11/30/1927, Vinton, Quebec

Tod Sloan was a Memorial Cup champion with the St. Michael's Majors in 1944–45 and took the Red Tilson Trophy as the OHA's most valuable player in 1946. The OHA phenom got his chance to play for the Toronto Maple Leafs in 1948–49, where he played half a season. He had another short stint in the minors before he was brought back to Toronto at the beginning of the 1950–51 season. He was impressive in the playoffs that year, helping to topple the Montreal Canadiens for the Stanley Cup.

Although a frail-looking player, Sloan was gritty. He was also a shifty skater who knew how to handle the puck. In 1955–56, he had his finest year on a line with George "Chief" Armstrong and Dick Duff. He led the team with 37 goals and made Second All-Star Team rating. "Tod is his own boss," said owner Conn Smythe. "He does what he likes with the puck. It took us a few years to discover that the best way to handle him is to leave him alone."

Sloan hurt his shoulder quite badly in December 1956, which greatly affected his production. At the end of the following season, he was dealt to every player's worst nightmare: Chicago. Like Jim Thomson before him, Sloan was traded on account of his involvement in the new NHL Players' Association, which Leafs GM Conn Smythe spat rail-hot lead about. Sloan returned to form with the Black Hawks, contributing to a Cup win in 1960–61, his last season.

After leaving the NHL in 1961, Sloan had his amateur status restored. He joined the Galt Terriers and played a part in a silver medal win at the World Championships the following year.

In 745 games, Sloan scored 220 goals and 482 points.

Peak Years   *1953–57*
Comparable Recent Player   *Owen Nolan*
In a Word   *TRICKY*

SID SMITH (Muff) Left Wing
5'10" 177
b. 7/11/1925 Toronto, Ontario

Sidney Smith led the Toronto Maple Leafs in scoring in his first full season (1949–50) with 45 points after scoring 55 goals and 112 points in 68 games with the AHL Pittsburgh Hornets. The following year, he scored 51 points, good for a place in the NHL's top 10. Always strong offensively, he was initially a one-dimensional player, good for a goal and precious little else. Under the defensive instruction of Leafs' head coach Joe Primeau and assistant coach King Clancy, however, Smith developed his all-around game. By 1955, he was one of the better two-way wingers in the NHL while leading his team in goals for four straight seasons.

He was not a particularly good skater and was not at all quick on the blades but was unusually deadly around the opposition net. He gobbled up rebounds and was shown to have a real knack for deflections. "The thing was to keep an eye on the puck coming in," he once explained. "Just make that slight deflection [to] throw the goalie off. He's playing it for the shot from the point." Smith was among the very best in the league with his team up a man, scoring 11 power-play goals in 1954–55. Following the retirement of Ted Kennedy, Smith was made captain of the Maple Leafs. After retiring in 1958, he hopped aboard the amateur Whitby Dunlops and contributed to a World Championship.

In 601 games, Smith was worth 186 goals, 369 points, three All-Star nominations, seven All-Star appearances, two Lady Byng trophies, and three Stanley Cup rings.

Peak Years   *1951–55*
Comparable Recent Player   *Luc Robitaille*
In a Word   *SNEAKY*

JIM THOMSON (Jeems) Defense
6'0" 190
b. 2/23/1927, Winnipeg, Manitoba

Jimmy Thomson, although possibly not as well known a name as some of the other great Leaf defensive greats, was a mutt, a "check first, ask questions later" player.

Thomson became a regular with the Leafs in 1946–47. He and Gus Mortson, who were business partners off the ice, formed a rollicking defensive duo on the ice for six seasons. Thomson matured into the picture of the quintessential stay-at-home defenseman. Although he wasn't the fleetest man afoot, he was exceedingly expert at the "grip and grab" technique, a tactic that earned him his share of penalties. Despite his focus on the defensive side of the game, he was a skilled play-maker.

Thomson was appointed team captain in 1956–57, but relinquished the "C" when Ted Kennedy retired in 1957. His involvement in the NHL Players' Association did not wash with King Leaf Conn Smythe. As a result, crotchety old Connie sold Thomson to the Chicago Black Hawks at the end of the 1956–57 season. The old war horse put in a year in Chicago before retiring. He made All-Star rating twice and appeared in the All-Star game seven times.

Peak Years   *1950–1954*
Comparable Recent Player   *Craig Ludwig*
In a Word   *FIRM*

The All-Stars

Pos	Player	Season	GP	G	A	PTS
D	Doug Harvey	1956–57	70	6	43	49
D	Red Kelly	1956–57	70	16	34	50
LW	Ted Lindsay	1956–57	70	30	55	85
C	Jean Beliveau	1958–59	64	45	46	91
RW	Gordie Howe	1952–53	70	49	46	95
			GP	GAA	ShO	
G	Jacques Plante	1955–56	64	1.86	7	

The Sixties

In a Flash

COMPOSITE REGULAR-SEASON STANDINGS
(JANUARY 1, 1960–DECEMBER 31, 1969)

National Hockey League

Club	GP	W	L	T	Pts	WPct	GF	GA
Montreal Canadiens	710	378	204	128	884	.623	2,349	1,806
Chicago Black Hawks	709	341	246	122	804	.567	2,231	1,860
Toronto Maple Leafs	709	339	254	116	794	.560	2,039	1,870
St. Louis Blues	185	82	67	36	200	.541	496	431
Detroit Red Wings	708	294	299	115	703	.496	2,099	2,113
New York Rangers	709	268	324	117	653	.461	2,009	2,193
Philadelphia Flyers	182	58	80	44	160	.440	426	498
Minnesota North Stars	182	54	88	40	148	.407	477	600
Boston Bruins	709	233	366	110	576	.406	2,033	2,482
Los Angeles Kings	180	61	95	24	146	.406	450	606
Pittsburgh Penguins	182	57	96	29	143	.393	455	564
Oakland Seals	184	53	98	33	139	.378	444	585

HELLOS

Wayne Gretzky *The Great One*	January 26, 1961
Doug Gilmour *Leafs & Blackhawks center*	June 25, 1963
Dominik Hasek *Goalie extraordinaire*	January 29, 1965
Mario Lemieux *Penguins superstar*	October 5, 1965
Patrick Roy *legendary Habs goalie*	October 5, 1965
Wendel Clark *Leafs star*	October 25, 1966

GOODBYES

Lester Patrick *Hockey innovator*	June 1, 1960
Carl Jung *Swiss psychologist*	June 6, 1961
John F. Kennedy *U.S. president*	November 22, 1963
Art Ross *Boston Bruins executive*	August 5, 1964
Winston Churchill *British prime minister*	January 24, 1965
Che Guevara *Argentine revolutionary*	October 9, 1967
Jack Adams *Detroit Red Wings boss*	May 1, 1968

REGULAR SEASON

BEST RECORD
1961–62 **Montreal Canadiens**, 42-14-14

WORST RECORD
1961–62 **Boston Bruins**, 15-47-8

BEST MINOR-LEAGUE RECORD
1967–68 **Clinton Comets** (Eastern Hockey League), 57-5-10

FAMOUS FIRSTS

TEAM TO WIN FIVE SUCCESSIVE STANLEY CUPS
Montreal Canadiens, April 14, 1960

FIVE-TIME HART TROPHY WINNER
Gordie Howe, 1959–60

GOALTENDER TO RECORD 400 CAREER VICTORIES
Terry Sawchuk, Toronto, 1964–65

PLAYER TO APPEAR IN 1,000 CAREER GAMES
Gordie Howe, Detroit, November 26, 1961

PLAYER TO REACH 600 CAREER GOALS
Gordie Howe, Detroit, 1965–66

NHL PLAYER TO SCORE MORE THAN 50 GOALS IN A SEASON
Bobby Hull, Chicago, 1965–66

PLAYER TO SCORE MORE THAN 100 POINTS IN A SEASON
Phil Esposito, Boston, 1968–69

DEFENSEMAN TO SCORE 500 CAREER POINTS
Bill Gadsby, Detroit, November 4, 1962

MISCELLANEOUS

MOST GOALS, SEASON
58   Bobby Hull, Chicago, 1968–69

MOST GOALS, DECADE
446   Bobby Hull, Chicago

MOST ASSISTS, SEASON
77   Phil Esposito, Boston, 1968–69

MOST ASSISTS, DECADE
530   Stan Mikita, Chicago

MOST POINTS, SEASON
126   Phil Esposito, Boston, 1968–69

MOST POINTS, DECADE
796   Stan Mikita, Chicago

COOLEST MIDDLE NAMES
Bob *Wellington* Dillabough
Kent *Gemmell* Douglas
Al *Wences* MacNeil
Joe *Boleslaw* Szura
Bob *Lomer* McCord
Dean *Sutherland* Prentice

COOLEST HANDLES
Gilles Marotte, "Captain Crunch"
Stan "Stosh" Mikita
Yvan Cournoyer, "Le Chinois,"

"The Roadrunner"
Bruce MacGregor, "The Redheaded Rocket"
Lorne "Gump" Worsley
Bob "Boomer" Baun
Claude Provost, "Secret Agent 14," "Pete"
Red Berenson, "The Red Baron"
Henri Richard, "The Pocket Rocket"
Don "Slip" McKenney
Claude Richard, "The Inside Pocket Rocket"

BIGGEST PLAYER
Pete Mahovlich, 6'5" 210

SMALLEST PLAYER
Len Haley, 5'6" 160

BEST SHOT
Bobby Hull had probably the hardest shot of all time.

BEST PASSER
Stan Mikita and Jean Beliveau were both pass-masters, smooth as butter on the attack. While Mikita might have the edge for tenacity and Beliveau for pure skill, this one's a pick-'em.

BEST STICK-HANDLER
J.C. Tremblay

BEST SKATER
Bobby Hull

WORST SKATER
Allan Stanley was slow as molasses in January. Although he was an incredibly consistent blue-liner, he moved like a turtle. His nickname was "Snowshoes."

FASTEST SKATER
Bobby Hull was brilliant at top flight with his golden blond hair and blazing red Hawks jersey.

BEST SNIPER
Bobby Hull

BEST INSTINCTS
Gordie Howe

BEST PENALTY-KILLER
Dave Keon was a dogged but clean competitor with an incredible skating ability. The little guy's genius for the kill was never more prominent than in the 1967 playoffs.

BEST BODY-CHECKER
Gilles Marotte used his 205-pound frame in a manner similar to Leo Boivin. Marotte could hit like a freight train.

BEST POKE-CHECKER
Jacques Laperriere

BEST SHOT-BLOCKER
Harry Howell

BEST GLOVE-HAND (GOALIE)
Eddie Giacomin, known as "Fast Eddie," was loved in New York for his acrobatic style.

MOST UNUSUAL GOALTENDING STYLE
Glenn Hall

BEST DEFENSIVE FORWARD
Claude Provost

WORST DEFENSIVE FORWARD
Yvan Cournoyer. For his first couple of years with the Montreal Canadiens, coach Toe Blake used him only on the power play, with good reason.

BEST SHADOW
Claude Provost proved in the 1965 finals against Bobby Hull and the Black Hawks that he was one of the finest shadows ever to play the game. His covering Hull like a family quilt was one of the keys to Montreal's Cup victory that year.

BEST FACE-OFF MAN
Whereas Ted Kennedy relied on positioning and footwork and Bobby Clarke would rely on smarts and dirty tricks, **Stan Mikita** used lightning-quick reflexes to cement a reputation as master of the draw.

BEST DEFENSIVE DEFENSEMAN
Harry Howell quietly persevered through 21 NHL seasons, plus three more in the WHA. After years of thankless toil with some awful New York Ranger teams, he was awarded the Norris Trophy in 1966–67.

BEST OFFENSIVE DEFENSEMAN
Pierre Pilote was the NHL's pre-eminent quarterback in the 1960s. Despite the presence of Bobby Hull, Pilote was perhaps the most important cog in the high-powered Chicago offense.

BEST ALL-AROUND PLAYER
It's easy to forget just how superb, how tenacious a fore-checker **Jean Beliveau** was, until you go back and review old *Hockey Night in Canada* game films. During the 1965 finals, when he won the first ever Conn Smythe Trophy as playoff MVP, Beliveau was a force both offensively and defensively.

BEST UTILITY PLAYER
Many older hockey fans will remember **Jimmy Roberts**'s superlative penalty-killing and defensive play. This loyal soldier was as effective at center or on the wing as he was on the blue-line.

STRONGEST PLAYER
Tim Horton

TOUGHEST PLAYER
John Ferguson

BEST FIGHTER

A three-way tie between **John Ferguson**, **Orland Kurtenbach**, and **Ted Harris**. Ferguson gets the edge because he was so fast and focused, and so damaging with his dukes.

ABLEST INSTIGATOR

Bryan "Bugsy" Watson

DIRTIEST PLAYER

Howie Young was bad news from the first time he skated with the Detroit Red Wings in 1961. In 1963, in a campaign of sheer mayhem, he earned a record 273 minutes in the sin bin. Scant days after he racked up 27 minutes in a single game on February 17, GM Sid Abel suspended him. By this time, a growing alcohol problem was affecting Young's performance and attendance at team meetings and practices.

CLEANEST PLAYER

Val Fonteyne was the cleanest player in NHL history: 26 penalty minutes in 820 games!

BEST CORNER-MAN

John Bucyk

BEST-LOOKING PLAYER

Rod Gilbert was tailor-made for the Big Apple with his model good looks. He was the NHL's answer to Joe Namath.

UGLIEST PLAYER

Lou Fontinato

BALDEST PLAYER

Doug Mohns

MUST UNDERRATED PLAYER

Norm Ullman

MOST CONSISTENT PLAYER

Norm Ullman, a star with the Detroit Red Wings, could hurt you any number of ways. For years, he maintained his ranking as one of the top scorers in the game while proving himself time and time again as one of the game's most conscientious diggers. Eddie Shack called Ullman the "hardest-working man in hockey."

MOST UNPREDICTABLE CAREER

Carl Brewer quit in 1965 — at the very peak of his career — regained his amateur status and played for the Canadian national team in the late 1960s, joined the IHL's Muskegon Mohawks for a season, hooked up with the Detroit Red Wings in 1969–70, then spent a couple of years with the St. Louis Blues. In 1972, he retired a second time, only to return a year later with the WHA's Toronto Toros, retired again in 1974, then made a 20-game comeback with the Maple Leafs in 1979–80, at the age of 41. Whew!

SMARTEST PLAYER

Carl Brewer

BIGGEST FLAKE

Eddie Shack

MOST HATED PLAYER

Ted Green. One of hockey's most vicious headhunters, his career was nearly terminated, ironically, by an act of violence. During a preseason game in 1969, Wayne Maki of the St. Louis Blues got his stick up on Green, fracturing his skull and nearly killing the Big Bad Bruin. Green was out of action for a year and, although he'd play nine more seasons, he was never the same player again.

MOST ADMIRED PLAYER

Jean Beliveau

BEST LINES

Team: Detroit Red Wings
LW: Frank Mahovlich
C: Alex Delvecchio
RW: Gordie Howe

Team: Montreal Canadiens
LW: Dickie Duff
C: Jean Beliveau
RW: Gilles Tremblay

Team: Chicago Black Hawks
LW: Doug Mohns
C: Stan Mikita
RW: Ken Wharram

HIGHEST-PAID PLAYER
Bobby Hull

MOST TRAGIC CAREER
Doug Barkley, a big redhead from Lethbridge, Alberta, was one of the NHL's top prospects in the late 1950s, labeled a "can't-miss" defenseman by the experts. The Detroit Red Wings brought Barkley along slowly and in 1962–63 he made his debut. After a strong rookie season, he was hailed as the next great blue-liner in the NHL. An unfortunate eye injury in January 1966 ended what might very well have been a brilliant hockey career.

WORST NHL AMATEUR DRAFT MISTAKE
Boston GM Hap Emms passed on Toronto Marlboro prodigy Brad Park, instead choosing Barry Gibbs. It boggles the mind to imagine Park and Bobby Orr on the same defense.

MOST LOPSIDED TRADE
On May 15, 1967, one of the greatest swindles in hockey history was finalized. Boston swung a deal with the Black Hawks that saw Phil Esposito, Ken Hodge, and Fred Stanfield travel to Beantown for Gilles Marotte, Pit Martin, and fringe goalie Jack Norris.

BIGGEST FLOPS
Rejean Houle. Toward the end of the decade, this Montreal Junior Canadien was touted as the big club's next great superstar. He was a fabulous skater, stick-handler, and play-maker, and was thought capable of taking over from Jean Beliveau as the next great Canadien. After Montreal selected Houle first overall in the 1969 Amateur Draft, things went downhill. The promising young star turned into a slightly-above-average checking winger.

BEST HEAD COACH
Toe Blake

BEST GENERAL MANAGER
Sammy Pollock

BEST SPORTSWRITER
Red Fisher

BEST BROADCASTER
Many can still remember **Danny Gallivan**'s colorful descriptions of seasons gone by. His unique turns of phrase — such "cannonading shot" and "Savardian spin-a-rama" — have left an indelible mark on the hockey lexicon. And who could forget his simple declaration after each goal: "The puck is in the net!"

BEST MINOR-LEAGUE PLAYER
Lou Jankowski

BEST STANLEY CUP FINAL
Toronto Maple Leafs vs. Montreal Canadiens, 1967. To this day the series remains the greatest all-Canadian Cup final ever staged. It was the icing on the cake in a year in which the nation marked its Centennial, the city of Montreal hosted a World's Fair, and national pride was at an all-time high.

IMPORTANT RULE CHANGES
- 1960–61
Teams allowed to dress 16 players plus goalie
- 1965–66
Teams must dress two goalies for each regular-season game.
- 1966–67
Substitution allowed on coincidental majors
- 1967–68
Curve on players' sticks limited to 1.5 inches

Big Blue

As the 1960s began, the Toronto Maple Leafs found themselves in an unfamiliar position. From the league's inception in 1917, right through the mid '50s, the Buds had been one of the NHL's powers. But the Detroit Red Wings came to the fore in the 1950s, and would vie with the Montreal Canadiens for league dominance. The Boston Bruins filled the void left by the Leafs, going to the Cup finals on three occasions during the decade.

Now the Leafs were rebuilding, having missed the playoffs in 1957 and 1958. The latter season was the first time a Toronto team had ever posted the worst record in the NHL. The 1958–59 season did not hold out much hope. The club had added Johnny Bower from Cleveland, defenseman Carl Brewer from their Marlboros Junior affiliate, and forwards Bert Olmstead from Montreal and Dave Creighton from the Rangers. Toronto also traded for defenseman Allan Stanley in October 1958. Stanley, who had been booed out of New York and largely ineffective in Beantown, blossomed alongside Tim Horton. Despite these additions, the team had a rocky start, winning only 5 of their first 20 games.

On November 28, club management canned coach Billy Reay and replaced him with GM George "Punch" Imlach, who'd been skipper of the Quebec Aces. Punch had an immediate impact. After dropping his debut 2–1 to the Chicago Black Hawks, Toronto went on a six-game unbeaten streak. But this early success was fleeting, as the Leafs shortly returned to their inconsistent ways. With five games left in the season, Toronto trailed the Rangers by seven points for the last playoff spot. And two of those last five games would be against New York.

Somehow, the Leafs managed to take both games. Heading into their final game, in Detroit, Toronto trailed the Rangers by a single point. After falling behind 2–0, the Leafs beat the Wings 6–4. The magical run, which would see them de-claw the Bruins in seven games in the semifinals, ended at the hands of the Montreal Canadiens, who pounded Toronto in the finals. Despite the painful defeat, the Leafs under Punch Imlach were suddenly a force to be reckoned with.

Prior to the 1959–60 season, Toronto acquired Johnny "Iron Man" Wilson from Detroit for Barry Cullen and Gary Aldcorn. A number of important Leafs, including Tim Horton, Dick Duff, Bob Pulford, and Ron Stewart, held out briefly for higher salaries, but the team managed to sign all of its players on time and looked forward to building on its strong finish the year before. By midseason, the Leafs were 17-12-6, good for 40 points and a tie for second place.

The Maple-Os finished the 1959–60 campaign in second place with a record of 35-26-9 for 79 points. After disposing of the Wings in the first round of the playoffs, Toronto hooked up with the Canadiens for a rematch of the finals from a year ago. Montreal devoured the Leafs in four straight games. This would be the last of an unprecedented five consecutive Cups for Montreal and their last appearance in the finals until 1965.

1966–67 Toronto Maple Leafs

The 1960–61 season saw only a few changes to Toronto's lineup. Perhaps the most important addition to the club came from the OHA's St. Michael's Majors. Dave Keon, a small, speedy center from Noranda, Quebec, would become an important cog in the Big Blue Machine. He was a superb checker who could score his share of goals. Soon thereafter, Toronto acquired Eddie Shack from the New York Rangers for Pat Hannigan and Johnny Wilson. Shack would bring toughness and loads of energy.

The story of the season was the fabulous Frank Mahovlich. By December 15 he had 27 goals (in 30 games) and had 36 after 41 games. Although he seemed a lock to break Maurice Richard's record of 50 goals in a season, he was slowed by injuries and tight checking and settled for a club record of 48.

Toronto had an excellent first half and only got stronger in the second. They streaked to the finish line with a 39-19-12 record for 90 points, only two behind first-place Montreal. Mahovlich made the First All-Star Team, as did Vezina Trophy winner Johnny Bower. Kelly grabbed the Lady Byng and Keon was named the league's top rookie. Despite a fine overall regular season, the Leafs failed to make any real noise in the playoffs. They bowed to Detroit in five games. The Wings would lose to Chicago in the finals. It was the Hawks' first Cup since 1938.

On November 23, 1961, Conn Smythe, who had controlled the Leafs for an eternity, sold controlling interest of Maple Leaf Gardens to his son Stafford, Harold Ballard, and John Bassett for $2 million. It was the end of one era and the beginning of another.

The Leafs were determined to erase the bitter taste left by the previous season's playoff performance. A strong regular season left them in second place with a 37-22-11 record. Mahovlich was fifth in league scoring with 33 goals and 71 points. Joining the "Big M" on the Second All-Star Team were Carl Brewer and Keon, who managed to nab the Lady Byng Trophy. Toronto squashed the Rangers in the semifinals to meet

Jean Beliveau (center) and Terry Sawchuk (left)

up with Chicago for the Cup. The Buds were up against Glenn Hall, Stan Mikita, Bobby Hull, and the rest of the golden boys, who were seeking their second straight world championship. Toronto took the first two games at home before dropping the next two in the Windy City. Game five back in Hogtown produced an 8–4 Toronto margin. Back in Chicago, Hull opened up game six with a ripper. Hawk fans littered the ice with debris and the ensuing delay allowed the Leafs to regain their composure. Goals by Dick Duff and Bob Nevin gave Toronto its first Cup since 1951.

As reigning champions, the Maple Leafs had the honor of hosting the 1962 All-Star Game, winning 4–1. The next day, papers around North America had it that Toronto had sold Mahovlich to the Black Hawks for $1 million. It seemed that Chicago owner Jim Norris had inquired about Mahovlich's availability and Harold Ballard had quoted him a price. After negotiating over drinks, the price was finalized at $1 million. The two men shook on it and Norris slapped down a $1,000 bill as a deposit. Elated, Norris gave Hawks GM Tommy Ivan a call, advising him to secure the funds. When news of the deal hit the media, angering and confusing Leaf faithful, Toronto execs quickly announced that their superstar winger was not for sale after all.

The Big M would go on to score 36 goals and earn a spot on the First All-Star Team. Keon nabbed his second straight Lady Byng, while defenseman Kent Douglas snagged the Calder Trophy as the league's top rookie. The 1962–63 edition was arguably the strongest Leaf team of the 1960s. Not only did they finish first in the regular season, but they also breezed through the playoffs, defeating Montreal in five games in the semifinals before dispatching Detroit in five for the silverware. Bower was sensational, allowing 16 goals in 10 playoff games. Gordie Howe was asked why his Wings were unable to solve the Leafs. "We tried," Howe sighed, "but it was like growling against thunder."

In 1963–64 the Leafs came crashing back down to Earth. After a solid first half, they fell into a rut. An 11–0 blowout at the hands of the Boston Bruins convinced Imlach he needed to shake things up. He dealt Duff, Nevin, Arnie Brown, Bill Collins, and Rod Seiling to New York for Andy Bathgate and Don McKenney. At the time, Bathgate was one of the NHL's top play-makers, a true offensive dynamo. He would jump-start the Leaf offense, which had been sputtering of late. Toronto went 9-4-2 in their last 15 games and finished with a 33-25-12 record. Bathgate finished fourth in scoring with 77 points, while both Horton and Mahovlich earned All-Star plaudits. Toronto was again matched up against the Canadiens in the first round. This time around, it took Toronto seven games to advance. In the finals, they would do

----

battle with the Red Wings for the second year in a row. This series also went the distance, with Toronto laying claim to their third Cup in as many years.

As a coach, Punch Imlach was very vocal, preferring to berate players instead of stroking their egos. This attribute did not sit well with many of the club's veterans. One player who seemed perpetually in Imlach's sights was Mahovlich. Punch rode the "Big M" mercilessly for not playing up to his supposed potential. Imlach's constant badgering is cited as one of the biggest reasons that Mahovlich — possibly the most talented individual to ever skate for Toronto — failed to become the "next Jean Beliveau," as many had him pegged early in his career. The Imlach–Mahovlich feud reached its apex in November 1964, when Mahovlich suffered a nervous breakdown. It's been argued that Imlach, the architect of the Leaf dynasty, was also the source of its downfall.

Drained from their arduous Cup run of the previous season, the Leafs never really got on track in 1964–65. Injuries abounded and they just didn't have enough in reserve. Former Detroit star Terry Sawchuk would alternate with Bower in goal, a system that seemed to work out well, as the two shared the Vezina Trophy. Toronto finished the season in fourth place with a 30-26-14 record. Although both Mahovlich and Brewer earned All-Star recognition, this was clearly a team in trouble, as was demonstrated in the playoffs, when Montreal ousted them in six games. The Canadiens would go all the way, ending Toronto's three-year grasp on the Cup.

Toronto's mini-dynasty came on the heels of the Canadiens' five straight Cups from 1956 through 1960. As such, it has been somewhat obscured. But it should be noted that, since the NHL was formed in 1917, teams have won three consecutive Stanley Cups only five times: the Leafs of 1947–49; Montreal's run of five between 1956 and 1960; Toronto again (1962–64); the Habs' late-'70s four-bagger (1976–79); and the New York Islanders run of 1980–83. Between 1959 and 1964, Toronto appeared in the Cup final five times.

The Hockey News, in its Collector's Edition 50th Anniversary issue, listed the top 10 NHL squads of all time, but none of the 1962–64 Leaf teams made the list. Yet if you compared the Leafs of this era with, say, the 1973–74 Philadelphia Flyers, who ranked ninth on the list, you'd get an argument from us. The Leafs had much more forward depth and owned a tighter four-man checking unit. Although not the equal of Bernie Parent, Bower was no slouch between the pipes. Here are the players who appeared on the three Toronto Cup-winners: George Armstrong, Johnny Bower, Carl Brewer, Tim Horton, Red Kelly, Dave Keon, Frank Mahovlich, Bob Pulford, Eddie Shack, Allan Stanley, Ron Stewart, Bobby Baun, and Eddie Litzenberger. Not too shabby.

Toronto was a finely crafted club, built to win when it mattered — in the spring. Despite winning three Cups in a row, the Leafs finished first in the regular season only once, in 1962–63. Here's to one of the most underrated dynasties in NHL history.

Dazed and Confused

Remember the movie *Dazed and Confused?* There's a scene in the movie when a bunch of kids get in a car and start smashing trash cans with assorted projectiles, including a bowling ball. Child's play? Not exactly.

Bob Pulford and Tim Horton of the Toronto Maple Leafs were charged with disturbing the peace in Quebec City for doing pretty much the same thing. The Buds were in town on September 22, 1963, to play the Quebec Aces in an exhibition match. Details on the situation are fuzzy but what is known is that the police stopped Pulford and Horton after the pair kicked over numerous garbage cans on the Grand Allée. The two future Hall of Famers were fined $50 apiece by Municipal Court Judge Emil Morin.

Me and My Shadow: The 1965 Finals

The fellows that wore the big red "CH" had just bested Punch Imlach's Toronto Maple Leafs in a bitterly fought six-game semifinal series. Another winter had come and gone and Chicago Black Hawk mega-star Bobby Hull had almost singlehandedly destroyed the Detroit Red Wings in the playoffs. It was April 1965. Lester B. Pearson was in charge in Ottawa and all was peachy-keen in half-thawed Canada. Even the beer ads were corny:

> *The Big Ale in the Big Land!*
> *Everywhere you go you'll find where people get together,*
> *One ale's the brand going up — not going down,*
> *Enjoy a Mol-son Export Ale*
> *If you like to drink an ale that gets your satisfaction,*
> *Ask for the brew with fla-vor, that's brewed — in the Big, Big Land*
> *Enjoy a Mol-son Export Ale*
> *The Big Ale in the Big Land, it's Molson Export Ale!*

The mid 1960s saw the beginning of what would become a truly senseless war in Vietnam as the United States neared a deadline set by the Soviet and Vietnamese governments for a cessation to all air strikes. According to Soviet Premier Kosygin, the Americans' predicted use of gas and napalm "may invite retaliation in kind." Canadian Prime Minister Pearson's initial pleas to Washington to choose flower over power in North Vietnam began drawing support from India, of all places.

Meanwhile in Canada, Manitoba's Red River was up to its old tricks, bursting forth in a spring thaw of raging proportions. Dykes were built and valley residents were bracing themselves for the worst.

Queen Elizabeth II's new eight-foot-tall portrait — she had recently commissioned an unknown British artist to make her beautiful — was raising eyebrows in the art community, drawing comments such as "Goya-like" and "simply awful."

Meanwhile, the Montreal Canadiens, hunting for their first Cup since 1960, were 7.5–6.5 favorites over the Hawks' powerhouse.

Amid the usual pre-series kibitzing came the announcement from Hawk management that star defenseman Pierre Pilote would probably be riding the pines with a shoulder injury. Kenny Wharram, the right winger on the "Scooter Line," was also not expected to start.

Although Glenn Hall had been The Man between the Chicago pipes for ages, head coach Billy Reay was toying with the possibility of using Denis DeJordy in game one of the finals. "We consider them about even and either of them may play the first game," Reay said.

Star center Stan Mikita, who was all but invisible against Detroit, received a great deal of support from Reay in the face of media criticisms. "Just because he wasn't scoring doesn't mean that Mikita wasn't playing well," he said. "We have to keep the puck out of our net and stay healthy. The Canadiens are well-rested — just long enough since Tuesday — to have the advantage."

Since the mid 1950s, little Hodge had toiled in the shadow of Jacques Plante, spending most of his time in the Canadiens' farm system. In June 1963, with Plante traded to the Rangers, Hodge finally got his big break. Gump came over from New York in a backup role.

The differences between the two puck-stoppers were vast, and rather entertaining. While Hodge seldom drank anything stronger than milkshakes, the Gumper liked the strong stuff. Hodge was always fretting about something, always looking for the shortcomings in his game, while the portly Worsley was about as happy-go-lucky as they come. Hodge counted his pennies; Worsley threw his money around like a drunken sailor. But there was one common between the two goalies: they were both loved by their teammates.

Les Canadiens were missing a key player in defenseman Jacques Laperriere, who had broken his leg in the semifinals against Toronto. Veteran Jean-Guy Talbot filled his spot, while Noel Picard would serve as the extra.

There was a huge buzz in the sports, and fashion, world about how Chicago's Golden Jet, Bobby Hull, appeared to be losing his hair and was growing "long, heavy sideburns, the like of which have never before been seen on a pro sport headliner." The Montreal *Gazette*'s Vern DeGeer commented, "I wouldn't be surprised if he's going to make a movie; there was talk of it a couple of years ago."

Game One

After Toe Blake had spent a week building up his decision to start Charlie Hodge in game one, it was Worsley who turned up in the Habs' nets. No one was more surprised than Gump. "Just before the game, the coach asked me how I felt," Worsley said. "I said I was all right and he said, 'Okay, you'll play.'" Blake denied the charge that it was a tactic he used to confuse the Hawks. "I changed my mind, just like a woman," he said.

The first period opened with the legendary Danny Gallivan doing the *Hockey Night in Canada* play-by-play and Keith Dancy providing color. About 7:20 into the match, Canadiens bruiser John Ferguson was nailed for elbowing rookie Doug Jarrett. The Chicago power-play unit of Hull, Phil Esposito, sickly-looking Camille Henry, and Chico Maki took the ice for the second time in the game.

Montreal did a fine job of containing the Hawks, succeeding in keeping the puck off Hull's stick. Kudos went to Claude Provost, who was all over Hull like a wet, smelly blanket. Although the first frame was a speedy one, there was no score. Chicago outshot Montreal 10–7. As the final whistle sounded, Eric Nesterenko tried to start something with Montreal toughie Ted Harris. Nesterenko wisely decided to skate away.

In the opening moments of the middle frame, Worsley robbed Hull on a breakaway. A minute later, it was Henri Richard taking a nice pass from Red Berenson and blasting a 30-footer past Glenn Hall. The lead wouldn't last long. At 4:47, Hull let loose a thundering slapper on the power play which Henry tipped in. Camille Henry was one of the NHL's greatest all-time power-play specialists. Fifteen of his 26 goals in 1964–65 came with the man advantage.

At 8:59 of the final session, with the score 2–2 (Ferguson had scored for Montreal, Matt Ravlich for Chicago), Yvan Cournoyer netted the game-winner for the Frenchmen after a pretty setup by big Jean Beliveau.

Mikita, "Diesel" Doug Mohns, and a young Johnny McKenzie showed some remarkable combination play and diligent corner-work. But the rest of the Hawks started to droop as a result of coach Reay's shortened bench. Hull was especially frustrated … and with little wonder! The Golden Boy had been shadowed almost every step of the way by the annoying but effective Provost, who limited him to only one shot on Worsley. "Joe [Provost] did a heck of a job on Hull," the Gumper clucked. "He checked him like crazy."

Overall, Montreal outshot Chicago 32–24.

Blake summed up the game somewhat tersely: "They can play a lot better than that and we'll have to play a whale of a lot better if we expect to win the series."

Chicago GM Tommy Ivan was left singing the blues after this one: "We missed Pilote on our power play. Of course, we did get two power-play goals but we didn't look too dangerous on the other two occasions when we had a man advantage."

Game Two

Talbot, Provost, Ted Harris, and Jimmy Roberts checked like hellcats as the Canadiens took the second game 2–0 on goals by Beliveau and Dick Duff. Beliveau, the first star for the second straight game, summed up the win with these words: "When you win 2–0 just about everybody has to be playing well. This was a little tougher game than last Saturday but we didn't give them many good scoring chances. At the same time, I still think we can skate better."

Worsley, who chalked up his first ever playoff shutout, kicking aside 18 shots, was jubilant after the game. "They played better but the guys checked them closer tonight."

Provost, assigned to shadow Chicago's Golden Jet once again, skated with Hull virtually all the way, annoying the high-flying Hawk to the point that he started running his opponents and taking stupid penalties. "If he's getting mad, that's okay

Marcel Bonin (right) and Jean-Guy Talbot

with me," Provost giggled. "That means I must be checking him pretty good. He was trying to give it to me a little bit but I don't mind, I've been hit before." Hull was asked if it was Provost's checking or his own playing that plagued his performance, to which the Golden Boy replied: "I imagine it's Provost." Blake was bubbling over with glee about Provost's work: "Claude Provost's two games against Hull have to be his best ever!"

Blake had a problem on his hands, despite the outcome of these first two games: since the hometown Hawks would now have the last line change before face-offs, it would be harder to get Provost on the ice during Hull's shifts. "It all depends on how fast and how well Provost can jump over the boards," Blake said, an indication that most of his changes would be made on the fly. "We've got another good checker in Jimmy Roberts. He doesn't have the sustained skating power of Provost, but he should be able to do a fair job in spurts."

Hull had his sideburns trimmed at the request of *Hockey Night in Canada*'s television sponsors, who thought they detracted from his all-Canadian image.

Game Three

The Chicagoans showed they still had some life in them, beating Montreal 3–1. Ironically, Ken Wharram and Pierre Pilote, until now watching from the sidelines, were the ones who ignited Chicago's return to form with big performances before a full house of more than 18,000. Wharram, who had been poison against the Canadiens in the regular season, connected for the winner during the third minute of the final frame. "It was one of the best goals I've seen Kenny score this season," Billy Reay smiled. Stan Mikita, who played by far his strongest game of the series, was impressed by Wharram's dekes. "The Gump is still looking for his underwear," Mikita said.

The teams matched markers 47 seconds apart in the second period, Ferguson for Montreal and big Phil Esposito for Chicago. According to Worsley, Espo kicked the puck in. The Gumper actually waddled out to center ice to argue his case with referee John Ashley. "Everybody in the rink saw him kick it in but the three stooges," Worsley groused after the game. "He steered it into the net."

Twenty-three seconds before the final siren, Gump became involved with the endzone fans after outbursts of fighting on the ice. The dumpy little guy claimed to have been struck by empty beer cups, coins, and finally by a slat from a Stadium seat. "That's when I blew it." Worsley tried to get at the taunting fans but was unable to overcome the glass partition.

Thanks to a pregame shot Pilote swore wasn't cortisone but a new wonder drug called DMSO (dimethyl sulfoxide), he went on to make a big difference. He was probably the sole reason the Canadiens were unable to control the puck in enemy territory. "It's some new kind of stuff, that burns like blazes," Pilote said of the medication used to numb his shoulder. "I guess I'll get to play again Sunday night."

Game Four

Hull popped in a pair of goals, including the winner, as Chicago trounced the Canadiens 5–1 in game four. Chicago struck for four goals in the final frame alone.

Hodge was in nets for Montreal, replacing Worsley. No, it wasn't the pennies and empty beer glasses that hurt Gump; it was a thigh injury he suffered during the pregame warmup. Hodge was caught napping on a mighty 70-foot slapper from Hull that went in for the winner just 26 seconds into the third.

Despite being outclassed, Montreal outshot the Black Hawks on this night, 26–25.

The Canadiens were their own worst enemy, racking up 15 penalties to Chicago's 8. Referee Vern Buffey seemed intimidated by the noisy Stadium crowd of more than 20,000 and the Hawks took advantage, falling almost every time they came in contact with a Canadien. Blake set a controlled tirade against Buffey from the bench; as the final siren sounded, he stormed out onto the ice and started mouthing off at Buffey. Trainer Andy Galley managed to calm down the steaming skipper. Outside the Montreal dressing room, Blake challenged the scribes: "Let me see how much guts you fellows have. You saw the game and the refereeing, so write about it."

Montreal GM Sam Pollock wasn't crying about the loss, although he refused to pull any punches: "All I ask is that the same circumstances prevail in Montreal on Tuesday. The crowd certainly influenced the referee tonight. There's something funny when a team that plays our type of hockey takes that many more penalties than the home team." Chicago enjoyed 10 power plays.

Game Five

Emotions ran high from the get-go in this one. In the opening frame, Nesterenko high sticked Ferguson at the Chicago end boards. The strapping Montreal winger lost it. The gloves flew into the air and, like a bolt of lightning, he tore into Nesterenko's face with a flurry of hooks, jabs, and crosses. The tall Hawk skulked from the ice like a frightened tot, his face a soft, bloody pulp. Ferguson's pummeling of Nesterenko seemed to demoralize Chicago, and it would prove to be the turning point in the series. Strangely, while Ferguson received a major for fighting, Nesterenko got only a double minor — two minutes for roughing and two for high sticking. Thoroughly disgusted, Ferguson slammed his stick against the side of the penalty box. Nesterenko, who would spend the rest of the first period in the Forum infirmary, took six stitches under his left eye.

Goals by Beliveau and Duff put Montreal up by two by the first bell.

Red Fisher asked former Montreal winger Floyd "Busher" Curry if he'd ever seen a harder right hand than the one that floored Nesterenko. Curry mentioned an instance in the late 1950s when Maurice Richard decked Ted Lindsay.

In the middle frame, Beliveau and J.C. Tremblay were brilliant. In a typically dazzling play, Beliveau skated down the right side and, behind the Chicago net, passed the puck back to Tremblay. The fleet rusher feathered the puck across to Bobby Rousseau, who whizzed a shot past Hall to make it 3–0 Montreal. In the third period, with Denis DeJordy spelling Hall in nets, Beliveau and Henri Richard counted to make it 5–0. Near the end of the period, following a flock of penalties, Tremblay stole the rubber at the Hawk blue-line, skated in alone and scored shorthanded to make it 6–0. Programs and toe rubbers littered the ice.

After the game, Ferguson commented on his scrap with Nesterenko: "That Nesterenko clipped me three or four times earlier on in the series and I told him he was going to get it. So tonight he got it. He whacked me on the back of the head with his stick again. What could I do but clout him? I don't know if that's the best punch I've ever thrown but it wasn't the worst." Ferguson went to say, "I don't know if it was the turning point but it sure spoiled Nesterenko's night."

Toe Blake said, "There was no turning point [in game five]. Our whole team was up for this one. Besides those Hawks have taken some good punches before." A stunned Billy Reay countered, "Geez, [the Canadiens] were flying so high they ought to have had saliva tests done on them. We just weren't in the game tonight."

After announcing his three game stars, Ted Lindsay noted that "the tremendous beating Nesterenko received from Ferguson certainly demoralized Chicago's spirits and affected the outcome of this game."

Lindsay's three stars of the game were Jean Beliveau (first star), Henri Richard, and Claude Provost.

Game Six

In a do-or-die scenario, Chicago came up with the goods against the Canadiens, edging them by a 2–1 count. Twelve-year veteran Doug Mohns became a Hawk hero at the nine-minute mark of the final period when an errant Mikita feed bounced off his left skate and past Hodge for the winner. "I missed the puck with my stick and it went in off my skate," said Mohns, who also figured on the first Chicago goal.

Elmer "Moose" Vasko, who scored only once in the regular season, netted his second career playoff marker. "The puck was bouncing and I wanted to make sure the puck hit both goalposts before it came out on the far side of the net," Vasko said. "Hodge was out of the play and didn't have a chance."

For the most part, Chicago came up with a strong performance, outshooting Montreal 24–22. "I think we deserved to win this one," Reay said afterwards. "If it hadn't been for Hodge's fine goaltending in the first two periods, we certainly wouldn't have been behind by a goal at that point."

At the beginning of the third, with the game knotted at one, a monstrously huge Stadium crowd of well over 20,000 began a thunderous chant of "Go Hawks Go!" "The fans just wouldn't let the Hawks die," Pollock said after the game, "but I think we played pretty well despite the loss; we should be able to beat them in the seventh game."

Blake was clearly irritated with the reporters and their leading questions about the officiating. After a particularly annoying question, he snarled: "I don't want to criticize anyone. Quit trying to get me to say things. You saw the game same as I did … Listen, I saw an extra Chicago man on the ice for 25 seconds and then [Terry] Harper gets a penalty for pulling Hull down. Did you see how many times Henri [Richard] was pulled down from behind?"

Heading into the winner-take-all seventh game, here's how the playoff scoring race was shaping up:

Player	Club	G	A	Pts
Bobby Hull	Chicago	10	7	17
Jean Beliveau	Montreal	7	7	14
Chico Maki	Chicago	3	9	12
Norm Ullman	Detroit	6	4	10

Henri Richard	Montreal	6	4	10
Bobby Rousseau	Montreal	5	5	10
Stan Mikita	Chicago	3	7	10
J.C. Tremblay	Montreal	1	9	10

Sportswriters had either Hull or Beliveau winning the Conn Smythe Trophy as playoff MVP, Hull because he was leading the scoring race despite being stuffed and cuffed by Montreal's checking crew.

Game Seven: Les Canadiens Sont Là!

In game seven at the Forum, Montreal snuffed out the Black Hawks 4–0. It was Montreal's first Stanley Cup in five seasons, but their sixth in 10 years under the guidance of Toe Blake. Beliveau, who would cop the first ever Conn Smythe Trophy, opened the scoring 14 seconds in. Goals by Duff, Richard, and Cournoyer before the end of the opening session brought Chicago's hopes of winning their second Cup of the '60s crashing to the ground. Provost and Jimmy Roberts, who checked like fiends throughout the game, disarmed the Hawks' big guns.

"I was glad to see the fourth one go into the net," Toe Blake said. "Gump made some big saves when it was 2–0 and one Chicago goal at that point might have made a difference in the game … This was the greatest championship of them all for me. We had no true superstars like the other five years and tonight, after we took the lead, the fellows never stopped skating or checking."

Reay offered "No excuses, no alibis. We were stoned, beaten by a better team. Skating is most of this game and they outskated us. They also seemed stronger at center than us … We've come in here three times during this series without scoring a goal and this is the club that scored the most goals during the regular season. That should tell the whole story."

"That first goal after 14 seconds sank us," according to Pierre Pilote. "I knew Dick Duff was going to fire it in there but nobody could move to stop it from getting to Beliveau. We also didn't penetrate their defense. Tremblay played a great series for them, I've never seen him play so well."

Forum organist Leo Duplessis played "Auld Lang Syne" as the victors and the vanquished shook hands at center ice. He swung into his rendition of "Prendre un Petit Coup" as Blake was hoisted above the Stanley Cup by his players, then into "Happy Days Are Here Again" as Beliveau carried the Cup around the rink. As the weary but jubilant Canadiens left the ice, a group of fans among the 15,740 in attendance lent their vocal support to the celebration, singing "Les Canadiens Sont Là."

Ferguson bounded around the Canadiens' dressing room like a gorilla under a banana tree, shaking hands with everyone. "Can you believe it?" he cried. "In the American league two years ago and now on the Stanley Cup team. Just great!"

Of all the Canadiens, though, Worsley was on the highest cloud. Having slaved and toiled for some bad teams in New York throughout the 1950s, he richly deserved his taste of champagne from the Cup. "It's hard to put into words just how I feel about this," he said between nervous puffs on a cigarette. "When you play in the minors you wonder sometimes if you'll ever get back. I guess I did."

> **Stanley Cup records broken during the 1965 finals:**
> • Blake's sixth Cup win behind the bench broke Hap Day's old record of five.
> • Most penalties in a playoff series — 136
> • Most penalty minutes in a playoff series by a team — 185 by Montreal

The 1965 finals were the litmus test for the Montreal Canadiens. As the Rocket Richard era began slowly to fade from memory, this Cup win was proof the "new" Habs of the '60s had arrived. General manager Sam Pollock had stuck with a core of veterans such as Beliveau, Henri Richard, and Provost, and built around them with the likes of Bobby Rousseau, Gilles and J.C. Tremblay, Jacques Laperriere, and a dumpy little goalie who loved beer and donuts — Gump Worsley.

This would be the beginning of a beautiful Cup run for Montreal, who would take three of the next four championships. If not for a surprise Cup win by Toronto in 1967, the Canadiens might have won five in a row for the second straight decade!

For their part, the Black Hawks were no slouches. They had pushed the Canadiens to seven games in the 1965 finals. The latter half of the decade would see them dominate the regular season, only to fold like a house of cards in the playoffs. Many would point to Reay's lax coaching style, arguing that if the Hawks had been a bit more disciplined there might be at least one more Stanley Cup banner hanging from the United Center rafters today.

No Fun for The Gumper

It was seven o'clock on a cold, blustery Monday morning in January 1966 as the Montreal Canadiens plodded into a coffee shop at Montreal's Dorval Airport. Trainer Andy Galley grinned like a chimpanzee as Gump Worsley sat down and turned up his sweaty palms to show all what happens when a yellowbelly flies the friendly skies.

Like most eastern cities that January, Boston was recovering from a weekend blizzard, and Toe Blake had been unable to contact Logan Airport to find out if the team's flight was grounded. Worsley, who hated flying, had his fingers crossed that the flight would be canceled and they'd come home by milk train. (On the trip down to Boston from Montreal, a freight had been good enough to transport the Canadiens. The Gumper enjoyed the leisurely trip, which stopped for donuts and coffee in Albany and a relaxed breakfast of bacon and eggs in Springfield. "Mmmm, I love them sinkers [donuts]," he drooled. "They aren't too great for my waistline, but boy, do they taste good!")

The Canadiens arrived at the airport to discover their flight hadn't been canceled. The Gumper (and a few others) shuddered as they watched a maintenance man sweep loads of snow off the plane's wings. Twenty minutes later, after several failed attempts to talk his way out of flying, Worsley gripped the arm of his seat as the plane taxied into position. While waiting his turn to take off, the pilot gunned the engines and there was a loud backfire as he cut them back to normal. "That's when I was ready to take off," Worsley whimpered afterwards.

Jean-Guy Talbot had the pleasure of sitting beside the Gumper during the flight, which went off without a hitch. "I don't think I'll be able to bowl now," Talbot chuckled, pointing to the bruised right arm Worsley had gripped for dear life.

While Worsley's teammates sympathized with their acrophobic goaltender, they couldn't help but rib him about it. "Believe me, it's never funny," Worsley protested. "I don't know what it is. I've tried talking myself out of it and have taken tranquilizers. I'd even try getting hypnotized, but I doubt if I'm smart enough for that." Jackie Jensen of the Boston Red Sox said Newk's fear of flying was one of the reasons he quit baseball.

Bruno

If a fellow knew his way around monstrous Chicago Stadium, he could save a lot of time getting from one dressing room to another. Leaving the press box, which hung just below the first balcony, he could double-time the stairs up to ice level, make a left turn and take a short flight of stairs to the visitors' dressing room. A few more stairs would lead to the storage basement and a clear passage to the Black Hawks' dressing room at the other end of the building. Without this shortcut, after a hockey game, when thousands of fans began elbowing their way through the corridors, he might be caught in a human traffic jam. But a reporter could get an awful scare if he hadn't heard of Bruno, perhaps the greatest "unknown" Chicago Black Hawk.

Bruno wasn't a player or a coach but a huge German Shepherd who barked as if he hadn't had a square meal in a month. This infamous Stadium doggie lived in an 8-by-8-foot cage, and he was known on occasion to escape his chicken-wire home. And after every game or attraction, it was time for Bruno to go to work with the Stadium's sleepy night watchman, Smokey Johnson. His duties included sniffing out those who hid in the building after games, planning on looting coin boxes.

"We drafted Bruno from St. Louis and Gus Kyle, the [St. Louis] Flyers' coach, claimed it killed his hockey team," Chicago publicity man Don Murphy said. "He had been working in St. Louis at an amusement park before it was demolished by a tornado and so the Hawks 'called him up' along with Doug Jarrett and Fred Stanfield!"

Only Smokey and three other people on staff at the Stadium were on speaking terms with Bruno. "We had to send them to school so they could work with him," Murphy said. "He's a lot better than having these guys with guns. They might wind up shooting each other."

Arthur Wirtz, then co-owner of the Black Hawks, had a way of his own with the dog. "He's crazy about Bruno and vice versa," Murphy gushed. "Every once in a while Wirtz whips down from the Bismarck Hotel downtown with a bag full of choice steaks."

The strange thing about Bruno for a number of years was that he was never formally "introduced" to any of the Black Hawk players. In 1965, after the team arrived back from a road trip by plane, Ken Wharram forgot about Bruno and stepped through the side door of the Stadium. The brave little winger might have lost an arm if Bruno hadn't been called off in time.

Arf, arf!

A New Era

When the Brooklyn Americans died after the 1941–42 season, the NHL became a six-team entity, with Boston, Chicago, Detroit, Montreal, New York Rangers, and Toronto the pieces of the "Original Six" puzzle. While the title was a misnomer — organized hockey pre-dates the birth of the oldest Original Six franchise by more than 20 years — these years represent for many hockey's golden era. Intense, often bloody, rivalries blossomed in the six-team league. With teams facing one another up to 14 times a season, there was ample time to develop grudges and nurse them. Detroit's Gordie Howe played the "revenge game" very well, often waiting months to exact his pound of flesh from a rival.

World War Two dampened the early years of the "new" NHL, as most wartime rosters were left as bare as Mother Hubbard's cupboard. The 1942–43 Bruins featured a player, left winger Bep Guidolin, who was a month from his 17th birthday when the season began. The New York Rangers lost so many players to military service that team bigwigs talked of closing up shop for a few years. Fortunately, this did not happen, but in 1943–44, they had an awful season, posting a 6-39-5 record. The best goalie they could come up with, Ken "Tubby" McAuley, allowed a league-record 310 goals in 50 games, for a whopping 6.20 goals-against average — still the highest ever! Eventually, the hostilities ended overseas, and the talent level not only returned to pre-war levels, it was enriched by the entry during the mid 1940s of such rookies as Rocket Richard, Gordie Howe, and Ted Kennedy.

Immediately after the war, there was a boom in minor-league hockey. Where there'd been only 13 clubs in two leagues in 1944–45, the next season saw the foundation of the United States Hockey League, the Pacific Coast Hockey League, the Quebec Senior Hockey League, the International Hockey League, and the Western Canada Senior Hockey League. The American league grew from eight to 10 teams. And representatives of both Philadelphia and Los Angeles had designs on securing NHL franchises. Len Peto and his Philadelphia group attempted to purchase the dormant Montreal Maroons franchise and move it to the City of Brotherly Love. Peto would ultimately fail to fulfill the conditions the NHL set out and his bid would fall as flat as week-old soda. The league cited travel problems — in those days it was a 39-hour train ride from Chicago to the coast — as the basis for rejecting L.A.'s application.

Frank Boucher, one of the more astute thinkers in the history of the game, proposed a massive expansion in 1951. According to the former Ranger star, a 12-team league, split into two divisions, was just around the corner. In an interview with *The Hockey News*, he outlined a plan calling for NHL rosters to be cut back to 15 players. The surplus, he reasoned, would stock the expansion teams. His vision looked something like this:

Eastern Division	**Western Division**
Boston	Buffalo
Montreal	Chicago
New York	Cincinnati

Ottawa	Cleveland
Quebec City	Detroit
Toronto	St. Louis

Interestingly enough, five of the six cities Boucher cited in 1951 as expansion sites would eventually host an NHL franchise, with varying degrees of success — Cincinnati was the lone exception. Boucher's forward-thinking plan also called for an amateur draft to be established as a way to break the monopoly certain teams had on talent — Montreal's stranglehold on Quebecois players, for instance, or Toronto's lock over Northern Ontario. The league's governors paid the notion no mind — it would not be until 1963 that the league instituted the Amateur Draft.

In 1952, James Hendy, general manager of the AHL's Barons, thought he would be the man to bring big-league hockey to Cleveland. Although NHL president Clarence Campbell spoke favorably of the idea, and Hendy fulfilled the league's initial requirements for financial backing and local ownership, the league ultimately turned thumbs-down — "not enough working capital," they decreed — and the NHL remained an elite domain of six teams.

During the 1950s, the nature of sport changed dramatically with the advent of air travel and coast-to-coast television. In August 1957, the New York Giants and Brooklyn Dodgers announced they were moving to San Francisco and Los Angeles, respectively. The Boston Braves had already moved to Milwaukee, and the Philadelphia A's to Kansas City; the sport was no longer concentrated along the Eastern Seaboard. In 1946, the NFL's Cleveland Rams moved to L.A., while the San Francisco 49ers had joined in 1950 when the league merged with the All-American Football Conference.

Hockey seemed unmoved by the changes sweeping the other major sports. But the Boston Bruins and Toronto Maple Leafs played a pair of preseason games in Los Angeles in 1960, and the size of the crowds was encouraging. Still, if the NHL brass had any expansion plans, they remained tight-lipped. In 1962, president Clarence Campbell broke the silence to say, "The league is not actively promoting or encouraging expansion of the numbers of its members at this time." Toronto major domo Conn Smythe threw in his two cents' worth: "There aren't enough players. Too many clubs are now short ... Take [Gordie] Howe away from Detroit and they'd have nothing."

Meanwhile, baseball had added teams in Los Angeles (which now had two clubs but no major-league ballparks), Washington (to replace the original franchise, which had moved to Minneapolis–St. Paul), Houston, and New York (to fill the void the Dodgers and Giants had left). In football, the upstart American Football League brought the game to non-NFL outposts such as Kansas City, Buffalo, Houston, and San Diego. Basketball also began to carve out western territory: in 1960 the Minneapolis Lakers moved to Los Angeles, while the Philadelphia Warriors shifted to San Francisco.

By 1964, Clarence Campbell had changed his tune. He now felt that "expansion is inevitable" and on March 11, 1965, the league announced it would expand, adding a new six-team division. Easy breezy. Deciding where the teams would come from was another kettle of fish.

A raft of cities threw their hats into the ring: Atlanta, Baltimore, Buffalo, Cleveland, L.A., Louisville, Minneapolis–St. Paul, Philadelphia, Pittsburgh, San Diego, San Francisco, Seattle, and Vancouver. League sources pegged six markets — Baltimore, L.A., Pittsburgh, San Francisco, St. Louis (which hadn't even applied for a franchise), and Vancouver — as the favorites. In February 1967, the league announced the winners, and Oakland would represent the Bay Area, while Baltimore and Vancouver were shut out in favor of Philly and the Twin Cities.

Baltimore's bid was done in by its arena. It featured a giant, permanent stage at one end, and it only seated about 12,500. New York Ranger president William Jennings said the league had outgrown rinks that size. The NHL was all in favor of bringing Baltimore aboard as long as the stage could be replaced with seats. But Baltimore's civic fathers refused, insisting the arena played host to a number of events that made use of the stage.

In September 1965, Campbell said excitedly that "It looks like Vancouver will go." The city was planning to build a new arena, which would cost an estimated $12 million. Early reports had the province of British Columbia pledging $6 million for the project, while the federal government would pitch in another $2 million. Then the province announced it was only willing to pony up $4 million, and even that amount would only be handed over when the federal government matched it. (The Canadian government help support sports franchises? Perish the thought.)

If the bid wasn't dead already, it was given a final stab when Cy McLean, head of B.C. Telephone, and legendary broadcaster Foster Hewitt traveled to New York to present their franchise application. McLean and Hewitt were sadly unprepared for the meeting, and did little to impress the expansion committee. There would be no hockey in Vancouver for now.

Now that the franchises had been awarded, there remained the question of who would play for the new clubs. After much wrangling, the NHL decided that an Expansion Draft would be held on June 6, 1967, in Montreal, giving the new teams only about four months to prepare. Each of the six new outfits would select 20 men from a list of players submitted by the Original Six teams. Each of the established clubs could protect one goalie and 11 skaters, and every time a team lost a player to the draft, it was allowed to protect one more. Terry Sawchuk was the first goalie selected, by the Kings, while Dave Balon was the first skater.

Los Angeles Kings

Los Angeles had a great minor-league hockey tradition, with the WHL Blades and the PCHL Monarchs. From the start, L.A., the largest market on the West Coast, would be the focal point of the Great Expansion. Owned by multimillionaire Jack Kent Cooke, the Kings burst out of the starting gates. They went undefeated in their first five games and were actually the last NHL club to lose a game in the 1967–68 season. Cooke, who had once played in the house band at a bar that Leafs legend Charlie Conacher owned, did things right when he built the Kings. He hired Red Kelly as coach, bought the AHL's Springfield Indians as a farm team, and drafted the great Sawchuk. Bill Flett and Ed Joyal provided the offense as Cooke's men finished second in their division before bowing out to Minnesota in the playoffs.

Minnesota North Stars

Minneapolis–St. Paul seemed a logical expansion site for many reasons. Minnesota was a high school and college hockey stronghold, and the NFL and Major League Baseball had successfully exploited the region. The spanking new Metropolitan Sports Center would be the home of the North Stars, who were run by Wren Blair, the man who had discovered Bobby Orr. Paced by the spectacular goaltending of Cesare Maniago and the timely scoring of Wayne Connelly and Ray Cullen, Minnesota scored a modest amount of success early on. After five seasons, the Stars' aggregate record sat at a respectable 129-173-80 for a .442 winning percentage.

Oakland Seals

Oakland was destined to be the misfit of the expansion bunch from day one. The franchise was headed by 28-year-old Barry Van Gerbig, a former Princeton varsity goalie and the backup to Jack McCartan on the gold medal–winning U.S. Olympic Team of 1960. Under his stewardship, the Seals would be known for promotional gimmickry, financial troubles, front-office instability, and on-ice impotence.

Van Gerbig owned parts of Standard Oil of New Jersey (now Exxon) and Union Carbide, as well as the Western league's San Francisco Seals. But the most important factor in his landing the franchise seems to be his close friendship with New York Ranger president Bill Jennings, who was on the NHL's expansion committee. His godfather, crooner Bing Crosby, was — don't laugh — part of the ownership group.

The league had its heart set on placing a club in the Bay Area, preferably in San Francisco. In fact, the NHL's television contract with CBS required there to be a team in northern California. But when "The City" — as the NBA's San Francisco Warriors' uniforms proclaimed — was unable to guarantee an adequate arena, all eyes were turned to Oakland, which boasted a brand-new arena but also had a smaller, poorer population.

The baby Oakland Seals named former Leaf and Canadiens star Bert Olmstead as their coach and general manager. They had selected quality players such as goalie Charlie Hodge, defenseman Bobby Baun, and Gerry Ehman, Bill Hicke, and Larry Cahan up front. But after racking up a record of 11-37-16, Olmstead was turfed in favor of former WHL star Gordie Fashoway. Attendance for the basement-dwelling Seals had sunk so low that there was talk of moving the team. The rumor mill had it that Labatt Breweries were offering a substantial sum to buy the club and move it to Vancouver. Any talk of a move was squelched at a league meeting in March 1968, where the owners voted 8-4 to leave the team in Oakland for the time being.

Philadelphia Flyers

Although conventional wisdom had it that Philadelphians would not support hockey, the Flyers would prove to be the most successful of the six expansion clubs of 1967. The boys in orange and black would play out of a brand-new arena, the Spectrum, coached by Keith "Bingo" Allen while former Leaf Bud Poile took on GM duties. Bernie Parent and Doug Favell, the youngest goalie combination in the NHL, were also the best pair among the six new teams. Brit Selby, Gary Dornhoefer, and Leon

Rochefort notched goals aplenty while 39-year-old Larry Zeidel, returning to the NHL after 13 years in the minors, solidified the defense. A first-place finish in the new West Division meant a quarterfinal match-up with the St. Louis Blues, who overcame the Flyers in seven games behind the brilliant goaltending of Glenn Hall.

Pittsburgh Penguins

At the turn of the twentieth century, Pittsburgh was one of the most important hockey centers in the U.S. It had been home to a team in the old International Professional league, and a local team, the Bankers, had played the Stanley Cup champion Montreal Wanderers in 1908 in the first "World Series of Hockey." And from 1925–26 through 1929–30, Pittsburgh would ice the Pirates, who in 212 regular-season contests had a miserable 67-122-23 record. The Pirates moved to Philadelphia in 1930 and the city of Pittsburgh would be left without big-league hockey … until 1967.

The expansion Penguins were coached in their first year by former NHL pivot George "Red" Sullivan. As the season opened, the Penguins were generally thought to have the most potent offense of the expansion teams, boasting Andy Bathgate, Earl Ingarfield, Val Fonteyne, and Ab McDonald. The player who would capture the hearts of Steeltown, though, was Les Binkley. The 31-year-old goaltender, the former Cleveland Baron, was good for six shutouts in the Penguins' inaugural campaign. Unfortunately, he broke his finger down the stretch and the Penguins would finish two points behind Minnesota for the final playoff spot.

St. Louis Blues

St. Louis was home to the NHL long before the Blues arrived in 1967. In 1934, there were the Eagles, who had transferred from Ottawa. Their folding a year later would give the hockey market back to the minor-league Flyers, who would last for almost 20 more years.

St. Louis was the final city to acquire a franchise in 1967. It is rumored that Arthur Wirtz, who owned the Chicago Black Hawks at the time, cleared St. Louis's path to the NHL personally. Wirtz controlled the city's arena, and he was looking to unload it. A team in St. Louis would provide him with a buyer for his rink as well as a natural geographic rival for his Hawks. The fact that St. Louis hadn't filed an official application did not seem to rankle the NHL's expansion committee, who reserved a coveted slot for the Missouri city. The Salomon family stepped forward to buy the club, but they were only allowed into the lodge when they agreed to take over the aging St. Louis Arena as well.

One of the necessary offshoots of the Great Expansion was the evolution of the Amateur Draft (renamed the Entry Draft in 1979). No longer would NHL teams have first crack at signing all Junior prospects, some as young as 14, within their areas and assigning them to club-sponsored Junior teams. The old guard would be forced to scout extensively for young talent, a situation that eventually had them tapping Europe and the U.S. high school and college systems. Teams that drafted well, like the Flyers and Canadiens, would become successful. Those that didn't, like Oakland, would have trouble fielding a competitive team.

On the ice, the Blues were tough. Built from the nets out, if not with an eye on the future, St. Louis had one of the stingiest defenses in the entire league. Glenn Hall, at 36, was the team's first netminder. Noel Picard and Al Arbour teamed with Barclay and Bob Plager on the Blues' blue-line. Up front, former University of Michigan star Gordon "Red" Berenson led a front line of Gerry Melnyk, Jimmy Roberts, and Frank St. Marseille.

A third-place finish gave St. Louis the honor of facing the Flyers in the quarter-finals. After grinding down Philadelphia in the full seven games, it was on to the North Stars, then to the Stanley Cup finals against the Montreal Canadiens, who swept them in four straight. A bitter defeat, but a delicious debut season.

Expansion teams really did not have all that much fun in 1967–68. Collectively, their record against the East Division, the so-called Original Six, was 40-86-18. Although none of the new teams finished above .500, the playoffs were entertaining, as all three West Division playoff series went the full seven games.

When expansion plans were discussed, the playoff format was one of the issues that needed to be resolved. One proposal had teams playing the first round within their division, then crossing over for the semifinals. But everybody knew the expansion teams were no match for the established clubs, and a raft of early playoff exits was no way to build interest in the new cities. Ultimately it was decided that the semifinals would be played within the division as well, thus guaranteeing an expansion team would be in the Stanley Cup finals.

It has been suggested that the NHL wanted to make sure expansion teams could make the finals because it would lead to a more lucrative TV contract — a plausible theory, since a U.S. network deal was one of the key factors driving the Great Expansion. CBS had been televising the occasional game since the 1950s, although never on a national level. NBC jumped on board for the 1966 playoffs, but could not agree with the NHL on a deal for the 1966–67 season. CBS jumped in, banking that the new, coast-to-coast NHL would deliver a major return on their investment.

Did the NHL do the right thing by expanding in 1967? Absolutely. Detractors may point out that only two of the "Second Six" franchises have won a Stanley Cup — the Flyers in 1974 and '75, the Penguins in 1991 and '92. Or they may point to the failure of the Oakland Seals (moved to Cleveland in 1976 before folding two seasons later) and Minnesota North Stars (moved to Dallas in 1993 after years of financial woes). But the Great Expansion dragged the NHL out of its regional status onto an

---

Expansion extended the careers of those already in the big league — Hall of Famers like Glenn Hall, Terry Sawchuk, Jacques Plante, Dickie Moore, and Doug Harvey all got in a few extra years. Players who'd never been quite good enough to crack an NHL lineup before 1967 also prospered. Consider Red Berenson, who'd scored 16 goals in 185 games over six seasons before St. Louis gave him a break in November 1967. He scored 35 goals, including six in one game, in 1968–69. Bill Goldsworthy, a Boston farmhand, would emerge as Minnesota's top sniper, potting 48 in 1973–74. Three goalies would emerge from relative obscurity: Minnesota's Cesare Maniago, Philly's Bernie Parent, and Pittsburgh's Les Binkley.

international stage. There will be 30 clubs in the NHL in the 2000–2001 season, representing states like Florida, Texas, North Carolina, and Tennessee. (If only Clarence Campbell had heeded Frank Boucher's advice 15 years before, today, fans might spend Saturday nights cheering the Stockholm Tre Kronor as they lock horns with the Tokyo Tornadoes.) The extra teams have led to an influx of talent from around the world. And it could be argued that the United States' 1996 win at the World Cup of Hockey would not have been possible if the NHL were still a six-team backwater, populated almost exclusively by Canadians.

Snap!shots

GEORGE ARMSTRONG (The Chief) Center/Right Wing
6'1" 195
b. 7/6/1930, Skead, Ontario

George Armstrong

George Armstrong was your basic jack-of-all-trades — a player who did not stand out in any one area yet was very solid in all facets of the game. Although the Chief, who scored a career-high 23 goals for the Toronto Maple Leafs in 1959–60, failed to garner a single All-Star nomination, he did make seven appearances in the NHL All-Star game.

Like many Leaf hopefuls, Armstrong played his Junior hockey with the Toronto Marlboros and won the Allan Cup with the Senior Marlies in 1949–50. After being shuffled in and out of the Leafs lineup for a couple of years, the big forward caught on for good in 1952–53. The youngster from northern Ontario's Nickel Belt made an impact almost immediately, playing brilliantly in the trenches and on the penalty kill. In 52 games, he scored 14 goals and a respectable 25 points.

Toronto named Armstrong, who was renowned for his leadership, team captain in 1957. He held the post until Dave Keon took over in 1969. Armstrong remains the only Leaf to captain four Stanley Cup champions. He retired after the 1969–70 campaign, but was coaxed out of retirement for the 1970–71 season. After 19 full seasons with the blue and white, "Army" decided to call it a career. In a club-record 1,187 games, he scored 296 goals and 713 points, playing a huge role in Toronto's four Cup wins between 1962 and 1967. "He did more for the Maple Leafs than any other hockey player who played for me," wrote Punch Imlach in *Hockey Is a Battle*.

Armstrong was elected to the Hockey Hall of Fame in 1975.

Peak Years   *1958–62*
In a Word   *MUD*

RALPH BACKSTROM Center
5'10" 170
b. 9/18/1937, Kirkland Lake, Ontario

During his last season as a Junior, Ralph Backstrom was generally thought to be the finest young hockey player in Canada. He counted 45 goals and 97 points on the Memorial Cup–winning Hull-Ottawa Canadiens of 1958. The young center was a fluid skater with blinding speed, polished play-making skills, hair-trigger reflexes on face-offs, and an impressive work ethic. In many ways, the perfect fit for Frank Selke's Montreal Canadiens.

In 1958, Backstrom was called up to the big team. He started out centering the fourth line between Claude Provost and either Don Marshall or Phil Goyette. The young trio, although bursting with offensive talent, was used as a checking line.

Backstrom would become a mainstay in Montreal; he was Selke's, and later Sam Pollock's, idea of the perfect player. Although he had the tools to be a first-line star and elite scorer, the selfless pivot put the team first and accepted his checking role. His reasoning was simple: "There were times in my career that I felt I could have played better statistically if I would have played on another [team] besides the Canadiens ... But there was nothing like the team success that the Canadiens had during the time I played with them ..."

Benefits notwithstanding, there came a time when he felt he had done all he could do in Montreal, and in early 1971 he approached Pollock and asked to be traded. "I got to a point in my career where I wanted to play somewhere else, preferably the west coast . . . " Backstrom was dealt to the Los Angeles Kings in exchange for Gord Labossiere and Ray Fortin.

After only a year in L.A., Backstrom was traded to the Chicago Black Hawks. After finishing out the 1972–73 season there, he jumped ship to the Chicago Cougars of the WHA. "They just made me an offer that I couldn't refuse," said Backstrom, who would win that league's Most Sportsmanlike Player award in 1974. "But today, I'm sorry that I jumped from the Black Hawks."

One of Backstrom's finest moments in hockey came in 1974 as a member of a WHA All-Star squad that played the Russians. Placed on a line between Bobby Hull and Gordie Howe, he really got the chance to shine.

In 1976, Backstrom retired from pro hockey to coach the University of Denver's hockey team. He spent a season as an assistant with the Kings before returning to the university level as a head coach. In 1985–86 he was named coach of the year in U.S. college hockey after he took his club to the semifinals of the NCAA championships.

Peak Years   *1964–68*
Comparable Current Player   *Alexei Yashin*
In a Word   *UNDERRATED*

JOHNNY BOWER (The China Wall) Goal
5'11" 189
b. 11/8/1924, Prince Albert, Saskatchewan

At 34, most goalies are playing out the final act of their careers, serving as backups or as mentors to the young hotshots. They certainly aren't just beginning their NHL careers. But Johnny Bower did.

Bower was hockey's Satchel Paige. Both men's real ages were open for debate, and both men amazed and dazzled fans and opponents alike with their ability to perform at an "advanced" age. After his discharge from the Canadian forces in 1945, Bower signed on with the AHL's Cleveland Barons. He would spend the next eight years in Cleveland, cementing his place as the AHL's top puck-stopper.

The New York Rangers couldn't help but notice Bower. They acquired the golden oldie, a master of the poke-check, for Emile "The Cat" Francis and Neil Strain in 1953. Despite putting in a solid performance for the middling club in 1953–54, Bower was returned to the minors, where he remained until June 1958 when Toronto, looking for someone to spell starter Ed Chadwick, secured Bower's rights. By the end of the 1958–59 season, Bower had backstopped a dramatic Leafs comeback in which they edged the Rangers for the final playoff spot. Bower would lead the Buds to the 1959 Stanley Cup finals.

Toronto was emerging as a contender as the 1960s opened. Bower's finest season overall was in 1960–61, when he won the Vezina Trophy and was named to the First All-Star Team. The playoffs were a huge disappointment, though, as Toronto was knocked out by the resurgent Detroit Red Wings. No matter; Toronto would go on to win the next three Stanley Cups with Bower in nets.

In 1964, Toronto acquired Terry Sawchuk. The two goaltending legends added another page to their respective legacies as they became the first goalies ever to share the Vezina Trophy. Sawchuk and Bower would team up one last time in 1967 for Toronto's last Stanley Cup win to date. The tandem was broken up when the L.A. Kings selected Sawchuk in the 1967 Expansion Draft. Bower put in two more years with the Leafs before retiring.

The lifetime numbers of the "China Wall" include a 2.52 goals-against average, a 250-195-90 record, and 37 shutouts in 552 regular-season games. Punch Imlach, who saw many a talent in his years as an NHL coach and general manager, thought of Bower as "the most remarkable hockey player I've ever seen."

Bower was inducted into the Hockey Hall of Fame in 1976.

Peak Years   *1960–1964*
In a Word   *AGELESS*

CARL BREWER Defense
5'9" 180
b. 10/21/1938, Toronto, Ontario

Years before Ken Dryden retired in mid-career to pursue a law degree, there was Carl Brewer. This prickly Toronto native, who was fluent in several languages, was one of hockey's intellectuals. Since he would not allow himself to be duped, he often found himself embroiled in conflicts with management and was a frequent holdout.

Brewer joined the Maple Leafs to stay in 1958–59. From the get-go, his quick skating, superb passing, and stick-handling caused problems for opponents. Then there was Brewer's quick temper, which, early in his career, caused him to take stupid penalties. He led the NHL in penalty minutes twice in his career. Brewer, Tim Horton, Bob Bauur, and Allan Stanley formed hockey's finest defensive troika in the 1960s. The three played together for seven years until Brewer retired.

Brewer was at constant odds with his coach and general manager, Punch Imlach. Prior to the 1964–65 season, Brewer "retired," officially with an eye toward finishing his education. This proved to be a mere negotiating ploy; he soon re-upped. The following summer, he pulled a similar stunt; this time, it was for real. The plucky defenseman took the year off and fought to regain his amateur status. After playing the 1966–67 campaign with the Canadian National Team, he moved to the IHL, where he took on player/coach duties for the Muskegon Mohawks. Brewer went overseas for 1968–69, playing a similar role with Finnish powerhouse IFK Helsinki.

In 1968, Brewer's rights were dealt to the Detroit Red Wings in the big Frank Mahovlich trade. Returning to North America for 1969–70, Brewer signed with the Winged Wheelers and showed up his detractors by earning a Second-Team All-Star nod. After short spells with the St. Louis Blues and in the WHA, he again called it quits.

Five years later, at the ripe old age of 41, he appeared in 20 games for the Leafs. The full effects of this stint would not be felt until years later, when he took the Leafs to court over unpaid back wages. Turns out Toronto had failed to terminate his contract. The brainy Brewer, having discovered a loophole, took the Maple Leafs to school one final time.

Hockey writer Stan Fischler summed up Brewer, the walking enigma, in this way:

> In a sport that treats iconoclasts like lepers, Carl Brewer was regarded by some hockey conservatives as an unmanageable kook who would have been better suited for the ministry or lighthouse work.

Peak Years   *1961–65*
In a Word   *BRAINY*

JOHN BUCYK (The Chief, Lurch, Digger) Left Wing
6'0" 215
b. 5/12/1935, Edmonton, Alberta

Boston Bruins GM Lynn Patrick fell in love with Johnny Bucyk the first time he laid his eyes on him late in 1954. Well, professionally. It took three years for Patrick to get young Bucyk into a Bruins uniform but when he did, a star was born.

Bucyk starred as a Junior with Bronco Horvath on the Edmonton Oil Kings, notching 29 goals and 67 points in 1953–54. Patrick was in the audience as the 19-year-old Bucyk, now a member of the WHL Edmonton Flyers, roared up and down the left side like a freight train. The Chief, who would go on to take the league's rookie-of-the-year award, supplemented two goals that night with an assortment of rock-ribbed bodychecks. Yes, thought Patrick, Bucyk was a "Bruin type" of man.

Detroit owned the big winger's rights, and he became a Wings regular in 1956. Patrick still had his eye on Bucyk, and he saw his chance when goalie Terry Sawchuk, who had walked out on the B's, asked to be traded back to the Red Wings. Patrick swapped the great goalie straight up for Bucyk, who would manage 112 points in his first two seasons as a Bruin.

Bucyk played on one of the most celebrated Boston lines in Bruin history. Teamed with Bronco Horvath and Vic Stasiuk, the trio formed the explosive "Uke Line."

The "Chief," so named because a Boston cartoonist thought he looked more like a Blackfoot Indian than a Ukrainian-Canadian, suffered through eight horrid seasons in Boston between 1959 and 1967, during which his B's failed to make the playoffs. Despite a lousy supporting cast, he managed to average more than 20 goals a season. It was said he could "mine the puck out of a crowd." His needle-threading passes on the power play are the stuff of Beantown legend. The big, stocky winger earned a reputation for hanging tough around the enemy net. "Lady Byng or not, I never knew anyone who could hit a guy harder than Chief, especially with a hip check," said teammate Bobby Orr.

As Boston began their resurgence in the late 1960s, it was the Chief who led the way. In 1970–71, playing alongside such stars as Orr, Esposito, and Hodge, Bucyk became the oldest player in NHL history to pot 50 goals. The man they called "Digger" earned Stanley Cup rings in 1970 and again in 1972.

When Old Man Bruin finally hung up his skates at the end of the 1977–78 NHL slate, he had racked up 556 goals and 1,369 points. He scored 20 goals or more in 16 of his 23 campaigns, an impressive record in any era.

Bucyk is a very worthy member of the Hockey Hall of Fame.

Peak Years   1963–67
In a Word   CHIEF

ALEX DELVECCHIO (Fats) Center
6'0" 195
b. 12/4/1932, Fort William, Ontario

It seems as if Alex Delvecchio was destined to play a supporting role throughout his hockey career. Although he played 22 full NHL seasons — all with the Detroit Red Wings — and racked up some impressive career numbers en route to the Hall of Fame, Delvecchio never broke through to become the star of the team.

When he joined the Red Wings in 1951–52, he became part of a dynasty in progress. Young hotshots like Gordie Howe, Ted Lindsay, Red Kelly, and Terry Sawchuk were already established names. As the first wave of stars passed from the scene, others came to take their place: the likes of Glenn Hall, Roger Crozier, Norm Ullman, and Frank Mahovlich would steal the spotlight. At the end of the 1970–71 season, Howe called it a career. Even then, the man they called "Fats" would be upstaged by Marcel Dionne, the diminutive scoring machine from the St. Catharines Black Hawks.

"Fats" joined his hometown Fort William Rangers at the tender age of 16 and showed enough in his two years there to suggest he had a future in the NHL. In 1950, he moved on to the Oshawa Generals, where he "blew up the spot," as they say.

Despite the pressure of being thrust into the midst of the Detroit juggernaut, the 19-year-old Delvecchio held down his spot on the second line with aplomb. In time, all of the big center's skills came to the fore. Outstanding play-maker; snappy wrist shot; clean and fair play; exceptional hockey smarts. Detroit's newest addition earned three Stanley Cup rings in his first four years. After the Wings' 1955 Cup win, Delvecchio would never sip champagne from the coveted mug.

Delvecchio scored 456 goals and 1,281 points in his 1,549 games (second-most all-time, natch, to Gordie Howe); two Second-Team All-Star selections; three Lady Byng Trophies. Despite his perpetual second-fiddle status, he made it to the Hockey Hall of Fame in 1977.

Peak Years   1960–1964
Comparable Current Player   Mike Modano
In a Word   EXCELLENT

JOHN FERGUSON Left Wing
6'0" 190
b. 9/5/1938, Vancouver, British Columbia

As a stickboy for the WHL's Vancouver Canucks, a young John Ferguson looked on in dismay as his team just sat and watched its star, Phil Maloney, get pummeled by perennial bad man Larry Zeidel. "I never again wanted to see any of my boys not back up a teammate in trouble," he would say one day. "You stand up for each other or you fall together." When he became a player in the AHL, he would give Zeidel a fearful beating as payback for the Maloney incident.

Ferguson would go on to take down the toughest the NHL had to offer as well — Ted Green, Eddie Shack, Kent Douglas. He broke Bobby Hull's jaw and Ken Schinkel's collarbone, and was once suspended for decking a linesman. After the Schinkel incident, New York Rangers trainer Frank Paice asked Ferguson how he did it. "A kiss," he replied with puckered lips. "I just gave him a kiss."

As a player, Ferguson was more than just a hired goon — he was inspiration personified. Only through pure fight and pluck did he actually make the NHL. After a successful stint in the AHL, he was called up to Montreal, where the Canadiens were being pushed around. He was meant to police the beat, which he did and more. He was deadly with his dukes. His punches came as a torrential rain upon his usually overwhelmed dancing partners. Ferguson played the role of hateful opponent to the max. If an "enemy" player walked into a restaurant where some Canadiens were dining, Ferguson would leave. He simply didn't believe in socializing with "the enemy."

Ferguson figured huge for Montreal in Stanley Cup wins in 1965, 1966, 1968, 1969, and 1971. After the 1970–71 campaign, he hung up his skates. On January 7, 1976, he was hired as coach/general manager of the New York Rangers. He signed a five-year deal with the WHA's Winnipeg Jets in November 1978, steering them into the NHL and through many ups and downs in the 1980s. His next stop was Ottawa, where he accepted a position as director of player personnel with the reborn Senators in March 1992. He would leave the club four years later over differences in team-building philosophy.

Peak Years   *1965–69*
Comparable Current Player   *Bob Probert*
In a Word   *SCARY*

ROD GILBERT (Hot Rod, Mr. Broadway) Right Wing
5'9" 175
b. 7/1/1941, Montreal, Quebec

Rodrique Gilbert overcame almost insurmountable odds to become a Hall of Fame right winger. Like Andy Bathgate before him, Gilbert worked his way up through youth hockey to a starring role with the Guelph Biltmores. During a game in 1961, he skated over a piece of debris on the ice and fell, somehow managing to sever his spinal cord. Two operations to correct the damage to his back almost left him without his left leg. Fortunately for hockey, he pulled through and made a full recovery. An excellent skater and stick-handler, he would put in almost 16 full seasons as a New York Ranger. In that time, he set or equaled no less than 20 team-scoring records. When he retired in 1978, he trailed only Gordie Howe in career points by an NHL right winger.

Gilbert was notoriously cocky as a rookie. He was slapped with the nickname "Hot Rod" for his tendency to hog the puck and shoot when he should have passed. As he matured, though, he learned the importance of setting up goals. "Assists have always meant a lot to me," he acknowledged. "An assist is as good as a goal. It means you've participated in the scoring of a goal for your team." Typical of his play-making style was his setup on a Phil Esposito goal in the 1977 All-Star Game in Vancouver. Gilbert dashed behind the net, took a jarring check from a defenseman, whirled around, and flipped the puck out front to his huge linemate, who slammed the puck in.

Playing on the "GAG Line" (it stood for the "Goal-A-Game" Line) with Jean Ratelle and bruising Vic Hadfield in 1971–72, Gilbert accumulated 43 goals, 97 points, and a First All-Star Team selection. He would play in eight All-Star games in his brilliant career. In 1976, he was awarded the Bill Masterton Trophy, recognizing the determination that helped him overcome back surgery and follow-up spinal fusion operations in 1961 and 1966 to become one of the most exciting hockey players of his time.

After a disagreement over salary with GM John Ferguson in 1977, Gilbert walked out on the Rangers for a week and a half. Ferguson, never one for sugar, spice, and everything nice, openly derided Gilbert as arrogant, egotistical, and vain. The flashy winger was coming to the end of the line as a Ranger.

After leaving hockey in the thick of the 1977–78 campaign, the suave Gilbert went on to pursue a career in a New York brokerage firm after a brief venture in the restaurant business.

In 1,065 games, Gilbert scored 406 goals and 1,021 points. He made it to the Hockey Hall of Fame in 1982.

Peak Years   *1968–72*
In a Word   *BROADWAY*

GLENN HALL (Mr. Goalie) Goal
5'11" 180
b. 10/3/1931, Humboldt, Saskatchewan

Clint Benedict flopped. Georges Vezina preferred to stand. And until Glenn Hall arrived on the scene, goalies played either of these two styles. Hall's style, known as the "butterfly," was a combination of the other two. Did it work? Well, his career statistics, and the number of current NHL goalies who use the "butterfly" style, suggest it does.

Born in Humboldt, Saskatchewan, in 1931, Hall quickly donned hockey's "tools of ignorance" for his school team. After a few years playing in and around his hometown, he got the call to play at the Junior level for the Windsor Spitfires of the OHA. From there, it was on to the WHL's powerhouse Edmonton Flyers, where he played alongside such future NHL luminaries as Bronco Horvath, Johnny Bucyk, and Norm Ullman. Hall's superb play did not go unnoticed by the parent Detroit Red Wings, who would call up the young phenom for short spells in 1952–53 and 1954–55. In his first eight NHL games, he posted an impressive 6-1-1 record.

The 1955–56 season was one of change in Detroit. After winning their third Stanley Cup in four years, the Wings decided to trade Terry Sawchuk to Boston. In the face of the enormous pressure that came with filling a legend's skates, Hall posted 12 shutouts and won the Calder Trophy. He would put in another solid season in the Motor City, but the Wings reacquired Sawchuk in June 1957, which meant "Mr. Goalie" was out. He was sent to Chicago with star winger Ted Lindsay for, —hold it!— Forbes Kennedy, Johnny Wilson, Hank Bassen, and Bill Preston. Hall spent 10 seasons in the Windy City, winning his only Stanley Cup in 1961. Between 1955 and 1962, he appeared in 502 consecutive regular-season games, not missing a minute of play during the streak (that's more than 30,000 straight minutes). Cal Ripken, eat your heart out! The advent of the two-goalie system in the early 1960s virtually guaranteed that Hall's record will never be broken.

Hall was drafted by the St. Louis Blues in the 1967 Expansion Draft and, although he was pushing 40, he showed no sign of slowing down. He posted goals-against averages of 2.48, 2.17, 2.91, and 2.42 before retiring after the 1970–71 season.

Hall claims he wasn't the nervous sort, but he would frequently throw up prior to games. Said one of his teammates, "Someday, [his] bucket should be in the Hall of Fame." The butterflies in his stomach certainly didn't affect his goaltending, as his career numbers will attest: over 16-plus seasons in the NHL, "Mr. Goalie" chalked up 84 shutouts, third-best on the all-time list; he was a First-Team All-Star seven times, won the Vezina Trophy twice, and took home the Conn Smythe Trophy for his play in the 1968 playoffs.

After retiring, Hall returned to his farm and was a goaltending consultant for several teams, most recently the Calgary Flames. He made the Hockey Hall of Fame in 1975.

Perhaps the most interesting tribute to "Mr. Goalie" comes from the pen of *Lions in Winter* author Chrys Goyens: "[Hall was] the type of goaltender who could turn back the Johnstown Flood for 60 minutes."

Peak Years   *1959–63*
Comparable Current Player   *Martin Brodeur*
In a Word   *GOALIE*

TIM HORTON Defense
5'10" 180
b. 1/12/1930, Cochrane, Ontario
d. 2/21/1974, St. Catharines, Ontario

For many, the name Tim Horton conjures up images of warm sun filtering through the window, a coffee, a Boston cream donut, and a slow read of the morning paper. But Tim Horton was once a living, breathing man, one of the top hockey players of his era. Defenseman Bob Goldham once said, "Watch Horton if you want a good idea of how defense should be played."

Tim Horton

Tim Horton once joked that he started his now-famous chain of coffee-and-donut shops because he spent too much of his salary on crullers. When Horton died in 1974 there were 40 donut shops in the chain. Twenty-five years later there were more than 1,700. Horton's business partner and owner of Store Number 1, Ron Joyce, also has an NHL connection — he's a part owner of the Calgary Flames and was involved with Hamilton, Ontario's unsuccessful bid to land an NHL expansion team in 1992.

Myles Gilbert Horton played his Junior hockey with the storied St. Michael's Majors. He completed his apprenticeship with the AHL's Pittsburgh Hornets, then the Toronto Maple Leafs' top farm team. Horton joined the big boys for good in 1952–53 and would anchor the Buds' blue-line for the next 17 years. He teamed with the likes of Allan Stanley, Bob Baun, and Carl Brewer to form perhaps the NHL's top defense corps throughout the 1960s. Although he would never capture a Norris Trophy, Horton was thrice named to the First All-Star Team (1964, 1968, and 1969).

In March 1970, Horton was shipped to the New York Rangers. He would play through the 1970–71 season in the Big Apple before putting in a year with Pittsburgh. He hooked up with Punch Imlach's Buffalo Sabres in 1972.

He was in the midst of his 22nd full season in the NHL (his 25th year as a pro!) when his life came to an abrupt end. In the early-morning hours of February 21, 1974, after a game, the big man was speeding down the Queen Elizabeth Way in his sports car en route to his home in Buffalo. He wouldn't make it: a horrific crash near St. Catharines, Ontario, claimed the life of one of hockey's greatest legends.

Strong beyond words, Horton would grab any forward foolish enough to invade his space on the ice and introduce him none too gently to the boards. In the words of Montreal Canadiens tough guy John Ferguson, "Horton's the hardest body-checker I've ever come up against. He's as strong as an ox and hits with terrific force." He was also a solid offensive threat and a strong skater with a cannon for a shot. Jacques Plante once said that Horton had "probably the toughest slapshot in the league."

Horton was elected to the Hall of Fame in 1977.

Peak Years   *1960–1964*
In a Word   *HERCULES*

HARRY HOWELL (Harry the Horse) Defense
6'1" 200
b. 12/28/1932, Hamilton, Ontario

Harry Howell joined the New York Rangers in 1952 via the club's productive OHA Junior affiliate, the Guelph Biltmores. At 22, the handsome boy from Canada's steel capital was made the youngest captain in Ranger history, although he relinquished the post two years later when the boos at Madison Square Garden became deafening.

Who could have known then that Howell would dress in the Broadway blue 1,194 times before being shipped to the California Seals and then the Los Angeles Kings? He was the cement that held the Rangers together for the better part of two decades — a take-charge leader on some very poor teams, and a player overlooked by the All-Star selectors until 1967 (the same season he took the Norris Trophy).

"Harry Howell," said longtime Ranger GM Emile Francis, "is one of the finest defensemen I've ever seen. He'll make fewer mistakes than any other defenseman and he'll also do more good things — like checking shots, stopping advances, and clearing pucks."

Howell, although as strong as a baby ox on his skates, rarely issued an illegal check. The consummate defender, he enjoyed crowding his opponent into the boards.

The NHL's top shot-blocker left the circuit in 1973 to take over as player-coach with the WHA's New York Raiders, who at midseason became the New Jersey Knights and, later, the San Diego Mariners.

Howell returned to the NHL in 1977, this time as assistant GM and director of operations for the Cleveland Barons. He moved on to the Minnesota North Stars when the Barons and Minnesota North Stars merged in 1978, and had a brief stint in the Twin Cities as a coach.

When named to the Hockey Hall of Fame in 1979, all Howell could say was: "I thought only the Bobby Orrs were named to the Hall of Fame."

Peak Years   1962–66
In a Word   ROCK

BOBBY HULL (The Golden Jet) Left Wing
5'10" 195
b. 1/3/1939, Point Anne, Ontario

If you were a defenseman, blink and he was past you. If you were a goalie, blink and you were back in the minors. Gifted with breakneck speed and an absolutely evil slap-shot, Robert Marvin Hull became the NHL's brightest star.

Hull's formative years were spent on the farm near Belleville, Ontario, where he developed a rock-hard body. His shot, which had its origin in his thick, powerful wrists, seemed more like a "high-velocity piece of lead," according to goaltending legend Jacques Plante. It was said a Hull slapshot could reach 120 miles per hour. And Hull could skate faster than anyone — he was once clocked at 29.7 m.p.h.

In 1957, after a couple of Junior seasons with the OHA's St. Catharines Teepees, he got the call to join the Chicago Black Hawks. His first season also saw the debut of Toronto Maple Leaf prodigy Frank Mahovlich, who won the Calder Trophy. But the 19-year-old Hull would have his day.

In 1959–60, only his third NHL campaign, Hull paced the NHL in goals and points. Two years later he would manage his first 50-goal effort. Back-to-back Hart trophies in 1964–65 and 1965–66 (when he scored an NHL-record 54 goals), left little doubt he was the world's best hockey player. During the 1960s, the Golden Jet was named eight times to the First All-Star Team; he scored 50 goals four times; and he snagged three Art Ross trophies to go with the two Harts in his trophy case. To no one's surprise, the Associated Press voted him hockey's player of the decade by a three-to-one margin.

A 50-goal, 93-point effort in 1971–72 was good enough to earn Hull his tenth nomination to the First All-Star Team. During the off-season, he could not agree on a contract with Black Hawk management. And now there was an alternative: a $2.75-million offer to coach and play for the Winnipeg Jets of the upstart World Hockey Association. Few seriously expected the Golden Jet to blast off, but they underestimated his stubbornness. On June 27, 1972, Hull put pen to paper.

Hull played six years alongside Swedish stars Ulf Nilsson and Anders Hedberg. His 77 goals in 1974–75 were an all-time high in major professional hockey. When the WHA collapsed in 1979, Hull followed his Winnipeg Jets back to the NHL. After just 18 games, Hull was moved to the Hartford Whalers, where the 41-year-old closed out his NHL career alongside Gordie Howe, 52, and Dave Keon, who was 40. Hull's plans to continue his career in 1980–81 with the New York Rangers were foiled by the Whalers.

Bobby Hull was a colossal talent. In his prime, his blood-red Hawks jersey set off his flowing golden mane, which seemed to light a path as he blew past entire teams. One sportswriter, when asked to imagine a one-on-one contest between Hull and the dazzling Montreal Canadiens legend Howie Morenz, proclaimed that "the only difference between them would be the colors of their sweaters."

The Golden Jet was inducted into the Hockey Hall of Fame in 1983.

Peak Years *1964–69*
In a Word *HOLLYWOOD*

DAVE KEON Center
5'9" 165
b. 3/22/1940, Noranda, Quebec

It would be interesting to see how Dave Keon would perform in today's NHL. Given his size (or lack thereof), he would no doubt be the sixth-round pick who achieves stardom by virtue of talent and dedication. "He's too small," the scouts might say before they were made to look like jabbering fools.

Keon, born in northern Quebec, opened his hockey career with the storied St. Michael's Majors, one of the Toronto Maple Leafs' feeder clubs. It would not be long before the speedy Keon was skating at the Gardens for the big club. And what a first impression he made! In his rookie season of 1960–61, he would take the Calder Trophy on the strength of a 20-goal, 45-point effort.

The little guy had also established himself as one of the NHL's top defensive forwards. He would later say, "If you can score three goals a game, you don't have to check. But I can't and no one else in this league can either. So, you have to play well defensively to keep your job." Former star defenseman Bill Gadsby remembers well Keon's defensive genius: "Trying to move the puck past Keon was about as easy as shaking your shadow in the sunshine."

In his second season, Keon won the Lady Byng Trophy (he also won it in 1963) and helped lead Toronto to its first Stanley Cup win since 1951. The Leafs would win the Cup in 1963 and again in 1964. Keon would save his best for 1967, when Toronto defeated the Montreal Canadiens in the finals. Although he managed only eight points in 12 playoff contests, his defensive play, penalty-killing, and brilliance at taking face-offs were invaluable. Red Fisher would later remark, "I don't know any player who did as much damage to the Montreal Canadiens as Dave Keon."

After 15 years in Toronto, Keon jumped to the renegade WHA. After stops in Minnesota and Indianapolis, he settled in with the New England Whalers. He would stay with the Whalers when they joined the NHL in 1979. After three more seasons as a Whaler, he decided to hang up his skates at age 42.

Keon was elected to the Hockey Hall of Fame in 1986.

Peak Years *1966–70*
Comparable Current Player *Guy Carbonneau*
In a Word *MOSQUITO*

JACQUES LAPERRIERE Defense
6'2" 190
b. 11/22/1941, Rouyn, Quebec

Jacques Laperriere caught on with the Montreal Canadiens for good in 1963–64, winning the Calder Trophy and earning his first of four NHL All-Star nods. The Canadiens won the Cup in his sophomore season and would win it three more times in the next four years. Laperriere bagged the Norris Trophy in 1966, distinguishing himself as a skillful, cool-headed player with a genius for controlling a game's flow. He was the first "big man" on the Canadiens defense since the departure of Doug Harvey to New York in 1961.

When Laperriere became the first rookie named to an NHL All-Star Team since World War Two, league president Clarence Campbell was heard to say, "Never in my years in professional hockey have I seen a young man take over and lead a team as Laperriere has done." The gawky, giraffe-like defenseman was doing the things many had expected of teammate J.C. Tremblay.

A serious knee injury ended Laperriere's career in 1974, but he maintained his association with the Canadiens as an assistant coach for the next two decades. Some say the real reason he called it quits was a long-simmering feud with head coach Scotty Bowman. Bowman had chewed out the 32-year-old defenseman after an 8–4 loss to the St. Louis Blues, throwing up his arms and screaming: "You're finished, hang up your skates — don't ruin your life and don't try to ruin mine."

In the summer of 1976, Laperriere sued the NHL and the Montreal Canadiens. He sought $50,000 in insurance benefits because of the injury to his left knee, which he'd suffered at the Habs' 1974 training camp. He claimed the injury prevented him from playing hockey for an entire year, and led to the premature end of his career. He settled out of court with both parties.

He also kept busy as coach of the Junior Canadiens, until a particularly ugly game against the Sorel Black Hawks, in which 334 minutes in penalties had been assessed. Quebec Major Junior league president Aime Constantin leveed $875 in fines and suspended five players in connection with a bench-clearing brawl. Laperriere abandoned his post, saying, "That's not my idea of hockey."

Laperriere got back into the NHL when Bob Berry hired him as assistant coach of the Montreal Canadiens in 1981. He would hold this position until he was fired, along with head coach Jacques Demers, in 1995.

Peak Years   *1966–70*
Comparable Current Player   Eric Desjardins
In a Word   METHODICAL

FRANK MAHOVLICH (The Big M, Gutch) Left Wing
6'1" 205
b. 1/10/1938, Timmins, Ontario

A strong argument can be made that Frank Mahovlich was the most physically talented man ever to sport the Toronto Maple Leaf colors. Others might contend that he was one of the laziest players ever to put on the blue and white.

Francis Mahovlich sharpened his skills on the ponds and rinks of Timmins, Ontario. The future "Big M" developed strong legs, which enabled him to skate with long, effortless strides. In 1954 he joined the St. Michael's Majors, where his game improved by leaps and bounds with each passing month. In 1956–57, after he was named the outstanding Junior player in the OHA, Mahovlich was called up to the Leafs for three games. He cracked the lineup in 1957–58, winning rookie-of-the-year honors.

After seasons of 20, 22, and 18 goals, the "Big M" had his breakout year in 1960–61. Through his first 41 games, he had 36 goals. Surely, thought the media, he would break Maurice Richard's record of 50. Unfortunately, injuries and pressure got to Mahovlich, who could manage only 12 goals in his final 29 games for a total of 48.

Mahovlich would remain an enigma wrapped inside a riddle for Leaf fans. After his breathtaking performance in 1960–61, he seemed poised to hit unseen scoring heights. Yet his goal production over the next four years dropped — to 33, 36, 26, and 23. At the time, these were exceptional numbers, yet there was no way the Big M could match the unrealistic expectations set when he scored 48.

Conventional wisdom said he lacked intensity. King Clancy said, "[Mahovlich] has the talent to be the greatest hockey player that ever lived if only he was a little meaner."

After 11 years, four Stanley Cups, and a nervous breakdown in Toronto, Mahovlich was shipped to the Detroit Red Wings. The trade seemed to invigorate the "Big M," who scored 49 goals in his first full season in Motown. In January 1971, he was traded to the Montreal Canadiens, where he hooked up with his brother, Pete. Montreal turned out to be some kind of tonic for Frank, who scored 41 points in his first 38 games. During the '71 playoffs, he led all scorers with 14 goals and 27 points in 20 games.

After the 1973–74 season, Mahovlich joined the Toronto Toros of the fledgling WHA. He followed the Toros when they moved to Birmingham, Alabama, in 1976, and put in two more seasons before retiring. He attempted a comeback with the Red Wings in 1979–80, but gave up three weeks into training camp.

Mahovlich, a nine-time All-Star, scored 533 goals and 1,103 points in 1,181 NHL games. The big man added 89 goals and 232 points in 237 WHA games. He made the Hockey Hall of Fame in 1981 and his 1998 appointment to the Canadian Senate put him back in the headlines.

Peak Years   *1961–65*
Comparable Current Player   *Mats Sundin*
In a Word   *BROODING*

STAN MIKITA (Stosh) Center
5'9" 165
b. 5/20/1940, Sokolce, Czechoslovakia

Stan Mikita, born Stanislaus Guoth, appeared in 1,394 NHL games, counting 541 goals and 1,467 points. The two-time league MVP was the first player to win three trophies in one season when he captured the Hart, Art Ross, and Lady Byng in 1967. He managed the "Triple Crown" again a year later.

Born in Czechoslovakia, young Stanislaus was sent by his family to live in St. Catharines, Ontario, with his uncle Joe Mikita in 1948. The eight-year-old boy adopted his uncle's last name. On this side of the Atlantic, he was taunted by classmates, who called him "DP" (for "displaced person"). Perhaps on account of some pent-up hostility, "Le Petit Diable" was always among the leaders in penalty minutes in his formative hockey years.

In 1958–59, he led the OHA in scoring despite playing only 45 games. When he joined the Chicago Black Hawks for good in the fall of 1959, it was evident that the 19-year-old Czech import had the makings of a star. But his apparent penchant for the penalty box mystified coaches, reporters, and fans alike. In 1965, he won his second straight scoring title despite spending 154 minutes in the sin bin. Two years later, though, he would incur only 12 minutes in 70 games. He credited his turnaround to his two-year-old daughter, Meg: "If a two-year old can see there's something wrong about it, why can't a 26-year-old find out why he has to be in that box all the time?"

In 1961, coach Rudy Pilous threw Mikita between Ken Wharram and Ab McDonald to form the original "Scooter Line." Doug Mohns ultimately replaced McDonald on the wing and the unit went on a tear. Between 1963–64 and 1967–68, Mikita led the league in scoring four times, earning a career-high 97 points (tying the NHL record) in 1966–67.

Mikita and teammate Bobby Hull were big fans of the slapshot. While Hull's was harder, Mikita's was no slouch. And although he wasn't the smoothest skater around, he was good at finding and exploiting holes in the enemy defense. Apart from his all-world offensive abilities, he was a diligent and untiring defensive force. Head coach

Billy Reay thought the world of Mikita: "[He] does more with everything he's got than any player I've ever seen."

After he sustained a back injury in February 1969, Mikita's skills eroded. Although he put up solid numbers throughout the 1970s, he was not the man he once was. He retired in 1980 after 21-plus years with the Hawks. He posted 14 consecutive 20-goal campaigns, managed two Harts, two Lady Byngs, four scoring crowns, eight All-Star nominations, and a Stanley Cup ring.

Mikita was inducted into the Hockey Hall of Fame in 1983.

Peak Years   1964–68
Comparable Current Player   Peter Forsberg
In a Word   THORNY

DOUG MOHNS (Diesel Doug)   Defense/Left Wing
6'0" 185
b. 12/13/1933, Capreol, Ontario

Douglas Mohns was not your average hockey player. While players like Red Kelly made seamless switches from defense to forward or vice versa, few could switch continually with no drop in performance. Mohns was one of those few. Was he a defenseman? A left winger? Neither. Both. With apologies to Kordell Stewart, Mohns was the original "Slash."

Mohns was an exceptional skater, always one of the game's fastest. He possessed a superb shot and had a special place in his heart for the physical game. He got his start in Barrie, Ontario, with the OHA Flyers. In 1953–54, his rookie season with the Boston Bruins, he managed 13 goals and 27 points. Although he was officially listed as a defenseman, he spent a fair chunk of his ice-time on left wing. By 1956–57, the B's had decided to make "Mohnsie" a full-time defender. He would not disappoint, tying the record for goals in a season by a defenseman with 20 in 1959–60.

Boston dealt Mohns after the 1963–64 season to the Chicago Black Hawks for Reggie Fleming and Ab McDonald. Early in the 1964–65 season, Mohns broke his foot and youngster Matt Ravlich took his place on the blue-line. When he recovered, Mohns discovered that he was more urgently needed up front. Coach Billy Reay threw the old veteran up front with Stan Mikita and Ken Wharram. This unit, known as the "Scooter Line," would go down as one of the top lines in Hawk history.

Mohns put in five seasons on the Chicago front line before returning to the defense. In 1971 he was traded with Terry Caffery to the Minnesota North Stars for Danny O'Shea, whose claim to fame would be a 1973 heart attack that ended his career when the NHL refused to give him medical clearance. After stops in Atlanta and Washington, Mohns decided to call it a career after the 1974–75 season, his 22nd in the big league.

Peak Years   1959–63
In a Word   LUSTY

PIERRE PILOTE (Mighty Mite) Defense
5'10" 178
b. 12/11/1931, Kenogami, Quebec

Pierre Pilote started his career with the St. Catharines Teepees, Chicago's top Junior squad, and moved on to the AHL's Buffalo Bisons. He cracked the big club's lineup for good in 1956. Although it took him a few years to blossom, the slim defenseman proved he was well worth the wait.

Pilote was one of the few blue-liners able to run with Bobby Hull & Company.

While others in his position might have tried to join the big-shooting Hawks in their seemingly endless hunt for goals, Pilote was happy to play the role of quarterback. He was surely one of the smartest play-makers of his time, a true craftsman. Although he wasn't blessed with blazing speed, Pilote had a remarkable ability to read and fake out his opponents, to stall them long enough for his big guns to get into scoring position. Then it was a quick zip over to Hull or Stan Mikita and bingo!

In 1961, Pilote tied Gordie Howe for the playoff scoring lead with 15 points in 12 games as Chicago captured its first Cup in 23 years. Between 1963 and 1965, he took home three consecutive Norris trophies. Heady stuff, especially considering that the only others to accomplish this feat were Doug Harvey and Bobby Orr. While 1960 through 1962 brought him Second-Team All-Star accolades, he made the First Team every year between 1963 and '67. Was there a better defenseman in the NHL in the 1960s than Pilote? Probably not.

Seeking more scoring depth, the Black Hawks dealt a 36-year-old Pilote to the Toronto Maple Leafs in May 1968 for Jim Pappin. Looking somewhat out of place in a Leafs uniform, Pilote managed to put together one more solid season before hanging up his skates for good after the 1968–69 season.

Pilote was inducted into the Hockey Hall of Fame in 1975.

Peak Years   *1960–1964*
In a Word   *CREATIVE*

CLAUDE PROVOST (Pete) Right Wing
5'9" 175
b. 9/17/1933, Montreal, Quebec
d. 4/17/1984, Miami, Florida

The Montreal Canadiens took the Stanley Cup in each of Claude Provost's first five seasons. After 15 years and 1,005 games in the NHL, he was worth 254 goals, 589 points, and nine championship rings. The all-time record for Cup rings is 11.

Provost was a choppy, frenetic skater whose legs, wide apart, seemed to surge in different directions. Although he looked like a frightened spider skittering down the ice, he was one of the hardest men in the NHL to knock off of his feet. His great speed and energy enabled him to shadow such ice-blazers as Chicago's Bobby Hull. Provost wasn't just a checker, though. In 1961–62, he scored 33 goals and 62 points.

During the 1961 All-Star Game, Provost noticed how extraordinarily short Gordie Howe's stick was. The tricky Frenchman switched to a shorter piece of lumber and the results were surprising — a tripling of his 1960–61 goal-scoring total, good for a tie for second place in the NHL with Howe and Frank Mahovlich. "I got all those goals but my checking was lousy," he said. "I'd rather check more and score less. It's better for the team."

It has been said that if it weren't for Bobby Hull, no one would know Provost's name. The 1965 Stanley Cup finals saw Toe Blake's defensive master do possibly the best single job of shadowing ever seen in the modern age — on one of the most explosive talents ever to play hockey. The Golden Jet was at the height of his powers when he lined up against Provost in this series. Although Hull had almost singlehandedly led Chicago to the finals, Provost was at his bloodsucking best. The number he did on Hull is perhaps the most important reason the Canadiens beat Chicago for the Cup.

The seamy-faced Provost called it quits in 1970. After a one-year stint as head coach of the QJHL's Rosemont Nationals in 1971, he seemed to miss playing and he tried a comeback with the Los Angeles Kings in 1971–72. The 38-year-old winger couldn't make the grade and retired for good.

One of Montreal's greatest soldiers died of a heart attack while playing tennis near his Miami, Florida, home in 1984.

Peak Years   *1961–65*
In a Word   *BLOODSUCKER*

BOB PULFORD (Pully, Clutch) Left Wing
5'11" 188
b. 3/31/1936, Newton Robinson, Ontario

In the late 1950s, the Toronto Maple Leafs were at a crossroads. After winning five Stanley Cups between 1945 and 1951, the blue and white had struggled, bottoming out in 1957–58 with a last-place finish. As control of the team passed from Conn Smythe to a group headed by his son Stafford, Harold Ballard, and John Bassett, out went the old Leafs — Sid Smith and Ted Kennedy, for instance — and in came a new generation — Frank Mahovlich, Carl Brewer, Dave Keon, and Robert Jesse Pulford.

Although his arrival in Toronto wasn't heralded by much pomp and ceremony, he would become one of the cornerstones of four Stanley Cup championship clubs in the 1960s. Pulford played his Junior hockey with the Toronto Marlboros. He was pressed into full-time service with the Leafs for the 1956–57 season, managing 11 goals and 22 points in 65 games. A tenacious winger, he teamed with Keon and George Armstrong to give Toronto a checking line unmatched in the NHL. Pulford was a truly superb penalty-killer, capable of thwarting an enemy power play and hurtling up the ice for a shorthanded marker. While not the speed-burning kind, he was a solid skater. And as his 281 goals over 1,079 games attests, he could score a bit, too.

Pulford would spend 14 years with the Maple Leafs. In September 1970, he was dealt to the Los Angeles Kings for Garry Monahan and Brian Murphy. He would spend two seasons in the purple and gold before moving to the front office. He took over the head coaching reins in L.A. for 1972–73, winning the Jack Adams Trophy as the NHL's top coach after his third season on the job. After five years in L.A., Pulford moved on to Chicago, where he was coach for a total of six seasons and general manager for 17.

Pulford is a member of the Hockey Hall of Fame.

Peak Years   *1963–67*
Comparable Current Player   *Rod Brind'Amour*
In a Word   *MUCKER*

HENRI RICHARD (The Pocket Rocket, Le Grand Canadien) Center
5'7" 160
b. 2/29/1936, Montreal, Quebec

In 1955, a young Henri Richard signed a two-year, $8,000 contract with the Montreal Canadiens. "Pay me what you think I'm worth," he had grinned. "I'm not worried about money. I just want to play with this team."

Montreal's newest star was a quiet guy, at first seemingly invisible in the loud, confident Canadiens dressing room. Sportswriter Dick Beddoes asked Toe Blake if he could interview the rookie, and the coach answered, "Sure, go ahead." Beddoes asked Blake, "Does he speak English?" Blake's comeback: "Hell, I don't know if he even speaks French."

Early in his career, Richard was described as being "puck lucky" on account of his ability to corral passes at top speed. Blake had his own opinion: "He's not puck lucky. He's smart enough to be where the puck is all the time … He sizes up how a play is going to go and then he gets there, and the first thing you know he's got the puck." On top of his extraordinary stick-handling skills, the little center had blazing speed, a good shot, and a keen sense of the defensive side of the game. He was the complete package.

Richard was one of the top offensive forces in the NHL throughout the 1960s. Although he was lucky to get 20 minutes of playing time a game, having to share pivot duties with the likes of Jean Beliveau and Ralph Backstrom, Richard was a major scoring threat. In 1957–58, he was second in league scoring with 28 goals and 80 points in 67 games. He would appear among the top 10 scorers in five of the next nine seasons.

Richard's competitiveness occasionally effected controversy in Montreal. During the 1971 Stanley Cup finals, he called head coach Al MacNeil the worst coach he had played under in his 16 years in the NHL. Richard's remark was twisted by the media into an English-French conflict and the little guy was forced to take it back. A year later, Richard and teammate Serge Savard got into a heated argument after a 9–1 win against the Vancouver Canucks. The shouting culminated in Richard's slapping Savard across the face. This particular disagreement came in the wake of a spicy Montreal *Gazette* story about certain players not being able to keep their night lives under control. Apparently, the idea of effecting a press ban in the dressing room was behind the argument.

In summer 1975, with another year still to go on a two-year contract, Richard retired. The Rocket's little brother summed up his wonderful career with these words: "After 20 years, a good thing is coming to an end."

His intelligence made Richard the ideal center. While he lacked the size or power of many of those around him, he had an accurate shot and could fake out the goalies almost as well as the great Beliveau. Opponents attested to Richard's great drive and his willingness to body the biggest men in the NHL. He was a fast, smooth, and pretty skater with an acceleration that often left defenders in tatters.

In 1,256 games, Richard scored 358 goals and 1,046 points. He sipped champagne from the Stanley Cup 11 times, more than any other player in history. He was inducted into the Hockey Hall of Fame in 1979.

Peak Years　　1961–65
Comparable Current Player　　Paul Kariya
In a Word　　MERCURY

EDDIE SHACK (The Entertainer) Left Wing
6'1" 200
b. 2/11/1937, Sudbury, Ontario

They say nickel is Sudbury's top export. But the best thing to come out of the northern Ontario city was a fast-skating, wise-cracking hustler (on and off the ice) by the name of Eddie Shack. Cries of "Clear the track, here comes Shack!" rocked the walls whenever the "Entertainer" was in the house.

Eddie Shack

Joining the Guelph Biltmores at the tender age of 15, Shack played five years as a Junior, using every minute of the time to hone his hockey skills. A league-leading 57 assists in 1956–57 proved that this young man was more than a common clown. He was also known as a bit of a tough guy. During one game in the minors, he got into a nasty brawl with veteran Larry "The Rock" Zeidel, one of the meanest fellows in hockey. After being ejected, they went to their respective dressing rooms, hit the showers, and returned to watch the rest of the game from the stands. A minute or two passed before Zeidel spotted Shack sitting down in the front row. Still sore at "The Entertainer," Zeidel came after him to finish their fight. "Shack was going to the NHL," Zeidel said, "and I [was] staying in the AHL and I [wouldn't] get another shot at him."

The New York Rangers assigned Shack to the Providence Reds in 1957–58, recalling him a year later. He never caught on with the Rangers, scoring only 16 goals in 141 games. He found his niche after a November 1960 trade to the Toronto Maple Leafs, with whom he earned four Stanley Cup rings. In May 1967 he was shipped to the Boston Bruins. He would make stops in Los Angeles, Buffalo, Pittsburgh, and Toronto again before waving goodbye to the NHL.

Shack was a wild man on the ice, a mischievous clown willing to do anything it took to win, or at least put on a good show. The man could play the game, though: he was the second player in NHL history (the first was Dean Prentice) to score 20 goals in a season for five different franchises. An exceptional skater, "Sweet Daddy Shackie" had speed, a hard shot, and a taste for the rough stuff. He might today be known as a "power forward." Since retiring, he has gained notoriety as a commercial pitchman for Canadian Tire, Speedy Muffler King, and the Pop Shoppe.

Peak Years   *1963–67*
Comparable Current Player   *Claude Lemieux*
In a Word   *CLOWN*

ALLAN STANLEY (Snowshoes, Sam, Big Allan) Defense
6'1" 170
b. 3/1/1926, Timmins, Ontario

How does a defenseman nicknamed "Snowshoes" last 21 years in the NHL before trudging through the front doors of the Hockey Hall of Fame? As Vince Lombardi once said, "The best in any field are simply brilliant at the basics." This pretty well summed up Allan Herbert Stanley, a slow, plodding, but remarkably effective blue-liner.

Allan, nephew of Hall-of-Fame PCHA and WCHL winger Barney, had stops with the Boston Olympics and Providence Reds before the latter team traded him to the New York Rangers in December 1948. The young defenseman was not the exciting type, a fact not lost on the fans, who suffered through 162 losses in his first five seasons. Stanley was booed so lustily, it began to affect him: "[The fans would] boo every time I touched the puck. Then they began to boo every time I got on the ice ... when I sat on the bench, they'd yell at me."

On November 23, 1954, the Rangers did Stanley a favor and dealt him to the Chicago Black Hawks. Only 111 games later, he was on the move again. This time it was to Boston, where the big guy began to hit his stride on the blue. A pair of 31-point seasons served notice to the hockey world that he was the real deal, not just some mucker.

At the relatively advanced age of 32, it seemed he was just coming into his prime. In October 1958, he was traded to the Toronto Maple Leafs for Jim Morrison. While Boston fans would grow desperate to "light a fire" under Morrison, Stanley "broke on through to the other side" in Toronto. Beside the likes of Tim Horton, Stanley became one of the NHL's top defenders.

Stanley would spend 10 years in Toronto, snagging four Stanley Cups and three Second-Team All-Star accolades. Throughout the years, he played an exceptional stay-at-home defensive game and had few peers in the "hockey smarts" department. He was drafted by the Philadelphia Flyers' Quebec City affiliate in the 1968 Reverse Draft and he played one year in the City of Brotherly Love before announcing his retirement.

Stanley was elected to the Hockey Hall of Fame in 1981.

Peak Years   *1958–62*
In a Word   *DRAINING*

J.C. TREMBLAY (J.C. Super Star) Defense
5'11" 175
b. 1/22/1939, Bagotville, Quebec
d. 12/7/1994

The great Red Fisher called Jean-Claude Tremblay the finest stick-handler of his era. The flashy defenseman's style was all about timing and control and he was at his very best when left alone to doodle with the puck as his forwards got in position to take a feed. Unfortunately, he played like a scared little girl against aggressive, hard-checking teams.

A 20-year-old Tremblay joined the Montreal Canadiens in 1959, full of spirit and confidence. It took until late 1961, though, for the young hotshot to nail down a full-time spot in the lineup.

The turning point in his professional career came during the 1965 Stanley Cup finals against Bobby Hull and the Chicago Black Hawks. With Jacques Laperriere down with a broken leg, Tremblay was called to step forward. He came through in a big way, playing 40 minutes a game and leading the Canadiens to their first championship in five years. As he later recalled: "The Canadiens had a shortage of defensemen in their Junior system. They just decided at the time to move me back to defense. It was certainly a good move for me." The tall, slender star's idol was Doug Harvey. "I learned all the tricks of the position just by watching Doug from the bench," said Tremblay.

Tremblay was never one to withhold an opinion. For years, he whined through the press about how his teammates never protected him like the Toronto Maple Leafs did Tim Horton, or the New York Rangers did young Brad Park. Tremblay's worst tantrum came just after the 1966 finals, after he was passed up for the Conn Smythe Trophy. Upon hearing the announcement, Tremblay threw towels around the dressing room, kicked over garbage cans, pummeled the wall with his fists, and finally burst into tears. Stupefied witnesses could hardly believe their eyes and ears — and on the night he and his team had won the Cup!

Why did Tremblay jump ship to the WHA Quebec Nordiques in August 1972? "Money, plain and simple," was his answer. "They were not paying me what I thought I was worth in Montreal at the time. I could have gone to the Los Angeles Sharks. That was the team that drafted me in the WHA. But Quebec traded to get my rights. I was the last hope of a big-name player jumping to their team. Plus moving to Quebec was just like moving to another French community for me."

Tremblay continued to sparkle in Quebec City, earning WHA First-Team All-Star nods in 1973, 1975, and 1976. He got his chance to face the Russians in 1974 when the WHA's best took on the cream of the Soviet Union. At the end of this tournament, the Russian coaches called Tremblay the most accomplished defenseman they had ever laid eyes on. The skinny Bagotville, Quebec, native would retire from the game after the 1978–79 season.

Peak Years   *1967–74*
Comparable Current Player   *Phil Housley*
In a Word   *PEACOCK*

NORM ULLMAN (Noisy, The Mechanical Man) Center
5'10" 185
b. 12/26/1935, Provost, Alberta

Norman Ullman broke into the NHL with the Detroit Red Wings in 1955. A strong, barreling skater noted for his durability, he would rank among the game's top skill players in a 20-year NHL career. He was a gritty, hard-nosed type, a classy player.

In only his second season, Ullman was put on a line with Gordie Howe and Ted Lindsay. The Red Wings finished first overall in 1956–57 as Ullman placed 10th in NHL scoring with 52 points. He would lead Detroit in goals in 1961, 1965, and 1966, topping the league with 42 in 1964–65.

Manager Jack Adams nicknamed Ullman "Noisy" because he was so terribly quiet and polite in the dressing room. On this count, Adams once said that Ullman reminded him of Charlie Gehringer, the Detroit Tigers' Hall-of-Fame second baseman: "They do everything so gracefully and make every move so well, that you many times underestimate them." Like Gehringer, Ullman performed with cold competence, without a trace of flamboyance.

On March 3, 1968, Ullman was packaged with Paul Henderson and Floyd Smith and sent to the Toronto Maple Leafs for Frank Mahovlich, Garry Unger, Pete Stemkowski, and the rights to Carl Brewer. The Leafs' head coach and general manager, Punch Imlach, called Ullman "the best center who ever played for me." High praise, indeed, seeing as Imlach had coached Jean Beliveau at the Senior level.

Ullman was always one of the best stick-handlers in the NHL. After a 1970 game against the Buffalo Sabres, he looked puzzled when asked if the referee had inspected his stick. "One of these nights," said his friend and fan, "the [referee] is going to peel the tape off your stick and find out where the magnet is hidden." The wonderful thing about Norm was that he was still at the top of his game in the early 1970s, when he was pushing 40.

Ullman remained in Toronto through 1974–75, whereupon he jumped to the WHA's Edmonton Oilers for $120,000 a season. He would close out his career in Edmonton two years later. His career NHL totals: 490 goals and 1,229 points in 1,410 games. He added 47 goals and 130 points in two WHA seasons. Sadly, the Provost, Alberta, native was never on a Stanley Cup–winner.

The man Eddie Shack called "the hardest-working guy in hockey" was given the greatest honor in hockey when he was inducted into the Hockey Hall of Fame in 1982.

Peak Years   *1962–66*
In a Word   *HOCKEY*

GUMP WORSLEY Goal
5'7" 180
b. 5/14/1929, Montreal, Quebec

"You show me a goalie who plays every game and I'll show you a guy who'll be swinging from a tree by the time the season is over." — Lorne "Gump" Worsley

After stops in seven cities, Gump Worsley was called up by the New York Rangers in 1952–53. Although he won rookie-of-the-year honors after posting a 3.06 goals-against average in 50 games, he was sent back down the following season, replaced by Johnny Bower. The guy a high school chum called "Gump" — because he resembled comic-strip character Andy Gump — would be back in 1954–55, playing nine more seasons in the Ranger cage behind some terrible lineups. During this part of his career, it was not uncommon for the stocky Montrealer to face 50 shots or more in a single game. When asked what NHL team gave him the most trouble, "The Rangers" was his sheepish reply.

On June 4, 1963, Worsley's fortunes turned 180 degrees when he was traded to the Montreal Canadiens in a multi-player deal that sent Jacques Plante to Manhattan. After spending most of the 1963–64 and 1964–65 seasons with the AHL Quebec Aces, recuperating from injuries, he would play a big role in Montreal's Stanley Cup win in 1965. He would share the 1966 Vezina Trophy with Charlie Hodge and help the Canadiens to their second straight Cup. After taking All-Star nods in 1966 and again in 1968, Worsley shared his second Vezina, this time with a young Rogie Vachon, posting six shutouts and a 1.98 goals-against average in 1967–68. That spring, Worsley won 11 of 12 playoff games to sip from the Cup once again.

As the 1960s came to a close, Worsley began complaining more often about the pressures of goaltending in Montreal. To no one's surprise, he walked out in protest of head coach Claude Ruel's practice methods. Worsley didn't stay unemployed for long, though; Montreal sold the portly puck-stopper on February 27, 1970, to the Minnesota North Stars. In early February 1973, the 44-year-old announced his retirement, only to be lured back by the North Stars for the 1973–74 campaign. He appeared in 29 games that year, posting a 3.22 average. He finally knuckled under on September 24, 1973, when he donned a goalie mask for the first time in his career. He would retire at the end of the season and made the Hockey Hall of Fame in 1980.

Peak Years   *1959–63*
In a Word   *LUMPY*

The All-Stars

Position	Player	Season	GP	G	A	PTS
D	Pierre Pilote	1963–64	70	7	46	53
D	Tim Horton	1961–62	70	10	28	38
LW	Bobby Hull	1965–66	65	54	43	97
C	Stan Mikita	1966–67	70	35	62	97
RW	Gordie Howe	1962–63	70	38	48	86
			GP	GAA	Sho	
G	Glenn Hall	1960–61	70	2.57	6	

The Seventies

In a Flash

COMPOSITE REGULAR-SEASON STANDINGS
(JANUARY 1, 1970–DECEMBER 31, 1979)

National Hockey League

Club	GP	W	L	T	Pts	WPct	GF	GA
Montreal Canadiens	790	501	159	130	1132	.716	3,282	2,040
Boston Bruins	787	487	189	111	1085	.689	3,314	2,295
Philadelphia Flyers	789	410	230	149	969	.614	2,782	2,159
Chicago Black Hawks	791	376	272	143	895	.566	2,585	2,239
Buffalo Sabres	750	357	261	132	846	.564	2,626	2,326
New York Rangers	789	383	286	120	886	.562	2,892	2,562
New York Islanders	590	265	215	110	640	.542	2,012	1,743
Toronto Maple Leafs	789	337	324	128	802	.508	2,642	2,562
Atlanta Flames	591	247	245	99	593	.502	1,892	1,869
Los Angeles Kings	790	311	351	128	750	.475	2,499	2,606
Quebec Nordiques	37	15	17	5	35	.473	114	125
Pittsburgh Penguins	790	302	347	141	745	.472	2,605	2,737
St. Louis Blues	790	286	376	128	700	.443	2,287	2,662
Detroit Red Wings	788	275	394	119	669	.425	2,419	2,870
Minnesota North Stars	789	265	397	127	657	.416	2,337	2,773
Vancouver Canucks	749	245	393	111	601	.401	2,249	2,783
Hartford Whalers	34	9	16	9	27	.397	111	126
Winnipeg Jets	38	12	22	4	28	.369	102	150
Edmonton Oilers	35	9	19	7	25	.357	120	155
Washington Capitals	437	93	281	63	249	.285	1,204	1,948
KC/Colorado	436	93	270	73	259	.297	1,188	176
Oak./Calif./Cleveland	673	176	390	107	459	.341	1,852	2,612

World Hockey Association

Club	GP	W	L	T	Pts	WPct	GF	GA
Houston Aeros	474	285	170	19	589	.621	1,928	1,541
Winnipeg Jets	555	302	227	26	630	.568	2,270	1,959
Quebec Nordiques	556	295	237	24	614	.552	2,274	2,121
Minn. Fighting Saints	293	154	127	12	320	.546	1,101	1,035
New England Whalers	555	281	236	38	600	.541	2,046	1,938
Clev./Minnesota	356	169	162	25	363	.510	1,198	1,169
NY/NY-NJ/San Diego	395	184	191	20	388	.491	1,484	1,488
Alberta/Edmonton Oilers	556	259	273	24	542	.487	1,976	2,026
Phoenix Roadrunners	238	106	114	18	230	.483	883	935
Cincinnati Stingers	321	142	164	15	299	.466	1,211	1,259
Ottawa/Tor./Birm.	556	242	286	28	512	.460	2,129	2,209
Phil./Van./Calgary	395	174	207	14	362	.458	1,381	1,498
Chicago Cougars	234	94	132	8	196	.419	777	880
Indianapolis Racers	344	118	202	24	260	.378	1,082	1,373
LA/Mich./Baltimore	234	83	141	10	176	.376	703	930
Denver Spurs/Ottawa Civics	41	14	26	1	29	.354	134	172

HELLOS

Pavel Bure *Russian Rocket*	March 31, 1971
Travis Weir	October 8, 1970
Eric Lindros *Flyers center*	February 28, 1973
Glenn Weir	October 28, 1973
Paul Kariya *Mighty Duck*	October 16, 1974
Jeff Chapman	October 2, 1975
Joe Thornton *Bruins center*	July 2, 1979

GOODBYES

Edouard "Newsy" Lalonde *Habs legend*	November 21, 1970
Gordon "Duke" Keats *early Toronto great*	January 16, 1971
Werner Heisenberg *German physicist*	February 1, 1976
Mao Tse-tung *Chinese statesman*	September 9, 1976
Joan Crawford *American actress*	May 13, 1977
Fred "Cyclone" Taylor *West Coast scoring ace*	June 9, 1979

REGULAR SEASON

BEST RECORD
1976–77 Montreal Canadiens, 60-8-12

WORST RECORD
1974–75 Washington Capitals, 8-67-5

BEST MINOR LEAGUE RECORD
1972–73 Syracuse Blazers (Eastern Hockey League), 63-9-4

FAMOUS FIRSTS

**NHL ROOKIE TO SCORE
MORE THAN 50 GOALS**
Mike Bossy, 1977–78 (53)

NHL PLAYER TO RECORD 1,000 ASSISTS
Gordie Howe, Detroit, October 29, 1970

**NHL PLAYER TO SCORE 100 POINTS IN A
SEASON WITH MORE THAN ONE TEAM**
Jean Ratelle, New York Rangers and Boston Bruins, 1975–76

**WHA PLAYER TO SCORE
10 POINTS IN A GAME**
Jim Harrison, Alberta, January 30, 1973

**DEFENSEMAN TO WIN
THE ART ROSS TROPHY**
Bobby Orr, Boston, 1969–70

**DEFENSEMAN TO SCORE
100 POINTS IN A SEASON**
Bobby Orr, Boston, 1969–70

**PLAYER TO WIN THE HART TROPHY IN
THREE CONSECUTIVE SEASONS**
Bobby Orr, Boston, 1970, '71, '72

**PLAYER TO SCORE
100 POINTS IN 6 SEASONS**
Phil Esposito

PERSON TO SIGN IN THE WHA
Vern Buffey, January 7, 1972

GOAL SCORED IN THE WHA
Ron Anderson, Alberta, October 11, 1972

TELEVISED WHA GAME ON U.S. TV
Winnipeg Jets vs. Minnesota Fighting Saints, January 7, 1973

**PENALTY-FREE GAME IN
PHILADELPHIA FLYERS HISTORY**
March 18, 1979

MISCELLANEOUS

MOST GOALS, SEASON
76 Phil Esposito, Boston, 1970–1971 (NHL)
77 Bobby Hull, Winnipeg, 1974–75 (WHA)

MOST GOALS, DECADE
506 Phil Esposito (NHL)
316 Marc Tardif (WHA)

MOST ASSISTS, SEASON
102 Bobby Orr, Boston, 1970–1971 (NHL)
106 Andre Lacroix, San Diego, 1974–75 (WHA)

MOST ASSISTS, DECADE
557 Phil Esposito (NHL)
547 Andre Lacroix (WHA)

MOST POINTS, SEASON
152 Phil Esposito, Boston, 1970–1971 (NHL)
154 Marc Tardif, Quebec, 1977–78 (WHA)

MOST POINTS, DECADE
1,063 Phil Esposito (NHL)
798 Andre Lacroix (WHA)

COOLEST MIDDLE NAMES
Danny *Mirl* Gare
Jean *Elmourt* Gilbert
Eddie *Lavern* Johnstone
Lanny *King* McDonald
Jan *Waldemar* Popeil
Fred *Edmondstone* Speck
Nick *Evlampios* Fotiu

COOLEST HANDLES
Borje Salming, "The Plastic Man"
Dave "Bammer" Langevin
Nick Fotiu, "Pieface," "Nicky Boy"
Claire Alexander, "The Orillia Milkman"
Barry "Bubba" Beck
Don "Cleaver" Lever
Jerry "King Kong" Korab
Frank "Seldom" Beaton
Joe Daley, "The Holy Goalie"
Mike Palmateer, "The Popcorn Kid"

BIGGEST PLAYER
Bill Bennett, 6'5" 235

SMALLEST PLAYER
Bobby Lalonde, 5'5" 155

BEST SHOT
Richard Martin had a truly devastating shot. Punch Imlach once called him "the best natural scorer I've ever seen in hockey."

BEST PASSER
Bobby Orr

BEST STICK-HANDLER
Gilbert Perreault

BEST SKATER
Bobby Orr

WORST SKATER
Dave Williams was so poor a skater that boss Harold Ballard hired a figure skater to come to Maple Leaf Gardens and coach Williams on the basics.

FASTEST SKATER
Yvan Cournoyer

BEST SNIPER
Phil Esposito

BEST ON-ICE INSTINCTS
Bobby Clarke was the NHL's answer to Pete Rose. Clarke accomplished so much in hockey with so little natural talent. The Flyers captain, who had incredible drive, spirit, work ethic, and instincts, could defeat you in so many ways.

BEST PENALTY-KILLER
Bob Gainey

BEST BODY-CHECKER
Barclay Plager

BEST POKE-CHECKER
J.C. Tremblay

BEST SHOT-BLOCKER
Borje Salming was called "The Plastic Man" by his Leaf teammates for his uncanny reach and ability to get in front of shots.

BEST GOALTENDER
Ken Dryden

BEST GLOVE-HAND (GOALIE)
Dan Bouchard

FINEST ATHLETE
Dale Tallon was Canada's national junior golf champ in 1969. He considered turning professional until the Vancouver Canucks made him their first pick in the 1970 NHL Amateur Draft. Tallon should have stuck with golf.

BEST DEFENSIVE FORWARD
Bob Gainey

WORST DEFENSIVE FORWARD
Rick MacLeish

BEST SHADOW
Craig Ramsay was nicknamed "Boris" by his peers because he played hockey like one of the many well-drilled Russian stars. Ramsay was a valuable part of the Buffalo Sabres into the 1980s, a master when it came to checking or positional play.

BEST FACE-OFF MAN
Mild-mannered Doug Jarvis was incredibly quick on the draw. Montreal coach Scotty Bowman remembered when he traded for Jarvis in 1975: "Roger Neilson, Doug's coach with the Peterborough Petes, told me that I was getting the best face-off man in hockey. He went on to say he meant in all of hockey, not just Junior."

BEST DEFENSIVE DEFENSEMAN
Bill White didn't reach the NHL until 1967, when he was the ripe old age of 28. He'd spent five years under the brutal Eddie Shore in Springfield. "Some people knock Shore, but he was one of the all-time greats on defense and he certainly taught me a lot," said White. "He didn't pay me much but he showed me plenty about playing defense."

BEST OFFENSIVE DEFENSEMAN
Bobby Orr

BEST ALL-AROUND PLAYER
Jacques Lemaire

BEST UTILITY PLAYER
Billy Reay used to call John Marks his "Johnny of all trades." The 1968 first-round pick was one of the top plumbers on the Chicago Black Hawks in the 1970s. He was

a super checker from any of the forward positions, could more than fight his way out of a wet paper bag, and was often called upon to fill in on the blue-line.

STRONGEST PLAYER
Walt Tkaczuk

TOUGHEST PLAYER
Barry Ashbee. The NHL's unluckiest player had to be the guy they called "Ashcan." Bobby Clarke once said his ex-teammate was "the strongest guy mentally I've ever seen." In 1972–73, Ashbee played the entire season with partially torn knee ligaments. The very next year, he sustained a chipped neck vertebrae, which sent sharp pains from his shoulders to his hands. Ashbee taped his arm snugly to his body, jammed his stick into his glove, and skated his way to a spot on the Second All-Star Team.

BEST FIGHTER
Nick Fotiu. In his book *The Hammer*, Dave Schultz said the Golden Gloves boxing champion from Rhode Island was the only man he was afraid to fight during his NHL career.

MOST ABLE INSTIGATOR
Bobby Clarke

DIRTIEST PLAYER
Bobby Clarke would do anything to win. *Anything*. Montreal Canadiens head coach Scotty Bowman once called the Flyers captain "the dirtiest player in hockey."

CLEANEST PLAYER
Butch Goring

BEST CORNER-MAN
Bob Gainey was the man the Soviets called "the world's best all-around hockey player."

BEST-LOOKING PLAYER
Garry Unger had that beautiful mop of long, golden hair. He was so pretty he looked like a Ken doll on the ice. The Detroit Red Wings traded him on account of his locks but he was "glad it happened because it got me to St. Louis."

UGLIEST PLAYER
Dave Williams

BALDEST PLAYER
Jim Morrison

MOST UNDERRATED PLAYER
Don Marcotte was one of Don Cherry's favorite players. The inimitable former head coach of the Bruins once said: "If they were going to send a hockey player to Mars, it would have to be Don Marcotte. They could watch how he plays and then mold hockey players that way."

MOST CONSISTENT PLAYER
Phil Esposito

SMARTEST PLAYER
Bobby Clarke

BIGGEST FLAKE
John Ferguson once called **Gilles Gratton** "Grattoony the Loony," and with good reason. The nutty goaltender, who saw action in St. Louis and New York, once explained his recurring abdominal pains by claiming that he was a reincarnated soldier from the Spanish Inquisition. "I've seen it in my mind," he told *The Hockey News* in 1977. "Was I a knight? No, just a simple soldier. But I was killed when I was run through with a lance."

MOST HATED PLAYER
Dave Schultz

MOST ADMIRED PLAYER
Bobby Orr

BEST LINES
Team: Winnipeg Jets (WHA)
LW: Bobby Hull
C: Ulf Nilsson
RW: Anders Hedberg

Team: Montreal Canadiens
LW: Steve Shutt
C: Jacques Lemaire
RW: Guy Lafleur

Team: New York Islanders
LW: Clark Gillies
C: Bryan Trottier
RW: Mike Bossy

Team: Toronto Maple Leafs
LW: Errol Thompson
C: Darryl Sittler
RW: Lanny McDonald

HIGHEST PAID PLAYER

Bobby Hull signed a 10-year deal worth $2.75 million with the WHA's Winnipeg Jets on June 27, 1972.

MOST TRAGIC CAREER

Bob Gassoff. This popular brawling defenseman for the St. Louis Blues was only 24 when he was killed in a motorcycle accident during the summer of 1977. His number was promptly retired.

PLAYER VERSUS TEAM

Ken Dryden vs. 1973–74 Montreal Canadiens
Dryden walked out on the Canadiens in September 1973 when he learned he wasn't going to be getting a raise. The bespectacled netminder "quit" hockey for a $135-a-week articling position at a Toronto law firm. Montreal GM Sam Pollock ultimately caved in and offered Dryden a three-year deal worth $200,000 a season.

MOST LOPSIDED TRADE

On May 22, 1970, Montreal Canadiens GM Sam Pollock traded Ernie Hicke and the Habs' Number 1 draft pick to the Oakland Seals for Francois Lacombe and the Seals' first-round choice in the '71 draft. Pollock predicted accurately that the Seals would finish last in 1970–1971, giving Montreal the first pick overall. This pick turned out to be none other than the fabulous Guy Lafleur.

BIGGEST FLOP

Greg Joly ranks as one of the most disappointing top-rated prospects in NHL history. The Calgary native was selected first overall in the 1974 Amateur Draft by the Washington Capitals, who touted him as "The kind of hockey player we want . . . He is the kind of rushing defenseman everybody has been looking for since Bobby Orr started . . ."

Joly would spend two sub-par seasons in Washington before being traded to the Detroit Red Wings. After a major wrist injury in 1979, his NHL career started a downward spiral. His NHL career lasted only 370 games (regular season and playoffs), in which he racked up just 97 points.

BEST HEAD COACH
Scotty Bowman

BEST GENERAL MANAGER
Sammy Pollock

BEST SPORTSWRITER
Dick Beddoes

BEST BROADCASTER
Danny Gallivan

BEST MINOR LEAGUE PLAYERS
Fred Speck (AHL)
Noel Price (AHL)
John Gravel (IHL)
Ron Wilson (IHL)
Ian McKegney (CHL)

BEST STANLEY CUP FINAL
1976 — Montreal Canadiens vs. Philadelphia Flyers
This series marked the dawning of one of the greatest dynasties in professional sports.

IMPORTANT RULE CHANGES

1970–1971
- Home teams must wear basic white sweaters; visitors to wear colored jerseys (though L.A. wore yellow and purple).
- Curvature of stick blades not to exceed 1/2 inch
- Minor penalty assessed against players who deliberately shoot a puck into stands

1971–72
- Teams may dress no more than 17 skaters and 2 goaltenders.

- Third man into an altercation automatically given a game misconduct

1972–73
- Minimum width of stick blade reduced to 2 inches from 2 1/2

1974–75
- Bench minor penalty assessed if a penalized player does not go directly to the penalty box

1976–77
- Player who instigates a fight gets a major penalty and a game misconduct.

1977–78
- Teams requesting stick measurement given a bench minor penalty if the measured stick is legal.

1979–80
- Players entering the NHL this season must wear a helmet.

Granny Loves Derek

O n the one hand he was a rough-and-tumble hockey player; on the other, he was a mod-haired, sharp-dressed, freewheeling bachelor. More than one blushing female considered him the "grooviest man alive" in the early 1970s. He was Derek Sanderson, the brash young center for the Boston Bruins.

During the 1970 Stanley Cup playoffs, Boston radio station WBZ came up with a gag promotion. They invited female listeners to say, in 103 words or less, why they would like a luncheon date with Sanderson at Bachelors III, a Boston night spot owned by the dashing hockeyist as well as another notable swinging athlete, Joe Namath.

Roughly 13,000 responses came in from more than 30 states as well as Canada. Applicants ranged from 8 to 83 years old. One of the youngest correspondents asked for "a date for my Mommy because Daddy doesn't take her out." The eldest suggested Derek "should have contact with a mature woman." A housewife and mother of three marked her envelope "sealed with a kiss." Another decorated her application with Xs and Os, representing "kisses and hugs for darling Derek." Yet another applicant said she had just left a convent and "what better way to get back into the swing of things" than a date with Sanderson. "I'd do anything for a free meal," wrote a New Jersey girl, indicating she was prepared to hitchhike to Boston to keep the date. Young ladies everywhere offered to "give up" any number of things, including "dull" boyfriends, a "right arm," and even "a week of anything you want."

The winner of the "Date Derek" contest turned out to be none other than 73-year-old Mabel Hocking, an avid hockey fan. Eventually, Sanderson and the grandmother of 12 met for dinner at Bachelors III.

Sanderson, a self-proclaimed connoisseur of women, was kind enough to impart this wisdom on the subject: "There are no better women in North America than in Montreal. Pittsburgh is terrible. The good cities are Los Angeles, San Francisco, Boston, New York, Montreal, and Toronto."

On another occasion, Sanderson explained, "My kind of girl has to be feminine, but she has to have a head on her shoulders and know what she's doing. I like a girl who is really good-looking, sensitive and soft . . . "

Those Nutty Plagers

D uring the 1970–1971 NBA season, Jerry West, the Los Angeles Lakers basketball legend and the guy they called "Mr. Clutch," had his nose broken for the ninth time in his career. Must have been some kind of record, no? Not so, said St. Louis Blues defenseman Bob Plager. Apparently, his brother Barclay busted his honker an amazing 10 times.

"Ten times on the button," Barclay confirmed. "On the nose, I mean."

In the early 1970s, the Plagers were the heart and soul of the Blues. They were a huge part of the tough defensive system set up by coach Scotty Bowman. All three came out of Kirkland Lake, Ontario, to join the St. Louis blue-line in the late 1960s.

Barclay and Bobby were original Blues and anchors of the team's defense corps, while Billy alternated between the NHL and the minors.

Those who booed and fought the Plagers were certainly happy to hear they were humans who got hurt, too. And boy, did the brothers get hurt!

Returning to Jerry West for a moment, the Lakers star once said the worst sensation he ever felt was on the many occasions they had to stick a needle into his broken nose. Barclay Plager had no problem relating to that: "Oh man, it's the most painful thing you can imagine. My last two came only three games apart. They stick these needles into all sorts of places on your nose to deaden it so they can take a hammer and whack it back into place, but they never do get it dead enough and you can feel that hammer in your brain for a month afterwards."

Upon further reflection, the big bruiser remembered something even more painful. "The worst was when I had three chest ribs pulled apart against Boston in 1970," he said. "I didn't know what had happened and I thought I'd had a heart attack. I hit a guy and twisted away and suddenly I felt this terrific pain in my chest and I couldn't breathe. All symptoms of a heart attack, which some others thought, too. When they found out what it was, they said they'd never seen anything like it. Not three ribs like that. I'm in medical history in that hospital."

Against the Vancouver Canucks during the 1970–1971 NHL campaign, Billy Plager's head was sliced open by a skate blade. He managed to struggle to his feet, but he crumpled when he noticed how profusely he was bleeding. Brother Bob had quite the opposite reaction: "When I saw the blood pouring from the kid's head, I knew he was all right. It was really sawdust he was losing, not blood. And, hey, no Plager is hurt when he gets hit on the head."

The Plagers were a colorful bunch, although some doubted their sanity. As Billy remembered, "They called our dad 'Squirrel' because everyone thought he raised three nuts. Dad never let us come crying to him. If we had something going on with each other or with other kids, we had to settle it ourselves."

Bob added, "We settled our differences with fights. We didn't have boxing gloves, so we'd wrap towels around our hands, then pull woolen socks over our fists and go to it in the backyard. Whoever won was right."

A Dirty Little Secret

In early 1971, promoter Dennis Murphy and attorney Gary Davidson set out to form the World Hockey Association. Finally the NHL would have competition, its first since the demise of the Western Canada Hockey League almost 50 years before. Most observers shook their heads in disbelief. Surely this new league was going to be an expensive, and foolish, undertaking. This so-called World Hockey Association actually thought itself fit to go toe-to-toe with the NHL, the top hockey league on the planet? Madness! Or was it?

The feeling [in the WHA] was totally different than anything I experienced in the National Hockey League. For so many years, the NHL owners treated their play-ers like cattle ... There was none of that crap in the WHA ... the WHA had a much better attitude than what I'd seen in the other league.

— Defenseman Paul Shmyr, who played in the NHL for Chicago, California, Minnesota, and Hartford, and in the WHA for Cleveland, San Diego, and Edmonton

During the summer of 1971, the WHA dream was becoming reality. Articles of incorporation were filed in Delaware on June 10, 1971, and the hunt was on for fran-chise owners. In time, Davidson and Murphy were introduced to "Wild" Bill Hunter of Edmonton, longtime owner of the Junior Edmonton Oil Kings, who was itching for a fresh challenge. Soon, Ben Hatskin of Winnipeg and Calgary's Scotty Munro were brought into the fold. These three would form the core of the new league.

It has been said that "WHA" really stood for "When Hull Arrived." In part, this was right on the money. The league was made when Bobby Hull signed with the Winnipeg Jets on June 27, 1972. For some time, the legendary Chicago Black Hawk had been feuding with management. The WHA owners were convinced Hull's pres-ence would guarantee credibility for their fledgling circuit, and they made his signing a group effort, raising a $1 million signing bonus. All told, Hull's 10-year deal was worth $2.75 million.

The Hawks took their star's defection very personally; they deleted his statistics from official team records, and assigned his Number 9 jersey to undistinguished defenseman Dale Tallon.

Once Hull jumped, the way was paved for such established NHLers as J.C. Tremblay, Bernie Parent, Gerry Cheevers, Derek Sanderson, and Ted Green, to cross over. NHL teams hoping to keep their stars had no choice but to match gold-plated WHA offers — the New York Rangers were a notable example, paying through the nose to prevent Vic Hadfield, Brad Park, and Rod Gilbert from becoming Cleveland Crusaders.

> *Nobody can tell me the WHA wasn't major-league hockey. In Houston, we won most of our exhibition games against NHL clubs. One year we challenged Detroit, but they wouldn't play us. And if you look back at the NHL scoring leaders in the first year after the merger, four of the top 10 scorers came from the WHA. It was damn good hockey.*
>
> *— Gordie Howe*

The WHA's inaugural season was no laughing matter. It had to survive opening-night cancellations, Zambonis falling through the ice, Derek Sanderson's eight-game WHA career, and owners who hadn't a clue how to run a hockey team. Still, the season wasn't a complete disaster. The league was getting by, its main assets being the novelty factor and the performances of such marquee players as Bobby Hull, Gerry Cheevers, and J.C. Tremblay. Although the NHL bigwigs had laughed when the WHA was formed, they were beginning to worry.

As soon as the novelty of the Hull signing began wearing off, the rebel league decided to go after none other than Gordie Howe. The old pro had apparently grown bored in retirement and was only too happy to sign with the Houston Aeros. Here, he would skate alongside sons Mark and Marty. Many derided Houston's 45-year-old acquisition, writing off the signing as a pathetic publicity stunt. Old Howe made fools of his critics with a 100-point championship season in 1973–74.

Wherever the two great Number nines, Howe and Hull, played, the media followed, and their road games were quite often sellouts. The league came to the end of its second campaign having improved considerably on its attendance figures.

In early 1974, the WHA filed a $50-million lawsuit against the NHL, claiming that it held a monopoly and was using "questionable trade methods." NHL president Clarence Campbell had no desire whatsoever to fight out this one before a judge so in February 1974 he settled out of court, paying the WHA $1.75 million to drop the suit. The WHA and NHL also agreed to schedule preseason games between teams from the two leagues.

Mystic Corn

On the night of February 25, 1973, before a game between the Ottawa Nationals and Alberta Oilers, the Ottawa trainer came across a half-eaten cob of corn outside the dressing room. He picked it up and tossed it to the first player he saw, joking that the cob was a good-luck charm. That player was Gavin Kirk, stuffed the cob into a spare glove. Ottawa beat the Oilers 2–1 on a fluke goal, and the Nationals players were more than convinced of the cob's "mystic power." For the next few weeks, Kirk kept the rotting cob in his glove. Before each game, it was the focus of a solemn ceremony during which six players would rub it for luck. The last player to rub would then pluck a single kernel of corn from the cob and throw it at goalie Ken Stephenson. However weird the ceremony sounded, it seemed to do the trick: Ottawa would take 12 of its last 13 games and clinch a playoff spot in its final outing of the 1972–73 season.

The WHA came along and paid us all a lot more money, but what was even more important was that it created so many new jobs for hockey players and gave them some leverage in negotiating. Today's players should thank the WHA for making it possible for them to earn the big money they're getting. Without that league, hockey would have been stuck in the dark ages for a long time.

— Val Fonteyne, left winger for Detroit, Pittsburgh, and the Rangers in the NHL, and the Alberta/Edmonton Oilers of the WHA

Teams tottering on the edge of bankruptcy, and going over the brink more than a few times, were the bane of the WHA. The New York Raiders, reorganized as the New York Golden Blades in 1973, dissolved early in 1973–74 after the new ownership in Manhattan ran out of cash. The league intervened, relocating the team in Cherry Hill, New Jersey, (near Philadelphia) where, as the Knights, they played out the year in a tiny minor league rink. The franchise's third year would see them in San Diego. The Los Angeles Sharks struggled through two years before investors stepped in and moved the club to Detroit. They'd be in Baltimore before the '74–75 season was over.

By the mid-1970s, an uneasy detente existed between the NHL and WHA, as the fledgling league showed no signs of fading away. But the upstarts continued to raid NHL rosters for high-profile talent, scoring another major coup in 1974 when the Toronto Toros landed former Leaf great Frank Mahovlich. They also signed the hero of the 1972 Summit Series, Paul Henderson.

Having seen the WHA get off the ground, Gary Davidson stepped down as president to focus on his new pet project, the World Football League. Dennis Murphy succeeded his partner on an interim basis.

The 1974–75 WHA season was a high-water mark. Gordie Howe led his Houston Aeros to a second consecutive championship; Bobby Hull scored 77 goals in 78 games — topping Phil Esposito's NHL record by one — and matched hockey's most distinguished feat — 50 goals in 50 games; and former Philadelphia Flyer Andre Lacroix rang up 106 assists, four better than Bobby Orr's 1970–71 record.

Meanwhile, WHA teams were developing a reputation as trailblazers when it came to scouting Europe for talent. The Winnipeg Jets acted first, inking Swedes Ulf Nilsson and Anders Hedberg to complement Bobby Hull. This threesome gelled almost instantly. Pound for pound, Nilsson was possibly the toughest Swede ever to play in North America. From his very first shift in the WHA, the 175-pounder was a target, but his willingness to put up his dukes went a long way toward destroying the myth of the "chicken Swedes." During Hedberg's heyday with the Jets, more than a few observers would compare his electrifying speed and explosive scoring ability to that of Montreal Canadiens megastar Guy Lafleur.

The Winnipeg Jets were simply dazzling, the very antithesis of the typical North American "dump and chase" team. The New England Whalers, originally based in Boston but now operating out of Hartford, followed Winnipeg's lead and picked up twin brothers Thommie and Christer Abrahamsson. Meanwhile, the Toronto Toros

---

What used to really irk me was when I'd run into NHL players who were always bad-mouthing the WHA for being weaker. They seemed to forget that it was because of our league that their salaries had more than doubled in just a few years.

— *Ralph Backstrom, the former Habs center who played for the Chicago Cougars and New England Whalers*

---

signed Czech defectors Vaclav "Big Ned" Nedomansky and Richard Farda. The WHA's focus on skill was a far cry from the blatant thuggery that was sweeping the big league, where the Philadelphia Flyers kicked and punched their way to Stanley Cups in 1974 and 1975.

Unfortunately, this trend the Flyers set would find its followers in the WHA. If 1974–75 epitomized skill, 1975–76 was the league's peak season for head-cracking. Clubs that saw fisticuffs as a way to sell tickets brought in such goons as Steve Sutherland, Rick Jodzio, and Jack Carlson. During the 1976 playoffs, a terrible event would cast a shadow over the league. In a match between the Calgary Cowboys and Quebec Nordiques, Calgary winger Rick Jodzio poleaxed the Nords' scoring star, Marc Tardif. The savage hit knocked Tardif out of the series, landing him in hospital with serious head injuries. It took a good number of policemen to put down the ensuing brawl.

The WHA's fourth year was in many ways the beginning of the end. Salaries had skyrocketed so high in such a short time that many clubs were neck-deep in red ink. The Chicago Cougars failed to answer the bell, leaving the league without a team in any of the top three U.S. markets. Minnesota withdrew 59 games into the 1975–76 season, outlasting the Denver Spurs-cum-Ottawa Civics, who perished after 41. Then in the summer of '76 the Toronto Toros moved to Birmingham, Alabama, while the Cleveland Crusaders moved to St. Paul, where they took the name of the old Minnesota Fighting Saints. They'd have no more luck than the original franchise, folding after 42 games. By the end of the 1976–77 campaign, the WHA had lost six franchises in only 15 months. It became glaringly obvious that the league would have to make peace with the NHL to survive.

In June 1977, Clarence Campbell stepped down as NHL president, handing the reins to John Ziegler. While the new boss was well aware of the WHA's problems, he was also concerned about the plight of a number of franchises in his own league, teams that had been sent reeling by the bidding wars. There already had been clandestine meetings between pro-merger figures from both leagues. Almost immediately after Ziegler took over as president, the first "official" merger talks were held.

One of the items tabled at the June 1977 meeting was a plan to combine some of the weaker NHL clubs to make room for WHA teams such as Cincinnati, Edmonton, Houston, New England, Quebec, and Winnipeg. Twelve of the 18 NHL owners voted in favor of a merger — unfortunately, this was two votes shy of the 75 percent needed to carry the motion.

The 1977–78 WHA season saw the league field just eight clubs — down from a high of 14 two years before. Established NHL stars were no longer jumping to the league, but the Howes — Gordie, Mark, and Marty — were the talk of the league when they left Houston for the New England Whalers, who came out of the gate like a house on fire. Winnipeg would ultimately take the season title with 50 wins. Victories over a Soviet All-Star squad and the Czech national team propelled Bobby Hull & Friends into a special category. In the words of Jets goalie Joe Daley, "Even though it was only an exhibition game against the Russians, beating them put the Winnipeg Jets up on a pedestal with some of the great teams in hockey history. We'll never know how good that Winnipeg team was, even with three championships, but for one night we were right up there with the best."

The "Plan B" blueprint for an NHL–WHA merger was far less ambitious than the first one. By this time the NHL had lost a team — the lowly Cleveland Barons (originally the Oakland Seals) merged with the Minnesota North Stars. Both teams had struggled on the ice and at the box office. The 17-team senior circuit was much in favor of adding three WHA clubs over two years, which would bring membership to an even 20. The early buzz had the Whalers and Oilers coming into the fold for 1978–79, to be followed a year later by the Jets. The WHA's Birmingham, Cincinnati, Houston, and Indianapolis teams would be paid to fold.

That left the Quebec Nordiques in limbo. Although the WHA insisted on the Nords' inclusion in the merger, the NHL balked. Quebec's rink, Le Colisee, was judged to be in need of extensive renovations to get it to an acceptable standard for the NHL. In any event, the idea of a merger was voted down for a second time.

The WHA's final season would be marked by the debut of a young man who'd been overlooked by NHL scouts. He was a skinny 17-year-old scoring wizard from the Ontario league's Soo Greyhounds: Wayne Gretzky. Nelson Skalbania's Indianapolis Racers signed the fresh-faced native of Brantford, Ontario, but he would play only eight games before the Racers folded. The Edmonton Oilers outbid the Winnipeg Jets for Gretzky, purchasing him for $800,000. The young center made an immediate impact with Edmonton, leading the team to its only appearance in the World finals.

Along with Gretzky, names like Michel Goulet, Mike Gartner, Rick Vaive, and Mark Messier made their WHA debuts in 1978–79. But it was the Gretzky factor that figured largest when the Winnipeg Jets, Edmonton Oilers, Quebec Nordiques, and Hartford Whalers entered the NHL.

WHA ALL-TIME LEADERS

Goals		Assists	
Marc Tardif	316	Andre Lacroix	547
Bobby Hull	303	J.C. Tremblay	358
Real Cloutier	283	Marc Tardif	350

Points		Penalty Minutes	
Andre Lacroix	798	Paul Baxter	962
Marc Tardif	666	Kim Clackson	932
Bobby Hull	638	Cam Connor	904

Goaltending Minutes		Shutouts	
Ernie Wakely	19,331	Ernie Wakely	16
Don McLeod	18,926	Gerry Cheevers	14
John Garrett	18,919	John Garrett	14

Wins		Goals-Against Average	
Joe Daley	167	Ron Graham	2.99
Richard Brodeur	165	Gerry Cheevers	3.12
Ernie Wakely	164	Jack Norris	3.16

WHA SINGLE-SEASON LEADERS

Goals		Assists	
Bobby Hull (1974–75)	77	Andre Lacroix (1974–75)	106
Real Cloutier (1978–79)	75	Ulf Nilsson (1974–75)	94
Marc Tardif (1975–76)	71	Ulf Nilsson (1977–78)	89
		Marc Tardif (1977–78)	89

Points		Penalty Minutes	
Marc Tardif (1977–78)	154	C. Brackenbury (1975–76)	365
Marc Tardif (1975–76)	148	Kim Clackson (1975–76)	351
Andre Lacroix (1974–75)	147	Gord Gallant (1975–76)	297

Goaltender Wins		Goals-Against Average	
Richard Brodeur (1975–76)	44	Don McLeod (1973–74)	2.56
Joe Daley (1975–76)	41	Michel Dion (1975–76)	2.74
Dave Dryden (1978–79)	41	Ron Grahame (1976–77)	2.74

WHA NICKNAMES

Michel "Plywood" Dubois
Wayne "Brinks" Gretzky
Dick "Goodyear" Proceviat

Wayne Muloin, "Mr. Guts"
Tom "Hawkeye" Webster
Ab McDonald, "Old McDonald"

Each of the four WHA clubs admitted to the NHL were allowed to protect only four players from their 1978–79 rosters. Any others whose rights belonged to NHL clubs reverted to their old teams. The Winnipeg Jets were hardest hit in this regard, as they lost star forward Kent Nilsson to the Atlanta Flames.

Bobby Hull, who had hung up his blades in 1979, returned to play for the Jets for one more year. Hartford featured 51-year-old Gordie Howe, returning eight years after his last NHL match, along with sons Marty and Mark. Also on the Whalers' roster was 39-year-old Dave Keon, back in the big leagues after four seasons in the WHA. Later in the season, Hull joined Howe and Keon on the Whalers.

Despite its short history, the WHA had lasting effects on the game. The competition for players drove the average salary to a level comparable to that in the other major sports. The WHA's signing of European players broke new ground — in 1972, more than 90 percent of the NHL's players were Canadian. WHA teams also adopted a more freewheeling, European-influenced style of play that would alter the NHL's direction in the 1980s.

---

*It bothers me that the WHA has never gotten the recognition it deserves . . .
I know there was a lot of animosity when the WHA was formed, but considering
what it accomplished in terms of opening up the game, creating jobs, and
making hockey more popular, I hope someday the NHL does the right thing and
acknowledges those contributions.*

— Ralph Backstrom

The WHA never got the credit it deserved in its day, and today, if it is remembered at all, it is often written off as a minor league, a novelty whose only claims to fame were Bobby Hull and blue pucks. Hockey historians like Murray Greig and Scott Adam Surgent have done much to make sure the league is not forgotten.

Chicago Blackhawks owner Bill Wirtz once estimated that increased spending for player salaries and minor league development, combined with legal bills and reduced attendance, cost the NHL $1 billion over the lifetime of the WHA. This might go far in explaining why the WHA is still somewhat of a taboo today. Pity.

No More Kate

The Broad Street Bullies were interested in much more than your lunch money. Consider their lineup: Andre "Moose" Dupont, the strong boy on defense; Dave "The Hammer" Schultz, the da Vinci of goons; Don "Big Bird" Saleski, a boy with a problem if ever there was one; Bob "Hound Dog" Kelly, walking proof that fingernails across a blackboard may not be the worst thing on earth after all; and of course, Bobby Clarke, leader of this fist brigade. The names are drenched in blood and sweat.

The Philadelphia Flyers wore their orange, black, and white with an enormous amount of pride, enough to have punched and hacked their way to back-to-back Stanley Cups in 1974 and 1975. But their secret weapon was World War Two–era belter Kate Smith, whose performance of "God Bless America" was heard before important games. Call it what you will, but her crooning seemed to awaken the sleeping dogs, lighting a fire under the rock-hard fanny of each and every Broad Street Bully.

In 1976, Philadelphia had just come through a tough semifinal series against the battling Boston Bruins, who were playing without the oft-injured Bobby Orr. Before that they'd played a brutal and bloody quarterfinal series with the Toronto Maple Leafs, which saw everything from criminal charges slapped on Saleski and Mel Bridgman, to Dave "Tiger" Williams biting Schultz and drawing blood, to 65-year-old Leaf fan George Crawford elbowing Schultz in the face. After the assault by the crazed sexagenarian, "The Hammer" held his nose in front of Gardens fans and was later heard to say, "It stinks."

The Montreal Canadiens, eliminated in the playoffs for the last two seasons, had retooled. Sophomore forwards Doug Risebrough and Mario Tremblay brought toughness to the lineup while rookie pivot Doug Jarvis was added as a face-off antidote to the awful Bobby Clarke. Montreal lined up three of the NHL's top defensemen in Larry Robinson, Serge Savard, and Guy Lapointe — known as "The Big Three" and "The Ministry of Defense." With Bernie Parent nursing an injury and brainy Ken Dryden kicking pucks out as if they were the size of beach balls, the Canadiens had a clear edge in nets going into the 1976 finals. Until now, the Bullies hadn't met a team equipped to stand up to them. It was time for a new era to begin.

Game One

Philadelphia 3 @ Montreal 4

Flyers head coach Fred "The Fog" Shero shocked fans with his decision to go with vastly underrated backup goalie Wayne Stephenson instead of the great Parent. Apparently, Parent had been horrid in the playoffs, with dicey performances against both the Toronto Maple Leafs and Boston Bruins and was not completely recovered from an earlier neck injury.

"Montreal will win the Stanley Cup . . . I'd bet my shirt on it."
— Henri Richard

Kate Smith

Period	Team	Scorer	Assists
1	Philadelphia	Reggie Leach	Bobby Clarke, Jack McIlhargey
1	Philadelphia	Ross Lonsberry	Mel Bridgman, Tom Bladon

The Canadiens, under pressure to win from fans and media, started off like scared kittens in a kennel of Dobermans. Leach, Philadelphia's top gun, nailed his 16th goal of the "second season," setting a new NHL record and giving the Bullies the lead only 21 seconds into the first period. A follow-up tally by trusty Ross Lonsberry put the "bad boys" up by two at the siren.

Period	Team	Scorer	Assists
2	Montreal	Jimmy Roberts	Bob Gainey, Doug Risebrough
2	Montreal	Larry Robinson	Pete Mahovlich, Guy Lafleur

In the middle frame, Montreal's speed came to the fore. Jack McIlhargey and Jim Watson were trapped at center ice on the Roberts goal, and Robinson caught Joe "Thundermouth" Watson with his pants down on a 2-on-1 rush. Going into the second intermission, the score was knotted at two.

Period	Team	Scorer	Assists
3	Philadelphia	Larry Goodenough	Gary Dornhoefer
3	Montreal	Jacques Lemaire	Bill Nyrop
3	Montreal	Guy Lapointe	Steve Shutt

Stephenson stood on his head long enough for Goodenough to break the deadlock on a pass from Dornhoefer. Lemaire tied the game up again with a backhander from the slot before Lapointe counted the winner.

Game Two

Philadelphia 1 @ Montreal 2

Ironically, at this point in the series it was the Bullies who were feeling physically overwhelmed by the Canadiens. At one point, big Larry Robinson bodied Gary Dornhoefer so hard that play had to be stopped to fix a section of the Forum boards.

Period	Team	Scorer	Assists
2	Montreal	Jacques Lemaire	

Lemaire picked Goodenough's pocket for a shorthanded score late in the middle session.

Period	Team	Scorer	Assists
3	Montreal	Guy Lafleur	
3	Philadelphia	Dave Schultz	Tom Bladon

The expert checking of Doug Jarvis, Jim Roberts, and Bob Gainey held Philly's big line of Clarke, Leach, and Bill Barber to one shot apiece. Jarvis rubbed it in by winning 14 of 18 draws from Clarke. A late goal by — of all people! — Schultz was too little, too late.

The "Big Three" was like a wall. After the game, Lonsberry said, "They're so big you can't go through them and so strong you can't get around them."

Game Three

Montreal 3 @ Philadelphia 2

In game three the Bullies would have the twin luxuries of fan support and the privilege of the last line change. Matching lines against Scotty Bowman, though, would prove to be a living hell for Shero.

Period	Team	Scorer	Assists
1	Montreal	Steve Shutt	Guy Lafleur
1	Philadelphia	Reggie Leach	Bobby Clarke, Larry Goodenough
1	Philadelphia	Reggie Leach	

Even after Stephenson missed Shutt's 70-foot knuckler, Philadelphia battled back. Clarke finally got free to dish out a lovely pass to Leach, who zipped in the tying goal. The "Riverton Rifle" scored again to put the Flyers ahead.

Period	Team	Scorer	Assists
2	Montreal	Steve Shutt	Guy Lafleur, Pete Mahovlich

Stephenson was brilliant, stumping Murray Wilson and Yvan Cournoyer on breakaways to keep the game tied. But as the seconds ticked away, Philadelphia was spending less and less time in the attacking zone.

Period	Team	Scorer	Assists
3	Montreal	Pierre Bouchard	Murray Wilson

At 9:16 of the final frame, defenseman Bouchard took a pass from Wilson and beat Stephenson with a 40-footer. The Bullies were cooked! Even with last change, Shero was having serious problems keeping Clarke's line away from the Jarvis unit. In desperation, he put his captain on a line with Ross Lonsberry and Gary Dornhoefer. Bowman responded by changing his lines on the fly, and he always managed to have a fresh mucker — Jarvis, Risebrough, or Lemaire — out on the ice. Said Shero later: "All I can do is give Clarke shorter shifts. But when I do that, I'm putting out a player who isn't as good. I don't have as many good swing-men as Bowman does."

Dave Schultz

Game Four

Montreal 5 @ Philadelphia 3

The defending champions had two days off to dread the thought of being swept. "I'd be embarrassed," said Terry Crisp. "We're too good for that." Schultz, on the other hand, was making excuses for their play: "Ever since the Toronto series, we can't help but be affected by all the publicity we got. If I take an extra penalty, it probably would hurt us."

"Win or Lose, You've Given Philly a Lot to be Proud Of" read the banner hanging from one of the upper-deck balconies. The fans, positive that their Bullies wouldn't go down without a fight, watched as their good-luck charm, Kate Smith, did her "God Bless America" routine in person before the opening face-off.

Period	Team	Scorer	Assists
1	Philadelphia	Reggie Leach	Mel Bridgman
1	Montreal	Steve Shutt	Yvan Cournoyer, Pete Mahovlich
1	Montreal	Pierre Bouchard	Doug Risebrough
1	Philadelphia	Bill Barber	Andre Dupont, Tom Bladon

Leach blasted a 45-footer past Dryden only 41 ticks into the game. Shutt and Bouchard responded for Montreal before Barber tipped one in to tie the affair at two.

Period	Team	Scorer	Assists
2	Philadelphia	Andre Dupont	Bill Barber, Bobby Clarke
2	Montreal	Yvan Cournoyer	Larry Robinson, Guy Lafleur

Dupont's power-play goal gave Philadelphia the lead early and, when Lemaire was whistled off for hooking, they had the opportunity to stuff in the insurance goal. Only 33 seconds later, though, Dornhoefer took a stupid penalty for hooking Doug Jarvis to the ice. When Lemaire returned to the ice, Cournoyer scored while the Flyers were still a man short.

"Philadelphia's injuries were starting to catch up with them [by the third period]. They were really dragging. I was sure we'd get the break eventually."

— *Pete Mahovlich*

Period	Team	Scorer	Assists
3	Montreal	Guy Lafleur	Pete Mahovlich, Steve Shutt
3	Montreal	Pete Mahovlich	Guy Lafleur, Steve Shutt

The last nail in the Flyers' coffin came after Dornhoefer had taken a swipe at a loose puck in the crease and hit Dryden's crossbar. It was time for Montreal's "Donut Line" to take over. Lafleur, Mahovlich, and Shutt were nothing short of dazzling for the rest of the game, with Lafleur scoring the winning goal with 5:42 left in the period. A minute after that, Mahovlich took a pretty feed from Lafleur and slapped in Montreal's insurance.

Montreal received a surprising ovation as captain Cournoyer skated around the Spectrum with the Cup held high. It had been much harder than most people thought to sweep the Bullies. Said Dryden amid the dressing-room celebrations: "Somewhere down the line, people will see that we won in four straight games and think that it was easy. But they [could] not be more wrong. If you'll notice, we're drinking our champagne sitting down."

The Flyers, meanwhile, were at a crossroads. "We'll be back after that Cup again next year," crowed Joe Watson. Then his voice dropped to a whisper: "But damn it, so probably will the Canadiens."

Broad Street Beating

In 1975, Dave "The Hammer" Schultz was the reigning heavyweight champion of the NHL. However, in an unusually violent Stanley Cup playoff semifinal series that year, the legend of David William Schultz was shattered. One of the most feared and respected enforcers the professional game had ever known was defrocked in full view of his shocked fans at the Philadelphia Spectrum.

Ironically, Schultz would get his comeuppance from a fellow native of the cereal-producing province of Saskatchewan. Clark Gillies was a huge, powerful rookie. Touted as a "a meaner Frank Mahovlich," Gillies had jumped directly from the 1974 Memorial Cup champion Regina Pats to earn a post on left wing with the New York Islanders.

Gillies and Schultz tangled twice in game five of the series. Eyewitness reports unanimously pegged Gillies, also known as "Jethro," as the winner of both. The first encounter was only a minor skirmish but, a few seconds before the final buzzer, young Gillies cleaned the league bully's clock. The clash was so one-sided that Flyers defenseman Andre Dupont jumped in to assist his fallen comrade and to save him from a worse drubbing. As Moose tangled with the big kid from Moose Jaw, Schultz stood off to the side, yelling "Hit him again, Dupe, hit him again!"

Snap!shots

BILL BARBER Left Wing
6'0" 195
b. 7/11/1952, Callander, Ontario

"Just happy to be here," Bill Barber often said. The big winger struggled through an assortment of injuries en route to a Hall of Fame career and a place in Philadelphia Flyers history as perhaps their greatest winger ever.

While other NHL wingers might have scored more goals and still others might have been better defensively, no one combined both sets of skills as completely as Barber. "I can't think of a winger in the NHL who was a better all-around hockey player," remembered Rick MacLeish. "I don't think there was one." Jay Greenberg, a veteran of the Philadelphia hockey beat, once summed up Barber: "[He] skated up and down the ice with the reliability of a metronome, and by dedicating his NHL career to blending in, he stood out. He had the soul of a grinder, but the talent of an artist."

Blessed with strong legs, major-league reflexes, and a great shot, Barber first made a splash with the OHA's Kitchener Rangers in 1969. Before long, he was one of the top five hockey prospects in North America. In the first round of the 1972 NHL Amateur Draft, he was taken by the up-and-coming Flyers. Although Barber was drafted as a center, Flyers head coach Fred Shero thought to plug him in at left wing beside team captain Bobby Clarke. Barber would score 30 goals and 64 points in his rookie campaign. "I was right out of Junior hockey as a fairly high scorer and trying just to hang on in the NHL," he recalled. "In the early part of my rookie season, Fred [Shero] allowed the team to go for goals, then swung the emphasis to defensive hockey. It was perfect for me. It's tough to build confidence that you can play in this league when you only work at checking assignments. But when I scored a few goals, I was ready when the swing to defensive play came."

Barber seemed to make good in any situation. On the power play, he was equally at home at the point or as the trigger-man. On a more dubious note, he was also an expert "diver," born with an actor's ability to convince referees he'd been fouled. He was a cornerstone of the Flyers' Stanley Cup wins in 1974 and '75.

Barber's knees started to break down in 1976, cutting short his career before he could reach such career milestones as 500 goals or 1,000 points. He underwent extensive knee surgery in April 1984, and was told it would be nine months before he could return to the ice, if at all. He tried, though, enduring excruciating pain — teammates recall his screams of anguish in the Flyers' dressing room. He would call it a career in the summer of 1984.

Barber is currently the head coach of the AHL Philadelphia Phantoms. "I wanted to be remembered as being capable of doing my job day in and day out, not just as a goal-scorer but as a good all-around player for every kind of situation."

Barber was inducted into the Hockey Hall of Fame in 1990.

Peak Years   1975–79
In a Word   MODEST

BOBBY CLARKE Center
5'10" 185
b. 8/13/1949, Flin Flon, Manitoba

There was something in the way Bobby Clarke played hockey that suggested he was playing for his soul. Few players in the NHL's 80-year history have poured so much of themselves into winning. To him, there was no excuse for losing.

Bobby Clarke

The key to Clarke's becoming a superstar was a remarkable work ethic, which he developed early. "Every kid in Flin Flon played hockey," remembered Clarke. "Some played three nights a week, some played four. I played every night. All I ever wanted to do was play hockey and I just played it the way I thought it had to be played."

During games, he would block everything else out. Nothing — big leads or hopeless deficits; January road games in half-empty arenas; illness, pain, or fatigue — could keep him from giving his all. His will bordered on the superhuman.

The Flin Flon native almost didn't make it to the NHL. Even though he led his Junior league in scoring two years in a row, general managers shied away from the 168-pounder because he had diabetes. The first round of the 1969 Amateur Draft went by without Clarke's name being called. Finally the Philadelphia Flyers picked him with the 17th pick overall.

Clarke was hardly swift or elusive but he always seemed to get the jump on the puck. His otherworldly corner work and face-off skills were his bread and butter. He only had an average shot, but until Wayne Gretzky came along the gritty Flyer was the best in the NHL at passing the puck. As a result, he racked up three 100-point seasons.

Although the Flyers generally protected their captain, Number 16 didn't always escape retaliation. By the time he retired in 1984, his face was a road map of the battles he had fought in the NHL. Each and every bump in the road told the tale of a fierce competitor who took the Flyers from mediocrity to the NHL penthouse. The club that won Stanley Cups in 1974 and 1975 remained a winner until the day he retired — and beyond.

On November 15, 1984, Flyer fans came out in droves for Bobby Clarke Night. For almost five minutes, fans at the Spectrum stood and cheered the greatest Flyer of them all.

Clarke was the top player in the game between the peak years of Bobby Orr and Guy Lafleur. He won MVP honors in 1973, 1975, and 1976. By the time he hung up his skates to become Philadelphia's new GM, he had racked up 852 assists and 1,210 points.

Clarke is a member of the Hockey Hall of Fame.

Peak Years   *1973–77*
In a Word   *WILLPOWER*

YVAN COURNOYER (Le Chinois, The Roadrunner, Mighty Mite) Right Wing
5'7" 178
b. 11/22/1943, Drummondville, Quebec

As a 15-year-old right winger with the Lachine Maroons, Yvan Cournoyer was the only francophone on an English-speaking team. Not knowing a word of English, the Drummondville native would slap the part of his body he wished to protect and the club's trainer would give him the appropriate piece of equipment. Though the little guy would eventually become bilingual, he did his best talking on the ice.

So great was Cournoyer's speed that he could appear to be in two places at once. Rookie Jacques Lemaire, seeing Cournoyer skate for the first time during a 1967 practice, thought Cournoyer was "some kind of laser beam."

Cournoyer was touted as "Montreal's next Rocket Richard" when he broke into the Canadiens lineup in 1964. Because of his desperate lack of back-checking skill, Toe Blake used the young speedball sparingly at first. In time, though, Cournoyer proved he could hold his own with the big boys. He retired with 428 goals and 10 Stanley Cup championships to his credit. He reached the 40-goal plateau four times, and became the Habs' captain in 1975.

Cournoyer was at his very best in the 1973 finals against the Chicago Black Hawks. Playing with pulled abdominal muscles, he would rack up 15 goals and 25 points in 17 playoff games and win the Conn Smythe Trophy.

After undergoing back surgery for the second time in his career and appearing in only 15 games in 1978–79, Cournoyer considered retiring. When he needed a hernia operation during the off-season, he decided to call it quits. "I have to be honest with myself," he said. "I could very well be physically affected and suffer the consequences the rest of my life if I was re-injured. It was a very hard decision to make but I think I just had to make it." The guy whom Ken Dryden once called the strongest man he'd ever seen in the corners went on to dabble in scouting, coaching, and the restaurant business.

Cournoyer was inducted into the Hockey Hall of Fame in 1982.

Peak Years   *1969–73*
In a Word   *BREAKAWAY*

KEN DRYDEN Goal
6'4" 205
b. 8/8/1947, Hamilton, Ontario

As remarkable as Ken Dryden's goaltending was — he seemed to weave order out of the anarchy that is a hockey game — he was also notable for his ambivalence toward the pro game.

A 1964 draft choice of the Boston Bruins, Dryden chose instead to go to Cornell University. During his three years there he ran up a 76-4-1 record to go with a 1.65 goals-against average, and earned All-America honors each year. In March 1969, Montreal general manager Sam Pollock, who'd traded for the lanky goalie's rights, made the first of several unsuccessful attempts to sign him. Each was greeted with a polite but firm rejection. "It was an interesting initial offer," Dryden would remember. "I expected Mr. Pollock to be much harsher with a take-it-or-leave-it approach."

Dryden wanted a multi-year deal worth $100,000 a year — an astronomical demand for the time, especially for someone with no NHL experience under his belt. But Dryden wasn't dying to play in the NHL. He made it clear to Pollock that a career in law was just as intriguing to him as a job in the Canadiens' net. "Yale and Harvard are the best schools in the country and if they'd accept me, I couldn't turn it down," he would say. "Hockey has been a part of my life for a long time. But the fact is, if negotiations break down it wouldn't break my heart. I'd be very pleased to go to law school."

Dryden played the 1969 season for the Canadian National Team, but Pollock eventually managed to sign the Hamilton native. He made his NHL debut in March 1971, replacing an injured Rogie Vachon. After playing in only a half-dozen regular-season games, the bookish Dryden gave one of the greatest playoff goaltending performances ever. Against all odds, the Habs upset the Boston Bruins — one of the most powerful offensive machines of all time — and then the Chicago Black Hawks to win the Stanley Cup. "The credit goes to their whole team," said Phil Esposito after the seventh game of the quarterfinals, "but if one man stood out, it was that bleeping octopus Dryden."

Dryden won the Conn Smythe Trophy for his efforts. Oddly, he was still considered a rookie in 1971–72, and he won the Calder Trophy that year. After winning the Vezina Trophy and another Cup in 1973, Dryden complained about his $78,000-a-year contract. "I can name six goaltenders who were higher paid than me last year and that sort of bothers me," he said later. "I don't see why this should be the case. Montreal is not impoverished. If other teams can [pay more], it seems to me they should be able to." Habs management felt there was nothing to discuss, so Dryden informed Pollock and team president Jacques Courtois that he would sit out the upcoming season. Later he would admit to feeling regretful — "It's sort of like turning your back on something you liked very much and felt very much a part of" — but in the meantime he began articling at the Toronto law firm of Osler, Hoskins, and Harcourt for a measly $135 a week.

In May 1974 the holdout was wooed back into the fold with a three-year deal worth a reported $200,000 a year. "I think what made me come back was the opportunity to come back," Dryden said. "There was no sudden change of heart on my part. I didn't know whether or not the opportunity to play here again would ever arise. When the chance came, I took it."

Dryden picked up right where he left off, leading the Canadiens to Cup wins in 1976, 1977, 1978, and 1979. But despite an impeccable resume — six Stanley Cups, five Vezina trophies, a 258-57-74 career record, six All-Star nominations — he had many detractors. Stan Fischler always claimed he was overrated and that he cracked under pressure. Others said he would be nowhere without the Habs' impenetrable defense, who prevented many decent shots from reaching Dryden. Hockey's most profound thinker countered that it took a lot of concentration to play behind a team like the Canadiens and that the pressure to win night after night was hellish.

In July 1979, after the Canadiens' fourth straight Cup win, Dryden called it a day. He was a month shy of his 32nd birthday and had only played seven full NHL seasons. He never looked back, embarking on a fascinating series of careers. He became the author of *The Game*, the most captivating book ever written about hockey. Between 1984 and '86 he was Ontario's Youth Commissioner, coordinating employment and training programs for young people. In May 1997 he was named president of the Toronto Maple Leafs.

Dryden is an esteemed member of the Hockey Hall of Fame.

Peak Years   *1974–78*
In a Word   *SCHOLAR*

PHIL ESPOSITO Center
6'1" 205
b. 2/20/1942, Sault Ste. Marie, Ontario

Phil Esposito made his NHL debut with the Chicago Black Hawks during the 1963–64 season. Over the next few years, the well-built center would prove both an effective scorer and play-maker. Playing mostly on a forward line between Bobby Hull and Chico Maki, Esposito posted modest seasons of 55, 53, and 61 points. By the end of the 1966–67 campaign, team brass concluded that the big lug would never be an elite player. "I got 23 goals, 27 goals, and 21 goals in my three years [in Chicago] so I hardly think I was trade material. But I didn't play too much in the playoffs after the first game [against Toronto] the year I was traded. I don't think Billy Reay had the confidence in me anymore."

The trade Esposito referred to took place on May 15, 1967. He, Ken Hodge, and Fred Stanfield were shipped to the Boston Bruins for Gilles Marotte, Pit Martin, and Jack Norris. It would become known as one of the most lopsided trades in hockey history.

Bruins coach Harry Sinden had a hunch the big center would be the perfect complement to young defenseman Bobby Orr, who was already showing promise as a playmaker. His hunch paid off: on March 2, 1969, Esposito became the first player in NHL history to notch 100 points in a single season. He hit the finish line with 49 goals and 126 points. Through the mid-1970s, Esposito was the dominant offensive player in the game. He took goal-scoring to cosmic levels, posting totals of 43, 76 (setting an NHL record), 66, 55, 68, and 61. By 1974, he had five Art Ross trophies, two Harts, six consecutive First All-Star Team nods, and two Stanley Cup rings. In September of 1972, he led Team Canada to a hard-fought victory over the dazzling Soviet national side. If not for his emotional speech after game four in Vancouver, many say Canada would have lost miserably.

Espo never considered his lack of a mean streak to be a liability. "I never went all over the ice looking to hit a guy," was the way he would put it. "It wasn't my style. I would go in the corners once in a while and I would avoid them most other times. Ken Hodge was really great in the corners and that was always our play. But I'm a little prejudiced about playing center ice. There was always too much work on the wing. I never liked wing."

Another rap against Esposito was that he was a subpar skater. Don't be fooled. Big men always seem to be moving slower on the ice than they really are. In truth, Esposito was a strong skater who could back-check when he wanted to. He was by no means a player who showed up only for power plays.

On November 7, 1975, Esposito was again the central figure in a multi-player blockbuster trade when the Bruins sent him to the New York Rangers along with Carol Vadnais for Brad Park, Jean Ratelle, and the unforgettable Joe Zanussi. Although the big center's best days were surely behind him, he would lead the Rangers in scoring four years in a row and help them reach the Stanley Cup finals in 1979. When he decided to retire in early 1981, his 717 goals and 1,590 points trailed only one other man: Gordie Howe.

Life after hockey for Esposito was no slow boat. The once-feared sniper served as the Rangers' GM (and, briefly, head coach) between 1986–87 and 1988–89. He would later help Tampa Bay land an NHL expansion team, and served as the Lightning's first ever GM.

Esposito is a member of the Hockey Hall of Fame.

Peak Years   *1969–73*
In a Word   *OPPORTUNIST*

TONY ESPOSITO (Tony O) Goal
5'11" 185
b. 4/23/1943, Sault Ste. Marie, Ontario

When Tony Esposito broke into the NHL with the Montreal Canadiens in 1968–69, he was known as "Phil Esposito's kid brother." But before long he would carve out his own niche in hockey history.

Tony was a late bloomer ("I didn't get too interested in playing on a team until I was in my late teens," he would recall years

Tony Esposito

later). He didn't play Junior hockey, but at the age of 19 he landed a hockey scholarship from Michigan Tech University. There, he earned a degree in business as well as three All-America nods on the ice. The Canadiens placed him on their negotiation list during his sophomore year, and when he graduated in 1967 he signed with the Habs, playing his first pro season for the WHL's Vancouver Canucks.

The Canucks finished last in the league in 1967–68, but Esposito stood out,

----

leading the league in games played, shutouts, and wins (and, for good measure, losses). He opened the next season with Montreal's farm team in Houston, but injuries to Canadiens regulars Gump Worsley and Rogie Vachon earned Esposito a promotion to the NHL, where in 13 games he posted two shutouts and a respectable 2.73 goals-against average.

In June 1969 the Canadiens left Esposito exposed in the Intra-League Draft, choosing to protect Vachon, the aging Worsley, and Phil Myre. The Chicago Black Hawks didn't hesitate to snap up the young hotshot. "I knew I'd be moving," he commented after the cut. "The Canadiens won the Stanley Cup with those goalies and decided to stick with them. I wasn't disappointed. All I wanted was a chance to show what I could do."

Chicago already had two solid goalies in Dave Dryden and Denis DeJordy, but the 26-year-old Esposito wowed everyone in training camp and won the starting job. His first year with the Hawks was nothing short of incredible: a 2.17 goals-against average, a league-leading 38 wins, and an incredible 15 shutouts! Suddenly, "Phil's kid brother" had become "Tony O," winner of both the Calder and Vezina trophies.

When asked about his butterfly goaltending style, Esposito laughed: "My job is stopping the puck and I don't really care how." He had remarkable reflexes and a real knack for clearing rebounds. Foot speed and hand-eye coordination were this goaltending legend's stock in trade.

Esposito backstopped Chicago to the Cup finals in 1971 and put up a career-best 1.77 GAA in 1971–72 to win another Vezina and another First-Team All-Star nomination. He shared puck-stopping duties with Ken Dryden on Team Canada during the 1972 Summit Series, and made it to the Cup finals again in 1973. His third Vezina came in 1973–74.

Tony remained the Hawks' top goalie for 15 years. When he retired in 1983–84, his 423 wins trailed only Terry Sawchuk's 447 and Jacques Plante's 434.

Esposito was inducted into the Hockey Hall of Fame in 1988. Since hanging up the skates, he has worked for the NHL Players Association and served in the front offices of the Pittsburgh Penguins and Tampa Bay Lightning.

Peak Years   *1970–74*
In a Word   *BUTTERFLY*

BOB GAINEY Left Wing
6'2" 200
b. 12/13/1953, Peterborough, Ontario

"It starts from the moment he gathers the puck in the graceful curve of his stick. Head up, eyes blazing like hot little coals, he gets beyond one man . . . then another, and by now there is no longer a crowd in Montreal Forum, but a noise engulfing it. This is Bob Gainey."
— *from Ken Dryden's* The Game

Gainey was one of the finest defensive forwards ever to have performed in the NHL. His stable, controlled presence on the ice was one of the biggest factors in the success of the Montreal Canadiens through the 1970s. In *The Game*, teammate Ken Dryden wrote: "If I could be a forward, I would want to be Bob Gainey."

Gainey's brilliance won him four consecutive Frank Selke trophies as the league's top defensive forward. Indeed, Gainey's marvelous combination of defensive and offensive skill spurred the creation of the Selke award in 1978. He also picked up a Conn Smythe Trophy in 1979, represented Canada in the 1976 and 1981 Canada Cups as well as the 1979 Challenge Cup, and earned berths on four NHL All-Star squads.

The Canadiens chose Gainey in the first round of the 1973 Amateur Draft. The tough, unobtrusive winger had finished 67th in the OHA scoring race, which had some critics questioning Montreal GM Sam Pollock's sanity. But as Gainey's Junior coach, Roger Neilson, would point out, Gainey "had given the checking role respectability." Said one Montreal *Star* reporter: "From his Junior days, where he was schooled in the finer points of defensive hockey, he has burnished and sophisticated that part of the game. It is against grinding, hitting, hard-working teams that Gainey reaches his zenith."

When he retired from the NHL in 1989, the man the Soviets once called "the world's best hockey player" spent a year in France as the playing coach of the Epinal club. In 1990 he returned to the NHL as head coach of the Minnesota North Stars. They went to the Stanley Cup finals in their first year under his tutelage. He added the GM portfolio in June 1992, a post he still holds today.

In 16 seasons as a Montreal Canadien, Gainey earned five Stanley Cup rings and the respect of the hockey world. He is a worthy member of the Hockey Hall of Fame.

Peak Years   *1977–81*
In a Word   *LABORER*

GUY LAFLEUR (The Flower, Le Demon Blond) Right Wing
6'0" 185
b. 9/20/1951, Thurso, Quebec

He was a Picasso on ice, weaving together seemingly impossible plays out of thin air the way a painter fills a blank canvas. The Flower was explosively fast, at least a stride swifter than his peers, and had amazing "ice vision." He changed direction sharply and smoothly, often making moves that left his foes flat-footed. He carried the puck on his stick as if it were fixed to the blade and was equally adept as a play-maker or a sniper. He was a spectacular athlete in a spectacular sport and it was a joy to see him in his full glory.

Lafleur learned to play hockey on frozen ponds and, during the summer, on the street, swapping a puck for a ragged tennis ball. So dedicated was he that he would sneak into a Thurso rink early in the morning and on Sundays to snatch extra ice-time. He would sleep in his hockey gear so he could get to the rink that much earlier in the morning. "When I was a kid all we saw on TV was the Canadiens and all I wanted to be was [Jean] Beliveau," remembered Lafleur, who wore Beliveau's Number 4 as a Junior with the Quebec Remparts. "We had one bleu, blanc, et rouge Canadiens sweater and I fought the others for the right to wear it. I dreaded to be drafted by any other team but the Canadiens and when they took me I was so happy."

In May 1970 Montreal GM Sam Pollock made sure he'd be able to get Lafleur. He dealt farmhand Ernie Hicke to the sad-sack Oakland Seals for their first pick in the 1971 Amateur Draft. The plan worked flawlessly: the Seals crossed the finish line in last place, and the Habs drafted first overall.

Lafleur had scored more than 100 goals in each of his last two amateur seasons, and was under immense pressure to deliver the goods immediately for the Canadiens. He was stepping into the roster slot just recently vacated by his childhood idol, the legendary Beliveau. When he scored less than 30 goals in each of his first three NHL seasons, the "flop" label was thrown around mercilessly. Then, in 1974–75, the young phenom came to life, scoring 53 goals and adding 66 helpers in 70 games. The Flower had arrived. "I think it was always there and it was maybe a matter of bringing it out," he said. "It was harder than I thought it would be and I had to try harder. I had lost but regained my confidence . . . I learned a lot from it, and learned how to relax."

The dazzling, and now helmetless, Lafleur blossomed into the NHL's most exciting, and dangerous performer. The Flower, who became a French Canadian icon, went on to score 50 or more goals in six consecutive seasons. Between 1974 and 1980, he won three Art Ross trophies, two Harts, a Conn Smythe, six First-Team All-Star nominations, and five Stanley Cup rings. Until Wayne Gretzky came along, Lafleur was the very definition of dominance in hockey.

Early in the 1984–85 season, Guy Lafleur made the decision to retire. "I saw the team was going well this year and thought it better to go out that way than when the team was in difficulty," he said. The Flower left the game as one of the most popular athletes to ever perform in Montreal. In 1988, his genius was rewarded with election to the Hockey Hall of Fame.

On September 26, 1988, Lafleur stunned the hockey world by signing as a free agent with the New York Rangers. Although the 37-year-old had lost a step, he still had the magic. In 67 games, he scored 18 goals and 45 points. He followed up the stint with a two-year finale back in Quebec City as a Nordique. He retired for good after the 1990–91 season with 560 goals and 1,353 points. Today, he is a goodwill ambassador for the Montreal Canadiens.

Peak Years   *1976–80*
In a Word   *ARTIST*

GUY LAPOINTE (Pointu) Defense
6'0" 205
b. 3/18/1948, Montreal, Quebec

Guy Gerard Lapointe played his Junior hockey with Maisonneuve, the Verdun Junior Maple Leafs, and the Montreal Junior Canadiens. He turned professional in 1968–69 with the Central League's Houston Apollos and was an AHL First-Team All-Star the following season with the Montreal Voyageurs.

Lapointe cracked the Montreal Canadiens' roster for good in 1970–1971. He would soon burst forth as a member of Montreal's famed "Big Three" (Lapointe, Larry Robinson, and Serge Savard), also known as the "Ministry of Defense." A skilled puck-handler and skater, big Lapointe was a force at both ends of the rink; he could body-check as well as he could score. His slapshot was hard, heavy, low, and accurate, generally considered one of the best in the game. He was an important part of the Canadiens' legendary power-play unit.

Lapointe's exploits as a dressing-room prankster are also the stuff of legend. During the 1972 Summit Series, he taped teammate Phil Esposito's shower sandals together with yards of sticky packing tape. Esposito, who was a superstitious chap, would not take his shower without his treasured sandals on his feet. He spent almost an hour unwinding the tape from them. There wasn't a single Canadien in the '70s who escaped having his shoes nailed to a dressing-room floor or bench.

Back when the big man was playing Junior hockey, players had to wear hats, ties, and coats. At a practice, Lapointe sneaked back into the dressing room and cut a hole in the top of almost every hat, including his own. He spared one hat only. When the rest of the team found out what had happened, they descended angrily on the confused soul whose hat didn't have a hole.

"When we would finish practice we would rush back into the dressing room before Guy got there . . ." recalled Montreal teammate Pierre Bouchard. "And nobody would leave the room to go out on the ice until they made sure that Guy had gone."

Lapointe was a key member of Team Canada at the historic 1972 Summit Series, as well as the first Canada Cup squad in 1976 and the 1979 Challenge Cup side. He earned four All-Star nominations and contributed to six Stanley Cup championships. In 1974–75 he hit a career high in goals with 28, and two years later had his best season with 76 points.

Lapointe was traded to the St. Louis Blues in March 1982, appearing in 62 games, before putting in one last season with the Boston Bruins. Since hanging up his skates in 1984, he has served as an assistant coach with the Quebec Nordiques, as general manager of the Longueil Chevaliers, and as an integral part of the Calgary Flames' scouting system.

In 884 games spread across 15 years, Lapointe scored 171 goals and 622 points. He was named to the Hockey Hall of Fame in 1993.

Peak Years   *1974–78*
In a Word   *JOKER*

REGGIE LEACH (The Riverton Rifle) Right Wing
6'0" 180
b. 4/23/1950, Riverton, Manitoba

Never serious about school as a boy, Reggie Leach lived for hockey. "I knew that was all there was for me," he recalled later. By age 13, he was skating among grown men in an Edmonton industrial hockey league when he was spotted by a Detroit Red Wings scout. Leach was signed to a contract with Detroit's junior club in Flin Flon, Manitoba. It was here that the young sniper struck up a friendship with the team's best, and most popular, player, Bobby Clarke. After Clarke went to the Philadelphia Flyers in the 1969 NHL Amateur Draft, Leach continued to improve, notching 65 goals for the Bombers in 1969–70 and becoming the Boston Bruins' first pick in 1970.

Leach's stay in Boston was uneventful, and in February 1972 he was dealt to the California Golden Seals for star defenseman Carol Vadnais. While he floundered on the West Coast, his old friend Clarke set the wheels in motion for a trade that would bring Leach to the Flyers. Clarke's new right winger contributed 45 goals in 1974–75, plus another eight in the playoffs, as the Flyers won their second consecutive Cup.

The 1975–76 campaign was Leach's breakthrough: he bagged 61 goals in powering Philadelphia to another finals appearance. This year, though, the Montreal Canadiens would take the Cup. Despite the loss, Leach (with 19 goals in 16 playoff matches) was awarded the Conn Smythe Trophy. "Clarke makes the bombs, and I drop them," explained Leach, whose 115-mile-an-hour shot struck fear into NHL goalies in the mid to late 1970s.

Leach wasn't the most motivated or coachable player, however. Fred Shero appealed to Clarke to get Leach fired up. He also tried to get the sullen winger to develop his defensive game. Leach though Shero was badgering him and his performance dropped off to just 24 goals in 1977–78. After the 1981–82 season, and the failure of two more coaches (Bob McCammon and Pat Quinn) to motivate him, Philadelphia dumped Leach on waivers. He was picked up by Detroit, for whom he scored 15 goals in 1982–83.

After retiring he joined Alcoholics Anonymous and began a grass-cutting job that turned into Reggie Leach's Sports Lawn Service. Today, he is sober and successful and has no regrets about his ups and downs as an NHL superstar.

Peak Years   *1975–79*
In a Word   *RIFLE*

JACQUES LEMAIRE (Coco) Center
5'10" 180
b. 9/7/1945, LaSalle, Quebec

Even though they'd lost 20 men to expansion, Montreal Canadiens skipper Toe Blake rated the roster for the Habs' 1967 training camp as one of the best he'd seen in a decade. "I think we have as many fine prospects as any year since I became coach," said Blake. According to Montreal *Gazette* sportswriter Pat Curran, the pick of the rookie litter was Jacques Gerard Lemaire, a 22-year-old center from north of Montreal. "We didn't consider Lemaire as our best prospect because he struggled quite a bit last season in the Central League," said Blake. "But he played very well in our exhibitions, especially killing penalties — well enough to stick around when the season started."

One of Lemaire's strongest points was his hard and heavy shot. "I try to keep it low and practice that way," he explained. "It's hard to score on rebounds off the goaler's chest." So hard was the young gun's shot that comparisons to Bobby Hull's were inevitable. "My father, he got me some pucks made out of steel and I used to practice shooting with these things," recalled Lemaire years later. "When I would play in a game after practicing like that, the regular puck would feel like a feather and it would go like hell."

All told, Lemaire starred in 12 brilliant seasons in Montreal and was generally considered underrated. He was the model of two-way play, as much a star at scoring goals as he was at preventing them. This eight-time Stanley Cup champion scored a total of 366 goals and 835 points. After retiring from the NHL in 1979, he went to play and later coach in Switzerland.

Lemaire took over from Bob Berry as Montreal's head coach during the 1983–84 season. He served in this capacity through the following season before taking a more "behind-the-scenes" role in the Canadiens organization. He acted as GM Serge Savard's right-hand man until the summer of 1993, when he accepted the head coaching job with the New Jersey Devils. "We looked for an individual who could immediately gain the respect of our players once he walked into that locker room," said Devils GM Lou Lamoriello. In New Jersey, Lemaire would introduce his new defensive system — now widely known as "The Trap." In 1995, he took his boys all the way to a Stanley Cup championship.

Today, Lemaire is back in the Canadiens organization, this time as a "special advisor" to GM Rejean Houle.

Lemaire was summed up best by broadcasting legend Danny Gallivan: "Jacques was an exceptional, intelligent player and exemplary, not only as a player but as an individual." Lemaire is a member of the Hockey Hall of Fame.

Peak Years   *1971–75*
In a Word   *MECHANICAL*

RICHARD MARTIN Left Wing
5'11" 179
b. 7/26/1951, Verdun, Quebec

For 10 NHL seasons, Rick Martin had the Midas touch. He was one of the purest shooters in the league during the 1970s. But his story also forces us to wonder what might have been.

In 1971 the Buffalo Sabres made Martin the fifth pick overall in the amateur draft. He stepped right into the Sabres' lineup and set a record for rookies by scoring 44 goals. Sabres boss Punch Imlach later commented: "I'd have taken him if I'd had the first draft choice." High praise when you consider that Guy Lafleur and Marcel Dionne were the first two selections in that '71 draft.

In September 1972, Martin was named to Team Canada in the Summit Series. But when he learned he wouldn't get a chance to play in the series, he left the team and hooked up with the Sabres at training camp. "I had a super-great attitude going [into] that '72 series," he would say four years later. "I wanted to play real bad. When they told me they wouldn't be using me, I felt I had to start thinking of myself, and the obligation I had to the Sabres. That's when I decided to come home. I was in super-excellent shape and I didn't want to lose any of it sitting in the stands over there when I could have been at training camp with Buffalo."

Martin's first nine NHL campaigns were impressive, to say the least. The owner of one of the most deadly shots of the 1970s averaged more than 40 goals a season, topping the 50-goal plateau twice. He represented one-third of "The French Connection," one of the most explosive line combinations in history. Teamed with the dazzling Gilbert Perreault and the slick Rene Robert on the explosive French Connection Line, Martin joined the NHL's elite class. The line propelled Buffalo to the upper echelon of the NHL, peaking with an appearance in the 1975 Stanley Cup finals.

"Playing with Rene and Gilbert was a lot of fun," recalled Martin years later. "There was very good chemistry on that line. We seemed to anticipate each other very well, and I knew if I got into the open they'd get the puck to me."

Martin suffered a career-ending knee injury during a November 9, 1980, game against the Washington Capitals, when he collided with goalie Mike Palmateer. "I had a semi-breakaway and got tripped at the blue-line and I got up at the top of the circle and [Palmateer] ran into me," recalled Martin. "I tore something but it didn't show up in the tests and I didn't have surgery for six months. I never played against Palmateer again and maybe that's a good thing because he would have had trouble ducking my shots."

Buffalo traded Martin to the Los Angeles Kings in March 1981. The once-feared sniper would play only four games in the purple and gold before retiring. "They said I'd be crippled by the time I was 40 if I continued to play," he said later. Since retiring, Martin has run his own restaurant, automotive shop, and trucking company. He has recently been involved in a gold-mining project in western Africa. A fitting industry for the man with the Midas touch.

Peak Years   *1973–77*
In a Word   *GUNNER*

LANNY McDONALD Right Wing
6'0" 185
b. 2/16/1953, Hanna, Alberta

When Lanny King McDonald was a kid growing up in Alberta, the time difference meant that *Hockey Night in Canada* started at six o'clock. He would wolf down his dinner while he watched his beloved Toronto Maple Leafs, led by his hero Dave Keon, on TV. "I fastened my eyes on Keon — up, down, zip. Supper was all hockey."

When McDonald joined Toronto in 1973, it was as if destiny was being fulfilled. The big winger had two years of standout Junior hockey under his belt when the Leafs chose him fourth overall in the amateur draft. Thanks to the patient coaching of Red Kelly and the leadership of his idol, Keon, McDonald got off on the right foot in the NHL. "Kelly is a fine coach," said McDonald. "[He] has no trouble communicating, lays it out so you really understand what he wants. Dave Keon has been super. He talks with me between every shift, points out my mistakes right at the time."

McDonald's first NHL goal gave the Leafs their first win in the Montreal Forum in three years. The marker was the first of many big ones he would score over the next 16 years. The hugely popular winger had a mustache like a walrus and one of the best wrist shots of the 1970s. Former Calgary Flames coach Bob Johnson raved about McDonald: "When he shoots, the puck just seems to go in the net."

McDonald was also noted for his generosity to his teammates. After notching his 400th goal, he was nagged by the feeling that the puck had actually gone in off teammate Ed Beers. Despite Beers's protests that it hadn't, McDonald was not satisfied. Watching a tape of the game at his home, he saw that the goal really wasn't his. The very next day, he called the NHL's official scorer and asked that credit for the goal be given to Beers. After taking a moment to recover from the shock, the scorer granted his request.

On May 25, 1989, during the deciding game of the Stanley Cup finals between Calgary and the Canadiens, McDonald returned to the ice after serving a penalty and blasted the rubber past goalie Patrick Roy to give his Flames a 2–1 lead. Calgary would hold on to their advantage and win the Cup. It was the last goal of McDonald's career. Almost immediately after the Cup celebrations wound down, he hung up his skates for good. "My decision, I'm sure, is not a great secret," he said through a few tears. "I've been hearing it for the last few months. I've had the time of my life and I wouldn't change a thing."

In 1,111 NHL games, McDonald was good for 500 goals and 1,006 points. He is a member of the Hockey Hall of Fame.

Peak Years 1976–80
In a Word MUSTACHE

TERRY O'REILLY (Mack Truck) Right Wing
6'1" 200
b. 6/7/1951, Niagara Falls, Ontario

At the age of 18, Terry O'Reilly was offered a scholarship to play for St. Louis University, then one of the top schools in the western U.S. when it came to college hockey. "They brought me to St. Louis, where the Bruins were playing the Blues that night," recalled O'Reilly, "and they foolishly gave me a ticket to the game." It was the era of Bobby Orr, Phil Esposito, and the Big Bad Bruins. Young O'Reilly was hooked. He decided to keep playing Junior hockey with the Oshawa Generals until his fondest dream came true in June 1971: he was drafted by none other than the Boston Bruins.

At O'Reilly's first training camp, he told a pack of hockey writers: "I'm not a real fancy right wing." He was right. If ever there was a meat-and-potatoes hockey player, it was O'Reilly, a big, aggressive kid with a lot to learn. "I was like a mouse in a maze," he recalled. "I kept bumping into barriers, making mistakes, but I kept going and kept learning until I found my way."

He handled his stick like an oversized broom and his skating was labored, but he had loads of heart. When people recall Don Cherry's lunch-bucket Bruins of the mid to late 1970s, O'Reilly's name invariably comes up. His crashing, bashing brand of hockey was complemented by a remarkable work ethic and a desire to see his foes not only defeated but crushed. He was the prototypical Bruin.

O'Reilly did whatever was asked of him, or died trying. He was all over the ice, checking, hitting, harassing, stealing, setting up plays, and sometimes even scoring a goal himself. He was a hustler, a one-man wrecking crew with a passion for the game that was contagious. Tommy McVie, a former head coach of the Washington Capitals, once said: "If we play against the Bruins 10 times we're going to have problems with [O'Reilly] 10 nights."

"I've dreaded this day," said Bruins GM Harry Sinden after the 1984–85 season. "I've lived in fear of the time when we had to face a season without Terry O'Reilly." At 34, the big winger was calling it quits.

Peak Years 1977–81
In a Word KNUCKLES

BOBBY ORR Defense
6'0" 197
b. 3/20/1948, Parry Sound, Ontario

Robert Orr's hockey career began in 1960, when he was only 12. The Boston Bruins' scouting staff discovered the 110-pound prodigy in an all-Ontario Bantam tournament. Two years later, the Bruins managed to ink the Parry Sounder to a Junior amateur contract, and they assigned him to the Oshawa Generals, where he would compete among players as old as 20. At 18 he joined the big team, signing for $60,000 plus bonuses over two years.

Even in the way he entered the league, Orr was different. In 1966, players just didn't hire lawyers to negotiate contracts. And Orr's agent was none other than the flamboyant Alan Eagleson.

As the brightest member of the lowly Bruins, Orr began immediately to show flashes of the explosive energy and on-ice genius that would mark his career. In 61 games, the young rushing phenom scored 13 times and added 28 assists en route to winning the Calder Trophy. He had unprecedented speed and balance on his skates, masterly control of the puck, and a deadly accurate shot. He led rush after rush for the resurgent B's.

Orr led the Bruins, who'd missed the playoffs seven years in a row prior to his arrival, to a pair of Stanley Cup wins — including, in 1970, their first in 29 years. The photograph of Orr's reaction to his Cup-winning goal against Glenn Hall is forever etched in our memories — the camera captured him flying through the air, having tripped over St. Louis's Noel Picard, his arms raised in celebration.

Number 4 won the Norris Trophy eight years in a row, the Hart Trophy three times, the Conn Smythe Trophy twice, and nine All-Star nominations. In an unprecedented feat for a blue-liner, Orr won the Art Ross Trophy as league scoring champion — twice!

During his second season, Orr was on the receiving end of a brutal hip check from Leafs defender Marcel Pronovost, tearing his left medial meniscus. He would go under the knife five times between 1968 and 1975. In June 1976, the ailing superstar signed on with the Chicago Black Hawks, but he appeared in only 20 games before needing a sixth round of knee surgery. After an unsuccessful eight-game comeback attempt in 1978–79, the great defenseman tearfully decided to hang up his skates. The Hockey Hall of Fame waived the traditional three-year waiting period and enshrined him immediately.

Was Orr the finest defenseman in NHL history? Probably. Was he the greatest player ever? Well, Don Cherry will certainly tell you so.

Peak Years   *1970–1974*
In a Word   *BLUR*

BERNIE PARENT Goal
5'10" 180
b. 4/3/1945, Montreal, Quebec

The youngest of seven children of a Montreal cement-machine operator, Bernie Parent got his start in hockey (sort of) by kicking out rubber balls while wearing galoshes. He would sign with one of the few youth teams not sponsored by the Canadiens, leaving him available for the Boston Bruins to claim him. After winning a Memorial Cup with the Niagara Falls Flyers in his last year as a Junior, the long-suffering B's called him up. For the first time in six years, Boston didn't finish last — they vaulted all the way to fifth. But in 1966–67, when Parent drank too many beers, stopped too few pucks, and heard about a thousand too many boo-birds, his inexperience and shaky confidence betrayed him. He

----

was sent down to the minors and left unprotected in the 1967 NHL Expansion Draft.

Philadelphia selected Parent, along with his Niagara Falls teammate and fellow Bruin castoff Doug Favell. The cage tandem were the Flyers' best players; many of the infant franchise's initial successes could be traced to the stellar work of these two. After four seasons, though, owner Ed Snider decided his team was settling for way too many ties and that its offense needed punching up. Parent was dealt away to Toronto in a three-way deal that saw Bruin prospect Rick MacLeish come to Philadelphia.

The young goaltending star was devastated at first, but he quickly saw the upside of his situation. The Leafs' lineup boasted 42-year-old legend Jacques Plante — Parent's childhood idol. The silver-haired Snake, as aloof and self-centered as ever, nonetheless took a shine to Parent, and set out to become his mentor. "He didn't really change my style," said Parent. "He just taught me how to use my own system."

Most notably, Plante taught Parent how best to approach the game mentally, and how to make the best use of his quick feet to improve his balance. Parent always seemed to know where the puck had the best chance of hitting him. Rather than flail at shots, he accepted them, cleanly snatching or deflecting the puck out of harm's way. His movements were economical and fluid. Such serenity seemed to rub off on his teammates and make them believe they couldn't lose with him in nets.

Parent couldn't see eye to eye with Leaf boss Harold Ballard, so he became one of the first name NHLers to jump to the WHA. He was the first, and only, player acquired by the Miami Screaming Eagles. When the Eagles failed to take off, Bernie found himself with the Philadelphia Blazers. After one season he announced that he wanted to return to the NHL, but would not play for the Leafs; Ed Snider jumped at the chance to reacquire him.

In 1973–74, Parent set NHL records for games (73) and wins (47), and chalked up 12 shutouts to go with a 2.02 goals-against average. "He was the best," said backup Bobby Taylor. "The only one who could come close was Glenn Hall. Bernie played 65 games a year and there would only be a handful of bad performances. The rest were not just good, but great. He was always there, like the sun rising in the east and setting in the west. His anticipation was just phenomenal. His feet were the key. He used them better than anybody."

Parent backstopped his Flyers to Stanley Cup wins in 1974 and '75, and he won the Conn Smythe Trophy in both seasons. Although two superb seasons (1973–74 and 1974–75) are not enough to consider the top puck-stopper of the 1970s, he was without doubt the most technically sound goalie since Jacques Plante. If not for injuries and a career-ending eye injury in 1979, he might have gone on to even greater glory in the 1980s.

Parent is a member of the Hockey Hall of Fame.

Peak Years   *1972–76*
In a Word   *TECHNICIAN*

BRAD PARK Defense
6'0" 200
b. 7/6/1948, Toronto, Ontario

Brad Park was a brilliant defender in an era laden with superstar blue-liners. Park had the misfortune to ply his trade at the same time as Bobby Orr and, later, Denis Potvin — he would play second fiddle throughout his career. In fact, Park's achievements are too easily overlooked: in his 17-year career the big man was named to the NHL's First All-Star Team five times, and twice more made the Second Team.

Park found stardom early, as a member of the OHA's Toronto Marlboros. He caught the eye of New York Rangers GM Emile Francis, who drafted him second overall in the 1966 Amateur Draft. "I have semi-secret plans to work Park in as our number-two point man behind Rod Gilbert. Brad gives you the puck and then takes it away from you. He's a smoothie out there and the most important thing is how he places his shots from the blue-line."

The hip-checking, baby-faced rearguard would remain the darling of Madison Square Garden for seven and a half years. By the time he was traded to the Bruins in November 1975, he was easily one of the National league's top two or three defenders.

In Boston, Park was teamed up on the power play with the great Bobby Orr. Like Orr, Park's career was severely hampered by knee problems. Nevertheless, he recovered from five major operations and four arthroscopic surgeries to become only the second blue-liner in NHL history to rack up 500 career assists.

In August 1983 Park signed as a free agent with the Detroit Red Wings. Bruins boss Harry Sinden was left fuming, convinced that Park had jumped the team. Park said he wanted out of Boston because he didn't want to go through what had happened to a couple of his old teammates, Wayne Cashman and Jean Ratelle, who in their last years as Bruins were left to rot on the bench as over-the-hill mongrels.

After the 1984–85 season, Park retired from the game. A stint as coach of the Wings was cut short after a controversial bench-clearing brawl on January 13, 1986 — he sent his entire team into the fray. Scotty Morrison, the NHL's head of officiating, suspended Park before Detroit management gave him his walking papers.

Park is a very worthy member of the Hockey Hall of Fame.

Peak Years   1973–77
In a Word   OUTSTANDING

GILBERT PERREAULT Center
6'1" 180
b. 11/13/1950, Victoriaville, Quebec

Hockey legend Bernie Geoffrion once said of Gilbert Perreault: "You could start a franchise with him." Which is precisely what the expansion Buffalo Sabres did in 1970. Perreault was already a star at age 18, a player known for his pretty skating as well as his power and finesse with the puck. He performed admirably as a center on the Montreal Junior Canadiens, leading the OHA side to Memorial Cups in 1969 and in 1970.

"I was a rink rat," recalled Perreault, a native of Jean Beliveau's hometown. "I hung around hockey all the time, helped scrape the ice, played wherever there was a chance. Jean Beliveau was my idol, he came from my town and his Montreal Canadiens were my team."

In Perreault's final year of Junior hockey (1969–70) he scored 51 goals and 121 points in only 54 games. Before the 1970 NHL Amateur Draft, the NHL's two newest franchises — Vancouver Canucks and Buffalo Sabres — spun a roulette wheel for the rights to the top pick. Buffalo boss Punch Imlach picked number 11, which turned out to be the winner, and Perreault became a Sabre.

Perreault's 38 goals and 72 points in his rookie season won him the Calder Trophy. In the fall of 1972 the young wizard was chosen to play for Canada in the Summit Series. He was used sparingly and, after only two games, he left Team Canada for the Sabres' training camp. Although he was criticized heavily for leaving Team Canada, called a traitor and a deserter, he came back with a 28-goal, 88-point effort between Richard Martin and Rene Robert on the brilliant new "French Connection" Line.

"Perreault's as unselfish as [Bobby] Orr and as much a team man as [Jean] Beliveau," said Imlach. "He has their sort of rare natural talent. He can skate as well as anyone ever could and can carry the puck on his stick as good as any. I've been around a lot of years and I've never seen a player with his speed and variety of shifts." Indeed, Perreault had a vast array of feints, fakes, and dekes. Hall of Fame referee Frank Udvari said it best: "I've never seen a player deke so many players out of their underwear — he made even the big players look ordinary in the All-Star Game."

Perreault took home the Lady Byng Trophy in 1973 and was twice a member of the Second All-Star Team. In 1975 his Sabres got to the Stanley Cup finals, where they were stopped in six games by the Philadelphia Flyers. In 16 seasons in the Sabre blue and gold, Perrault scored 512 goals and 1,326 points. The Sabres retired his Number 11 jersey in 1990, the year he was inducted into the Hall of Fame.

Peak Years   *1976–80*
In a Word   *PANACHE*

JEAN RATELLE Center
6'1" 180
b. 10/3/1940, Lac St. Jean, Quebec

Jean Ratelle played his Junior hockey with the OHA's Guelph Biltmore "Mad Hatters." A game program from those days described Ratelle as "the Montreal smoothie," an apt description.

The pride of Lac St. Jean made his NHL debut in 1960–1961, but it wasn't until the '64–65 campaign that he found a niche with the New York Rangers. Beginning in 1967–68, he worked between Rod Gilbert and Vic Hadfield on the famed "Goal-a-Game" or "GAG" Line, and strung together four 70-point seasons. In 1971–72 he cranked it up a notch, putting up 109 points in just 63 games. According to Emile Francis, then the Rangers' GM, "Jean deserves to be rated along with Stan Mikita and Jean Beliveau as one of the NHL's best centres. He's the most consistent player I've ever seen."

Ratelle helped Canada best the Soviets in the 1972 Summit Series, tallying a goal and three assists in six games. Although he would never win a Stanley Cup, he did reach the finals with New York in 1972, and the Boston Bruins in 1977 and '78. Hall of Fame defender Brad Park, who played with Ratelle in New York and Boston, described him as "our straight arrow. Ratelle is without a doubt the model hockey player, totally dedicated to the sport and the team. He's just a beautiful player."

In November 1975, the Boston Bruins traded for Ratelle and Brad Park. By the end of the 1975–76 campaign, Ratelle had 105 points and his second Lady Byng Trophy. Bruin teammate Wayne Cashman once gushed, "Jean Ratelle is the special player in this league because he brings so much dignity to the game."

Ratelle decided to call it a career after the 1980–81 season. Since then, he has done coaching and scouting stints in the Boston organization. Despite all the success he'd enjoyed in hockey, the "old smoothie" had one regret: "I'd trade almost everything for one Stanley Cup."

"He functions on a different level from the rest of us," someone once said of Jean Ratelle. "He's the kind of man we'd all like to be." This classy center scored 491 goals and 1,267 points in his career.

Ratelle is a member of the Hockey Hall of Fame.

Peak Years   *1969–73*
In a Word   *EXQUISITE*

LARRY ROBINSON (Big Bird) Defense
6'3" 210
b. 6/2/1951, Winchester, Ontario

In the 1971 Amateur Draft, the Montreal Canadiens thrice passed over a tall, raw-boned defender by the name of Larry Clark Robinson. When their fourth pick, the 20th overall, came up, Montreal finally gave him the nod. He would enjoy the longest career of any player chosen in that draft.

Robinson was assigned to Montreal's farm team, the Nova Scotia Voyageurs. He helped the "Vees" win the Calder Cup (the AHL championship trophy) in 1972. Halfway through the 1972–73 season he was declared ready for prime time. Before long he, along with Serge Savard and Guy Lapointe, would become part of an ultra-talented Habs defense corps known as "The Big Three."

Robinson played for 17 years in Montreal and saw playoff action in every one of those seasons. The "Big Bird," whose game was all about skating, passing, and puck control, was awarded the Conn Smythe Trophy in 1978. This member of six Stanley Cup teams was smooth and fast on his blades, an imposing presence, and a quarter-back of colossal ability. Robinson could use his dukes, too. "There have been many tough guys in the NHL who could stamp out trouble but usually they had to beat up somebody to do it," said coach Scotty Bowman. "In Larry's case, he would just skate into the middle of any trouble or confusion on the ice and things would straighten out automatically."

Robinson wound up his career in 1991–92 as a Los Angeles King. He scored 208 goals and 958 points over his brilliant career. Internationally, he was an important member of Team Canada at the 1976, 1981, and 1984 Canada Cup tournaments.

After retiring, Robinson concentrated on maintaining his stable of world-class polo horses and Montreal-area garages, before joining the New Jersey Devils as an assistant coach under his ex-teammate Jacques Lemaire. He helped guide the Devils to a Cup in 1995, and went on to serve as head coach of the Kings until the end of the 1998–99 season.

Robinson is a member of the Hockey Hall of Fame.

Peak Years   *1976–80*
In a Word   *TOWER*

BORJE SALMING (BJ, The King, King Salmon, The Plastic Man) Defense
6'1" 193
b. 4/17/1951, Kiruna, Sweden

For 17 NHL winters, Borje Salming was one of the finest two-way defenders around. As the first European-trained player to make an impact in the NHL, Salming paved the way for today's European dominance of the league.

Salming spent his formative hockey years with the Kiruna AIF Junior squad. He was bright enough even then to represent his area in the national TV-Puck Junior competition and skate on the Swedish National Junior Team. In 1968, he helped the Swedes finish in second place at the Junior European Cup tournament in West Germany. From there, it was off to the Gavel-based Brynas club of the Swedish Elite League, where he was a factor in the league championships in 1971 and 1972. Following the 1972–73 season, after dazzling performances in the 1972 and 1973 World Hockey Championships, he was voted the most valuable hockey player in Sweden.

Toronto Maple Leafs scout Gerry McNamara first noticed Salming during an exhibition match against the touring Barrie Flyers. The big defender's skill and fearlessness

---

impressed McNamara immediately. On May 12, 1973, Salming and Inge Hammarstrom agreed to join the Leafs. In his rookie season, Salming racked up 39 points and handled the rough stuff more than admirably. By the end of his second year, the Second-Team All-Star was among the NHL's elite blue-liners.

Toronto's best defenseman for many years combined remarkable puck-handling talent with airtight defensive play. Many critics went so far as to say that Salming, and not Larry Robinson or Denis Potvin, was the top defender in the NHL in the late 1970s. "After seeing Salming through five games in this series, I'd have to say he's the best, which makes him better than Robinson," said Philadelphia skipper Fred Shero after a playoff series against the Leafs. "Salming is an absolutely superb skater because he seems to be moving sideways much of the time, plus [he has] that great balance . . ."

Salming reached a number of milestones as the Leafs' elder statesman in the 1980s. On January 4, 1988, he became the first European player to appear in 1,000 NHL games. When he left the Leafs for the Detroit Red Wings after the 1988–89 season, he was the club's career leader in goals (148) and assists (620) by a defenseman. After a year in Motown the gravelly-voiced blue-liner continued his career with AIK Solna of the Swedish Elite Division. He hung up his skates at age 41, early in the 1992–93 campaign.

In 1,148 NHL games over 17 seasons, Salming scored 150 goals and 787 points. Among his accomplishments are six All-Star nominations and a place in the Hockey Hall of Fame.

Peak Years   1977–81
In a Word   IMPECCABLE

SERGE SAVARD (Le Senateur, Uncle Serge) Defense
6'2" 210
b. 1/22/1946, Montreal, Quebec

Serge Savard

Serge Savard punched in 16 seasons of Hall of Fame hockey with the Montreal Canadiens and the Winnipeg Jets. The big, easy-going defender had his first taste of stardom in 1969, when he earned the Conn Smythe Trophy. Savard would become an integral part of a Montreal powerhouse. In 14 seasons with the Flying Frenchmen, he won the Stanley Cup eight times, the last four in a row. He was also a key member of the 1972 Team Canada side that beat the Soviet Nationals and was on the ice when Paul Henderson scored his famous game eight winner.

Early in his career, Savard's game was one of skating, puck-control, and defensive excellence. Like J.C. Tremblay before him, Savard knew how to set a game's tempo. In the mid 1970s, with Tremblay in the World Hockey Association and Jacques Laperriere retiring, Savard became the elder statesman on the blue-line. During the latter half of the decade, the man whose silky smooth play inspired the term "Savardian Spin-a-rama" was one-third of what is still considered possibly the finest defensive trio ever assembled. Savard, Larry Robinson, and Guy Lapointe were called "The Big Three."

In October 1981, Winnipeg Jets manager John Ferguson claimed his ex-teammate in the waiver draft. "It cost me $2,500 to draft him and I gambled with the $2,500 because he was simply the best player in the waiver draft," Ferguson said.

"He's going to help the Jets," said Lapointe. "Heck, he could still have helped us." Winnipeg had failed to make the playoffs in its first two NHL seasons. With Savard on the roster, the Jets earned 80 points and made the post-season at last.

In 1983 the Canadiens fired general manager Irv Grundman, and Savard took his place. The once-great club was a mess. "Serge knows that he is under a lot of pressure and that he has to produce," Canadiens president Ronald Corey said. "We have a five-year plan. I hope we can win before then but this is not something you can turn around overnight."

Twelve years and two Cups later, Savard was axed in favor of Rejean Houle in yet another Corey cleanup. As Montreal's fortunes took a turn for the worse in the 1990s, Montreal fans began wondering if Corey should have been the one swept out of the organization.

Savard is a member of the Hockey Hall of Fame.

Peak Years   1974–78
In a Word   MELLOW

STEVE SHUTT Left Wing
5'11" 185
b. 7/1/1952, Toronto, Ontario

To look at Steve Shutt, you wouldn't have marked him a hockey player, much less a sharp-shooting winger. He was scrawny, skated like an egg-beater, wore a kooky Jofa helmet, and looked like a happy little Martian. But boy, could he shoot!

Stephen John Shutt was a standout with the Toronto Marlboros — in 1970–1971 he scored 70 times — before being drafted fourth overall by the Canadiens in 1972. He scored 30 goals in 1974–75 on a line with Pete Mahovlich and Guy Lafleur. The next season, he upped his output to 45 and earned a spot on Team Canada in the first Canada Cup tournament. He reached his peak in 1976–77, when he scored 60 goals, establishing a record for goals by a left winger that stood for 16 years.

A winner of five Stanley Cups in Montreal, Shutt could shoot with uncanny accuracy using either his wrist shot or a slapshot. He was especially skilled at working the slot for deflections and gobbling up rebounds.

On November 18, 1984, the 32-year-old Shutt was traded to Los Angeles for future considerations. The Canadiens claimed him in the 1985 Waiver Draft, but he made it clear he'd had enough of hockey: "I'm retiring. I don't want to fight any more for a job with the Canadiens and I don't want to play in another city. Now I want to get out."

In early August of 1993, he was brought back into the Canadiens' fold as a special assistant to skipper Jacques Demers. It was thought that the ex-sniper's presence would somehow breathe life into Montreal's floundering offense. "I'm a firm believer that you can teach people how to score," he said, "not actually how to put the puck in the net, but simply being in the right place at the right time." When the Canadiens failed to grasp his teachings, he left the club to work as a TV commentator.

Shutt is a member of the Hockey Hall of Fame.

Peak Years   1976–80
In a Word   UNLIKELY

DARRYL SITTLER Center
6'0" 190
b. 9/18/1950, Kitchener, Ontario

Darryl Sittler

It was a long, hard road from the main street of St. Jacobs, Ontario, to the captaincy of the Toronto Maple Leafs. As a boy, Darryl Sittler would push a two-wheeled cart throughout his hometown, cleaning the streets for cash. You can bet he used the money to buy hockey equipment. The hard-working youngster made his way up the hockey ladder, all the way to the London Nationals of the OHA. It was only a short hop from Junior "A" to the Toronto Maple Leafs, who took him eighth overall in the 1970 Amateur Draft.

Although his numbers in his first two seasons were poor, he busted out in 1972–73 with 29 goals and 77 points. When Toronto captain Dave Keon jumped to the WHA in 1975, Sittler was given the "C." As the 24-year-old's fortunes rose, so did those of the club. From 1975 until 1978, the Leafs made steady progress in their mission to return to the top of the heap. Although Sittler would not headline any Cup victory parades in Toronto, he would lead the Leafs to a level of excellence they hadn't known in almost 10 years.

On the night of February 7, 1976, he shocked the hockey world, and probably even himself, when he shook down the Boston Bruins for six goals and four assists. He would hit career highs in 1977–78 with 45 goals and 117 points.

The return of Punch Imlach as Toronto GM in 1979 led to much dissension in the dressing room; it resulted in Lanny McDonald being unceremoniously shipped to the Colorado Rockies on December 29, 1979. Sittler was disgusted, and he resigned his captaincy in protest. Although he would take the "C" back for the 1980–1981 campaign, he too was dealt away, to Philadelphia on January 20, 1982. He remained a Flyer through the 1983–84 season, and spent one last year with the Detroit Red Wings. He retired with 484 goals and 1,121 points, good for 15th place on the NHL's all-time scoring list.

Sittler was elected to the Hockey Hall of Fame in 1989. He would ultimately return to the Leafs organization — after the death of owner Harold Ballard — as an assistant to GM Cliff Fletcher. He works in the organization to this day in marketing, community relations, and alumni relations.

Peak Years   *1976–80*
In a Word   *SPECIAL*

The All-Stars

Position	Player	Season	GP	G	A	PTS
D	Bobby Orr	1970–71	78	37	102	139
D	Denis Potvin	1978–79	73	31	70	101
LW	Bob Gainey	1978–79	79	20	18	38
C	Phil Esposito	1970–71	78	76	76	152
RW	Guy Lafleur	1976–77	80	56	80	136
				GAA	ShO	
G	Ken Dryden	1975–76		2.03	8	

The Eighties

In a Flash

COMPOSITE REGULAR-SEASON STANDINGS
(JANUARY 1, 1980–DECEMBER 31, 1989)

National Hockey League

Club	GP	W	L	T	Pts	WPct	GF	GA
Edmonton Oilers	725	420	215	90	930	.641	3,526	2,749
Philadelphia Flyers	725	410	231	84	904	.623	2,934	2,376
Montreal Canadiens	724	396	227	101	893	.617	2,887	2,275
New York Islanders	726	385	256	85	855	.589	2,939	2,475
Boston Bruins	724	373	261	90	836	.577	2,832	2,424
Atlanta/Calgary Flames	725	359	261	105	823	.568	3,059	2,724
Washington Capitals	721	352	266	103	807	.560	2,723	2,462
Buffalo Sabres	722	342	267	113	797	.552	2,743	2,485
Quebec Nordiques	721	318	305	98	734	.509	2,846	2,725
St. Louis Blues	722	307	309	106	720	.499	2,679	2,713
New York Rangers	723	315	320	88	718	.497	2,755	2,761
Chicago Blackhawks	723	314	319	90	718	.497	2,764	2,872
Minnesota North Stars	727	290	306	131	711	.489	2,707	2,752
Los Angeles Kings	723	275	345	103	653	.452	2,876	3,145
Hartford Whalers	725	273	364	88	634	.437	2,590	2,945
Winnipeg Jets	719	262	361	96	620	.431	2,674	3,082
Vancouver Canucks	722	255	356	111	621	.430	2,569	2,839
Pittsburgh Penguins	722	259	384	79	597	.413	2,643	3,102
Detroit Red Wings	724	244	381	99	587	.405	2,548	3,000
Toronto Maple Leafs	725	228	410	87	543	.374	2,611	3,204
Colorado Rockies/New Jersey Devils	724	206	429	89	501	.346	2,367	3,141

HELLOS

Nick Carter, *Backstreet Boy*	January 28, 1980
Vincent Lecavalier, *NHL up-and-comer*	April 21, 1980
David Legwand, *NHL prospect*	August 17, 1980
Britney Spears, *pop diva*	December 2, 1981
Jason Spezza, *future NHL star*	June 13, 1983
Zachary Hanson, *wee pop artist*	October 22, 1985

GOODBYES

John Lennon, *British rock legend*	December 8, 1980
Max Bentley, *Hawk legend*	January 19, 1984
Richard Burton, *British actor*	August 5, 1984
Eddie Shore, *Bruin great*	March 16, 1985
Frank "King" Clancy, *Toronto favorite*	November 8, 1986
Mervyn "Red" Dutton, *hockey legend*	March 15, 1987

REGULAR SEASON

BEST RECORD
1983–84 Edmonton Oilers, 57-18-5

WORST RECORD
1980–81 Winnipeg Jets, 9-57-14

BEST NON-NHL RECORD
1987–88 Muskegon Lumberjacks (IHL), 58-14-10

FAMOUS FIRSTS

AMERICAN-BORN NHLᴇʀ TO SCORE 100 POINTS IN A SEASON
Neal Broten, 105 (1985–86)

NHL DEFENSEMAN TO SCORE 1,000 POINTS
Denis Potvin (1986–87)

NHL PLAYER TO SCORE 200 POINTS IN A SEASON
Wayne Gretzky, 212 (1981–82)

MISCELLANEOUS

MOST GOALS, SEASON
92   Wayne Gretzky (1981–82)

MOST ASSISTS, SEASON
163   Wayne Gretzky (1985–86)

MOST POINTS, SEASON
215   Wayne Gretzky (1985–86)

MOST GOALS, DECADE
637   Wayne Gretzky

MOST ASSISTS, DECADE
1,200   Wayne Gretzky

MOST POINTS, DECADE
1,837   Wayne Gretzky

COOLEST MIDDLE NAMES
Neal *Lamoy* Broten
Marcel *Elphege* Dionne
Mark *Anatole* Osborne
Brent *Bolin* Sutter
Behn *Bevan* Wilson

COOLEST HANDLES
Mike "Red Dog" Allison
Dan Daoust, "Dangerous Danny"
Marcel "Little Beaver" Dionne
Nick Fotiu, "Nicky Boy"
Ed "Boxcar" Hospodar
Tom "Cowboy" Laidlaw
Ken "The Rat" Linseman
Tom "The Bomb" Lysiak
Rich Preston, "Cool Hand Luke"
Risto Siltanen, "The Incredible Hulk"

BIGGEST PLAYER
Kjell Samuelsson, 6'6" 235

SMALLEST PLAYER
Jean-Francois Sauve, 5'6" 175

BEST SHOT
Mike Bossy

BEST PASSER
Wayne Gretzky is the all-time king of the pass. The man who needs no introduction racked up better than 100 assists in 11 of his first 12 NHL seasons for a total of 1,424. His combination plays with the likes of Jari Kurri and the blazing Paul Coffey were deadly.

BEST INSTINCTS
Wayne Gretzky has shown the uncanny ability to know exactly where everybody is on the ice at all times. He was a slippery, unhittable point-pig.

BEST STICK-HANDLER
Denis Savard would have been a perfect fit beside the likes of Guy Lafleur in Montreal. The Canadiens, however, passed up Savard on account of his size. The little guy dazzled Chicago Blackhawk fans for years with his stunning collection of dekes, feints, and dipsy-doodles. He also had red-hot speed, which made him a constant breakaway threat.

BEST SKATER
Paul Coffey

WORST SKATER
Tim Kerr was a four-time 50-goal scorer for the Philadelphia Flyers in the 1980s but an exceedingly poor bladesman.

FASTEST SKATER
Mike Gartner

BEST SNIPER
Mike Bossy scored 362 goals in 461 games between 1980–81 and 1985–86. Although Wayne Gretzky scored more goals in Edmonton, Bossy was the most dangerous man around the net for many years. As his own goalie, Billy Smith, said, "I've faced them all and Mike's shot is the toughest to handle."

BEST PENALTY-KILLER
Guy Carbonneau

BEST BODY-CHECKER
Denis Potvin

BEST SHOT-BLOCKER
Kevin Lowe

BEST GOALTENDER
Grant Fuhr backstopped the Edmonton Oilers to Stanley Cups in 1984, 1985, 1987, and 1988. While never at the top of the goaltenders' statistical pile, he earned a reputation as a clutch performer.

BEST GLOVE-HAND (GOALIE)
Grant Fuhr

MOST UNUSUAL GOALTENDING STYLE
Patrick Roy

FINEST ATHLETE
Mike Gartner

BEST DEFENSIVE FORWARD
Guy Carbonneau

WORST DEFENSIVE FORWARD
Kent Nilsson was a complete zero on the back-check. Broadcaster Jiggs McDonald once said, "I watched Kent for a full season and I can say that he doesn't like to play hurt."

BEST SHADOW
Steve Kasper wasn't called "The Friendly Ghost" just because of his last name. Wayne Gretzky was rendered pointless on many a night facing him.

BEST DEFENSIVE DEFENSEMAN
Rod Langway came to the Washington Capitals from Montreal in September 1982 and turned around his new team. The man who hated to be embarrassed led the

Capitals to win totals of 39, 48, 46, and 50 in his first four seasons. Quite a departure for the club that since its birth in 1974 had racked up an abominable 163-375-102 record.

BEST OFFENSIVE DEFENSEMAN
Paul Coffey notched 669 points in 532 regular-season games in Edmonton.

BEST ALL-AROUND PLAYER
Mark Messier was possibly the biggest reason the Edmonton Oilers won Stanley Cups in 1984, 1985, 1987, 1988, and 1990. A bone-crushing physical presence, he matured into one of the NHL's top offensive threats. Edmonton's second choice in the 1979 Entry Draft topped the 100-point plateau four times in the 1980s.

STRONGEST PLAYER
Clark Gillies was like a dormant volcano. Opposing players steered clear of the New York Islanders' man-mountain. In the 1980 playoffs, Boston Bruin tough Terry O'Reilly took on big Gillies three times and, well, lost. As former NHL goalie John Garrett once put it, "It's not wise to aggravate that man."

TOUGHEST PLAYER
Mark Messier

BEST FIGHTER
John Kordic was for years the most feared brawler in the bigs. The big man lost his life in the wake of his wild party lifestyle.

MOST ABLE INSTIGATOR
Ken Linseman

DIRTIEST PLAYER
Ken Linseman wasn't called "The Rat" for nothing. According to then Los Angeles King Dave Lewis, Linseman "likes to instigate but he never finishes off what he's doing. He'll give a guy a stick in the back and then call a teammate over."

CLEANEST PLAYER
Marcel Dionne

BEST CORNER-MAN

John Tonelli was one of the true unsung heroes of the New York Islanders dynasty (1980–1983). Possessing an uncanny knack for digging out the puck in close quarters, he was an intimidating physical presence.

BEST-LOOKING PLAYER

Paul Coffey fit in well with comb-and-mirror hogs Wayne Gretzky and Jari Kurri in Edmonton.

UGLIEST PLAYER

Dave "Tiger" Williams served as the NHL's Great Amphibious Man for years. He was one of the scariest, most intimidating men in the league in the days of Dave "The Hammer" Schultz and Terry O'Reilly, the Tasmanian Devil.

FACE-OFF MAN

Doug Jarvis

BALDEST PLAYER

Brian Bellows

MUST UNDERRATED PLAYER

Bernie Federko

MOST CONSISTENT PLAYER

Wayne Gretzky

MOST TRAGIC CAREER

Pelle Lindbergh was on his way to being Philadelphia's next great goaltender. Promise ended in tragedy, when he crashed his Porsche into a wall, killing him instantly.

MOST UNPREDICTABLE CAREER

Wendel Clark

SMARTEST PLAYER

Wayne Gretzky was not just another pretty face. Harry Neale once said, "Coming up ice, Gretzky is thoroughly unpredictable. He is like the soccer player who kicks the ball into open space and suddenly a teammate is there. His anticipation is uncanny. He knows the area and is totally aware."

MOST HATED PLAYER

Dave Williams was as much beast as he was human. The man who incurred almost 4,000 penalty minutes in the NHL could not only fight but could bite. "In a playoff game," tough guy Dave Schultz recalled, "Williams bit me on the cheek then pulled my hair and then head-butted me." In the 1980 playoffs, Williams was suspended for swatting Buffalo Sabres head coach Scotty Bowman.

MOST ADMIRED PLAYER

Wayne Gretzky quickly became hockey's poster boy. Opponents gave him room and sports editors across North America gave him front pages.

BEST LINES

Team: Edmonton Oilers
LW: Mark Messier
C: Wayne Gretzky
RW: Jari Kurri

Team: New York Islanders
LW: Clark Gillies
C: Bryan Trottier
RW: Mike Bossy

Team: Los Angeles Kings
LW: Charlie Simmer
C: Marcel Dionne
RW: Dave Taylor

The Edmonton Oilers of the mid-1980s was an offensive machine. Gretzky, Messier, Anderson, Paul Coffey, and Jari Kurri formed the nucleus of a frighteningly efficient offensive team.

PLAYER VERSUS TEAM

Paul Coffey vs. Edmonton Oilers, 1987. Coffey held out for more money when he saw the pay raises teammates Mark Messier and Wayne Gretzky received. Coffey was eventually traded to the Pittsburgh Penguins.

MOST LOPSIDED TRADE

The Vancouver Canucks traded future superstar Cam Neely and a first-round pick to Boston for aging Barry Pederson. The Bruins used the Canuck pick to select solid defenseman Glen Wesley. Pederson was soon out of the league. In 1994, the Whalers acquired Wesley for three first-round picks.

The 1995 pick, defenseman Kyle McLaren, has been a strong addition to the Bruins and will pick up where Ray Bourque leaves off. The 1997 pick, Sergei Samsonov, won the 1998 Calder Trophy. So, in retrospect, the Canucks traded Cam Neely, Sergei Samsonov, and Kyle McLaren for Barry Pederson. Yikes!

BIGGEST FLOP
Doug Wickenheiser was selected by the Montreal Canadiens over Denis Savard in the 1980 NHL Entry Draft. Wickenheiser enjoyed moderate success in 10 professional seasons, but Savard became one of the most dominant offensive players of the modern era.

BEST HEAD COACH
Al Arbour gave the New York Islanders the space they needed to mature. This thoughtful, methodical man stayed behind the Isles bench in some capacity until 1994, and handed the reins over to Terry Simpson from 1986–87 to 1987–88. Arbour's career coaching record in

Al Arbour

1,815 regular-season and playoff games is 904-663-248 for an outstanding .566 winning percentage.

BEST GENERAL MANAGER
Bill Torrey, New York Islanders

BEST SPORTSWRITER
Michael Farber, *Montreal Gazette*

BEST BROADCASTER
Bob Cole has been the boomingest, most exciting voice in hockey in the past 20 years. The CBC has been lucky to have him aboard. Honorable mention in the area of game presentation must go to The Sports Network's John Wells, whose deep, rich voice and poise behind the camera helped make TSN an internationally respected sports channel. Wells is an esteemed member of the Canadian Broadcasting Hall of Fame.

BEST SEASON
1988–89. **Mario Lemieux** came within a point of the magical 200-point plateau. Wayne Gretzky was dealt to sunny California. Guy Lafleur made a comeback with the New York Rangers, scoring 18 goals and 45 points in 67 games. The Flames brought the Stanley Cup to Calgary for the first time ever.

BEST STANLEY CUP FINAL
1986. The Montreal Canadiens and **Calgary Flames** squared off in the first all-Canadian final since 1967. Twenty-year-old Canadiens goalie Patrick Roy, with a 1.92 goals-against average in the playoffs, became the first rookie since Harry Lumley in 1945 to record a shutout in the finals. In addition to a Stanley Cup ring, Roy took home the Conn Smythe Trophy as playoff MVP.

IMPORTANT RULE CHANGES

1982–83
• Clubs permitted to dress 18 skaters and 2 goalies

1983–84
• Five-minute sudden-death overtime established for all regular-season ties

1985–86
• Substitutions allowed on coincidental minor penalties

Tiger's Rap Sheet

*"My nose has been broken so many times,
I don't even smell or breathe through it anymore."*
— *Tiger Williams*

David James Williams, a 5'11" 190-pound Weyburn, Saskatchewan, boy, was the inspirational leader of the Toronto Maple Leafs from the mid to late-1970s and a fierce player for the Canucks in the 1980s. Williams, the guy people called "Tiger," couldn't skate or shoot very well but was a very hard worker. Oh, and he loved to bust skulls.

Examining the mile-long NHL rap sheet on Williams is a task in itself. He made a name for himself by refusing to shake hands in the playoffs, and of course his ride-on-his-stick celebration skate after scoring a goal. Let's take a look at the career of the Tiger.

On August 16, 1974, Williams and Terry Ruskowski, his teammate on the WHL Swift Current Broncos, pleaded guilty to three charges of common assault. Williams, who had signed with the Toronto Maple Leafs, was fined $300 plus court costs while Ruskowski, who had recently come to terms with the WHA Houston Aeros, was slapped with a $150 fine. Williams was also originally charged with causing a disturbance and assaulting a police officer but the former charge was dropped. In passing sentence, Judge Howard Boyce said that the two players "disgraced themselves."

On January 7, 1975, Williams finally got his call from the Leafs. He took over on the wing for long-time anti-hero Eddie Shack, who was immediately shuffled off to the Oklahoma Blazers. The early scouting report on Tiger: "Williams can't skate, move very well, or shoot very well, but he can fight and he's just itching to put a little fight in the Leafs."

On April 11, 1975, in the first round of the playoffs, Williams got into a stick-swinging duel with Los Angeles Kings' tough guy Dave Hutchison, earning himself a two-game suspension to be served at the beginning of the 1975–76 season. Big Hutchison was slapped with a five-game hitch while his teammate, Gene Carr, got two games for spitting on Williams. NHL president Clarence Campbell said the degree of violence in the duel "was terrifying and it is fortunate that no blows were struck."

On September 17, 1975, Williams beat up teammate Pat Boutette, repeatedly bashing the plucky center's head against the glass before they exchanged punches. When Lanny McDonald tried to break up the fight, Williams gave him a good one across the chops.

Tiger Williams

"Teams send tapes every time I do something. Bryan O'Neill has a set of tapes on me that MGM would be proud of."
— *Tiger Williams*

King Clancy, ever the little goon-master, was heard to say from the gondola of Maple Leaf Gardens: "It's good to see spirit like that. I'm telling you, Williams has improved a helluva lot . . . Boutette is no slouch either."

On April 22, 1976, in a playoff match against the hated Philadelphia Flyers, Williams was accused of biting enforcer Dave Schultz. Clarence Campbell emerged from the Flyers' dressing room after the game with the words, saying, "I had a good look at Schultz's wounds. It's no joke. It's pretty serious. There is no doubt — there were teeth marks." When the *Toronto Sun*'s George Gross asked Campbell whose teeth marks they were, Campbell replied, "Williams bit him." When other newsmen asked Campbell if he had checked the fillings of Williams' teeth to be sure he was the culprit, Campbell retorted, "Let's just say I know it was Williams."

On October 20, 1976, Pittsburgh Penguins' defenseman Dennis Owchar needed 46 stitches to close a gash on his head after Williams struck him with his stick. Williams was later charged with assault by Attorney-General Roy McMurtry. About a year later, Williams went to trial to plead his case. His lawyer opened the hearing by debating the admissibility of a videotape recording the Williams–Owchar incident as evidence. A ruling was ultimately postponed and by the end of the first day of proceedings, *Toronto Star* reporter Jim Kernaghan published a quote from Williams that caused quite a stir: "Owchar can keep his stitches for his grandchildren."

At the hearing, young girls vied for good seats, giggling and nudging each other when Tiger entered the courtroom. The tape showed that Owchar had body-checked Williams in an attempt to stop his rush on goal and in the collision, Williams had spun around and brought his stick down on Owchar's head. To the shock and dismay of all in the courtroom, Williams' stick blade had shattered from the force of the blow to Owchar's head. Judge Hugh Locke ruled that sections of the Williams–Owchar assault, shown on videotape in slow motion, weren't reflective of the speed of the game of hockey and that the tape was prejudicial. Judge Locke acquitted Williams, allowing him "the benefit of the doubt" in stating that he "may or may not have intended to take a final swipe" at Owchar. According to Locke, there was "no satisfactory evidence" that Williams had made a deliberate attempt to injure Owchar.

Williams was in hot water again on February 15, 1979. Assault charges were laid following a New Year's Day dispute in downtown Toronto. Apparently, the set-to began while Williams and another man had an incident while driving. A court date was set for May 11 but the case was eventually thrown out of court.

"I'm sorry Randy [Carlyle] got hurt but he should have been wearing a helmet. He has that beautiful blond hair and is waiting for a shampoo commercial to come along."
— *Tiger Williams*

On April 11, 1980, this time decked out in the black, gold, and white of the Vancouver Canucks, Williams had another of his many run-ins with NHL vice-president Bryan O'Neill. Buffalo Sabres' skipper Scotty Bowman was clipped on the side of the head by Williams' stick while standing behind the bench as Williams collided with a Sabre player. As Bowman fell, several Sabres rushed at Williams. Rick Dudley grabbed

---

"I have my friends and what they think has value to me. The rest? Draw your own conclusions because I really don't give a f—."
— Tiger Williams

Williams near the Vancouver blue-line. Referee Bryan Lewis tossed Dudley out of the game with a fighting major and game misconduct. Tiger was not penalized.

After reviewing the videotapes of the Williams–Bowman incident, O'Neill announced he was suspending Tiger for one game. "I didn't know [Bowman] got hit," Williams growled. "I just remember taking their guy into the boards and both sticks went over. I don't know which stick hit Bowman."

On October 19, 1982, Mr. O'Neill's favorite whipping boy struck again. During a game against the New York Islanders, Williams got into a stick-swinging duel with Isles' goalie Billy Smith. Tiger, who conked Smith on the head, was furious at the seven-game suspension handed to him four days later. "The league buried their head like an ostrich on the whole issue!" he roared. "What I did to Smith was wrong, I'll admit that . . . Smith should get life." This was by no means Smith's first brush with controversy. In the 1980 playoffs, he butt-ended Buffalo's Lindy Ruff with his stick. In these 1982 playoffs, his casualty list included Tiger, Wayne Gretzky, and Canucks' captain Stan Smyl.

In Williams–Smith Part II, on January 29, 1983, Tiger got even. This was the first game between the Islanders and Canucks since October of the previous year, when Williams and Smith had last got into it. The return battle did not disappoint. A Williams slapshot hit Smith square in the throat. Smith was furious. The two players brawled. In the wake of the scrap, Williams was given a minor, a major, and two game misconducts by referee Denis Morel. Smith was slapped with two minor penalties.

"I used to respect Tiger because he always went after guys on a one-on-one basis," said Smith after the game. "But not after he tried to elbow me in the throat after I was injured. He doesn't show much class. He even had his hands on my throat. That's a little tacky. But, that cost them another hockey game, and that shows he's an idiot."

On November 4, 1983, Bryan O'Neill continued his rampage on Williams. In an October 30 game between the Canucks and Flames, Williams held his stick across the

---

"When I first started with the Kings, I was scared of [Williams], and always looking out for him. Then, after being with the team, I found out that he's one of the nicest guys, and he never made fun of us when we spoke French."
— Luc Robitaille

----

neck of Flames' defenseman Paul Baxter as the two lay on the ice. Said O'Neill, "After considering the facts of this incident, it is my judgment that the actions of [Williams] were unacceptable and potentially dangerous." O'Neill slapped Tiger with an eight-game suspension.

On December 20, 1983, after getting wind of some negative remarks written about him, Williams tossed a Vancouver sportswriter out of the Canucks' dressing room.

St. Louis 1983 Draft Guide: N/A

"With their first selection of the 1983 NHL Entry Draft, the St. Louis Blues select . . . no one." In one of the strangest occurrences in NHL draft history, the Blues decided not to participate in the 1983 grab-bag.

Okay, let's try to make sense of this one. In 1980–81, St. Louis finished first in the Smythe Division with 107 points. The following year, their overall production dropped by 35 points. A report surfaced that the Blues were losing almost $2 million a year. They tumbled to 65 points in 1982–83. It took Hal Dean, chairman of Ralston Purina and club owner, a while to realize that his money-burning franchise was no longer a desirable enterprise. Dean attempted to get rid of the Blues. Before long, a group from Saskatoon stepped forward to purchase the team and move it to the Canadian prairies. Just when everything seemed to be in place, the NHL blocked the sale. Flustered, the Ralston group packed up and left, leaving the club with the league.

With the ownership situation in utter chaos, the Blues were unable to partake in the 1983 Entry Draft. In total, they would miss out on 10 picks. Among the players that could have been theirs that year: Brian Bradley, Bob Essensa, Rick Tocchet, Sergei Makarov, and some goalie by the name of Dominik Hasek. Ever heard of him?

A Flower Wilts

Guy Damien Lafleur was a true Flying Frenchman, a man with little or no concept of slow and steady wins the race. Before the Wayne Gretzky era, at a time when 50 goals was still a magical number, there was Lafleur, as much a man of pride as one of sheer genius. The young wizard they called "Flower" would build on an unparalleled Junior career, one that saw him score better than 100 goals in two consecutive seasons.

Lafleur was the "next one" in a long line of French-Canadian hockey icons. He played a game of stops, starts, jerks, lunges, and fakes. In his first nine seasons in the big league, he earned three scoring crowns and five Stanley Cup rings. In 677 regular-season games in that span, he racked up an astounding 941 points for an average of 1.4 per game. But, as with all players, he couldn't be a star forever. Although the curtain wouldn't come down on his career overnight, there came a point when the writing was on the wall — in big, block letters.

On the night of March 24, 1981, Lafleur had dinner and drinks in downtown Montreal with teammate Robert Picard. As the night wound down, Lafleur bade his chum goodnight and climbed into his 1981 Cadillac Seville. At about two o'clock in the morning, as he was motoring down the 2&20 highway, he fell asleep at the wheel.

His car left the road at considerable speed and rammed into a fence. In the crash, a signpost ran through his front windshield, severing his earlobe. A quarter of an inch to the left and Lafleur would have been kabob! He was whisked to hospital where, other than a cut ear, he was found to be perfectly fine.

The car accident couldn't have come at a worse time for Lafleur. On the ice, things weren't going well at all. After six straight 119-plus point seasons, Lafleur was losing his grip on the top rung. Lafleur had been in a funk since Pat Boutette of the Hartford Whalers rocked him out of the 1980 playoffs. For the first time in his brilliant career, he was getting injured. Included in a lengthy list of rips, pulls, and tears was a bad knee, which made him apprehensive on his skates where before he had been nothing short of volcanic. A report said that Lafleur tumbled down the stairs of a Montreal discotheque, a charge he denied heatedly. All told, Lafleur missed 29 games in the 1980–81 season, six more than the total he missed in the seven previous seasons combined. Off the ice, Lafleur's marriage was said to have been under great strain. Overall, the life of Quebec's "Demon Blond" was not the bowl of cherries it once was.

Lafleur was eager to get back into the swing of things after the accident, but he was going through a tough time emotionally. "You really think about it after you get so close to being dead," he said. "I pass more time with my family [now]. If I go out now, I go out with my wife. That's where I really changed. You find out your best friends are your family, not the people who try to hurt you, to make you lose everything you've got."

Lafleur finished the 1980–81 season with only 27 goals and 70 points, a far cry from the 50-goal, 100-point seasons he and his legion of worshipers had grown accustomed to. In the 1981 playoffs, he was just not himself. He earned one measly assist in three games. He was hardly the Flower of old.

Teammate Larry Robinson was understandably worried. "It drives me crazy sometimes. Injuries are part of the game. Flower's in the same situation I was. We went probably six or seven years without getting hurt for more than two or three games here and there . . . there have been so many injuries. It becomes very frustrating sometimes."

The 1981–82 season brought a mountain of possibilities. Lafleur still had hope. Montreal was a solid team, albeit much more defensive-minded than in years past. These sweet vibes would not last long, however. On September 20, 1981, at the beginning of training camp, Lafleur missed a mandatory practice. Coach Bob Berry fined Lafleur and sent him home. As the season progressed, Lafleur found himself playing less and less. But the more he and others like Pierre Larouche complained about their dwindling ice-time, the less management seemed to listen. The Canadiens were playing under a new "system." Georges-Hebert Germain wrote in *Overtime*, "The flamboyant attacks, improvisation, this jazz on the ice was no longer wanted. Lafleur was supposed to play sensibly and follow well-orchestrated scores. In this system, Lafleur no longer had his old place. He wasn't sure he wanted to play this way." In 66 games in 1981–82, the Flower was good for 27 goals and 84 points. It was a respectable total, a 14-point improvement on the previous season. Just not Lafleuresque. The following two seasons yielded totals of 76 and 70 points.

Some believe that the 70-point, 33-year-old Lafleur of 1983–84 was the same

Lafleur who won scoring crowns. In one game in January 1984 he played 14 minutes, hardly star ice-time. If you play it out, however, 70 points in 14 minutes per game becomes 125 points at 25 minutes per game. However, star or no star, there was method to co-coach Jacques Lemaire's madness: "Before putting a Guy Lafleur on the bench, you have to think about it. When I did it, it was for the good of the team. I was also trying to motivate Guy a little more, and I know when I did it, he came back and played one of his best games. It was a spark of the Guy Lafleur everybody knows."

So was it ice-time or aging that had Lafleur on the shelf by the mid-1980s? Probably a combination of the two. In November 1984, Al Strachan, a sportswriter with the Toronto *Globe and Mail*, parceled up the Lafleur enigma: "Inside, he was being torn apart. The fierce pride that had made him the best in the game also prevented him from accepting the fact that he could no longer dominate." Pretty packaging, no sale. Although Strachan was not wrong, he wasn't right either. The truth is that Lafleur was in excellent condition well into the 1980s. He may very well have dominated into the 1980s had playing conditions been more agreeable.

Upon hearing of Lafleur's first retirement in late 1984, Edmonton Oilers' GM Glen Sather's ears perked up. "If he wanted to come out of retirement," said Sather, "I'd certainly find a place for him." And with this, we ask ourselves the question: Was Lafleur really washed up in 1984? Or did he just not buy what Montreal GM Serge Savard called the "new image" of Les Glorieux?

The answers to these questions are blindingly obvious. Lafleur made a comeback in 1988 at the age of 37, and played respectably: proof enough that the Flower still had it, and would have been even better four years before.

One Dynasty after Another

Hockey is always a main priority in your life, but you can fit it in with others which are just as important — your family, your values . . . except one, when hockey is the only thing that matters. It is the instant when you pick up the Stanley Cup for the first time. Everything else is forgotten in that moment.
— Bryan Trottier

The 1980s were not kind to the Canadiens in general. Following the 1979 playoffs, the Stanley Cup–champion Montreal Canadiens lost two important pieces of their dynasty puzzle when Ken Dryden and Jacques Lemaire flew the coop. Dryden, the 31-year-old goalkeeper and lawyer, simply had other games to play, while Lemaire, although still a potent forward at age 33, opted for a coaching position in Switzerland. By mid-decade, Guy Lafleur, Steve Shutt, Guy Lapointe, and Serge Savard were gone by trade, waiver draft, or unceremonious dumping. From the breathtaking heights of their dynasty, Montreal was suddenly and hopelessly mediocre. The Flying Frenchmen had become a well-meaning defensive side with little to offer either fan or tradition.

A hole opened up in the NHL, one where the Cup was anyone's to win. Enter the Isles and Oilers.

First came the Isles, a big, blue blanket of stifling defense, stellar goaltending, and timely scoring. The franchise didn't get off to a great start in the NHL, recording a 12-60-6 record in its inaugural 1972–73 season. With dedicated winners like GM Bill Torrey and coach/resident brainiac Al Arbour on their side, however, the Isles wouldn't be a laughingstock for long. Draft additions such as Denis Potvin, Bryan Trottier, and sniper Mike Bossy helped turn the Islanders into a hockey powerhouse. Before long, they were a feared up-and-coming team in the NHL. Even enemy Philadelphia Flyers' center Bobby Clarke commented that his own team, a bruising crew, was scared of the Islanders.

In 1975–76, New York had their breakout season, racking up 42 wins and 101 points in 80 games. By 1980, they won their first of four Stanley Cup championships.

Meanwhile, the Alberta, later to be Edmonton, Oilers, went 38-37-3 in 1972-73 and featured players like 86-point center Jim Harrison and NHL oldies Val Fonteyne, Eddie Joyal, and Bill Hicke. In November 1978, Edmonton sent a chunk of cash to the Indianapolis Racers for Peter Driscoll, goalie Ed Mio, and the rights to Wayne Gretzky. Although only a teen at the time, Gretzky made an immediate impact with the big boys, scoring 43 goals and 104 points in 72 games as a WHA Oiler. The bony whiz-kid made the leap to the NHL when Edmonton joined the big league for the 1979–80 campaign, scoring 51 goals and 137 points, good for second place in scoring and his first of eight consecutive Hart trophies. However good Gretzky was, however, it was not yet Edmonton's time. They were still far too young. They would have to learn how to win first.

From 1979–80 through 1982–83, the New York Islanders put on a winning clinic. In the span of four years, the big blue wave from Long Island racked up 183 wins, 415 points, and four Stanley Cup championships. Mike Bossy, Bryan Trottier, and Denis Potvin headlined a lunch-bucket crew, a diligent pack of grinders, battlers, and skilled trench-mutts. That's not to say the supporting cast was a collection of hard-working no-talents — quite the opposite. Behind Bossy, Trottier, and Potvin skated many players who on any other club would've been go-to guys.

First, there was Clark Gillies, a regular member of the "Long Island Electrical Company" unit with Trottier and Bossy. Here was a veritable mountain of a man, a huge, smoldering, black-bearded player strong enough to break an ordinary man in two. Gillies could score, too. His best year came in 1978–79 when he was worth 91 points. Throw speedy checker Butch Goring, all-purpose Bob Bourne, battling Bob Nystrom, hard-rock defender Dave "Bammer" Langevin, and big stay-at-home Ken Morrow, and the Long Island crew was a force. Need a goal? Ask Bossy or Trottier. Need to protect a one-goal lead late in the third? Send out Goring to stick to someone. Need a big hit to rally the troops? Have a talk with Nystrom — the Viking would be sure to deliver.

That's great, you might say. But what about goaltending? How about Billy Smith? Within this squat, cranky ball of flesh and fire lay the heart of the team. Vicious? Without apology. Cocky? Without question. A winner? Without a doubt. In the playoffs from 1980 through 1983, the foul net-monkey ran up a kingly 57-13 record with four shutouts and a 2.64 goals-against average. Smith was a champion.

Coming into the 1983–84 season, the Isles began thinking of a fifth Cup in as many years. And why not? Why not go for another, thought some of the more ambitious Islander players? Why not one-up the Canadiens of a few years back and equal the all-time record by stealing a fifth consecutive Cup? After all, they had swept the young Oilers in 1983. But the Oilers wouldn't give up so easily.

In the fall of 1983, Gretzky and crew had no Cups to their credit. Not a blessed one. Sure, Gretzky had seasons of 137, 164, 212, and 196 points under his belt, but he didn't have that snazzy rock on his finger. Talk about pressure.

In 1983–84, the Great One turned the NHL upside-down once again, to the tune of 87 goals and 118 assists! Gretzky and the Oilers rolled to a 57-18-5 record, tops in the NHL, and were the odds-on favorite to topple the aging New York Islanders in the post-season. But what about the Oilers' checkered playoff history? What of Edmonton's first-round playoff exit in 1982 at the hands of the Los Angeles Kings after running up an 111-point season? "We just weren't ready to win," insisted Gretzky. "We were talented, but we didn't have the right attitude to cope with adversity. We hadn't grown up." Maybe so. But the Isles weren't about to roll over and die. Edmonton had its work cut out for them in 1984.

As the 1984 post-season wore on, the New York Islanders came under a strange funk. In the past, this pack of war dogs had thrived on pressure and hard work, but something was different this time around. During their Drive for Five, Big Blue was not playing well. Some sportswriters thought this was just a ploy. They thought the Isles were rolling over and playing dead to lull their opponents to sleep. Michael Farber, then with the *Montreal Gazette*, stated, "Somehow, the Islanders will conspire to play with one hand tied behind their backs or locked in a safe, drawing predictions of imminent doom. Do not believe it." New York had tricked other teams before with this routine. But don't think for a second that young Gretzky and his Oilers were fooled. New York and Edmonton battled in the Stanley Cup finals, and the Oilers were ready.

In game one, not a lot happened. It was the kind of defensive/goaltending duel we all love so much. The Islanders successfully hog-tied Gretzky. At the end of 60 minutes, the Great One had but two measly shots on goal.

Period	Team	Scorer	Assists
3	Oilers	Kevin McClelland	Pat Hughes, Dave Hunter

This one goal, from who Michael Farber called "an unconscionable goal-scorer," was all the Oilers would need. Edmonton goalie Grant Fuhr was spectacular.

The Oilers killed off all five Islanders power plays. Edmonton skipper Glen Sather, knowing the Isles were injured and fatigued, used four lines, sending out fresh skaters to wear down the Isles.

Fiery New York keeper Billy Smith, oft the recipient of bad press for his chops and hacks on crease-invaders, was the whipping boy of the Edmonton press. The Edmonton media had the ill-tempered goalie down as "Mister Obnoxious," "Jack the Ripper," and "a creep."

But four-time Stanley Cup champions do not roll over and die in the finals, no matter how tired they may be. New York didn't just beat the Oilers in game two, they stomped them.

Period	Team	Scorer	Assists
1	Islanders	Bryan Trottier	Mike Bossy, Paul Boutilier
1	Islanders	Greg Gilbert	Pat LaFontaine, Stefan Persson
1	Oilers	Randy Gregg	Kevin McClelland
1	Islanders	Clark Gillies	Anders Kallur

It didn't take long for New York to sink their teeth into the Oilers. A late first-period goal by big Gillies had the Isles up by two with 40 minutes to go.

2	Islanders	Bryan Trottier	Brent Sutter, Pat Flatley
2	Islanders	Clark Gillies	Denis Potvin, Mike Bossy

Good old Bryan Trottier. Leave it up to that Cup-hog to rub salt in his enemy's wounds! With 20 minutes to go, it was Big Blue all the way.

3	Islanders	Clark Gillies	Bryan Trottier, Paul Boutilier

On a feed from our friend Bryan, Gillies had his hat-trick. But wait a minute! Shouldn't Gretzky have scored by now? Come on now, Gillies had three and the Great One couldn't even scrape together an assist? New York was doing exactly what it set out to do: check Gretzky into the ice. Islanders fans chanted "M-I-C-K-E-Y M-O-U-S-E!" in response to Gretzky's comment earlier in the season that the New Jersey Devils were a "Mickey Mouse operation" and threw beer on the Edmonton bench. The Isles were grinding Gretzky into a fine silt. So far so good for Al Arbour and his hounds. The Islanders won 6–1.

In the space of 60 minutes in game three, the good-look, no-hit pretty boys from Edmonton completely turned the tide of the 1984 finals. Tim Burke of the *Montreal Gazette* noted, "Seldom has a team, better known as the league's glamorous wunderkinds than champions, grown up as fast as the Oilers did last night." Indeed, nothing would keep Gretzky's Oilers from victory on this night.

Period	Team	Scorer	Assists
1	Islanders	Clark Gillies	Pat Flatley, Brent Sutter
1	Oilers	Kevin Lowe	Glenn Anderson, Willy Lindstrom

Sometimes it takes the war horses to jump start a slumbering hockey team. Edmonton was snoozing, and the alarm clock was defender Kevin Lowe, hardly a goal-scoring genius. No matter. At this point, the Oilers would take anything they could get.

2	Islanders	Clark Gillies	Bryan Trottier, Mike Bossy
2	Oilers	Mark Messier	Lee Fogolin
2	Oilers	Glenn Anderson	Charlie Huddy, Wayne Gretzky
2	Oilers	Paul Coffey	Pat Hughes, Ken Linseman

After yet another goal by Gillies, Edmonton put their foot down, notching three goals to make the score 4–2 by the second intermission. Oh, and did you notice who recorded his first point of the finals?

3	Oilers	Mark Messier	Kevin McClelland, Charlie Huddy
3	Oilers	Kevin McClelland	Dave Lumley
3	Oilers	Dave Semenko	Jari Kurri, Wayne Gretzky

The Islanders were in deep trouble. The only damper for Edmonton was that Grant Fuhr was forced to leave the game with eight minutes to go because of injury. He wouldn't be back for the rest of the finals. The Oilers rolled to a 7–2 win.

In game four, the Oilers ran up a 7–2 score for the second game in a row, this time with 24-year-old Andy Moog in nets. Headlining this show was none other than the Great Gretzky, who broke out of his funk with two nifty goals in the game.

Period	Team	Scorer	Assists
1	Oilers	Wayne Gretzky	Dave Semenko, Jari Kurri
1	Oilers	Willy Lindstrom	Glenn Anderson
1	Islanders	Brent Sutter	Greg Gilbert, Ken Morrow
1	Oilers	Mark Messier	

A Gretzky breakaway marker only 1:53 into the game set the tone for this one while a late one by Messier put the Oilers up comfortably going into the dressing room.

2	Oilers	Willy Lindstrom	Mark Messier, Paul Coffey
2	Oilers	Pat Conacher	Pat Hughes
2	Oilers	Paul Coffey	Jari Kurri, Dave Semenko
2	Islanders	Pat Flatley	Clark Gillies, Stefan Persson

The New York Islanders, winners of four consecutive Stanley Cup championships, were about ready to die.

3	Oilers	Wayne Gretzky	

Although the outcome of the match was no longer in doubt, the Oilers had reason to cheer when their prince counted his second goal of the evening. Wayne was back! Woe to the boys from Long Island!

"I can't remember the last time we played so poorly in back-to-back games," moaned coach Arbour. "I mean, this is the Stanley Cup final, isn't it?"

This was a huge win for the Oilers. But Gretzky wasn't ready to pop open the bubbly just yet. "We want to be excited and enthused over what's been happening," he said. "We're happy we're leading 3-1 but that hockey team is a four-time champion. If we think we're in, we're in trouble. We haven't won anything yet."

Game five wasn't pretty. The New York Islanders, for years the most feared team in the NHL, went down to defeat on the night of May 19, 1984, without so much as a whimper. Sure, they managed to score twice in the game but, really, they were finished from the opening face-off. Sad.

Period	Team	Scorer	Assists
1	Oilers	Wayne Gretzky	Jari Kurri
1	Oilers	Wayne Gretzky	Jari Kurri

Having allowed two goals to the Great One, Smith was yanked and replaced in the Islander goal by Rollie Melanson. This was the beginning of the end.

2	Oilers	Ken Linseman	Charlie Huddy, Wayne Gretzky
2	Oilers	Jari Kurri	Paul Coffey, Glenn Anderson

At the end of 40 minutes, it was 4–0 Edmonton. Nothing more to say.

3	Islanders	Pat LaFontaine	Pat Flatley, Clark Gillies
3	Islanders	Pat LaFontaine	Clark Gillies
3	Oilers	Dave Lumley	

Two scores by young LaFontaine, too little, too late. Edmonton wins, 5–2. Wrote George Vescey of the *New York Times*, "In the runway to [New York's] dressing-room, Butch Goring kicked a festive-looking balloon, but it was too late to change a thing: the Islanders' marvelous four-year bubble had been burst."

"This is the most disappointed I've ever felt in my career," groaned Mike Bossy. "It's a crushing defeat!" Denis Potvin was somewhat less despairing than his teammate. "When I leave this building," he said, "I'm going to hold my head high." Without question, winning four straight Stanley Cups is something to be proud of.

Ahhhhh . . . Fischler!

After [Patrick] Roy's 1986 Stanley Cup heroics, perhaps the [Montreal Canadiens] figured they had the second coming of Georges Vezina. He looks more like Charlie Brown.
— *Stan Fischler*, Inside Sports, June 1987

Nudie North Star

In 1987, Ciccarelli lived in a quiet part of Minneapolis, Minnesota. A nice "family" neighborhood where the doggies barked and the kiddies made mud pies. Apparently, the star North Star had stomach problems one morning and was in his bathroom. Suddenly, there was a strange noise from outside the Ciccarelli home, one loud enough to compel him to go out to his garage wearing only socks and a sweatshirt. According to one eyewitness, Ciccarelli opened a side door and took a step or two outside au naturel, raw as a clam! He spotted a van about 200 feet away and panicked: "I immediately withdrew back to the garage at that time and police officers suddenly darted into the doorway, apparently from behind my garage, and arrested me for indecent exposure."

The cops were said to have taken pictures of Ciccarelli standing in the front yard of his $300,000 home wearing his socks and a sweatshirt. He was released after being slapped with a misdemeanor charge. North Stars' GM Lou Nanne, no doubt stifling a giggle, put in a good word for his star winger: "The charge certainly isn't indicative of Dino's behavior. If there is anything to it, we will certainly give Dino any kind of assistance he needs."

Ciccarelli had his day in court — fully clothed. His lawyer, Ron Simon, painted the picture of an innocent nudist: "[Ciccarelli] does admit that he frequently walks around the house in a nude or semi-nude state. The biggest problem is that the complaint suggests he's some kind of sexual pervert or deviant."

Ciccarelli pleaded guilty to indecent exposure, ready to move on with his life. The damage? Probation, $200 in court costs, and shame.

"I may never play in a game like this. I doubt I'll ever play with Wayne Gretzky and Mario Lemieux again. I still can't believe I played in this game."
— *Rick Tocchet, after Team Canada's 1987 Canada Cup victory over the Soviets*

Cry Me a River

On August 9, 1988, Wayne Gretzky sat at an Edmonton press conference bawling his eyes out. It had been less than a month since his marriage to American actress and bombshell Janet Jones and less than three months since he had led his Oilers to their fourth Stanley Cup title in five years.

In one of hockey's all-time shockers, Gretzky was shipped to the Los Angeles Kings with Marty McSorley, Mike Krushelnyski, and minor-leaguer John Miner for Jimmy Carson, Martin Gelinas, three first-round draft picks, the rights to minor-league defenseman Craig Redmond, and $15 million US. But why? Gretzky had almost 1,700 points, an average of 185 points a season, eight Hart trophies, seven First All-Star Team selections, seven scoring titles, and four Stanley Cup rings. Gretzky had first heard of a rumored trade only hours after helping the Oilers to the Cup in the summer of 1988. At the club's celebration dinner, Wayne's father, Walter, let him in on a huge secret: he was being shuffled off to La-La Land. The only reason he wasn't told about the impending trade earlier was because he was in the middle of leading the Oilers through the playoffs and the news might have distracted him. In the book *Gretzky*, Edmonton's most celebrated citizen described his reaction:

> I couldn't believe it, but I could tell from my Dad's expression that it was true. The team wanted to trade me? The team that just two hours before I'd helped to win its fourth Stanley Cup in the last five years? The team that was still young enough to win another three or four in a row? The team I supposed I'd retire with? Amazing how fast you can lose your appetite.

The cash-strapped Oilers owner Peter Pocklington had been looking to ship off his prize pig for a couple of years. His other business interests — land development, cars, oil — were in serious trouble and he'd liquidated personal assets and put up the Oilers as collateral against a loan. After rumors of Gretzky moving on to Detroit, New York, and Vancouver, Pocklington sent Gretzky down the West Coast.

Was this the untimely end of Wayne Gretzky as the NHL's top performer and drawing card? Was Pocklington really dumping Gretzky because the dynamic center's best years had come and gone? No.

Hey, [Gretzky] belongs in L.A. He's the greatest. I'm definitely going to get season tickets.
— Magic Johnson, Los Angeles Laker

Los Angeles. That means I can fly to L.A. and check out the women.
— Brent Gretzky, Wayne's kid brother

As if on cue from a movie director, the "Great One" scored on his first shot as a King. In 539 regular-season matches in the City of Angels, he scored 246 goals and 918 points for an average of just over 1.7 points per game. He eventually surrendered his status as the most dominant player in the game to Pittsburgh's Mario Lemieux, but Gretzky remained one of hockey's most consistent producers. In 1993, after a fairly disappointing regular season, he exploded for 40 points in 24 playoff matches in leading L.A. to the finals against the Montreal Canadiens. The Cup came to rest in the Montreal Forum, but Gretzky had proven himself. He wasn't washed up. At 32 years of age, he was past his peak but was still far from ready for the rocking chair.

Wayne vs. Mario

Wayne Gretzky was a skinny little fellow from Brantford, Ontario. He was the most unlikely of heroes: just six feet tall, weighing 150 pounds soaking wet with change in his pockets. As for strength, well, he would have trouble out-benchpressing a 12-year-old. Who was to know this little bag of bones would become maybe the greatest offensive player in NHL history?

Next came Mario Lemieux. From his days as a Laval Titan in the early 1980s, the hockey world had him marked as the next "Great One." In 1983–84, the boy who towered over the rest, who skated and stick-handled around his would-be checkers as if they were pylons, scored 133 goals and 282 points in 70 games in the Quebec juniors. Lemieux grew into one of the most dominant forces in the history of the game. Bobby Orr once said, "On sheer ability, Mario is good enough to win scoring titles with a broken stick. On pure talent, he's the best there is."

Gretzky. Lemieux. Two men, two styles, two legends. Who was better?

Over their careers, Gretzky wins. Who would dare argue against 3,000 points, 10 scoring crowns, and four Stanley Cup rings?

For Lemieux, health (chronic back pain, Hodgkin's Disease) was always a factor. Like Orr before him, Super Mario's performance depended largely on his health, on whether or not he could even bend down to lace up his skates. Gretzky described a day in the life of Lemieux:

> About three weeks into the '89–90 season, he started a consecutive-points streak that looked unstoppable. By about the thirtieth game, I figured my streak of fifty-one was history. He wasn't just getting a point a game, he was getting three or four. But he suffered a herniated disc in his back somewhere in there and you could see it was killing him . . . The personal and

Wayne Gretzky

media attention are hard enough when you're trying to break a record, but when your body wants to be lying in a swimming pool full of ice it's even tougher. Finally, after forty-six straight games, Mario played two periods against the New York Rangers and was in so much pain he couldn't come back to the ice. The streak was over.

Armed with good health, Gretzky racked up incredible point totals and took down record after record. But was he, at his peak, as dominant as Lemieux? Which of these two monstrous talents has the higher peak value? Let's figure it out.

In 1983–84, Gretzky scored 87 goals and 118 assists in 74 regular-season games before powering his razzle-dazzle Edmonton Oilers to their first ever Cup win. Although Gretzky's 205 points was 10 shy of his 1985–86 total, it was likely his finest season overall. Gretzky was worth 20 power-play goals, a record 12 short-handed goals, a First All-Star Team nod, a Hart Trophy, an Art Ross, and a Stanley Cup ring. He was truly at the peak of his breathtaking power.

Lemieux, on the other hand, did something in 1992–93 that no one before or since has been able to do: he came back from cancer to win the NHL scoring race. He missed 20 games receiving treatment for and recuperating from Hodgkin's Disease, a form of cancer. At one point, he was so far behind the Buffalo Sabres' Pat LaFontaine in the scoring race that it was unlikely Lemieux would take the crown. But, against all odds, Lemieux tossed the slinkier, bonier LaFontaine aside and laid claim to the scoring title with 69 goals and 91 assists in only 60 games! In 1992–93 Lemieux was at the top of his game.

Let's do the math: 160 points in 60 games is worth 197 in 74 games, so Lemieux's 1992–93 effort falls short of Gretzky's 1983–84 total by eight points, right? Well, what if we were to consider that in 1983–84, there were 7.8 goals and 12.8 assists in the average 60-minute game? And that in 1992–93, there were 7.25 goals and 11.9 assists in the average game? Not much of a difference, right? You'd be surprised. In 1983–84, goals were almost 8 percent easier to come by than they were in 1992–93. The percentage for assists is about the same. Let's transport 1992–93 Lemieux to 1983–84, a time of neon bracelets and stirrup pants:

	GP	G	A
Lemieux	60	74.2	97.9

Now let's say Lemieux played 74 games, the same number Gretzky played in that same year:

	GP	G	A	Pts
Lemieux	74	92	121	213
Gretzky	74	87	118	205

Super Mario comes out on top!

Of course, there's no way we can say without a doubt that Lemieux would have scored 213 points in 74 games in 1983–84. But with good health and a little bit of luck, the NHL record books might have looked a lot different. Gretzky is hands-down the greatest offensive force the game of hockey has ever known, but Lemieux was likely the talent of the century.

Mario Lemieux is a fine example of what mighta been in hockey. If not for his sore back and illness, that he played much of his 10 years in the league in excruciating pain, Mario Lemieux and not Wayne Gretzky might have had all the records listed under his name.

----

*Snap!*shots

GLENN ANDERSON Right Wing
6'1" 190
b. 10/2/1960, Vancouver, British Columbia

Glenn Anderson got his start in hockey with the Bellingham Blazers of the British Columbia Junior Hockey League in 1977–78. He scored 62 goals that year, but was still a raw talent. He passed through Denver and Seattle and had a stint on the Canadian Olympic Team. He was selected 69th overall in the 1979 Entry Draft by Edmonton. In 1980–81 with the Oilers, he came up with 30 goals and 53 points in 58 games.

Anderson emerged as a force in only his second season when he finished 11th in NHL scoring. Although not nearly as offensively dynamic as teammate Wayne Gretzky, Anderson nonetheless struck fear into opposition goalies. Not only did he have the raw skills — speed, skating, big shot — but he had a great big mean streak. Teammate Kevin Lowe once commented on Anderson's abrasive playing style: "Andy does it in an unassuming fashion. He's very subtle. But anyone who wants to take advantage of him will pay the price."

The player the *Hockey News* once referred to as "kamikaze" hit the 50-goal mark in 1983–84 and again in 1985–86. He scored a high of 105 points in 1981–82. He took part in the Canada Cup in 1984 and 1987 and played in Rendez-Vous in 1987. Oilers' co-coach John Muckler, for one, was high on the fiery right winger: "He's a gifted skater and a daredevil. He goes to the net as well as anybody in the NHL. He drives to the net and when you're playing against him, you have to be leery of him. You never know what's going to happen. He loses control."

In September 1991, Anderson was sent to the Toronto Maple Leafs with Grant Fuhr in a blockbuster deal. Although Anderson did not have the 50-goal gun anymore, he was still a dangerous offensive threat. After seasons of 24 and 22 goals, he was dealt near the end of the 1993–94 season to the New York Rangers for Mike Gartner. He and other former Oilers helped the Rangers win their first Stanley Cup in 54 years. It was Anderson's sixth championship ring.

Anderson's days in the NHL were numbered. After stints on the Canadian National Team, the St. Louis Blues, and again with the Oilers, Anderson came to the end of the hockey trail. In 1,129 games, the left-shooting right winger famous for his angled charge on net scored 498 goals and 1,099 assists.

Peak Years   *1984–88*
In a Word   *BRAVADO*

MIKE BOSSY Right Wing
6'0" 185
b. 1/22/1957, Montreal, Quebec

Michael Bossy smoked a pack of cigarettes a day throughout most of his career. He used a 54-inch hockey stick, long by most standards. His teammates bugged him about anything from his soft playing style to his big honker. But Bossy matured into one of the deadliest shooters the game has ever known.

Bossy got his start in hockey with the Quebec Major Junior Laval National club at the tender age of 16. From day one, the boy seemed destined for greatness. In almost 300 total games in the QMJHL, Bossy managed 338 goals and 602 points. Drafted 15th overall by the New York Islanders in the 1977 Amateur Draft, he took his place to the right of Bryan Trottier, a hard-nosed center. Together, the two men were dynamite. In

1977–78, Trottier reeled in 123 points while the 21-year-old Bossy scored 53 times in 73 games. Coach Al Arbour was, of course, very pleased: "Trots and Bossy, what a pair! I remember when we put them together for the first time. They were made for one another: it was obvious right away."

With Bossy and Trottier on the first line, the Islanders won four straight Stanley Cups. The two were inseparable on the ice. Trottier, the quintessential all-around talent, always managed to find Bossy on the ice. It was as if they had a psychic connection.

However dandy a player Trottier was, Bossy was the star attraction. Arbour couldn't remember the last time he'd seen a talent as great as Bossy: "When he shoots, it doesn't even look like he touches the puck. He swoops on it like a jai alai player would. He's got the quickest hands I've ever seen on a hockey player, even quicker than Rocket Richard's." In 752 games, Bossy scored 573 goals and 1,126 points.

Among Bossy's accomplishments are three Lady Byng trophies, a Conn Smythe, two goal-scoring crowns, eight All-Star selections, and four Stanley Cup rings. He became a worthy member of the Hockey Hall of Fame in 1991. What a shame that Bossy, one of the purest scorers in the history of the game, was railroaded into early retirement by chronic back pain in 1987.

Peak Years *1980–1984*
In a Word *LETHAL*

RAYMOND BOURQUE Defense
5'11" 210
b. 12/28/1960, Montreal, Quebec

First there was Eddie Shore, a seething, scowling bloodbowler from hockey's Missing Tooth Era. Then there was Bobby Orr, who, with one part razzle and one part dazzle, revolutionized the role of the defenseman. Finally, there was Raymond Jean Bourque, the latest of the great Boston Bruin defenders. And for the Boston Bruins, who took him eighth overall in the 1979 Entry Draft, he couldn't have come along at a better time.

Since the departure of Orr three years earlier, the team had been in dire need of a front-line quarterback. While Brad Park was one of the top defensemen around, he was not getting any younger. Bourque had managed 56 goals and 220 points in 204 games in the Quebec juniors. "[Bourque] can shoot so well," gushed Bruin defenseman Mike Milbury in October 1979. "He can skate. He's quick. He can pass. He has everything . . . I'd have to compare him to Denis Potvin. It won't take long before he's as good as Potvin."

Bourque's first season in the NHL went well. He played the full 80 games, setting a new record for points by a rookie defenseman with 65. This, on top of some great defensive work and a +52 rating, brought him the Calder Trophy and his first of 18 All-Star nods. Very impressive. In the playoffs, he led his 46-21-13 Bruins through 10 games, scoring two goals and 11 points in a losing cause. In the next few years, Bourque steadily improved. In 1983–84, he equaled Denis Potvin's goal total of 31 in one season.

Bourque was one of those rare players who has everything. His shot ranked among the best in the NHL while his point-control was nothing short of incredible. He was deadly on the power play, especially alongside rough-and-tumble sniper Cam Neely. Few in hockey history had the mix of skating, passing, checking, and shooting that Bourque had in his prime.

On December 3, 1987, the Bruins held Phil Esposito Night to honor the former scoring star. It was a major event as Esposito was to be only the seventh player in club history to have his jersey number retired. Midway through the ceremonies, Bourque met Esposito at center ice, took off his #7 jersey, and handed it to him. Underneath,

Bourque wore his now equally famous #77. "All I could say when I saw Raymond in that '77' was 'Raymond, thank you,'" said Esposito later. "I had no idea."

Bourque continued to work hard despite his club's failure to take the Stanley Cup. Through the 1998–99 season, the five-time Norris Trophy winner had almost 1,500 points. He has seen action in three Canada Cup tournaments, 18 All-Star games, and an Olympic tournament. His plaque will look very nice in the Hockey Hall of Fame.

Peak Years   1987–91
In a Word   ROCK

GUY CARBONNEAU Center
5'11" 185
b. 3/18/1960, Sept-Iles, Quebec

Of the dozens of hockey stars to come out of the province of Quebec, perhaps no one made such a dramatic shift from offense to defense on entering the NHL as Guy Carbonneau. This tall, slim center started with the Chicoutimi Sagueneens in late 1976 at the age of 16. Improving by the day, he followed up a 141-point season with 72 goals and 182 points in 72 games in 1979–80. The Montreal Canadiens, who were always looking for more speed and skill, found Carbonneau an attractive possibility. The Canadiens drafted Carbonneau 44th overall in the 1979 Entry Draft.

In the wake of four straight Stanley Cup championships in the 1970s, Montreal devoted itself to building a more defensively minded outfit. With the departure of several key players, the timing couldn't have been better for Carbonneau. He fit into the new check-first-ask-questions-later system in Montreal, the one that would eventually make high-octane players like Guy Lafleur obsolete. Carbonneau was willing to check, and check, and check. Carbonneau had a unique blend of speed, skill, and defensive ability. Playing with the likes of Mario Tremblay, Mats Naslund, Bobby Smith, and Mike McPhee, Carbonneau blossomed into possibly the top defensive forward of his time. He could also score — he had point totals of 47, 54, 57, and 56 in his first four seasons. In Montreal's successful Stanley Cup run in 1986, Carbonneau played brilliantly, scoring 12 points in 20 playoffs games and checking like a madman. In 1993, he figured huge in another championship. In August 1994, after 12 seasons in Montreal, he was traded to the St. Louis Blues. A little over a year later, he was shipped off to the Dallas Stars.

In his prime, Carbonneau was one of those players who could hurt you in more than one way. Patrick Roy owes more than one of his shutouts to the shot-blocking genius of Carbonneau. The checking center from Sept-Iles, Quebec, was worth over 200 goals, three Selke trophies, and three Stanley Cup rings.

Peak Years   1987–91
In a Word   AIRTIGHT

DINO CICCARELLI Right Wing
5'10" 185
b. 2/8/1960, Sarnia, Ontario

Coaches love fireplugs. They love the hustle, the fire, the determination, the desire to win at all costs. Dino Ciccarelli was just this kind of player. A former Junior hockey coach called the gritty right winger a "scavenger," which wasn't an insult. Scavenger or not, the Sarnia, Ontario, native was good for upwards of a goal a game in three Junior seasons. At the beginning of the 1978–79 season, the London Knight broke his leg. A 40-inch steel rod was put into his leg. There was doubt in hockey circles that Ciccarelli would overcome this injury.

Because of his average size and his broken leg, Ciccarelli was passed over in the NHL draft. "In my mind," he would recall later, "I figured I was done. When I look back, I have really got to thank my parents, my landlady and landlord in London [Ontario] . . . and my London Knight trainer Don Brankley. I was ready to pack it in and they said to keep with it."

In September 1979, despite the risk, the Minnesota North Stars signed Ciccarelli as a free agent. The feisty gunner made an immediate splash with his new team. After appearing in 32 games in 1980–81, Ciccarelli scored 55 goals and 106 points in 76 games in 1981–82. Over the next seven seasons, he scored a total of 271 goals. Although never a natural All-Star selection, he did make All-Star appearances in 1982, 1983, 1989, and 1997.

Although not the fastest winger afoot, Ciccarelli had a truckload of heart. He was a nuisance in front of the net. His goals were seldom pretty, but his coaches had few complaints. He topped the 50-goal and 100-point plateaus in 1981–82 and again in 1986–87, scoring 30 or more goals 11 times.

Ciccarelli was traded in March 1989 to the Washington Capitals with Bob Rouse for Mike Gartner and Larry Murphy. He made stops with the Detroit Red Wings, Tampa Bay Lightning, and Florida Panthers. Although, like any other player, his production slipped with age, he never lost his competitive edge.

In 20 NHL seasons, Ciccarelli scored well over 600 goals and 1,000 points.

Peak Years   *1984–88*
In a Word   *HUSTLER*

PAUL COFFEY Defense
6'0" 190
b. 6/1/1961, Weston, Ontario

The Edmonton Oilers selected Paul Coffey sixth overall in the 1980 NHL Entry Draft. Coffey had just finished thrashing the Ontario Hockey Association to the tune of 29 goals and 102 points in less than 80 games. Coffey and his blinding speed, good shot, and superb play-making abilities were a perfect fit for Wayne Gretzky and his merry band of cherry-pickers. At 19 years of age, he was ready to become the Oilers' quarterback.

In 1980–81, the rookie Weston, Ontario, native was good for nine goals and 32 points. Over the next three seasons, he steadily improved, posting point totals of 89, 96, and 126. By the mid-1980s, Coffey was considered by many to be the NHL's premier defender. He was surely one of the speediest men in the history of the game.

Toronto Sun sportswriter Jim O'Leary said of Coffey, "He moves like a marble on a hardwood floor." Certainly, Coffey could skate, pass, and shoot, but many saw him as little more than a center playing the blue-line. They thought of him as a defensive liability, a hockey player out for the goals and glory. In 1985, Montreal Canadiens' tough boy Chris Nilan screamed at Coffey, "Hey Coffey, how does it feel to go around the NHL knowing that [Washington Capitals defenseman] Rod Langway is a better defenseman than you are?" Coffey responded, "Hey Nilan, how does it feel going around the NHL knowing that there are 500 guys better than you?" Coffey had no illusions about his weaknesses in the physical side of the game, but he wasn't about to break down to the taunts. He proved himself defensively, playing a magnificent two-way game in the 1987 Canada Cup tournament.

Coffey had three Stanley Cup rings, five All-Star nods, and two Norris trophies under his belt by the time he was dealt to Pittsburgh in 1987. He has since played in several NHL cities, including Los Angeles, Detroit, Hartford, Philadelphia, Chicago, and Carolina. A brilliant career has yielded him over 1,000 assists and 1,487 points. He may not have been the complete package like Bobby Orr or Denis Potvin, but Coffey was one of the top defensemen ever. He's a shoo-in for induction into the Hockey Hall of Fame.

Peak Years *1985–89*
In a Word *SCINTILLATING*

MARCEL DIONNE (Little Beaver) Center
5'9" 190
b. 8/3/1951, Drummondville, Quebec

Most discussions of the highest-flying French Canadians in hockey history include Maurice Richard, Jean Beliveau, Guy Lafleur, and Mario Lemieux. All four of these legends carved out brilliant NHL careers with flash, flair, and a pinch of pizzazz. One peek at the record books, however, reveals that Marcel Dionne, and not one of the above, holds all career scoring marks for French Canadians. It's hard to believe that the guy who looked more like a chubby ice-cream salesman than a hockey player tops French Canada's list of high flyers.

Fame descended on Dionne early in life. When he was but a little gaffer playing midget hockey in Quebec, fans shoved scraps of paper at him to autograph. As a Junior with the St. Catharines Black Hawks, Dionne won back-to-back Eddie Power trophies as the OHA's top scorer and was named to the All-Star team in 1970 and 1971. He stood beside Guy Lafleur of the Quebec League as one of the top two amateur players in North America. By the spring of 1971, the big argument was over which of the two boys was better.

By the time he reached the NHL, the "Little Beaver" was ready to go. He was selected second overall by the Detroit Red Wings in the 1971 Entry Draft. He counted 366 points over his first four seasons with Detroit.

With a helmeted Lafleur stinking it up with the Montreal Canadiens, Dionne looked like the pick of the litter. Things in Detroit would soon turn sour for the young messiah, however. Mounting pressure from media and team management left him with a bad taste in his mouth, so in May 1975 he signed on with Jack Kent Cooke's Los Angeles Kings. "There's no figure Marcel would have taken from Detroit," Alan Eagleson, Dionne's agent, commented at the time. "Leaving Detroit isn't a question of dollars." So, with the flick of a pen Dionne was headed to the West Coast. Decked out in the Kings' purple, yellow, and white, he soon eclipsed Butch Goring as the club's star player. Dionne later starred between Charlie Simmer and Dave Taylor on the "Triple Crown" line, one of the most devastating forward line combinations in NHL history.

Having endured major trade rumors in 1983 and 1984, the Drummondville native finally had his fill of L.A., and on March 9, 1987, he asked Kings' owner Jerry Buss for a trade. At the trade deadline, New York Rangers' GM Phil Esposito acquired Dionne for Bobby Carpenter and Tom Laidlaw. "I asked for the trade but in a way I'm surprised to be going," said Dionne soon afterward. "But I want to thank [L.A. GM] Rogie [Vachon] for giving me this opportunity. You always feel confident when you're going to another team."

In almost 20 seasons in the NHL, Dionne scored 731 goals and 1,771 points. He earned two Lady Byng trophies, an Art Ross Trophy, and four All-Star Team nominations. He was elected to the Hockey Hall of Fame in 1992. He still ranks third all-time in career points, behind Gretzky and Howe.

Peak Years *1979–83*
In a Word *OFFENSE*

BERNIE FEDERKO (The Magician) Center
6'0" 178
b. 5/12/1956, Foam Lake, Saskatchewan

He wasn't as flashy as Wayne Gretzky. He wasn't as fast as Mike Gartner. He didn't have the moves of Denis Savard, the strength of Mark Messier, or the toughness and will of Bryan Trottier. But Bernie Federko was a star. The St. Louis Blues made him their first pick, seventh overall, in the 1976 draft.

Federko was a star in hockey from the beginning. In just over 200 games as a Saskatoon Blade between 1973 and 1976, the brainy center managed 133 goals and 344 points for an average of 1.7 points per game.

The 1978–79 season marked the beginning of the Federko era in St. Louis. The man they called the Magician recorded 31 goals and 95 points in 74 games. After recording point totals of 94, 104, 92, and 84 in the following four seasons, the Blues' brightest luminary since Red Berenson put up three straight 100-point efforts. He had a 21-point effort in the 1986 playoffs.

Teammates, peers, and management sang Federko's praises. He was an elite scorer through the first half of the 1980s, and he was a modest, quiet, clean player. "[He'd] been so good for so long," said Blues GM Ron Caron in 1986, "and yet he still [played] in silence. But he always [played]." Many think that Gretzky was the first player to consistently set up goals from behind the enemy net, but Federko did it from the start. Despite his overall lack of speed, he was tricky and had loads of smarts.

In the summer of 1989, after 13 seasons in St. Louis, Federko was dealt to the Detroit Red Wings. The aging star managed 57 points in his last season and probably could have put in another season or two in the Motor City, but he decided to retire. In 1,000 games over 14 seasons in the NHL, the Foam Lake, Saskatchewan, native scored 369 goals to go with 761 assists. Although he failed to win the Stanley Cup and often played in the shadows of the NHL's prettier players, Federko was a true champion.

Peak Years   *1981–85*
In a Word   *WHIZ*

GRANT FUHR Goal
5'9" 190
b. 9/28/1962, Spruce Grove, Alberta

Grant Fuhr got his start in hockey with the Victoria Cougars of the WHL in 1979. Over the next two seasons, Fuhr recorded six shutouts, 78 wins, and a goals-against of under 3.00. In the 1981 NHL Entry Draft, the Edmonton Oilers selected Fuhr eighth overall.

Fuhr appeared in 48 games in 1981–82, ending the season with a 3.31 GAA and a remarkable 28-5-14 record. After this impressive rookie campaign, in which he earned a spot on the Second All-Star Team, Fuhr took a wrong turn. In 32 games in 1982–83, he was 13-12-5 with a 4.29 GAA. In early 1983, sick of all the bad press surrounding his ineptitude, he lashed out. "Edmonton fans are totally horse—! I couldn't care less about Edmonton fans. They're all a bunch of jerks!" The pudgy young goalie regretted his words. After making a formal public apology, he resolved to get his game back on track.

It didn't take Fuhr long to find his stride behind the amazing Oiler skaters. In 1984, he posted an 11-4 record in the playoffs to lead his team to their first ever Stanley Cup championship. A year later, he was equally impressive in taking the Oilers to their second straight Cup. By the mid-1980s, he was at his peak. "I don't feel any pressure," he said in 1986. "Everybody is playing his best, then you have to turn around and do it again the next night. That's my idea of fun."

Fuhr led the Oilers to additional Cups in 1987 and 1988, bringing his total to four. He had a combined 56-14 record in the four Cup runs, numbers that compare favorably to goaltending legend Ken Dryden, who in a four-year Cup run with the Montreal Canadiens between 1976 and 1979 ran up a 48-10 record. Fuhr's attitude was always "Play Now, Think Later." As Oiler teammate and friend Wayne Gretzky once said: "Grant never gets excited. He never gets mad. He never gets happy. His attitude to anything is just, 'Oh well.'"

In September 1991, with Bill Ranford in the wings, Fuhr was traded to the Toronto Maple Leafs. He has since made stops in Buffalo and Los Angeles. In St. Louis, his career was rejuvenated. In 1995–96, the old veteran appeared in 79 games, posting a 2.87 GAA and a 30-28-16 record.

In almost 20 NHL seasons, Fuhr has almost 400 wins. He is a Vezina Trophy winner and a five-time Stanley Cup champion.

Peak Years   *1984–88*
In a Word   *BULLETPROOF*

MIKE GARTNER Right Wing
6'0" 187
b. 10/29/1959, Ottawa, Ontario

In the 1979 Entry Draft, the Washington Capitals selected Mike Gartner, a fast-skating winger from Niagara Falls of the OHA. The pick was definitely a step in the right direction for the Capitals, who had been a losing team since their inaugural season of 1974–75. Gartner was a winner, a modest but effective scoring winger who would eventually top the 700-goal mark.

The thing that impressed people from the very start about Gartner was his incredible speed. "I have a God-given ability to skate," said Washington's young buck. "I haven't really worked on my legs at all during my career. [The speed] is just there although I do remember my dad sending me to a power-skating school when I was a kid. Maybe that helped the natural talent." In 77 games in 1979–80, the 20-year-old scored 36 goals and 68 points. He scored 48 goals the following season, placing him in the upper echelon of NHL scorers.

Over the next few years, Washington went through a remarkable transformation. The old losing attitude was replaced by fresh, healthy optimism. Dennis Maruk and Rod Langway joined Gartner in picking the franchise up out of the ashes into respectability. In 1982–83, after eight seasons of losing hockey, the Washington Capitals were 39-25-16 for 94 points. Again, Gartner was solid, scoring 38 goals and 76 points. In 1984–85, he enjoyed his finest offensive season, scoring 50 goals with 52 assists, putting him in the top 10 in scoring.

In March 1989, Gartner was traded to the Minnesota North Stars in a deal for Dino Ciccarelli. Only a year later, he moved to the New York Rangers. In the Big Apple, the fleet winger experienced a revival of his waning career. In almost four seasons, he scored 173 goals, averaging 40 a year. He was traded to the Toronto Maple Leafs for Glenn Anderson in the spring of 1994, scant months before the Rangers went on to win the Stanley Cup. He ended his career as a Phoenix Coyote. In almost 20 years in the NHL, Gartner scored 708 goals and 1,335 points.

Peak Years   *1983–87*
In a Word   *FLEET*

MICHEL GOULET Left Wing
6'1" 195
b. 4/21/1960, Peribonka, Quebec

In the 1979 NHL Entry Draft, the Quebec Nordiques, who had just made the jump from the WHA, selected Michel Goulet with their inaugural first-round pick. Goulet was a strong skater with a superb shot, who threw his body around and played well defensively. Goulet was the complete package.

Goulet improved steadily through his first three seasons, recording point totals of 54, 71, and 84. In 1982–83 he broke out, scoring 57 goals and 48 assists. Nordique fans, who chanted "Gou! Gou! Gou!" during games, loved him. "What the Quebecois want," wrote Bob Kravitz of *Sports Illustrated* in 1985, "is the 'savoir faire' and the end-to-end rushes and the wild goal-scoring celebrations that [Guy] Lafleur and [Maurice Richard] provided in Montreal. What they get from Goulet is 'extraordinaire' unfortunately hidden under a thick layer of 'ordinaire.'"

Goulet was not the flashy type. He was not the kind of player who brought you up out of your chair. In the face of Nordique president Marcel Aubut's gibberish that Goulet was "the new Guy Lafleur of Quebec," the big winger plodded on. He followed up his brilliant 1982–83 season with goal totals of 56, 55, 53, 49, and 48. Goulet had four 100-point seasons, four world tournaments, and five All-Star nominations between 1983 and 1988.

Goulet spent almost 11 seasons with the Nordiques, but never came close to winning the Stanley Cup.

In March 1990, an aging Goulet was traded to the Chicago Blackhawks. In the Windy City, Goulet regained his All-Star form, ringing off point totals of 65 and 63 in 1990 and 1991. Goulet came through a serious medical crisis in 1990 when he underwent laser treatment to correct a rapid heart beat. After the 1993–94 season, the big man from small-town Quebec hung up his skates. In 1,089 NHL games, Goulet had scored 548 goals and 1,152 assists. He was inducted into the Hall of Fame in 1998.

Peak Years   1983–87
In a Word   MARKSMAN

WAYNE GRETZKY (The Great One) Center
6'0" 180
b. 1/26/1981, Brantford, Ontario

Wayne Gretzky

What can be said about Wayne Gretzky that hasn't already been said? From a modest house at 42 Varadi Avenue in the sleepy town of Brantford, Ontario, came the most dominant offensive force in the history of organized hockey. While some may make the argument that Gordie Howe played for 1,000 more years or that Mario Lemieux could score a goal while carrying a baby elephant on his back, Gretzky has proven himself time and time again. He is the Great One.

Gretzky entered the major leagues with the Edmonton Oilers, who in 1979 made the jump from the mortally wounded WHA to the NHL. The impact of this skinny little guy on the National League was immediate and shocking. In his first season in the NHL, he managed 51 goals and 137 points. Amazing! Who was this kid? Where did he come from? In the space of one season, he had ripped the Mr. Big title from the hands of Montreal Canadiens' legend Guy Lafleur, eclipsing the Flower's best single season point total by a tick. *Globe and Mail* writer Allen Abel was as confused as everyone else:

Naked, the Great Gretzky does not look like the next Bobby Hull. Sheaves of shaggy gold hair tickle his shoulders. A mustache is fighting to break through his upper lip, and losing. You've seen physiques like his in Charles Atlas ads, above the caption 'Before.' His lean face is ravaged by acne. Lord knows the lad can afford Stridex Medicated Pads.

Gretzky took the NHL by storm. The little boy Quebec City hockey fans used to call "Le Grand" and "Tornado" had grown into the NHL — and how! He went from 137 points in his first season to 164 to a record 212 in 1981–82. Coming into the mid-1980s, Gretzky was at the peak of his colossal powers. Over the next little while, there would be Stanley Cups aplenty. The Oilers shook off the seemingly indomitable New York Islanders in 1984 for their first ever Cup and came through again in 1985, 1987, and 1988. In the last of these "Gretzky" Cups, the Great One was particularly impressive in rebounding from a "sub-par" 149-point season to cop the Conn Smythe Trophy.

On August 9, 1988, only a few months after taking Edmonton to its fourth Cup in five years, Gretzky was traded to the Los Angeles Kings. Although quite shaken by the deal, the Great One came through big in the City of Angels. Hockey, which had always been some kind of a joke in southern California, took on new life. The Great One's image was marketed to one of the largest centers in the United States, and to great effect. By 1990, the game was never more popular. Even Hollywood celebrities were snapping up tickets to what had become the hottest game in town. Gretzky rang off point totals of 168, 142, 163, and 121 in his first four seasons as a King. In 1993, he caught fire in the playoffs to lead Los Angeles to the Cup finals. Although the Kings would ultimately succumb to the Montreal Canadiens, hockey had officially arrived in Los Angeles. The *Toronto Sun*'s John Robertson knocked hockey's golden boy:

> [Gretzky's] too perfect. Just once I'd like to see him score on his own net. Or shoot from a bad angle when he should have passed. Or take a dumb penalty. Or go on TV with a booger hanging from his nose . . . He darts up the ice like Bambi stalking a butterfly. Genuine hockey heroes should not have weak chins and high-pitched voices.

Indeed, Gretzky was the NHL's poster boy, the hockey hero of a new generation of fans. He has broken virtually every offensive record known to man, scoring close to 3,000 points in 20 years in the NHL. Who else but the Great One would have more assists than any other player in hockey history has points? Add to that 10 Art Ross trophies, five Lady Byngs, nine Harts, two Conn Smythes, and four championship rings — enough hardware to open up a store. He starred for 21 winters in two professional leagues, four Canada Cup tournaments, a World Cup tournament, and an Olympic Games tournament. Not bad for a skinny little fellow from southwestern Ontario.

After much reflection, the Great One decided to retire at the end of the 1998–99 campaign. His much-hyped retirement ceremony took up most of a Sunday afternoon before a game between the Rangers and the Penguins. Before that game, league commissioner Gary Bettman retired Gretzky's legendary #99 league-wide. Gretzky will join the rest of hockey's best in the Hockey Hall of Fame in November 1999.

Peak Years   *1983–87*
In a Word   *OTHERWORLDLY*

DALE HAWERCHUK (Ducky) Center/Left Wing
5'11" 190
b. 4/4/1963, Toronto, Ontario

Dale Hawerchuk starred amid all the hustle and bustle of the 1980s, in the thick of the Wayne Gretzky craze. As a result, Hawerchuk has been relegated to a place in hockey history unbecoming of someone so talented. While this may not be fair, it is indeed the result of having starred at the same time as Gretzky, who was the most dominant player in the history of the sport.

Hawerchuk was a star long before entering the NHL. As a Cornwall Royal, he tore up the Quebec League, scoring 81 goals and 183 points in 72 games in 1980–81. He was taken first overall by the Winnipeg Jets in the 1981 Entry Draft. Expectations ran high. "He's the best right now," said Jim Gregory of the NHL Scouting Bureau. "They say he can't skate too well," added scout George Armstrong, "but that's what they said about Wayne Gretzky." In his first nine games, Hawerchuk scored eight goals and 14 points. Not bad. Not bad at all. Overall, his rookie season of 1981–82 was an extremely successful one — 45 goals and 103 points in the full 80 games. The Toronto native was well on his way to NHL stardom.

As is often the case with players of Hawerchuk's caliber, there came an inhuman amount of pressure to perform and lead the team to the Cup. By late 1983, the young buck was stressed. "He was trying so hard that at times he was overtrying," said then-Jets coach Barry Long. "When I took over as coach, I told him I just wanted him to be Dale Hawerchuk. I didn't want him trying to be a Wayne Gretzky or a Mike Bossy." Although Hawerchuk failed to lead the Jets anywhere near the hallowed Stanley Cup, he definitely led them to respectability. The franchise that had suffered through a 9-57-14 record in 1980–81 was suddenly a .500 club, somewhere between good and solid. Bear in mind that where Gretzky had the luxury of playing with the likes of Paul Coffey, Mark Messier, Jari Kurri, and Glenn Anderson, Hawerchuk was really the only superstar in Winnipeg.

In the summer of 1990, after nine seasons as a Jet, Hawerchuk was moved to the Buffalo Sabres. During his time in Buffalo and later in St. Louis and Philadelphia he took on more of a defensive role. He had his last great offensive seasons between 1992 and 1994. After that, he slowed down. He retired after the 1996–97 season at the age of 34.

Peak Years   1984–88
In a Word   PRODIGY

PHIL HOUSLEY Defense
5'10" 185
b. 3/9/1964, St. Paul, Minnesota

In the 1982 NHL Entry Draft, the Buffalo Sabres selected a fresh, red-haired American kid by the name of Housley. Rex MacLeod of the *Toronto Star* said that, "with his cherubic, unmarked face and thatch of red hair, he stands out among the scarred, beat-up pros like a streaker in a hotel lobby." Phil Housley entered the NHL gifted with blinding speed, excellent play-making ability, and split-second reflexes. Although no one dared compare him to hockey legend Bobby Orr so prematurely, the similarities in their raw skills were difficult to ignore. Shortly after being drafted, Housley spoke on this matter with an anonymous doubter, as reported in the *Toronto Star*:

Housley:	I'm going to be as good as Orr.
Doubter:	Those are [going to be] big shoes to fill.
Housley:	I've got big feet.

Housley got right to work in the big league. In his rookie season of 1982–83, he was worth 19 goals and 66 points in 77 games. Orr had 25 less in his first year. Housley followed up this early brilliance with a 31-goal effort in 1983–84. By mid-decade, many had Housley as one of the top offensive performers in the game. Strangely, he would receive his only All-Star nomination in 1992 as a member of the Winnipeg Jets. He was hard-pressed to overcome the stiff competition he faced in Ray Bourque, Paul Coffey, Rod Langway, and Mark Howe.

Housley continued his point-scoring tear throughout the rest of the 1980s. In all, he would score 20 or more goals in a season seven times and top the 50-point plateau in each of his first 11 seasons. Since being traded to Winnipeg in 1990, he has made stops in St. Louis, Calgary, New Jersey, and Washington.

Peak Years   *1988–92*
In a Word   *SWEETIE*

JARI KURRI Right Wing
6'1" 195
b. 5/18/1960, Helsinki, Finland

On the way to building a dynasty, the Edmonton Oilers did well in selecting Finnish winger Jari Kurri 69th overall in the 1980 NHL Entry Draft. The 20-year-old Helsinki boy came in handy. In his rookie season, 1980–81, he scored 32 goals and 75 points in 75 games, serving notice to the rest of the NHL. The Oilers also had Mark Messier, Paul Coffey, Glenn Anderson and, of course, the incomparable Wayne Gretzky, who had just concluded a 164-point campaign of his own. Yes, the Edmonton Oilers were on their way.

Kurri could do it all. He had excellent speed, enough natural instinct to ultimately earn a regular spot on Gretzky's right flank, a generous pinch of defensive awareness, and a shot rivaling that of Mike Bossy. Kurri steadily improved over the next few seasons and had his official coming-out party during the 1984 Stanley Cup playoffs, when he scored 14 goals and 28 points to help bring Edmonton their first ever NHL championship. In 1984–85, he stepped it up, scoring 71 goals in the regular season before scoring 19 times in 18 playoff games in another successful Oiler Cup run. By the time he was traded to Los Angeles (via a deal with the Flyers), he had scored almost 500 goals, secured five All-Star nominations, and earned five Cup rings.

After a few moderately fruitful campaigns as a Los Angeles King, Kurri, who had suddenly become one of the better defensive forwards in the NHL, was traded to the New York Rangers. He also played for the Anaheim Mighty Ducks and the Colorado Avalanche. He scored 601 career goals.

Peak Years   *1984–88*
In a Word   *GOALS*

ROD LANGWAY (Rocket Rod) Defense
6'3" 218
b. 5/3/1957, Maag, Formosa (now Taiwan)

Rod Langway, a fine physical specimen, got his break in the NHL with the Montreal Canadiens in 1978–79. He was good for only seven points in 45 games that year, but he played well enough to crack the lineup. The *Boston Globe*'s Bob Duffy said, "He removes his gloves, and it seems miraculous that his fingers haven't drowned inside. The white bands of protective tape on his wrists appear welded in place. As he looks down to inspect the gloves, a waterfall pours from his curly blond hair."

What impressed many from the early going was the big boy's confidence, the fact that he wasn't in awe of the champions around him. His play improved over the next couple of years. He became one of the most coveted defenders in the game. Langway was willing to fight the messy battles, to get down into the muddiest quarters of a game and get dirty. He was a warrior, a huge man. He knew he would never be the next Bobby Orr, so he mastered the stay-at-home style. "You can call me whatever you want," he once said. "I'm old-style. I know that. And I know my limitations."

In September 1982, Montreal sent Langway to Washington with Doug Jarvis, Craig Laughlin, and Brian Engblom for Ryan Walter and Rick Green. From there, it was all uphill for Langway. Having escaped the crippling Canadian taxes and the shadows of over 70 years' worth of ghosts in Montreal, he was at last free to perfect his craft. While the big man was no Paul Coffey, he was a strong, steady skater with a burning desire to win. Management looked on with delight as their newest stallion shored up the defense and brought about a winning attitude. By the mid-1980s, the Capitals were a force to be reckoned with. Combining timely scoring with a stifling defense, the franchise soared to 50 wins in 1985–86. Suddenly, hockey pundits everywhere were eye-balling Langway. "The Oilers would survive without Coffey," said former Philadelphia Flyers coach Fred Shero, "but not the Caps without Langway."

Although Langway would never revisit his Montreal Stanley Cup memories of 1979, he forged a great career for himself. He remained a Capital for the rest of his playing days, and retired at the end of the 1992–93 season. In 15 years as an NHLer, he managed three All-Star nominations, two consecutive Norris trophies (in 1983 and 1984), and a Stanley Cup ring. He is one of hockey's true forgotten heroes.

Peak Years   1982–86
In a Word   OX

RICK MIDDLETON (Slick) Right Wing
5'11" 170
b. 12/4/1953, Toronto, Ontario

Rick Middleton made his mark in the NHL as a Boston Bruin, but he started out as property of the New York Rangers. The Rangers selected Middleton 14th overall in the 1973 draft. The talented winger dug his heels in quickly. In his second season, 1975–76, he scored 24 goals and 50 points. In May 1976, he was shipped to Boston in exchange for aging war horse Ken Hodge. Things looked up for Rick Middleton.

By 1976, the Bruins were rebuilding. Phil Esposito was gone. Bobby Orr was also gone. It was time for a change in Boston. Middleton joined Brad Park, Jean Ratelle, Terry O'Reilly, and, of course, coach Don Cherry in returning the B's to the Stanley Cup finals.

Middleton was talented enough to be a star but was not considered among the best players of his day. There was little the Toronto native couldn't do on the ice, but the Marcel Dionnes and Mark Messiers grabbed most of the headlines. Middleton was less flashy. He was methodical, more of a thinking man's player, though he was very fast, and he had excellent passing and shooting skills. As a working man's star, Middleton was loved by the fans.

But Middleton was not a second-class star. From 1978–79 on, he racked up point totals of 86, 92, 103, 94, 96, and 105. The man they called "Slick" could not lead his B's to a Cup, but he played hard. The Bruins never finished below .500 with Middleton on the team.

In 14 seasons in the big leagues, Middleton scored 448 goals and just under 1,000 points. He was the Bruins' most valuable forward for the first half of the 1980s.

Peak Years   1979–83
In a Word   CONSTANT

LARRY MURPHY Defense
6'2" 210
b. 3/8/1961, Scarborough, Ontario

Larry Murphy is often discussed among the most underrated players in NHL history. Murphy took limited natural ability and built an impressive 19-year career with it. Here's a player who, without pomp and circumstance, topped the 1,000 point mark. A player who, despite never being at the top of his profession, managed five 20-goal seasons, three All-Star nominations, and four Stanley Cup rings. Not as exciting as Paul Coffey, you ask? Not as masterful as Ray Bourque? No matter. Four Cup rings. Murphy must've been doing something right.

Murphy, a hot prospect coming out of Junior hockey, was selected fourth overall by the Los Angeles Kings in the 1980 NHL Entry Draft. Southern California's newest young gun did not disappoint. He played the full 80 games in his rookie season of 1980–81, scoring 16 goals and 76 points. By the end of the 1982–83 season, the Scarborough native was considered one of the top offensive defensemen in the league. In October 1983, just as he was beginning to get used to Los Angeles, the Kings traded Murphy to the Washington Capitals for Ken Houston and Brian Engblom.

In Washington, Murphy got the chance to play with Rod Langway and Mike Gartner. Together, this fearsome threesome turned the franchise around. Langway may have been the team's leader, but Murphy was their quarterback. Murphy marshaled the troops on the power play, setting up goals and scoring some of his own. He wasn't the fleetest player afoot, but he had keen instincts. In 453 games as a Capital, he was good for 85 goals and 344 points for an average of 15-46-61 a season.

In late 1990, after a short stint with the Minnesota North Stars, Murphy joined Mario Lemieux and the Pittsburgh Penguins. Murphy played a huge role in bringing the Cup to the Steel City in 1991 and again in 1992. After four and a half seasons in Pittsburgh, the big defenseman moved on to the Toronto Maple Leafs and the Detroit Red Wings. He won his third and fourth Cups in 1997 and 1998 on the Wings defense corps.

Murphy is one of the few NHL defensemen with over 1,000 points to his credit.

Peak Years   1986–90
In a Word   SOBER

DENIS POTVIN Defense
6'0" 205
b. 10/29/1953, Ottawa, Ontario

Only seconds before the Islanders Bill Torrey and Co. were about to select Denis Potvin first overall in the 1973 draft, to put the most promising defenseman since Bobby Orr in a New York Islanders uniform, along came Montreal Canadiens GM Sam Pollock. Trader Sam wanted to strike a deal for the top pick. Having Larry Robinson, Serge Savard, and Guy Lapointe on defense was not enough for Pollock. The Islanders held firm and selected Potvin. The

Denis Potvin

dynamic, strong defender became an Islander.

There was tremendous hype surrounding Potvin during his rookie season of 1973–74. He was happy not to be in Montreal, where the pressure to perform would have been excruciating. But he was still expected to excel on the Island. "I'm not Bobby Orr and I know it," he insisted. "You can't compare us anyway because our styles are different . . . I just hope I can accomplish some of the things Orr has done, but in my own way."

Potvin was a throwback to the time of Canadiens' legend Doug Harvey, a big, powerful rusher with remarkable play-making ability and a cannon for a shot. Much like Harvey, and Ray Bourque after him, Potvin controlled games. He could rush up the ice and set up one of his high-octane forwards. If the Isles needed a boost, he could crash an enemy forward into the boards so hard the whole building would shake. He was one of the finest rushing defensemen of the modern era, and one of the most punishing hitters ever to play. Under his leadership, the Islanders reached dynasty status.

Potvin spent his entire 15-year career on Long Island. He earned three Norris trophies, a Calder, had seven All-Star nominations, four Cup rings, 310 goals, and over 1,000 points. He became a worthy member of the Hockey Hall of Fame in 1991.

Peak Years   *1978–82*
In a Word   *WRECKER*

DENIS SAVARD Center
5'10" 175
b. 2/4/1961, Pointe Gatineau, Quebec

Denis Savard shuffled, faded, deked, and faked his way to well over 1,000 NHL games. He was yet another in the seemingly endless parade of French Canadian greats.

When the 1980 Entry Draft rolled around, everyone had the little wizard going to the Canadiens first overall. Wrong. In one of the biggest draft day blunders ever, Montreal selected

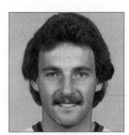

Denis Savard

Doug Wickenheiser first overall. On the brink of tears, Savard went third to the Chicago Black Hawks. Wickenheiser scored 111 goals and 276 points in his career. Savard scored 473 goals and had 1,338 points.

In Denis Savard, the Hawks had the speediest, most exciting player in hockey. While Wayne Gretzky was tricky and Mike Bossy was deadly, Savard was a party on skates. Unlike most other players, the little guy was able to change gears at will. His ability to stop and start mid-stride made him exciting to watch. "When Savard gets the puck," said NHL coach Roger Neilson, "he can turn on a dime and drive you crazy. This is how important he is to the Black Hawks; if the other club can't contain him in a game, that will be the difference in winning or losing." But Savard wasn't just a skater. He could score, too. A 75-point rookie season was followed by totals of 32-87-119 and 35-86-121. By the end of the 1982–83 campaign, he had joined the NHL's elite ranks. His finest season came in 1987–88 when he potted 44 goals and added 87 assists.

In the summer of 1990, the Canadiens, to make amends for snubbing Savard in 1980, secured his rights in exchange for defenseman Chris Chelios and a second-round draft pick. Savard spent three seasons in Montreal, living out his lifelong dream of playing for the bleu, blanc, et rouge. In his final season in Montreal, the Canadiens won the Stanley Cup. In July 1993, Savard was signed by the Tampa Bay Lightning. After less than two years there, he was traded back to Chicago. He retired as a Hawk at the end of the 1996–97 season.

Peak Years   *1983–87*
In a Word   *SENSATIONAL*

BILLY SMITH (Bad Billy/The Hatchet Man) Goal
5'10" 185
b. 12/12/1950, Perth, Ontario

Few in the history of hockey have had a hotter desire to win than William John Smith. Smith was drafted by the Los Angeles Kings in the 1970 NHL draft. The New York Islanders claimed him in the 1972 expansion draft. No one knew it at the time, but the stocky, ill-tempered goalie would backstop the Isles to four Stanley Cups.

The Islanders were a pathetic outfit in their inaugural season of 1972–73. Smith went 7-24-3 that season with a 4.16 goals-against average — hardly championship numbers. However, with a gradual influx of talent via trades and draft picks, the Isles became a feared unit. In 1977–78, Smith went 20-8-8 with a 2.65 GAA. By 1979, he was one of the top goalies in the league.

Smith was one of hockey's great battlers. "In the 30 years I've played and coached professional hockey," said Don Cherry, "there's never been a player who wanted to win as bad as [Smith] . . . you won't find a better money goalie. And that goes for the great ones like Terry Sawchuk and Glenn Hall. If you don't believe it, look at the record."

One thing that set Smith apart from his peers was his temper. He played his game the old-fashioned way, butt-ending, punching, hacking, and pushing to make his point. Smith didn't tolerate anyone infringing on his space — his crease was his castle. Players like Lindy Ruff, Tiger Williams, and even Wayne Gretzky found out the hard way what happens when someone bugged Billy when he was tending his cage.

Smith backstopped the Islanders to Cups in 1980, 1981, 1982, and 1983, running up a playoff record of 57-13 and a 2.64 GAA — good in an era when even the top goalies surrendered three goals a game. Smith was perhaps every bit as important as Potvin, Bossy, and Trottier in the Islanders' dynasty. He was a money performer, a goalie who gave his club just enough to win.

Smith retired an Islander at the end of the 1988–89 season. In 680 games, the fiery goaltender went 305-223-105 with 22 shutouts and a 3.17 GAA. He became a worthy member of the Hockey Hall of Fame in 1993.

Peak Years   *1978–82*
In a Word   *OGRE*

PETER STASTNY Center
6'1" 200
b. 9/18/1956, Bratislava, Czechoslovakia

Before Jaromir Jagr hit the ranks of the NHL in 1990, the pride of Czechoslovakia was Peter Stastny of the Quebec Nordiques. "The play here is harder," said Peter of the NHL. "The quality average of the league is better. All the teams have very good players. They are strong, they can skate, and they have good shots. In Czechoslovakia, there are [only] four or five very good teams that can represent the country." Few were surprised when the big, muscular Slovak ran over many of his North American counterparts. In 77 games in a Calder-winning 1980–81 season, Stastny scored 39 goals and 109 points. In 1981–82, brothers Peter, Anton, and Marian were worth a combined 107 goals and 300 points.

Peter Stastny was without a doubt the best of the Stastny boys. He could expertly shoot, skate, check, and pass the puck. Hockey opened up in the 1980s, and Stastny was in his element. He topped the 100-point plateau in seven of his first eight seasons in the big league, topping out at 46 goals and 139 points in 1981–82.

In March 1990, after almost 10 full seasons in Quebec City, Stastny was dealt to the New Jersey Devils for Craig Wolanin and future considerations. He was approaching his mid-30s, but he did himself proud in New Jersey in a two-way role. What he had lost in speed and scoring touch he more than made up for in defensive ability. After a few years, the aging superstar signed on with the St. Louis Blues. He retired at the end of the 1994–95 season with 450 goals and 1,239 points in just under 1,000 games.

Peak Years   *1981–85*
In a Word   *OUTSTANDING*

BRYAN TROTTIER (Trots) Center
5'11" 195
b. 7/17/1956, Val Marie, Saskatchewan

Bryan Trottier

In the 1974 NHL amateur draft, Isles' GM Bill Torrey selected Bryan Trottier, a rough, hard-driving kid from western Canada. It was a wise choice. By the end of his first professional season, the Saskatchewan native had 32 goals and 95 points. "The thing that gets me about [Trottier] is his coolness," said then Philadelphia Flyers' coach Fred Shero. "Hell, he's just a baby and he's out there with grown men who are trying to take the puck from him and the kid doesn't get nervous."

Trottier could've played in any era. He was a rare mix of speed, skating, checking, passing, and shooting ability. He was also a fabulous hitter. He was never the biggest man in the NHL, but he didn't back down from anybody. His fire, his burning desire to win, figured big in the New York Islanders' run of four straight Stanley Cups between 1980 and 1983.

At his peak, there were few who could play at Trottier's level. The feisty center, who had the extreme pleasure of skating between Mike Bossy and big Clark Gillies, was among the NHL's elite producers. Between 1977–78 and 1983–84, he rang off six seasons of 100 points or more. His best offensive season came in 1978–79, when he was worth 47 goals and a league-best 134 points.

With the rise of the Edmonton Oilers in the mid-1980s, the Islanders sunk into mediocrity. Some retired, some moved on, and still others simply lost the desire to win. After nearly 10 years as one of the world's premier hockey players, Trottier seemed to be losing his passion. Yes, he was hitting 30, but the Islanders were rebuilding. In the summer of 1990, Trottier signed with the Pittsburgh Penguins. In the Steel City, he won his fifth and sixth Cups. He retired at the end of the 1993–94 campaign.

Trottier's former teammate Billy MacMillan said he had "magic hands and magic feet." He was one of the greatest all-around talents ever to play in the NHL. In 1,279 games, he scored 524 goals and 1,425 points. He became a member of the Hockey Hall of Fame in 1997.

Peak Years   *1979–83*
In a Word   *VIKING*

The All-Stars

Pos	Player	Season	GP	G	A	PTS
D	Ray Bourque	1986–87	78	23	72	95
D	Paul Coffey	1985–86	79	48	90	138
LW	Mark Messier	1983–84	77	37	64	101
C	Wayne Gretzky	1983–84	74	87	118	205
RW	Mike Bossy	1981–82	80	64	83	147
			GP	GAA	ShO	
G	Grant Fuhr	1987–88	75	3.43	4	

The Nineties

In a Flash

COMPOSITE REGULAR-SEASON STANDINGS
(JANUARY 1, 1990–APRIL 20, 1999)

National Hockey League

Club	GP	W	L	T	Pts	WPct	GF	GA
Detroit Red Wings	745	406	243	96	908	.609	2,733	2,172
Pittsburgh Penguins	746	390	269	87	867	.581	2,810	2,494
New Jersey Devils	744	375	263	106	856	.575	2,369	2,042
Boston Bruins	745	369	277	99	837	.562	2,442	2,241
St. Louis Blues	745	359	286	100	818	.549	2,427	2,263
New York Rangers	744	352	293	99	803	.540	2,455	2,246
Montreal Canadiens	742	348	290	104	800	.539	2,363	2,186
Chicago Blackhawks	744	347	293	104	798	.536	2,276	2,056
Philadelphia Flyers	744	345	291	108	798	.536	2,442	2,289
Minnesota North Stars/Dallas Stars	743	346	300	97	789	.531	2,306	2,199
Buffalo Sabres	744	333	281	112	778	.523	2,376	2,170
Washington Capitals	746	347	319	80	774	.519	2,348	2,208
Calgary Flames	744	333	308	103	769	.517	2,497	2,337
Quebec Nordiques/Colorado Avalanche	746	331	319	96	758	.508	2,498	2,481
Toronto Maple Leafs	743	319	336	88	726	.489	2,280	2,408
Winnipeg Jets/Phoenix Coyotes	747	307	348	92	706	.473	2,357	2,492
Vancouver Canucks	745	303	343	99	705	.473	2,381	2,516
Los Angeles Kings	746	300	343	103	703	.471	2,452	2,586
Edmonton Oilers	744	292	364	88	672	.452	2,300	2,550
Hartford Whalers/Carolina Hurricanes	745	281	367	97	659	.442	2,138	2,427
Florida Panthers	460	183	192	85	451	.490	1,236	1,279
New York Islanders	744	249	378	95	593	.399	2,278	2,477
Nashville Predators	82	28	47	7	63	.384	190	261
Tampa Bay Lightning	544	176	306	62	414	.381	1,374	1,783
San Jose Sharks	624	192	362	70	454	.364	1,688	2,241
Ottawa Senators	544	160	316	68	388	.357	1,369	1,870

GOODBYES

Harold Ballard, *Toronto Maple Leafs owner*	April 11, 1990
Earl Seibert, *Hall of Fame defenseman*	May 12, 1990
Bob Johnson, *NHL coach*	November 26, 1991
Ace Bailey, *Leaf winger*	April 7, 1992
Reggie Lewis, *Boston Celtics forward*	July 27, 1993
Lady Diana Spencer, *Britain's sweetheart*	August 31, 1997
Toe Blake, *Hab icon*	May 17, 1995
Joe DiMaggio, *American baseball legend*	March 8, 1999
Frank Sinatra, *American music legend*	May 14, 1998
Syl Apps, *Leaf legend*	December 24, 1998

REGULAR SEASON

BEST RECORD

1995–96 Detroit Red Wings. This edition of the Wings ran up a 62-13-7 record before flunking out short of the Stanley Cup. Their points total dropped by 37 the following season, but their Cup hunt was successful.

WORST RECORD

1992–93 Ottawa Senators, 10-70-4

BEST MINOR LEAGUE RECORDS

1992–93 San Diego Gulls (IHL), 62-12-132, with 8 OT losses
1997–98 Columbus Cottonmouths (CHL), 51-13-108, with 6 shoot-out losses
1997–98 San Diego Gulls (WCHL), 53-10-107, with 1 shoot-out loss

FAMOUS FIRSTS

NHL COMMISSIONER

Gary Bettman

TEAM WITH THREE 20-GOAL DEFENSEMEN

1992–93 Washington Capitals (Sylvain Cote, Kevin Hatcher, Al Iafrate)

TEAMMATES TO SCORE 50TH GOAL IN SAME GAME

Mario Lemieux and Kevin Stevens (3/21/1993)

U.S.–BORN CONN SMYTHE TROPHY WINNER

Brian Leetch

RUSSIAN HART TROPHY WINNER

Sergei Fedorov

FAMOUS LASTS

LAST GOAL AT THE MONTREAL FORUM

Andrei Kovalenko (3/11/1996)

LAST GOAL AT MAPLE LEAF GARDENS

Bob Probert (2/13/1999)

MISCELLANEOUS

MOST GOALS, SEASON

86   Brett Hull, 1990–1991

MOST GOALS, DECADE

473   Brett Hull

MOST ASSISTS, SEASON

122   Wayne Gretzky, 1990–1991

MOST ASSISTS, DECADE

722   Wayne Gretzky

MOST POINTS, SEASON

163   Wayne Gretzky, 1990–1991

MOST POINTS, DECADE

958   Wayne Gretzky

COOLEST MIDDLE NAMES

David *Anaclethe* Emma
Byron *Jaromir* Dafoe
Mike *Chene* Donnelly

COOLEST HANDLES

Eddie "The Eagle" Belfour
Pavel Bure, "The Russian Rocket"
Mariusz Czerkawski, "The Polish Prince"
Doug Gilmour, "Killer"
Dominik Hasek, "The Dominator"
Vladimir Konstantinov, "The Impaler"
Andrei Kovalenko, "The Russian Tank"
Eric Lindros, "The Big E"
Krzysztof Oliwa, "The Polish Pug"
Teemu Selanne, "The Finnish Flash"

BIGGEST PLAYER

Zdeno Chara, 6'9" 255

SMALLEST PLAYER

Theoren Fleury, 5'6" 180

BEST SHOT

Al MacInnis. "There's hard and then there's MacInnis hard," said former goalie Mike Liut.

BEST PASSER

Wayne Gretzky had eyes in the back of his head. He was quite simply the finest passer in the history of the sport. He had almost 2,000 assists over 20 years.

Jaromir Jagr

BEST STICKHANDLER
Jaromir Jagr

BEST SKATER
Sergei Fedorov looks like he's an inch above the ice when in full flight. A dazzling performer.

WORST SKATER
Dave Andreychuk

FASTEST SKATER
Pavel Bure

BEST SNIPER
Teemu Selanne

BEST ON-ICE INSTINCTS
Wayne Gretzky

BEST PENALTY-KILLER
Guy Carbonneau

BEST BODY-CHECKER
Eric Lindros

BEST POKE-CHECKER
Kjell Samuelsson. At 6'6" tall, this big Swede resembles an octopus on the ice.

BEST SHOT-BLOCKER
Craig Ludwig wore extra-large shin pads to help block the rubber.

BEST GLOVE-HAND (GOALIE)
Curtis Joseph

MOST UNUSUAL GOALTENDING STYLE
Dominik Hasek played net like a fish out of water.

FINEST ATHLETE
Brian Savage, Eric Lindros, and Rod Brind'Amour. This one's a pick 'em. All three men are physical specimens.

BEST DEFENSIVE FORWARDS
Sergei Fedorov, Michael Peca, and Jere Lehtinen

WORST DEFENSIVE FORWARD
Vladimir Ruzicka stunk it up in the NHL for five seasons in the early 1990s before moving back to his native Czech Republic.

BEST SHADOW
Esa Tikkanen

BEST DEFENSIVE DEFENSEMAN
Scott Stevens

BEST OFFENSIVE DEFENSEMAN
Brian Leetch

BEST ALL-AROUND PLAYER
Peter Forsberg. If Sergei Fedorov didn't disappear every few months, we might have chosen him in this category. Forsberg is the top player in the NHL right now.

BEST UTILITY PLAYER
Kelly Miller

STRONGEST PLAYER
Eric Lindros. At 6'5" tall and over 230 pounds, the "Big E" is one of the most towering men in a towering NHL. About the only man in the league who's had the nerve to tangle with Lindros was New Jersey Devils' defenseman Scott Stevens, himself a big man.

TOUGHEST PLAYER
Chris Chelios

BEST FIGHTER
Tony Twist

MOST ABLE INSTIGATOR
Claude Lemieux

DIRTIEST PLAYER
Bryan Marchment has put more than a few people on the DL with his brand of knee-to-knee hockey.

CLEANEST PLAYER
Paul Kariya

BEST CORNER-MAN
Brendan Shanahan has elbows Gordie Howe could be proud of.

BEST-LOOKING PLAYER
Adam Oates

UGLIEST PLAYER
Gino Odjick

BALDEST PLAYER
Mark Messier

MOST UNDERRATED PLAYER
Joe Sakic can skate through a whole career almost unnoticed. Ask Hall of Famer Norm Ullman how that feels. Sure, Sakic's had his front pages and won a Conn Smythe Trophy, but with the higher profile that players like Eric Lindros and Dominik Hasek have received, he's been left in the shadows.

MOST CONSISTENT PLAYER
Steve Yzerman

MOST UNPREDICTABLE CAREER
Vladimir Malakhov was nicknamed "Magic Man" for his propensity to disappear. He looks like Ray Bourque for a couple of games, then he vanishes like Houdini. The Montreal Canadiens have been pulling out their hair trying to answer the Malakhov Question.

SMARTEST PLAYER
Steve Yzerman

BIGGEST FLAKE
Brendan Shanahan once claimed in a media guide that he was Ireland's backup goalie in the 1994 World Cup of Soccer.

MOST HATED PLAYER
Ulf Samuelsson

MOST ADMIRED PLAYER
Wayne Gretzky. Since Wilf Paiement retired, have you seen anyone else wearing #99 on their jersey outside of beer leagues?

BEST LINES
Team: Philadelphia Flyers
LW: John LeClair
C: Eric Lindros
RW: Mikael Renberg

Team: Colorado Avalanche
LW: Valeri Kamensky
C: Peter Forsberg
RW: Claude Lemieux

Team: Vancouver Canucks
LW: Alexander Mogilny
C: Trevor Linden
RW: Pavel Bure

Team: Anaheim Mighty Ducks
LW: Paul Kariya
C: Steve Rucchin
RW: Teemu Selanne

Team: St. Louis Blues
LW: Brendan Shanahan
C: Adam Oates
RW: Brett Hull

HIGHEST PAID
Sergei Fedorov earned $28 million in 1997–98.

MOST TRAGIC CAREER
Mario Lemieux. Back problems and a bout with Hodgkin's Disease cut down "Super Mario" in his prime.

PLAYER VERSUS TEAM
Eric Lindros vs. Quebec Nordiques

MOST LOPSIDED TRADE
The Montreal Canadiens traded John LeClair, Eric Desjardins, and Gilbert Dionne to the Philadelphia Flyers for Mark Recchi and a third-round pick on February 9, 1995. Recchi for Desjardins, straight-up, would have been a reasonable trade, but to include LeClair, a future superstar, made no sense. This deal became even more lop-sided when Recchi was reacquired by Philadelphia for Dainius Zubrus and draft picks late in the 1998–99 season. Who else but Montreal's bigwigs could pull this one off and still claim to be in control of the ship?

BIGGEST FLOP
Alexandre Daigle

BEST HEAD COACH
Pat Burns turned around both the Toronto Maple Leafs and Boston Bruins in the space of about five years. The key to the former cop's success as an NHL coach is his belief in hard work and persistence. He is also the only coach to win the Adams Award with three different teams.

BEST GENERAL MANAGER
Glen Sather

BEST SPORTSWRITER
Michael Farber of *Sports Illustrated* and the *Montreal Gazette*

BEST BROADCASTER
Mike Lange, Pittsburgh Penguins. "Well, scratch my back with a hacksaw!"

BEST MINOR LEAGUE PLAYERS
Trevor Jobe
Kevin Kerr
Peter White
Nick Vitucci

BEST STANLEY CUP FINAL
1994, Vancouver vs. New York Rangers. One of the only Cup finals in the 1990s that was not over before it began. The Rangers broke a 54-year jinx.

IMPORTANT RULE CHANGES
1990–1991
- Goal lines, blue-lines, and defensive zone face-off circles and markings moved out one foot from end boards, creating more room in the offensive zone and shrinking neutral zone by two feet

1991–92
- Video replay employed
- Goal disallowed if attacking team player in crease

1993–94
- Game misconduct for instigating a fight

1996–97
- Maximum stick length increased to 63 inches

1998–99
- Two-referee system instituted
- Goal lines, blue-lines, defensive zone face-off circles and markings moved out another two feet from end boards, creating even more room in offensive zone and shrinking neutral zone by four feet
- Goal crease shrunk to 6 x 8 feet

Koo Koo Lindros

The Eric Lindros story starts back in 1988–89, when he was playing for the St. Michael's Buzzers, a Junior B team in Ontario. The 15-year-old Lindros played well, racking up 67 points and 193 penalty minutes in only 37 games. He was eventually called up to the Canadian National Team, with whom he'd count his first international goal. In the 1989 midget draft, Sault Ste. Marie Greyhounds GM Sherry Bassin ignored the warnings of the Lindros family and drafted Eric first overall. The Lindros family had repeatedly warned Bassin that Lindros would never play in the Soo as the Greyhounds' long road trips would hamper young Eric's education. At the time, the Ontario Hockey League (OHL) had a rule that teams could not trade their first-round draft picks for a year after they selected a player. Ed Olczyk and Pat LaFontaine had previously been victims of this rule. Big Lindros was determined not to become the next victim. He resigned himself to the fact that he would never join the Greyhounds, so he joined Detroit Compuware, a Tier II team in the Great Lakes Junior circuit, where he dominated, scoring 52 points in 14 games.

The OHL knew Lindros was a huge drawing card. A villain, capable of taking apart teams either by magic or by brute force. Not wanting to lose him to the NCAA, the OHL simply changed the rules. From then on, an OHL team would be able to trade its first-round pick, as long as it did so between January 1 and January 10. The Greyhounds immediately sent Lindros to the Oshawa Generals for a package of players, draft picks, and $80,000. The Generals paid a heavy price, but it soon paid dividends. Hockey's newest rising star led the Generals to the Memorial Cup in 1990.

Lindros was also fast becoming a sought-after commodity in the hockey collectibles market. At the time, hockey cards were considered the next great investment. Collectors gambled on young talent, hoping he would be the next Gretzky, the second Lemieux. Score, a Texas-based sports-card company, signed Lindros as a spokesman. He became the first Canadian Junior player to be featured in an NHL-licensed trading-card set. Score, it seems, invented ways to get him on their cards. They even featured him in their 1990 baseball collection as a tip of the hat to the time the hockey star took batting practice with the Toronto Blue Jays.

Lindros scored 149 points and won the Red Tilson Trophy as OHL MVP. In 1991, he was the NHL's most sought-after draft-eligible prospect. The Nordiques selected him first overall in the entry draft, despite countless warnings that he would not sign with Quebec. His reasons for shunning the Nordiques were not without merit: a poorly talented club; an extremely high provincial tax rate on top of the insane federal tax rate; an unstable provincial political climate; and less future endorsement potential. When Quebec GM Pierre Page called Lindros's name, Lindros rose from his seat in Buffalo's Memorial Auditorium and accepted congratulations from his family. As he approached the stage, the building was abuzz. Would he don the Nordiques sweater and hat in keeping with tradition? No. He was coy. Rather than put on the sweater, he smiled and waved to the drooling media.

Having spurned Quebec, Lindros had to figure out where he was going to spend the 1991–92 season. He really didn't want to return to Junior hockey — he had nothing left to prove. So, the powers that be in Canadian hockey tipped their hat to the talented center and selected him to play on the 1991 Canada Cup team. He was to be the only non-NHLer on a team that featured greats Wayne Gretzky and Mark Messier. Lindros showed quickly that he belonged, scoring three goals in eight games and hitting everything in sight. The thundering youth knocked Swedish defenseman Ulf Samuelsson out of the tournament.

After the Canada Cup, Lindros returned to the Generals, scoring 31 points in 13 games. It was obvious that he did not belong in the OHL, that he was more than ready for the big league. He joined the Canadian National Team, a side preparing for the upcoming Olympics in Albertville, France. Other NHLers, such as Sean Burke, had used the national team to stay in shape during their holdouts. He showed the world just how ready he was for the NHL by storming through the team's pre-Olympic schedule. And on the Olympic stage, he did nothing to sully his reputation. He notched 11 points in eight contests and scored the winning goal in a medal-round shoot-out against upstart Germany. The Canadian team advanced to the gold medal game, where they were put down by the Unified Team.

Desperate to bring Lindros into the fold, Quebec offered him a reported $55 million over 10 years. No dice. The Big E stood firm. "If they offered me $100 million a year, I would not play for them," he said. Many observers felt he was insane to turn down Quebec's offer, but Lindros insisted that money was not an issue. "[The Nordiques] didn't want to win. I don't think everyone in their organization had the same goal: winning the Stanley Cup."

Following the Olympics, rumors began flying that Lindros was about to sign with a European team or with the San Diego Gulls of the IHL. Fred Comrie, owner of the Gulls, offered Lindros a $2.5 million deal — $500,000 to play the last quarter of the 1991–92 campaign and $2 million for the 1992–93 season. Agent Rick Curran and Lindros backed away from the offer, however. If Lindros had signed with the Gulls, the Nordiques would have held his rights indefinitely. At the 1993 draft, the Nords could have declared him a defected player, and retained his rights.

Entering draft day 1992, Quebec was busting to deal Lindros. The organization knew that the kid wasn't bluffing when he said he wouldn't play for them. They also knew that the longer they held onto their prize pig, the less leverage they would have in a trade. If Lindros wasn't dealt or signed before draft day 1993, he would simply re-enter the draft pool. So, in June 1992, at the Montreal Forum, Nordiques president Marcel Aubut finally traded Lindros.

This is where it gets messy. *Aubut traded his boy to two different teams!* He reached a deal with the Philadelphia Flyers and then made another deal with the New York Rangers. The Flyers and Rangers were outraged and went straight to the league's bigwigs. With the future of the "Next One" in peril, the NHL was forced to take action. They called in arbitrator Larry Bertuzzi to mediate the dispute and decide where Lindros would be playing hockey in 1992–93. Either deal Bertuzzi decided, one team would be guaranteed a victory: Quebec.

The Flyers had offered defensemen Kerry Huffman and Steve Duchesne, goalie Ron Hextall, forwards Peter Forsberg, Mike Ricci, and Chris Simon, and cash and draft picks. The Rangers' package consisted of Alexei Kovalev, Tony Amonte, Doug Weight, John Vanbiesbrouck, and cash and draft picks.

A crucial factor in Bertuzzi's decision involved the Lindros family home telephone number. Aubut maintained through the ordeal that he would give the number only to the team with which he had struck a deal. Bertuzzi discovered that Aubut had given the Flyers the number shortly after 11 a.m. on June 20, 1992. Flyers president Jay Snider had given Lindros a ding-a-ling and welcomed him to the organization. New York, on the other hand, was never given the number.

Bertuzzi decided in favor of Philadelphia.

The Lindros–Quebec feud had been settled. The Big E would be playing in the NHL in 1992–93. Mere weeks after becoming an official member of the Flyers, he signed a six-year, $21-million (U.S.) contract. Lindros and the Flyers opened the new Philadelphia era against Mario Lemieux and his reigning Stanley Cup champion Pittsburgh Penguins. Lindros got right down to work, scoring his first NHL goal in a 3–3 tie. His fourth game was much more interesting, however. The Flyers entered Le Colisee to play the Nordiques. Quebec fans flapped vulgar signs and cursed Lindros. Despite two goals from Lindros, Quebec prevailed 6–3. At several points in the game, fans littered the ice with everything from golf balls to baby soothers, bullets to batteries. Some fans wore diapers.

Lindros was a good fit for the Flyers. On a line with Mark Recchi and Brent Fedyk, he was fast becoming the force that everyone had predicted he would become. But in a November 22, 1992, game against the Buffalo Sabres, he injured his left knee. He was told to stay off the ice for a few weeks. After a week in the press box, he asked for permission to return home for the weekend. The Flyers granted his request, and he made the trek back to Toronto.

On Saturday, November 29, Lindros and his friends decided to hit the bars to enjoy the weekend. They decided on Koo Koo Bananas, a bar in Whitby, Ontario.

Eric Lindros (center) with Pierre Page (left) and Pierre Gauthier

From all accounts, the beer flowed freely on this night. After a few brews, Lindros decided to hit the dance floor. Amid the merriment, he ran into Marie Lynn Nunney, a 24-year-old factory worker. According to Nunney, Lindros elbowed her to get more room on the floor. Nunney wouldn't budge. Nunney claims that Lindros poured beer on her. When she turned around, he allegedly spat beer in her face. Nunney pressed assault charges against Lindros. The Big E's face was plastered on front pages across North America. On December 4, Lindros returned to Toronto and turned himself in to the authorities. In the following days, opinions varied on his guilt. Was he a cocky, spoiled brat? Or was he a victim of an attention-seeker? Eventually, he was cleared of all charges.

Lindros returned to the Philadelphia lineup in mid-December. On January 9, 1993, the Flyers traveled to New York to face the Rangers. Philadelphia's 4–3 victory was the 1,000th win in franchise history. The big news, though, came after the game. Lindros and a friend from Toronto went out to a New York night spot following the game. Lindros's friend got involved in a skirmish. Lindros showed up for the following night's game with a bad knee.

Flyer management, clearly unimpressed, hinted that their star might be better off by living with an older teammate instead of by himself. Lindros scowled: "This is just ridiculous. Why do I need a roommate?"

In the big guy's absence, Philadelphia was mortal. When he returned, the team still continued to struggle, playing .500 hockey until ringing off wins in their final eight games. The Flyers finished the season with a 36-37-11 record, fifth in the Patrick Division and out of the playoff picture for the fourth straight season. Lindros finished with 41 goals and 75 points in 61 games and was third in Calder voting.

It's now been 10 years since Lindros was traded to the Philadelphia Flyers. So, who won the trade? Well, Quebec, who moved to Colorado in 1995, won the Stanley Cup in 1996 — one more Cup than the Lindros-era Flyers have won since the deal. But Lindros is only 26 and probably will have a few more cracks at Lord Stanley's mug. Still, considering all the variables, Quebec/Colorado won the deal.

The Lindros trade brought Quebec Peter Forsberg, one of the top players in the game today. They also acquired Mike Ricci and biff-and-bash Chris Simon. Ricci and Simon are now on other teams, but they played integral roles on the Colorado Avalanche's 1996 Cup-winning team. The Lindros deal gave Quebec more depth on offense. Ron Hextall became Quebec's top goalie in 1992–93 before he was peddled to the New York Islanders with a draft pick (Todd Bertuzzi) for Mark Fitzpatrick and a draft pick (Adam Deadmarsh). Steve Duchesne was also a Nordique for one season. He held out prior to the 1993–94 campaign and was eventually dealt to the St. Louis Blues with Denis Chasse for Garth Butcher, Ron Sutter, and Bob Bassen. Bassen departed as a free agent in 1995. Butcher was packaged with Mats Sundin and sent to the Toronto Maple Leafs for Wendel Clark and Sylvain Lefebvre. Sutter was dealt to the Islanders for Uwe Krupp and a swap of first rounders. Quebec chose goalie Jocelyn Thibault with their pick (from the Lindros deal). Clark was in Quebec for only a year when he was shipped off to the Islanders for Claude Lemieux, a Conn Smythe Trophy winner the year before with the New Jersey Devils. Keeping up? Good.

At the time, the Nordiques/Avalanche lacked a proven playoff goalie to go along with their forward depth. Has there been a better money goalie in this era than Patrick Roy? No. Avalanche GM Pierre Lacroix probably never thought Roy would leave Montreal. But in a nationally televised debacle against the Detroit Red Wings, then-Canadiens skipper Mario Tremblay left Roy to fend for himself in a blowout. Roy screamed at team president Ronald Corey that he had played his last game as a Canadien. And he had. The Avalanche came calling. Roy wasn't cheap. Lacroix had to give up Thibault and Martin Rucinsky and Andrei Kovalenko, two budding young forwards. Lacroix was hesitant to give up on his young goalie, but Montreal insisted that any deal involving Roy would also have to involve Thibault. Lacroix pulled the trigger on the deal, also acquiring Mike Keane, a tough two-way forward who had fallen out of favor with the local media.

As good as the Nordiques would have been with Lindros, it's doubtful they would have won the Cup with him.

Lightning Storm

The Tampa Bay Lightning joined the NHL in 1992–93, alongside the Ottawa Senators. The Lightning played their first ever game on October 7, 1992, against the defending Campbell Conference–champion Chicago Blackhawks. In front of a sellout crowd of 10,425 in Expo Hall, the Lightning exploded to a 7–3 victory. Chris Kontos, former Los Angeles Kings' playoff hero, had four of Tampa Bay's seven markers. Defenseman Joe Reekie added four assists.

It was an incredible debut for what has so far been a mediocre outfit. Here's to a lift in Tampa Bay's fortunes in the years to come. Heck, the only way to go now is up.

Roy of Kings

As arguably the most exciting second season of the decade, the 1993 Stanley Cup playoffs featured upsets, upsets, more upsets, and phenomenal play from some of hockey's elite performers. Coming into the playoffs, the Pittsburgh Penguins, Boston Bruins, Chicago Blackhawks, Quebec Nordiques, and Detroit Red Wings were favorites. These squads had the top five records in the regular season. But none of these teams reached the finals, and only the Penguins would even make the second round. Strange? Indeed.

If the first round was a Broadway play, it might have been named "Upset at Tiffany's." Of the eight series, only two higher-seeded teams managed to win out. In Adams Division action, the Buffalo Sabres had three overtime victories, and Sabre announcer Rick Jeanneret shouted "Mayday!" when Brad May ended a game in overtime, to sweep the heavily favored Bruins. Meanwhile, the Battle of Quebec raged one last time. The Quebec Nordiques and Montreal Canadiens were evenly matched on the season, with Quebec finishing two points ahead of Les Glorieux. Game one, in

Quebec's Colisee, went to the Nords in overtime on a Scott Young marker. By the end of the second match, Quebec was up 2–0. The Canadiens were eyeing their golf equipment nervously. Game three was another OT adventure, but this time Vincent Damphousse ended the game for Montreal. Suddenly, the Canadiens were back in it. They would not lose an overtime game the rest of the playoffs. Bolstered by their game three win, Montreal took the next three matches to win the series in six.

In Patrick Division action, Mario Lemieux and his mighty Pittsburgh Penguins were up against the New Jersey Devils, while the Washington Capitals had the upstart New York Islanders in their face. Pittsburgh disposed of the Devils in five. The Caps–Isles series was far more interesting. Washington started off well, taking the opener 3–1. The Isles came back to reclaim home-ice advantage when Brian Mullen counted in double overtime in game two. After two games on Long Island, New York found itself with a 3-1 series stranglehold. In game five in Landover, Maryland, the Capitals staved off elimination with a 6–4 win. Islander fans were pumped for the sixth match, anticipating the team's first playoff series victory since 1987. New York led the Capitals 4–3 late in the final frame when Pierre Turgeon zipped in an insurance marker. Nassau Coliseum erupted. Soon, though, the fans went eerily silent. As Turgeon celebrated his goal, gritty Washington forward Dale Hunter leveled him with a bone-crunching check. Hunter later justified the hit by claiming that he didn't see the puck go in the net. No matter — the damage had already been done. The Isles had taken the series. Turgeon was out of commission for most of the following playoff series with a separated shoulder. As for Hunter, he was suspended for the first 21 games of the 1993–94 season.

Over in the Smythe Division, the Vancouver Canucks were up against the Winnipeg Jets, while the Calgary Flames faced Wayne Gretzky and his Los Angeles Kings. The Canucks polished off the pesky Jets in six, while Gretzky, playing with a cracked rib, led the Kings past the Flames, also in six games.

The Norris Division semifinals featured two upsets. The Chicago Blackhawks, behind the stellar play of defender Chris Chelios, center Jeremy Roenick, and goalie Ed Belfour, were expected to steam roll the St. Louis Blues. But, as you well know, life is full of surprises. The Hawks didn't win a game in the series. In the other Norris series, the Detroit Red Wings had the rough and ready Toronto Maple Leafs on their hands. Sparked by dynamic Doug Gilmour, the Leafs were looking to pull off the upset of the year. The situation was bleak for Toronto when the Wings took the first two games. Back in Toronto, though, the Maple Leafs squared things up with 4–2 and 3–2 victories. In game five, the tide turned. An OT marker by Mike Foligno had Toronto sitting pretty. In the sixth contest Maple Leaf Gardens rocked. The long-suffering Leaf fans could smell victory. Detroit, however, wasn't going to curl up and die. They won game six, 7–3, setting up game seven at Joe Louis Arena for all the marbles. Late in the final frame of the final game, with the Wings up 3–2, the indomitable Gilmour beat Tim Cheveldae to send the game into OT. Only 2:35 into the extra frame, little Nikolai Borschevsky tipped home a Bob Rouse shot to send Toronto into the second round for the first time since 1987.

In the Adams Division final, the Buffalo Sabres tangled with the Montreal Canadiens. Montreal won at home in game one, 4–3. A Guy Carbonneau OT winner in game two provided the Canadiens with another 4–3 victory. Back in Buffalo, Montreal won with a pair of 4–3 OT victories. It was the first time since 1970 that every game in a playoff series had the same final score.

In the Patrick Division final, Pittsburgh was heavily favored to smash the under-manned Islanders, who were without Turgeon. But hold on! The teams split the first four games before a 6–3 Penguin victory put New York on the ropes. A 7–5 Isles victory in game six did little to dampen the enthusiasm of Pittsburgh fans, who fully expected Lemieux to finish off the Isles in game seven. But someone forgot to tell the Islanders to bring their doormat costumes. Turgeon, though not at full power, was in uniform and the game was tied 3–3 going into OT. It was goal or golf. In 5:16 of the extra session, Islander Dave Volek slapped one by Penguins goalie Tom Barrasso.

In the Campbell Conference, St. Louis, Toronto, Vancouver, and Los Angeles were still alive. The Blues–Leafs series was a war of attrition. The first two games, played in Toronto, led to mass sleep-deprivation among Toronto's hockey faithful, which was growing. The opener featured a clutch of unbelievable Curtis Joseph saves and a gaggle of blown scoring opportunities by Leafs' grinder Mark Osborne. The game rolled into double OT, and just when it seemed Toronto would never beat Cujo, Gilmour scored on a dramatic wraparound at 23:16. Game two lasted only 13 seconds less than the opener. This time, the Blues won. An ill-advised pinch by Leaf defender Rouse led to a Jeff Brown marker. The series was tied. Cheered on by fist-pumping GM Ron Caron, St. Louis took the often pivotal third game by a 4–3 count. Toronto, with their backs against the wall, roared back to win games four and five. A 2–1 Blues' victory in game six set up a do-or-die situation at a stormy Maple Leaf Gardens. The game was anticlimactic, with Toronto cruising to a 6–0 victory.

Meanwhile, in the Prince of Wales showdowns, Montreal went toe to toe with the Cinderella Islanders. Few pegged the Islanders to get out of the first round, but here they were, four wins away from the Big Show. Montreal, winners of 14 of their past 16 playoff encounters at the Forum, made it 16 of 18 and seven straight with two wins to open the series. The second game was won by Stephan Lebeau, who scored in double OT to give the Canadiens their sixth straight overtime win in the 1993 playoffs. In game three, the Canadiens extended their streak to seven games as Guy Carbonneau chalked up an OT marker. Up three games to none, the Canadiens let their guard down and allowed New York to win a game. No matter. A 5–2 Canadiens victory in game five flushed New York's Cup hopes down the toilet.

By now, much of Canada had gone Cup crazy. The Canadiens and Maple Leafs were among the NHL's final four. Legions of hockey fans dreamed of a Cup final between the two storied clubs to commemorate the 75th anniversary of the league. One man, however, was hell-bent on crushing Canada's fantasy: Wayne Gretzky.

Although a Leaf fan growing up, the world's most popular hockey player had known remarkable success against Toronto at the Gardens, counting 77 points in 30 regular-season games in Toronto. In the 1993 playoffs, he continued his Leaf-killing ways.

For his stellar efforts in the 1993 playoffs, Patrick Roy was awarded the second Conn Smythe Trophy of his storied career. In doing so, the quirky keeper joined legendary Bobby Orr, Bernie Parent, Wayne Gretzky, and Mario Lemieux as the only players in NHL history to win the award twice.

Toronto showed no signs of fatigue in game one, zapping the Kings 4–1. Toward the end of the game, Los Angeles defender Marty McSorley leveled Gilmour, prompting Wendel Clark to come to his teammate's rescue. This tilt set the tone for a long, trying series. The Kings won the game, 3–2, and they took the series lead with a 4–2 win back in Inglewood, California. Toronto, however, wouldn't die without a fight. Two Leaf wins put the Kings on the ropes, one punch away from a knockout. Then came game six, a sad night for Leaf fans everywhere. Three Clark goals had

Toronto and the Kings going into extra time with everything on the line. In the heat of battle, Gretzky high sticked Gilmour, drawing blood. Was it intentional or accidental? Who knows for sure? Whatever way you look at it, Gretzky should have been penalized for drawing blood. Seconds later, the Great One, parked on Potvin's doorstep, back-handed the winner past the Cat. Toronto was headed for yet another seventh game.

Patrick Roy

During the series, noted hockey columnist Bob McKenzie of the *Toronto Star* remarked that Gretzky was skating "as if he were carrying a piano on his back." Gretzky got wind of McKenzie's comments before he took the ice for game seven. The King's last words before that game: "This piano man's still got one more tune to play." And how! The Great One scored three times and added an assist to lead Los Angeles to a 5–4 win. The Leafs were done.

The surging Kings squared off against Montreal and their quest for a 24th Stanley Cup championship. Talk about your contrasts — this was Los Angeles' first Cup final, Montreal's 34th!

The Kings came out like grizzled Cup veterans in game one. At the end of the night, Montreal's eight-game home winning streak was broken and the Kings had themselves a 4–1 victory. Gretzky had a goal and three assists to lead the charge.

The Kings nearly won two straight in Montreal, but for McSorley's stick. Yes, his stick. In what proved to be the turning point of the series, Canadiens' coach Jacques Demers asked for a stick measurement on the hulking blue-liner. Montreal's one-in-a-

Ahhhhh . . . Fischler!

"With Craig Janney at center, Bill Ranford in goal, and Vincent Lecavalier everywhere, Phil Esposito has both a playoff contender for the Tampa Bay Lightning and a job-saver for himself." — Stan Fischler, *The Hockey News*, July 1998 (Esposito lost his job a few months later, Ranford and Janney were dealt, and the Lightning went on to finish dead last.)

million horse came in. McSorley's stick was an illegal length. Eric Desjardins sent the game into overtime on the ensuing power play. Only 51 seconds into OT, Desjardins scored again, completing the first ever hat-trick by a defenseman in a Cup final. Montreal's incredible OT string was intact! Kings coach Barry Melrose was not impressed with Demers. "I don't believe in winning that way," Melrose said after the game.

Montreal beat Los Angeles again, thanks to John LeClair. The huge forward scored 34 seconds into OT to give Montreal a 3–2 victory in game three, and the series lead. Patrick Roy, the story of the 1993 playoffs with his spectacular goaltending, put on a show-stopping performance in game four. In OT, he robbed Tomas Sandstrom of a sure goal, rubbing salt in his foe's wounds by winking at him. At 14:37 of the extra frame, LeClair wove his way around a maze of fallen players in front of the Kings net and fired the winner past Kings' goalie Kelly Hrudey. Montreal headed home with a 3-1 series lead.

On June 9, 1993, the Montreal Forum was filled to the rafters. Most of the fans were there to see their beloved Canadiens polish off Los Angeles in a spectacular finale. But the Kings were spent. Roy was marvelous in his cage once again in game five, as Montreal went on to win, 4–1. Montreal hoisted the Cup once again.

Out with the Old

In the 1990s, salaries escalated to stratospheric levels. Canadian clubs packed up and went stateside. The FoxTrak puck turned televised hockey games into a light show. Expansion teams popped up in Miami, Tampa Bay, Anaheim, and Nashville. And, of course, the last four Original Six arenas closed their doors forever.

When you ask hockey fans where they would like to see a hockey game, more than likely they would say the Montreal Forum, or Maple Leaf Gardens. Not the Molson Centre or the Air Canada Centre. They prefer tradition, history, and atmosphere over luxury boxes, huge concession stands, and luxurious snacks. Sadly, the economic reality of hockey in the 1990s and the move to trend over tradition dictated that hockey rinks should have luxury boxes and more seating. We lost rowdy Chicago Stadium, electric Boston Garden, the classy Montreal Forum, and storied Maple Leaf Gardens in Toronto.

Chicago Stadium was the first dinosaur to become extinct in hockey's glorious new era. Among other events, the old Stadium was the only NHL arena ever to host an NFL playoff game, the 1932 NFL Championship between the Chicago Bears and the Portsmouth Spartans. Red Grange scored the game's only touchdown in a 9–0 Bear win. Home to the world's most obnoxious organ, the Stadium had housed the Hawks since 1929. The final game was played on April 28, 1994, a 1–0 loss to the Toronto Maple Leafs. Mike Gartner scored the final goal in the building.

Next up was Boston Garden, which opened its doors in 1928 with a fight between French featherweight boxing champion Andre Routis and Dick "Honeyboy" Finnegan from nearby Dorchester, Massachusetts. Over the next 67 years, the building played host to 19 NBA championships and 16 Stanley Cup finals. The home of

Skalde on the Move

The life of a professional hockey player is filled with uncertainty. A demotion to the minors or a trade can send a player's life into disarray. Forward Jarrod Skalde survived his 1997–98 adventure, racking up frequent-flyer miles in the process.

Skalde, a former Junior teammate of Eric Lindros in Oshawa, was a second-round pick of New Jersey in the 1989 Entry Draft. He spent part of three seasons with the Devils before Anaheim claimed him in the 1993 expansion draft. He spent time with the Ducks and Calgary, and often spent long periods in the IHL and AHL. He was signed by San Jose in August 1997.

The Sharks sent Skalde to Kentucky of the AHL after training camp, but he was recalled after six games. He stayed with the Sharks until January 8, 1998, when he was claimed by Chicago on waivers. Two weeks later, when the Hawks tried to send him down, the Sharks re-claimed him. Four days later, Dallas claimed him on waivers from San Jose. He played only one game with the Stars when he was once again placed on waivers. Chicago claimed him once again. After three games with the Hawks, he was placed on waivers and the Sharks claimed him once again.

The final tally: 30 games, 4 goals, 7 assists, 18 penalty minutes, 5 waiver claims, and a serious case of jet lag.

vaunted parquet floor, Red Auerbach's victory cigars, the Beanpot, Eddie Shore's infamous hit on Ace Bailey, and the so-called Gallery Gods, the Garden closed its doors to professional sports on May 14, 1995, when the New Jersey Devils defeated the Bruins 3–2.

As historic as the Stadium and Garden were, they had nothing on the Montreal Forum, home to the Maroons and later the Canadiens. The Forum, which opened in 1924, was the oldest of the Original Six arenas and was the most important, historically. The Canadiens, who were the building's most celebrated tenant, clinched many a Cup at the Forum. Perhaps the most exciting game in Forum history took place on December 31, 1975, when the Canadiens and the Soviet Union's Central Red Army side skated to a 3–3 draw. The final game at the Forum was played on March 11, 1996. The Canadiens stuffed the Dallas Stars that night by a 4–1 count. Following the game, a ceremony was held featuring all of the club's living legends. Jean Beliveau and Bernie Geoffrion were well received, but Maurice Richard stole the show. When the Rocket's

Oilers vs. Bears

In December 1998, the Edmonton Oilers were struggling. When a Russian circus came to town, team officials scheduled a three-on-three game against some of the circus performers. The idea was to pit Oilers Mikhail Shtalenkov, Andrei Kovalenko, and Boris Mironov against their countrymen. Make that countrybears. You see, the circus performers were bears.

Allan Maki of the Toronto *Globe and Mail* said, "The bears, who wore skates and helmets and looked about as mobile as Vancouver Canucks' defenceman Dana Murzyn, took on the Oilers trio and were beaten like a rug."

Shtalenkov was asked if he was scared the bears would attack him. He said, "No." He gave a big smile when he heard the reporter's next question: "Did any of the bears score on you?"

name was announced, the Forum shook for 10 minutes. It was a fitting end for the old Forum.

On February 13, 1999, the Toronto Maple Leafs played their last game inside their venerable Gardens. Their opponent that day, as it had been in the building's first game on November 12, 1931, was the Chicago Blackhawks. Chicago's Mush Marsh, who scored the first goal in Gardens history, was on hand to drop the ceremonial face-off 67 years later. Chicago took the first game at the Gardens 2–1 and was also victorious in the last one, 6–2. The Leafs also held a long ceremony to honor their past stars but were roundly slammed for failing to live up to the standard set by the Forum closing. There is a simple explanation for this, however — the Canadiens have a much deeper hockey tradition than the Leafs. While Montreal could march out Richard, Beliveau, and Geoffrion, Toronto's hugest ovations were for Red Horner, Darryl Sittler, and Borje Salming. Nevertheless, 15,726 fans were happy to have been on hand to close out the old building.

Chicago Stadium, Boston Garden, Maple Leaf Gardens, and the Montreal Forum were replaced, respectively, by the United Center, FleetCenter, Air Canada Centre, and Molson Centre.

Chokers No More

As a franchise, the Detroit Red Wings compare well to the 1950s Brooklyn Dodgers, perennial bridesmaids. The familiar refrain 'round the borough of Brooklyn every October was "Get 'em next year!" Not until they won their first World Series in 1955 did Brooklyn's Bums get that monkey off their back. Only months earlier, the Wings had won their fourth Stanley Cup in six years. This power-house team, fronted by Gordie Howe, Ted Lindsay, Red Kelly, and Terry Sawchuk, seemed certain to strike again. Little did anyone know that when Lindsay hoisted Lord Stanley's mug on April 14, 1955, it would be over 42 years before the Motor City would see their beloved Wings in the championship again.

Jack Adams, "The Old Exhorter," was both the architect and the ruin of the Wings dynasty in the 1950s. After the 1955 Cup win, he sent Sawchuk to the Boston Bruins in order to make room for a young Glenn Hall, his top goaltending prospect. Only two years later, Adams reacquired Sawchuk, surrendering in return a young buck by the name of Johnny Bucyk. Adams then dealt Hall and Lindsay to the sad-sack Chicago Black Hawks for Forbes Kennedy, Johnny Wilson, and two minor leaguers. It was all downhill from there. Although the Wings of the 1960s were solid, still anchored by Howe, they couldn't put it all together. In the 1960s alone, they lost four Cup finals. When the NHL expanded in 1967–68, all life seemed to be sucked out of the franchise. Between 1966–67 and 1982–83, Detroit qualified for the post-season only twice, a record of futility even the San Jose Sharks can chuckle at. Howe once commented on the sad state of affairs: "They just got rid of so much great talent. They made bad trades, the people didn't come up through the system, and they made more bad trades trying to fill the holes."

The 1970s and early 1980s were downright ugly for Detroit. Just when hope seemed right around the corner, management would either trade away (see Marcel Dionne) or lose to serious injury (see Mickey Redmond) their top talent. A quick check of their top draft picks between 1972 and 1981 reveals a weakness in scouting: Pierre Guite, Terry Richardson, Bill Lochead, Rick Lapointe, Fred Williams, Dale McCourt, Willie Huber, Mike Foligno, Mike Blaisdell, Claude Loiselle. Some, like McCourt, Huber, and Foligno, became good players, but were traded away. So what were Detroit's great brains doing? Trying to draft future Leafs?

In 1982, Mike Ilitch, owner of Little Caesar's Pizza, purchased the Wings from the Norris family. One of his first moves as new owner was to name Jimmy Devellano his GM. For the first time in a long while, the future was brighter in Detroit.

The 1983 NHL Entry Draft was all about hotshot center Steve Yzerman, who was snapped up by Detroit. The kid they called "Stevie Y" brought an enthusiasm and winning attitude the Wings hadn't had for a donkey's age. He and his 87 points paced the club to a third-place finish and a playoff berth in 1983–84. In the first round, Detroit faced the St. Louis Blues and managed a split in St. Louis. The Blues, however, took both games in Detroit in overtime to knock the Wings out of the Cup hunt. The following season brought about an almost identical result: third-place finish, capped off by an early post-season exit, this time at the hands of Denis Savard and his Chicago Blackhawks.

Ilitch spent big money on free agents in the summer of 1985, inking college stars Adam Oates, Chris Cichocki, Tim Friday, and Dale Krentz and one-year wonder Warren Young. Only Oates panned out, though he had his best years with St. Louis. Yzerman cracked his collarbone midway through 1985–86 and missed the final 29 games of the campaign. Without their young dynamo, the Wings sputtered their way

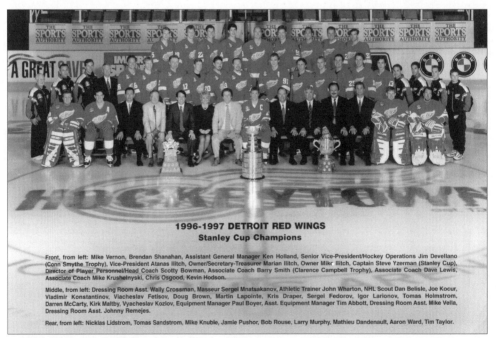

1996-1997 DETROIT RED WINGS
Stanley Cup Champions

Front, from left: Mike Vernon, Brendan Shanahan, Assistant General Manager Ken Holland, Senior Vice-President/Hockey Operations Jim Devellano (Conn Smythe Trophy), Vice-President Atanas Ilitch, Owner/Secretary-Treasurer Marian Ilitch, Owner Mike Ilitch, Captain Steve Yzerman (Stanley Cup), Director of Player Personnel/Head Coach Scotty Bowman, Associate Coach Barry Smith (Clarence Campbell Trophy), Associate Coach Dave Lewis, Associate Coach Mike Krushelnyski, Chris Osgood, Kevin Hodson.

Middle, from left: Dressing Room Asst. Wally Crossman, Masseur Sergei Mnatsakanov, Athletic Trainer John Wharton, NHL Scout Dan Belisle, Joe Kocur, Vladimir Konstantinov, Viacheslav Fetisov, Doug Brown, Martin Lapointe, Kris Draper, Sergei Fedorov, Igor Larionov, Tomas Holmstrom, Darren McCarty, Kirk Maltby, Vyacheslav Kozlov, Equipment Manager Paul Boyer, Asst. Equipment Manager Tim Abbott, Dressing Room Asst. Mike Vella, Dressing Room Asst. Johnny Remejes.

Rear, from left: Nicklas Lidstrom, Tomas Sandstrom, Mike Knuble, Jamie Pushor, Bob Rouse, Larry Murphy, Mathieu Dandenault, Aaron Ward, Tim Taylor.

1996–97 Detroit Red Wings

to a ghastly 17-57-6 record. It was their worst season in franchise history.

With Yzerman back in the mix for the 1986–87 season, things were looking up. The Wings finished a respectable, albeit mediocre, 34-36-10. In the playoffs, they knocked off Chicago and Toronto before succumbing to the eventual champs, the Oilers.

Detroit rolled through the Norris Division in 1987–88 and ended up in first place by 17 points. They crushed Toronto and St. Louis before losing to Edmonton in the Conference finals once again. The rest of the Norris caught up to the Wings in 1988–89 — they finished in first by a mere two points. Yzerman had a career year, scoring 65 goals and 155 points. Detroit again fizzled in the playoffs, however. Chicago knocked off the Wings in six games. In 1989–90, the Wings returned to their losing ways and finished out of the playoffs. Yzerman was not to blame, though. He potted 62 goals and 127 points to once again finish third in the NHL scoring race.

At the beginning of the nineties, Detroit finished behind the Chicago Blackhawks in the regular season. The Wings finished third in the Norris in 1990–91 before dropping a seven-game heartbreaker to St. Louis in the playoffs. The following year, the Wings made top spot, second in the NHL, and beat the Minnesota North Stars to face Chicago in the division finals. Four games later, though, the Red Wings were sipping iced tea on the golf course.

It was fast becoming apparent that Detroit lacked the heart, the intestinal fortitude to go deep when it counted. While their regular-season records were usually impressive, their post-season history was a sick joke. Sadly, the Wings did little to turn it around over the next few campaigns.

In 1992–93, Yzerman returned to super scorer form, tallying 137 points. Detroit finished with 103 points for second in the Norris and fifth in the league. In the post-season, the Wings met up with a Toronto team that many felt wouldn't provide Detroit with a challenge. But the Leafs surprised the Wings in seven games.

It got worse for Detroit in 1993–94. A first-place finish in the Western Conference matched the Wings up against the San Jose Sharks, a team that had won only 11 games the year before. Few gave the Sharks a chance to win even one game against Detroit, a club led by Yzerman and Hart Trophy–winner Sergei Fedorov. In game one, San Jose knocked off Detroit, 5–4. The Sharks were for real! To everyone's surprise, the little team from central California extended the series to a seventh game. Late in the third period of game seven, Sharks' center Jamie Baker intercepted a clearing attempt by rookie goalie Chris Osgood, and tallied the game- and series-winning marker. Those amazing Red Wings were out — again!

The playoff monkey was nearly knocked off Detroit's back in 1994–95. A lockout shortened the season to 48 games and the Wings captured the President's Trophy as regular-season champions. Mike Vernon came aboard from the Calgary Flames to provide the Wings with a big-time playoff goaltender. No doubt refreshed by the long break between seasons, Detroit cruised past the Dallas Stars, and dropped San Jose and Chicago to reach the Cup finals for the first time since 1966, against the New Jersey Devils. After losing a close one in game one, the Wings found themselves up 2–1 midway through the final frame of game two. Smooth-skating Devil defenseman Scott Niedermayer went end to end with the rubber. He took a shot that bounced off the end boards back to his stick. The young buck made no mistake on his second opportunity. Rookie Devil forward Jim Dowd notched the game-winner eight minutes later. Detroit was down yet again. Back in New Jersey and Meadowlands Arena, the powerful Devils put the Red Wings out of their misery.

After the 1995–96 season, Detroit fans wondered if their team would ever drink from Lord Stanley's mug again. After rumbling through the regular season to 131 points in 82 games, the Wings stuffed the Winnipeg Jets before cuffing the St. Louis Blues in double OT of game seven. But Detroit still had to face the Colorado Avalanche. Bolstered by the addition of proven playoff performers Patrick Roy and Claude Lemieux, Colorado beat back the Wings in an out-and-out war for the silverware and NHL bragging rights.

At the beginning of the 1996–97 campaign, many hockey pundits had Colorado pegged as hockey's latest and greatest dynasty. But what of Detroit? The 1997 Red Wings, for all of their recent success, were slammed for their lack of mental and physical toughness. The Wings? Ha! the critics mocked. They were nothing more than hockey's New York Knicks. A bunch of chokers. But the pundits were proven wrong.

In the off-season, Detroit rid themselves of winger Dino Ciccarelli, citing his age and his penchant for taking silly penalties. To some, this move was surprising. Ciccarelli did take dumb penalties now and then, but his feistiness and clutch goal-scoring would be hard to replace. At about the same time, Hartford was having trouble with tough winger Brendan Shanahan, who was finding it increasingly difficult to play for a pretender. Before long, Whaler brass put their star on the market. Detroit wasted little time in making a play for him. For Primeau, Coffey, and a draft pick, Shanny was theirs. They paid a steep price, for sure, but the deal paid dividends. The big Irish-Canadian provided the Wings with muscle, leadership, and big-goal potential on the wing they had lost in releasing Ciccarelli.

With Vernon and Osgood in goal, Konstantinov and Lidstrom on the blue-line, and Yzerman, Fedorov, and Shanahan up front, this was a team built for success. But plumbers like Joey Kocur, Kris Draper, and Kirk Maltby (the Grind Line) kept the Wings in many games. If Fedorov and Yzerman were off their game, Bowman substituted Darren McCarty, Igor Larionov, or Doug Brown to mix it up a bit.

Colorado and Detroit found themselves in the thick of a white-hot rivalry. On March 26, 1997, the bigger, badder Red Wings squashed the NHL champions. Hulking Darren McCarty stalked and thrashed Claude Lemieux, who had rearranged Kris Draper's face with a malicious check from behind in the 1996 Conference finals. McCarty hammered away on Lemieux, even as he lay on the ice. To rub salt in Colorado's hurt ego, McCarty potted the game-winner in extra time. In one match, Detroit had hurtled to the top of the NHL pack. The Wings were whipping boys no longer.

The Wings finished the regular season with 94 points, good enough for third place in the Western Conference. In the first round, they faced St. Louis, the club they knocked out the previous spring. The ghouls of past Wing failures reared their ugly heads in game one. Grant Fuhr was phenomenal in the Blues' net, turning aside everything Detroit sent his way. Brett Hull called game two a "game with no rhythm" as the referees whistled down even the slightest infractions. The Wings prevailed, 2–1. Back in St. Louis, the two teams traded wins. With fears of suffering yet another playoff collapse, the Red Wings came through with a big 5–2 win before taking the series with a 3–1 victory in game six. The Anaheim Mighty Ducks, led by Paul Kariya and Teemu Selanne, now stood in the Wings' way. Anaheim had knocked off the Phoenix Coyotes and were seeking to derail Detroit as the Sharks had done three years earlier. It was not to be. The series was over in four games, although it was a close series. Three of the games were decided in overtime, one in double OT, and one in triple OT. The only non-OT game of the series, the third, was tied at three in the final frame when Sergei Fedorov and Slava Kozlov chipped in goals. When Shanahan scored in double OT of game four, Detroit moved on to the Conference finals to meet Patrick Roy and the hated Avalanche.

Colorado was eager to repeat as champion, but the mighty Wings stood in the way. The Avalanche roared to the series lead at home, 2–1. In game two, Colorado took an early 2–0 lead only to lose out 4–2. Game three, a Detroit win, featured exceptional goalkeeping from Mike Vernon and two Kozlov goals. The Wings destroyed Colorado 6–0 in game four. The Avalanche did not roll over and die, however. They bashed the Wings 6–0 in game five. But back in the Motor City, Vernon and Fedorov were at their dazzling best in a 3–1 Wing victory. At last, after years of failure and embarrassment, Detroit was going back to the Big Dance.

Meanwhile, the Philadelphia Flyers, who had put up impressive regular-season numbers, were weak in several areas. Many of their skaters were slow. Their goaltending was questionable at best. Despite these concerns, the odds-makers had the Flyers as the favorites heading into the NHL's 80th Stanley Cup final. Detroit exploited their opposition's weaknesses in routing the Flyers. Almost from the opening face-off, it was clear Philadelphia didn't have the speed to skate with the Wings, or the muscle to keep rugged Kocur and Shanahan from buzzing around their net. Ron Hextall was shaky on long shots. With this in mind, coach Bowman ordered his men to fire on Hextall from all angles and distances. Hextall surrendered soft goals to Fedorov and Yzerman in a 4–2 Detroit victory in game one. In game two, Philadelphia put Garth Snow in net, but it didn't make a difference. The Wings went home with a 2–0 series lead. A 6–1 Detroit victory gave Flyers' coach Terry Murray fuel to reprimand his team as chokers and quitters.

Joe Louis Arena was a madhouse in game four. Vernon was stopping everything and McCarty beat Hextall on an end-to-end rush. Detroit defeated the Flyers, 2–1. The Cup was returned to the Motor City for the first time in over 40 years.

Detroit was excited, but also relieved. Diehard Wings supporter Matt McCooeye explained: "It was more a feeling of relief, rather than happiness. It was like 42 years of monkeys had been lifted from our backs." Vernon was rewarded with the Conn Smythe Trophy though many put up an argument on Fedorov's behalf. The Detroiters won because they played as a team. Grinders picked up the slack when the big guns were silent and Bowman's left-wing lock had the Flyers completely baffled.

Only a week after the Cup win, tragedy struck the Detroit camp. On the way home from a golf tournament, a limousine containing Vladimir Konstantinov, Slava Fetisov, and team masseur Sergei Mnatsakanov crashed into a tree. Fetisov emerged with minor cuts and bruises. Konstantinov and Mnatsakanov were not so lucky. The pair survived, but their respective careers were finished. Just like that, the Wings went from sitting on top of the world to rock-bottom.

With Konstantinov recuperating from his severe injuries, few gave Detroit much of a chance to repeat as champions. The Flyers and Devils were the favorites. Yet, against all odds, Detroit finished third overall on the 1997–98 regular season and fought through six-game wars with Phoenix, St. Louis, and Dallas to reach the finals once again. This time, they were up against the Washington Capitals, who had knocked off Dominik Hasek and the Buffalo Sabres. Olaf Kolzig, the Capitals' goalie, was outstanding, but Detroit was simply too strong. A second straight sweep in the finals gave the Wings their second straight Cup. At the conclusion of game four, Konstantinov was wheeled out onto the ice for the celebrations. Although no longer able to play hockey, he was still a loved member of the team.

Detroit did it. They shook off 40 years of failure. No longer would opposing rinks be filled with chants of "1955!" No longer would Detroit players be labeled as "chokers." The Motor City men had exorcised their demons.

Hey, Chicago . . . 1961!

The Red Wings Take Flight

In the era of big money and 11th-hour deals, it's interesting to note how the Red Wings of the late 1990s were built. Jim Devellano, who was brought on board in 1982, made it known that the club would be rebuilding through the draft (the free agent fiasco of 1985 notwithstanding). Over the next few seasons, Detroit netted Shawn Burr, Steve Chiasson, Tim Cheveldae, Joe Murphy, and Adam Graves, all of whom would wear the red and white. Devellano snagged players who would play major roles on the 1997 and 1998 Cup teams.

In the 1983 draft, Detroit scooped up Yzerman, their catalyst for 15 years, as well as knuckle-boy Joey Kocur. Kocur was the team's enforcer until he was dealt to the New York Rangers in 1991. In December 1996, the Wings brought Kocur back to town in an attempt to inject toughness into their lineup. His leadership and physical play figured huge in the team's Cup success.

The 1989 draft may have been Detroit's best as they selected Nicklas Lidstrom, Sergei Fedorov, Dallas Drake, and Vladimir Konstantinov. The following year, they brought Keith Primeau aboard, as well as Slava Kozlov. Then came Martin Lapointe, Chris Osgood, Darren McCarty, and Tomas Holmstrom. All would be key ingredients in the coming Hockeytown dynasty.

But the draft could take them only so far. Great teams must be able to add the right pieces to the puzzle at exactly the right time. Luckily, Detroit did just that. They needed experienced defenders who could move the puck, so they picked up Slava Fetisov and Larry Murphy. They needed a steady, stay-at-home rearguard, so they signed veteran Bob Rouse. They dealt sniper Ray Sheppard to San Jose for Igor Larionov to add experience on the third line. They added Kris Draper, Doug Brown, and Kirk Maltby to upgrade their third and fourth lines.

As the 1990s dragged on, it became obvious that Detroit was lacking two things: a proven playoff goalie and a bona fide power forward. With the development of Lidstrom and Konstantinov, Chiasson became expendable and was dealt to the Calgary Flames for 1989 Cup standout goalie Mike Vernon. Vernon quickly ended the goalie question. Detroit picked up Brendan Shanahan from the Whalers for a steep price.

All of these moves paid off. The team gelled in 1997, and the rest is history.

A Real Pain in the Crease

There have been many controversial goals in NHL playoff history, some real doozies. In 1966, Henri Richard of the Habs slid headfirst along the ice with the puck on his stick right into Detroit netminder Roger Crozier, potting the Cup-winning goal. In 1973, the Pocket Rocket again notched a controversial Cup-winner in overtime, past Tony Esposito.

In June 1999, the NHL played its last Stanley Cup championship series of the twentieth century, between Ken Hitchcock's Dallas Stars and Lindy Ruff's Buffalo Sabres. With Buffalo trying to force a game seven, the game went into overtime. The Stars' Brett Hull swatted in the game- and Cup-winner past Dominik Hasek. The Sabres protested, screaming "No goal!" but referee Terry Gregson made no effort to have the goal reviewed. The goal stood and the Stars hung on to win the Cup.

Ruff, Hasek, and anyone who eats Buffalo wings started screaming bloody murder.

"I wanted Bettman to answer the question why [Hull's goal] was not reviewed," said Ruff. "And really, he just turned his back on me like he knew this might be a tainted goal and there was no answer for it."

"I'm very bitter because what happened. It's a shame," commented Dominik Hasek.

"You don't want to sit here and complain about things that are too late. I think it's a case where they don't have the nerve after all the celebration to call the goal back," cried Sabre forward Michael Peca.

The newspapers had a field day with this debacle. Jack Todd of the *Montreal Gazette* said, "Face it: the crease rule has no reason to live. The rule was born with good intentions. It didn't work. End of story . . . Hull did not interfere with Dominik Hasek, so without the crease rule no one would have filed the meekest protest . . . The solution? Deep six the crease rule now. Call goalie interference tightly when it applies. And apologize profusely to the Sabres and their fans."

Damien Cox of the *Toronto Star* added, "Forget the Buffalo Sabres. Feel sorry for the Dallas Stars. Their title is tainted. And they should blame Gary Bettman . . . Hull . . . never had control [of the puck]. He was fishing, along with several others, for a loose puck in a goalmouth scramble."

Jack Todd's suggestions became prophetic, for two days after the goal was scored, the NHL eliminated video goal-judge reviews for man-in-the-crease violations. Bettman simply said, "We're relying too much on replay for goal decisions." He also said that "the absolute right call" was made on Hull's goal, but other than that, he would not address the controversy. He left that up to Colin Campbell and Bryan Lewis, the NHL supervisor of officials.

"The rule was absolutely, correctly applied," said Lewis. "Everyone understands it was the right call." The official response from the league was that it didn't matter if Hull had his skate in the crease or not, but that he had full control of the puck.

Baloney. Hull never had control of the puck and the goal never should have stood, according to NHL rules. But that really isn't the argument here. The real problem is that a stupid rule created a tainted Stanley Cup win. Hull's "goal" stood, the Stars won the Cup, and there is nothing that anyone can do about that after the fact.

Congratulations, NHL! Congratulations, Mr. Bettman! You've wrapped up a momentous century of Stanley Cup playoff hockey in a fine way.

Gretzky Calls It a Career

All around the world, hockey fans refused to believe. He was bluffing. He had to play another year, because the 2000 All-Star Game would be played in Toronto. But this was no bluff. All of the rationalizing in the world could not stop Wayne Gretzky from playing his final NHL game on April 18, 1999, against the Pittsburgh Penguins.

Three days earlier, after a game in Ottawa, Gretzky had stated that Sunday's game would be his last. Most of hockey had anticipated Gretzky's official announcement before he made it.

Following the final buzzer in Ottawa, the Corel Centre remained full. Ottawa's fans and most of the Senators stuck around to applaud Gretzky in what would prove to be his final hockey game in Canada.

Madison Square Garden was electric on that fateful spring afternoon. A short pregame ceremony featured NHL Commissioner Gary Bettman, Gretzky's family, Mario Lemieux, and Mark Messier. Gretzky was presented with a Mercedes and a big-screen TV. With the formalities out of the way, it was time to get Gretzky's Last Stand underway.

While the game meant nothing for the Rangers, it did have playoff implications for other teams. If the Penguins were to grab a victory, they would vault ahead of Buffalo for the seventh playoff spot if the Sabres lost to Washington that afternoon. A Dominik Hasek shutout of the Caps made this a moot point.

From the opening face-off, both teams seemed tentative. Gretzky dipped into his bag of tricks, creating several scoring chances. The game was scoreless after one period of play.

In the second period, the teams had played for just over twelve minutes when former Ranger Alexei Kovalev finished off a pretty three-way passing play from Alexei Morozov and Robert Lang. The goal quieted the Garden crowd, which buzzed only when Gretzky took his shift. Possibly feeling the pressure of playing in the Great One's final game, the Rangers blasted 24 shots at Barrasso without solving him.

At 18:15, referee Bill McCreary whistled Jaromir Jagr for tripping. Seventy seconds into the power play, the puck came to Gretzky along the boards. Using his remarkable peripheral vision, Gretzky found the trailer, Brian Leetch, who hit a wide-open Mathieu Schneider with a perfect pass. Schneider made no mistake. CBC's cameras immediately flashed to Wayne's wife, Janet, and to Lemieux. Play-by-play man Bob Cole spoke the immortal words: "Yes, Janet, he's got a point. Yes, Mario, he's got a point."

By this time, the 18,200 in Madison Square Garden and the 4.3 million people watching across North America on CBC and Fox realized that they were about to witness Gretzky's final period of NHL hockey. Buzz throughout the arena reached immeasurable heights every time Gretzky touched the puck. Would he get a goal?

With 90 seconds left in the third period, the Garden crowd began chanting "Gretzky!" begging for their hero to return to the ice. With 55 seconds to go, Gretzky jumped over the boards to the roar of the crowd. At the 40-secondmark, play was whistled dead.

One by one, the Garden crowd began to rise, giving Gretzky a standing ovation. Ranger coach John Muckler called a timeout to allow Gretzky to savor the moment. When the puck was finally dropped, the two teams played out the remainder of regulation, which ended with the two teams knotted at one. The game went into overtime.

Could Gretzky summon up enough magic to give his fans one last memory? Lamentably, no. At 1:22 of the extra session, Jagr took a feed from Morozov to end the game and Gretzky's career. The MSG crowd was stunned at first, but then rose to their feet to salute their hero. The Penguins, to a man, sought out the Great One to shake his hand, and, with MSG rocking, gave Gretzky the ultimate tribute, banging their sticks on the ice in appreciation.

Just like that, it was over. 1,487 regular-season NHL games. 894 goals. 1,963 assists. 2,857 points. A legacy never to be forgotten.

How fitting, as the NHL enters the next millennium, that Jaromir Jagr, the player the league hopes will fill Gretzky's skates, scored the goal that ended Gretzky's career. Call it fate. Call it symbolic. Call it whatever you want. The greatest player the NHL has ever seen has retired. We'll miss you, Wayne.

----

*Snap!*shots

ED BELFOUR (The Eagle) Goal
5'11" 182
b. 4/21/1965, Carman, Manitoba

A relative unknown with only one year of college hockey experience, Eddie Belfour became the NHL's top goalie in the early 1990s. Possessed of a lightning-quick glove hand and using the butterfly style, the Manitoba native won Vezina trophies in 1991 and 1993 and backstopped his Chicago Blackhawks to the Stanley Cup finals in 1992 and the Dallas Stars to a Cup win in 1999.

 Belfour came to the University of North Dakota in 1986–87 by way of the Manitoba Junior Hockey League and quickly established himself as one of the NCAA's top keepers, earning First-Team All-WCHA honors. The Hawks moved quickly to sign the young goalie. He spent 1987–88 with Saginaw of the IHL and joined the big boys in the Windy City for 23 games the following season. Determined to improve his game, Belfour joined the Canadian National Team in 1989 before rejoining Chicago for the 1990 playoffs. Although at first expected to ride the pines as the team's third goalie behind Greg Millen and Jacques Cloutier, Belfour was thrown into the fray in game two of the opening round series. In all, he saw action in nine playoff contests, playing well enough to clinch the starting job the following season. The 1990–91 campaign was a storybook season for Eddie the Eagle — he captured both the Calder and the Vezina trophies, the first goalie to accomplish the feat since Tom Barrasso in 1983–84. The playoffs were another story, however, as Belfour and the ChiHawks were eliminated in the first round.

 Belfour avoided the sophomore jinx in 1991–92 in leading Chicago to a berth in the finals. Unfortunately, Mario Lemieux and the powerhouse Pittsburgh Penguins dumped the Hawks in four. Belfour grabbed another Vezina in 1992–93, he couldn't take the Blackhawks very far in the post-season. Despite being a leading Cup contender, Chicago didn't win a single game. People began to say Belfour couldn't win the big game.

 In January 1997, the soon-to-be-unrestricted free agent was dealt to the San Jose Sharks. His life as a Shark lasted a mere 13 games. He was signed by the up-and-coming Dallas Stars in July 1998. Backstopping the defense-obsessed Stars revitalized the Eagle's career but the question remained: Can Belfour take a team to the Stanley Cup championship? The answer is yes. He led the Stars to the 1999 Stanley Cup.

Peak Years *1991–95*
In a Word *INTENSE*

MARTIN BRODEUR Goal
6'1" 205
b. 5/6/1972, Montreal, Quebec

At first, Martin Brodeur, a first-round selection (20th overall) by the New Jersey Devils in the 1990 NHL Entry Draft, was seen as second-string material. He tended nets in four games with the Devils in 1991–92, but spent 1992–93 with Utica of the AHL. Coming into the 1993–94 season, the young netminder was mired in third place on New Jersey's goalie depth chart behind Chris Terreri and Peter Sidorkiewicz. By the end of the season, however, Brodeur was a Calder Trophy winner and the Devils' top keeper.

 In 1994–95, Brodeur established himself as one of hockey's elite performers. A strike-shortened 48-game campaign proved a mere primer for the playoffs. He was 16-4 with a playoff-tops 1.67 goals-against average in backstopping the franchise to its first ever Stanley Cup championship. Brodeur crumbled under the immense expectations that followed his amazing playoff performance. His Devils missed the post-season in 1995–96. The big goalie bounced back the following season and if not for Buffalo's Dominik Hasek, Brodeur would have won the Vezina Trophy. He had to content himself with the Jennings Trophy and the fact that his 1.88 GAA was the first sub-1.90 GAA (minimum 25 games) since Philadelphia's Bernie Parent did it in 1973–74. Brodeur even managed to score a goal against the Montreal Canadiens in the playoffs. Brodeur followed up with a 1.89 GAA effort and another Jennings Trophy in 1997–98. Unfortunately, New Jersey was bounced in the opening round of the playoffs by the upstart Ottawa Senators.

Brodeur plays a textbook style in net, always upright and in good position to face shooters. This almost military style sometimes yields rebounds. Fortunately, New Jersey's top-flight defense makes sure their keeper only has to make the first save.

What sets Brodeur apart from most other goalies is his coolness under fire. Brodeur does his best work with the weight of the hockey world on his shoulders. Television analyst and former NHL defender Brian Engblom once said, "Martin Brodeur makes goaltending look easy."

Peak Years   *1996–99*
In a Word   *POISE*

PAVEL BURE (The Russian Rocket) Right Wing
5'10" 189
b. 3/31/1971, Moscow, USSR

Quite possibly the most heralded Russian prospect ever, Pavel Bure was selected by the Vancouver Canucks 113th overall in the 1989 NHL Entry Draft. After being drafted, the boy who would become the "Russian Rocket" put in two more years with the Russian Red Army, potting 35 goals in 44 games in his final season with the team, 1990–91. He finally made his way over to Vancouver, and when he did, NHL fans soon knew what all the fuss was about. His skating. His shot. With a 34-goal, Calder Trophy–winning year under his belt, Bure erupted in 1992–93 with 60 goals and 110 points. He reached the 60-goal plateau again in 1993–94 and powered his Canucks to within a hair of winning a Stanley Cup.

After the Cup run of 1994, Bure and the Canucks seemed sluggish. After a nondescript lockout-shortened 1994–95 season, through speculation that his work ethic was waning, Bure entered a tough time in his career. In 1995–96, after only 15 games, he tore his ACL and took a seat for the rest of the schedule. He potted only 23 goals in 63 games the following season. Had the injury robbed Bure of his blistering speed?

The Russian Rocket bounced back huge in 1997–98, scoring 51 goals on the season and putting on a show in the Nagano Olympics with nine goals in six games. But with the season coming to an end, Bure insisted that the Canucks trade him. He stated that he'd never play in Vancouver again. Vancouver GM Brian Burke finally dealt the speedy winger to the Florida Panthers in January 1999 for a package headlined by young blue-liner Ed Jovanovski. Bure was an instant hit in Florida, scoring 13 times in his first 11 games. Unfortunately, he once again succumbed to injury, this time to his knee, and his 1998–99 season was over.

Can the Russian Rocket bounce back again and turn his career around? Only time will tell.

Peak Years   *1994–98*
In a Word   *BLAST*

CHRIS CHELIOS Defense
6'1"   190
b. 1/25/1962, Chicago, Illinois

Chris Chelios

Chris Chelios has plied his trade like a rusty backdoor that creaks incessantly in a windstorm. He has been an instigator, an irritant. Not a dirty irritant like Ulf Samuelsson, mind you (though fiery goaltender Ron Hextall would beg to differ. Hextall attacked Chelios in the 1987 playoffs after Chelios hammered Philadelphia Flyers' forward Brian Propp into the boards.)

Chelios can play. Three Norris trophies are testament to the big defender's ability. Although not your classic rushing defenseman, he had all the passing, skating, and shooting skills to quarterback an offense. His bread and butter, though, has been the physical game.

The tough-as-nails Chelios opened his hockey career with the Wisconsin Badgers of the NCAA. The Montreal Canadiens selected him 40th overall in the 1981 NHL Entry Draft and eagerly awaited his arrival after a stint with the U.S. National Team in the 1984 Olympic Games. In his first full season, he racked up 55 assists and took a spot on the NHL All-Rookie Team. In 1988–89, he was worth 73 points and a Norris Trophy.

June 29, 1990, stands as one of the saddest days in Montreal hockey history. The Canadiens had lived with their poor decision to skip over Denis Savard in the draft for about 10 years. They were determined to acquire Savard, it seemed, at any price. That price turned out to be Chelios. Savard spent three mediocre seasons with the Canadiens. Chelios, on the other hand, won two Norris trophies in a long and storied stint in the Windy City.

In Montreal, Chelios made one All-Star Team. As a member of the Chicago Blackhawks, he made three First Teams and two Second Teams. In Chicago, he teamed with defenders such as Steve Smith, Gary Suter, and Eric Weinrich to anchor one of hockey's top defense corps throughout the 1990s. Chelios was a major factor in bringing the Hawks up against the Cup-winning Penguins in 1992.

At the 1999 trading deadline, the Blackhawks traded Chelios to the mighty Detroit Red Wings for young defender Anders Eriksson and draft picks. The Wings, who also secured the rights to Wendel Clark and Bill Ranford on the same day, set themselves for a strong, but unsuccessful, run at a third consecutive Cup championship. Chelios is one of the greatest defensemen of the last 25 years.

Peak Years   *1990–1994*
In a Word   *FEARLESS*

SERGEI FEDOROV Center
6'1"   200
b. 12/13/1969, Pskov, USSR

Pavel Bure, Alexander Mogilny, and Sergei Fedorov were once a dominant line on the Soviet Junior team. But another "KLM line" they would not become. It was a new era. Russians were skating west to ply their trade in the NHL. Mogilny was the first to leave, defecting during the 1989 Goodwill Games. Bure was a vaunted prospect for years. The relative unknown of the three, Fedorov, just might have been the best all-around player of the trio.

Signed by the Detroit Red Wings for 1990–91, Fedorov ended up with 31 goals, 79 points, and a place on the All-Rookie Team. Two solid years later, he was one of the

NHL's young stars. In 1993–94, the former Red Army star exploded for 56 goals and 120 points and was honored with the Hart and Selke trophies. After returning to earth for the shortened 1994–95 season, Fedorov came back to life in the post-season with a playoff-high 24 points. He returned to the 100-point plateau in 1995–96 with 107 and took his second Selke Trophy. By now, Fedorov and Peter Forsberg were generally considered to be hockey's finest two-way players. Mark Recchi once said of Fedorov, "He's got the tools, the speed [and] the panache to be MVP another three or four times." In 1996–97, the Russian speedster was inconsistent, posting only 63 points in 74 games. He did manage to put up another solid playoff performance, however, scoring 20 points as Detroit captured their first Stanley Cup since 1955. ·

Prior to the 1997–98 season, Fedorov was among a long list of big-name holdouts, and skipped training camp and the first part of the season. At around mid-season, Fedorov signed an offer sheet with the Carolina Hurricanes. Despite the $38-million price tag, the Red Wings were not about to let their young star get away. They quickly moved to match Carolina's offer, and Fedorov was back in a Wings uniform. Hockeytown fans greeted their rebellious Russian with mixed emotions. Fedorov won them over in helping bring Detroit a second straight Cup in 1998. With Yzerman winding up his career, the Red Wings will become Fedorov's team in the new millennium.

Peak Years   *1993–97*
In a Word   *DYNAMO*

THEOREN FLEURY Right Wing
5'6"   180
b. 6/29/1968, Oxbow, Saskatchewan

Fleury. Who woulda thunk it? He's too small, the experts said. Several NHL personnel directors said he'd never make the NHL. But you can never measure the size of a man's heart.

The Calgary Flames selected Fleury, a WHL star with the Moose Jaw Warriors, 166th overall in the 1987 Entry Draft. "A lot of clubs eliminated him on account of his size," noted Flames scout Ian McKenzie. Calgary was willing to gamble on the small man with the huge heart. The Flames assigned their budding star to their IHL affiliate club in Salt Lake City. When he scored 37 goals in 40 games, he was promoted to the big leagues.

In 1989, Fleury unloaded onto the NHL scene, scoring nearly a point a game in his 36-game rookie season. That spring, the Flames landed their first ever Stanley Cup championship. Two years later, Fleury had his first 50-goal, 100-point season. Although his numbers dipped slightly in 1991–92, he came back with a vengeance with another 100-point performance the following season. Cliff Fletcher, the man who drafted Fleury, once commented that "Fleury defies logic just by the way that he can play with the size he has."

The little titan's next three seasons were point-a-game efforts. As economic conditions worsened for Canadian clubs, Calgary was forced to chop salaries. Fleury escaped the chopping block, at first. His stay of execution wouldn't last forever, though. With Fleury approaching unrestricted free-agent status at the end of the 1998–99 season and insistent on testing the free-agent waters, Calgary sent him to the Colorado Avalanche for Rene Corbet, Wade Belak, and Robyn Regher. The move to Denver rejuvenated Fleury's career. He fit right in with Peter Forsberg, Joe Sakic, and Patrick Roy. And why not? Theo Fleury is a star.

After the Dallas Stars knocked out Colorado in the 1999 semifinals, Fleury became an attractive free-agent proposition. The New York Rangers came calling, inking him to

----

a $24-million dollar contract. He has a big job to do, trying to fill the gap left by Wayne Gretzky's retirement.

Peak Years   *1993–97*
In a Word   *DAVID*

PETER FORSBERG (Peter the Great/Foppa) Center
6'0"   190
b. 7/20/1973, Ornskoldsvik, Sweden

Admit it — you had no idea who Peter Forsberg was when he was taken sixth overall by the Philadelphia Flyers in the 1991 Entry Draft. You still didn't know who he was when he was dealt to Quebec in the Eric Lindros trade in 1992. The 1993 World Junior Championships probably opened your eyes a bit — 31 points in seven games will do that to you. When Forsberg earned the 1995 Calder Trophy, the whole world knew who he was.

Many liken Forsberg to former Chicago Black Hawk dynamo Stan Mikita. Forsberg became the best all-around player in the NHL in the late 1990s. There really isn't much the young star can't do.

In 1995–96, Peter was worth 116 points. A point-a-game player in the playoffs in 1996, he led his Colorado Avalanche to their first ever Stanley Cup championship. He didn't quite have Hart Trophy numbers — yet. Mario Lemieux was still in the way. In 1996–97 he endured a 30-point drop in production. Was he falling apart? Hardly. He missed 17 games to injury.

Since Forsberg became a Nord/Av in the Lindros deal, critics have shouted that he's no Lindros. They're right — he's better! He has a Cup win, and he's a better two-way player. He's a complete player, and he produces.

"There is nothing Forsberg can't do," gushed noted *New York Daily News* sports-writer Sherry Ross.

Peak Years   *1997–99*
In a Word   *PROTOTYPE*

RON FRANCIS   Center
6'3"   200
b. 3/1/1963, Sault Ste. Marie, Ontario

Ron Francis began his hockey career there with the OHL Greyhounds. In 1981, he was drafted fourth overall by the Hartford Whalers and was inserted into the lineup immediately. The young sniper was being groomed to take over from Blaine Stoughton and Mike Rogers, Hartford's big guns at the time. Francis averaged less than a point a game only once in his 10 years in Connecticut. He was more than just a scorer, however. He was an exceptional defensive forward with a knack for face-offs, and had a soft passing touch. Former Whalers' coach Rick Ley once commented that Francis was "easily one of the best all-around players in the game." In 1991, Ley removed the captain's "C" from Francis's jersey. Soon, he was traded to Pittsburgh with Grant Jennings and Ulf Samuelsson to the Pittsburgh Penguins for John Cullen, Zarley Zalapski, and Jeff Parker.

Before Francis arrived, the Penguins were an offensive juggernaut with a tendency to strain under the tight checking required in the playoffs. Francis changed the complexion of the team almost overnight, bringing aboard leadership and a two-way conscience. Pittsburgh won the Cup in 1991 and again in 1992. As a Penguin, the big man played inspired hockey. He posted some of the best numbers of his career, including a career-high 119 points in 1995–96. After seven years in Steeltown, though, it was time to move on. In 1998 Francis signed with the Carolina Hurricanes.

It took Ron Francis 10 years in the NHL to get noticed. Back-to-back Stanley Cups earned him the recognition he so richly deserved.

Peak Years   *1989–93*
In a Word   *FOOTSOLDIER*

DOUG GILMOUR (Killer) Center
5'11" 175
b. 6/25/1963, Kingston, Ontario

"Dougie plays like he owes us," former Toronto Maple Leafs' coach Pat Burns once said. How very true. Doug Gilmour gives it everything he has on the ice, and then some.

In 1980, "Killer" took over from Dale Hawerchuk as the leader of the Cornwall Royals. Gilmour was a part of the 1981 Memorial Cup–winning squad. Two years later, he challenged Hawerchuk's team scoring record but came up just short.

Gilmour was selected 134th overall by the St. Louis Blues in the 1982 NHL Entry Draft and joined the club for the 1983–84 season. He had his coming-out party in the 1986 playoffs, when he led all scorers with 21 points. The following year, he erupted for 105 points. After pouring in 86 points in 1987–88, he was sent to the Calgary Flames in a seven-player deal. In his first year with the Flames, they won the Stanley Cup. The abrasive center chipped in 22 points.

After two more solid seasons in Calgary, Gilmour was involved in "The Trade." In the single biggest deal in NHL history, Calgary dealt Gilmour to the Toronto Maple Leafs. The legend of Doug Gilmour was born in Toronto. When he arrived, the Leafs were a weak club with deficiencies in almost every area of the game. He became the nucleus of a winning franchise with a new-found pride.

Toronto fans will never forget the 1992–93 season. A 32-point improvement in the standings and 127 points from Gilmour were precursors to the playoffs. The Leafs failed to reach the Cup finals, but hockey fever was back in Hogtown. Gilmour's 35-point playoff performance was a major factor in this revitalization. In the 1993–94 season, Toronto won its first 10 games en route to the Cup semifinals. Gilmour and his Leafs played hard, but fell just short of the mark.

As the club's magic began running out, so did Gilmour's. Two years of carrying the Leafs had worn him down. Nagging injuries were taking their toll. In 1997, Toronto dealt their hero to the New Jersey Devils for prospects. Gilmour couldn't quite rekindle the same playoff magic with the Devils, however. After two sub-par years in New Jersey, he signed a huge free-agent deal with the Chicago Blackhawks.

Gilmour is a special player, a player who can rally his teammates. He's not the smooth, speedy type of player, but he's a relentless attacker, both offensively and defensively. If you need a goal, he sets one up. If you need an emotional lift, he delivers a big hit. Either way, you're glad Killer is on your side.

Peak Years   *1989–93*
In a Word   *HEART*

DOMINIK HASEK (The Dominator/The King)   Goal
5'11" 165
b. 1/29/1965, Pardubice, Czechoslovakia

The Dominik Hasek story would make for a nice made-for-TV special. Hasek was drafted 207th overall in 1983, but played nine years in the Czechoslovakian league. He came to North America only after refusing to play in an important game for the Czech Army Team. In his first three years he was shuttled between Chicago and Indianapolis of the IHL. In his first year in the NHL, he wanted to head home, claiming that he was not good enough to make it. A year later, he was traded to the Buffalo Sabres for fellow goalie Stephane Beauregard.

In 1993–94, Hasek caught a break when Grant Fuhr, Buffalo's regular goalie, was struggling. Five years later, Wayne Gretzky called Hasek "the greatest player in the game today."

What happened? The skinny keeper always had the talent. What he lacked early on was an opportunity to show off his stuff. The year he joined the Chicago Blackhawks, starter Ed Belfour enjoyed a dream rookie season. Hasek backed up Belfour for two years before moving to Buffalo. In western New York, he found himself sharing the net with former All-Star Daren Puppa. Then Buffalo acquired Grant Fuhr from the Toronto Maple Leafs for Puppa, Dave Andreychuk, and a first-round pick. The next season, with Fuhr playing poorly, Hasek was thrown in. He was rock-solid, and Fuhr never got his job back. The man who started the season as a backup won the Vezina Trophy with a 1.95 goals-against average, seven shutouts, and an amazing .930 save percentage. In the lockout-shortened 1994–95 campaign, Hasek repeated as top goalie. After an off-season in 1995–96, he bounced back to win the Hart Trophy and his third Vezina in four years. Hasek won his fourth Vezina in 1997–98 and his second consecutive Hart. Hasek staked his claim as hockey's top goalie of the 1990s by leading his underdog Czech Republic side to a gold medal at the 1998 Olympics in Nagano. And he won his fifth Vezina in 1998–99.

Keith Tkachuk said, "If Buffalo doesn't win a Cup, [Hasek will] still be considered one of the greatest. He's probably the only guy that could get away with it." And to think Hasek was pushing 30 when he earned a regular spot in the NHL. To this day, no one knows how he does it. He has all the grace of a harpooned seal on the ice.

Peak Years   *1994–98*
In a Word   *GUMBY*

BRETT HULL (The Golden Brett/The Silver Jet) Right Wing
5'10" 201
b. 8/9/1964, Belleville, Ontario

How would you know without looking at them? The body? No. Father was cut, son is more doughy. Skating? No again. Father was a rocket, son not even close. How about the shot? Ah, the shot. Vintage Hull. Any hockey-playing son of Bobby Hull was destined to be a goal-scorer anyway, not a Selke Trophy candidate.

Brett Hull made a name for himself in 1983–84 with the Penticton Knights of the British Columbia Junior League when he shattered the league scoring record with 105 goals in 56 games. From there, it was off to the University of Minnesota–Duluth, where he was worth 84 goals over two seasons with the Bulldogs. He signed on with the Calgary Flames after they took him 117th overall in the 1984 draft. After his NCAA season was over, he appeared in two playoff games with the Flames in 1986. In 1986–87, young Hull was the top rookie in the AHL and received a late season call-up to the big club.

In 1987–88, Hull played his first full season in the NHL. He counted 26 goals in 52 games for the Flames before he was traded to the St. Louis Blues with Steve Bozek for Rob Ramage and Rick Wamsley. Calgary would live to regret the deal, and how! Hull scored 41 goals in 1988–89, while the Flames were busy winning the Stanley Cup. Hull scored 72, 86, and 70 over the next three years for the Blues as Adam Oates' right winger. Meanwhile, Calgary stumbled. Hull's 86 goals in 1990–91 put him in select company — with Wayne Gretzky and Mario Lemieux — as one of the only players ever to have scored 80 goals in a season.

Hull's production dropped over the next five years in St. Louis. He became increasingly frustrated with the team's lack of post-season success and clashed with coaches Mike Keenan and Joel Quenneville about everything. When Hull dropped down to an unheard-of 27 goals in 1997–98, his end in St. Louis was near. Seeking a change, the 33-year-old sniper did what many thought impossible a few years before: he left St. Louis, bolting the Blues for the up-and-coming Dallas Stars. Hull's new club, although a perennial Cup contender, was in desperate need of a finisher, a go-to guy. Hull would be a perfect fit. Or would he?

Many of hockey's self-appointed experts questioned how the individualistic Hull would fare as a member of the team-oriented Stars. Dallas earned the President's Trophy in 1998–99 and scored a controversial overtime winner to give Dallas the 1999 Stanley Cup over the Buffalo Sabres.

Although not the force his father Bobby was in hockey, Brett Hull is one of the game's all-time most dangerous snipers. He will someday join his father in the Hockey Hall of Fame.

Peak Years   *1990–1994*
In a Word   *PRODIGAL SON*

JAROMIR JAGR (Mario Jr.) Right Wing
6'2" 228
b. 2/15/1972, Kladno, Czechoslovakia

Jaromir Jagr always wanted to be a professional hockey player. At age nine, the precocious kid did 1,000 squats a day to improve his skating strength. A few years later, he paid goalies to stay after practice to field his shots. By age 18, he was in the NHL with Mario Lemieux and the Pittsburgh Penguins.

Two years with Poldi Kladno in the Czech league made Jagr a household name among NHL scouts and the unknown member of the "Big Five," five players (Jagr, Mike Ricci, Petr Nedved, Keith Primeau, and Owen Nolan) all capable of being the first player selected in the 1990 NHL Entry Draft. Pittsburgh selected Jagr fifth overall, while Owen Nolan went first to the Quebec Nordiques. If that same draft was held today, there is no question who the Quebec Nordiques/Colorado Avalanche would take with their first pick.

Jagr showed himself remarkably well when thrust onto the NHL scene in 1990–91. Under Lemieux's tutelage, Jagr scored 27 goals and 57 points in his rookie season and the Penguins won their first ever Stanley Cup championship. Jagr's production improved the following year, but his play in the 1992 playoffs marked him as a soon-to-be superstar and the heir apparent to Lemieux's throne. Jagr scored 11 goals and 24 points in 21 games in the 1992 playoffs to help Pittsburgh win its second straight Cup. He had seasons of 94 and 99 points, and won his first Art Ross Trophy with 70 points in 48 games in the strike-shortened 1994–95 season.

Teamed with Lemieux in 1995–96 full-time, Jagr erupted for 62 goals and 149 points, second in the league behind his mentor. Lemieux played one more season in the NHL, and Jagr inherited his role as the leader of the Pens. He did not disappoint in his new role, leading the NHL with 35 goals and 102 points in 1997–98, the lowest total for an Art Ross winner in a non-shortened NHL season since Stan Mikita's 87 in 1967–68. Jagr took home another Art Ross in 1998–99, winning by a substantial margin. Without question, Jagr is the most explosive offensive force in hockey.

Peak Years   *1997–99*
In a Word   *MANCHILD*

PAUL KARIYA   Left Wing
5'11" 180
b. 10/16/1974, Vancouver, British Columbia

Paul Kariya has shown promise since his three-point games with the BCJHL Penticton Panthers. Was he too small for the NHL? Too frail? In 1992–93, the shifty forward, with the University of Maine, scored 93 points in 36 games and took the Hobey Baker Trophy as the top U.S. collegiate player. Still, when the 1993 NHL Entry Draft rolled around, Kariya was not the consensus number one pick. The 1993 draft had an A-list of prospects, including Alexandre Daigle and Chris Pronger. No one was sure who would be drafted when. Kariya was selected fourth by the Anaheim Mighty Ducks.

Kariya wasn't in a hurry to hook up with the Ducks, who were a weak team at the time. The young hotshot decided to finish his education at Maine, keeping himself sharp by playing with the Black Bears, on the Canadian National Team, and in the 1994 Olympics in Lillehammer, Norway.

Kariya joined Anaheim for the 1994–95 season. He struggled at first, but came on at the end to average nearly a point a game. In the lockout-shortened season he scored 39 points in 47 games, good enough for a spot on the NHL All-Rookie Team. The following season, with Winnipeg import Teemu Selanne coming on board, Kariya erupted for 50 goals, 108 points, and a spot on the First All-Star Team. The fun continued for the explosive winger in 1996–97. Despite missing 13 games to injury, Kariya managed 99 points. "Oh my god, he's fun to watch," gushed Philadelphia Flyer superstar Eric Lindros. What really stood out about Kariya's game was how coolly he performs in the close checking NHL. While Wayne Gretzky and Denis Savard played in a free, open league, Kariya plays in an NHL of hooks, checks, and top-notch goaltending. Like Gretzky and Savard, Kariya has incredible passing and shooting skills.

With two exceptional seasons under his belt, Kariya, now a member of the NHL's elite, was after more money. Unfortunately, Disney, who owned the Mighty Ducks, played it cool. At an impasse, Kariya missed almost half of the 1997–98 campaign. Only 22 games into his return, a concussion forced him to sit out the remainder of the season. Is Kariya strong enough to rebound from injury? Is he tough enough? He returned to his game better than ever, this time with an edge to his game.

Kariya is climbing back to his post as the NHL's next great player. He was a First-Team All-Star in 1998–99.

Peak Years   *1998–99*
In a Word   *HUMMINGBIRD*

PAT LaFONTAINE   Center
5'10" 182
b. 2/22/1965, St. Louis, Missouri

As a teenager, Pat LaFontaine was a scoring genius, with a knack for threading the needle. The smallish center ran roughshod through every league he played in. At 16, he played for Detroit Compuware and scored 175 goals and 324 points in 79 games. The following season, he moved on to the Verdun Junior Canadiens and his numbers "slipped" noticeably. His goal production dropped. He scored only 104 goals, and only 234 points. Gee whiz, was the kid burned out at 17? The New York Islanders overlooked the kid's clearly diminishing skills and selected him third overall in the 1983 NHL Entry Draft behind perennial underachievers Brian Lawton and Sylvain Turgeon. At the conclusion of the 1984 Olympics in Sarajevo, LaFontaine signed with the Isles and scored 13 goals in his first 15 games. By the late 1980s, he was ready to take over from an aging Bryan Trottier as the team's dynamo.

LaFontaine scored 47, 45, 54, and 41 goals in the next four years, and was a hair's width from superstar status. Yet just when the St. Louis native was beginning to feel his oats, he was traded to the Buffalo Sabres for a package that included Pierre Turgeon.

In Buffalo, LaFontaine's game came together. Teamed with Russian sensation Alexander Mogilny, LaFontaine put up 93 points in 57 games in 1991–92 before a broken jaw knocked him out of commission. The following season, he was worth 53 goals and 148 points. Rick Jeanneret's calls of "La, La, La, LaFontaine" filled the airwaves of western New York and southern Ontario. LaFontaine was named to the Second All-Star Team.

Knee surgery knocked LaFontaine out of all but 38 games over the following two seasons before he fought back with a 91-point effort in 1995–96. Just when he was getting back on track, injury came a-calling once again. This one would ultimately end his career. In a game against the Pittsburgh Penguins early in the 1996–97 season, he sustained a severe concussion in a collision with defender Francois Leroux. LaFontaine tried to come back but was having problems with his memory. "Anyone who knows me knows my first priority in life isn't hockey but being a father to my three children and a good husband to my wife," he said. "I would never do anything to jeopardize that." In a move to unload their breakable star, Buffalo dealt LaFontaine to the New York Rangers for a second-round draft pick. He played only one year on Broadway before calling it a career.

Peak Years   *1989–93*
In a Word   *SUPERB*

JOHN LeCLAIR (Marmaduke)   Left Wing
6'3"   225
b. 7/5/1969, St. Albans, Vermont

Big John LeClair, the first Vermonter ever to play in the NHL, did not follow the typical route to his dream. He was cut from his high school hockey team each year until his senior year when, having finally made it, he proceeded to average nearly four points a game. From there, it was on to the University of Vermont, where he played four years.

The Montreal Canadiens, who drafted him in the second round of the 1987 NHL Entry Draft, were made to wait until he closed out his collegiate career before they could get their hands on him. He appeared in 10 games for the Canadiens in 1990–91 and would spend the next three years teasing Montreal fans with flashes of brilliance, including two overtime winners in the 1993 Stanley Cup finals. LeClair has speed, size, strength, and a wicked shot, but he couldn't put it together for the Canadiens.

Frustrated, the Canadiens sent their lumbering winger with Eric Desjardins and Gilbert Dionne to the Philadelphia Flyers for Mark Recchi and considerations. It is a deal Montreal would live to regret. As a member of the Flyers, LeClair blossomed into the total package, a player Pittsburgh sportswriter Dave Molinari termed "the prototype NHL forward." Teamed with Eric Lindros and Mikael Renberg on the "Legion of Doom" line, LeClair scored 25 goals in his first 37 games in the City of Brotherly Love.

LeClair broke the 50-goal mark in each of his next three seasons and will no doubt score many more before hanging up his huge skates.

Peak Years   *1996–99*
In a Word   *REDWOOD*

BRIAN LEETCH Defense
5'11" 190
b. 3/3/1968, Corpus Christi, Texas

You wouldn't think the town of Corpus Christi, Texas, would produce an all-world NHL defenseman. Somehow, it did. Brian Leetch played one season with the Boston College Golden Eagles, followed by a year with the United States National Team and the 1988 U.S. Olympic Team. The New York Rangers had selected Leetch with the ninth overall pick in the 1986 Entry Draft. He made the jump to the NHL for 17 games in 1987–88. The early reviews were positive. Leetch could skate circles around most of his opponents, set up the brilliant play, and put the puck in the net. He was just the kind of talent the Rangers were looking for.

Leetch scored 23 goals and 71 points in 1988–89, and was handed the Calder Trophy as the NHL's top rookie.

After an off-year in 1989–90, Leetch rebounded for 16 goals and 88 points the following season. In 1991–92, Leetch won the Norris Trophy and became the first defender in Rangers history to rack up 100 points in a season. He was injured for much of 1992–93, but would bounce back the following year. In the 1994 playoffs, he led all scorers with 34 points and scooped the Conn Smythe Trophy as his Rangers won their first Stanley Cup championship in over 50 years.

Over the next few seasons, Leetch averaged nearly a point a game. In 1997, he took his second Norris. In 1997–98, both he and the Rangers struggled. Leetch had the crummiest season of his brilliant career, finishing with a horrid plus/minus of –36. In 1998–99, he showed himself much better, with 55 points.

Peak Years   *1993–97*
In a Word   *IMPACT*

MARIO LEMIEUX (Super Mario/Le Magnifique) Center
6'4" 210
b. 10/5/1965, Montreal, Quebec

Mario Lemieux was Pittsburgh's hockey savior, and was the only real threat to Wayne Gretzky as the league's best player since the mid-1980s. Lemieux wasn't just another scoring star, however. He was colossal. He was unlike anyone before him.

Mario Lemieux

Lemieux's fantastic voyage began in the Quebec town of Laval, where he spent three years sharpening his hockey skills. The 1983–84 campaign was one to remember for Lemieux, who shattered all Quebec League scoring records with 133 goals and 282 points in 70 games. His final regular-season game with Laval yielded him six goals and five assists. He was unquestionably the pick of the litter in the 1984 NHL Entry Draft.

Every team angled to get their hands on him. The Montreal Canadiens struck a deal with the Hartford Whalers to get their first-round pick, but because Hartford ended up not in last place, the Canadiens would not get their man (they still did okay, surprising the hockey world by selecting defenseman Petr Svoboda). The Quebec Nordiques offered all three Stastny brothers, while the Minnesota North Stars offered all 12 of their draft picks. However attractive these offers were, Pittsburgh stood firm and drafted Lemieux.

Lemieux scored a goal on his first shift in the NHL in 1984–85 after stripping Boston Bruins defender Ray Bourque of the puck. Lemieux added 42 more in his rookie season, finishing with 100 points and the Calder Trophy under his arm. He posted years of 141 and 107 points in the next two seasons — solid numbers, but not earth-shattering.

Before the 1986–87 campaign, Lemieux was part of Canada's Canada Cup team. The final matched Team Canada against the Russians. The series came down to a third game. With the score tied, Lemieux took a pass from Wayne Gretzky and beat goalie Sergei Mylnikov for the winner. Lemieux silenced his critics in 1987–88 when he scored 70 goals and 168 points. He had become the first player since 1979–80, other than Gretzky, to top the NHL scoring race. Lemieux also took the Hart Trophy, another Gretzky-only award since 1979–80. Lemieux followed up with 85 goals and 199 points in 1988–89. Penguin coach Eddie Johnston said, "Not taking anything away from Gretzky but if Mario hadn't been sick, he could have averaged 200 points a season."

Sadly, the man they called "Super Mario" was unable to remain healthy. In 1990, it was a herniated disc in his back. He managed a remarkable 123 points in 1989–90 despite missing 21 games. In July 1990, he underwent surgery and developed an infection in his back. The infection forced him to sit out the first 50 games of the 1990–91 season. Fully rested from a short season, he exploded in the playoffs for 44 points. He was named playoff MVP as the Penguins grabbed their first ever Stanley Cup championship. In 1991–92, nagging injuries cost Lemieux 16 games. Despite sustaining shoulder and hand injuries, he managed to nab his third scoring title and lead Pittsburgh to its second straight Cup.

The 1992–93 season was Lemieux's most trying. In January 1993, with the big man cruising to his fourth Art Ross Trophy, he was diagnosed with Hodgkin's Disease, a form of cancer. Many wondered whether or not Lemieux would ever play again. Fortunately, he did. Despite missing 20 games recuperating, he returned and roared past Pat LaFontaine to grab the scoring title, and of course he won the Hart Trophy. The playoffs, however, were a different story. The Penguins, who were heavily favored to win their third Cup in a row, met the New York Islanders in the second round. The underdog Isles extended the series to a seventh game and put Pittsburgh away on a goal by Dave Volek.

Lemieux played only 22 games in 1993–94 and missed the entire 1994–95 season with chronic back pain and follow-up cancer treatment. He returned with a vengeance in 1995–96, scoring 69 goals and 161 points for his fifth scoring crown. The following season was no different. His 122 points paced the rest of the league. Lemieux, who announced that the 1996–97 campaign would be his last, beat Philadelphia Flyers' goalie Garth Snow on a breakaway in his last game.

The final tally for Lemieux: 745 games, 613 goals, 881 assists, 1,494 points. Mike Gartner, a 700-goal scorer in the NHL, remarked: "If Mario had been healthy his whole career, he might have scored 1,000 goals." Indeed, if Lemieux had been healthy throughout his 12-year career, the history books might've looked a lot different.

Lemieux was inducted into the Hockey Hall of Fame in 1997. The standard induction waiting period was waived, of course.

Peak Years   *1991–95*
In a Word   *MEGA-TALENT*

NICKLAS LIDSTROM (Saint Nick) Defense
6'2"   185
b. 4/28/1970, Vasteras, Sweden

In the 1989 NHL Entry Draft, Neil Smith, director of Detroit Red Wings scouting, practically had to beg GM Jimmy Devellano to select defenseman Nicklas Lidstrom. The Wings are no doubt glad Smith was so persuasive. He later claimed, "If we would have waited another year, he would have gained a lot more exposure."

Lidstrom is what Wing skipper Scotty Bowman refers to as a low-maintenance player. Simply put, you don't notice Lidstrom until he's won a game for you. He is not as noticeable as, say, Brian Leetch, as he doesn't play that dazzling end-to-end game. Nonetheless, most GMs in the NHL would probably take Lidstrom's solid, dependable, all-around game over Leetch's breathtaking rushes.

That's not to say Lidstrom has been a dud on offense. Point totals of 67, 57, 59, and 57 from 1995–96 through 1998–99 tell of a defenseman with more than enough skill to make it in the NHL.

Lidstrom joined Detroit for the 1991–92 campaign and was an almost immediate hit in the Motor City. Altogether, he and fellow 1989 draftees Sergei Fedorov and Vladimir Konstantinov ushered in an exciting era of youth and vitality in Detroit.

In eight years, Lidstrom has been the model of consistency. Detroit can count on him to play it solid at both ends of the rink. His consistency has made him a fan favorite. Darren McCarthy, his Red Wing teammate, once remarked, "[Lidstrom] always seemed to be the forgotten guy." Indeed, his lack of flash probably cost him the 1998 Norris Trophy, which went to the Los Angeles Kings Rob Blake.

Lidstrom continued to play quietly and efficiently in 1998–99 as Detroit unsuccessfully went after its third straight Stanley Cup.

Peak Years   *1996–99*
In a Word   *DEFENDER*

ERIC LINDROS (The Big E/Eric the Great) Center
6'4"   235
b. 2/28/1973, London, Ontario

Eric Lindros

The weight of expectations put on the shoulders of young Eric Lindros would've caused a lesser man to crack. Not Lindros. The big kid reached superstardom in the NHL, using his gargantuan size, deadly shot, and ability to deliver glass-shattering hits.

After a stint with the Junior B St. Michael's Buzzers, Lindros dominated the OHL as a member of the Oshawa Generals. Coming into the 1991 NHL Entry Draft, he was the overwhelming favorite to go first overall. One teensy problem: the first selection was owned by the Quebec Nordiques, the one NHL club Lindros refused to play for. The Nordiques called the big center's bluff and drafted him nonetheless. They spent the following season listening to Lindros tell them over and over again that he wouldn't change his mind. At long last, Quebec decided to trade their brooding star. Nordiques president Marcel Aubut traded Lindros to the Philadelphia Flyers before cutting a separate deal with the New York Rangers. It took an arbitrator to decide that "The Big E" was going to Philadelphia.

Lindros followed up a 41-goal rookie season with 44 goals and 97 points in 1993–94. He won the Hart Trophy in a lockout-shortened 1994–95 season and would post 47 goals and a career-best 115 points the following season on a line with Montreal import John LeClair. In 1997, Lindros and his Flyers made it to the Stanley Cup finals only to lose out to the Detroit Red Wings. The following season was a season of injuries for Lindros.

Expectations for Lindros and the Flyers were high once again for 1998–99 after the acquisition of John Vanbiesbrouck put a theoretical end to their past goaltending woes. Philadelphia rolled through the early part of the season before going into a funk. Late in the schedule, Lindros suffered a collapsed lung. The Flyers lost to the Maple Leafs in the first round of the 1999 playoffs without Lindros.

The big bruiser has suffered through a numbers of injuries. The player Flyers' GM Bob Clarke once referred to as an "apartment building" has had shaky foundations. Perhaps the new millennium will be kinder to Lindros.

Peak Years   *1998–99*
In a Word   *BRUTE*

AL MacINNIS (Chopper) Defense
6'2" 195
b. 7/11/1963, Inverness, Nova Scotia

At first, Al MacInnis was nothing more than "The Shot." You know the one — 100 mph-plus. MacInnis had goalies quaking in their boots, had shot-blockers cringing. Former keeper Mike Liut once confessed that "when MacInnis shot, I closed my eyes and prayed [the puck] didn't hit me." MacInnis, a perennial Norris Trophy candidate, began his career as a power-play specialist. He honed his shot during countless hours of blasting pucks against a barn door in his hometown of Inverness.

MacInnis was drafted 15th overall by the Calgary Flames in the 1981 Entry Draft. With his Junior eligibility running low, he split the 1983–84 season between the Flames and the CHL Colorado Flames. While he had a mighty shot, he lacked all-around skill. Even in his first few years as a Flame, he was a defensive liability. Not until 1986–87 was the big defender recognized as one of the league's best. His defensive game, although still not great, was steadily improving. His offensive production, meanwhile, was going through the roof.

MacInnis made a name for himself in the 1989 Stanley Cup playoffs, scoring seven goals and adding 31 points and winning the Conn Smythe Trophy as the Flames won it all. In 1990–91, he scored 28 times and added 75 assists to become the first Flame blue-liner to record 100 points in a single season.

In July 1994, MacInnis was traded to the St. Louis Blues, where he and sniper Brett Hull teamed up to give opposing goalies nightmares. Age was creeping up on MacInnis, though, and his production dipped with each passing season in St. Louis. He turned it around in 1998–99, when he led NHL defensemen in scoring and took home his first Norris Trophy.

Peak Years   *1988–92*
In a Word   *BLASTER*

MARK MESSIER (Moose) Center/Left Wing
6'1" 205
b. 1/18/1961, Edmonton, Alberta

Mark Messier and Wayne Gretzky have been linked throughout their respective careers. They won four Stanley Cups together with the Edmonton Oilers, and were reunited as New York Rangers. But only when this duo was split up did Messier receive the recognition he so richly deserved.

Messier's only Junior hockey experience was seven playoff games with the WHL

Portland Winter Hawks in 1977–78. Soon thereafter, he signed up for a 10-game tryout with Indianapolis. The Racers folded before Messier's 10 games were up. He was subsequently picked up by the Cincinnati Stingers, for whom he scored all of one goal and 11 points in 47 games.

The young moose went to the Edmonton Oilers 48th overall in the 1979 NHL Entry Draft. In Edmonton, Messier hooked up with Gretzky once again. While the boy wonder was battling Los Angeles Kings' star Marcel Dionne for the scoring title, Messier was on his way to a 33-point season. He erupted in 1981–82 for 50 goals. He was quickly establishing himself as one of the NHL's most dominant all-around talents, combining a natural touch around the net with a rough and rumbling style. He became the unquestioned leader of the Oilers, the king of the clubhouse. Glen Sather admitted: "Wayne had a huge influence on this team. But he wasn't the one to stand up in the dressing room and get everyone going. Mark was the one who did that."

Messier was named playoff MVP in 1984 as Edmonton captured its first ever Stanley Cup. Injuries knocked him out of the lineup for stretches of the next couple of seasons and his production suffered. He bounced back with seasons of 107 and 111 points as Edmonton won their third and fourth Cups. After the 1987–88 season, Gretzky was traded to Los Angeles, leaving Messier to guide the Good Ship Oiler on his own. In 1989–90, he scored 45 goals and 129 points en route to leading Edmonton to another Cup. In October 1991, he was sent to the New York Rangers for Bernie Nicholls, Steven Rice, and Louie DeBrusk. He became the second ever player (after Gretzky) to win Hart trophies with two different clubs with a 107-point performance in 1991–92. Overall, New York was a better team because of him. In 1994, for the first time in 54 years, the Rangers won the Stanley Cup.

After six seasons in the Ranger blue, Messier became an unrestricted free agent. Although most people figured he would re-sign with New York, he inked a deal with the Vancouver Canucks. From the get-go, there was a lot of pressure put on the aging star to bail out the sinking Canucks. Unfortunately, he was unable to turn it around in Vancouver. He struggled through nagging injuries in 1997–98 to post one of the lousiest seasons of his professional career. He bounced back somewhat the following year, but the Canucks drifted deeper into oblivion.

Messier's stint in Vancouver notwithstanding, Messier has shown himself to be one of the game's truly great leaders. He has been an all-around star, a man with as much ability in the passing and shooting part of the game as in the crash-and-bash aspects. In 20 years of NHL service, Moose has been worth over 600 goals and 1,000 assists. He is a shoo-in for the Hockey Hall of Fame.

Peak Years   *1986–90*
In a Word   *POWERHOUSE*

CAM NEELY   Right Wing
6'1"   215
b. 6/6/1965, Comox, British Columbia

What might have been? People will forever ask that question about Cam Neely. What if cheap-shot artist Ulf Samuelsson hadn't knee-checked Neely on the thigh in the 1991 conference finals? Surely, the robust winger would have scored 500 goals instead of the 395 he ended up with.

Neely was drafted by the Vancouver Canucks in the first round of the 1983 NHL Entry Draft. He put in three seasons with the Canucks before team brass, who decided he wasn't developing quickly enough, traded him and a first-round pick (who became standout defenseman Glen Wesley) to the Boston Bruins in exchange for Barry

Pederson. Neely flourished in Beantown, netting 36 goals in his first season and 42 a year later. Was he just another scorer? Nope. Neely was the very definition of a power winger. Although not the fastest man on skates, he was one of the most powerful men in the league. Standing over six feet tall and weighing almost 220 pounds, he was a huge physical presence on the ice, especially in front of the net. In the slot, Neely was immovable. Defenders soon learned that trying to clear him from the crease was an exercise in futility. In 1989–90, the big man logged his first 50-goal season, finishing with 55. He followed up in 1990–91 with 51 more. Then came the Samuelsson incident in the playoffs. Neely played only 22 games over two years following the hit.

Neely followed a rigorous training program and returned with a vengeance in 1993–94. Despite being unable to play more than 49 games, the big brute scored 50 goals. For his efforts, he took Second All-Star Team honors and the Bill Masterton Trophy. But over the next two seasons, he appeared in only 91 games. After the 1995–96 campaign, Boston's feared sniper announced his retirement.

Perhaps Don Cherry is right. Perhaps fighting should not only be tolerated but actually pushed as a way of keeping cheap-shot artists like Ulf Samuelsson in check. What better way to deter these cowardly tactics?

In 726 games in the NHL, Neely scored almost 400 goals. The possibility of his ever making the Hockey Hall of Fame has been somewhat hamstrung. Keep your fingers crossed.

Peak Years   *1988–92*
In a Word   *CURSED*

ADAM OATES   Center
5'11" 185
b. 8/27/1962, Weston, Ontario

"I know that Adam is an unbelievable play-maker. He does a lot of things extremely well. He plays good defensive hockey and he's great on face-offs." These are the words of former Boston Bruins' star Cam Neely on Adam Oates. Neely's quote sheds light on a part of Oates' game that so many people overlook. Many people see him as a passer, an offensive player. In truth, he is so much more.

From the campus of Rensselaer Polytechnic Institute in Rhode Island, Oates was signed by the Detroit Red Wings in a collegiate bonanza in June 1985. It took the muscular center a few years to adapt to the NHL game, but by 1988–89 he was one of the NHL's top passers with 62 assists. At the end of that season, he was sent to the St. Louis Blues with Paul MacLean for Bernie Federko and Tony McKegney. The Red Wings probably wished they'd never made that deal.

In St. Louis, Oates was paired with Brett Hull. Together, the two players flourished. With the son of Bobby Hull on his right side, Oates posted assist totals of 79 and 90. Midway through his third season in St. Louis, he was shipped to the Boston Bruins for Craig Janney and Stephane Quintal. Hull for one was not happy with the move and went as far as calling Oates "the NHL's best passer this side of Wayne Gretzky. I'm nothing without him."

In Boston, Oates was counted on to take on a big chunk of the scoring load. While as a Blue there were Hull and Brendan Shanahan to help him shoulder the offense, Boston had just lost Cam Neely to injury and was in great need of a blue-chip producer. In Oates' first full season as a Bruin, he scored 45 goals and 142 points. With Neely's return the following season, Oates racked up another 80 helpers. He had quietly become one of the NHL's most consistently prolific play-makers. He was the only player to finish in the top 10 in scoring every season between 1989–90 and 1994–95.

In March 1997, Oates was traded to the Washington Capitals. With his help, the Capitals made it all the way to the Stanley Cup finals in 1998.

Peak Years   *1990–1994*
In a Word   *ASSISTANT*

PATRICK ROY (St. Patrick) Goal
6'0"   192
b. 10/5/1965, Quebec City, Quebec

Patrick Roy

Some have argued that Patrick Roy did for Quebec goaltending what Mario Lemieux did for Quebec skaters, that he inspired a generation of imitators. Look at the goalies in and around the NHL today: Martin Brodeur, Felix Potvin, Roberto Luongo — all inspired by Roy and his butterfly style.

Looking at Roy's statistics with the Granby Bisons, one has to wonder how he became so great. Goals-against averages of 6.26, 4.44, and 5.55 don't exactly send scouts rushing off to phone their general managers. But he achieved these numbers in Quebec's Junior league, a league in which Vladimir Ruzicka could win the Selke Trophy. The Montreal Canadiens must have seen something in Roy when they took him 51st overall in the 1984 NHL Entry Draft. It stands as one of the few brilliant moves the organization has made since the crazy Cup days of the late 1970s.

Roy was handed the starting job for the 1985–86 season and acquitted himself well. Despite being in poor physical condition ("He probably couldn't do one pushup," joked a team official) he amazed in the playoffs. Unfazed by the razzing of opposition crowds, the skinny kid from Quebec City led the Canadiens to their 23rd Stanley Cup championship. He won the Conn Smythe Trophy for his brilliance.

Roy's legend grew. He won Vezinas in 1989, 1990, and again in 1992. Between the first and last of these trophies, he ran up a cumulative record of 125-58-25. In 1988–89, he backstopped the Canadiens to another appearance in the Cup finals. This time, however, the Calgary Flames prevailed. No matter. Coming into the 1990s, he was the best goaltender in the world.

In 1992–93, Roy had one of his worst regular seasons. Against the Quebec Nordiques in the first round of the playoffs, many wrote him and the Canadiens off. This is when he stepped it up, played at the highest level of his career. Montreal captured their 24th Cup, thanks largely to his genius between the pipes. In 20 playoff games, he went 16-4 with a 2.13 GAA and a sparkling .929 save percentage.

Only two and a half years after that latest championship, Roy was unceremoniously shipped out of Montreal. Humiliated in front of a national TV audience in a rout at the hands of the Detroit Red Wings, he demanded to be traded. After about a week, the Canadiens dealt their beloved keeper to the Colorado Avalanche. Bolstered by the addition of the era's top playoff goalie, Colorado went on to win the Stanley Cup, Roy's third. His solid play has continued through the end of the decade. He now has over 400 career wins.

Kevin Allen of *USA Today* may have put it best when he said: "Roy is a cocky, arrogant athlete who somehow manages not to offend either his friends or his foes. He's the Muhammad Ali of hockey."

Patrick Roy is a lock for the Hockey Hall of Fame.

Peak Years   *1989–93*
In a Word   *MIRACLE*

JOE SAKIC   Center
5'11" 185
b. 7/7/1969, Burnaby, British Columbia

The Quebec Nordiques had two draft picks in the first round of the 1987 NHL Entry
Draft. With their first pick, they snapped up hotshot Junior defenseman Bryan Fogarty.
Six picks later, they took Joe Sakic, a boy with all the makings of a superstar. The fol-
lowing year, Sakic was the Canadian Major Junior Player of the Year. And Fogarty? His
NHL career lasted 156 games.

Sakic joined the Nordiques in 1988–89 as the team was beginning a steep drop to
the NHL basement. He was worth 62 points in his rookie season. His production
jumped 40 points the following season as the Nordiques finished a year-long free fall
with 31 measly points. As the club grabbed future stars in the draft (Mats Sundin,
Owen Nolan), Sakic's production began to rise. Sakic was the lone star on a bad team, a
100-point man with several All-Star appearances to his credit.

By 1992–93, Quebec had become a solid squad and bona fide playoff contender.
Sakic, with 105 points, was second on the team in scoring behind Sundin's 114. But
Quebec could not get by Patrick Roy and the Canadiens in the post-season. Sakic's pro-
duction remained stable in 1993–94, though Quebec missed the playoffs. In a lockout-
shortened 1994–95 season, his 62 points were good enough for fourth place in the
NHL scoring race. The Nordiques seemed ready for a long playoff run but were done in
by weak goaltending and some questionable calls in their first round series against the
New York Rangers.

In 1995–96, Sakic, who moved with the Nordiques to Colorado, scored 51 goals
and a career-best 120 points. He won the Conn Smythe Trophy as the Avalanche won
the Stanley Cup in their first year in the Rockies.

After the 1996–97 season, Sakic became a restricted free agent and was immediately inked by the Rangers to a three-year $21-million pact. Colorado immediately (and
wisely) matched the offer. Club GM Pierre Lacroix would later comment, "I knew five
seconds after the Rangers signed Joe [that] we would find a way, some way, to match
[the offer]. There never was any doubt with him." Sakic remains one of the NHL's elite
performers.

Peak Years   1993–97
In a Word   PERFORMER

TEEMU SELANNE (The Finnish Flash) Right Wing
6'0" 200
b. 7/3/1970, Helsinki, Finland

Teemu Selanne played five years in his native Finland before coming over to the NHL
in 1992. Many NHL coaches are now wishing that he had just stayed there. When
asked how to stop him, Edmonton Oilers' assistant Bob McCammon ventured, "You
hijack Anaheim's plane or just kidnap Teemu when he's scheduled to play your team."
Calgary Flames head coach Brian Sutter offered, "You can never shut him down completely. He's just too good."

Selanne was drafted 10th overall by the Winnipeg Jets in the 1988 NHL Entry
Draft. He spent the next four years tearing up the Finnish leagues before hopping
aboard the Jets. Selanne didn't need an adjustment period. The Finnish Flash exploded
onto the hockey scene. He annihilated Mike Bossy's rookie goal-scoring record of 53 by
23 goals! On the strength of such a remarkable rookie season, Selanne took home the
Calder Trophy and First-Team All-Star honors.

During his sophomore season, Selanne suffered a career-threatening injury to his Achilles' tendon. Many wondered if he would ever completely recover his blazing speed. In 1994–95 he scored only 22 goals in 45 games, and the quality of his play was in question. In February 1996, he was traded to the Anaheim Mighty Ducks for Oleg Tverdovsky and Chad Kilger. Anaheim teamed Selanne with their boy wonder, Paul Kariya, which paid immediate dividends. The Finnish Flash, far from being damaged goods, finished the 1995–96 season with 40 goals and 108 points.

The Selanne magic returned in full force in 1996–97. Teamed with Kariya for the full year, Selanne counted 51 goals and 58 assists for 109 points. For the second time in his career, he was a First-Team All-Star and the Ducks advanced to the second round of the playoffs. Kariya played only 22 games in 1997–98 due to a holdout and injuries, so Selanne was forced to shoulder Anaheim's scoring load. His 52 goals topped all NHL scorers, but it wasn't enough to lift the Ducks into the post-season. In 1998–99, Selanne showed no signs of slowing down any time soon. He scored 47 goals and 107 points, and became the first winner of the Rocket Richard Trophy for the most goals in the regular season.

Selanne is no one-trick pony. His main weapon is his speed. "Selanne's speed is unbelievable. He's as dangerous a player as there is in the NHL," remarked Philadelphia Flyers GM Bob Clarke. But Selanne is also as strong as a bull and isn't afraid to throw every last one of his 200 pounds around. For a sniper, he passes the puck remarkably well. He should be a star in the NHL well into the next decade.

Peak Years   *1996–99*
In a Word   *TURBO*

BRENDAN SHANAHAN Left Wing
6'3" 218
b. 1/23/1969, Mimico, Ontario

Did you know that Brendan Shanahan was the backup goalkeeper for Ireland in the 1994 World Cup of Soccer? And that he made his movie debut in *Forrest Gump*? Or that he was a ball-boy in the 1994 U.S. Open of tennis? Well, if you believe what "Shanny" puts on his media guide surveys . . .

Shanahan opened his career with the New Jersey Devils in 1987–88 after being taken second overall in the 1987 NHL Entry Draft. Only 18, he had trouble adjusting to the pace of the professional game. Fortunately, he showed enough potential to remain with the Devils all year. Young Shanahan was a rugged 30-goal scorer by 1990, but he hadn't yet hit his peak. Blessed with size, scoring touch, and razor-sharp elbows, the Mimico, Ontario, native was one of New Jersey's go-to guys. Unfortunately, the swamps of the Garden State wouldn't be home to big Shanahan for much longer. Prior to the 1991–92 campaign, Shanahan signed with the St. Louis Blues, who were forced to part with Scott Stevens as compensation.

Although Shanahan was good for 33 goals in his first season as a Blue, many felt that someone who cost them Scott Stevens ought to score more. The big winger would, eventually. In 1992–93, Shanahan lit up the lamp 51 times and 52 more times the following season, when he was named to the First All-Star Team. Within a year, he was on the move again. This time, it was off to Hartford in exchange for young blue-liner Chris Pronger. Shanahan tallied 44 goals for the Whalers in 1995–96 and St. Louis fans screamed bloody murder. But Hartford hardly got to know Shanahan before he was gone. Not really one to complain, he simply wanted to be on a winner.

In October 1996, he was sent to the Detroit Red Wings for Paul Coffey, Keith Primeau, and a first-round pick. Although many thought this to have been a steep price, few today will argue that the Wings didn't get bang for their buck in Shanahan. Detroit, perpetually lacking in toughness on the wings and leadership in the club-house, was a different team with Shanny aboard. No longer would star Wings get pushed around. Shanahan scored 46 times in 1996–97 and was instrumental in Detroit's successful first Stanley Cup win since 1955. In 1997–98, Shanahan's goal total dropped off, but he was a big factor in a second straight Cup championship in the Motor City.

Peak Years   1993–97
In a Word   HARDY

SCOTT STEVENS   Defense
6'2"   215
b. 4/1/1964, Kitchener, Ontario

Scott Stevens is an opposing forward's worst nightmare. Just when you thought it was safe to cross the blue-line you see the trainer coming at you with smelling salts. Stevens is one of hockey's most punishing hitters. In the words of sportswriter Jeff Gordon, "Stevens strives to physically eliminate his man. Every forward in the league fears his hip-check."

Stevens has been a perennial Norris Trophy runner-up. Ever since stepping onto Capital Center ice in 1982 by way of the Kitchener Rangers, Stevens has been one of hockey's top all-around defenders. Not only is he exceptional in his own end, clearing the slot and hanging up forwards to dry, he can score, too. He's put up point totals of 78, 72, 68, and 65 points. Somehow, his all-around game has been ignored by Norris Trophy voters, who seem more in tune with the one-way stylings of Brian Leetch and Paul Coffey. He led the New Jersey Devils to the Stanley Cup in 1995.

Stevens is a huge presence on the ice and never backs down from the game's rougher side. He hits as well as any defender in the NHL (just ask Eric Lindros) without sacrificing his sound defensive positioning.

In a perfect world, Stevens would have won at least one Norris Trophy by now. Instead, he'll have to content himself with dreams of making the Hockey Hall of Fame after he hangs up his blades. Besides, who needs the Norris when you've got a Stanley Cup ring on your finger?

Peak Years   1990–1994
In a Word   CONCRETE

STEVE YZERMAN (Stevie Y) Center
5'11"   185
b. 5/9/1965, Cranbrook, British Columbia

Few players are as universally appreciated as Steve Yzerman. From his NHL debut in 1983, he has proven to be an exceptional offensive force, the most brilliant of Detroit's Red Wings. He came into his own in 1987–88, scoring 102 points before a bad knee cut his season short.

The boy they call "Stevie Y" put it all together the following year, scoring 65 goals and 155 points while improving his defensive game. This was the second of six straight 100-point campaigns for the Cranbrook, British Columbia, native. Despite losing 26 games with a herniated disc in his neck in 1993–94, Yzerman still managed to put up 82 points.

Thanks to the presence of other more flashy players in the NHL, Yzerman never made a post-season All-Star Team. The bigger knock, though, was in his inability to steer Detroit to a Stanley Cup championship. In the early to mid-1990s, the Wings were perennial post-season chokers, an army without a mission. The Red Wings answered their critics by winning the Cup in 1997. Suddenly, the man the armchair GMs loved to ride was lifted up as one of the game's elite performers. Funny how opinions change.

The Red Wings didn't have the greatest time in the 1997–98 regular-season. But all too often, noted skipper Scotty Bowman, teams wore themselves out in the regular-season only to fade away in the playoffs. Not the Wings. Not this year. Yzerman stepped up his game in the second season to lead his boys to their second straight Cup. For all his extra efforts, 24 points and a sea of perspiration, he was handed the Conn Smythe Trophy.

Yzerman takes us back to the old days, when hockey players worked hard for their money and even harder for the chance to touch the Stanley Cup. He is one of that rare breed of skills players who can leave defensemen sucking dust, make the perfect shot, orchestrate elaborate scoring plays, and hold off would-be goal-scorers. He is the finest hockey talent to play in the Motor City since the days of Gordie Howe, Alex Delvecchio, and Norm Ullman. Yzerman is a shoo-in for the Hockey Hall of Fame.

Peak Years   *1989–93*
In a Word   *LONG-SUFFERING*

The All-Stars

Pos	Player	Season	GP	G	A	PTS
D	Ray Bourque	1990–91	76	21	73	94
D	Chris Chelios	1992–93	84	15	58	73
LW	John LeClair	1997–98	82	51	36	87
C	Mario Lemieux	1992–93	60	69	91	160
RW	Jaromir Jagr	1995–96	82	62	87	149
			GP	**GAA**	**ShO**	
G	Patrick Roy	1991–92	67	2.36	5	

Appendix
I

THE STANLEY CUP: A RETROSPECTIVE

1893

Montreal AAA.

The Winged Wheelers are awarded the Cup by virtue of winning the regular-season championship of the Amateur Hockey Association of Canada.

1894

Montreal AAA defeat Montreal Victorias (3–2) and Ottawa Capitals (3–1)

AAA forward Billy Barlow notches the first goal in Stanley Cup history.

1895

Montreal Victorias, as AHAC league champs, take possession of the Cup after the AAA defeat Queen's University to keep the Cup in the AHAC's hands.

1896 (February)

Winnipeg Victorias defeat Montreal Victorias (2–0)

For the first time, the Cup leaves Montreal. Winnipeg netminder Whitey Merritt is the first in Stanley Cup history to don pads.

1896 (December)

Montreal Victorias defeat Winnipeg Victorias (6–5)

Montreal's Vics reclaim Lord Stanley's mug. Little Ernie McLea scores the first hat trick in Stanley Cup history for the victors.

1897

Montreal Victorias defeat Ottawa Capitals (15–2)

Montreal so thoroughly dominates the Central Canada Hockey Association champs that the scheduled second game is not played.

1898

Montreal Victorias

The champs were so dominant that no challengers came forward during the 1897–98 campaign.

1899 (February)

Montreal Victorias defeat Winnipeg Victorias (2–1, 3–2)

When referee Findlay doesn't expel Bob McDougall after the latter severely injures Winnipeg star Tony Gingras in game two, the Prairie Boys refuse to continue.

1899 (March)

Montreal Shamrocks defeat Queen's University (6–2)

The Shamrocks win the Canadian Amateur Hockey League championship, finally wresting the Cup from the Vics. Future barrister Flip Trihey's hat trick helps sink the helpless Golden Gaels.

1900

Montreal Shamrocks defeat Winnipeg Victorias (4–3, 2–3, 5–4) and Halifax Crescents (10–2, 11–0)

Led by Flip Trihey's seven goals, the Shamrocks defeat Winnipeg in a series played during the regular season. The Maritimers were destroyed a fortnight later.

1901

Winnipeg Victorias defeat Montreal Shamrocks (4–3, 2–1)

Dan Bain's overtime winner in game two returns the Cup to Manitoba for the first time since 1896.

1902 (January)

Winnipeg Victorias defeat Toronto Wellingtons (5–3, 5–3)

The Hogtowners are no match for the Flett brothers and Tony Gingras, who lead the Prairie Boys to a successful Cup defense.

1902 (March)

Montreal AAA defeat Winnipeg Victorias (0–1, 5–0, 2–1)

Challenging for the Cup for the first time in eight years, the "Little Men of Iron" silence the huge Winnipeg crowd with a gritty three-game victory.

1903 (February)

Montreal AAA defeat Winnipeg Victorias (8–1, 2–2, 2–4, 5–1)

Winnipeg is no match for the sniping of Jack Marshall, who totals seven goals in four games.

1903 (March)

Ottawa Silver Seven defeat Montreal Victorias (9–1 total goals) and Rat Portage Thistles (6–2, 4–2)

Frank McGee knifes through the defenses of Montreal and Rat Portage for seven goals, leading the Silver Seven to their first Stanley Cup win and title defense, respectively.

1904

Ottawa Silver Seven defeat Winnipeg Rowing Club (9–1, 2–6, 2–0), Toronto Marlboros (6–3, 11–2), Montreal Wanderers (Wanderers refuse to continue after a 5–5 tie), and Brandon (6–3, 9–3)

Despite facing four challenges, the Silver Seven still manage to keep their mitts on the Cup. McGee contributes 21 goals in eight games, including two five-goal performances.

1905

Ottawa Silver Seven defeat Dawson City Nuggets (9–2, 23–2) and Rat Portage Thistles (3–9, 4–2, 5–4)

After throttling the Yukoners, the Silver Seven are humbled by Rat Portage, 9–3, in the first game of their challenge. However, as great teams often do, Ottawa bounces back to win the next two games and keep the Cup in the nation's capital.

1906 (February)

Ottawa Silver Seven defeat Queen's University (16–7, 12–7) and Smiths Falls (6–5, 8–2)
The Silver Seven continue to dominate, crushing Queen's University before humbling Smiths Falls, a town the Weir brothers once called home.

1906 (March)

Montreal Wanderers defeat Ottawa Silver Seven (12–10 total goals). Also defeat New Glasgow (10–3, 7–2) prior to 1906–07 campaign
The Wanderers put an end to Ottawa's stranglehold on the Cup in a total-goals series that sees Ottawa bounce back from a 10–1 deficit to tie the series before finally succumbing.

1907 (January)

Kenora Thistles defeat Montreal Wanderers (4–2, 8–6)
Bolstered by the addition of Art Ross, the Thistles beat the star-laden Wanderers, thus becoming the smallest city, population-wise, ever to capture the Stanley Cup.

1907 (March)

Montreal Wanderers defeat Kenora Thistles (12–8 total goals)
The Wanderers waste little time in reclaiming the Cup from Kenora. Ernie Russell pots five goals in the two-game, total-goals series, to return the Cup to Mount Royal.

1908

Montreal Wanderers defeat Ottawa Victorias (9–3, 13–1), Winnipeg Maple Leafs (11–5, 9–3), and Toronto Professionals (6–4). Also defeat Edmonton Eskimos (13–10 total goals) prior to 1908–09 campaign
Emulating the 1904 performance of their staunch rivals, the Ottawa Silver Seven, the Wanderers accept four challenges and turn aside all comers.

1909

Ottawa Senators
As Eastern Canada Hockey Association champs, Ottawa takes over the Stanley Cup. A challenge from the Winnipeg Shamrocks' comes too late in the season, but during the 1909–10 season the Sens defend their title against Galt (12–3, 3–1) and Edmonton Eskimos (8–4, 13–7).

1910

Montreal Wanderers defeat Berlin Dutchmen (7–3)
Ernie Russell continues his big-game excellence, tallying four goals against the champions of the Ontario Professional league.

1911

Ottawa Senators defeat Galt (7–4) and Port Arthur (13–4)
After ransacking the NHA, the Senators have little trouble with their Cup challengers. Marty Walsh puts up a ten-spot in the rout of Port Arthur.

1912
Quebec Bulldogs defeat Moncton (9–3, 8–0)
Jack McDonald scores nine goals in Quebec's two-game dispatching of the Maritimers.

1913
Quebec Bulldogs defeat Sydney Millionaires (14–3, 6–2)
For the second straight year, a Maritime club travels west, only to have their head handed to them on a platter by Quebec's Bulldogs. Joe Malone pops nine goals in the opener.

1914
Toronto Blueshirts defeat Victoria Aristocrats (5–2, 6–5, 2–1)
Toronto finally can claim a Cup winner as the Blueshirts, led by the steady goalkeeping of Harry "Hap" Holmes, knock off the Pacific Coast Hockey Association champs.

1915
Vancouver Millionaires defeat Ottawa Senators (6–2, 8–3, 12–3)
The Left Coast takes home its first Cup as the Millionaires knock off the powerhouse Senators in three games. Cyclone Taylor scores six times in the three-game affair.

1916
Montreal Canadiens defeat Portland Rosebuds (0–2, 2–1, 6–3, 5–6, 2–1)
The beginning of the series is shrouded in controversy as Moose Johnson makes his return to Montreal. Once the series gets under way, Georges Vezina and Didier Pitre lead the Habs to their first-ever Stanley Cup.

1917
Seattle Metropolitans defeat Montreal Canadiens (4–8, 6–1, 4–1, 9–1)
After they beat the reigning Stanley Cup champs, the Metropolitans become the first American team to hoist Lord Stanley's mug.

1918
Toronto Arenas defeat Vancouver Millionaires (5–3, 4–6, 6–3, 1–8, 2–1)
Toronto becomes the first NHL team to capture the Cup.

1919
No Winner
The series features the Montreal Canadiens and Seattle Metropolitans, but is halted by an influenza epidemic that claims the life of Canadiens defenseman "Bad" Joe Hall.

1920
Ottawa Senators defeat Seattle Metropolitans (3–2, 3–0, 1–3, 2–5, 6–1)
For the first time in nine years, the Cup is claimed by Ottawa. The Senators overcome Frank Foyston's six goals, as goalie Clint Benedict stonewalls the rest of the Mets over the five-game series.

1921

Ottawa Senators defeat Vancouver Millionaires (1–3, 4–3, 3–2, 2–3, 2–1)
What a team! The Senators starters include Clint Benedict, Eddie Gerard, Buck Boucher, Sprague Cleghorn, Frank Nighbor, Jack Darragh, and Cy Denneny. Future Hall of Famer Punch Broadbent is a sub!

1922

Toronto St. Patricks defeat Vancouver Millionaires (3–4, 2–1, 0–3, 6–0, 5–1)
Down two games to one, the St. Pats fight back and blow the Millionaires out in the final two games of the series by a combined score of 11–1. Babe Dye had nine goals in the five-game series.

1923

Ottawa Senators first defeat the Vancouver Maroons (1–0, 1–4, 3–2, 5–1), then finish off the Edmonton Eskimos (2–1, 1–0)
After defeating the Habs in a bloody NHL final, the Senators travel west, bruised and battered, to face Vancouver and Edmonton. With his teammates out of fuel, Benedict does his imitation of a brick wall and leads the Sens to their third Cup in four years.

1924

Montreal Canadiens defeat the Vancouver Maroons (3–2, 2–1), then go on to beat the Calgary Tigers (6–1, 3–0)
Vezina flashes the form he had displayed in 1916, allowing the Habs to capture their second Stanley Cup.

1925

Victoria Cougars defeat Montreal Canadiens (5–2, 3–1, 2–4, 6–1)
The Cougars become the last non-NHL team to win the Stanley Cup.

1926

Montreal Maroons defeat Victoria Cougars (3–0, 3–0, 2–3, 2–0)
This series represents the last time a non-NHL team will play for the Stanley Cup. It is also Clint Benedict's fourth and final Cup triumph.

1927

Ottawa Senators defeat Boston Bruins (0–0, 3–1, 1–1, 3–1)
Ottawa's last Stanley Cup win. In game four, Boston defenseman Billy Coutu's attack on referee Jerry LaFlamme mars the series. Coutu gets a life suspension from the NHL.

1928

New York Rangers defeat Montreal Maroons (0–2, 2–1, 0–2, 1–0, 2–1)
The Rangers' winning goalie in game two is their manager–coach, the ageless Lester Patrick.

1929

Boston Bruins defeat New York Rangers (2–0, 2–1)
Tiny Thompson shuts down the Rangers' potent line of Frank Boucher and the Cook

brothers as the Bruins capture their first Stanley Cup. It's the first time both finalists are from the U.S.

1930

Montreal Canadiens defeat Boston Bruins (3–0, 4–3)
The Habs, who finished 26 points behind the Beantowners in the regular season, ride George Hainsworth's netminding to a mind-bending upset of the Bruins.

1931

Montreal Canadiens defeat Chicago Black Hawks (2–1, 1–2, 2–3, 4–2, 2–0)
Montreal comes back from a 2–1 series deficit to edge the Hawks for their second consecutive Stanley Cup. Johnny "Black Cat" Gagnon contributes four goals in the final.

1932

Toronto Maple Leafs defeat New York Rangers (6–4, 6–2, 6–4)
With scores resembling a tennis match, the Maple Leafs break the Habs' two-year Cup streak. Busher Jackson, goalless in the first two playoff series, scores five goals in the three-game final.

1933

New York Rangers defeat Toronto Maple Leafs (5–1, 3–1, 2–3, 1–0)
In a rematch of the 1932 final, the Rangers ride the faultless combination play of the Cook-Boucher-Cook line, Cecil Dillon's magnificent sniping, and Andy Aitkenhead's solid netminding to victory.

1934

Chicago Black Hawks defeat Detroit Red Wings (2–1, 4–1, 2–5, 1–0)
Hawks keeper Charlie Gardiner stands on his head, especially in game four, leading the Hawks to their first-ever Cup. Tragically, Gardiner will pass away a few months later.

1935

Montreal Maroons defeat Toronto Maple Leafs (3–2, 3–1, 4–1)
The Maroons waste little time in dispatching the favored Maple Leafs. Baldy Northcott leads all playoff scorers with four goals, counting twice against the Maple-Os.

1936

Detroit Red Wings defeat Toronto Maple Leafs (3–1, 9–4, 3–4, 3–2)
The Red Wings become the last of the Original Six franchises to win a Cup as they dispose of the Leafs in four games.

1937

Detroit Red Wings defeat New York Rangers (1–5, 4–2, 0–1, 1–0, 3–0)
The Motowners make it two straight.

1938

Chicago Black Hawks defeat Toronto Maple Leafs (3–1, 1–5, 2–1, 4–1)
Quite possibly the worst team to capture Lord Stanley's mug, the Hawks finish the

regular season with a record of 14-25-9. Somehow, they manage to knock off the Habs, Amerks, and Leafs to win the Cup.

1939
Boston Bruins defeat Toronto Maple Leafs (2–1, 2–3, 3–1, 2–0, 3–1)
The Leafs lose their fourth Cup final in five years in the first best-of-seven series. Calder and Vezina winner Frankie Brimsek stars in the Beantown cage.

1940
New York Rangers defeat Toronto Maple Leafs (2–1, 6–2, 1–2, 0–3, 2–1, 3–2)
With the series tied at two, the Rangers get OT winners from Muzz Patrick and Bryan Hextall to win their last Stanley Cup for more than 50 years.

1941
Boston Bruins defeat Detroit Red Wings (3–2, 2–1, 4–2, 3–1)
The Bruins' defeat of the Red Wings is the first four-game sweep in Stanley Cup history.

1942
Toronto Maple Leafs defeat Detroit Red Wings (2–3, 2–4, 2–5, 4–3, 9–3, 3–0, 3–1)
After losing six Cup finals in eight years during the 1930s, it looks as if Toronto will lose another one as the Red Wings take a 3–0 series lead. But the Leafs win the next four games, becoming the only team in Stanley Cup final history to come back from a 3–0 deficit.

1943
Detroit Red Wings defeat Boston Bruins (6–2, 4–3, 4–0, 2–0)
Johnny Mowers shuts out the Beantowners twice, while Mud Bruneteau and Don "The Count" Grosso each count hat tricks in the final, as the Wings win the Cup for the first time since 1937.

1944
Montreal Canadiens defeat Chicago Black Hawks (5–1, 3–1, 3–2, 5–4)
The only club not decimated by World War II, the Habs have no trouble knocking off the Hawks in four games. Rocket Richard scores five goals in the final and 12 in the playoffs.

1945
Toronto Maple Leafs defeat Detroit Red Wings (1–0, 2–0, 1–0, 3–5, 0–2, 0–1, 2–1)
Frank "Ulcers" McCool makes the 1945 playoffs his personal showcase, accumulating four shutouts and keeping his cool as the Leafs almost blow a 3–0 series lead, holding on for a 2–1 game seven victory to claim their second Cup of the decade.

1946
Montreal Canadiens defeat Boston Bruins (4–3, 3–2, 4–2, 2–3, 6–3)
The Punch Line is unstoppable throughout the playoffs, counting 41 points in nine games, leading the Habs past the Hawks and Bruins.

1947

Toronto Maple Leafs defeat Montreal Canadiens (0–6, 4–0, 4–2, 2–1, 1–3, 2–1)
A six-game triumph over the Habs gives the Leafs their first of three consecutive Stanley Cups. Turk Broda outduels Bill Durnan, proving to be the difference in the series.

1948

Toronto Maple Leafs defeat Detroit Red Wings (5–3, 4–2, 2–0, 7–2)
Toronto rolls over the Wings in what is supposed to be a close series. Syl Apps closes out his glorious career with a goal in game four, the last of his career.

1949

Toronto Maple Leafs defeat Detroit Red Wings (3–2, 3–1, 3–1, 3–1)
Another year. Another Cup. Another sweep of Detroit. The Leafs become the first NHL team to win three Stanley Cups in a row. Broda is phenomenal once again, allowing but five goals in the final.

1950

Detroit Red Wings defeat New York Rangers (4–1, 1–3, 4–0, 3–4, 1–2, 5–4, 4–3)
The Wings lose their young star Gordie Howe in the semifinals against Toronto, but they still have Pete Babando. Babando, who played only one year with the Wings, scored at 8:31 of the second overtime in game seven to give the Wings the Cup.

1951

Toronto Maple Leafs defeat Montreal Canadiens (3–2, 2–3, 2–1, 3–2, 3–2)
All five games go into overtime. Leafs defenseman Bill Barilko scored at 2:53 of overtime in Game Five to give the Leafs the Cup. He would pass away in a plane crash later that summer.

1952

Detroit Red Wings defeat Montreal Canadiens (3–1, 2–1, 3–0, 3–0)
The Red Wings were at their most dominant, sweeping the playoffs in eight games. Terry Sawchuk surrendered a mere five goals in eight playoff games, posting four shutouts.

1953

Montreal Canadiens defeat Boston Bruins (4–2, 1–4, 3–0, 7–3, 1–0)
Elmer Lach's overtime goal, his only marker of the playoffs, at 1:22 of overtime in Game Five, gave the Canadiens their first Stanley Cup in seven years.

1954

Detroit Red Wings defeat Montreal Canadiens (3–1, 1–3, 5–2, 2–0, 0–1, 1–4, 2–1)
The Habs looked good to overcome a 3–1 deficit in the final, until a Tony Leswick shot hit Doug Harvey and fluttered past a hopeless Gerry McNeil at 4:29 of overtime to give the Red Wings their third Cup in five years.

1955

Detroit Red Wings defeat Montreal Canadiens (4–2, 7–1, 2–4, 3–5, 5–1, 3–6, 3–1)
The Wings' Cup win of 1955 will always remain tainted in the eyes of Montrealers.

Rocket Richard was suspended for the playoffs for punching a linesman. Without their heart and soul, the Habs could not muster a victory in game seven and the Red Wings had their second straight Cup.

1956
Montreal Canadiens defeat Detroit Red Wings (6–4, 5–1, 1–3, 3–0, 3–1)
The dynasty begins. Jean Beliveau scored seven goals in the final and Jacques Plante allowed five goals in the final four games to give the Habs the first of their five consecutive Stanley Cups.

1957
Montreal Canadiens defeat Boston Bruins (5–1, 1–0, 4–2, 0–2, 5–1)
Quite possibly the greatest team the NHL has ever seen. Bernie Geoffrion tallied 18 points throughout the playoffs, while Rocket Richard contributed eight goals.

1958
Montreal Canadiens defeat Boston Bruins (2–1, 2–5, 3–0, 1–3, 3–2, 5–3)
Don Simmons did his darnedest to keep the Bruins in the series, posting a .928 playoff save percentage. However, Jacques Plante's save percentage was .937 and the Habs hoisted the Cup for the third straight year.

1959
Montreal Canadiens defeat Toronto Maple Leafs (5–3, 3–1, 2–3, 3–2, 5–3)
The heroes for the Habs this time around were Dickie Moore (17 playoff points) and the bear wrestler, Marcel Bonin (15 points). Four straight Cups and counting . . .

1960
Montreal Canadiens defeat Toronto Maple Leafs (4–2, 2–1, 5–2, 4–0)
Five straight Stanley Cups! They did it in style, sweeping the playoffs in eight games, equalling the feat of the 1952 Detroit Red Wings.

1961
Chicago Black Hawks defeat Detroit Red Wings (3–2, 1–3, 3–1, 1–2, 6–3, 5–1)
After knocking off the Habs in six games, Chicago disposed of the Red Wings in another six-game series. It would be their last Stanley Cup.

1962
Toronto Maple Leafs defeat Chicago Black Hawks (4–1, 3–2, 0–3, 1–4, 8–4, 2–1)
Eleven years after their last Cup win, the Leafs knocked off the Hawks in six games to hoist the Mug once again. Bob Nevin and Dick Duff scored in the third period of game six to erase a 1–0 Hawks lead and give them the Cup.

1963
Toronto Maple Leafs defeat Detroit Red Wings (4–2, 4–2, 2–3, 4–2, 3–1)
In Gordie Howe and Norm Ullman (16 points each), the Red Wings had the leading playoff scorers. However, the Leafs had Johnny Bower, who stonewalled the prolific Detroit attack en route to the Leafs' second straight Cup win.

1964
Toronto Maple Leafs defeat Detroit Red Wings (3–2, 3–4, 3–4, 4–2, 1–2, 4–3, 4–0)
It appeared that the Leafs were heading down to a series defeat, but Bobby Baun scored in overtime to win Game Six for the Leafs. Johnny Bower shutout the Wings in game seven and the Leafs had their third straight Stanley Cup.

1965
Montreal Canadiens defeat Chicago Black Hawks (3–2, 2–0, 1–3, 1–5, 6–0, 1–2, 4–0)
Gump Worsley and Charlie Hodge split goaltending duties in the final. Worsley got the game seven start and shutout the Hawks 4–0.

1966
Montreal Canadiens defeat Detroit Red Wings (2–3, 2–5, 4–2, 2–1, 5–1, 3–2)
The Habs became the first team to ever lose the first two games of a Cup final at home and come back to win the next four games.

1967
Toronto Maple Leafs defeat Montreal Canadiens (2–6, 3–0, 3–2, 2–6, 4–1, 3–1)
The "Geriatric Gang" overcame all their problems and quieted all the naysayers by knocking off the Habs in six games. The final Stanley Cup of the "Original Six" era would also be the Leafs' final Cup.

1968
Montreal Canadiens defeat St. Louis Blues (3–2, 1–0, 4–3, 3–2)
Even though the Habs swept the Blues, all four games were decided by one goal and two games went into overtime.

1969
Montreal Canadiens defeat St. Louis Blues (3–1, 3–1, 4–0, 2–1)
Basically a carbon copy of the 1968 final. Serge Savard's rock-solid blueline play earned him the Conn Smythe Trophy as playoff MVP.

1970
Boston Bruins defeat St. Louis Blues (6–1, 6–2, 4–1, 4–3)
The Cup-winning goal came in overtime of game four. Bobby Orr scored while he was being tripped by Noel Picard, creating one of the most famous images in hockey history.

1971
Montreal Canadiens defeat Chicago Black Hawks (1–2, 3–5, 4–2, 5–2, 0–2, 4–3, 3–2)
Ken Dryden was the playoff hero, stoning the powerhouse Bruins in the first round. He had only appeared in six NHL games prior to the 1971 playoffs. The Habs knocked off Minnesota and then disposed of the Hawks in a hard-fought seven-game series.

1972
Boston Bruins defeat New York Rangers (6–5, 2–1, 2–5, 3–2, 2–3, 3–0)
The Bruins went 12–3 on their successful Stanley Cup run in 1972, led by the tandem of Phil Esposito and Bobby Orr. Many people feel that the Bruins of the '70s could have rivaled the Habs of the late '50s in the dynasty department.

1973

Montreal Canadiens defeat Chicago Black Hawks (8–3, 4–1, 4–7, 4–0, 7–8, 6–4)
The Habs captured their eleventh Cup in 18 years with a six-game triumph over the Black Hawks. This would be Henri Richard's eleventh and final Cup.

1974

Philadelphia Flyers defeat Boston Bruins (2–3, 3–2, 4–1, 4–2, 1–5, 1–0)
The first expansion club to capture the Cup, the Philadelphia Flyers were built on brawn. Bernie Parent was magnificent between the pipes and was awarded the Conn Smythe Trophy.

1975

Philadelphia Flyers defeat Buffalo Sabres (4–1, 2–1, 4–5, 2–4, 5–1, 2–0)
The Flyers made it two in a row with their six-game triumph over the Sabres. Parent made it back-to-back Conn Smythes, becoming the first player to accomplish that feat.

1976

Montreal Canadiens defeat Philadelphia Flyers (4–3, 2–1, 3–2, 5–3)
The cleverly crafted Canadiens destroyed any thoughts of a Flyer three-peat with a four-game destruction. It was the first of four straight Cups for the Habs.

1977

Montreal Canadiens defeat Boston Bruins (7–3, 3–0, 4–2, 2–1)
Another year, another sweep for the Habs. They lost only two games during the play-offs and were led by Guy Lafleur's 26 playoff points and Ken Dryden's four shutouts.

1978

Montreal Canadiens defeat Boston Bruins (4–1, 3–2, 0–4, 3–4, 4–1, 4–1)
The Habs capture their third straight Cup with their second consecutive finals triumph over the Bruins. Larry Robinson was awarded the Conn Smythe Trophy for his playoff-leading 17 assists and solid defensive play.

1979

Montreal Canadiens defeat New York Rangers (1–4, 6–2, 4–1, 4–3, 4–1)
The Habs' main competition came in the semi-finals when they needed a late Guy Lafleur goal to send the game into OT, where Yvon Lambert ended the series. They met the Cinderella Rangers in the final and spotted them a game before cruising to a five-game series victory.

1980

New York Islanders defeat Philadelphia Flyers (4–3, 3–8, 6–2, 5–2, 3–6, 5–4)
From one dynasty to the next. Bobby Nystrom's OT winner in Game Six gave the Islanders the first of their four consecutive Stanley Cups.

1981

New York Islanders defeat Minnesota North Stars (6–3, 6–3, 7–5, 2–4, 5–1)
Minnesota knocked off Boston, Buffalo, and Calgary to reach the finals, where they

were promptly destroyed by the precise Islanders. Mike Bossy's 35 playoff points set the NHL playoff record.

1982

New York Islanders defeat Vancouver Canucks (6–5, 6–4, 3–0, 3–1)
The hockey world was riveted by "King" Richard Brodeur and the Vancouver Canucks and their magical run deep into the 1982 playoffs. The Islanders made sure to bring them back to earth with a four-game sweep.

1983

New York Islanders defeat Edmonton Oilers (2–0, 6–3, 5–1, 4–2)
Experience met youth in the 1983 final and experience won out. Billy Smith foiled Wayne Gretzky and the free-wheeling Oilers, allowing only six goals in the four-game sweep.

1984

Edmonton Oilers defeat New York Islanders (1–0, 1–6, 7–2, 7–2, 5–2)
Gretzky gets his first Cup! The Oilers knocked off the Islanders in five games to become the first ex-WHA club to win the Stanley Cup.

1985

Edmonton Oilers defeat Philadelphia Flyers (1–4, 3–1, 4–3, 5–3, 8–3)
Wayne Gretzky shattered all playoff records, tallying 47 points in a dominant playoff performance. In the final, the Oilers dropped the first game before roaring back to take the next four and their second straight Cup.

1986

Montreal Canadiens defeat Calgary Flames (2–5, 3–2, 5–3, 1–0, 4–3)
Riding the magnificent goaltending of rookie Patrick Roy and a little luck, the Canadiens captured their first Cup in seven years. The dynastic Oilers were knocked off in the quarterfinals when rookie defenseman Steve Smith banked an errant clearance off of Grant Fuhr for an own goal.

1987

Edmonton Oilers defeat Philadelphia Flyers (4–2, 3–2, 3–5, 4–1, 3–4, 2–3, 3–1)
The Oilers returned to glory, capturing their third Cup in the first seven-game Cup final since 1971. Flyer rookie goaltender Ron Hextall captured the Conn Smythe Trophy in a losing cause.

1988

Edmonton Oilers defeat Boston Bruins (2–1, 4–2, 6–3, 3–3, 6–3)
Game Four was suspended in the second period due to a power failure at the Boston Garden. It mattered little, as the Oilers wrapped up their second straight Cup two days later in Edmonton.

1989

Calgary Flames defeat Montreal Canadiens (3–2, 2–4, 3–4, 4–2, 3–2, 4–2)
With their Game Six victory in Montreal, the Flames became the first visiting team to win the Stanley Cup in the Montreal Forum.

1990

Edmonton Oilers defeat Boston Bruins (3–2, 7–2, 1–2, 5–1, 4–1)

The Oilers captured their fifth Cup in seven years with their five-game defeat of the Boston Bruins. Bill Ranford, incredible between the Oiler pipes, scored the Conn Smythe Trophy.

1991

Pittsburgh Penguins defeat Minnesota North Stars (4–5, 4–1, 1–3, 5–3, 6–4, 8–0)

The Penguins captured their first-ever Stanley Cup in the "Rock and Roll, Part Two" final. Mario Lemieux, who would snag the Conn Smythe, scored 12 points in the final.

1992

Pittsburgh Penguins defeat Chicago Blackhawks (5–4, 3–1, 1–0, 6–5)

The Penguins won their final 11 games in the playoffs to capture their second consecutive Cup. They survived a scare in the first round from Washington, who took a 3–1 series lead before dropping the next three.

1993

Montreal Canadiens defeat Los Angeles Kings (1–4, 3–2, 4–3, 3–2, 4–1)

The Canadiens won ten consecutive overtime games to win their first Stanley Cup since 1986. Patrick Roy was at his best, garnering Conn Smythe honors.

1994

New York Rangers defeat Vancouver Canucks (2–3, 3–1, 5–1, 4–2, 3–6, 1–4, 3–2)

The 54-year wait is over! Mark Messier takes the Rangers on his back and leads them to the promised land. The Ranger win energizes hockey in the United States.

1995

New Jersey Devils defeat Detroit Red Wings (2–1, 4–2, 5–2, 5–2)

Derided for playing the neutral-zone trap, the Devils thumbed their nose at hockey's establishment by sweeping the Red Wings and hoisting their first-ever Stanley Cup.

1996

Colorado Avalanche defeat Florida Panthers (3–1, 8–1, 3–2, 1–0)

The Avalanche, in their first season in Denver, added money goalie Patrick Roy and swept aside the upstart Florida Panthers in the final. The Cup-winning goal was scored in triple overtime of Game Four by Uwe Krupp.

1997

Detroit Red Wings defeat Philadelphia Flyers (4–2, 4–2, 6–1, 2–1)

The Red Wings, seemingly cursed in the playoffs, won their first Cup since 1955 with a four-game sweep of the favored Philadelphia Flyers. Mike Vernon's clutch goaltending earned him the Conn Smythe Trophy.

1998

Detroit Red Wings defeat Washington Capitals (2–1, 5–4, 2–1, 4–1)

The Cup final was another letdown as the Capitals proved to be no match for the Red

Wings. Steve Yzerman was the Wings leader throughout the playoffs and copped Conn Smythe honors.

1999

Dallas Stars defeat Buffalo Sabres (2–3, 4–2, 2–1, 1–2, 2–0, 2–1)

A controversial finish, without question. Brett Hull scored 14:51 into the third overtime period of game six to give Dallas their first Cup. The controversy arose since Hull's skate was in the crease when he scored, which some viewed as a violation of the crease rule. Nevertheless, the goal stood.

Appendix II

Authors' All-Time Teams

Glenn Weir

GOAL

Patrick Roy

Not as polished as Jacques Plante. Not as durable as Glenn Hall. Not as smart as Ken Dryden. Not as ferocious as Terry Sawchuk. But who cares? He is worth three Stanley Cup championships as of 1999 and is fast approaching the record for career wins.

And to think he won one of his Cups behind a Keystone Kops defense in Montreal.

DEFENSE

Doug Harvey

This one's a no-brainer.

DEFENSE

Bobby Orr

Again, there's not much to say on this one.

CENTER

Mario Lemieux

Sorry, Gretzky fans. Although I love the Great One too, I cannot in good faith take him as the best center ever — scoring records, streamers, balloons, ribbons, and all — over possibly the most gifted player in hockey history. Had Super Mario been healthy, you probably would've seen a lot more than his best, 199 points in a season.

LEFT WING

Bobby Hull

Can you imagine the Golden Jet taking feeds from Lemieux, Orr, and Harvey? Talk about frying your mind!

RIGHT WING

Gordie Howe/Maurice Richard

Please forgive me — I can't decide. I guess I'm just another in the long line of fence-sitters on the eternal Richard–Howe question. Sorry.

HEAD COACH

Scotty Bowman

How many Stanley Cup rings does the old master have now?

Jeff Chapman

GOAL

Clint Benedict

I'll be the black sheep of hockey historians on this one. Benedict's statistics don't lie, however. Kudos to Terry Sawchuk, Jacques Plante, Patrick Roy, and Chuck Gardiner, but have any of them won eight Vezina trophies in nine years? "Praying Benny" didn't either (because it wasn't awarded), but, using the award criteria, I find that he would have. This at a time when the great Paddy Moran, Bert Lindsay, Hap Holmes, and Georges Vezina himself were playing — a pretty select group. He's definitely been passed over by historians.

DEFENSE

Doug Harvey

He controlled the game from his position like no one since Eddie Shore.

DEFENSE

Bobby Orr

He was Gretzky on the blue-line, the first defenseman to win the Art Ross.

CENTER

Wayne Gretzky

The guy scored more assists than anyone else had points!

LEFT WING

Mario Lemieux

Not really a winger but one of my top three forwards, so he's on my team! He was the most physically talented player ever seen. If Lemieux hadn't suffered back problems and that unfortunate bout with Hodgkin's disease, he would have seriously challenged Wayne Gretzky's numbers. Former coach Eddie Johnston once said, "If he hadn't been sick, he might have averaged 200 points a season."

RIGHT WING

Gordie Howe

Mr. Hockey. The finest all-around player the game has ever seen. Wayne Gretzky and Mario Lemieux were more dominant offensively, but Howe had the mean streak and physical dimension on top.

COACH

Toe Blake

He made the successful transition from star player to star coach, and coached the Montreal Canadiens to five straight Stanley Cups in the 1950s. A master of psychology, Blake always knew when to give it to his players and when to take it easy. A genius.

Travis Weir

GOAL

Patrick Roy

The greatest I've ever seen. No goalie has done what he has done on teams with such soft defensemen in front of him. What he did in the 1986 and especially the 1993 playoffs was pure magic.

DEFENSE

Doug Harvey

The guy who blazed the trail for all other blue-liners since the 1950s. The shoulders on which a dynasty rested.

DEFENSE

Bobby Orr

He was brilliance personified. He took the trail Harvey blazed and changed the way we look at the position.

CENTER

Wayne Gretzky

I don't need to say anything here.

LEFT WING

Maurice Richard

The purest goal-scorer in hockey history. The Rocket is hockey in Montreal and in the province of Quebec.

RIGHT WING

Gordie Howe

The Old Man. He did it all, with class and humility. That's not to say he couldn't break you with a goal, a pass, or a bone-shattering elbow.

HEAD COACH

Toe Blake

Imagine having Rocket Richard, Jean Beliveau, Bernie Geoffrion, Jacques Plante, Henri Richard, and Doug Harvey on your team. Well, Blake did in the late 1950s and managed to keep them all happy at the same time. He played the dual role of dad and team psychologist.